T0256484

Trust and Crime in Information Societies

Disclaimer

The chapters that make up this book were commissioned by Foresight, part of the Office of Science and Technology, to inform the Cyber Trust and Crime Prevention project that has been looking at the possible societal impact of future generations of information technology over the next 10 to 15 years. All of the chapters, excluding the three short discussion or review chapters in Part 4, have been peer-reviewed and stand on their own merits. The latter either fill small gaps in the coverage of the science reviews or address some specific points as a stimulus for further debate. In all cases, the views are those of the authors. While the Office of Science and Technology commissioned the work, the findings are independent of government and do not constitute government policy.

Trust and Crime in Information Societies

Edited by

Robin Mansell

London School of Economics and Political Science

and

Brian S. Collins

Cranfield University

Edward Elgar
Cheltenham, UK • Northampton, MA, USA

Published by
Edward Elgar Publishing Limited
Glensanda House
Montpellier Parade
Cheltenham
Glos GL50 1UA
UK

Edward Elgar Publishing, Inc.
136 West Street
Suite 202
Northampton
Massachusetts 01060
USA

A catalogue record for this book
is available from the British Library

ISBN 1 84542 177 9

Printed and bound in Great Britain by MPG Books Ltd, Bodmin, Cornwall

Contents

Figures

Tables

Boxes

Contributors

Nick Allum, Lecturer, Department of Sociology, University of Surrey

James Backhouse, Director, IS Integrity Group, Department of Information Systems, London School of Economics and Political Science

Ayse Bener, Lecturer, Department of Computer Engineering, Bogazici University, Istanbul

Jonathan Cave, Senior Lecturer, Department of Economics, University of Warwick

Narisa Chauvidul-Aw, Senior Financial Analyst, Red Bull UK

Brian S. Collins, Professor and Head, Department of Information Systems, Royal Military College of Sciences, Cranfield University

William H. Dutton, Professor and Director, Oxford Internet Institute, University of Oxford

John Edwards, Head of International Communications Practice, Herbert Smith, London

George Gaskell, Professor, Methodology Institute, London School of Economics and Political Science

Jonathan Jackson, Lecturer, Methodology Institute, London School of Economics and Political Science

Nicholas R. Jennings, Professor of Computer Science, School of Electronics and Computer Science, University of Southampton

Cliff Jones, Professor of Computing Science, School of Computing Science, University of Newcastle upon Tyne

Sir David King, Chief Scientific Adviser to UK government and Head of the Office of Science and Technology, London

Robin Mansell, Dixons Chair in New Media and the Internet, Department of Media and Communications, London School of Economics and Political Science

Kieron O'Hara, Senior Research Fellow, Intelligence, Agents, Multimedia Group, School of Electronics and Computer Science, University of Southampton

Fred Piper, Professor of Mathematics and Director, Information Security Group, Royal Holloway, University of London

Charles D. Raab, Professor of Government, School of Social and Political Studies, University of Edinburgh

Sarvapali D. Ramchurn, PhD student, School of Electronics and Computer Science, University of Southampton

Brian Randell, Emeritus Professor and Senior Research Investigator, School of Computing Science, University of Newcastle upon Tyne

Matthew J.B. Robshaw, Reader in Information Security, Information Security Group, Royal Holloway, University of London

M. Angela Sasse, Professor of Human-Centred Technology, Department of Computer Science, University College London

Scarlet Schwiderski-Grosche, Lecturer, Information Security Group, Royal Holloway, University of London

Nigel Shadbolt, Professor of Artificial Intelligence, Intelligence, Agents, Multimedia Group, School of Electronics and Computer Science, University of Southampton

Adrian Shepherd, Survey Research Officer, Oxford Internet Institute, University of Oxford

W. Edward Steinmueller, Professor of Information and Communication Technology Policy, SPRU – Science and Technology Policy Research, University of Sussex

Frederick Wamala, Post-Doctoral Researcher, IS Integrity Group, Department of Information Systems, London School of Economics and Political Science

Robert Willison, Assistant Professor, Department of Informatics, Copenhagen Business School

Abbreviations and acronyms

AA	Automobile Association
ACPO	Association of Chief Police Officers
AD	Active Directory
AKT	Advanced Knowledge Technologies (project)
AmI	Ambient Intelligence
AMSD	Accompanying Measure on System Dependability
APECKS	Adaptive Presentation Environment for Collaborative Knowledge Structuring
ARPANET	Advanced Research Projects Agency Network (US)
ASICS	Application-Specific Integrated Circuits
ATG	Advanced Technologies Group
ATM	Automated Teller Machine
B2B	Business to Business
BBB	Better Business Bureau
BSE	Bovine Spongiform Encephalopathy
BSI	Bundesamt für Sicherheit in der Informationstechnik
CA	Certification Authority
CAA	Civil Aviation Authority
CBS	Computer-based Systems
CCTV	Closed Circuit Television
CDA	Cmputer Data Authentication
CEN	Comité Européen de Normalisation
CMC	Computer Mediated Communication
CoE	Council of Europe
COHSE	Conceptual Open Hypermedia Services Environment
CRS	Credential Recovery Systems
DARPA	Defense Advanced Research Projects Agency (US)
DAML+OIL	DARPA Agent Markup Language + Ontology Inference Layer
DDA	Dynamic Data Authentication
DIRC	Interdisciplinary Research Collaboration Dependability of Computer-Based Systems (EPSRC Project, UK)
DPA	Data Protection Act (UK)
DRM	Digital Rights Management

DSR	Dynamic Signature Recognition
ED	Enumeration Districts
EPSRC	Engineering and Physical Sciences Research Council
ESC	Extended Static Checkers
ESRC	Economic and Social Research Council
FIPA	Foundation for Intelligent Physical Agents
FIPS	Fair Information Principles
FOAF	Friend-of-a-Friend
FTC	Federal Trade Commission (US)
GD	Global Desktop
GM	Genetically Modified
GDP	Gross Domestic Product
GSM	Global System for Mobile Communications
GUI	Graphical User Interface
GWH	Goodwill Hunting
HCI	Human Computer Interaction
HTML	HyperText Markup Language
ICANN	International Corporation for Assigned Names and Numbers
ICT	Information and Communication Technologies
ID	Identity
IP	Internet Protocol
IPR	Intellectual Property Rights
IS	Information System
IT	Information Technology
ISO	International Organization for Standardization
ISP	Internet Service Provider
IST	Information Society Technologies
ISTAG	Information Society Technologies Advisory Group
KT	Knowledge Technologies
MAFTIA	Malicious and Accidental Fault Tolerance for Internet Applications
MITI	Ministry of International Trade and Industry (Japan)
MMOG	Massively Multiplayer Online Game
MOO	Multi-user Domain, Object Oriented
MUD	Multi-user Domain/Multi-user Dungeon (gaming)
NATS	National Air Traffic Service
NGSCB	Next-Generation Secure Computing Base
NSF	National Science Foundation (US)
OASIS	Organically Assured and Survivable Information System
OII	Oxford Internet Institute
OECD	Organisation for Economic Cooperation and Development
OST	Office of Science and Technology

OxIS	Oxford Internet Survey
P3P	Platform for Privacy Preferences
PC	Personal Computer
PDA	Personal Digital Assistant
PETS	Privacy Enhancing Technologies
PGP	Pretty Good Privacy
PIA	Privacy Impact Assessment
PICT	Programme on Information and Communication Technologies (UK)
PIN	Personal Identification Number
PISA	Privacy Incorporated Software Agent
PIU	Performance and Innovation Unit (UK)
PKI	Public Key Infrastructure
RDF	Resource Description Framework
RFID	Radio Frequency Identification
RSA	Rivest, Shamir and Adleman
SARF	Social Amplification of Risk Framework
SCP	Structure, Conduct and Performance
SDA	Static Data Authentication
SDS	System Design System
SES	Socio-economic Status
SIM	Security Identity Module
SVS	Salient Value Similarity
SW	Semantic Web
TCPA	Trusted Computing Platform Alliance
TFT	Tit-for-Tat
UML	Universal Markup Language
URI	Uniform Resource Identifiers
URL	Uniform Resource Locator
W3C	World Wide Web Consortium
WIP	World Internet Protocol
XML	eXtensible Markup Language
Y2K	Year 2000

Foreword

Sir David King

The importance of information and communications technologies (ICTs) to the people of the United Kingdom and to the UK's economic well-being is widely accepted. Most people use mobile phones, and increasing numbers are using the Internet to obtain information, make purchases and access public services. ICTs enhance the quality of life and are a key part of the knowledge economy. The pace of technological change remains fast: smart objects, intelligent software, new forms of pervasive computing and other developments will continue to give us new possibilities. It is rarely clear precisely what form these possibilities will take, or how people will want to use them. At the same time, some aspects of ICT, such as the structure of the Internet, are essentially well established, but their profound effects are changing as they work their way through the economy.

The Foresight programme, run within the Office of Science and Technology (OST), creates challenging visions of the future to inform decisions being taken today. The work in this book represents an exploration of the science base, that was carried out as part of a Foresight project on Cyber Trust and Crime Prevention. This project, part of Foresight's rolling programme, aimed to explore the implications and applications of ICTs. The team was given the space and encouragement to look beyond normal planning horizons, in order to provide insight and tools for decision making.

As in other Foresight projects, the Cyber Trust and Crime Prevention team started by bringing together a wide range of researchers – from philosophy to systems design, and from encryption to economics. These academics identified the areas of science and the humanities that they felt would be important in creating the cyberworld and in understanding it. The project team commissioned reviews of the research in these areas, aiming to establish a clearer picture of the knowledge base, key themes and uncertainties. These reviews were peer-reviewed.

Working with experts in business and government, the project team then stepped forward to 2018 to create visions of the future that would help to bring the implications of ICT to life. The scenarios for 2018, and the gaming process developed to test them, brought to the fore the implications of ICT across a vast range of areas where it will have significant impact.

This book represents the complete set of scientific reviews, together with some papers that were developed during the lifetime of the project as 'thinkpieces'. All have helped to inform the work of the project and subsequent continuing actions by a variety of stakeholders.

I am delighted that the scientific reviews are being published together here, representing as they do a fascinatingly broad and cross-disciplinary look at some of the key issues affecting the ways in which today's complex social and technological systems are evolving. Further project material, including the scenarios, is available through the Foresight website, http://www.foresight.gov.uk

1 Introduction

Robin Mansell and Brian S. Collins[1]

1.1 INFORMATION SOCIETY FUTURES

The future of today's information societies is contingent upon the evolution of cyberspace as a complex human and technical system. The structure of the Internet is favouring fragmentation into many loosely connected cyber communities that are governed by a range of different principles. This renders cyberspace subject to highly unpredictable emergent behaviours and makes the consequences of efforts to prevent crime very difficult to predict. This is especially so when such efforts are targeted at particularly unstable components of the system. In some areas, however, there is sufficient stability and understanding of relationships within the system to justify actions aimed at improving crime prevention.

The Internet, its future and the experiences of those using it have become subjects of enquiry for nearly every academic discipline. As its reach has become global, the Internet has become the focus of a growing amount of 'research in the wild' and the subject of argument over the values that should govern its development currently and in the future.[2] Our main concerns in this volume are with the relationships that exist between cyber trust and crime prevention, and some of the key interrelationships between the human and technical components of cyberspace.[3] These connections too also with others relating to how actions that might be taken in relation to other aspects of policy might interact with actions relating to cyber trust and crime prevention.

The chapters in this book are based on papers commissioned by the UK government's Foresight project on Cyber Trust and Crime Prevention.[4] This project, which was formally completed in mid-2004, aimed to explore the application and implications of new generations of information and communication technologies (ICTs) in selected areas that will present future opportunities and challenges for crime prevention. In the course of this project consideration was given to the possible drivers of the evolution of cyberspace, to the opportunities created by innovations in technology, to the threats and barriers to cyberspace development, and to the feasibility of various crime prevention measures. Such measures will play some part in governing interactions between people and their machines, and within a globally networked 'machine'.

The continuing development of cyberspace raises issues that are fundamental to individual and collective human safety and security. One of the challenges of the project was to distil lessons from the scientific evidence base and to highlight areas where there are gaps that warrant more research. The authors of the chapters comprising this volume draw upon research within the sciences, the social sciences and the field of engineering. Each of the chapters highlights current understanding of issues that will affect the evolution of cyberspace and the future effectiveness of crime prevention measures. In this introductory chapter, we explain why particular technologies were selected for investigation in the project and give reasons for our focus on such issues as risk, trust and trustworthiness, privacy, security and ethics alongside technology.

As in other areas of technological innovation it is important to assess whether new criminal opportunities will arise from cyberspace developments. One means of making such an assessment is to examine some of the key features of cyberspace to determine the extent to which the predisposition for anyone to commit a crime will increase, and how far the new resources available will enable this. It is also necessary to examine what the incentives are for developers of the cyberspace system to adopt measures that will make cyberspace a less attractive medium for criminals and those who promote crime, for example by preventing the provision of 'inside' information, passwords and tools, and encouraging users not to be careless about their own security.

In a Foresight project of this kind, it is essential to restrict the scope of the enquiry in order to move beyond speculative claims about the likely consequences of cyberspace developments for crime prevention strategies. The principal technologies considered during the project were those that play a major role in managing human and software agent identities and authenticity in cyberspace, in delivering cyber system robustness and dependability, in augmenting the security of cyberspace and in contributing to information assurance and knowledge management.

The topics for the state-of-the-art reviews of the existing scientific literature were chosen by an expert panel. This volume provides an entry point to theoretical and empirical work in the topic areas shown in Figure 1.1. The figure depicts some of the key components and issue areas in the cyberspace system. Each of these is recursively related to the others, forming a highly complex system that is populated by many different agents, both human and non-human.

Figure 1.1 Cyber trust and crime prevention: web of components

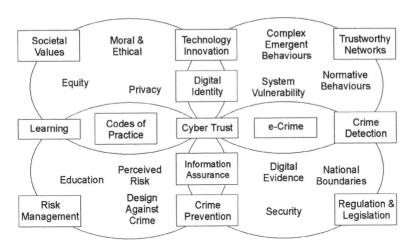

At any given time, there will be dominant organizing themes in the spread of cyberspace networks. In 2004, even as the open source software movement was gaining ground, cyberspace technologies were organized largely around corporate and home desktop computing, and the 'Wintel' or Microsoft Windows and Intel microchip model predominated. Mobile communication was undergoing the transition to its third generation in which data services are delivered alongside voice services. The ICT industry as a whole was experiencing a period of instability and the Internet Protocol (IP) was becoming established as the global networking standard, presenting new issues for the pace of innovation throughout the ICT industry and for the competitiveness of both smaller and larger ICT-producing and -using firms. At the content end of the ICT spectrum there was no leading model for the distribution of digital products or for payments. There was much debate about the viability of conventions with respect to intellectual property protection alongside measures to promote open access to information and new models fostering open source software developments, that is, a global information commons. In the commercial domains of cyberspace, many new electronic services were emerging and markets for many of these services were growing rapidly, suggesting that a relatively stable structure would emerge.

The current and future trends in the development of cyberspace technologies were examined in the Cyber Trust and Crime Prevention project in a variety of contexts and with respect to the many social, technical and ethical issues that they raise. Analysis of the potential threats to human safety and security in a pervasive cyberspace environment is complicated by uncertainty about how people will perceive its associated risks, whether or not they perceive it as trustworthy, and whether or not they behave as if it were trustworthy. The public's perception of risk has been examined in terms of risks from exposure to technological dangers such as radioactivity, pollution and other hazards. However, the public's perception of cyberspace risk has received relatively little attention, despite the considerable work on risk relating to financial markets in the business community. Much of the information people receive about cyberspace risk comes from the media and a growing variety of Internet-based sources of imagery and symbols. All of this information is further translated by multiple actors and is interpreted in different ways with consequences that we are only beginning to understand.

It is important to acknowledge, nevertheless, that concepts of risk and trust are important for understanding the future development of the cyberspace system. Today's social and technical systems are being created in an environment of chance and risk. This environment embraces interdependent systems of production, consumption, governance and control. It is giving rise to new perceptions of risk and to new meanings and interpretations of developments in cyberspace. People assess risks as being more or less serious depending upon how they weigh their consequences. This has substantial implications for the viability of crime prevention strategies.

Identification of a threat or danger associated with cyberspace and the appraisal of its possible consequences also raises ethical issues and the need to consider how new criminal opportunities give rise to the need for new principles, responsibilities and accountabilities. There is considerable uncertainty about how trust in the offline world transfers into cyberspace and about the trustworthiness of the components of the cyberspace system. For instance, problems and perceived dangers may be seen as a failure either of the technical system or of the system designers and users to take steps to prevent crime or to reduce the vulnerabilities in the system. It is essential, therefore, to understand the relationships between human factors, and risk and trust if a relatively secure cyberspace system is to develop in the future. Risk and trust, the trustworthiness of the cyberspace system and the feasibility of crime prevention strategies were considered in the Foresight project in relation to questions such as:

- Which cyber trust issues will be of dominant concern – what will be the new kinds of vulnerability and how will the risks of cyberspace be perceived?
- How will the overall structure of the emerging system drive the uptake of cyber trust technologies?

- What kinds of interventions might be made to influence the system's dynamics for the purpose of improving cyber trust and crime prevention?

The contributors to this volume demonstrate that addressing these questions within existing paradigms of trust, security and technology will not suffice to alleviate concerns about the potential threats of cyberspace. In many instances new frameworks that, as far as possible, take into account the distinctive features of cyberspace, are suggested with signposts indicating the kinds of cross-disciplinary research that will be needed.

The issues addressed in the Foresight Cyber Trust and Crime Prevention project are not the only important or relevant ones for the future, but their weight has been signalled by many of those concerned with the increasing potential for identity fraud, changes in the balance between private and public information needs, the role of trust in society and the interfaces between technological innovation and society that the cyber system offers.[5]

1.2 STRUCTURE OF THE BOOK

This book is organized in four main parts. In Part 1, State of the Art, we provide a synthesis of the lessons about cyber trust and crime prevention that can be drawn from the existing scientific evidence.

In Part 2, Future Cyberspace Systems, the focus is on some of the key issues that are likely to influence the future of the cyberspace system including its dependability, architecture and means of handling identities and authentication procedures. Two important areas of technological innovation are the subject of in-depth examination: knowledge technologies and the semantic web,[6] and agent-based software deployment.

In Part 3, Experiencing Cyberspace, we turn to evidence on the ways that people appear to experience cyberspace. The themes in this part centre on risk and trust and the social, organizational and technical challenges of the spread of the Internet and experiences of using it in a variety of social and commercial contexts.

Part 4, Commentary, comprises a set of three short chapters each focusing on a limited theme or issue that emerged in the course of the Foresight project. The first addresses issues around the institutions that influence cyberspace markets, trust and the accumulation of social capital; the second tackles positions on ethical issues and their relationship to cyber trust; and the third offers insight into some of the legal considerations with respect to principles and practices in the digital age.

1.3 CONCLUSION

As the information societies of the twenty-first century are being constructed, it is increasingly being acknowledged that the whole of the cyberspace system is subject to emergent and unpredictable system behaviour. The contributors to this volume show why developments in cyberspace technologies and the social system are giving rise to new opportunities for crime. Strategies will be needed to minimize these opportunities, and such strategies clearly will involve numerous choices. The solutions for improving cyber trust and crime prevention in a future pervasive cyberspace environment will differ from those in use today.

In Chapter 2 we provide a synthesis of the numerous issues and problems facing those seeking to strengthen strategies for crime prevention. The analysis in Chapter 2 and the state-of-the-art reviews of existing research in subsequent chapters demonstrate that there is a serious deployment gap with respect to the software development methods and procedures used in the construction of the technical components of cyberspace. Improved levels of dependability require greater attention to the commercial issues that influence customer willingness to invest in more reliable ICT systems and in training and education.

We discuss issues concerning the appropriate means of authenticating identity in the light of changes in the design of secure technologies and in the social practices and cultural norms of information assurance. We indicate the way that the development and application of 'criminal opportunity' models can inform future crime prevention strategies and show how the field of ICT forensics is influencing the design of data management tools that will be necessary for evidence gathering.

Perceptions of risk and trust in cyberspace are fundamentally important in understanding the way members of the public appraise risk and uncertainty. We examine these concepts from a variety of theoretical and empirical vantage points. These generally indicate that people's perceptions of risk may be amplified or attenuated depending on a large number of social and technical factors. These factors vary depending on whether enquiries into issues of trust and trustworthiness involve person-to-person, person-to-system or system-to-system trust.

We review developments in software agent-based systems and knowledge technologies and the semantic web to illustrate the tactics for fostering trust that are being considered, and the social dynamics and learning processes involved in cyberspace risk perception and trusting behaviour. We also consider the ethical issues that inform choices about whether or not to intervene in cyberspace to achieve improved protection against crime.

We consider the economic incentives for investing in the deployment of more trustworthy networks and applications, and the interactions between different legislative and self-regulatory approaches that govern cyberspace, especially in the case of privacy protection and security.

A key conclusion that emerges from our review of the existing scientific evidence is that it is relatively weak in important areas that bear on cyber trust and crime prevention. However, we suggest that critical reasoning can be applied to reach judgements about appropriate strategies for crime prevention and about 'acceptable' and 'unacceptable' levels of the trustworthiness of the cyberspace system.

Collaborative and cross-disciplinary research is needed to harness the considerable breadth of expertise that is available in the UK and elsewhere. New crime prevention measures will be more effective if they are complemented by such research and by measures that enable people to achieve a better awareness of when and when not to trust in the cyberspace system.

NOTES

1   We would like to thank all those who contributed to the production of this book. We are especially grateful to Dr Claire Craig and Dr Miles Yarrington of the Office of Science and Technology Foresight Team for encouraging us to undertake the work necessary to prepare the manuscript. Thanks go to Martin Ince for managing the contractual process, for his editorial comments generally and his contribution to Chapter 15. Cynthia Little provided her superb editing skills, Peter Morris contributed the graphics, and Jennifer Moss contributed comments during the final stages of manuscript preparation. Our thinking has been influenced by the many comments and observations made by members of the Cyber Trust and Crime Prevention project's stakeholder group and its advisory group. We are very grateful to them all. A considerable number of academics participated in the peer review process and we thank them all for the careful consideration they gave to earlier versions of the chapters. We especially thank all the authors for their responsiveness throughout the manuscript preparation stage. Finally, thanks to Dymphna Evans, our editor at Edward Elgar Publishing, for her assistance and support. We, the editors, are ultimately responsible for this book and for any errors or omissions.

2   'Research in the wild' is a phrase coined by Michel Callon to distinguish science undertaken in a laboratory from enquiry performed by concerned groups, see Callon (2003, p. 61).

3   We refer to 'cyberspace', that is, a 'space' in which electronic information processing and communication occur. This term signifies various activities – social and technical – that occur in the electronic environments enabled by digital technologies. Cyberspace is not homogeneous and is constantly changing. Not only are the technologies deployed in many different ways, but also the exploitation of them by various social groups differs considerably. We use the term without detailing specific technologies or applications (that is, open distributed and relatively closed networks; proprietary and open source software).

4   Office of Science and Technology, see http://www.foresight.gov.uk/ accessed 17 April 2004.

5   See Royal Society (2003).

6   Knowledge technologies (KT) and semantic web (SW) are used in the literature; see Chapters 5 and 6 for definitions and a discussion.

REFERENCES

Callon, M. (2003), 'The Increasing Involvement of Concerned Groups in R&D Policies: What Lessons for Public Powers?', in A. Geuna, A.J. Salter and W.E. Steinmueller (eds), *Science and Innovation: Rethinking the Rationales for Funding and Governance*, Cheltenham: Edward Elgar, pp. 30-68.

Royal Society (2003), 'Potential Wealth-creating Developments from Research in Security: The Next Decade', Royal Society Science, City, Industry Dialogue, Information and Communication Technologies to Enhance the Quality of Life, report on a seminar held 2 June, London.

Part 1   State of the art

The chapter in this part provides highlights of the state-of-the-art science that is relevant to our assessment of the questions and issues examined by the Foresight Cyber Trust and Crime Prevention project. In Chapter 2, Brian Collins and Robin Mansell draw upon the chapters comprising the other parts of this volume. This first chapter provides a brief introduction to the technologies of cyberspace in Section 2.2. It then goes on to examine key issues that arise in constructing and using the large-scale networking technologies that are available today and that will provide the infrastructure and services for future information societies (Section 2.3).

Section 2.3 draws together the main topics covered in the chapters that follow. Issues of system dependability and software engineering are considered, together with the need for procedures for verification and authentication of identity. The difficulties involved in securing cyberspace environments and in managing risks are discussed in the light of various crime prevention strategies. Several approaches to the analysis of risk and trust as they bear on cyberspace and crime prevention are highlighted. These draw on disciplinary perspectives, including computer science, economics and psychology, and on work in the fields of computer-mediated communication and human-computer interaction. The need for ethical consideration of interventions in cyberspace aimed at crime prevention is also considered.

Two key areas of innovation in cyberspace technologies are highlighted. The first is the deployment of software agent-based systems within cyberspace, and the second is the development of knowledge technologies and the semantic web. These are both crucial to next generation Internet developments. Insights on trust are highlighted, based on new empirical evidence about trust and the Internet gained from a survey conducted in the UK. Consideration is also given to the cyberspace markets and policy contexts in which crime prevention strategies must operate. The structure of emerging markets is considered in terms of the incentives in the market for investment in trustworthy cyberspace systems. Finally, a brief review of the legislative environment sets the scene for a consideration of privacy protection and its social and technical features.

Chapter 2 concludes (Section 2.4) with a discussion of some of the uncertainties about the potential trade-offs that will have to be considered as efforts are made to secure cyberspace environments in the future. This chapter is intended as a guide for readers to the discussions that are of particular interest to them in Parts 2 and 3 of this volume. The structure of Chapter 2 is different from that of the succeeding chapters because of its synthetic nature. However, it enables the state-of-the-art science reviews to be grouped in a way that is intended to facilitate the reader's access to the large amount of material in this volume.

2 Cyber trust and crime prevention

Brian S. Collins and Robin Mansell[1]

2.1 INTRODUCTION

Cyberspace is global in its reach. In the UK and elsewhere, many solutions for crime prevention could be introduced through public or private initiatives. Many of these solutions, however, will require internationally coordinated action if they are to be effective. In the UK the science and engineering foundation is strong both in key technical areas as well as with respect to problems and issues that are the concerns of the legal profession, the social sciences and the humanities. This provides a strong basis for leadership internationally.

The evolution of cyberspace is a subject of great controversy. There are divergent views about whether the UK has a competitive advantage in developing technologies that will be trusted by the majority of their users and whether there is a need for government initiatives to ensure that technologies that are trustworthy emerge. There are similarly divergent views about the need to constrain cyberspace developments in order to limit the potential for destructive attack, strengthen collective security and limit privacy invasions. The scientific evidence base cannot be applied to resolve all of these controversies. However, it can help to clarify how the human and technical components of cyberspace relate to each other. Our review of the main issues raised in this volume is designed to suggest how the interventions in cyberspace of various actors are likely to reverberate throughout the social and technical system.

In the UK, Foresight projects are designed to produce challenging visions of the future with the aim of ensuring that the strategies of the day are effective. The Cyber Trust and Crime Prevention project explored the application and implications of the new generation of information and communication technologies (ICTs) across a variety of areas and the possibilities and challenges they bring for crime prevention in the future. These areas included identity and authenticity, system robustness and dependability, security and information assurance, and privacy and surveillance. All are crucial to our understanding of how risk is perceived and trust is fostered within complex social and technical systems. In this chapter we highlight the key interrelationships between the human and technical components of cyberspace.

This chapter is based on the state-of-the-art science reviews commissioned for the Cyber Trust and Crime Prevention project. The ten chapters in Parts 2 and 3 of this volume provide authoritative reference material and a foundation for further research and debate.[2] Each chapter examines the current state of knowledge in a selected area as well as highlighting future research needed to clarify and improve the knowledge base in the future. Part 4 consists of three short notes written by experts who were invited to comment on a specific topic.[3]

Section 2.2 provides a brief discussion of the technologies of cyberspace. In Section 2.3 we reflect on the lessons that can be drawn from existing research in relation to the future context in which crime prevention strategies will evolve. In Section 2.4 we conclude by emphasizing areas where measures could be taken to develop more trustworthy cyberspace systems that could strengthen crime prevention strategies. The overriding concern is to minimize the potential for cyberspace to develop in ways that create new opportunities for physical and cyber crime.

2.2 THE TECHNOLOGIES OF CYBERSPACE

'Technology' can refer to the components of cyberspace, such as its hardware and software, or to the social values, norms, practices and institutions of cyberspace. 'Cyberspace' refers to interconnected networks or the spaces within which electronic communications take place, and this term has become synonymous with the Internet and the World Wide Web and their use by the public (Skibell 2002).[4] Those who invent, design and implement the ICTs that underpin cyberspace generally agree that much needs to be done to build confidence both in people and in the 'mechanics' of cyberspace.

Analyses of the technical and possible market developments in the field of pervasive computing and trustworthy ICT systems show that some of the technologies are relatively mature and well understood, but still evolving. Other technologies are immature, but their evolution is reasonably predictable while still others are in the 'blue-skies' research phase (Sharpe 2003; Sharpe and Zaba 2004). The technologies range from those used for pattern recognition and cognitive modelling to those supporting network connectivity and broadband access. They include various kinds of software, service platforms and service functionalities.

We focus particularly on the development of complex software systems and the technologies used to establish identity and to authenticate users of cyberspace. We look specifically at developments in software agent-based computing, and knowledge technologies and the semantic web. All of these technologies play a crucial role in the emergence of 'pervasive' or 'ubiquitous' computing and the spread of networks of 'ambient intelligence' (see Box 2.1). These technologies also play a major role in the extent to which such issues as risk, trust, privacy and security, and also ethical issues, become important in crime prevention strategies.

As is suggested in Box 2.1, the majority of cyberspace users do not have a good understanding of current security requirements. As the European Commission's Advisory Group on Information Society Technologies (IST) has suggested, the solutions for improving cyber trust and crime prevention in a pervasive computing or ambient intelligence environment are likely to be quite different from those in use today.

Box 2.1 Ambient intelligence and the security paradigm

'In the ISTAG [Information Society Technologies Advisory Group] concept of Ambient Intelligence, intelligence is pervasive and unobtrusive in the environment. The environment is sensitive to the presence of living people in it, and supports their activities. People, physical entities, and their agents and services share this new space, which encompasses both the physical and virtual worlds – the Ambient Intelligent Space – or AmI Space.

Security in this space will require solutions very different from those of today's systems which are predicated on relatively stable, well-defined, consistent configurations, contexts, and participants to the security arrangements. ... This new paradigm will be characterized by 'conformable' security, in which the degree and nature of security associated with any particular type of action will change over time and with changing circumstances and with changing available information so as to suit the context. ... within the existing security paradigm there are significant outstanding problems that inhibit development of information society markets. The majority of potential users of services and products have, at best, a poor understanding of security, which leads to caution and, at worst, severe distrust. They need comprehensible mechanisms in which they can have confidence ...' (European Commission, IST Advisory Group 2002, pp. 3-4)

The commercial setting in which ICT evolution is occurring is subject to the dynamics of the interactions between the players (governments, citizens and consumers, civil society organizations of many kinds, and businesses) and the choices made with respect to regulations, standards and the role of the market. These, in turn, are strongly influenced by changes in the motivations and actions of those that seek to minimize criminal opportunities through crime prevention, and those that seek to exploit emerging technologies to support existing and new forms of criminal activity. In an emergent and evolving system, such as cyberspace where there is an 'arms race' between offenders and crime preventers, a key strategic issue is 'how to live with it and how to ensure that the balance is tilted as far as possible, for as much of the time as possible, in favour of preventers' (Ekblom 1999, p. 47).

Crime prevention in the context of cyberspace means reducing the risk of the occurrence of crime and the potential seriousness of crime and disorder that may occur either in the online or the offline world (Ekblom 2002, 2003). To achieve this, it is necessary to identify the problems and their causes. Given the relatively recent and rapid development of cyberspace it is not surprising that there are very substantial uncertainties about what problems will emerge and how they can be tackled. It is clear, however, that cyberspace entails new opportunities for crime because its reliance on networks and communication is such that criminal events may be distributed across geographical space and through time in many new ways.

Cyberspace enables new computer systems and data capture methods, which may be vulnerable to attack, but also may offer innovative means of responding to criminal activity. Just as the cyberspace system design itself is evolving and adaptive, giving rise to new forms of criminal opportunity, so also are the tactics and strategies of potential offenders (Ekblom 1997). The answer to the evolutionary arms race involving cyberspace technologies will undoubtedly lead to new technical design considerations, but their feasibility will depend on changing social, cultural, political and economic priorities as well as on a number of crucial ethical considerations.

In a dynamic socio-technical system of this kind, the components of cyberspace often acquire a self-reinforcing structure. The motivations of the different players in society will be such that as new ICTs are implemented, parts of the system may become quite stable for a period of time. The significance of this is that the future use of ICTs will be inextricably bound up with systems that coordinate a large number of technologies within agreed interfaces and standards, which themselves will experience periods of transient stability. These will evolve from generation to generation; as the technology shifts, the various responses of players will change their respective motivations and actions.

The range of technologies – technical and social – that is central to the emergent properties of cyberspace is vast.[5] In this book, emphasis is given to those areas and developments that were seen as being the most important as a result of consultations during the Cyber Trust and Crime Prevention project. Many of the problems that give rise to perceptions of risk and the insecurity of cyberspace are not new, but crime prevention in the light of developments in cyberspace does have some new dimensions. This particularly applies to such areas as the management of digital identities, the processes and tools used to enable reciprocity in cyberspace, and the properties that are required to enable humans to place trust in technology systems, that is, in part, the trustworthiness of such systems.

The scope of the issues examined in this book is informed by an analysis of previous studies in closely related areas. Although trust, assurance, security and dependability as aspects of cyberspace developments have been mentioned in earlier works, crime prevention itself has not been an explicit focus. In addition, there are differences in focus in the studies of cyberspace-related developments conducted in the US and in Europe as suggested by the following extract:

> The US studies tended to be more focused on technological and managerial solutions to the challenges. European studies addressed these issues but discussed more extensively the societal context and had more explicit visions of the desired societal end-state. This perhaps reflects a US focus on managing the risks consequent on market led developments compared to the European attempt to direct and shape these developments. It may also reflect an embedded US view that ICT developments (mainly US-led) are broadly positive, compared to a more sceptical European view that is more concerned about the economic, social and political changes they will entail. (Cremonini et al. 2003, p. 8)

The European emphasis on the economic, social and political implications of cyberspace technologies is reflected in the state-of-the-art science reviews commissioned by the Cyber Trust and Crime Prevention project. Pervasive computing will give rise to the need for new paradigms for managing uncertainty, the perceived and actual risks of cyberspace, and the trustworthiness of the cyberspace system.

The technical and human components of cyberspace form a complex emergent system that is subject to periods of instability and stability. Historically, studies of innovation and techno-economic change give evidence of periods of instability and stability as technical and human or social systems interact in new ways. There is no reason to expect the cyberspace system to differ in this respect (Freeman and Louça 2001; Perez 2002). Addressing questions about cyber trust and crime prevention within existing paradigms, however, will not suffice to alleviate concerns about threats in this environment. The contributors to this volume call for a stronger cross-disciplinary research effort that will build a better foundation for understanding key facets of the technical and human dimensions of cyberspace.[6]

2.3 CYBER TRUST AND CRIME PREVENTION: KEY ISSUES AND LESSONS

In this section, we provide a synthesis of the key issues and lessons that are raised in the chapters that follow. These are distilled to reveal where there are gaps in understanding, and to highlight the areas of consensus or controversy over future developments. We emphasize those areas where there is a need for measures to encourage more trustworthy cyberspace systems and improved strategies for crime prevention. In most cases, such measures will need to be underpinned by a stronger cross-disciplinary research effort.

The observation that cyberspace is a complex human and technical system is being accepted increasingly by experts and non-experts alike. What is less readily acknowledged or understood by stakeholders, including cyberspace system developers and users, is that the whole of this system is subject to unpredictable emergent behaviour, which may yield unintended results. This means that the balance between the anticipation of, and scanning for, new problems that provoke reactions is likely to favour the latter. More will need to be invested in searching for new forms of criminal activity, enabling versatile responses and ensuring that, in cases where remedies fail, there is sufficient redundancy in the system.

This means that at any given time, parts of the system will be relatively stable while other parts will not.[7] In addition, there will always be ambiguity surrounding the interpretation of research results. This is because the co-evolving components of cyberspace may combine to deliver a large number of possible outcomes, many of which will not have been anticipated. This observation has particular consequences for interventions aimed at improved crime prevention because interventions for other purposes may confound crime prevention. Nevertheless, there is sufficient evidence from existing studies of cyberspace developments and, more generally, from research in related areas of science and technology, to draw inferences about the outcomes associated with the most likely future developments. In the face of uncertainty and the need to strengthen the evidence base in key areas, decisions about the most effective crime prevention strategies must be considered in the light of ethical considerations and principles that are derived from plausible theories.

The existing scientific evidence can be applied to clarify some of the interdependencies between the human and technical components of cyberspace, especially in areas that have achieved a degree of stability. This suggests how interventions in cyberspace are likely to reverberate throughout the social and technical system, both locally and globally. The chapters in this volume demonstrate that nearly every area of cyberspace technology development and the components of the social system present new opportunities for criminal activity. Strategies to mitigate these involve numerous trade-offs and choices, some of which we consider here.

As the dynamics of the cyberspace system unfold, much will need to be done to build confidence both in people and in the 'mechanics' of cyberspace. As electronic services of all kinds continue to evolve, people will appraise cyberspace threats in different ways and ascribe to them quite different meanings. The variety of responses will depend on the way various people value the consequences of perceived threats. Therefore, a better understanding of the relationships between human factors, risk and trust is essential for the future security of cyberspace.

So far, relatively little attention has been given to analysis of the public perceptions of cyberspace risk. This is a major gap in the evidence base.[8] We can infer, however, from studies of the public perception of risk in other fields of science and technology that a set of complex risk factors is involved. This research indicates that future problems in and perceived dangers from cyberspace could be interpreted by the public as a failure of the technical system, as a failure on the part of system designers and users or as a failure in the governance model. It is also essential to bear in mind that reported perceptions of risk may not be aligned with the trust that people actually place in cyberspace technologies or in the individuals (and software agents) and institutions that govern cyberspace.

It is clear from research undertaken by organizations across Europe that the solutions to improving cyber trust and crime prevention in a pervasive computing environment will be quite different from those in use today. There will be a need for a new paradigm for cyberspace security, even in the face of the current situation in which the majority of potential users of cyberspace services and products have a poor understanding of security.

In Chapter 1 of this volume we posed several questions:

- Which cyber trust issues will be of dominant concern – what will be the new kinds of vulnerability and how will the risks of cyberspace be perceived?
- How will the overall structure of the emerging system drive the uptake of cyber trust technologies?
- What kinds of interventions might be made to influence the system's dynamics for the purpose of improving cyber trust and crime prevention?

Some answers to these questions are provided in the discussion that follows, but it is important to remember that addressing these questions within existing paradigms of trust, security and technology is unlikely to be enough to alleviate concerns about potential threats in this environment. A strengthened cross-disciplinary research effort is needed to create a better foundation for understanding important facets of the technical and human dimensions of cyberspace.

2.3.1 Dependable Software Systems and Commercial Issues

Part 2 of this volume focuses on constructing and using cyberspace systems. Technological innovations could affect many elements of the mesh of interacting and mutually dependent aspects of cyber trust and crime prevention. The dependability of pervasive and complex computing systems has a clear impact both on security and on risk. Recent thinking about the way large-scale pervasive computing systems are being developed emphasizes technical and human issues and the importance of managing risk and trust in cyberspace. There is a need to examine assumptions about the work organization of software engineering teams and collaborations between developers and between developers and end-users.

In Chapter 3 Cliff Jones and Brian Randell examine the dependability of pervasive and complex computing systems. Their analysis indicates that a deployment gap exists between software development methods and procedures, which are currently insufficiently robust to produce a more trustworthy network infrastructure and service applications. The dependability or 'trustworthiness' of a computer system refers to the ability to avoid computer system failures beyond an 'acceptable' level.

One key issue then is the level of failure that in the eyes of users would be regarded as being unacceptable. Another is the management of the software engineering process in which there are numerous dependencies and constraints. In response to the first issue, Jones and Randell argue that there is a need to develop fault prevention and removal techniques to maintain satisfactory service in the face of attacks on networks. In relation to management, there must be good project leadership and close involvement of the customer to ensure that the system meets required levels of dependability, and standards must be established against which system performance can be measured.

In large-scale software engineering projects there must be flexibility in the development process to allow responses to specific customer requirements and changes in the external environment. This means that it is essential that appropriately educated and experienced people work on the design and implementation of large software projects in order to avoid low levels of system dependability. If future networked computer systems are to attain higher levels of dependability or trustworthiness, considerably greater attention will need to be given both to commercial issues, which influence customer willingness to invest in such systems, and risk management.

Improved ways of managing the components of large-scale software projects will be needed. Whether these components are developed using proprietary or open source software code, and whether they rely on reusable code, the problems of managing the aggregation/disaggregation processes will remain.

It may become technically feasible to develop warrantable software and systems. This would require a software system development approach that: (1) enables the likely impact on system dependability of all design and deployment decisions and activities to be assessed throughout the system lifecycle; and (2) caters for system adaptation and the realities of huge, rapidly evolving, pervasive systems (see Chapter 3).

In this context the commercial relationship between those who commission a project and its developers and deliverers involves financial, functional and time risks, all of which need to be managed in an equitable manner. Contracting regimes may be based on fixed price or cost plus arrangements, but because of the difficulties of estimation and resource allocation and unexpected component integration problems, adherence to a rigid structure of contracting regimes often contributes to the failure of such projects. 'Best practice' codes can play a role, but adjustments and flexibility are needed in conjunction with a change manager with a very high level of expertise, experience and education.

Incentives for all parties involved in complex software projects to adopt best practice are essential, as is the maintenance of an intimate collaborative relationship on all aspects of a software project (Collins 2004). In addition to the methods for managing those risks related to technical, financial and timescale aspects, software development introduces two additional risks. The first involves estimation. The lack of any physical constraints raises considerable uncertainty as to how long a complex piece of software will take to develop.

To address this risk there is a need to achieve a balance between delivering functionality within the expected time and cost while not bounding the creativity of the software developer to deliver functional code. At present software development is seen as a mix of art and science. The challenge for software engineers in attempting to provide solutions to large complex problems is that the solution will also inevitably be very complex.

In addition the processes by which such complex artefacts are created are themselves complicated and ill-defined. Concentration on the modularity of functionality is leading to a neglect of the connectivity between the software modules (see Box 2.2).

Box 2.2 A holistic view of modularity

A holistic view of modularity and the links between modules is essential if the implicit decomposition that modularity implies is to be successful. Several engineering disciplines adopt holistic approaches to the design of large complex structures, including software engineering. While there are no physical laws, and the constraints are less rigorous and less well-shared within the project, it might benefit software engineering methods if the holistic approaches of other disciplines are evaluated for their applicability in the software engineering process (Collins 2004).

The second specific risk in large-scale software lies in the difficulty of accurately describing the relationship between critical elements of the requirements. The use of prototyping, rapid application development approaches or other approaches to risk reduction in areas of critical uncertainty within a project is essential. It is, in the main, people who write software. There is research ongoing looking at how software could be used to generate software, but up to now automatic software generation tools have not met with widespread success. For the foreseeable future, people will continue to play a critical role in the generation of software.

Greater efforts are needed to encourage a holistic view of software engineering in order to reduce the risks of software unreliability. Alongside this, there are divergent views about whether open source software developments will produce software that has greater reliability and dependability when employed on a large scale and as a component of hybrid proprietary and open source applications.

Achieving greater dependability of complex ICT systems in the future will require greater investment in training and education. On a global scale training in software engineering and computer science is increasing, but in the UK is on the wane. Efforts to improve this situation are being made by a number of bodies, but the skills and expertise available to British industry in this field are declining. The key issue is appropriate education to produce graduates that are capable of participating effectively in the development of large complex software projects (Collins 2004).

The skills base necessary to develop trustworthy software requires a body of experienced professionals who are appropriately certified or chartered. It also requires recognition from employers that it is imperative they recruit experienced people to work on projects to develop software. To ensure that such people are available, the overall qualifications of the labour pool must be continuously upgraded. Also there must be greater awareness of vulnerabilities among those who invest in the components of cyberspace systems. This would create stronger incentives to introduce measures aimed at reducing cyberspace system vulnerabilities.

A survey carried out by the UK Department of Trade and Industry and PricewaterhouseCoopers in April 2004 indicated a rapidly growing dependency in British industry and commerce on critical information held in computer systems and a general increase in the use of the Internet and the web in business.[9] These factors combined to give rise to an increase in security incidents of all types even though there was heightened awareness of the need for good security. This survey indicated the need for improvements across the board if businesses are to maintain or improve the dependability of services derived from the use of such systems.

Dependable pervasive systems will be constructed out of multiple existing systems and will also need to be highly adaptable. Most will embody human beings as system 'components'. The successful design and deployment of such systems is a major challenge that calls for expertise and socio-technical as well as technical dependability.

Cross-disciplinary approaches to research and operations are essential if any inroads are to be made in this field. Those that undertake research within technical and procedural disciplines that presently concentrate on particular types of systems, their dependability attributes, types of faults and means for achieving dependability, must interact with those researchers that tackle socio-technical issues, including design, usability, functionality specification, acceptable levels of failure, recovery modes and incident management, as well as 'best practice' and innovative approaches to project management and software engineering throughout the whole of the life cycle. If the practice of software engineering is strengthened by measures that enhance the dependability or trustworthiness of software systems, the opportunities for criminal attack or accidental failures could be minimized (see Chapter 3).

Those taking leadership in standards setting with respect to the testing and certification of all aspects of dependable systems, including autonomous software agents, could gain competitive advantage. If processes and systems are accredited by a national standards body, and this accreditation is seen elsewhere as having value, then practices, procedures and technical designs – especially with respect to networks and software – could spread rapidly producing externalities and a strong potential for global impact. However, for this to happen cyberspace systems developers and users would need to see a reasonable financial return, given the additional costs of more dependable systems. This suggests the need for investigation of the economic incentives that will arise in future markets and the links between these incentives, people's perceptions of risk and their willingness to trust networks despite their relatively low levels of dependability.

2.3.2 Managing Identity(ies) in Cyberspace

One of the most significant issues for crime prevention is the fact that in cyberspace users may choose to maintain their anonymity. In addition, new issues will be raised in areas where identification of users is essential for commercial services, or for access to such items as health records and income tax returns or for crime prevention, for example, the appropriate means of authentication of identity. In Parts 2 and 3 of this volume we have included reviews of the many instances where people, devices or digital data need to be identified and authenticated (see Chapters 4 and 10). In Chapter 4, Fred Piper, Matthew Robshaw and Scarlet Schwiderski-Grosche show how users (including computers, software agents, information objects and people) can be authenticated, based on something they own, something they know or something they are. The success of all these techniques, whether used alone or in combination, depends on the assumption that there has been an initial, accurate identification and then reliance being placed on that assumption. If the original identification is not conducted properly then there is a risk of error in later identification. There is also an assumption that a reliable trustworthy infrastructure is available over which the identification process is carried out. The engineering of solutions that make these assumptions valid is a non-trivial process, especially on the scale of the population of a nation.

Passwords, encryption and biometrics can be used to support a number of means of identification. The last offers a direct means of authentication but, even in this case, there is a risk of error insofar as no two biometric templates match perfectly. In using this type of authentication a Type 1 error may occur such that the system fails to recognize a valid user, or a Type 2 error may occur where the system accepts an impostor. The likelihood of such errors has implications for the usability of cyberspace systems and for the extent of actual and perceived risk. Decisions in this area will influence the perceived trustworthiness of the service applications that are supported by the cyberspace infrastructure, and raise questions about people's attitudes towards the use of biometrics.[10] One means of addressing this area will be to examine empirically how people respond to specific measures and how they perceive the trade-offs between intrusion and protection, and their respective benefits and costs. Use of biometrics will mean that it will not be possible to maintain multiple core identities for a given purpose without introducing considerable system and process complexity (see Chapter 4).

Identification is usually thought of in relation to people, to establish links with their rights to services or assets. When the services and assets are also in a digital form (documents, software that provides processes for financial services, money online, personal data held on government computers or movies bought online) the identity of these digital objects and processes also becomes a very important issue. This is not only to establish that the transaction is legal, carried out appropriately and with proper controls where necessary, but also to establish evidence for investigation or prosecution where criminal activity is suspected. These aspects of identification and identity management are poorly understood, in spite of the subject matter having been discussed for a long time both technically and socially (Collins 1996).

2.3.3 Cyberspace Usability, Risk Management and Security

Changes in the design of secure technologies and in social practices and cultural norms of information assurance influence the effectiveness of strategies to reduce crime and the threats arising from changes in information handling procedures. User identification and authentication mechanisms have an impact on security and, in addition, are tightly bound to tokens, passwords, encryption and the usability of these mechanisms by human agents.[11] Empirical research demonstrates that despite the availability of mechanisms that can be used to authenticate the identity of cyberspace users, many of these are hard to use or are rendered ineffective because of the demands they make on users. Unless users are given training in the use of those mechanisms that are available, human error will render them of little benefit (see Chapters 10 and 11).

In Chapter 10, Angela Sasse argues that the usability of such mechanisms as passwords, tokens and encryption depends on the organizational processes and the workflows that are involved as well as on the extent to which users believe themselves to be at risk. Similarly, in Chapter 11 James Backhouse and his colleagues summarize studies of organizational and behavioural change, demonstrating that effective risk management requires the development of a 'culture of security' where end-users, rather than their physically present or distant managers, take responsibility for monitoring risks and acting appropriately.[12] Although information security management codes have been developed, the complexity of cyberspace systems and the dangers of unwanted intrusion or attack mean that there will be an increasing need for the interoperation of management policies and new frameworks to ensure that security measures become more closely integrated into business processes. However, as Backhouse et al. point out, business models need to take account of different cultural practices which may lead to unanticipated system vulnerabilities. In parallel with the need for new approaches to software engineering and the design of large complex software systems, there is a need to foster 'persuasive design' techniques that reward cyberspace users for good security habits (see Chapter 10).

A key lesson from empirical research on security mechanisms and behaviours is that appropriate and effective security must be an integral part of the socio-technical system. Security needs to be integrated into all cyberspace development approaches. A central focus for crime prevention strategies may be the point at which people directly interface with the digital world. Research on cyberspace market evolution also suggests that as the cyberspace system evolves, a major area of development concerns the technical interfaces and standards that are used. These interfaces and standards are the vulnerable points in cyberspace in terms of security, and the risks associated with them will either be amplified or attenuated in the future (see Chapter 11).

The vast scale and scope of cyberspace also highlights the need to achieve greater reliability in the authentication of information and digital documentation, which may be accompanied by metadata describing a document's use and functionality. This raises issues of digital rights management (DRM), data and information ownership, identity and privacy. As agent software is used in an increasingly large number of cyberspace applications, the necessity for identification and authentication of software and data objects as well as people, as indicated above, will grow in importance.

There will continue to be a need for research into the security of technology and the effectiveness of identification processes used for important everyday processes. The questions that must be addressed on an ongoing basis are: (1) How much 'security' or 'strength' is appropriate? (2) What is the appropriate balance between procedural approaches and architectural solutions to reduce the risk of vulnerabilities arising as a result of human behaviour? (3) What kinds of education programmes could be used to highlight the need for compliance with local security policies?[13]

2.3.4 Cyberspace and Crime Prevention Strategies

Crime occurs in many forms and one way of depicting generic crime problems and solutions as a guide for future crime prevention strategies in cyberspace is within the misdeeds and security framework (see Table 2.1) This could be modified as further consideration is given to the risks encountered in cyberspace.

Cyberspace developments of this kind could be addressed in the context of crime prevention strategies through the further elaboration of 'criminal opportunity' models. Felson's (1987) routine activity theory, for example, has been used to encourage those responsible for crime prevention to consider the physical and virtual locations and times in everyday life when potential offenders are likely to become motivated by contact with vulnerable crime targets, especially in the absence of 'capable guardians' (see Chapter

11). In an extension of this model, efforts are being made to develop crime prevention activities to reduce the likelihood of the 'conjunction of criminal opportunity' (Ekblom 2003; Rogerson and Pease 2003).

Table 2.1 Cyberspace developments and risk and security measures

Misdeeds	Actions supporting security
Misappropriated (theft)	Secured against theft
Mistreated (damaged or injured)	Safeguarded against damage
Misused (for crime, including counter measures against prevention or enforcement)	Shielded against misuse
Mishandled (fraud, counterfeiting, smuggling, illegal divulgence)	Supporting – justice, crime reduction, community safety (facilitating arrest, forensics, identification, punishment, reassurance)
Misbehaved (disorder and antisocial behaviour)	Scam-proofed
Mistaken (false alarms, wrongful accusation, leading to miscarriage)	'Sivilized' – conducive to good behaviour
Mistrusted (non-reporting of crime to authorities)	Straightening adverse side-effects

Source: Adapted from Ekblom (2004a).

The conjunction of criminal opportunity model provides a means of systematically considering the conditions necessary for a crime to occur and the possibilities for prevention. It focuses both on the predispositions of potential offenders and on the immediate characteristics of the crime situation – in this case the online and offline situation of cyberspace users and the systems within which they operate (Ekblom 2002, 2003). With respect to the situation, the model signposts many factors that encourage crime. Crime prevention can be defined as an intervention that tackles the causes of criminal events to reduce the risk of their occurrence and/or the potential seriousness of their consequences. The causes of crime can be complex, but also remote and fairly weak. However, immediate causes are reducible to 11 generic precursors which act through common aspects of crime situations and of criminals – whether in the physical world or in cyberspace.

The conjunction of criminal opportunity occurs when a predisposed, motivated and equipped offender encounters, seeks or engineers a crime situation involving human, material or informational targets, enclosures (such as a building or a firewall), a wider environment (such as a shopping centre or a financial system) and people (or intelligent software agents), which are acting in diverse ways as crime preventers or promoters (see Table 2.2).

Table 2.2 Generic precursors of crime

Potential offender	Crime situation
Presence (including virtual) in crime situation without leaving traces	Target of crime (person, company, government; material goods, systems, information) that is vulnerable, attractive or provocative
Perception of risk, effort, reward and conscience and consequent decisions	Enclosure (safe, building, firewall) that is vulnerable, contains targets
Resources for crime (skills, weapons, knowledge, equipment, access to supporting network; *modus operandi* to maximize reward and minimize risk and effort, creating a crime opportunity)	Wider environment (town centre, airport, computerized financial system) that contains targets, generates conflict; favours concealment, ambush and escape over surveillance and pursuit
Readiness to offend (motivation, emotion, influenced by current life circumstances)	Absence of preventers (people or intelligent software) that make crimes less likely to happen
Lack of skills to avoid committing crime (literacy, social skills)	Presence of promoters (people, intelligent software) that make crime more likely, including careless individuals, reckless designers/manufacturers, deliberate fences and criminal service providers
Predisposition to criminality (personality, ideology)	

Source: Adapted from Ekblom (2004b).

Preventive interventions can act by interrupting, diverting or weakening any of these causes. Understanding these resources for offending is important because they influence the situation that crime preventers confront and the strength of the offender's predisposition and motivation to commit a crime (Ekblom and Tilley 2000).

Trust fits into this framework in several ways. An Internet shopper who is too trusting may act as a careless or negligent crime promoter, as may a system designer. Conversely, being an effective crime preventer means being equipped with appropriate applications and systems. Offenders exploit misplaced trust, sometimes to an expert degree, and are aided by software-

and hardware-based resources, for example, 'skimming' devices planted into cash machines to clone cards.

Efforts to improve the security of complex information systems often rely on the use of risk analysis to justify the cost of designing and implementing security features. The concept of a criminal opportunity can be used to understand the means of reducing crime opportunities in organizational contexts where threats to security are raised by dishonest staff (see Chapter 11); for example, the opportunities available to potential inside perpetrators of network-related crimes.

These approaches could be extended to examine the organizational contexts and behavioural characteristics that are most likely to give rise to criminal opportunities. Notwithstanding the development of these approaches, answers to questions about acceptable levels of dependability and trade-offs require an understanding of the nature of trusting behaviour among human and software agents and of the actual and perceived risk associated with cyberspace.

A key area in this context is ICT forensics. Data held on storage devices, such as the ubiquitous hard disk, can be put to criminal use. If they can be identified and authenticated, these data can provide evidence of malfeasance. In this context, the problem of identifying 'the original' is difficult and finding solutions to this problem is often glossed over. In the future, as the scale of cyberspace systems increases, the sheer volume of distributed stored data may overwhelm the capacity of the law enforcement agencies. As data management tools are developed, they are not likely to have the processes of auditability and traceability incorporated in them as required for evidence gathering. It will be necessary, therefore, to document these requirements, which in turn will require stakeholder collaboration to reach agreement on the principles and standards to be met.

As data are increasingly likely to be stored in jurisdictions beyond the reach of national law enforcement agencies, some form of international code of practice will be needed to enable access to data by the agencies involved in crime detection and criminal prosecutions. If the match between these data and a suspect with seemingly appropriate spatial, logical and temporal proof is insufficiently strong, the data will not stand up in court as evidence.[14] One objective in using forensic data could be to establish sufficient strength of 'binding' or linkage to allow other physical investigations to be instigated that would add to this evidence. This would require collaboration between system designers and legal and law enforcement specialists on an international scale.

The availability and growth in the use of mobile and transportable miniature mass storage devices that use strong encryption are very likely to expand enormously over the coming years. Reliance on the analysis of log files to identify when and where specific devices have accessed or are accessing systems and networks, and being able very rapidly and accurately to track subsequent use, seem the only means at present for tracing illegal activities. As the volume of encrypted material within which the criminal can conceal his or her activities increases, it is possible that where data are shown to be encrypted and not legitimate, they could be used to justify further investigations. Whether the public or private sector would be willing to bear the costs of very expensive tracking or endure rapidly spreading unprosecutable crime is an urgent subject for debate.

Forensic tools are being developed by a very small number of academic groups and companies to meet specific needs. Without some collaboration with their developers, the ability of investigators and computer forensic experts to maintain parity with the environment within which the data under investigation are used and stored, will be limited. The ability to carry out forensic investigations will need to be seen as a legitimate requirement placed on a system or application design if this situation is not to become worse. All of these issues need to be discussed, but it is unclear who should initiate it. There is some indication that cyberspace users do not want to know in advance of any potential weaknesses. Nevertheless, there is a need to consider what balance could be struck between evidential – investigative – preventative computer forensics, and the risks and benefits of the various options.

Up to now there has been little fundamental research into the issues of the scale of cyberspace and the criminal use of data, especially that stored outside the jurisdictions of law enforcement agencies, and the ethical, social, economic and legal strategies that might be adopted. There is a need for cross-disciplinary research in the area of ICT forensics and cyber-evidence management. Enhancement of trustworthiness itself will reduce the likelihood of malfeasance by temptation, but without strong cyber policing, the determined criminal will find in the use of ICTs and the applications that will be running on the Internet, a 'honey pot' of opportunity and illegal gain.

2.3.5 Trust and Risk in Cyberspace

The trustworthiness of the 'space' implemented by the use of pervasive ICTs will only be enhanced when we have a deeper understanding of how knowledge, the currency of the knowledge society and the economy, can be managed throughout its life cycle, both by people and agents, interactively and collaboratively, in such a way that outcomes of transactions and interactions are predictable, at least generically, and are perceived as being reasonably safe. To achieve this it will be necessary for the barriers to criminal or socially unacceptable use of ICTs to be sufficiently high to minimize opportunities for unpredictable interactions associated with behaviours that are not socially valued. The way system components interact dynamically to add value to society, and the way critical technologies support social processes that may lead to cyberspace crime prevention both need to be understood from a variety of perspectives.

The extent to which people are likely to accept government intervention or controls over their behaviour in cyberspace depends upon whether they are informed about the potential risks of cyberspace and whether they perceive themselves to be at risk. It is unclear whether the technical possibility of risk in cyberspace is the same as the reality of the perception and experience of risk. We are in the early stages of creating an evidence base to assess whether people act according to their perceptions of risk or their experience of actual incidents in cyberspace. These factors influence people's willingness to place their trust in cyberspace. As in other areas of technological innovation, cyberspace is being developed in an environment that Beck (1992) and Giddens (1991) have called the 'risk society'.

Many assumptions about trust and risk in cyberspace are made by technology developers and users. These assumptions are examined in Part 3 in order to understand why there are divergent views about person-to-person, person-to-system and system-to-system trust in cyberspace and to suggest some implications for crime prevention.

There is a growing body of literature that provides insight into whether the technical possibility of risk in cyberspace is the same as the perception and actual experience of risk. We can gain insight into perceptions of risk in cyberspace by drawing upon research into the way members of the public have been found to appraise uncertainty and the risks associated with scientific and technological innovations (see Chapters 7 and 8). In Chapter 8, Jonathan Jackson, Nick Allum and George Gaskell review research indicating that the social meaning of a risk will influence its salience and the way uncertainty is judged. People's perceptions of risk are related to their cultural and social values, their attitudes to blame, their morality and how they view an event, such as an intrusion, that reveals their identity in cyberspace. In addition, the attitude of the public towards experts and regulators can be expected to influence the way cyberspace risks are interpreted. Risk perception is also intimately linked to levels of trust.

These observations rely on theories and empirical research in the fields of cognitive psychology, psychometric analysis and studies of risk and emotion (see Chapter 8). There is also evidence from studies in the field of media and communications that people's perceptions of risk are strongly influenced by the symbols within their social networks and in the media's reporting of events. There is empirical evidence based on people's stories about their perceptions of risk that suggests that whereas experts see risks as chains of cause and effect, laypeople tend to see them in a social context of relationships. Research is needed to assess the importance of these observations for cyberspace and crime prevention. This body of research helps to explain why probabilistic analyses of actual risk may vary considerably from analyses that take the context of cyberspace experience into account in a qualitative way.

It is also important to distinguish between reported perceptions of trust and the way in which people actually conduct their lives. We have little evidence of the extent of inconsistency between reports of mistrust in individuals or institutions and the capacity to place trust in various parts of the socio-technical system (O'Neill 2002).

The literature on risk perception suggests that perceived risk may be amplified or attenuated depending on a large number of socio-technical factors. The Social Amplification of Risk Framework (SARF) has been developed as a means of integrating disparate approaches to risk (Kasperson et al. 2003; and see Chapter 8). The SARF:

> ... aims to examine broadly, and in social and historical context, how risk and risk events interact with psychological, social, institutional, and cultural processes in ways that amplify and attenuate risk perceptions and concerns, and thereby shape risk behavior, influence institutional processes, and affect risk consequences. (Pidgeon et al. 2003, p. 2)

Debate among adherents to different positions with regard to the risks people will encounter or perceive in cyberspace are informed by very different knowledge claims (Callon 2003; Rosa 2003). The SARF could be further developed to understand why some risks associated with cyberspace attract particular social and political attention (risk amplification), even when experts judge them to be relatively unimportant. Application of the SARF could produce a new frame in which to evaluate the likely effectiveness of crime prevention strategies.

We know that trust is a means for alleviating risks, but there is little empirical research on the conditions under which people are prepared to trust others in cyberspace or to trust in the trustworthiness of cyberspace systems. Yet, with the spread of access to global networks, it is clear that in many circumstances people are willing to trust in each other in cyberspace and in the notion that system-to-system interdependencies and relationships are trustworthy. Empirical research in the fields of human–computer interaction and computer-mediated communication is beginning to provide insight into person-to-person and person-to-system trust in cyberspace as indicated by Angela Sasse in Chapter 10. Key variables influencing trust include: the number of actors involved; the types of actors; whether relationships are conducted synchronously or asynchronously; the availability of trust-warranting properties and signals to convey those properties; prior experience and the propensity to trust; and the perceived benefits and risks of trusting behaviour.

It is clear that growing numbers of interactions are occurring between people who have never met 'in real life', and exchanges of a social and commercial nature are increasing, indicating that whatever the explanation of the basis for trust, people do act as if they trust 'virtual' others in many instances. For example, in the commercial world, people are buying and selling goods from each other on eBay, spending hours playing computer games and dating via instant messaging. Massively Multiplayer Online Games (MMOGs) involve increasing numbers of people in buying and selling imaginary 'property' and avatars. Games-players have invented a currency for exchange, the total value of which in 2001 was estimated as equivalent to the gross domestic product (GDP) of a relatively wealthy country (Tyrrell 2004). More and more government services are being provided online, giving rise to new means of accessing information and of communicating between all the actors in the social system. These relationships are possible only to the extent that people behave as if they trust in each other and in the systems they use.

It seems that as more information exchanges are mediated by technology, the responsibility for supporting trust will increasingly fall on cyberspace system designers and operators. Studies of trusting behaviour provide suggestions for the types of factors that are likely to influence software agent-based behaviour in contexts where system-to-system trust must be established. However, most of the research in this area is conducted using stylized game-theoretic models, which limit the number of variables that can be examined in a given 'game' and are difficult to populate with data reflecting the experiences of cyberspace users.[15]

Economic analysis suggests that the propensity to trust another person or software agent is partly informed by expectations (see Chapters 12 and 13). In Chapter 12, Jonathan Cave demonstrates how agents' expectations can be modelled probabilistically to provide insight into the likelihood that choices about whether or not to trust will yield various outcomes. Such game-theoretic approaches assume that an agent's decision to participate in a game involves trust that the other actor(s) will behave as expected. The outcomes of the games are influenced by the completeness of the institutional framework (laws, rules and standards), by the completeness of the information available to the agents in the game and the network structure of the game that is established at the outset (see Chapter 12).

One application of this approach is a coordination game in which it is feasible to establish whether high or low trust equilibria will emerge if all the agents interact in a fully connected network according to a prespecified set of rules, and definitions of trustworthiness. One of the assumptions in this approach is that the players engaged in a game will act rationally and this allows their behaviour to be predicted. This approach facilitates understanding of the consequences of precautions that may be taken to avoid crime in the face of externalities. Research in this area helps to demonstrate when such measures are likely to affect the risk to others and when it is appropriate to transfer the cost of protection to others, that is, from the cyberspace system developer to the end-user firm or the consumer. This work suggests that it is the distribution rather than the level of trust that supports the setting of priorities for establishing trust relationships and establishes a structure for negotiating the distribution of liabilities arising from cyberspace interactions (see Chapter 12).

In recent years there has been a revival of the concept of social capital in which trust is a major component. This concept can be applied to examine the positive effects expected from networks of trusted agents. Drawn from studies in sociology, human geography and economics, it has been suggested that societies with a more complex and dense pattern of networked social relations may benefit from lower transaction costs and stronger assumptions about whether agents will act opportunistically. Edward Steinmueller suggests in Chapter 13 that this approach could be extended in the future to examine the way networks or webs of trust emerge in virtual communities of various kinds. There is a need to better understand how social capital can be fostered in cyberspace.

Just as there is uncertainty about how best to design and operate trustworthy or dependable cyberspace systems, the trusting behaviour and trustworthiness of human and software agents are not clearly understood. In the light of this uncertainty, it is important to consider cyber trust and crime prevention issues in terms of the ethical issues, especially with respect to identity, anonymity and privacy. In cases where the evidence base is weak, we also need to rely on principles derived from plausible theories. We have seen that cyberspace security systems often require identity authentication, but the Internet is currently designed to facilitate the way people can 'play' with their identity. This will remain the case as long as the design and architecture of the Internet provides for anonymous communications.[16]

2.3.6 Ethical Considerations for Cyberspace

Views are divided about the ethical justification for interventions in cyberspace that seek to limit this potential. From an ethical standpoint, this suggests the need for a forum in which those who remain sceptical of the need for security interventions to prevent crime indicate their requirement for justification of changes that might limit the scope for anonymity. However, in Chapters 8 and 14 evidence is presented demonstrating why it is so difficult to discuss these key issues in generic open forums. The principal difficulties are the extent to which different meanings become attached to the perceptions of risk and danger, uncertainty about how the media are likely to influence opinion in this area, and the strongly polarized views about the origins and appropriate future of the Internet.

Kieron O'Hara argues in Chapter 14 with respect to these polarized views about the Internet, that while some seek to place the burden of proof on those that wish to alter the libertarian and open principles underpinning the Internet as we know it today, others argue that although recognizing certain privileged activities such as science or commerce must be able to continue in a secure way, liberty and openness are the important values. The judgements, however, might be made by those with political power, in which case the trade-offs between individual privacy and the benefits of greater collective security would need to be taken account of in such a way that specific issues would be considered and assessed as transparently as possible.

From a moral standpoint, some regard trust as the effect of good behaviour while others regard it as being the cause of good behaviour. Some argue that liberty and openness are essential and non-negotiable in cyberspace; others want to alter the design of cyberspace to make inappropriate behaviour more difficult (O'Hara 2004 and see Chapter 14). Different views about the moral arguments supporting different approaches to crime prevention strategies for cyberspace hinge on the extent to which actors are presumed to be rational and are likely to act to maximize their own self-interest. In an environment where there are multiple complete or partial identities, standard assumptions about what motivates actors need, at the very least, to be carefully scrutinized.

This argument mirrors a major ethical debate about the purpose of the Internet and the limits of its regulation. Castells (2001) and others argue that openness is deeply embedded in the architecture of the Internet.[17] They suggest that cyberspace technology is inherently supportive of values such as passion, freedom, social worth, caring and creativity; values that are prevalent within the 'hacker' community. They argue that these values need to be defended in the face of efforts to achieve control for purposes such as crime prevention.

Others such as O'Siochru and Constanza-Chock (2003) and Surman and Reilly (2003) suggest that the picture is more complicated. While evidence shows that civil society organizations are making much greater use of cyberspace tools, the extent to which such use is dependent upon maintaining all of the original features of the Internet's architecture is unclear. In addition, many uses of the Internet may be associated with actions across the spectrum of values and political aims. The relationships between the spread of the Internet and issues of privacy, vulnerability and security in the broader context of ethical and political considerations, mainly in the US, have been examined (Latham 2003). In the UK and with a more international orientation, empirical work has been undertaken on the use of the Internet for criminal activities, but it tends to focus on near-term developments and technologies rather than on the technological landscape that is likely to emerge in future decades (Thomas and Loader 2000; Wall 2001).

Having originated in the West, the Internet has a Western bias, which tends to inform debate and policies for crime prevention. On the one hand, it can be argued that actors should be allowed to pursue their conception of what is 'good' (if this does not interfere with others). On the other hand, it can be argued that there should be no departure from Western principles and their implications for crime or cyber terrorism. It is also possible, however, to argue that the key issue is the privileges that people should have in cyberspace, thus enabling debate about this to become a political problem that may be addressed through compromise and various social policy measures (see Chapter 14).

Positions on this issue are closely linked to the role of the media and strategies for building awareness of the risks in cyberspace, and about trust and the trustworthiness of cyberspace. As with other issues where there is uncertainty and a possibility of the amplification of risk, if there is to be informed and reasoned debate about these issues then citizens must be well informed about cyber trust and crime prevention issues.

Technologists sometimes make a distinction between the 'real' world and cyberspace. The spaces and means of access may be quite different, but research increasingly shows that many aspects of human behaviour remain constant (Mansell and Steinmueller 2000).[18] It seems unlikely that the majority of people will alter their basic behaviours, ethical stances and morality when they enter cyberspace. In fact although criminals – or those who seek to exploit others – will think of new forms of attack, most people are likely to find ways of translating conventionally understood norms and practices into cyberspace. When people understand that there are certain ethical and moral requirements, they may be more likely to adopt and demand them. Helping them to acquire that understanding is a key challenge for crime prevention.

For this reason, we need to consider the ethical standpoint from which it is feasible to argue that interventions in cyberspace to improve crime prevention are reasonable. O'Neill argues that a critical approach to practical reason 'does not take the expression of the basic norms of a community or of one's own personal commitments as intrinsically rational' (O'Neill 2000, p. 26). Instead, the standards for taking action should be whether the guidance provided to those with a capacity to act can be recommended universally without damage to others, and whether they can be understood. Any measures to secure cyberspace through building trust and trustworthy systems raise numerous ethical issues, and discussions are needed to discern the interesting ways in which standard ethical concepts map onto cyberspace (see Chapter 14).

The government, the private sector, citizens and civil society groups – as well as the traditional and alternative media outlets – will continue to draw attention to many of the problems and issues in this area.[19] The debates that ensue will not all be based on reasoned argument, and the provenance of some of the information upon which these debates rely may be difficult or impossible to trace. However, as awareness of cyberspace risk and vulnerability continues to spread, there are growing numbers of forums (national and international) that are seeking to foster critical and reasoned debate and to adopt measures to tackle specific issues. This highlights the importance of ongoing monitoring by governments and other actors of opportunities to facilitate such debates such that consideration is given to the feasibility and appropriateness of actions proposed to limit crime.

Existing theory and empirical evidence do not support unambiguous conclusions in this area. This is to be expected given the emergent properties of a complex system. Similarly, there are a substantial number of models and perspectives on trust and trustworthiness in cyberspace, but these enable relatively few inferences to be drawn about trust and trustworthiness. One of the difficulties of translating the results of existing research into practical solutions for crime prevention is that many conceptual frameworks and models are based on strict parameters and assumptions, and some approaches do not lend themselves to empirical verification.

Those that can be analysed empirically often yield results that are open to different interpretations depending on views about how opinions are influenced by the media and other psychological and sociological factors. In addition, even though the use of computers and the Internet has reached a reasonably high level in the UK, the more advanced components of cyberspace systems have yet to diffuse widely. Globally too, usage is very uneven and interactions are widely dispersed, in many cases adding to the difficulties involved in understanding trust and risk perception and the ethical issues raised with respect to interventions in cyberspace. This area is another major gap in the evidence base necessary to support more effective crime prevention strategies.

2.3.7 New Cyberspace Technologies and Trust

Various models of trust are being applied in two important areas of technical development – knowledge technologies and the semantic web, and software agent-based systems (see Chapters 5 and 6). These areas are likely to be critical for the development of cyberspace. The authors of Chapters 5 and 6 examine how concepts of trust and risk are being modelled and whether there is reason to be concerned about knowledge management and the information aspects of cyberspace.

Knowledge technologies and the semantic web are enabled by technological developments that allow much more intelligent machine engagement with the documents, services and other objects on the World Wide Web. Kieron O'Hara and Nigel Shadbolt show in Chapter 5 how they manipulate and create knowledge – that is, usable information – within a context. Developments in this area illustrate how concepts of trust are being applied that influence the future utility of cyberspace in providing users access to structured, contextually sensitive mechanisms and services that potentially allow them to work, live and interact in virtual communities that contain some of the social properties available to them in the real world.

Many modern computer applications are open distributed systems in which the (very many) constituent components are spread throughout a network in a decentralized control regime that is subject to constant change throughout the system's lifetime. Examples include peer-to-peer computing, the semantic web, the grid,[20] web services, e-business, m-commerce, autonomic computing, and pervasive computing environments. In all of these cases there is a need to have autonomous components that act and interact in flexible ways in order to achieve their design objectives in uncertain and dynamic environments. Given this, as Sarvapali Ramchurn and Nicholas Jennings indicate in Chapter 6, agent-based computing has been advocated as the natural computation model for such systems.

Work on knowledge technologies and on the semantic web requires a certain degree of trust in the means of ensuring that the input to knowledge and information manipulation processes are trustworthy (see Chapter 5). The available tactics for imbuing trust include transparency, ownership rules, the means to extend trust between sub-networks, certification, restriction of entry, formal methods, calculations, interrogation and knowledge management. Research in this area shows that each of these tactics has costs and benefits and that they must be combined with effective trust management strategies for the software systems – including the use of metadata and ontologies for trust requirements. Use of all of these tactics raises questions with respect to identity, anonymity and privacy.

Effective procedures for maintaining knowledge bases will need to be developed to ensure that as sharing of knowledge in a controlled way becomes a major influence on commercial and social behaviour, the sources used are maintained and exploited in ways that ensure they can be trusted. At present the end-user's perspective on these issues is not well understood.

If cyberspace systems are to become more dependable and secure there will need to be changes in the design and implementation of the ICT components that take account of high level protocols for reciprocity. Agent-based computing is regarded as a means of achieving this. Software agents have to trust each other in order to minimize the uncertainty associated with their interactions and take account of individual and system-level trust (see Chapter 6). In both cases, there is a need for protocols that ensure the software and human agents will find no better option than telling the truth and interacting honestly with each other. This is a major challenge for the future.

A problem related to research aimed at examining end-user perceptions of trust and the trustworthiness of cyberspace is that it is difficult to define trust in a way that is meaningful for survey respondents. This problem is addressed by William Dutton and Adrian Shepherd in Chapter 7 in their analysis of confidence and risk on the Internet. Definitions based on rational expectations and game theoretic models are difficult to apply in social surveys. However, trust can be defined as: 'a firm belief in the reliability or truth or strength etc. of a person or thing. ... *a confident expectation. ...* reliance on the truth of a statement etc., without examination' (Pearsall and Trumble 1996, p. 1546). The Oxford Internet Institute used this definition when it conducted the first large-scale survey of Internet use in the UK in 2003. Some of the results with respect to issues of cyber trust are summarized in Box 2.3.

Box 2.3 Results of first Oxford Internet Survey

Results based on a survey of 2030 respondents aged 14 and upwards in the UK showed that well over half – 59 per cent were using the Internet. Experience on the Internet tends to engender a higher level of cyber trust. Users of the Internet have more certainty and more confidence in the information and people they can access than do non-users, and many non-users have no opinion about the Internet's trustworthiness. Greater proximity to the Internet tends to instil more trust to some extent. Those who use the Internet more, for example for shopping online, are somewhat more likely to expose themselves to spam, email and other bad experiences. This tends to undermine trust in the Internet and raise concerns about risks. Those with more formal education tend to be somewhat more sceptical of the information and people accessible on the Internet, but also somewhat less concerned about the risks of Internet use (see Chapter 7).

The survey results suggest that the relationship between information about the Internet and uncertainty and trust varies along many dimensions, including the extent of experience in using online forms of communication (see Chapter 7). Trust appears to be enhanced as people learn more about the technology, but experience over time may also create new uncertainties and perceptions of risk. Individuals with more formal education tend to be somewhat more sceptical of the information and people accessible via the Internet, but also somewhat less concerned about the risks of Internet use. Evidence and analysis are needed to gain a better understanding of the underlying social dynamics and learning processes that are involved.

The problems associated with the 'digital divide' are likely to persist even when people have obtained access to cyberspace. Evidence from the Oxford Internet Survey suggests that there is lower trust of the Internet among categories of users such as the less affluent or the disabled (see Chapter 7). For these groups, experience in using the Internet has a particularly disproportionate positive impact, increasing their trust in the Internet and lessening their preconceived concerns about risks. Education and exposure to the Internet may offer a general strategy for coping with the risks and threats to the perceived trustworthiness of this technology. However, education and exposure to the Internet are skewed towards higher socio-economic groups. As a result, these strategies could actually reinforce the digital divide in access to the Internet. Other survey data (MORI 2003) suggest that there is considerable public ignorance about what happens to personal data when they are used by public agencies. Overall, there is a gap in the evidence base in this area partly because of the lack of comparable and systematic data.

2.3.8 Cyberspace Market Evolution, the Policy Context and Privacy

Incentives for investing in the deployment of more trustworthy networks and applications depend substantially on the dynamics of the market and how markets interact with legislation (and its enforcement) and policy intervention. Research on the economic dynamics of the evolution of cyberspace technology and service markets is reviewed in Chapter 12 and the interaction of these features with policy measures and the legislative environment is considered in Chapter 9, with a special emphasis on privacy protection. A key observation about market dynamics and the changing legislative policy context is that the development of cyberspace is a global phenomenon. In the future, monitoring global developments will continue to be very important. Effective monitoring across a wide range of issues is essential for effective national crime prevention strategies.

The special characteristics of these markets are an important consideration in understanding how cyberspace technologies will evolve and whether there will be incentives to invest in more dependable and secure systems. Industrial structure, conduct and performance analysis can be used to address this issue. The analysis in Chapter 12 by Jonathan Cave shows how asymmetrical information between firms and their customers can produce customer lock-in, often leading to the emergence of dominant firms. Firms will use trust in a variety of ways, sometimes to achieve a form of lock-in to the market, which is in a 'low-trust equilibrium' in which there are few incentives to invest in more dependable systems.

In cases where there are few suppliers competing in the market, a small number of supplier firms can influence the rate of investment in new technologies through their influence over supply and price. In addition, the analysis in Chapter 12 suggests that when firms compete in electronic marketplaces they encounter new opportunities for using anonymity in ways that make their participation in potentially collusive agreements difficult to detect. At the same time, new technologies can be used by firms to monitor customer behaviour and allegiance to firms because of the customer-related information that is available as a result of new information management systems.

The way that the various components of market exchanges in cyberspace may favour concentration is suggested in Box 2.4.

Box 2.4 Forces for cyberspace market concentration

Achieving trust in cyberspace payments favours the prominence of financial intermediaries. This may become a force for increasing market concentration. A firm's prominence also increases risk by making a larger target for fraudulent activities, that is, 'phishing' attacks on online banking sites and transactions service providers (*Independent* 2003). Market prominence may reinforce concentration in the fulfilment phase where the selling party may be located in another (even an unknown) jurisdiction in which pursuing consumers' rights may be difficult or expensive. The follow-up stage of relations with consumers also highlights the importance of signalling. Verified information (for example, quality certification by independent third parties) or assurance may advantage players with greater capacities to invest in these signals. This may favour increased market concentration (see Chapter 12).

From the customer's perspective, the analysis of cyberspace markets highlights the way new technologies may increase competition by augmenting consumer search capabilities through the use of search engines as intermediaries. However, intermediaries may not act solely in the consumer's interest, given the economic incentives that drive their operations. In addition, in areas such as financial intermediation and electronic payment systems, greater trust may enable such intermediaries to encourage increasing market concentration. Cyber trust agents are essential if effective competition in electronic markets is to be fostered, but it remains uncertain whether the market for certification services will grow rapidly in the future (see Chapter 12).

The demand for security solutions will be influenced strongly by the costs involved in switching between cyberspace security products on the market. Economic analysis suggests that the sustainability of trust relationships in cyberspace markets may actually depend on asymmetry among the participants. 'Improvements' or measures designed to enhance the security of cyberspace products, leading to greater symmetry in the marketplace, may actually undermine trust. This indicates again that it is the distribution of trust rather than its level that is central to future economic outcomes and whether they foster technologies that reduce or exacerbate cyberspace vulnerabilities (see Chapter 12).

The evolution of the UK's crime prevention strategies will, in part, result from international cooperation. Some observers are concerned that the spread of global networks is outstripping the pace of law makers (Goodman et al. 2002). Although considerable international work is under way in this area, there are few signs that there will be efforts to adopt a formal treaty (Bryen 2002). This means that there is unlikely to be a clear international framework within which to consider the implications of crime prevention strategies for privacy as cyberspace develops.

In the European Union a very high priority is being given to ensuring that Europe achieves competitiveness in the global knowledge-based economy. The Union's Lisbon strategy outlined policies, measures and actions that are expected to strengthen Europe's performance by accelerating the transition to the knowledge-based economy, 'while preserving – and modernizing – Europe's unique social welfare model and decoupling economic growth from environmental damage' (European Commission 2003, p. 31). This intention to stimulate economic growth depends partly on leadership in the development and use of ICTs in ways that are both efficient and socially valued.

In some areas, such as technical standards and organizational practices to achieve improved risk management and crime reduction, the UK is well placed to take the lead. It is argued by some that any measures (formal legislative or self-regulatory) that might discourage the early commercial introduction of advanced applications, but which have not been fully certified for dependability, could slow the pace of ICT innovation and reduce the competitiveness of the European economy. Others argue that it is essential to create economic incentives for cyber-technology suppliers and end-users to invest in greater levels of dependability and security even if this may slow the rate of diffusion of the most advanced technologies.

The parameters of the European Union's existing legislative framework, which affects decisions about cyber trust and crime prevention, are complex and involve numerous interdependencies (RAND Europe 2003a, b). At the European Union level, relevant legislation comes from directives on privacy and electronic communications, electronic commerce, telecommunications, data protection and consumer policy. As European legislation is transposed into the UK's legislation, its combination with specific laws in which the UK retains full national jurisdiction is creating a veritable jungle of law making.[21]

These combinations can produce contradictory outcomes: in some cases they foster greater privacy protection, while in others they sanction measures that, for crime prevention purposes, alter the extent to which information about individuals is revealed.

This issue is considered in Chapter 9 by Charles Raab. Given that perceptions about privacy are closely related to the acceptance of measures to enhance the security of cyberspace, the question as to whether the prevailing 'privacy paradigm' is consistent with the need to assess the requirements for improved crime prevention strategies is a crucial one.

Privacy protection, in particular, relies on many international instruments, national legislation, self-regulatory or voluntary tools, and privacy enhancing technologies or PETs (see Chapter 9). Research in this area suggests that PETs cannot provide a 'magic bullet' to solve privacy problems or address issues of identity authentication. It is much more likely that a mix of instruments will have to be applied to protect privacy alongside instruments and technologies that are consistent with equity considerations and the collective interests of society.

Given the complexity of cyberspace and varying levels of dependability or trustworthiness, future developments will create new possibilities for opportunistic crime and for privacy intrusions. Although technical solutions to provide communications and transactions with rigorous authentication may eventually provide a foundation for a higher level of trust in cyberspace, they will also create new threats to privacy. One possibility is, as suggested by John Edwards in Chapter 15, to encourage the development of relatively fine-grained 'digital principles' to complement the security and privacy guidelines developed by organizations such as the OECD (2002). Such self-regulatory arrangements might build on developments in autonomous software agent computing, but will raise issues of privacy protection and surveillance.

Surveys in many Western countries suggest that people generally have high and increasing levels of concern about privacy (Bennett 1992; Bennett and Raab 2003; and see Chapter 9). While this could be attributed to reports from various pressure groups or to press coverage of data protection issues, the important point in the context of cyber trust and crime prevention is that discussions about privacy generally presume that balance is the main feature of policy responses aimed at protecting individual interests in privacy and other rights and responsibilities.

This view has been criticized by those who believe that insufficient weight is given in the conventional privacy paradigm to collective or community interests. In the future it will be necessary to examine distributional issues and equity concerns within the conventional privacy paradigm. This will mean examining who enjoys what privacy and why. This view is another feature of the 'digital divide', suggesting that insofar as there are inequalities in the distribution of privacy protection, the issues need to be treated as a social policy concern.

Very little is known about the distribution of privacy protection in terms of typical socio-economic and demographic categories. Empirical research is needed on this issue. The results would enable privacy protection to be treated as an element of social policy. It could then be debated, together with collective security, in terms of alternatives, such as public or private provision, the costs and benefits, rights and entitlements, and the best way to secure privacy. This is important given that crime prevention will be used to protect citizens from infringements of their privacy, for example as a result of the theft of their identities. Better understanding of the distributional characteristics of privacy protection would provide an evidence base for considering whether inequalities can be justified and whether public policy and its implementation can alter them (see Chapter 9).

This raises the issue of how much information about our identities is required for crime prevention purposes and what should constitute informed consent (see Box 2.5). Research indicates that some people have low levels of trust in those who currently and in the future will manage their personal data in both the public and private sectors.

Box 2.5 Identity and identity cards

Supporters of compulsory identity cards in the UK maintain that around 90 per cent of the population already carry identifying information on plastic cards, and an identity (ID) card would be more convenient resulting in the necessity for fewer cards to be carried. Card holders exercise 'informed consent' regarding their cards. However, combining information on one card would potentially facilitate the linking together of different pieces of information about an individual's identity. The implications of this need to be considered in the light of the fact that consent to reveal a 'piece of ourselves' in one context does not necessarily imply consent in another context (Rogerson and Pease 2003).

In addition, few of the most frequently used websites meet basic privacy standards (Electronic Privacy Information Centre 1997). Although cookies can be disabled, most people do not have the technical expertise to do this and know little about firewalls and other protection mechanisms (Rogerson and Pease 2003). Many of the tools being developed for use in cyberspace, such as encryption, digital signatures, digital pseudonyms and anonymous re-mailers, are also available to criminals and terrorists. It may also be the case that too great a focus on limiting encryption may be at the expense of more effective, yet less intrusive, crime prevention interventions. This may also apply to the excessive use of closed circuit television (CCTV) surveillance as discussed in Box 2.6.

Ekblom (1996) argues that the goal should be to reduce crime to 'tolerable' levels, while Kleinig (2000) suggests that a level of crime must be tolerated if it cannot be diminished without incurring unacceptable privacy intrusions. What is 'unacceptable' is partly a matter for empirical research into citizens' beliefs and preferences, but it is also a matter for ethical debate.

Box 2.6 CCTV surveillance and crime prevention

Unimaginative implementation of CCTV may be contributing to concerns associated with the extension of its use. Von Hirsch (2000) recommends that CCTV should be limited to the tracking of activity within a specific location over time, providing a record of activity for inspection when, and only when, an offence is known to have taken place. Constant surveillance involves growing intrusion of privacy and the crime prevention benefits need to be sufficiently high to justify this and also should directly benefit those being monitored. The effectiveness of CCTV as a crime prevention mechanism has not been empirically demonstrated (Welsh and Farrington 2002). The use of CCTV may lead to more self-policing as people aim to avoid being wrongly identified as criminals (Palmer 2000). CCTV can be used to track individuals using human or software agents to identify faces, suspicious behaviour or a potentially criminal 'gait'. This raises issues of the ethics of crime prevention and whether class or other interests shape efforts designed to prevent crimes (Rogerson and Pease 2003).

There are different interests and vantage points as to what constitutes 'acceptable' and 'unacceptable' levels of protection, as suggested by the following:

> there is evidence that citizens are reacting to new anti-terrorism surveillance measures by calling for more checks and balances within their own democratic state structures. However, market agents are utilizing new technologies to collect personal data, mostly in the absence of effective enforcement of privacy protection legislation, in order to financially benefit from their further processing and use. (IPTS 2003, p. 19)

Crime prevention measures to tackle crime linked to global networks in the future will rely on models that yield predictions and crime scenarios (Levi 2001). The perception of risk in cyberspace and of the acceptability of using intrusive technologies to monitor potentially criminal behaviour may become amplified or may be attenuated depending on a wide variety of factors, many of which have come to light as a result of the review of existing scientific evidence. It seems clear, however, that much more will need to be done to ensure that cyberspace developments do not lead to the exacerbation of existing criminal opportunities or to new ones.

Charles Raab suggests in Chapter 9 that the development of a Privacy Impact Assessment (PIA) methodology would provide a basis for assessing the actual or potential effects that an activity or policy may have for individual privacy (Raab 1995; Stewart 1996). Further development could help to answer questions such as whether we should see cyberspace and various practices as being safe until proven dangerous, or dangerous until proven safe. A system where the role of the 'precautionary principle' in privacy protection is more explicit could become increasingly important (European Commission 2000; European Union Council 1999; and see Chapter 9), especially if consideration is given to how and when (and when not) to apply it. Measures will be needed to resolve tensions between individual privacy and collective security and to assess the adequacy and enforceability of data protection and freedom of information legislation. Resolution of ethical issues in the contexts where privacy issues come to the fore will play a key role in determining the acceptability of crime prevention measures.

2.4 CONCLUSION: LESSONS FOR THE FUTURE

The scientific evidence yields insights into the way technical innovation is intersecting with human capacities for learning about cyberspace developments. In each of the areas addressed in this book there are uncertainties about the trade-offs that will accompany future human and technical measures to develop more dependable and secure cyberspace systems to minimize the risk of new 'conjunctions of criminal opportunity'. Some of these trade-offs are summarized in Table 2.3.

Table 2.3 Cyberspace and the potential trade-off

Software dependability	User requirements, cost and complexity
Identification	Anonymity
Authentication of software, data objects and people	Privacy protection
Type 1 false rejection errors	Type 2 false acceptance errors
Cyberspace security	Cyberspace usability
Risk	Trust and trustworthiness
Libertarian, open networks	Network control, surveillance
Informed debate	Risk amplification
Individual privacy	Collective interest
Liability	Risk and cost
Security	Economic growth and innovation

The literature on risk and trust formation and their relationships to the design and implementation of cyberspace systems emphasizes the importance of values, reciprocity, information management, and human and technical capabilities.

Available research is inconclusive with respect to the implications of interventions in cyberspace by those who seek to minimize crime. Given the relatively weak scientific evidence in key areas, there is a need to consider the ethical positions associated with crime prevention measures and to draw inferences about their impact. In some of the areas addressed in this book, the lack of systematic and comparable quantitative evidence means the foundation for evidence-based decision making will be weak. In these areas, it will be important to consider the ethical positions and to reach equitable judgements. Critical reasoning can be applied to reach such assessments – subject to review as new evidence accumulates – about 'acceptable' and 'unacceptable' levels of trustworthiness in relation to the cyberspace system. This is essential for evaluations of the distributional issues associated with intrusive privacy protection measures and of the benefits of crime protection.

It is clear that:

- Improved crime prevention in cyberspace depends upon a better understanding of human motivations and practices and the way these are embedded within complex cyberspace systems.
- Problems facing crime preventers will not be solved by improved technology alone; enforcement of behavioural change consistent with 'good' behaviour in cyberspace will require enabling people to do the 'right' thing easily, with substantial implications for the usability and cost of cyberspace technologies.
- Trust in cyberspace can be fostered in both technical and non-technical ways; the options need to be considered in the light of studies of risk perception and the actual risk encountered in cyberspace and in the wider situation.
- Crime prevention measures for cyberspace will need to receive widespread consent nationally and internationally if they are to be effective.
- The dependability of future cyberspace systems and the extent to which they ensure human safety and well-being are matters of human choice; understanding the human and non-human relationships often requires an assumption that it is feasible to believe that agents, both human and technological, will act or, in the case of the latter, will have been designed and implemented to act, in rational or at least quasi-rational ways.

The scale of the challenge facing government policy makers is vast. The speed at which the machinery of government operates can be slow relative to the rate of technological change, and further slowing of the decision-making process due to the need to adopt international solutions may create a larger problem. There are also concerns about introducing legislative and governance solutions, which may manage risks more effectively, but stifle innovation and competitiveness. When new measures are introduced they interact with other measures, often giving rise to unexpected outcomes that may be inconsistent with policy – or indeed with changing social mores.

No 'future-proof' set of measures can be put in place through unilateral action because the positions of stakeholders continuously change and are thus insufficiently clear. Partnerships will be needed between the public and private sectors, working with civil society representatives, to create an accepted framework for cyber trust and crime prevention. Lessons must be learned from policy and regulatory initiatives and the corresponding failures and successes of these initiatives. In this chapter we have highlighted several research frameworks (new frameworks for dependable software engineering, the criminal opportunity models, the social amplification of risk framework and the privacy impact assessment framework) that could be further developed and interconnected to increase understanding of security measures and crime prevention strategies. Crime prevention, especially in cyberspace, occurs in a rapidly changing technical, economic and social context where unforeseeable properties emerge. The key knowledge about what works as a crime prevention strategy is a wasting asset that must be constantly replenished if crime preventers are to innovate faster than criminals.

Our synthesis of the existing scientific evidence in the areas covered in this book identifies gaps in research that is under way in the UK. It is clear that cross-disciplinary investigation is needed on the dependability and trustworthiness of all aspects of the cyberspace system. There is in particular a need to promote cyberspace system design that enables users to manage their privacy and security, and enables crimes to be prevented or detected. System design methodologies are needed that will encourage greater system reliability and robustness, while maintaining a degree of transparency for users. It will be necessary to ensure appropriate levels of investment in research and development in cyberspace systems, advanced knowledge services, information management and engineering approaches as well as in information assurance initiatives. There will also be a need for a collaborative approach across the research community that will harness the considerable breadth of expertise that is available, and help to overcome existing fragmentation.

Research needs to be complemented by investment in adequate levels of education to build awareness of cyberspace developments and crime prevention measures. Such measures must be sensitive to local contexts and cultures. Many ethical issues are raised by innovations in ICTs and these must be debated in the future. Cyberspace must not become exclusive to only the 'experts', thereby exacerbating 'digital divides'. Building confidence in the information provided by government about the risks to those who encounter cyberspace and about the trustworthiness of cyberspace systems is essential. The social and economic threats from the social fragmentation and exclusion that will arise if some groups take up the new technologies and benefit from them, but others do not, must also be examined.

The complexity of cyberspace and its emergent properties means that it will be essential to develop methodologies for testing when changes in the human and technical system are likely to create new vulnerabilities. Only in this way will it be feasible to encourage alternative action. The greatest challenge in the future will be managing emergent properties and vulnerabilities in ways that respect changing individual and collective values.

NOTES

1   This review of the main arguments in this book draws on the state-of-the-art science reviews that follow. We are grateful to the authors of subsequent chapters for allowing us to draw upon their work. The views incorporated in this chapter are not necessarily those of any institution. We accept full responsibility for the views expressed in this chapter and for any errors or omissions.

2   This chapter and the science reviews, Chapters 3 to 12 of this book, were peer-reviewed by a minimum of two anonymous referees who are acknowledged experts in their respective fields. The authors of this chapter thank all those who participated in the review process and acknowledge the comments that were received and fed back to the contributors to this volume.

3   Chapters 13 to 15 were commissioned to address key areas that came to light as a result of discussion among participants in the Foresight project and are not intended to provide comprehensive reviews in the style of the preceding chapters.

4   And see Castells (2001), Gibson (1984) and Mitchell (1996).

5   'Social technology' is terminology often used in the social sciences, including the social studies of technology and sociological literatures. For instance, Foucault (1970) uses the term 'technology' to refer to technologies of the self and governance structures and processes; see also Rose (1999). Others use this terminology to refer to aspects of the social system that either become embedded in a technical system by virtue of design choices that reflect alternative values or, alternatively, represent the discourses, processes and procedures that are used to develop and implement the components of a technical system (see Pinch 1992).

6   Throughout, we use the term 'cross-disciplinary' to encompass those who favour multi-disciplinary or inter-disciplinary research; what we intend is stronger cooperation based upon excellence in research located in many different disciplines.

7   The OST Foresight programme examined complex systems within the framework of the Foresight Cognitive Systems Project, see Austin et al. (2003) for a review.

8   OST Foresight was commissioning research reviews in this area in the spring of 2004. There is some research on perceptions of risk with respect to the Y2K (Year 2000) issue (Pidgeon et al. 2003) and on risk management, particularly in the financial services sector (see Chapter 11).

9   http://www.pwc.com/Extweb/service.nsf/

10 Biometric solutions using iris recognition that do not rely upon the use of a data template are being developed. If the method is scaleable (and the signs are encouraging) this has potential. However, usability studies show that there will be a small percentage of the population for whom this will not be feasible (see Chapter 10).

11 See also Frith and Blakemore (2003), McClue (2003), Morris et al. (2003) and O'Hara et al. (2003) for Foresight research on memory and cognition.

12 For empirical data on high-tech crime in the UK see National Hi-Tech Crime Unit (2004), which indicates that from a sample of 105 business employees the following computer-related crimes were identified as serious: sabotage of data or networks 91per cent; virus attacks 90 per cent; financial fraud 88 per cent; theft of proprietary information 86 per cent; attacks, for example Denial of Service 79 per cent, theft of laptops 76 per cent, unauthorized website access or misuse 75 per cent, spoofing attacks 74 per cent, theft of other hardware 71 per cent, telecommunications fraud 55 per cent, telecoms eavesdropping 48 per cent, and active wiretapping 43 per cent.

13 The European Commission has launched a 'preparatory action', 'Towards a programme to advance European security through Research and Technology', IP/04/145, Brussels, 5 February 2004. The programme covers: improving situation awareness; optimizing security and protection of networked systems; protecting against terrorism; enhancing crisis management; and achieving interoperability and integrated systems for information and communication.

14 Current advice on the management of computer crime-related evidence is contained in the ACPO (Association of Chief Police Officers) guidelines which can be found at http://www.nhtcu.org/ACPO%20Guide%20v3.0.pdf accessed 17 April 2004.

15 See von Neuman and Morgenstern (1944).

16 Since the Internet and its platforms are subject to continuous evolution, it is important to distinguish analytically here between the public and private spaces that can be created, the changes in the IP with respect to quality of service and other features, and the differences in the requirements for security of various industry sectors, government services, and public spaces frequented by citizens and civil society groups.

17 See for example Himanen (2001), Lessig (1999), Miller (2003) and Naughton (1999).

18 See also Hawkins et al. (1999) and Silverstone (2003).

19 There are growing numbers of articles in the press focusing, for instance, on the impact of anti-spam laws in the US, use of software for anti-terrorism surveillance and the privacy and freedom of speech issues that are raised. The subjects for future research suggested by this volume indicate that information control and assurance, together with the overall stability of the cyberspace system, will continue to provide a focus for, and give rise to, debate.

20 The 'grid' refers to efforts to build the next generation computing infrastructure providing intensive computation and analysis of shared large-scale databases, from hundreds of terabytes to petabytes, across widely distributed scientific communities, see http://eu-datagrid.web.cern.Ch/eu-datagrid/, accessed 17 April 2004, for an example of one project.

21 See European Commission (1999, 2000, 2002a, b); European Union Council (1999) and United Kingdom Government (1990, 1998a, b, 2000a, b, c, 2003).

REFERENCES

Austin, J., Cliff, D., Ghanea-Hercock, R. and Wright, A. (2003), 'Large-Scale, Small-Scale Systems', *Foresight Cognitive Systems Research Review*, http://www.foresight.gov.uk/cognitive.html accessed 17 Apr. 04.

Beck, U. (1992), *Risk Society: Towards a New Modernity*, London: Sage.

Bennett, C.J. (1992), *Regulating Privacy: Data Protection and Public Policy in Europe and the United States*, Ithaca NY: Cornell University Press.

Bennett, C.J. and Raab, C.D. (2003), *The Governance of Privacy: Policy Instruments in Global Perspective*, Aldershot: Ashgate.

Bryen, S. (2002), 'A Collective Security Approach to Protecting the Global Critical Infrastructure', ITU Workshop on Creating Trust in Critical Network Infrastructures', Seoul, 20-22 May,
http://www.itu.int/osg/spu/ni/security/docs/cni.09.doc accessed 17 Apr. 04.

Callon, M. (2003), 'The Increasing Involvement of Concerned Groups in R&D Policies: What Lessons for Public Powers?', in A. Geuna, A.J. Salter and W.E. Steinmueller (eds), *Science and Innovation: Rethinking the Rationales for Funding and Governance*, Cheltenham: Edward Elgar, pp. 30-68.

Castells, M. (2001), *The Internet Galaxy: Reflections on the Internet, Business, and Society*, Oxford: Oxford University Press.

Collins, B.S. (1996), 'Practicalities of Information Management' in D. Best (ed.), *The Fourth Resource: Information and Its Management,* London: ASLIB/Gower, pp. 115-27.Collins, B.S. (2004), 'Submission to the Royal Academy of Engineering on Complex Software Projects', London, January.

Cremonini, L., Rathmell, A. and Wagner, C. (2003), 'Cyber Trust and Crime Prevention – Foresight Overview', Annotated Briefing prepared for Office of Science and Technology, UK, by RAND Europe, July.

Ekblom, P. (1996), 'Towards a Discipline of Crime Prevention: A Systematic Approach to its Nature, Range and Concepts', in T. Bennett (ed.), *Preventing Crime and Disorder: Targeting Strategies and Responsibilities*, Cambridge: Institute of Criminology, pp. 47-9.

Ekblom, P. (1997), 'Gearing Up Against Crime: A Dynamic Framework to Help Designers Keep Up with the Adaptive Criminal in a Changing World, *International Journal of Risk, Security and Crime Prevention* 2(4): 249-65.

Ekblom, P. (1999), 'Can We Make Crime Prevention Adaptive by Learning from Other Evolutionary Struggles?', *Studies on Crime Prevention* 8(1): 27-51.

Ekblom, P. (2002), 'Future Imperfect: Preparing for the Crimes to Come', *Criminal Justice Matters* 46(Winter): 38-40.

Ekblom, P. (2003), 'The Conjunction of Criminal Opportunity: A Framework for Crime Reduction', Home Office Crime and Policing Group, Research Development and Statistics Directorate, London, 3 March, http://www.crimereduction.gov.uk/learningzone/cco.htm#1 accessed 17 Apr. 04.

Ekblom, P. (2004a in press), 'How to Police the Future: Scanning for Scientific and Technological Innovations which Generate Potential

Threats and Opportunities in Crime, Policing and Crime Reduction', in M. Smith and N. Tiley (eds), *Crime Science: Prevention and Detection*, Cullhompton, Devon: Willan.

Ekblom, P. (2004b) 'The Conjunction of Criminal Opportunity', developed between 2001 and 2004, http://www.crimereduction.gov.uk/learningzone/cco.htm accessed 17 Apr. 04.

Ekblom, P. and Tilley, N. (2000), 'Going Equipped: Criminology, Situational Crime Prevention and the Resourceful Offender', *British Journal of Criminology* 40(3): 376-98.

Electronic Privacy Information Centre (1997), 'Surfer Beware: Personal Privacy and the Internet', June, http://www.epic.org/reports/surfer-beware.html accessed 17 Apr. 04.

European Commission (1999), *The Telecommunications Data Protection Directive (97/66/EC) and the Telecommunications (Data Protection and Privacy) Regulations 1999 (SI 1999 No. 2093)*, http://www.dti.gov.uk/industries/ecommunications/directive_on_privacy_electronic_communications_200258ec.html#overview accessed 17 Apr. 04.

European Commission (2000), 'EU's Communication on Precautionary Principle', Brussels, 2 February, http://www.gdrc.org/u-gov/precaution-4.html accessed 17 Apr. 04.

European Commission (2002a), *The Directive on Privacy and Electronic Communications (2002/58/EC)*, http://www.dti.gov.uk/industries/ecommunications/directive_on_privacy_electronic_communications_200258ec.html accessed 17 Apr. 04.

European Commission (2002b), *The Electronic Commerce Directive (00/31/EC) & the Electronic Commerce (EC Directive) Regulations 2002 (SI 2002 No. 2013 UK)*, http://www.dti.gov.uk/industries/ecommunications/electronic_commerce_directive_0031ec.html accessed 17 Apr. 04.

European Commission (2003), *Third European Report on Science & Technology Indicators 2003 – Towards a Knowledge-based Economy*, Brussels, http://www.cordis.lu/indicators/third_report.htm accessed 17 Apr. 04.

European Commission, IST Advisory Group (2002), 'IST Advisory Group – Trust, Dependability, Security and Privacy for IST in FP6', June, http://www.mcst.org.mt/public/01_Sixth%20Framework%20Programme/02_Information%20Society%20Technologies/Reports%20and%20Publications/istag_kk4402464encfull.pdf accessed 17 Apr. 04.

European Union Council (1999), 'Council Resolution of 28 June 1999 on Community Consumer Policy 1999 to 2001' (1999/C 206/01), *Official*

Journal of the European Communities, 21 July.

Felson, M. (1987), *Crime and Everyday Life*, Thousand Oaks CA: Pine Forge Press.

Foucault, M. (1970), *The Order of Things: An Archaeology of the Human Science*, translation of *Les Mots et les Choses* (1966), New York: Pantheon Books.

Freeman, C. and Louçà, F. (2001), *As Time Goes By: From the Industrial Revolutions to the Information Revolution*, Oxford: Oxford University Press.

Frith, U. and Blakemore, S.-J. (2003), 'Social Cognition', *Foresight Cognitive Systems Project, Research Review*,
http://www.foresight.gov.uk/ accessed 17 Apr. 04.

Gibson, W. (1984), *Neuromancer*, New York: Ace Books.

Giddens, A. (1991), *Modernity and Self-identity: Self and Society in the Late Modern Age*, Stanford CA: Stanford University Press.

Goodman, S.E., Hassebroek, P.B., King, D. and Ozment, A. (2002), 'International Coordination to Increase the Security of Critical Network Infrastructures', ITU Workshop on Creating Trust in Critical Network Infrastructures', Seoul, 20-22 May, CNI/04,
http://www.itu.int/osg/spu/ni/security/docs/cni.04.doc accessed 17 Apr. 04.

Hawkins, R.W., Mansell, R. and Steinmueller, W.E. (1999), 'Toward Digital Intermediation in the Information Society', *Journal of Economic Issues* 33(2): 383-91.

Himanen, P. (2001), *The Hacker Ethic*, New York: Random House.

Institute for Prospective Technological Studies (IPTS) (2003), 'Security and Privacy for the Citizen in the Post-September 11 Digital Age: A Prospective Overview', Technical Report Series, IPTS, Seville, July.

Kasperson, J.X., Kasperson, R.E., Pidgeon, N. and Slovic, P. (2003), 'The Social Amplification of Risk: Assessing Fifteen Years of Research and Theory', in N. Pidgeon, R.E. Kasperson and P. Slovic (eds), *The Social Amplification of Risk*, Cambridge: Cambridge University Press, pp. 13-46.

Kleinig, J. (2000), 'The Burdens of Situational Crime Prevention', in A. von Hirsh, D. Garland and A. Wakefield (eds), *Ethical and Social Perspectives on Situational Crime Prevention*, London: Hart, pp. 37-58.

Latham, R. (ed.) (2003) *From Bombs and Bandwidth: The Emerging Relationship Between Information Technology and Society*, New York: New Press.

Lessig, L. (1999), *Code and Other Laws of Cyberspace*, New York: Basic Books.

Levi, M. (2001), '"Between the Risk and the Reality Falls the Shadow":

Evidence and Urban Legends in Computer Fraud', in D.S. Wall (ed.), *Crime and the Internet*, London: Routledge, pp. 44-58.

Mansell, R. and Steinmueller, W.E. (2000), *Mobilizing the Information Society: Strategies for Growth and Opportunity*, Oxford, Oxford University Press.

McClue, A. (2003), 'Nationwide Ditches Iris and Fingerprint Biometrics', 23 September, http://www.silicon.com/software/security/0,39024655,10006129,00.htm accessed 17 Apr. 04.

Miller, P. (2003), 'The See-through Society: Openness and the Future of the Internet', note prepared for the Foresight Cyber Trust and Crime Prevention Project, DEMOS, London.

Mitchell, W.J. (1996), *City of Bits: Space, Place and the Infobahn*, Cambridge MA: MIT Press.

MORI (2003), 'Privacy and Data-Sharing: Survey of Public Awareness and Perceptions', Research Study Conducted for Department for Constitutional Affairs, Market and Opinion Research International, London.

Morris, R., Hitch, G., Graham, K., and Bussey, T. (2003), 'Learning and Memory', Foresight Cognitive Systems Project, Research Review, http://www.foresight.gov.uk/ accessed 17 Apr. 04.

National Hi-Tech Crime Unit (2004) 'Hi-Tech Crime: The Impact on UK Business, Report by the National Hi-Tech Crime Unit', London, http://www.nhtcu.org/ accessed 17 Apr. 04.

Naughton, J. (1999), *A Brief History of the Future*, London: Phoenix.

OECD (2002), 'Guidelines for the Security of Information Systems and Networks: Towards a Culture of Security', OECD, Paris.

O'Hara, K. (2004), *Trust: From Socrates to Spin*, Cambridge: Icon Books.

O'Hara, K., Hall, W., van Rijsbergen, K. and Shadbolt, N. (2003), 'Memory, Reasoning and Learning', Foresight Cognitive Systems Project, Research Review, http://www.foresight.gov.uk/ accessed 17 Apr. 04.

O'Neill, O. (2000), *Bounds of Justice,* Cambridge: Cambridge University Press.

O'Neill, O. (2002), *Autonomy and Trust in Bioethics,* Cambridge: Cambridge University Press.

O'Siochru, S. and Constanza-Chock, S. (2003), 'Global Governance of Information and Communication Technologies: Implications for Transnational Civil Society Networking', prepared for the Social Science Research Council, New York, http://www.ssrc.org/programs/itic/governance_report/index.page accessed 17 Apr. 04.

Palmer, G. (2000), 'The New Spectacle of Crime', in D. Thomas and B.D.

Loader (eds), *Cybercrime Law Enforcement, Security and Surveillance in the Information Age*, London: Routledge, pp. 85-102.

Pearsall, J. and Trumble, B. (eds) (1996), *The Oxford English Reference Dictionary*, 2nd edn, Oxford: Oxford University Press.

Perez, C. (2002), *Technological Revolutions and Financial Capital: The Dynamics of Bubbles and Golden Ages*, Cheltenham: Edward Elgar.

Pidgeon, N., Kasperson, R.E. and Slovic, P. (eds) (2003), *The Social Amplification of Risk,* Cambridge: Cambridge University Press.

Pinch, T.J. (1992), 'Opening Black Boxes: Science, Technology and Society', *Social Studies of Science* 22(3): 487-510.

Raab, C.D. (1995), 'Connecting Orwell to Athens? Information Superhighways and the Privacy Debate', in W. van de Donk, I. Snellen and P. Tops (eds), *Orwell in Athens: A Perspective on Informatization and Democracy*, Amsterdam: IOS Press, pp. 195-211.

RAND Europe (2003a), 'Handbook of Legislative Procedures of Computer and Network Misuse in EU Countries for Assisting Computer Security Incident Response Teams (CSIRTs)',
http://www.iaac.org.uk/csirt/csirtWS-flyer.pdf accessed 17 Apr. 04.

RAND Europe (2003b), 'Benchmarking Security and Trust in Europe and the US', Statistical Indicators Benchmarking the Information Society (SIBIS), report by L. Cremonini and L. Valeri, IST-2000-26276, EC IST Programme, Santa Monica CA,
http://www.rand.org/publications/MR/MR1736/MR1736.pdf accessed 17 Apr. 04.

Rogerson, M. and Pease, K. (2003), 'Privacy, Identity and Crime Prevention', note prepared for the Foresight Cyber Trust and Crime Prevention Project, University of Huddersfield.

Rosa, E. (2003), 'The Logical Structure of the Social Amplification of Risk Framework (SARF): Metatheoretical Foundations and Policy Implications', in N. Pidgeon, R.E. Kasperson and P. Slovic (eds), *The Social Amplification of Risk,* Cambridge: Cambridge University Press, pp. 47-79.

Rose, N. (1999), *Governing the Soul*, London: Free Association Books.

Sharpe, B. (2003), 'Foresight Cognitive Systems Project – Applications and Impact', DTI Foresight Report for the Cognitive Systems Project, The Appliance Studio Ltd, September,
http://www.foresight.gov.uk/cognitive.html accessed 17 Apr. 04.

Sharpe, B. and Zaba, S. (2004), 'CTCP Technology: Forward Look', The Appliance Studio Ltd, report prepared for the Foresight Cyber Trust and Crime Prevention Project, London.

Silverstone, R. (2003), 'Media and Technology in the Everyday Life of European Societies', Final Deliverable, The European Media and

Technology in Everyday Life Network, 2000-2003,
http://www.lse.ac.uk/collections/EMTEL/main1.html accessed 17 Apr.
04.

Skibell, R. (2002), 'The Myth of the Computer Hacker', *Information,
Communication & Society* 5(3): 336-56.

Stewart, B. (1996), 'Privacy Impact Assessments', *Privacy Law and Policy
Reporter, Vol. 3-4,*
http://www.austlii.edu.au/journals/PLPR/1996/39.html accessed 17 Apr.
04.

Surman, M. and Reilly, K. (2003), 'Appropriating the Internet for Social
Change: Towards the Strategic Use of Networked Technologies by
Transnational Civil Society Organizations', prepared for the Social
Science Research Council, New York,
http://www.ssrc.org/programs/itic/civ_soc_report/index.page accessed 17
Apr. 04.

The Independent (2003), 'Gone Phishing', 17 December.

Thomas, D. and Loader, B.D. (eds) (2000), *Cybercrime: Law Enforcement,
Security and Surveillance in the Information Age,* London: Routledge.

Tyrrell, P. (2004), 'Realities of a Virtual Economy', *FT.com*, 1 January.

United Kingdom Government (1990), 'Computer Misuse Act 1990',
http://www.hmso.gov.uk/acts/acts1990/Ukpga_19900018_en_1.htm
accessed 17 Apr. 04.

United Kingdom Government (1998a), 'Data Protection Act 1988',
http://www.hmso.gov.uk/acts/acts1998/19980029.htm accessed 17 Apr.
04.

United Kingdom Government (1998b), 'The Human Rights Act 1998',
http://www.hmso.gov.uk/acts/acts1998/19980042.htm accessed 17 Apr.
04.

United Kingdom Government (2000a), 'The Telecommunications (Lawful
Business Practice) (Interception of Communications) Regulations 2000',
http://www.hmso.gov.uk/si/si2000/20002699.htm accessed 17 Apr. 04.

United Kingdom Government (2000b), 'Electronic Communications Act
2000', Chapter c.7,
http://www.uk-legislation.hmso.gov.uk/acts/acts2000/20000007.htm
accessed 17 Apr. 04.

United Kingdom Government (2000c), 'Regulation of Investigatory Powers
Act 2000',
http://www.hmso.gov.uk/acts/acts2000/20000023.htm accessed 17 Apr.
04.

United Kingdom Government (2003), 'Statutory Instrument 2003 No. 2426,
The Privacy and Electronic Communications (EC Directive) Regulations
2003', http://www.hmso.gov.uk/si/si2003/20032426.htm accessed 17

Apr. 04.

von Hirsch (2000), 'The Ethics of Public Television Surveillance,' in A. von Hirsch, D. Garland and A. Wakefield (eds), *Ethical and Social Perspectives on Situational Crime Prevention*, London: Hart, pp. 59-76.

von Neuman, J. and Morgenstern, O. (1944), *Theory of Games and Economic Behavior*, Princeton NJ: Princeton University Press.

Wall, D.S. (ed.) (2001), *Crime and the Internet,* London: Routledge.

Welsh, B.C. and Farrington, D.P. (2002), 'Crime Prevention Effects of Closed Circuit Television: A Systematic Review', Home Office Research Study 252, London.

Part 2   Future cyberspace systems

This Part focuses on the human and technical considerations involved in the construction of future cyberspace systems.

In Chapter 3, Cliff Jones and Brian Randell focus on the key social and technical factors that are influencing the dependability of pervasive, large-scale computer systems. In Chapter 4, Fred Piper, Matt Robshaw and Scarlet Schwiderski-Grosche turn their attention to the controversies and issues surrounding identity verification and authentication in cyberspace. The Foresight project expert panel selected two rapidly changing technologies for in-depth consideration. The first, the development of knowledge technologies and the semantic web, is examined in Chapter 5 by Kieron O'Hara and Nigel Shadbolt and the second, innovations in software agent-based computing, is considered in Chapter 6 by Sarvapali Ramchurn and Nicholas Jennings.

3 Dependable pervasive systems

Cliff Jones and Brian Randell

3.1 INTRODUCTION

Virtually all aspects of society in the UK and other developed countries are now dependent, to a greater or lesser degree, on computer systems and networks. For example, a US National Research Council Report (Schneider 1999) states:

> The nation's security and economy rely on infrastructures for communication, finance, energy distribution, and transportation – all increasingly dependent on networked information systems. When these networked information systems perform badly or do not work at all, they put life, liberty, and property at risk. Interrupting service can threaten lives and property; destroying information or changing it improperly can disrupt the work of governments and corporations; and disclosing secrets can embarrass people or hurt organizations. The widespread interconnection of networked information systems allows outages and disruptions to spread from one system to others; it enables attacks to be waged anonymously and from a safe distance; and it compounds the difficulty of understanding and controlling these systems (p. i).

A report from the US National Academy of Science (Estrin 2001) states:

> Information technology (IT) is on the verge of another revolution. Driven by the increasing capabilities and ever declining costs of computing and communications devices, IT is being embedded into a growing range of physical devices linked together through networks and will become ever more pervasive as the component technologies become smaller, faster, and cheaper. These changes are sometimes obvious – in pagers and Internet-enabled cell phones, for example – but often IT is buried inside larger (or smaller) systems in ways that are not easily visible to end users (p. 1).

It is easy to bemoan the fact that computer systems are less dependable than one might want, but it is essential to understand that large networked computer systems are among the most complex things that the human race has created. The huge advances in the short history of computing must not be forgotten. Progress on hardware, as shown by the continued validity of

'Moore's Law',[1] has delivered platforms on which many major software applications have been successfully constructed. No human (design) activity can be expected to progress at the same rate; this accounts for many of the dependability complaints, but the techniques and tools available today have made it possible to produce software and systems with impressive functionality that do, in many cases, eventually work adequately dependably, though their development all too often incurs major schedule and cost over-runs. However, there is a huge deployment gap, with many organizations using technical and management methods that are far from 'best practice' with regard to both the effectiveness of system development and the quality of the resulting systems.

The current situation looks set to become more precarious: present trends and predictions indicate that huge, even globally distributed, networked computer systems, perhaps involving everything from super-computers and large server 'farms' to myriads of small mobile computers and tiny embedded devices, are likely to become highly pervasive. In many cases such systems will be required by governments, large industrial organizations and, indeed, society at large, to function highly dependably and essentially continuously. This would be the consequence should various industrial and government plans such as the European Commission's e-Europe initiative (European Commission 2002) come to fruition. Such plans have been formulated despite the fact that the envisaged systems are likely to be far more complex than today's typical large systems. Hence questions as to how and at what cost, and indeed whether, such systems can be developed so as to have acceptable functionality and dependability, and thus gain the trust of the people affected by them, are matters of great importance.

This chapter analyses this situation, concentrating mainly on issues related to software. In Section 3.2 we summarize the current state of the art concerning the overall subject of system dependability, a term that encompasses such characteristics as reliability, security, safety, availability and so on. According to needs and circumstances, some appropriate balance of such characteristics will be needed for a given system to be regarded as 'trustworthy', that is, dependable, by its users and owners. In Section 3.3 we describe some general research goals that we believe are among those that will be fundamental to ensuring that in the future we will have computer systems whose dependability is commensurate with the requirements that are implied by present policies and trends. In the conclusion (Section 3.4) we highlight opportunities for interdisciplinary research.

3.2 STATE OF THE ART

The present situation is perhaps best illustrated by the following sample facts and statistics regarding the costs of undependability:

- The average cost per hour of computer system downtime across 30 domains, such as banking, manufacturing, retail, health insurances, securities and reservations, has recently been estimated at nearly US$950,000 by the US Association of Contingency Planners.[2]
- The French Insurer's Association has estimated that the yearly cost of computer failures is 1.5–1.8 bn euro, of which slightly more than half is due to deliberately induced faults, for example by hackers and corrupt insiders (Laprie 1999).
- The Standish Group's 'Chaos Chronicles' report for 2003 analysed over 13,000 IT projects and estimated that nearly 70 per cent either failed completely or were 'challenged' that is, although completed and operational, exceeded their budget and time estimates and had less functionality than originally specified. This led to their estimate that in 2002 the US 'wasted $55 billion in cancelled and over-run IT projects, compared with a total IT spend of $255 billion' (quoted in the July 2003 report on 'Government IT Projects', Pearce 2003, p. 3).
- The Pearce (2003, p. 1) report states that in the UK: 'Over the past five years, high profile IT difficulties have affected the Child Support Agency, Passport Office, Criminal Records Bureau, Inland Revenue, National Air Traffic Service (NATS) and the Department of Work and Pensions, among others.'
- The AMSD Overall Dependability Roadmap (AMSD Roadmap 2003) cites a recent UK survey of 1,027 projects, which reported that only 130 (12.7 per cent) succeeded. Many of these projects were maintenance or data-conversion projects – of the more than 500 development projects in the sample surveyed, only three (0.6 per cent) succeeded.
- A UK Department of Trade and Industry and PricewaterhouseCoopers survey indicated rapidly growing dependency on critical information held in computer systems and increasing use of the Internet and the Web in British businesses.

This situation would undoubtedly be considerably improved if all project developments were carried out using the levels of technical and managerial expertise that some of the best developments exhibit. However, merely encouraging the take-up of today's best practice, though it would greatly help the current generation of systems, will not suffice in the future, given the changes these coming years will undoubtedly bring.

These changes will occur, in part, because of the plans referred to above – but also because of the continuing headlong pace of technological development. To get some feel for what the next ten years will bring, one need merely think of the situation ten years ago, when a typical PC (personal computer) ran at 50 Mhertz, and had perhaps 4 Mbytes of memory and a 100 Mbyte disk. Regarding wide area data communication, for most network users a 9,600 bps telephone modem was the norm – and a new and little-known scheme called the World Wide Web was only just starting to attract attention in parts of the research community.

We therefore concentrate in this chapter on current and especially future dependability issues related to large complex distributed systems – both the problems of dependably constructing such systems, that is, of producing systems to match their functional and dependability specifications within time and budget constraints, and the problems of actually achieving adequate operational dependability from such systems when they are deployed.

Such systems are rarely constructed *de novo*, but rather are built up from earlier systems. Indeed, they are often actually constructed out of multiple pre-existing systems; hence the term 'systems-of-systems'. Moreover, there is almost always a requirement for systems to be capable of being adapted so as to match changes in requirements – such as changed functionality and changes in system environments – and there is likely to be an increasing need for systems that can themselves evolve, for example in order to serve a dynamic environment constituted by large numbers of mobile devices moving into and out of range.

Most of the systems of concern embody human beings as, in effect, system 'components', though sometimes such humans become actively involved only when things go wrong with the computers and their communication. We term such systems 'computer-based systems'. The various types of components have rather different failure characteristics: (1) hardware suffers mainly from ageing and wear, although logical design errors do sometimes persist in deployed hardware (see, for example, Avizienis and He 1999 and van Campenhout et al. 2000); (2) it is mainly software that suffers from residual design and implementation errors, since this is, quite appropriately, where most of the logical complexity of a typical system resides; and (3) human beings (users, operators, maintenance personnel and outsiders) can at times, through ignorance, incompetence or malevolence, cause untold damage. Malevolent activities can range from acts of petty vandalism by amateur hackers, through the efforts of expert and highly devious virus creators, to well-resourced and highly sophisticated attacks by terrorists and enemy states. The successful design and deployment of a major computer-based system, and indeed of any system that interacts directly with humans, thus calls for socio-technical as well as technical expertise, a point we return to in Section 3.4.

The task of developing a complex computer system involves human beings, possibly in large numbers, aided by extensive computer facilities that provide means of recording and analysing specifications, and compiling and evaluating detailed designs. These facilities and their users in fact constitute what we term a 'system-design system'.[3] As indicated earlier, in this chapter we concern ourselves with the dependability of the system-building process, which will be crucial to the timely production of acceptable systems, that is, of such system-design systems, as well as that of the resulting complex system-of-systems and computer-based systems. However, issues regarding the provision of the networking infrastructure that such systems will be built upon and will depend on, fall outside the scope of this chapter.

3.2.1 Concepts and Definitions

The topic of dependability or trustworthiness cannot be tackled adequately without a careful identification of the basic concepts involved and their definitions.[4] The choice of the terms is less important; it is the clarification of basic concepts that matters. 'The *dependability* or, equivalently, *trustworthiness*, of a computing system can be defined as the "the ability of a system to avoid failures that are more frequent or more severe, and outage durations that are longer, than is acceptable"' (Avizienis et al. 2001, p. 2).

We need to distinguish between three basic concepts: failure, error and fault. A given system, operating in some particular environment, may fail in the sense that some other system makes or could, in principle, have made a judgement that the activity or inactivity of the given system constitutes *failure*.

The judgemental system may be an automated system, a human being, the relevant judicial authority or whatever. It may or may not have a fully detailed system specification to guide it, though evidently one would expect such a document to be available to guide the system construction task. Different judgemental systems might, of course, come to different decisions regarding whether and how the given system has failed or might fail in the future in differing circumstances and from different stakeholders' viewpoints. The crucial issue might concern the accuracy of the results that are produced, the continuity or timeliness of service, and the success with which sensitive information is kept private.

Moreover, such a judgemental system might itself fail in the eyes of some other judgemental system, a possibility that is well understood by the legal system, with its hierarchy of courts. So, we have a (recursive) notion of 'failure', which clearly is a relative rather than an absolute notion. So, then, is the concept of dependability.

From the notion of failure, we move on to discuss and distinguish between what we term errors and faults. An *error* is that part of the system state that is liable to lead to subsequent failure; an error affecting the service that is being provided by a system is an indication that a failure occurs or has occurred. The adjudged or hypothesized cause of an error is a *fault*.

Note that an error may be judged to have multiple causes, and does not necessarily lead to a failure; for example error recovery might be attempted successfully and failure averted.

Thus a failure occurs when an error 'passes through' the system–user interface and affects the service delivered by the system; a system being composed of components that are themselves systems. The manifestation of failures, faults and errors follows a 'fundamental chain':

... → failure → fault → error → failure → fault → ...

Such chains can exist within systems. System failures might be due to faults that exist because, for example, of the failure of a component to meet its specification. However, these chains also exist between systems. For instance a failure of a system-design system might result in the wrong choice of component being made in the system that is being designed, resulting in a fault in this latter system that leads eventually to its failure. Also, a system might fail because of the inputs that it receives from some other system with which it is interacting, though ideally it will be capable of checking its inputs thoroughly enough to minimize such failures.

It is essential to have separate terms for the three essentially different concepts – 'fault', 'error' and 'failure' – since otherwise one cannot deal properly with the complexities and realities of failure-prone components being assembled together in possibly incorrect ways, so resulting in systems which in reality will still be somewhat failure-prone. Moreover, with the sort of system we are concerned with here, there are likely to be uncertainties and arguments about system boundaries. The very complexity of the system (and its specification, if it has one) can be a major problem. Judgements as to possible causes or consequences of failure can be subtle and disputable and any provisions for preventing faults from causing failures are themselves almost certainly fallible.

The above definitions, in clarifying the distinction in particular between fault and failure, lead to the identification of the four basic means of obtaining and establishing high dependability, that is, minimizing the frequency and seriousness of failures, namely:

* fault prevention: prevention of the occurrence or introduction of

faults, in particular, via the use of rigorous design methods;

- fault tolerance: the means of delivery of correct service in the presence of faults;
- fault removal: that is, verification and validation, aimed at reducing the number or severity of faults; and
- fault forecasting: system evaluation, via estimation of the present number, the future incidence and the likely consequences of faults.

In the absence of (successful) fault tolerance, failures may occur and will presumably need to be tolerated somehow by the encompassing (possibly socio-technical) system. However, this notion of 'failure tolerance' is just fault tolerance at the next system level.

One of the most important lessons from work over many years on system dependability is the fact that fault prevention, removal and tolerance should not be regarded as alternatives, but rather as complementary technologies, all of which have a role to play, and whose effective combination is crucial – with fault forecasting being used to evaluate the degree of success that is being achieved. Moreover, and this is not so well understood: (1) all four of these dependability technologies are as relevant to the system design implementation and deployment process, that is, to system-design systems, as they are to the systems that are being produced; and (2) in many situations effective use of the strategies calls for the exercise of socio-technical as well as technical expertise. These two lessons guide the structuring and content of what follows.

3.2.2 Current Systems and Current Abilities

The European Commission's Accompanying Measure on System Dependability (AMSD) Overall Dependability Roadmap (AMSD Roadmap 2003) estimates that for large and complex computer systems, namely those involving 1 million–100 million lines of code, current development techniques, that is, system-design systems, can at best produce systems that achieve a level of reliability in the range 10 to 100 failures per year.

In fact, in some ways the system dependability situation has been getting worse rather than improving in recent years. Quoting the AMSD Roadmap, 'the availability that was typically achievable by (wired) telecommunication services, and computer systems in the 90s was 99.999% to 99.9%. Now cellular phone services, and web-based services, typically achieve an availability of only 99% to 90%' (AMSD Roadmap 2003, p. 31). One can speculate that this is in part because of both greater overall system complexity, but also the move away from a highly regulated economic environment made up of major, often nationally-owned, companies that were required by their governments to meet stringent reliability and availability standards.

It is extremely difficult to obtain any objective, let alone quantitative, assessments of the present state of the art with respect to system security. However, the AMSD Roadmap states that:

> the increasing number of breaches that is indicated by industry and government surveys and statistics on cyber-crime is already impacting on user trust and confidence and hence take-up. For example, the EU project Statistical Indicators for Benchmarking the Information Society (SIBIS) indicates that perceived online risks are deterring large numbers of consumers from making online transactions. (AMSD Roadmap 2003, Vol. 3, p. 30)

Schneier's book *Secrets and Lies: Digital Security in a Networked World* (Schneier 2000) starts with an alarmingly long list of security breaches reported during only the first week of March 2000, and goes on to say:

> Digital security tends to rely wholly on prevention: cryptography, firewalls and so forth. There's generally no detection and there's almost never any response or auditing. A prevention-only strategy only works if the prevention mechanisms are perfect; otherwise someone will figure how to get around them. Most of the attacks and vulnerabilities listed ... were the result of bypassing the prevention mechanisms. (p. 412)

In fact both Schneier and Anderson (1994) state that the great majority of reported security problems are due to the undependability of the underlying technical infrastructure, and especially the socio-technical environment, rather than to deficiencies of the cryptographic and other security mechanisms employed.

Moving on to consider systems-of-systems, this concept is not a new one, but has been given much impetus in recent years by various industry-led standardization efforts. Currently, the major emphasis is on the web services approach, which facilitates the use of web-servers by other computers, not just by human users of web browsers. By such means major pre-existing computing services can be taken advantage of in constructing new systems-of-systems (Narayanan and McIlraith 2002). An example that is commonly used to explain this approach is that of constructing a general travel agent enquiry service out of a set of separate pre-existing enquiry services operated by various hotel companies and airlines.

The web services approach to constructing systems-of-systems takes advantage of XML (eXtensible Markup Language) and allied technologies for defining and structuring the formats of data messages sent to and received from web-servers. As a result, large numbers of industry teams are now working on establishing special XML-based standards, each intended for use within a particular application sector. However, defining the exact meaning of such messages, as opposed to just their formats, and dealing with inter-sector incompatibilities, remain difficult, and hence a likely source of future systems-of-systems failures, as is any inability on the part of the designers to establish the exact specification of the services offered by a pre-existing system that has to be incorporated into their system-of-systems.

Perhaps the biggest problems at present concern: (1) systems-of-systems whose component systems belong to separate, even mutually suspicious organizations, perhaps operating under different legal jurisdictions; (2) systems-of-systems that need to be created quickly but have only a temporary existence, in support of what the military term 'dynamic coalitions', or their commercial counterparts; and (3) 'accidental' systems-of-systems, ones that have come into existence through almost haphazard system interconnections that have subsequently proved so useful as to create a system upon which large numbers of users have become dependent.

Regarding general computer-based systems, the whole subject area is in an early state, with comparatively little socio-technical expertise being available to guide system development, which thus tends to be treated as a solely technical challenge. However, with specialized computer-based systems in the arena of safety-critical control, for example, the situation is somewhat better. There have been studies in this arena of how best to partition the overall task between humans and computers so as to reduce the probability of failures due to misunderstandings across the human–machine interface, and to make best use of the greatly differing abilities that humans and computers have with respect to: (1) following complicated detailed sequences of instructions; and (2) recognizing that a situation is both novel and potentially dangerous. Elsewhere there have been a number of major failures, due to the little-understood realities of computer-based systems, which have even led to complete project cancellations. For example, it is all too easy to specify and implement a would-be highly secure computer-based system whose technical security features are completely nullified by the workarounds that users find themselves having to adopt if they are going to get their work done.

There are already a number of major government and industry initiatives, especially in the US, aimed at improving the present situation. These include projects by IBM on Autonomic Computing,[5] Microsoft on Trustworthy Computing,[6] the Defense Advanced Research Projects Agency's (DARPA) Organically Assured and Survivable Information Systems (OASIS) Program[7] and National Science Foundation's (NSF) Trusted Computing Program.[8]

3.2.3 Current Usage of the Dependability Technologies

A system typically can fail in several – possibly many – different ways, and these failures can be of widely varying severity as far as the system's environment is concerned. Thus, it is important to design systems so as at least to minimize the frequency of serious failures and, where possible, to set up or to modify system environments so as to avoid undue dependency on the more demanding functions expected of a system. Indeed, minimizing dependency can be as important as maximizing dependability. Unfortunately these issues are not always well understood.

These issues are equally important within systems, where they take the form of architectural design strategies concerning: (1) the positioning of system interfaces, especially between humans and computers; (2) the structuring of system activity so as to limit error propagation – for example, via techniques that can be seen as generalizations of the concept of a database transaction; and (3) the assessment of what dependence can be safely placed where, that is, which components can be 'trusted', in some appropriate sense, a crucial aspect of the task of 'risk management'.

Successful resolution of such issues provides an excellent starting point for making good use of the four dependability technologies, which we now deal with in succession.

3.2.3.1 Fault prevention
The task of fault prevention centres on extremely careful, well-documented and well-managed processes for specifying a system's required functionality, and so-called 'non-functionalities', in particular dependability, and then making the myriad decisions, from architectural to detailed coding choices, that constitute the full development process – one that will of necessity be tentative and iterative, and which may continue well after initial versions of a system are first fielded. This process is aided, particularly in the case of software, by the appropriate use of well-supported modularization and information-hiding techniques, rigorous design conventions and so on, while techniques such as shielding and radiation-hardening can prevent the introduction of operational physical faults into hardware systems.

With software, the production task needed in order to generate multiple instances of a software component is essentially finished once all design and implementation decisions have been taken (and confirmed), given the trivial ease with which one can generate accurate copies. Production of an actual hardware system, however, involves extremely challenging manufacturing processes that also can introduce faults if great care is not taken.

Additional complications arise when what is being designed is a generic system, from which a version of the system intended for a particular environment and set of circumstances has to be produced by some 'configuration process', indeed an activity which may need to be repeated in order to adapt a system to changing needs. However, this is in reality just a continuation of the design and implementation process, and hence equally an arena in which fault prevention has a major role to play, though with the additional difficulty of needing to confirm that the system's basic functionality actually admits of being configured and reconfigured as required.

Europe in general and the UK in particular have made major contributions to formal development methods for systems (especially software).[9] Used sensibly, such formal methods can produce systems, such as the French Réseau Express Régional train control software, that are (known to be) highly reliable (Guiho and Hennebert 1990). Furthermore, as for example Praxis' use of formal methods on a Civil Aviation Authority (CAA) air traffic control system has shown, the resulting software can be of significantly higher quality, but can also be produced more quickly and at lower cost than is typical of the much less rigorous techniques that are employed in many other parts of the software industry. Several other European software and systems companies have reported similar findings.

None of this should really be surprising: any significant engineering task requires documentation and justification and the mark of an engineering discipline is the use of mathematically based methods. What is surprising is that such methods are not more widely applied in software design, at least for relatively modest systems and system components. Lessons that need to be learned by formal methods researchers include the fact that that there is a cost–benefit trade-off in the mathematical sophistication expected of users, and the fact that pictorial representations can both have firm semantic foundations and be readily accepted. From the user's side, it is true that as increasing percentages of practitioners have sound engineering training, and possibly formal engineering professional status, this will result in a culture which will more readily accept new (formally based) notations, especially if these are well supported and integrated with conventional software engineering tools (Rushby 2000).

This is not, however, to claim that current formal methods and their tools are readily applicable to large and complex systems in their entirety. Indeed, a review commissioned by the German Bundesamt für Sicherheit in der Informationstechnik (BSI), is reported in the AMSD Overall Dependability Roadmap as having given the following rough estimates of their present limits:

- Equivalence checking of 1 million gate application-specific integrated circuits (ASICs).
- Model checking of 1,000 latches at a time, using techniques for modularizing and looking at components, for example there are claims of verifying large (10^{20}) state spaces.

- Software verification from design to code of ~80K lines of code.
- Simple formally verified compilers for special purpose languages.
- Static analysis of >150K lines of code.
- Specification and modelling of >30,000 lines of specification.

This does not mean that completely formal methods have no part to play in the development of large systems; rather that they are likely to be confined, for some time to come, to small highly critical areas and to higher architectural levels of systems. A major issue for wider use is tool support.

A separate, equally important issue, given the very frequent requirement to adapt existing systems, is that there is a need to find means of adaptation that at least preserve existing dependability levels and which make good use of the existing rigorous design documentation and arguments. The present situation in which, for example, a security certification is typically valid for only a single hardware and software configuration, and in which formal validation typically has to start from scratch after any significant change is made, will have to be improved greatly if formal methods are to contribute to making adaptation a dependable and cost-effective process.

3.2.3.2 Fault removal

Fault removal is employed during both system development and system deployment – in the former case it can form an integral part of a formal engineering approach. A first level of such fault removal relates to faults of a general nature, such as deadlocks or buffer overflows; the more challenging level relates to system-specific faults, that is, ones that are related to the particular requirements placed on a system.

Though terminology varies, it is typical to distinguish between the task of validating a system specification, that is, establishing that it is consistent with the requirements that are placed on the system, and that of verifying that a system adheres to its specification. Validation and verification can take place at all stages of development and deployment, though the aim is to perform both at the earliest stage possible. One can distinguish between static verification, which involves inspecting or analysing the system without actually exercising it, and dynamic verification, which involves exercising the system on symbolic or actual inputs. This latter approach, system testing or 'debugging', is in fact often the primary means by which confidence in a system is achieved. Validation and verification can be fully integrated into a formal development process and, if well supported by tools, can greatly encourage the industrial take-up of such processes.

Tools cannot replace the need for thought, but they can increase the effectiveness of the design intuitions and inspections. An interesting case study is the ready acceptance of model-checking tools. Some model-checking systems can be used to detect critical timing problems such as 'deadlocks'; other systems check that logical (often temporal) assertions are true of executions of a system. At least in their initial forms, model-checking tools worked on the executable code of a system. Their attraction is that one can deploy them on the final product; but this is also their weakness: they do not help construct a correct implementation, they only help locate errors. A badly architected system will never be made dependable by work at the final stages of development.

Another example of tools that help locate errors is the class of extended static checkers (ESC). Hoare (2002) reports significant progress with the adoption of assertions within Microsoft where ESC tools support their use. To gain the full benefit of such formal approaches they must, however, be used early in the development process where the key architectural decisions are made – and recorded as abstractions of the detailed code – which affect related issues such as usability and security, rather than just as an adjunct to detailed implementation.

For many years much if not most fault removal has been done through various forms of conventional system testing. There is a large and active academic and industrial test community, whose activities range from the development and use of sophisticated tool-supported techniques for selecting and automatically processing test cases, down to simply making *alpha* and *beta* versions of software available to large, perhaps very large, numbers of customers, so as to receive bug reports from them. Clearly, this latter approach is of little relevance to one-off systems.

Ideally, the result of using fault prevention and removal techniques, especially highly formal ones, is a correct system, that is, one that is completely free of design faults by the time it is deployed. In practice, even with relatively small software systems, intended for safety-critical applications and developed using highly-prescribed well-tooled techniques, the fault density (faults per thousand lines of code) is rarely less than one – though significantly better than this can be achieved by taking extreme care, and it has been claimed that some Space Shuttle software had less than 0.01 faults per thousand lines of code (AMSD Roadmap 2003). But such statistics relate to systems that are far less complex than the ones that concern us in this chapter, systems whose deployment must surely also involve extensive reliance on fault removal and/or fault tolerance.

3.2.3.3 Fault tolerance
The subject of fault tolerance originated in the earliest days of computing, and was aimed at reducing the frequency and/or seriousness of system failures due to operational hardware faults. The provision of means of tolerating operational hardware and environmental faults, whether at a

detailed level, for example via the use of error detecting and correcting codes, or at an architectural level via the use of replicated major components, which indeed replicated complete computers, is now comparatively well understood and well supported by design methods and tools. One interesting current example of the successful use of such fault tolerance on a well-known system with a huge global user base is that made by Google, which uses massively replicated processor and storage facilities in order to minimize system downtime and unavailability of any of its huge web archive (Ghemawat et al. 2003).

Tolerance of software design faults is not so well developed, but is achieved in some areas. These include database systems, whose facilities for logging and rerunning transactions have been shown to cope with a significant fraction of any residual software bugs, and safety-critical systems, such as the Boeing 777 flight control system, which employs redundant, diversely designed, software modules (Yeh 1999), but also – to a degree at least – in a number of well-known standard desktop applications by means of run time assertions, restart facilities and so on.

Fault tolerance in system-of-systems is typically provided using additional software components, in particular in the form of 'wrappers', that is, software that surrounds an existing system and, for example, augments its means of error detection and tries to cope with any disparities between the service it provides and that expected by the rest of the system-of-systems (Anderson et al. 2003).

Computer-based systems can suffer from any of the problems that can afflict more confined computer systems, but are also vulnerable to many others because of the involvement of humans. A computer system can perfectly match its specification, but the overall system can fail if unrealistic expectations are put on operators, for example a response to many alarms in an extremely short time. A general problem with systems, such as those that help operators control nuclear power plants, is to ensure that users can gain a clear picture of the 'state' of the physical system they are supposed to be monitoring. On the other hand, the human 'components' of a computer-based system may have critical roles to play in assuring that failures of the computer systems within the computer-based system are detected and recovered from.

Regarding the use of fault tolerance during the system design process, many of the tasks involved in developing a system gain such dependability as they possess by exploiting redundancy and diversity. For example, checking the consistency of a design with a specification, providing they have been produced 'independently', whether this checking is undertaken manually or automatically, can assist greatly in locating errors in each. However, a specification that has been generated automatically from a design, or a design that has been synthesized from a specification, contributes little to the task of finding and removing faults from either the specification or the design, though the chances of their being consistent with each other will presumably be enhanced by such automation – whereas redundant diverse specifications have been shown to be very effective (Anderson 1999). Activities such as model-checking and static analysis can all be viewed as contributing to the dependability, via fault tolerance, of the system-design system within which they are employed.

In such wider systems, the problems of fault tolerance, indeed the problems of dependability in general, are socio-technical problems. This is especially the case when it is necessary to take into account the possibility of faults arising from malicious behaviour, whether by insiders or by external attackers. However, the present state of the art with respect to the dependability of complex computer-based systems is at an early stage of development.

The idea of employing fault tolerance to enhance system security is not new (Dobson and Randell 1986), but is still a subject of research, for example by the recent European Union Information Society Technology Malicious and Accidental Fault Tolerance for Internet Applications (MAFTIA) project (Powell et al. 2001)[10] and elements of the DARPA OASIS Program, mentioned above. The aim of such research is to find means, either by fault masking or by error detection and recovery, of continuing to provide a useful level of secure service despite the fact that attackers are exploiting some vulnerability that has been discovered and not yet remedied. Fault masking might, for example, involve the use of multiple diverse redundant sub-systems, so that service could continue as long as only a minority had been compromised by the attacker; intrusion detection is a form of error detection, though at present, in practice, any subsequent recovery is still largely manual. But the discipline of choosing the goals for would-be secure systems in such a way that their human and organizational environments will be able to tolerate the systems' inevitable occasional failures is already of current practical importance, though rarely followed (Schneier 2000).

3.2.3.4 Fault forecasting

Quoting from an Appendix to the AMSD Overall Dependability Roadmap (Littlewood et al. 2003, p. 91):

> Underpinning almost all work on dependability evaluation must be a realisation of the 'inevitability of uncertainty' – in the processes we use to build systems, in the behaviour of the systems themselves. We cannot predict with certainty how dependable a system will be, even if we use the best process (e.g. as mandated in a standard); we cannot predict with certainty the failure behaviour of a system. Dependability evaluation is thus an evaluation in the face of uncertainty and will generally involve probability ... An exception to this observation concerns those

circumstances where formal verification of certain dependability properties is possible – e.g. proof that a certain class of failure is impossible under certain prescribed circumstances. However ... the possibility of fallibility of the proof process needs to be addressed ...

The quantitative estimation of operational hardware dependability, at least for relatively small assemblages of hardware components, even in sophisticated fault-tolerant architectures, is a well-established field, well supplied with powerful tools, based for example on Stochastic Petri Nets, for example Möbius, a next generation software modelling tool,[11] and SURF-2, a dependability evaluation tool.[12] The accuracy of the results obtained naturally depends on the accuracy of the component dependability statistics used, and the correctness of any assumptions made, for example, that faults will occur essentially independently.

The basic difficulty underlying all forms of evaluation of large computer systems, in particular that of estimating their dependability, is their discrete nature and complexity. One dare not assume that their logical design is fault-free, and thus conventional engineering concepts such as 'strength' or 'safety factor' are not available, and enumeration of all relevant possibilities, though in theory required, is in fact totally infeasible.

Statistical experiments aimed at estimating the number of design faults remaining in a complex software component, let alone the frequencies with which any such fault might be activated, need extremely large samples and are crucially dependent on the faithfulness with which the statistical sample mirrors, with respect to the effects of the unknown design faults, the characteristics of real operation. The present situation is that though – with considerable effort – software components of relatively modest size and complexity, such as are typically used for safety-critical control applications, can be built that in operation show every sign of achieving extremely high dependability, say 10^{-9} probability of failure on demand, it is rarely feasible to justify claims beyond say 10^{-3} or at most 10^{-4} by such methods.

Quantitative evaluation of the dependability of the various activities carried out within a system-design system is particularly difficult, and rarely attempted. It is, for example, far easier to assume (unjustifiably) that once the design of some component has been 'proved' correct, or model-checking has been completed, that these processes were themselves carried out faultlessly, rather than to come up with some credible numerical estimate of the probability of this being the case.

In practice, one has to settle for a 'dependability case'[13] which brings together all the available evidence about a system and the processes that were involved in its construction and validation. The unsolved problem is that of knowing how to combine this evidence, in order to come up with an overall estimation that is itself dependable. Thus, perhaps not surprisingly, one approach is to try to make the system evaluation process itself fault-tolerant, by constructing the dependability case out of a 'multi-legged' argument (Bloomfield and Littlewood 2003), and providing some believable evidence that there is sufficient diversity and independence between the various 'legs' of the argument such that, although each on its own may be insufficiently strong, their combination will be persuasive.

At bottom, the fundamental problem is that of identifying all the assumptions that have been made, for example that particular faults will never occur together, that an alleged proof is in fact correct, that a specification is complete and fully appropriate, that the compilation process did not introduce any errors, that two processes really are highly diverse, and so on, and then of justifying these assumptions.

3.2.4 Drivers

Moore's Law facilitates the prediction of future hardware capabilities and costs, that is, of the direct impacts of technological developments. But the indirect impacts, for example of the new markets that will be created, the new functions that will be found feasible and attractive to automate, are much more difficult to predict and the impacts are likely to be at least as great in practice. The creation of these new functions, perhaps in the form of entirely new applications or types of device, will, however, be greatly influenced by certain factors which, though not unique to the ICT industry, are unusually significant.

In particular, much of the software industry, at least those parts of the industry that are concerned with commodity software, is inherently likely to result in the creation of so-called 'natural monopolies' because, other than for one-off or specialized software, costs are greatly dominated by those of development rather than manufacturing. Thus, in such situations it is difficult to compete with any company that gains a dominant position in a particular market.

The economics of this situation are, however, at least in part of the software world, complicated by the emergence of the open source movement, which some have argued will have a beneficial influence regarding system dependability, especially security. There is thus a particular pressure to be 'first to market', usually at the expense of dependability. Add to this the fact that outside particular closely regulated market areas, for example those concerned with specialized safety-critical or security-critical systems, much software can currently be sold with little regard for issues of product liability, and it is clear why to date ordinary market forces are often not very effective in ensuring that dependability concerns are properly valued.[14]

Instead, government policies, and perhaps social and media pressures, may prove at least as significant. One can readily trace several recent US industrial initiatives at least in part to public post-September 11 pressure placed directly on the companies by the US government. In addition, factors such as the relative weight given to the protection of personal privacy versus law enforcement considerations and how issues of cross-border legal jurisdiction develop, may also greatly influence how system dependability issues are treated in the future.

Another non-technical influence on what levels of system dependability will be achieved is the current fashion for efficiency gains. This often results in over-optimization: running very close to capacity margins makes load fluctuations much more likely causes of system failure, and arguments for the provision of extensive protective redundancy can fall on deaf ears. This particular point applies to all sorts of systems, not just computer systems of course, but with computer systems it is exacerbated because of the difficulty in predicting and quantifying dependability gains.

Finally, an even more direct driver is the seemingly ever-increasing level of malicious and fraudulent behaviour aimed at computing systems – to say nothing of possible serious terrorist attacks. The future impact of planned and possible further law enforcement measures, both on offenders and on system providers, is extremely difficult to foresee.

3.2.5 Pervasiveness

As computers become ever smaller and cheaper, it is becoming feasible to integrate them into ever more things and ever more aspects of life and commerce. At the same time there are now many ways of interconnecting computers over various distances and effective means of reaching agreement on protocol standards, largely based on the Internet Protocol (IP).

Thus, the quotation attributed to Lamport,[15] 'A distributed system is one in which the failure of a computer you didn't even know existed can render your own computer unusable', was but a harbinger of things to come.

One can now, for example, imagine situations in which computers one does not know one is wearing or carrying are involved in large-scale dependability problems that are adversely affecting huge numbers of people that one has never heard of. Indeed, there are predictions of 'everything being connected to everything', and of 'disappearing computers', which have led to interest in the many new commercial opportunities and – in some quarters – grave concerns about possible loss of privacy.

More generally there is the question of how effectively the environment which is pervaded by computers can tolerate any serious overall system failures – in other words of the extent to which this environment has become dependent on these pervasive systems. The telephone system can be regarded as representing an early, at least somewhat pervasive system. Isolated and temporary failures of small parts of this system, for example affecting individual subscribers, were relatively common and acceptable. However, incidents such as the one that brought down almost the whole of the US East Coast telephone system for many hours as a result of a cascading set of faults (arising during a system upgrade) provides a dramatic foretaste of what might happen in future (Kemp 1990).

Pervasive computing implies dynamic groups of 'computation facilities' that are in communication. Unlike the problem of 'network partitioning', this means, for example, that each individual node has no concept of say 'half of the nodes being reachable'. Thus, there is a real challenge of knowing which nodes are trying to do what. Add to this the fact that there will be trusted and untrusted partners and you get (playground-like) pictures of a node realizing that it is surrounded by untrusted nodes. Obviously this whole picture is unbelievably dynamic. This raises challenges of what is the 'purpose' of a node and where does this purpose come from? All of these practical problems need theory beneath them to really underpin them.

3.3 FUTURE DIRECTIONS

Technology and, in particular, R&D forecasts often attempt to predict breakthroughs as well as incremental technological developments, and ignore many types of possible (socio)-technical failures and their consequences. However, there is unlikely to be a magic bullet to solve the problems of system dependability. Major improvements in the general dependability of the large-scale systems that are now being created can be achieved simply via the full employment of best practice and the industrialization of current and already planned future research. Nevertheless, even widespread use of the best methods available today will not suffice for the systems of the future. Thus, this section identifies a number of specific long-term challenges for research.

3.3.1 Long-Term Research Targets

3.3.1.1 Dependability-explicit systems and system-design systems
Current approaches to the design of dependable complex computer systems are in some ways analogous to the early methods for designing real-time systems, that is, systems whose operations have to conform to stringent timing constraints. These early methods were essentially iterative, in that only by completing a version of the system could it be found whether possibly extensive redesign was needed in order to ensure that timing

constraints would be met. Imagine that an aircraft design team had to build a first example of their new plane before they could find whether it met overall weight constraints!

In mentioning these analogies, a worthwhile, but highly challenging long-term goal for dependability research immediately suggests itself – that of incorporating effective concern for the achievement of any necessary dependability targets into the full system life cycle. This involves: (1) identifying explicit dependability requirements before a system is specified and designed; (2) gathering dependability information and estimates concerning system components, and of the estimated effect on system dependability of any use of the various development and adaptation tools and techniques; and (3) exploiting this information throughout the development process, and during system deployment, in order to provide dependability-related guidance to all design and adaptation decisions.

The notion, therefore, is to annotate all design information files (specifications, algorithms, code and so on) with dependability-related meta-information, and to use and update this meta-information as the files themselves are processed by validation and verification tools and so on, using meta-level operations associated with these tools that carry forward the dependability estimation process. Such meta-information is likely to be composite and in part qualitative; and the task of determining how it should be processed will be far from straightforward, compared even to the processing of timing information during the design of a real-time system. Thus, this research aim is both challenging and worthwhile.

The record of the meta-level operations performed during system development on the dependability information will provide a trace of the dependability-related decisions and actions taken during design, thereby resulting in the construction of a 'dependability case', which could be used to support the design work, provide traceable evidence regarding the dependability of the system, or support a formal safety or security case, prior to system deployment. Any subsequent system adaptation will be equally well informed regarding the impact of any proposed subsequent changes to the system.

A separate, but related, goal should be to create and provide tool support for a process model, that is, a set of rules governing the way in which the overall development process is carried out, which ensures that all four dependability technologies (fault prevention, removal, tolerance and forecasting) are properly employed throughout system development – that is, that the system-design system is itself well designed to be highly dependable (Kaâniche et al. 2002). This would be done by (1) considering the activities related to the four dependability technologies as explicitly forming four distinct fundamental processes, within a comprehensive development model;

and (2) providing a tool environment which guides and constrains the interactions among these processes, and with all the other processes, for example requirements definition, specification and implementation, which make up the overall development process.

Achievement of these two goals taken together would turn the process of developing complex computer systems that meet given dependability requirements into one that, via its explicit concern for dependability, is much more akin to a true engineering process than at present.

3.3.1.2 Cost-effective formal methods

The use of formal methods tends to be confined to safety-critical applications. We have already argued above that this need not be the case. But it is clear that any development process (or system-design system) that creates a poor system and then tries to improve the quality either by testing or by formally based approaches is doomed to discard much work: scrap-and-rework is the productivity drain of large system design. The temptation to believe that things can be put right later is greater with software than elsewhere in engineering because there is no physical artifact going into the bin.

The crucial step towards cost-effective use of formal methods is to use them throughout the development process. They can be of particular value in developing robust fault tolerance mechanisms. There is a significant challenge here for tool builders in that support is required that keeps track of the entire development process and can support changes to requirements in the sense that the impact of changes is clear and that unaffected parts of a system do not need to be revalidated.

Another key challenge in the area of tools is to develop common interfaces so that tools themselves can coexist. There are also some difficult research problems that are being addressed such as finding ways to use design abstractions to reduce model checking and testing. The argument that testing cannot prove that a complex system is correct is well known, but this observation does not indicate that testing is unnecessary. In fact, running a single test case establishes a result about a class of executions; the missing argument is about the size of that class. What is required is a means of combining the use of testing and formal reasoning (Bernot et al. 1991; Marre 1999). Earlier research on 'symbolic execution', 'abstract interpretation' and 'partial evaluation' is relevant to this aim, but there is a clear and urgent need for more research on a theory of testing.

It is clear that ensuring the effective use of formal methods, and of the tools that support them, involves socio-technical as well as technical research. In the area of concurrent and real-time systems there is a research challenge to find adequately compositional approaches. This requires a full awareness of interference, which is what makes compositionality difficult to achieve with concurrency. It is also clear that a full study of mobility is required to provide an underpinning of the sort of ubiquitous computing that is envisaged above. Furthermore, most interesting security issues are non-compositional and this poses additional questions for research, alongside those caused by the problems of information flow analysis and control in a world of open evolving networks of mobile as well as fixed devices. It is all too obvious that any system that is not closed to outside signals will attract the unwelcome attention of malicious attacks. Even the World Wide Web is plagued with worms, viruses and so on. The sort of systems described above, which are built from dynamic coalitions, will need to be much better architected than the Web if malicious attacks are not to render them unusable.

3.3.1.3 Architecture theory

Systems architecture concerns the way in which a system is constructed out of appropriately specified components and the means of component interconnection to be employed. A well-chosen system architecture will result in a cost-effective and high-quality product. Architectural-level reasoning about dependability has the merit of counteracting the situation in which system dependability concerns currently tend to be left until the later stages of system design and to result in solutions that are hidden within the detailed system design and implementation. There is now an initial body of work on architecting dependable systems and on tool support for specifying, analysing and constructing systems from existing components, building in part on the notion of architecture description languages (Shaw and Garlan 1996) as a contribution to ways of classifying systems designs. This encompasses research on, for example, the dependability of system-of-systems based on web services (Tartanoglu et al. 2003), and on providing means of tolerating intrusions (Veríssimo et al. 2003). It must also be recognized that the architecture of a system might have to reflect the need to assess the system dependability as well as to maximize that dependability.

It is imperative that such research makes further progress because of the importance of the overall architecture in the understandability and fault-containment properties of a system, whether the resulting dependability mechanisms are integral across an entire architecture or contained within particular architectural components. However, though the structure even of the technical part of a system should be designed carefully from the earliest stages, this is certainly not an argument for pure top-down design. Indeed, one of the key issues with architecture concerns the need for it to evolve as requirements change, not just to facilitate detailed changes that leave the architecture intact (Jones et al. 2003).

3.3.1.4 Adaptability

There is a danger of misinterpreting the previous three sections as implying that the problems of trustworthy pervasive systems are those of how to create systems *de novo* that can be trusted to meet a prespecified set of new dependability requirements. In some cases this will indeed be what is needed – though incremental procurement may well often be the best way to obtain such systems, so that system adaptability will be an important issue even in such circumstances. However, the more common problem, especially as far as very large and complex systems are concerned, is that the new system will have to be built starting from a situation in which there already exist various systems that are being depended upon, more or less successfully, by various sets of users whose needs will continue to have to be met during any change-over period. One can draw an analogy to the road construction world: traffic has to continue to flow somehow, even while major road construction projects are being undertaken, and wherever existing facilities still have a useful role to play, they have to be preserved and remain usable if possible.

The problems of (1) making use of pre-existing designs and, more specifically, dependability cases (in particular existing validation and verification data), in producing a new variant of an existing system, and (2) those of dependably changing over to the use of the new system, possibly without significant interruption to service, are thus of great significance. Ideally, the required adaptations will be confined to the internal activity of particular system components. In practice, there will often be a need to adapt existing interfaces and to do so dependably – a much more difficult problem (Jones et al. 2003). However, the extreme case of adaptability is the system that evolves automatically in response to changes in its environment. Such a property will become of increasing importance in the dynamic world of pervasive systems involving large numbers of mobile component systems – and maintaining dependability during such evolution will be a challenging research goal.

Realistically, adaptation and evolution activities will at times fail, so a further challenge is to integrate system change and exception handling facilities to facilitate recovery following such failures, both internal to the system and, when necessary, involving the human activities into which the system is integrated.

A particular class of evolutionary activity concerns fault removal. This can be undertaken either before a system is deployed or when faults are identified during operation. It has typically been regarded as an at least partly manual activity. However, there are now research programmes aimed at automating identification and even repair of faults in operational systems – that is, building what are sometimes called 'self-healing' or 'autonomic' systems. To what extent these aims are practical remains to be determined.

3.3.1.5 Building the right (computer-based) system

Even if it were the case that we routinely built programs that perfectly satisfy their specifications, the difficulty would often remain of getting the specification itself right. Risk management strategies constitute one approach to this issue – these involve assessments (albeit using rather coarse scales) of the likelihood and severity of the consequences of system failure and of the effectiveness of means by which such failures might be tolerated, and thus provide decision criteria that can be applied to many dependability requirements. This approach forms the basis for many security standards.

Similarly, there are major research challenges in order to construct dependable computer-based systems. Notions of, for example, trust and responsibility, which inform the day-to-day operation of an environment such as a hospital or a government department, are elusive and must be fully understood and recorded if a supportive system is to be specified. Furthermore, one must be able to reason about the activities of parties that might wish to disrupt a new system. The Engineering and Physical Sciences Research Council (EPSRC) Interdisciplinary Research Collaboration on the Dependability of Computer-Based Systems (DIRC)[16] is active in this area, but much more needs to be done.

Today, most computer systems are deeply embedded within groups of humans. What the Moore's Law reduction in hardware cost and size has given is ubiquity and closeness to the users. Nearly all professionals, and a huge percentage of manual workers, could not do their job without computers. But many of these computer systems are ill thought out and difficult to use. In many cases, the system is designed with scant attention to – or understanding of – the needs and capabilities of the user. In the highly professional contexts that DIRC has been investigating such as the National Health Service or National Air Traffic Service (NATS) there are crucial relationships of trust and responsibility that must be fully understood if a system is ever to be deployed successfully.

There has been a considerable amount of work dating back to Enid Mumford's early 'participative design' approach (Mumford and Henshall 1979), and including the more careful applications of Universal Markup Language (UML) 'use cases', on understanding the needs of users, but there is still a considerable research gap in finding ways of describing notions such as trust and responsibility. These fundamental notions are of particular importance when planning a system that will change the way people work: one cannot just infer the specification from current practices, but nor should one ignore the key functions and relationships of the people whose work will be affected by a new system.

There appears to be an inevitable feedback loop that the more dependable computing systems become, the more dependence is placed on them, that is, the more they will be trusted. The more dependable a major system is, the more any eventual failure is an emergency situation – and trust, which typically will have been built up gradually, will be lost abruptly. Similarly, when for whatever reason – perhaps a subconscious 'guesstimate' of the likely frequency or cost to them personally of failures, a run of bad publicity and so on – a person or whole population is unwilling to place significant trust in a system, the use he or she is willing to make of it, given any choice in the matter, may well be far from sufficient to justify the cost incurred in constructing the system. There is, thus, a need for interdisciplinary work on how appropriate levels of trust can be built up, nurtured and, when necessary, regained. Of evident close relevance to this is the whole subject of risk assessment and management. Research is needed on methods for user-oriented risk assessments that address regulatory, legal and liability issues, as well as direct system requirements.

A closely related issue is that consideration of the wider system context is typically essential in order to determine an appropriate system specification – to identify what demands the environment will place on the system and what constraints might need to be exercised and strategies followed, outside the system – in order to achieve a satisfactory level of overall dependability. For example excessive demand for a system that is a shared resource may not be controllable by the system itself, but instead may have to be controlled outside the system. If this demand originates with people, the wider context together with the computer system can be regarded as a computer-based system whose overall dependability is at stake, again implying the need for a socio-technical approach to the problem.

3.3.2 The Overall Aims

The foregoing discussion aims not just to identify a set of high-priority technical dependability research topics. Rather, and more importantly, the aim is to ensure that research that is carried out will be effective. It should relate well to the realities of government and industry as well as to evident technological trends and to the realities of systems in which human beings are frequently as important a part of system dependability problems and their solutions as are technical matters concerning hardware, software and communication.

We do not suggest that the task of developing and deploying trustworthy pervasive systems can be one that becomes entirely guided by formal and quantitative considerations, even when supported by tools that cope effectively with requirements for system adaptability. However, it is possible that enough progress can be made so that conventional business practices and market forces will start to play a dominant and effective role in ensuring that governments, industry and society are provided with systems of the required size and functionality, whose dependability matches the dependence that has to be placed on them. Therefore, rather than provide a set of specific and rather arbitrary quantitative goals for various dependability-related research targets, we suggest that it is more appropriate to have as an overall goal:

- the generation of dependability techniques and tools which, when supported by appropriate policy and training initiatives, enable the UK software and systems industry involved in creating complex networked systems to offer warranted software and services, even for pervasive computer-based systems and systems-of-systems.

Complementary goals are then those of seeking to ensure that:

- dependability research is pursued in such a manner as to take full cognizance of the consequences of the human involvement, both as (accidental and malevolent) sources of dependability problems, and of dependability solutions, in computer-based systems and system-design systems; and that

- in such research, whether aimed at the problems of developing or of deploying complex pervasive systems, fault prevention, fault removal and fault tolerance are regarded as complementary strategies, whose effective combination is crucial, and fault forecasting is used to evaluate the degree of success that is being achieved.

3.4 OPPORTUNITIES FOR CROSS-DISCIPLINARITY

Quoting again from the AMSD Overall Dependability Roadmap:

> There is a need for interdisciplinarity among the various technical communities whose work – whether they realize it or not – is highly related to overall system dependability. Many of the technical disciplines focus very narrowly on particular types/levels of systems, dependability attributes, types of fault, and means for achieving dependability. For example, only in recent years has a (small part) of the security community started acknowledging the importance of fault tolerance. In addition to this technical-interdisciplinarity there is a need for multi-disciplinarity in the sense of socio-technical interdisciplinarity. (AMSD 2003, Part 3, p. 14)

The need for such interdisciplinary research and activity in the area of achieving dependable systems is already clear today when one considers major applications such as those envisaged in medical records, electronically mediated voting, or defence systems involving military personnel working in complex coalitions, for example. Furthermore, our national infrastructure is at risk if we fail to take an interdisciplinary view of the capabilities of potential attackers.

Serious though these issues are, we face even larger challenges in the immediate future. We are faced with the impact of the observation that, as dependability increases, society increases its dependence on the technology. Furthermore, the continued progress along the lines of Moore's Law is making it possible to deploy huge numbers of computing devices which will themselves form coalitions. These virtuous coalitions will face attack from large numbers of computation units launched by malicious forces.

We need interdisciplinary teams to design systems and to study their development processes. We need to find ways to facilitate effective collaboration within such teams. There is a need to harness sociologists, psychologists and economists and those working in related disciplines, for example by building on the efforts by the Economic and Social Research Council's (ESRC) Programme on Information and Communication Technologies (PICT) (Dutton and Peltu 1996) and its subsequent programmes, to promote such interdisciplinarity. We also need to harness work being pursued in the dependability arena by the EPSRC's Interdisciplinary Research Collaboration on the Dependability of Computer-Based Systems (DIRC), referred to above.

NOTES

1   In 1965 Gordon Moore of Intel noted that the number of transistors per integrated circuit was doubling every year. This situation lasted until the 1970s, when the doubling slowed down to every 18 months, but this still dramatic rate of progress has continued ever since and shows every sign of going on for some years to come. Similar improvements are occurring in storage and network technologies, presaging continued spectacular improvements in system costs and performance.
2   See http://www.acp-wa-state.org/Downtime_Costs.doc accessed 17 April 2004.
3   The task undertaken by a system-design system is, of course, both a management and a combined technical and socio-technical challenge – this chapter concentrates on the latter challenge – which when handled inadequately can greatly exacerbate the management challenge. Note, this is a special class of computer-based system; in fact all three categories – computer-based system, system-design system and system-of-systems – overlap.
4   Here we provide only a very brief outline of these concepts – fuller accounts can be found in Laprie (1991) and Randell (2000).
5   See http://www-3.ibm.com/autonomic/index.shtml accessed 17 April 2004.
6   See http://www.microsoft.com/security/whitepapers/secure_platform.asp accessed 17 April 2004.
7   See http://www.darpa.mil/ipto/programs/oasis/goals.htm accessed 17 April 2004.
8   See http://www.cise.nsf.gov/fndg/pubs/display2.cfm?pub_id=5370 accessed 17 April 2004.
9   Surveys of this area are provided by for example Clarke and Wing (1996) and van Lamsweerde (2000).

10 See http://www.newcastle.research.ec.org/maftia/ accessed 17 April 2004.
11 See http://www.crhc.uiuc.edu/PERFORM/mobius-software.html accessed 17 April 2004.
12 See http://www.laas.fr/surf/ accessed 17 Apr. 04.
13 The notion of a 'dependability' case is an obvious generalization of the now well-accepted idea of a 'safetycase'.
14 For example it would appear that the present problems of wholesale virus propagation largely stem from the fact that Microsoft's email systems ignore (in favour of functionality and 'user convenience') the restrictive rules in RFC 1341 (see http://www.faqs.org/rfcs/rfc1341.html accessed 17 April 2004), the 1992 MIME standard for email attachments, which were specifically aimed at reducing the danger of transmitting rogue programs through the mail.
15 See http://research.microsoft.com/users/lamport/pubs/distributed-system.txt accessed 17 April 2004.
16 See http://www.dirc.org.uk accessed 17 April 2004.

REFERENCES

AMSD Roadmap (2003), *A Dependability Roadmap for the Information Society in Europe*, Accompanying Measure on System Dependability (AMSD) IST-2001-37553 - Work-package 1: Overall Dependability Road-mapping. Deliverable D1.1, http://www.am-sd.org accessed 17 Apr. 04.

Anderson, R. (1994), 'Why Cryptosystems Fail', *Communications of the ACM* 37(11): 32-40. An extended version (1999), http://www.cl.cam.ac.uk/users/rja14/wcf.html) accessed 17 Apr. 04.

Anderson, R. (1999), 'How to Cheat at the Lottery (or, Massively Parallel Requirements Engineering)', in *Proceedings of the Computer Security Applications Conference (ACSAC'99)*, Phoenix, AZ, New York: IEEE Computer Society Press,
http://csdl.computer.org/comp/proceedings/acsac/1999/0346/00/0346000 1abs.htm accessed 17 Apr. 04.

Anderson, T. Feng, M., Riddle, S. and Ramonousky, A. (2003), 'Protective Wrapper Development: A Case Study', in *Proceedings of the 2nd International Conference on COTS-Based Software Systems Conference (ICCBSS 2003)*, Ottawa, 10-12 February, LNCS 2580, pp. 1-15.

Avizienis, A. and He, Y. (1999), 'Microprocessor Entomology: A Taxonomy of Design Faults in COTS Microprocessors', in *Proceedings of Dependable Computing for Critical Applications (DCCA '99)*, 6-8 January, San Jose, CA, New York: IEEE Computer Society Press, pp. 3-23.

Avizienis, A., Laprie, J. and Randell, B. (2001), 'Fundamental Concepts of Computer System Dependability', IARP/IEEE-RAS Workshop on Robot Dependability: Technological Challenge of Dependable Robots in Human Environments, Seoul, 21-22 May,
http://www.cs.virginia.edu/~jck/cs651/papers/laprie.taxonomy.pdf

accessed 5 May 04.

Bernot, G., Gaudel, M.-C. and Marre, B (1991), 'Software Testing Based on Formal Specifications: A Theory and a Tool', *Software Engineering Journal* 6(6): 387-405.

Bloomfield, R.E. and Littlewood, B. (2003), 'Multi-Legged Arguments: The Impact of Diversity upon Confidence in Dependability Arguments', in *Proceedings of the Conference on Dependable Systems and Networks,* 22-25 June, San Francisco CA, New York: IEEE Computer Society Press, pp. 25-34, http://csdl.computer.org/comp/proceedings/dsn/2003/1952/00/19520025abs.htm accessed 17 Apr. 04.

Clarke, E.M. and Wing, J.M. (1996), 'Formal Methods: State of the Art and Future Directions', *ACM Computing Surveys* 28(4): 626-43.

Dobson, J.E. and Randell, B. (1986), 'Building Reliable Secure Systems out of Unreliable Insecure Components', in *Proceedings of the Conference on Security and Privacy,* Oakland CA, April, New York: IEEE Computer Society Press, pp. 187-93, http://www.cs.ncl.ac.uk/research/pubs/inproceedings/papers/355.pdf accessed 17 Apr. 04.

Dutton, W.H. and Peltu, M. (eds) (1996), *Information and Communication Technologies: Visions and Realities*, Oxford: Oxford University Press.

Estrin, D.L. (ed.) (2001), *Embedded, Everywhere: A Research Agenda for Networked Systems of Embedded Computers*, Washington DC: Computer Science and Technology Board, National Academy of Science, http://www7.nationalacademies.org/cstb/pub_embedded.html accessed 17 Apr. 04.

European Commission (2002), *e-Europe 2005 Action Plan: An Information Society for All*, COM(2002) 263 final, Brussels: European Commission, http://europa.eu.int/information_society/eeurope/news_library/documents/eeurope2005/eeurope2005_en.pdf accessed 17 Apr. 04.

Ghemawat, S., Gobioff, H. and Leung, S.-T. (2003), 'The Google File System', in *Proceedings of the 19th Symposium on Operating System Principles (SOSP-2003),* 19-22 October, New York: ACM Press, http://www.cs.rochester.edu/sosp2003/papers/p125-ghemawat.pdf accessed 17 Apr. 04.

Guiho, G. and Hennebert, C. (1990), 'SACEM Software Validation', in *Proceedings. of the 12th International Conference on Software Engineering*, 26-30 March, Nice, New York: IEEE Computer Society Press, pp. 186-91, http://portal.acm.org/citation.cfm?id=100321&dl=ACM&coll=portal accessed 17 Apr. 04.

Hoare, C.A.R. (2002), 'Assertions in Programming: From Scientific Theory to Engineering Practice (Keynote Speech)', in *Proceedings of Soft-Ware 2002: Computing in an Imperfect World, First International Conference, Soft-Ware 2002 (Lecture Notes in Computer Science 2311),* 8-10 April, Belfast, Berlin: Springer, pp. 350-1.

Jones, C., Periorellis, P., Romanovsky, A. and Welsh, I. (2003), 'Structured Handling of On-Line Interface Upgrades in Integrating Dependable Systems of Systems', in *Proceedings of the Scientific Engineering for Distributed Java Applications International Workshop (FIDJI 2002),* Luxembourg, Berlin: Springer-Verlag, pp. 73-86, http://www.cs.ncl.ac.uk/research/pubs/inproceedings/papers/418.pdf accessed 17 Apr. 04.

Kaâniche, M., Laprie, J.-C. and Blanquart, J.P. (2002), 'A Framework for Dependability Engineering of Critical Computing Systems', *Safety Science* 40(9): 731-52.

Kemp, D.H. (1990), 'Technical Background on AT&T's Network Slowdown, January 15, 1990', *The Risks Digest,* 9(63), http://catless.ncl.ac.uk/Risks/9.63.html#subj3 accessed 17 Apr. 04.

Laprie, J.C. (ed.) (1991), *Dependability: Basic Concepts and Associated Terminology, Dependable Computing and Fault-Tolerant Systems,* Berlin: Springer-Verlag.

Laprie, J.C. (1999), 'Dependability of Software-Based Critical Systems', in D.R. Avresky (ed.), *Dependable Network Computing,* Dordrecht: Kluwer Academic Publishers, pp. 3-9.

Littlewood, B., Bloomfield, R. and Laprie, J.C. (2003), 'Trends in System Evaluation (Vol. 3, Appendix F)', in M. Masera and R. Bloomfield (eds), *A Dependability Roadmap for the Information Society in Europe,* Accompanying Measure on System Dependability (AMSD) IST-2001-37553 - Work-package 1: Overall Dependability Road-mapping. Deliverable D1.1, pp. 91-4, http://www.am-sd.org accessed 17 Apr. 04.

Marre, B. (1999), 'Symbolic Techniques for Test Data Selection from Formal Specifications', in J.M. Wing, J. Woodcock, and J. Davies (eds), *Formal Methods 99,* Toulouse, September, Berlin: Springer-Verlag, pp. 1708-9.

Mumford, E. and Henshall, D. (1979), *A Participative Approach to Computer Systems Design: A Case Study of the Introduction of a New Computer System,* London: Associated Business Press.

Narayanan, S. and McIlraith, S.A. (2002), 'Simulation, Verification and Automated Composition of Web services', in *Proceedings of the 11th International Conference on the World Wide Web (WWW'2002),* Honolulu, 8 May, New York: ACM Press, http://portal.acm.org/citation.cfm?id=511457&dl=ACM&coll=portal accessed 17 Apr. 04.

Pearce, S. (2003), *Government IT Projects, Report 200*, London: Parliamentary Office of Science and Technology.

Powell, D., Adelsbach, A., Cachin, C., Creese, S., Dacier, M., Deswarte, Y., McCutcheon, T., Neves, N., Pfitzmann, B., Randell, B., Stroud, R., Veríssimo, P. and Waidner, M. (2001), 'MAFTIA (Malicious- and Accidental-Fault Tolerance for Internet Applications)', in *Supplement of the 2001 International Conference on Dependable Systems and Networks*, Göteburg, New York: IEEE Computer Society Press, pp. D32-D35.

Randell, B. (2000), 'Facing up to Faults (Turing Memorial Lecture)', *Computer Journal* 43(2): 95-106, http://www.cs.ncl.ac.uk/research/pubs/articles/papers/245.pdf accessed 17 Apr. 04.

Rushby, J. (2000), 'Disappearing Formal Methods', in *Proc. High-Assurance Systems Engineering Symposium (HASE-5), 15-17 November, Albuquerque NM*, New York: ACM Press, pp. 95-6, http://csdl.computer.org/comp/proceedings/hase/2000/0927/00/0927toc.htm

Schneider, F.B. (ed.) (1999), *Trust in Cyberspace: Report of the Committee on Information Systems Trustworthiness, Computer Science and Telecommunications Board, Commission on Physical Sciences, Mathematics, and Applications*, National Research Council, Washington DC: National Academy Press, http://www.nap.edu/readingroom/books/trust/ accessed 17 Apr. 04.

Schneier, B. (2000), *Secrets and Lies: Digital Security in a Networked World*, Hoboken NJ: John Wiley & Sons.

Shaw, M. and Garlan, D. (1996), *Software Architecture: Perspectives on an Emerging Discipline*, New York: Prentice Hall.

Tartanoglu, F., Issarny, V., Levy, N. and Romanovsky, A. (2003), 'Dependability in the Web Services Architecture', in R. D. Lemos, C. Gacek and A. Romanovsky (eds), *Architecting Dependable Systems, LNCS-2677*, Berlin: Springer, pp. 89-108, http://www-rocq.inria.fr/arles/doc/doc.html accessed 17 Apr. 04.

van Campenhout, D., Mudge, T. and Hayes, J.P. (2000), 'Collection and Analysis of Microprocessor Design Errors', *IEEE Design and Test* 17(4): 51-60.

van Lamsweerde, A. (2000), 'Formal Specification: A Roadmap', in *Proceedings of Conference on The Future of Software Engineering, Limerick*, New York: ACM Press, pp. 147-59, http://portal.acm.org/citation.cfm?id=336546&dl=ACM&coll=portal accessed 17 Apr. 04.

Veríssimo, P., Neves, N.F. and Correia, M. (2003), 'Intrusion-Tolerant Architectures: Concepts and Design', in R.D. Lemos, C. Gacek and A.

Romanovsky (eds), *Architecting Dependable Systems,* LNCS-2677, Berlin: Springer, pp. 4-36, http://www-rocq.inria.fr/arles/doc/doc.html accessed 17 Apr. 04.

Yeh, Y.C.B. (1999), 'Design Considerations in Boeing 777 Fly-By-Wire Computers', in *Proceedings of 3rd IEEE International High-Assurance Systems Engineering Symposium,* 13-14 November, Washington DC, New York: IEEE Computer Society Press, http://csdl.computer.org/comp/proceedings/hase/1998/9221/00/92210064 abs.htm accessed 17 Apr. 04.

4 Identities and authentication

Fred Piper, Matthew J.B. Robshaw and Scarlet Schwiderski-Grosche

4.1 INTRODUCTION

As the automation of business and the use of electronic forms of communication increase, we are challenged with finding equivalents to such basic security and crime prevention features as face-to-face recognition and handwritten signatures. Although the technology is changing rapidly, when two people communicate electronically, for instance by email, they have usually lost the important facility of face-to-face recognition and need some other means of identifying each other. Similarly, while shoppers in the high street have confidence in the authenticity of the identities of the major stores that they frequent, it is not so easy for Internet shoppers to have confidence in the authenticity of a store's website.

Our focus in this chapter will be the identification and authentication of what we term primary objects, whether these be a person, a device or even digital data. This is an area of major concern to government and business, and weaknesses in currently used mechanisms allow exploitation by criminals. Many solutions have been proposed. Most are appropriate for certain environments and inappropriate for others. However, it is not always clear that the importance and/or magnitude of the problem are appreciated and there are many situations where systems are insecure and identity theft is a danger. It is perhaps worth noting that in some communities the terms 'identification' and 'authentication' are essentially synonymous. However, this is not true for biometrics where there is a very specific technical distinction (see Section 4.7).

We also discuss more speculative aspects of the overall authentication mechanism and consider the role of the infrastructure in supporting our applications and security mechanisms. Throughout industry there are islands of progress in securing different aspects of the information infrastructure. However, the issues are complex and, as yet, not particularly well formulated. Nevertheless, we believe that developments in the future will highlight many of these issues and help move the community towards developing a broader understanding of the problem and its solution.

4.2 AUTHENTICATION AND IDENTIFICATION IN CONTEXT

Before we can discuss the problems associated with identification and authentication in the electronic world we should consider some of the limitations of the techniques used in the pre-electronic age. Suppose for instance, that you look up someone's telephone number in a directory and dial it. If someone answers and claims to be that person, then can you be sure that they are the person you wish to contact? The realistic answer is yes, almost certainly. However, it is worthwhile to stress the assumptions you are making. The first is that your contact is the only person likely to pick up the phone and claim to be them. This, of course, may not be true. Even if the number is correct there may be two people at the same address with identical names, for example, mother and daughter. The phone call may have been rerouted by a criminal to an impostor who is deliberately impersonating the person you wish to contact. The second assumption is that the number in the directory is accurate. This is almost certainly true if you are relying on a paper version of the directory that has been published by, for instance, the telephone company, and it would certainly be difficult for fraudsters to change people's entries. However, the same may not be true if you are relying on an electronic copy of the directory where obtaining assurance that the information has not been altered might be much more difficult.

There are three classic ways for a user to authenticate themselves to a system, which may be a computer, a network or another individual. They are: (1) something they own; (2) something they know; and (3) something they are (that is, a personal characteristic). Combinations of two or three authentication mechanisms are common, giving what is termed two- or three-factor authentication. Typically the 'something owned' might be some form of token. If that token has some form of processing capability, for example a smart card, then the something known might be a password to activate the device. The personal characteristic is likely to be some form of biometric, such as a fingerprint, and this might also be used as an activation process for a smart card. As we will see later, it is common for a smart card to have encryption capabilities and to contain cryptographic keys. The authentication process may then involve sophisticated protocols between the card and the authenticating device.

Before any of these techniques can be used, there must be an identification of the user to ensure that they have, in fact, been given the correct object or knowledge, or that the characteristic being associated with them is, in fact, theirs. This process is fundamentally important and is one that is frequently overlooked. The problems associated with establishing someone's identity are significant and this is an area that needs considerable research. Most of the commonly used authentication techniques assume that there has been an initial, accurate identification, and rely on that assumption. Authentication techniques that rely on something owned and/or something known cannot authenticate the individual. All that they do is equate the individual with either the knowledge or possession. If the original identification is not conducted properly then obvious disaster looms. Even if the identification process is accurate, there is always the danger that impostors may either obtain the knowledge or capture the token.

4.3 EXAMPLES AND POTENTIAL PROBLEMS

Your front door key authenticates you as an authorized entrant to the lock and allows you entry to your home. Similarly, a password may authenticate you to your computer and allow you to log on to the system. However, in neither case is the individual being authenticated. Anyone who has possession of the correct key or knows your password will also be accepted. In the case of door keys it is, of course, common for many people to have copies of the same key and, unless some crime is committed, there is no need to be able to determine which of the legitimate key holders opened the door. The situation with passwords is different and, usually, passwords are intended to be unique to specific users.

A common authentication mechanism for shoppers is the use of a credit card with the holder's signature on a white stripe on the back of the card. The card will usually contain the issuer's logo plus a hologram to make counterfeiting difficult. The authentication process is simple. When the user makes a purchase they sign a docket and the retailer compares the signature on the docket with that on the card. When this form of authentication was first introduced the standard way of distributing these cards was to use the postal system and to request the user to sign the stripe as soon as they received the card. This led to an obvious attack. If someone intercepted a card during its postal transmission they could write the cardholder's name (in their own handwriting, of course) on the white stripe. They would then present the card to a retailer and, after completing a purchase, write the cardholder's name on the docket. The two 'signatures', the one on the card and the one on the docket, would agree and the retailer would allow the impostor to walk away with the goods. It is important to note here that the imposter is not actually forging the real user's signature. In fact they have never seen it. What they are doing is exploiting a weakness in the card distribution infrastructure to get the real user's name, written in the imposter's handwriting, established as authentic. Having a more secure distribution system easily thwarts the attack. Many modern cards also incorporate the user's photo as an extra security check.

An example of a combination of something known and something owned is the process associated with withdrawing cash from automatic teller machines (ATMs). When debit cards are used at ATMs, the card is inserted into the ATM and the customer enters a (secret) personal identification number (PIN). The system then checks that the PIN entered is the one allocated to the account identified by the details encoded on the card's magnetic stripe. Because the human is taken out of the authentication process, the logo and hologram are not relevant and attackers can make 'white cards' which, to the human eye, are clearly identifiable as forgeries but which contain the correct magnetic stripe details and are, therefore, accepted by the network. The security of the authentication system depends on the user keeping their PIN secret. It is worth noting that while the user is authenticated by the network, the user has no way of authenticating the system. This provides an example of one-way authentication and can lead to problems involving 'dummy' ATMs (Anderson 1994).

In the next few sections we introduce and discuss some of the fundamental technologies used for identification and authentication. We will begin with the simple password and then move through the use of cryptographic technologies to biometrics.

Throughout, though, we should keep in mind why we are doing this. In the traditional non-digital world we are constantly performing very sophisticated identification and authentication decisions without realizing it. Our eyes and minds are remarkably adept at recognizing visual clues – from people to objects – and the calculations we perform are remarkably complex to replicate on a computer. Yet, in cyberspace, we are robbed of this remarkable skill and it is for this reason that we find the need to introduce a replacement set of complex calculations to prove our identity to one another.

4.4 PASSWORDS

The aim of identification (which is sometimes described as entity authentication within the cryptographic community; Menezes et al. 1996) is to provide real-time assurance that some entity (a person or a device) is the one claimed. Suppose that a user wishes to authenticate him or herself to some authenticating server so that he or she can receive some service. In the subsequent text we sometimes refer to that user as the claimant, and we use the notion of 'authenticating server' in a general way to indicate any device that authenticates them.

The fixed password is perhaps the most common way of authenticating a user to a device such as a personal computer (PC). At the time of authentication, the user is identified by a user-name and prompted to enter a password. The system compares the entered password against the expected response and reacts accordingly.

It is clear that, at the very least, a fixed password system is vulnerable to interception and replay. The extent of the risk to which the system is exposed will depend on the deployment. If passwords are being transmitted across an unprotected network the risk is greater than with a closed system where there are limited opportunities for eavesdropping.

Since user-chosen passwords are memorable, they are likely to contain some inherent structure. Widely available password crackers, perhaps based on a dictionary search, appear to achieve a surprisingly high success rate when attacking user-chosen passwords. To help provide additional protection, some proposals deploy machine-generated passwords, but these are not especially popular. In fact, such approaches can sometimes be counter-productive since a password that is difficult to remember[1] is sometimes written down, which might degrade the overall security of the system.

A third point of weakness with password-based entity authentication is that a user's password must be stored within the system. Depending on the system and the deployment, this can be done in different ways. To reduce the risks of compromise, it is common practice to store not the password, but the image of the password after it has been processed through a one-way function. A one-way function is a computational process which is easy to perform in one direction, but difficult to reverse (see Menezes et al. 1996). Thus, the image of the user-supplied password can be compared with the stored image of the password. So, even if the password file is stolen or compromised in some way, it remains difficult to reverse the images of the passwords to recover the original passwords.

While there are substantial problems with password-based authentication – and these problems mean that passwords are considered a weak form of authentication – it should be noted that passwords are very familiar and offer a wide degree of user acceptability and convenience. Added to this, administration safeguards can be used to ensure that user-chosen passwords satisfy certain criteria to help set a minimum level of password acceptability. Users can also be forced to change their passwords at regular intervals, and systems often lock-down after a specific number of unsuccessful login attempts.

As a particular form of password, we have already mentioned the PIN. We are very familiar with this mechanism from the banking industry, but the PIN is little more than a short, restricted password. As far as password-based authentication is concerned, the PIN would appear to offer very little security. However, such PIN-based authentication does not depend on the PIN alone. The PIN is typically used in a two-factor authentication system and it is used in conjunction with the bank (or ATM) card. The user is only authenticated if they have the right card and they know the correct PIN.

Certainly fixed passwords have many good attributes – most particularly the simplicity and cost of administration – but the risk of password discovery, interception and/or replay might be too great in some deployments. The one-time password is a move towards a stronger means of authentication.

In a one-time password scheme, a user's password may only be valid for a short time frame, perhaps for 30 seconds or one minute. After this time the password changes. Thus, the window of opportunity for an attacker is greatly reduced since an intercepted password is unlikely to be of use in the future. All that we require is that the sequence of passwords should not be easy to predict after witnessing or intercepting a (potentially large) set of past passwords.

Such a one-time password scheme will require a moderate level of computational complexity and, to provide this, the user will typically be given a token. There are a variety of schemes available, but one of the largest deployments is probably RSA SecurID.[2] The RSA SecurID technology can be provided in a variety of form-factors, but most typical deployments will involve a tamper-resistant card. The card is issued to a specific user and each card contains a secret quantity, which is also held at the authenticating server. The one-time password is computed as a complex function of the physical time, the unknown secret stored in the card and, optionally, a user-supplied PIN. The password on the token display should then match the password anticipated by the server.

Such tokens have an inherent cost of deployment in terms of manufacturing the cards and supporting the infrastructure. User acceptability is reasonably high and products like RSA SecurID are likely to provide a good level of security when compared to fixed passwords. Interestingly, such technology can also be deployed in software and is supported on a variety of platforms including some mobile phones. In this way, the cost of card deployment is mitigated, and the mobile phone can be used as a convenient channel for deployment. In some sense, the phone itself becomes the token.

Even though the window of opportunity for interception and replay might be reduced with a one-time password mechanism, it is still not referred to as strong authentication. For this we require some real-time interaction and we will need to use some cryptographic algorithms.

4.5 INTERACTIVE AUTHENTICATION

We now move on to consider stronger forms of authentication. Instead of transferring a password (or a short-lived password) as a means of authentication, the authenticating server and the claimant (typically a card or token) perform some protocol or exchange of messages. In general terms, the server sends a challenge to the token and a cryptographic computation takes place within the card or token. The result is sent back to the server for verification. The cryptographic computation can be based on secret (symmetric) key or public (asymmetric) key techniques.

In classical cryptography, the two participants in a cryptographic exchange share the same secret key. Such algorithms are referred to as secret key or symmetric algorithms. While there is now a wide variety of algorithms for achieving both confidentiality and authentication, it can be difficult to guarantee that both participants have the same key.

Public key or asymmetric cryptography allows two participants in a cryptographic exchange to possess different keys. Such systems are designed so that knowledge of one key (the public key) does not allow an adversary to recover the other (the private key). This is a very powerful property and permits a range of interesting applications. As well as providing encryption capabilities – where the sender of a message uses the receiver's public key and only the intended receiver can recover the encrypted message[3] – public key techniques can be used to provide what are termed digital signatures. Here, the signer of an electronic document performs a computation on the document using their own private key – this is an action only the signer of the document can perform – while the widely available public key can be used by anyone to verify that signature.

Of course, public key cryptography is not free of its own unique problems. In particular, ensuring the availability of authenticated, valid, public keys is a significant problem and one that has proved to be practically tractable in only a few specific areas of deployment. Such a supporting infrastructure is referred to as a public key infrastructure, or PKI.

Cryptographic algorithms are typically classified as shown in Table 4.1.

Table 4.1 Classification of cryptographic algorithms

	Confidentiality	Authentication
Secret key (symmetric) cryptography	Block ciphers Stream ciphers	Message authentication Codes
Public key (asymmetric) cryptography	Public key encryption	Digital signatures

4.5.1 Using Symmetric Techniques

There are a number of systems where authentication relies on the use of a secret that is shared between the two entities. In these systems the authentication may be one way, but there may also be the possibility of mutual, or two-way, authentication, where each entity authenticates the other. The basic principle is that two entities share a secret key that they believe is known only to them. The integrity of the authentication process is dependent on this key remaining secret. As a consequence, it will typically be delivered to the user in the form of a tamper-resistant token. Each participant regards the use of that secret as identifying the other.

It is worth noting that any mutual authentication scheme that relies on parties sharing keys can only be suitable for use between parties who trust each other. Furthermore, if one-way authentication is being provided then the verifier will need to be sure of the identity of the other party before agreeing to share a secret with them. Thus, for these systems, the original identification is likely to have taken place before the system is established. (For instance it might involve two personal friends who have known each other for a long time.) This is unlikely to be true in an e-commerce situation.

A variety of techniques is available to perform secret key-based authentication. For instance, in order to establish the identity of their partner an entity might issue a random number as a challenge, which the entity claiming to be the partner will encrypt using the shared secret as a key. If the result of decrypting the response with the shared secret key gives the original challenge, then the identity of the partner is authenticated. This kind of interaction is referred to as a challenge–response protocol.

One of the most widespread deployments of a version of secret key challenge-response is in global system for mobile communications (GSM) phones. The phone's security identity module (SIM) card is a tamper-resistant module that contains a secret. This is used in a challenge–response authentication protocol when the phone authenticates itself to the network.

When compared to passwords and one-time passwords, we can see why challenge–response authentication is a stronger mechanism. Instead of the claimant sending a currently valid password (which might then be reused over a limited period) the server challenges the claimant to perform some cryptographic computation that can only be accomplished with possession of the secret key. It is this element of timeliness that adds additional strength to the authentication process.

Like the move to one-time passwords, the need to deploy tamper-resistant tokens and the need to manage secret keys make the deployment of such mechanisms more expensive than a simple password-based approach. The computational resources for a secret key-based challenge–response protocol are likely to be more substantial than the simpler algorithms that might be deployed in cheaper one-time password tokens. And again, like one-time passwords, it is common to combine such a token-based authentication method with a user-PIN to authenticate the holder of the token.

4.5.2 Using Asymmetric Techniques

Once we have moved on to more computationally sophisticated tokens, a variety of technologies becomes available. One problem with a secret key-based solution is that, by necessity, there is a direct prior relationship between the authenticating server and the claimant token, since they both need to share the same secret key.

When we move to public key techniques we can deploy tokens that contain both the public and private key for that token. To verify some cryptographic operation, the public key can be sent (together with the transformed challenge) to the authenticating server. The entire computation can, therefore, be verified without any direct pre-existing relationship between the verifying server and the claimant token. While this simple description motivates the potential desirability of a public key-based solution, it also exhibits a minor sleight-of-hand. While there need not be a direct link between the claimant token and the authenticating server, we do require an indirect link, which allows the authenticity of the token's public key to be verified by the server. This indirect link is often provided by a PKI.

The basic principles involved when using public key cryptography are fairly straightforward. A user is associated with a pair of numbers. The first, the private key, can be used solely by that user and use of that number then effectively identifies that user. Thus, your private key has become essentially your electronic identity. The second, the public key, can be used by anyone to verify that the private key has been used. However, it is extremely difficult to determine the private key from the public key. In the real world there are a number of ways in which people can impersonate each other. A recent high-profile case involved the theft of a passport by someone who resembled the passport photo of the legitimate holder. When public key cryptography is being used there are at least two different ways in which user A might try to impersonate user B. They might either obtain B's private key or they might try substituting their public key for that of B. The protection of private keys relies on strong algorithms and strong physical protection for the key. The prevention of public key substitution is not so straightforward and the most common current solution involves the use of a trusted third party, called a certification authority (CA). Users identify themselves to the CA which then uses its own private key to sign an 'electronic certificate' binding the user to their public key value. Third parties can then check the signature using the

CA's public key and be confident that the CA is confirming that they have identified the user and confirmed the value of the user's public key. There are a number of protocols for using public keys to authenticate users. However, clearly, these rely on the accuracy and trustworthiness of the original identification performed by the CA.

Public key techniques can be used to provide encryption and digital signature capabilities and both can be used in a challenge–response protocol. As a consequence, many different proposals are available. The major downside in a move to public key techniques is the increase in computational resources required. Any claimant token is required to perform a computation involving the private key from the key pair since the cryptographic operation provides proof of the possession of the private key. The most widely deployed public key cryptographic algorithm is RSA, but the private key operation for this algorithm is computationally intensive. This means that tokens supporting RSA in this way need to be quite computationally sophisticated and this can put up the cost of deployment.

The most high-profile description of a public key challenge–response authentication protocol is perhaps that contained in the EMV specifications.[4] These specifications include a range of security techniques for the credit card industry and these are based on digital signatures. While we do not need to look at the details of these techniques, the simplest, static data authentication (SDA), would be used to authenticate data stored on the card. However, the remaining two, dynamic data authentication (DDA) and combined data authentication (CDA) would be used to provide assurance that a given card contains a specific private key. In the end, the most appropriate choice of protocol for deployment will be a business decision that depends on the sophistication of the adversary, the level of fraud anticipated, the security required, and the estimated cost of deployment.

Thus, in moving to asymmetric cryptography, we have replaced the management of secret keys (for secret key-based challenge–response authentication protocols) by the management of public keys. To some observers this might be viewed as no real gain. However, we have gained in the form of the deployment, which can now be much more open. A token can be issued by a different administrative entity to the one that performs the authentication. Provided there is an adequate PKI linking administrative domains in an appropriate way, authentication can proceed in a flexible and fluid way.

4.5.3 Public Key-based Identification Protocols

An alternative to challenge–response protocols based on public key techniques (which are computationally intensive) might be to use what are termed public key-based interactive identification protocols (Menezes et al. 1996). However, we will not go into any details on these techniques in this chapter. Suffice it to say that such techniques offer a very different set of algorithms and protocols to those that have already been discussed. Nevertheless, they can still be used to provide strong authentication, and they typically do so with less computational complexity. This can result in the need for less-sophisticated cards or tokens, which, in turn, can lead to cheaper deployment.

Of course, we do not get something for nothing. The algorithms and protocols we use do not provide public key encryption nor do they provide digital signatures. However, they remain public key techniques since the two participants in the interaction possess different keys. So, while they provide entity authentication at a particular instant, interactive identification protocols are much less versatile than the algorithms typically used in challenge–response protocols. Nevertheless, the reduction in computational complexity in these schemes means that interactive identification protocols are used in a range of practical deployments.

4.5.4 Summary

We summarize the different identification (entity-authentication) mechanisms we have discussed in Table 4.2.

Table 4.2 Summary of identification (entity-authentication) mechanisms

Technique	Pros	Cons
Fixed passwords	Familiar Simple to use Simple administration	Vulnerable to simple dictionary attacks, interception, replay. Closed-system deployment
One-time passwords	Simple to use Relatively simple administration Less vulnerable to replay attacks	Typically needs a hardware-token plus supporting infrastructure. Closed-system deployment
Challenge–response (secret key)	Simple to use Relatively simple administration Cryptographically strong	Typically needs a hardware-token plus supporting infrastructure. More complicated interaction than one-time passwords. Closed-system deployment
Challenge–response (public key)	Simple to use Cryptographically strong. Open-system deployment possible	Typically needs hardware token plus supporting infrastructure. Administration can be involved; protocols can be computationally intensive
Identification protocols	Simple to use Cryptographically strong Open-system deployment possible. Computationally cheaper than PK challenge–response	Typically needs hardware token plus supporting infrastructure. Administration can be involved. Less cryptographically versatile than PK challenge–response

4.6 DOCUMENT (DATA) AUTHENTICATION

There are (at least) three easily recognized scenarios where authentication is used: to authenticate a document, to authenticate a device and to authenticate a person. In this section, we focus on document authentication.

Document authentication is an important application of cryptographic techniques (Menezes et al. 1996; Stinson 2002). In many situations it is the authenticity of information that is far more important than its confidentiality. In this chapter we use the term 'document' in a particularly broad way. Not only do we use it to cover the simple electronic representation of physical documents, but also to include other forms of digital information such as that carried on a bank card, or executable code downloaded into a device, or virtual and dynamic documents that might contain links to temporary resources on the Internet or might be generated dynamically using temporary data stored on some server.

Depending on the form of the document being authenticated, different techniques are available. If a secret key-based infrastructure is viable, then we might use message authentication codes for this form of data authentication. Here, the sender and receiver share a secret key and the sender enters the data and the secret key into an authentication algorithm to produce a cryptographic check sum which, clearly, depends on the data and the shared secret key. The receiver performs the same calculation using the received message and compares the value that they calculate with the value sent with the message. If these two values agree then the receiver accepts the message as being authentic in the sense that it is from the partner and has not been illegally changed.

However, given the nature of document distribution (that is, that one copy of a document might need to be authenticated by many recipients) public key techniques – digital signatures – would typically be more useful.

When considering the authentication of a document the complexity of the document can have a significant impact. When we sign a stand-alone electronic document, or some executable code, then it is (reasonably) obvious what we intend the signature to cover and what we intend the signature to mean. However, if a document were to contain links to, or be generated by, other temporary resources, then while the implication behind the signature might be obvious, its execution and continued validity can introduce some significant problems.

4.7 BIOMETRIC AUTHENTICATION

The only authentication techniques that attempt to authenticate a user directly, as opposed to relying on devices or knowledge assigned to that user, are biometrics. The term 'biometrics' is derived from the Greek words *bio* (life) and *metric* (to measure). The field of biometrics is the measurement and statistical analysis of biological data. As we have already noted, the problem associated with authentication methods that are either knowledge based (something that you know) or token based (something that you have) is that they can be passed on to others, or can be lost, stolen or forgotten, and therefore do not truly authenticate a person. This is different with biometric authentication methods; they cannot be passed on to others and losing them is pretty difficult (and even if the feature is 'lost', it cannot be used by somebody else). However, impersonation by forgery may be possible.

In biometrics, identification is a statement of who the user is and authentication is the process by which a claimed identity is verified. Identification, therefore, means to find the user in a group of users (a one-to-many comparison) and authentication means to verify the user's identity (a one-to-one comparison). A typical example of identification is matching a fingerprint found at a crime scene to a forensics database, and an example of authentication is withdrawing money from an ATM, where a person claims an identity by inserting a debit or credit card and that claimed identity can be verified by providing a biometric sample (or indeed a PIN).

In a biometric system, a personal characteristic, such as a fingerprint, is used and the basic assumption of the authentication process is that a person's fingerprint identifies them uniquely or, more accurately, that the probability of two people having identical fingerprints is so small that it can be safely assumed to be zero. In a typical biometric system, a user will give a number of copies of the chosen biometric which are converted into bit patterns and stored on a template. When that user wishes to authenticate to the system they provide a copy of the chosen biometric and that copy is compared to the template. If the copy provided is 'close enough' to the template then the user is authenticated. A fundamental problem with applying biometrics is the determination of what is acceptable as close enough. If the demands are too stringent then the likelihood of the correct user being rejected may become too high. If, on the other hand, it is too lax then impostors will be accepted. From the security perspective it must be noted that the template needs protection since, if that can be altered, then the system fails. It is also important to recognize that the person needs to be identified correctly before providing the biometric. Otherwise the wrong person will be identified when that biometric is presented at any later date.

In fact the term 'biometrics' has been generalized slightly from its original concept and we now talk about static and dynamic biometrics. While there are many techniques that are in differing states of technological advance, the main biometric methods in use today are the following:

1.   fingerprint recognition
2.   hand geometry reading
3.   iris scan
4.   retinal scan
5.   face recognition
6.   signature dynamics
7.   speech recognition

Biometric methods 1 to 5 are so-called static biometric methods (also physiological biometric methods); they depend on human features that are always present and which are fixed and do not change (at least in theory). Biometric methods 6 and 7 are so-called dynamic biometric methods (also behavioural biometric methods); they are related to a certain action of the user, to a behavioural habit. In order to be applicable for authentication, a biometric method must fulfil the general requirements shown in Table 4.3. Different biometric methods fulfil these requirements to a different extent. However, it should be said that current technology is such that no biometric method fulfils all the requirements to the fullest extent.

Table 4.3 Requirements for authentication

Universality	Each person should have the characteristic
Uniqueness	No two persons should have the same characteristic
Permanence	The characteristic should neither change nor be altered
Collectability	The characteristic can be measured quantitatively
Performance	The characteristic can be efficiently measured in terms of accuracy, speed, robustness and resource requirements
Acceptability	The characteristic should be acceptable to the public
Circumvention	There should be no easy way to fool the system

Before a biometric system can be used, the user has to enrol, providing the system with their biometric reference data. These data can be stored in a centralized or distributed database or on a smart card (the latter may be preferable in terms of security). The identification process (deciding whether a user belongs to the set of registered users) or verification process (deciding whether the user is who he/she claims to be) works as follows.

First, the biometric data are captured at the sensor. The biometric features are extracted and then, depending on the biometric method applied, a biometric template is produced. This biometric template is matched with one (in the case of verification) or many (in the case of identification) reference templates and an acceptance decision is made. Only the first two steps take place when the user enrols in the system.

It is important to note that no two biometric templates match 100 per cent. Instead, the similarity between the two has to be calculated. In order to make a decision, a certain threshold is defined which maximizes the acceptance rate for authorized users and minimizes the acceptance rate for impostors. Two types of error are defined to measure the performance of biometric systems:

Type 1: The system fails to recognize a valid user (false rejections).
Type 2: The system accepts an impostor (false acceptance).

While there is not necessarily a precise link between the two error rates, in practice they are typically linked. When the false rejection rate is kept small, the false acceptance rate tends to rise and vice versa. The equal error rate denotes the case where the false rejection rate and the false acceptance rate are the same. This equal error rate is often the manufacturer's default setting of a biometric system. However, the acceptable rate for errors of either type depends on the application, and the acceptability of precise threshold values will vary. For instance, when access control to a high-security location is required, it is likely that a relatively high level of Type 1 errors will be acceptable provided that the chances of a Type 2 error are essentially zero. On the other hand, when an application does not require very high security, but when the smooth operation of the system for the valid user is important, then the Type 1 error rate will be kept small and a higher Type 2 error rate may be tolerated.

The application domains for biometric authentication coincide with the applications domains of conventional authentication methods. They include access control to networks, physical access control to sites, entity identification, and time and attendance control. Some applications that have attracted recent attention in the media include passports and identity cards. Many airports now issue smart cards with biometric templates to allow speedy checks at immigration. In the US the biometric is typically either hand geometry or fingerprint, while at Heathrow Airport in the UK it is iris recognition.

Despite the fact that different authentication methods are frequently adequate for their purpose, they display obvious security limitations. Tokens can be lost or stolen and passwords and PINs can be guessed or copied. The use of biometrics can, at least in theory, remove some of these insecurities. Today we have reached the situation where some biometric authentication techniques have become quite advanced, with hardware and software technology reaching a sophisticated level. This is especially true in the dominant fingerprint recognition market (which accounts for about two-thirds of the overall biometric market). However, it is not clear that there is yet any reliable consistency in biometric products. Indeed, there seem to be other major inhibitors that might prevent the widespread use of this technology, including user privacy concerns and low acceptance by the public. These two issues are related because user privacy concerns are one reason why biometrics experience a low acceptance by the public. Another reason is a perceived health threat (for example, from scanning of a retina or through direct contact with an unhygienic fingerprint sensor).

As opposed to conventional authentication methods, a biometric feature is bound to the user and cannot be removed without causing physical harm. This is a major advantage of biometrics, but it also leads to user privacy concerns. First, biometric features are often publicly available, such as photographs or fingerprints. Hence, it is not the biometric feature as such that can be used in biometric systems, but the fact that it comes from the live user. Biometric user templates, therefore, need to be secured to the highest degree, otherwise there is the risk that the user becomes trackable or that confidential user data are compromised. Depending on the biometric technology, this can include information on the user's health: for example an image of the user's retina can reveal cardiovascular diseases.

Biometric systems consist of hardware, namely the sensors, and software for recognition. Moreover, biometric systems need to be integrated with existing systems and applications. There is, therefore, a significant research industry built around a variety of problems. With regard to the hardware, there is constant pressure to increase its reliability while maintaining low costs and maintenance. Reliability is also an issue with the software, particularly in terms of keeping the Type 1 and Type 2 error rates low while increasing the performance.

Security issues are very important and it seems that the main research contribution in security relates to system integration. Because the transmission of biometric data between different system components is one of the main weaknesses of a biometric system, much research is devoted to integrating a sensor (generally a fingerprint) onto a smart card and performing the whole recognition process on the card, without any biometric data ever leaving the card. However, although smart cards that contain sensors do exist, it appears that they are not yet sufficiently powerful to perform the whole recognition process.

The infrastructure surrounding biometric deployment such as the storage of biometric templates (in databases or on smart cards) raises many security issues, as does the secure transmission of biometric data during the authentication process. Note that the biometric data are transmitted from the sensor to the feature extractor and then to the matching module and on to the application. All these transmissions need to be secured. Even though we might be attempting to minimize Type 1 and Type 2 errors, we will need to provide alternatives for users who inadvertently fail or are unable to use a given biometric test.

In an ideal world, where we assume that all the security problems of biometrics are solved, including the privacy issues, the user could use a single biometric authentication mechanism for all authentication purposes. The best solution might be to have the reference data (templates) stored on a smart card or another device that the user can carry. Further, the sensor and all phases of the recognition process might be integrated into this single device (smart card or pen). In this case, the biometric data of the user would never have to leave the secure environment of the user.

Biometric methods have the potential to make our life easier because the information being checked is part of us and always with us. This also has the potential to increase the security, although considerable research still needs to be conducted before this is achieved. As a slight justification for this assertion we note that there are very few products on the market where the transmissions between sensor and matching module are secured.

No discussion about the security of biometrics would be complete, however, without reference to the work of Matsumoto who used sweets called 'gummy fingers' to create forged fingerprints. This is an important piece of work that shook the biometrics community, and a description of what he did can be found in his presentation 'Impact of Artificial Gummy Fingers on Fingerprint Systems'.[5] This particularly highlights the issue of liveness detection; it is critical that the template used at both registration and authentication is from a live user![6]

4.8 PROCESSES AND INFRASTRUCTURE

In some sense, the issues we have addressed are ones of primary object identification and authentication. A much more subtle, and in many ways more complex, set of issues arises when we consider secondary levels of authenticity and trustworthiness.

What do we mean by this? Authenticating (or identifying) a specific entity – a human or a computational device – is a very specific problem. Underpinning our solutions to this problem we often made the assumption that the supporting infrastructure would be trustworthy and that it would behave as intended. Without this trust it is difficult to imagine that any solutions would be viable and we tend to ignore, or at best acknowledge and then ignore, this issue.

One of the very obvious places where we are forced to address this issue, and which we have continually alluded to throughout this chapter, is the issue of enrolment and registration. It has to be acknowledged that all the very wonderful security mechanisms we have mentioned in this chapter could be easily compromised by something as simple as a failure in the administration procedure. We consider this in more detail in Section 4.10. However, this reliance on additional mechanisms, that often lie outside the scope of our technical solutions, should give us a rather uncomfortable feeling.

Thus, we need to be sure to pinpoint where technology is not enough, and it seems that many security problems occur when the human being directly interfaces to the digital world. This happens at user registration. An obvious second example is when a user is prompted for action by some application. For instance, when certificate verification fails after pointing a web browser to some secure site, how is the user supposed to react if (say) a certificate is rejected because it is being used either before the date of validity or after? How is the uneducated user supposed to react to this? Even better, how is the educated user supposed to react to this?

It would seem to require, therefore, a rather significant leap of faith to assume that the whole system will necessarily work as intended. Indeed, as more rights are managed and conferred by digital means – for instance with the use of digital identification cards as a way of providing access to services – the stakes are raised and the illicit gains of fraudulent behaviour increase.

These examples are merely prompts for discussion. There are, in fact, many different aspects involved in considering the trustworthiness of the infrastructure. Gradually, safeguards for the infrastructure are being introduced, but in a piecemeal manner. There is a wide range of industry bodies working to protect their particular parts of the digital fabric. Here we list a few diverse issues:

- We are already in a position where our consumer devices – PCs, PDAs (personal digital assistants) and mobile phones – can import code that changes their functionality. To help decide between good and potentially malicious code, initiatives such as code-signing have been developed that allow a device to digitally verify the authenticity of a particular application.
- Smart card manufacturers spend millions of dollars every year in research on the best ways to provide additional security features on the cards they produce. The whole integrity of a smart card-based solution is dependent on the fact that the smart card offers a secure storage and computation environment.
- Computing initiatives such as Microsoft's NGSCB (Next-Generation Secure Computing Base), formerly called Palladium (Microsoft 2003) and TCPA (Trusted Computing Platform Alliance) (TCG 2002) attempt to provide a secure and trusted computing environment.

- There are industry initiatives to promote good engineering and secure coding practices. How can we be sure that good security implementation practices are used within deployments?

It is the control of information that is fast becoming the issue of our times. Ubiquitous computing and ad hoc networking mean that our personal information can be increasingly used without our knowledge. We might delegate our devices to authenticate on our behalf as they seek out wireless-based interactions with other devices in the room. Yet it is not always clear that this is to the user's advantage if the user is concerned about their privacy. In a different field, what is the best way to authenticate dynamic documents that either point to transitory information or use transitory information in their construction?

Thus, the use to which we put information is an increasing concern. One step forward has been the introduction of meta-data where information has a description of its own use and functionality attached. An extension of the very same concern occupies the minds of executives of companies providing information for our entertainment (that is, music and videos). The use and potential misuse of this information drives the whole area of digital rights management (DRM) and, very interestingly, leads us full circle to the issue of registration. Indeed, one DRM solution that is much touted is to effectively 'register' the devices on which information can be accessed. Note that, unlike the case of human registration where there is no digital interface, registering a device is technically rather straightforward despite the formidable privacy and consumer-acceptance issues involved.

We might also broaden the concept of trustworthiness to include reliability. Catastrophic failures are usually easy to detect and, more often than not, to fix. What can be harder to sort out are the problems that are intermittent, thereby leading to degradation rather than an outright failure in service. In the case of a communications infrastructure it is hard to imagine at what stage a loss of service would become noticeable. Would a network operating at 50 per cent efficiency be noticeably slow to the user? Depending on the network and the application, perhaps not. Would a network operating at 50 per cent efficiency lead to measurable losses if accumulated over a sufficiently long time? Depending on the network and the application, perhaps so.

We feel that it is particularly important to begin to speculate on the continued robustness of the supporting infrastructure. As agent software is increasingly used for workflow, middleware and automatic negotiation, the identification and authentication of software and data objects as well as people will grow in importance.

4.9 THE PROBLEM OF ORIGINAL IDENTIFICATION

Suppose for the moment that we are confident that we know the identity of Mrs Mary Smith. If her son wanted his identity to be John Smith son of Mrs Mary Smith, then there is only one stage of his life at which we can have total confidence in this claim. That is while the umbilical cord is still joining John to his mother Mary.

As soon as the cord is cut, procedures are required to ensure that there is some form of binding between John and his identity. If these procedures go wrong, for whatever reason, then either someone else will have John's identity or John will have the wrong identity, or both. If we wish to be confident that John Smith has the correct identity for the rest of his life, it could be argued that the binding must take place while the umbilical cord still provides an undeniable physical link between the two parties. Two obvious options that are often discussed are: taking a DNA sample, or the physical insertion into the baby John Smith's body of a microchip containing his identity. If the DNA sample is taken then procedures are still needed to ensure that the record that associates the DNA sample with John Smith is accurate and cannot be altered at any time during John Smith's lifetime. If the chip is inserted into John's body then there need to be assurances that this cannot be removed or replaced by another person and that the information stored on the chip cannot later be changed via remote access.

If either of these two options is to be given serious consideration then it will be necessary to explore people's attitudes to such perceived intrusive measures as taking DNA samples or inserting chips at birth. Another research area is the likely physical consequences of implanting chips in someone's body for life plus, of course, the durability of the chip.

The example of John and Mary Smith plus the proposal of two somewhat extreme solutions are included to illustrate a point rather than to discuss a specific situation. Indeed, many would argue that there are very few occasions when anyone would deliberately steal a baby's identity and that less severe solutions are sufficient to prevent accidental mix-ups. Be that as it may, there is no doubt that the general problem of identifying 'the original' is difficult and frequently overlooked. One area where it is particularly relevant concerns the concept of digital evidence. If, for example, a digital image is to be produced as evidence then it will be necessary to protect it from alteration. However, if the digital image is obtained using a digital camera then a question that needs to be answered is how do we know that the image for which the protection was provided is the original? If the protection, for example, a digital signature, is constructed and attached inside the camera then we need assurances about the tamper-resistance of the camera. If, on the other hand, it is applied using another device then we will need to rely on procedures to ensure that it was not changed before the protection was applied.

The problems associated with establishing identity are frequently ignored in many discussions relating to, for instance, the issuance of passports, digital certificates and all the authentication techniques that rely on biometrics. Most of the current methods of establishing identity seem to depend on the fact that that person's identity has already been established somewhere else. Each new process is merely endorsing the old one. For instance, a passport application requires the production of a birth certificate. If the birth certificate is not the correct one for the person claiming the identity, then the passport may be issued to the wrong person. Similarly, any record associating a biometric template with a specific individual has a built-in assumption that the identity of the person was correct at the time that the biometric samples were taken. We could go on and produce numerous examples where the ability to impersonate someone at some point in the registration stage implies the ability to steal their identity and impersonate them for life.

In this chapter we have looked at a number of identification and authentication techniques. If they are to be trusted then it is vital that the process of what we might call original identification is adequate. This is an area where much research is needed. In addition to the necessary technical research into the security of the technology, more basic research is needed into the effectiveness of the identification processes used for important, everyday processes, such as passport applications and bank account or credit card applications, including their costs and failure rates.

4.10 CONCLUSION

With regard to the identification and authentication of primary subjects cryptography is, at present, the only 'strong' mechanism available to us. It is now in widespread use and helps to support a wide range of identification and authentication mechanisms. However, we should not be in complete thrall to the technology since there may well be situations where it can be subverted or used as a tool for denial of service.

As with all security solutions, an outstanding question is how much 'security' or 'strength' is enough, and in what parts of the identification and authentication process is it essential to use 'very strong' methods? We also note the requirement that procedural approaches and architectural solutions (separation of duties) be used to significantly reduce the risk of social engineering vulnerabilities in what might otherwise be 'trustworthy' processes.

Finally, we observe that the increased reliance on the automatic creation and distribution of information, in all its guises, places interesting and novel requirements on the trustworthiness and reliability of the supporting infrastructure.

NOTES

1   Some software is claimed to generate high-quality yet pronounceable passwords.
2   See http://www.rsasecurity.com/products/securid/, accessed 17 April 2004; note RSA is the acronym for Rivest, Shamir & Adleman.
3   In a little more detail, it is typical to use encryption with a public key cryptosystem when it is necessary to agree on a symmetric key between users since this is a faster way of encrypting bulk data.
4   See EMVCo. (2000).
5   Available via http://www.itu.int/itudoc/itu-t/workshop/security/present/s5p4.pdf accessed 17 April 2004.
6   For more detailed information on biometrics, see Jain et al. (2003) and Woodward (2003). Also, there are several independent organizations focusing on biometrics, namely the International Biometric Group, http://www.biometricgroup.com/, The Biometric Consortium, http://www.biometrics.org/ and the Association for Biometrics (see http://www.afb.org.uk/ all accessed 17 April 2004.

REFERENCES

Anderson, R. (1994), 'Why Cryptosystems Fail', *Communications of the ACM* 37(11): 32-40.

EMVCo (2000), The EMV4.0 Specifications, www.emvco.org, accessed 17 Apr. 04.

Jain, A.K, Maltoni, D. and Maio, D. (2003), *Handbook of Fingerprint Recognition*, New York: Springer-Verlag.

Menezes, A., Van Oorschot, P. and Vanstone, S. (1996), *The Handbook of Applied Cryptography*, London: CRC Press.

Microsoft (2003), *NGSCB: Trusted Computing Base and Software Authentication*, Microsoft Corporation, Windows Platform Design Notes.

Stinson, D. (2002), *Cryptography: Theory and Practice*, 2nd edn, London: CRC Press.

TCG (2002), *Trusted Computing Platform Alliance (TCPA) Main Specification*, Version 1.1b, The Trusted Computing Group, Portland, February, http://www.trustedcomputing.org/home, accessed 17 Apr. 04.

Woodward, J. (2003), *Biometrics and Strong Authentication*, Emeryville CA: Osborne/McGraw-Hill.

5   Knowledge technologies and the semantic web

Kieron O'Hara and Nigel Shadbolt[1]

5.1 INTRODUCTION

In this chapter, we discuss cyber trust issues relevant to knowledge technologies and the new area of development, the semantic web (Berners-Lee et al. 2001). Knowledge technologies are technologies enabled by recent technological developments that allow much more intelligent machine engagement with the documents, services and other objects on the World Wide Web. They manipulate and create knowledge, that is, usable information. The major fault lines for trust management are in making sure that the input to knowledge manipulation processes is trustworthy and in ensuring that the processes themselves are trustworthy. Their limits and margins for error must be known and predictable.

There are many ways of creating or maintaining trust in this domain. We set out a number of approaches or 'tactics for trust'. These include: allowing scrutiny; maintaining transparency; transferring ownership from experts to stakeholders; exploiting the minimal transitivity of trust; and requiring evidence of identity, provenance and certification. Above and beyond these, we suggest restricting interactions to a small set of agents; using formal methods to make data less 'scruffy'; using 'calculi of trust' to determine when and when not to place trust; using new technologies to allow interrogation of and dialogue with agents; replicating computational processes; and using knowledge technologies to manage knowledge more effectively.

These tactics need to be combined in active trust management strategies. It is important to maintain agile policies for managing trust, including the collection of rich sets of meta-data about knowledge sources and agents and ontologies for expressing trust requirements. It is essential to maintain the distinction between trust and trustworthiness, so that signalling trustworthiness does not become detached from trustworthiness itself. It is necessary to ensure that functionality is not sacrificed to trustworthiness. And finally, privacy has to be sufficiently protected so as not to undermine trust.

The discussion in this chapter leads to suggestions for many opportunities for interdisciplinary research collaboration. These include determining the extent of the distinction between online and offline trust; examining whether a utilitarian or a moral notion of online trust is appropriate; understanding the nature of trustworthy knowledge acquisition; investigating why personalized interactions are perceived as more trustworthy; examining how brands and reputations contribute to trust; and considering how effective procedures for the maintenance of knowledge bases can be developed.

The semantic web, conceived as an extension to the World Wide Web, is a potentially large area for Internet development. The Web is, of course, massive, containing in 2002 about 2.5 billion fixed documents – 550 billion documents in all, when databases and other information sources that users can access via web forms are added into the total, between them holding 7.5 million gigabytes of data (O'Hara 2002a). The Web is now so large that the various navigation tools, including hyperlinks and search engines, are coming under increasing strain. This is leading to pressure to move to the semantic web, which, for the eXtensible Markup Language (XML), the Resource Description Framework (RDF) and ontologies, allows systems many more inferential possibilities than the World Wide Web, whose underlying language, the Hypertext Markup Language (HTML), is more concerned with looks than content.

There is no way of knowing whether the semantic web will take off as the Web did; much will depend on whether the tools and formalisms devised are as successful at selling the concept to the heterogeneous band of users that would be essential to its large-scale take up. In 2004, the semantic web had not decisively left its home in the computer science department. However, this chapter will remain relevant because many of the claims within it will apply to the Web as well and because, however the Web is upgraded, its sheer size dictates that various functionalities, such as intelligent search and the customization of content, will inevitably be developed in some form.

We focus our analysis in this chapter on likely developments over a five- to ten-year horizon. This is a very uncertain field and the technology could develop in a number of ways. However, we focus on the likely development of the Web and the semantic web, given the current direction of technology and the existing set of problems on the Web.

This chapter is structured as follows. We begin by scoping our enquiry. Section 5.2 sets out our assumptions about trust. This is not intended to be an in-depth contribution to philosophy or sociology; neither is it intended to undercut other discussions of trust that appear in this volume. Rather, the aim is to set out our preliminary understanding of the concept of trust that underlies our argument in this chapter. Section 5.3 briefly sets out the technological background of the semantic web, and Section 5.4 introduces the concept of knowledge technologies.

The creation of trust can happen at many levels; individual technologies can attempt to be trusted or trustworthy, or it may be that groups of people and organizations set up institutions for the wider purveyance of trust. Accordingly, our discussion of trust treats these levels separately. Section 5.5 looks at the possible ways of promoting trust that individual designers might be able to use; we call these the 'tactics' of trust-creation. We, therefore, claim that the issues surrounding trust at a wider level are relevant to 'strategies' of trust-creation (strategies that might involve the artful deployment and combination of more than one of the tactics of trust). We discuss these in Section 5.6. Bringing strategies into the discussion implicitly suggests that many aspects of cyber trust stretch beyond the abilities of individual designers to address them and, therefore, that cyber trust is a problem that a number of disciplines can throw light upon. The interdisciplinary aspects of the problems and likely solutions are discussed in Section 5.7.

5.2 TRUST

We begin with a brief overview of our understanding of the concept of trust. As we focus on the important semantic web notions of services and technologies, we will be looking at ways of ensuring that inputs to and outputs from such services and technologies are trustworthy. We make the assumption, common to many commentators, that there are strong analogies between online and offline trust (Corritore et al. 2003).

We give less attention to trust as a security issue. Clearly trust has an important security dimension, but secure infrastructures are not covered in this chapter (see Chapter 3 in this volume). The key issue for the semantic web, as with the World Wide Web, is that services deliver reliable output, which may be as much a social issue as a security one. The semantic web and knowledge technologies do not seem to raise any particular security issues peculiar to themselves (the security issues pertaining to e-commerce, largely with respect to transactions and transfers of monies, are the central security issues for the web; see Camp 2000).

In general, information downloaded from the Web tends to be fairly reliable. Given the number of people posting information, this in itself is a minor miracle. The World Wide Web is a major source of information for many people – academics obviously, but also for various more or less naive users who download often introductory information about, for example, their medical, financial or legal problems. While the majority of this information is relatively reliable, impartial or explicit about its partiality, web users are generally trusting of it. The trick will be to keep this information reliable in future generations. The issue is much more a social than a security one.

To define terms, trust is at minimum a binary relation, between someone or something that does the trusting, and someone or something that is trusted. We will call the actor that trusts the principal, and the actor that is trusted the agent. In this chapter we will make no distinction between principals or agents that are human and those that are 'artificial'. We will equally make no distinction between principals or agents that are individuals and those that are institutions. In other words, we assume that the human notion of trust is usefully exportable, if only metaphorically, into these non-human realms. This is a controversial assumption, argued against by Hardin (1999), for example. A defence of the assumption for practical purposes can be found in O'Hara (2004a) and Corritore et al. (2003).

Furthermore, the trust of a principal in an agent is generally context-bounded, so the agent is trusted to do something; this something may be open-ended, or it may be quite specific (Grandison and Sloman 2000). This extra context is not essential to trust, because trust can be across the board. But, in World Wide Web and semantic web contexts in general, there is some contextual limitation of the scope of trust. In the terms employed by Corritore et al (2003), World Wide Web and semantic web contexts generally produce specific trust as opposed to general trust.

5.2.1 Functions of Trust

Much discussion of trust begins with a functional definition.[2] In a survey of empirical research on cyber trust, it has been noted that conceptualizations of cyber trust are often conflicting, which has militated against comparisons and the synthesis of results (Grabner-Kräuter and Kaluscha 2003). The multi-dimensional and, indeed, second-order nature of the trust construct is clearly a problem. O'Hara (2004a) discusses some of the difficulties of defining trust and some of the anomalies that crop up when trust is defined rigidly. He argues that a better methodological approach is to define the sphere of life or society in which the author or audience is interested and then to try to trace all the various trust-like phenomena that impinge upon that sphere. Most areas will be affected, not only by trust, but by other phenomena such as risk, expectation or inclusion in moral communities that are very hard to disentangle from trust. It is, therefore, unsurprising that different conceptions of trust should produce a range of functional characterizations (Misztal 1996).

The most common approach with respect to cyber trust is the definition of trust as an epistemological construct that reduces complexity and/or transaction costs in conditions of uncertainty, generally following Niklas Luhmann (1979). Interactions with other actors are rendered simpler because the trusting actor simply foregoes the necessity of investigating other actors' credentials or of putting in place systems of performance metrics, invigilation regimes or management structures. In an uncertain situation, the trusting actor simply behaves as if there is more certainty than there actually is, and therefore is absolved from having to perform all the extra tasks that uncertainty would have loaded upon it.

This is an important function of trust and we follow the majority of commentators in making this assumption (Grabner-Kräuter and Kaluscha 2003). In a context where many of the interactions are either commercially based (e-commerce), or where the aim is to create a cooperative environment, for example, creating and acting on a plan involving a number of autonomous agents, then trust is likely to be a central complexity-reduction strategy.

However, particularly where the Internet is concerned, there are other functions of trust that deserve consideration. For instance, we might also follow Emile Durkheim (1893) and Talcott Parsons (1949) in looking at the role of trust in projecting a consensus of values and thereby helping to integrate a community. In communities with a moral dimension, which are held together by a set of values, trust often plays the role of signalling inclusion into that moral community. Much empirical survey evidence from offline contexts seems to suggest that trust is an inclusive, value-based capacity (Uslaner 2002). In such contexts then, trust, far from being the effect of extended displays of trustworthy behaviour, acts as a cause of trustworthiness (O'Hara 2004a).

This is extremely relevant to the Internet as a whole. Thanks in part to its development in academic circles, the Internet is a very value-laden space and the extension of the Internet, via the Web, to non-academic contexts, including political and commercial contexts, has caused a substantial cultural clash – where so-called 'newbies' are looked down upon by the 'founding fathers'. In general, the governing values of the Internet among its creators are anarchistic, based on liberty and free expression. Such values have helped the technical development of the Internet quite dramatically (for example, with the open source software movement), but equally have made the (so far successful) grafting of a commercial marketplace onto the Internet somewhat fraught.

In many ways, these two interpretations of the notion of trust pull against each other, and ways of extending the first notion may prevent the extension of the second, and vice versa (Lessig 1999). Nevertheless, each function of trust should,as far as possible,be respected in a value-laden space such as the Internet and – depending on its course of development – the semantic web.

5.2.2 Properties of Trust

Trust is often best characterized by its functions. However, it tends to be recognizable by its properties. As trust is generally desirable, the exploitation of these properties to achieve trust would, if feasible, be a very useful development. However, trust, being a second-order phenomenon, is rarely as reproducible as that.

One tactic is to devise axioms that reproduce some of trust's properties, particularly its limited transitivity (see Section 5.5.7). It has been argued that trust is not transitive (Povey 1999) – it certainly is not completely so, but it, nevertheless, exhibits some transitive properties, even if these are unpredictable and often unintentional (Grandison and Sloman 2000). Basically these properties are dependent on the main observed property of trust, which is that it builds up slowly and is dissipated quickly. In general, an agent must prove that it is trustworthy by meeting expectations (which may be moral or merely practical) within understood parameters.

The extent of the trust, the number of tasks for which the agent is trusted, will also be limited – the agent is trusted to do something, not trusted unrestrictedly. In other words, trust is usually specific to a particular task, or function or promoted service. If an actor is trusted, then this is usually shorthand for the actor's being trusted for a specific implicit task or set of tasks. Such models of trust may help in the development of automated systems for trust management and trust creation (Grandison and Sloman 2000).

5.2.2.1 The non-specificity of trust
Unfortunately, the triggering condition for trust is highly non-specific. There are no answers to such questions as:

- How many times does the agent have to achieve the task before it is trusted?
- Under what range of circumstances does the agent have to achieve the task?
- What set of interests should characterize the agent?

The last question, about interests, is noteworthy. If it is in the agent's own interests – independent of the principal's interests, and of the agent's interests to be trusted – to perform the task, then it may be that trusting the agent to perform the task would be premature (Hardin 1999). What must happen is that the agent's interests must somehow become aligned with those of the principal. This may happen with the explicit alteration of the agent's interests, for example by the principal paying it a fee. Or the agent might be altruistic. Or it might be that the interests of the agent can be manipulated by the principal. Whatever the case, the performance of the task is in the principal's interests – this is why it has to trust the agent – and in order for the principal to trust the agent, it has to be confident that the agent's interests and its own are suitably aligned.

As Corritore et al. (2003) argue, trust can come in various shapes with very different properties – which is another way of saying that the properties of trust are highly unpredictable or that modelling trust in general may well be inappropriate or indeed impossible. For example, Corritore et al. draw a distinction between slow trust, built up over time (and therefore relatively rationally based), and quick trust, which occurs when relationships are created and then cease to exist within a short time-frame (for example, when a team is assembled to perform a specific task). They also distinguish between cognitive trust, where the principal has good rational reasons for trusting, and emotional trust, where it does not. These distinctions can be helpful, but they may simply reduce to the proposition that trust can be rational or not and that it may build up quickly or slowly.

5.2.2.2 The withdrawal of trust

The loss of trust is more straightforward. Failure to perform the task, in apparently appropriate circumstances, will in general result in the forfeiture of trust by the agent in that respect (and possibly in other respects too). This is not to say that trust will necessarily be lost, but that it is liable to be lost. It is also possible that a suitable explanation of the failure from the agent, or an explanation of why the circumstances were inappropriate for trust, will save the situation.

Trust, though, need not be all or nothing (Grandison and Sloman 2000); it may be associated with a level, for example, a real number between 0 and 1. In that case, withdrawal of trust may mean a decline in the value assigned to this parameter, but not necessarily to 0.

Principals must have knowledge of the agents they are trusting. This is one example where trust, when it operates smoothly, takes on transitive properties: trust transfers through intermediaries between the actors at each end of the chain. This clearly does not always happen; hence, our caveat that trust is only partly or occasionally transitive.

The performance of many tasks is organized by brokers or project managers. For instance, a principal A might trust an agent B with the performance of some task, while B's contribution is to decompose the task into subtasks and to assign the subtasks to trusted agents of B's own (towards which B now acts as principal). A knows nothing of the other agents. The situation is as depicted in Figure 5.1. If one of B's agents, for example C, fails to perform the task, then A does not cease to trust C, of whose existence it may not even be aware. It ceases to trust B; the untrustworthiness of B's agents transfers back to B.

Figure 5.1 Proxy agents

Indeed, many of the mechanisms that are used to promote trust do so at the cost of massively increasing risk. For example, consider the use of institutions to spread trust. In such a circumstance an institution takes on the role of certifying trustworthiness and, therefore, the principal has access to many more agents in whom it can trust. The institution has to have power and sanction over those it certifies. There is still a primitive trust arrangement, but now the principal trusts the institution to certify responsibly. This division of labour, illustrated in Figure 5.2, is held to be vital for the spread of trust through even moderately complex societies (Fukuyama 1995).

However, as has been argued elsewhere (O'Hara 2004a), such an arrangement also dramatically increases systemic risk. Where a principal trusts an agent through personal acquaintance, a betrayal results in the withdrawal of trust from that agent. Where a principal trusts an agent as a result of a certificate from an institution, a betrayal might well result in the principal withdrawing trust from all agents certified by that institution (in the absence of a further reason to preserve trust in any individual cases).

Trust via institutions has been called global trust and trust via personal acquaintance local trust (O'Hara 2004a).

Figure 5.2 Spreading trust via institutions

Trust via personal acquaintance

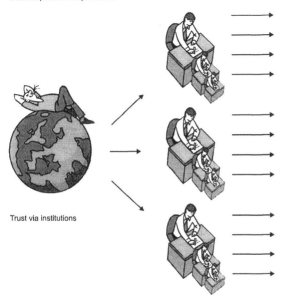

Trust via institutions

5.2.2.3 Trust and contracts

Trust is in many respects similar to contracts. If A trusts B, then B claims that it will bring about some state of affairs in A's interests; A then investigates no further, but will behave as if B's claims were true (for example it will plan for the future on that basis). If A has a contract with B saying the same thing, then it will equally behave as if B's claims were true. In neither case does A have any proof that B will carry out its claims; in neither case does A have any power to bring the state of affairs about itself. So the similarity lies in the fact that A has no power to bring some state of affairs about, yet is able to plan for a world in which that state of affairs obtains. With a contract, of course, A has recourse to law should B renege, which will allow A to impose some sanctions (though not necessarily to bring the state of affairs about). In the case of trust, the only sanction against B's reneging is for A to cease to trust B, and to publicize the reneging.

However, there are two important dissimilarities with contracts that should be noted. First, trust is much more flexible than contracts. A contract usually specifies background conditions that must obtain for the contract to be valid. An allowable defence against breach of contract is that the contract was not valid at the time of the breach (independently of intentions).

Second, contracts can crowd trust out. Where contracts are binding, recent empirical studies have shown that trust relations tend not to evolve. Where a certification approach (see Section 5.5.4) involves tightly determined sanctions and powers for the certification authority, then trust may be inhibited (Spiekermann et al. 2001). Trust, being risky, tends to evolve only when there are no other mechanisms for addressing the inherent uncertainty in the situation. Non-binding contracts, on the other hand, tend not to inhibit the development of trust (Malhotra and Murnighan 2002).

5.2.2.4 Trust and knowledge
A related point concerns knowledge. Trust is a rational strategy under uncertainty. One obvious way of increasing trust and reducing risk is to reduce the uncertainty, that is, to perform some investigation of the agent. If we rely too heavily on this strategy, however, then trust relationships will not develop. They will not need to develop if the uncertainty and risk are reduced to minimal levels. Under such circumstances, the investigation would have used up a lot of work and demanded navigation through highly complex situations; as the need for trust decreased, then so would the benefits from trusting have become unavailable. Removing uncertainty altogether takes away risk, but at the potentially high cost of the investigation.

5.2.2.5 Trust and risk
There is an interesting, yet underspecified relationship between trust and risk – in general, they have a roughly inverse relationship. People are less inclined to trust when risk is high, and so this should be taken into account. For instance, people risk money and resources in e-commerce applications and so may be less inclined to trust even though the level of security is usually higher than in other applications. There has been little work linking trust management and risk management (Grandison and Sloman 2000).

5.2.2.6 Distrust
The topic of distrust should be mentioned briefly, although it is not addressed

further in this chapter. Most treatments of trust implicitly include distrust, which, consequently, need not be treated separately. However, it should be noted that distrust is not simply related to trust. In particular, it would be wrong to assume that distrust is analysable as trust in a complementary piece of behaviour. If I distrust you to pay me back, it is not the case that I trust you not to pay me back. In particular, Grandison and Sloman (2000) must be wrong to define distrust as 'the lack of firm belief in the competence of an entity to act dependably, securely and reliably within a specified context' (which is the complement of their definition of trust). This definition makes no distinction between, say, a randomly-chosen person whom I do not know and, therefore, have no firm beliefs about at all, and a known betrayer about whom I harbour firm beliefs about his or her untrustworthiness. I distrust the latter, but it seems correct to say I neither trust nor distrust the former.

5.3 THE SEMANTIC WEB

The semantic web is the potential successor to the World Wide Web. As the Web has increased in size, the mechanisms for navigating through it are coming under increasing strain. The move to the semantic web is expected to enable more intelligent navigation and customization of content. For those unfamiliar with the principles underlying the semantic web, an appendix at the end of this chapter provides a short introduction.

Trust has always been envisaged as a key factor in the structure of the semantic web. Figure 5.3, developed by Berners-Lee, shows how the various layers of the semantic web are supported. Each layer 'makes sense' of the layers below. XML tells the computer what the Unicode data encoding and the universal resource identifiers (URIs) refer to; RDF tells it how they are related; ontologies give a meaningful context for these types and relations, creating a holistic 'web' of meaning (see Quine and Ullian 1970). There would be no point in having this language without logic to make inferences; no point in making the inferences without a proof theory to ensure that the inferences are valid; and no point in producing the proofs without trust in the system as a whole.

With these formalisms and structures, the semantic web provides an environment in which a computer can behave intelligently; compare this to the Web, where the system of HTML plus web addresses allows the illusion that the whole Web is lodged on the current machine. But the data remain uninterpreted. Trust is not required, because the machine is inactive.

Figure 5.3 The layered view of the semantic web

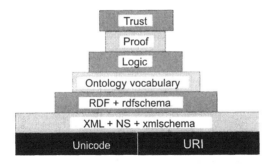

Source: Adapted from Koivunen and Miller (2002, p. 34).

There are two important points with respect to the semantic web and trust that we need to note at this stage. First, like the Web, the semantic web is designed for anyone to operate in; the semantic web should be a space in which political activity, commercial activity and leisure activity can coexist with the inevitable scientific activity. Again, as with the Web, the expectation has to be that semantic web users are heterogeneous and that the data in the semantic web are 'scruffy'.

The emphasis therefore needs to be on formalisms and mechanisms that can cope with such 'scruffiness'. For example, ontologies probably need to be partial, flexible and interoperable, rather than highly principled and fixed. But this scruffiness may also make trust a little more complicated to produce. It may be – and the evidence for this is small and equivocal – that there is an epistemological version of Gresham's Law, that bad knowledge will drive out good. For example, if datasets are going to be large and relatively 'noisy', then the inferences drawn from them will be correspondingly riskier. Risk parameters will be computable, but equally these will tend to be disregarded, especially outside scientific or otherwise statistically literate communities. As a result, the chances of information being seriously misleading may well be relatively high.

The second point concerns the current circumstances of the semantic web, which is at a fairly early stage. It is an emerging technology, and one that is intended to develop a high profile. There may be a trade-off between developing technologies that exploit the expressivity of the semantic web, and those that are provably trustworthy. Getting useful – and usable – structures, formalisms and tools off the ground, now may be more important than fostering trust across any kind of representative cross-section of the heterogeneous group of potential semantic web users. This is not to say that such a trade-off is inevitable, only that, for a short period of time at least, it may be a sensible strategy for semantic web development.

In fact, the incidence of errors may actually affect trust. Corritore et al. (2003) have a prominent role for credibility and error-proneness in their model of online trust.[3] It may be that smoothly functioning systems or easy-to-navigate websites are necessary if not sufficient conditions for trust. Having technologies that work may well be an essential priority even for those who value trust highly. Professionalism is also valued by users; Corritore et al. cite more studies that show that cues that have an impact on user perceptions of trustworthiness include ease of navigation, good use of visual design elements, professional images of products, freedom from grammatical errors or typos, a professional look to the website, ease of search and ease of carrying out transactions. Indeed, website design is a quite major determinant of trustworthiness for lay users as compared to experts who look at information quality (Stanford et al. 2002).

5.4 KNOWLEDGE TECHNOLOGIES

The semantic web provides a very helpful context for the development of knowledge technologies, that is, those technologies whose aim is to transform information into knowledge, or usable information (O'Hara 2002a). Knowledge technologies are technologies that transform information so that it can be an input to some problem-solving process. Typical of such technologies are those that enable significance to be extracted from stores of information; these include ontologies, systems for enabling or automating the production of annotations or metadata for information sources or systems for information extraction from natural language.

Another important class of knowledge technologies are those that enable the transfer of information around an organization, providing knowledge sharing services for instance, enabling the identification and distribution of knowledge. These might include discussion spaces for documents or communication systems for remote or asynchronous meetings.

Following the account of the UK's Advanced Knowledge Technologies (AKT) project,[4] we assume a (rough) knowledge lifecycle including the following stages: acquisition, modelling, retrieval, reuse, publishing and maintenance.

A knowledge technology would be expected to contribute to the manipulation of knowledge in one or more of these stages. Trust impinges on such technologies in two ways. First of all, given the scruffiness of the worlds in which such technologies flourish, one problem is how to ensure that knowledge technologies operate on trustworthy data. Second, given that the input data are trustworthy, how can we trust the processes underlying the knowledge technologies themselves, in order that we can trust the output?

5.4.1 Epistemological Functions of Technology

The trend, particularly since the economic downturn in 2001, is for organizations to focus less on technology installation and on reconfiguring themselves, and to switch the focus to services (*The Economist* 2003). Knowledge technologies and the semantic web are very much in this mould. When the service ethos is combined with the epistemological advances that knowledge technologies and the semantic web make possible, the result is knowledge services. Knowledge services provide knowledge-based analyses through the medium of the Web, for example, using ontologies for data capture and integration or for user modelling for customizing content for the reader. Meta-level brokering services are also interesting in this context; such services could provide and integrate a suite of services required for a particular organizational context.

An alternative scenario for knowledge technologies, though rooted also in organizational sense-making and consensus creation, would be the development of technologies for enhancing collaborative work for workers dispersed remotely through space and time. Various intelligent aids to communication could, for example, integrate multimedia representations of meetings, combining movies with PowerPoint and supporting facilities such as querying with something very close to natural language, given sufficiently rich, probably ontology-driven, annotation of the material.

5.4.2 Trust in Content and Input

In many cases, knowledge technologies will be extrapolating structures from vast quantities of heterogeneous data with a great number of sources (for example where knowledge services are extracting information from web page text and generalizing over that information). In such cases, where the range of information sources is messy, the knowledge technologies must trust in the reliability of the majority of the sources so that any misleading or out-of-date data are swamped by reliable data and appear only as noise. For instance, if a system is taking information from the web pages of a department's professors to form a picture of the department's publication records, then the extent to which the system must ensure that the pages are up to date will depend crucially on the extent to which the system has to present the truth. Are there sanctions that will apply if the system produces an inaccuracy? If there are no sanctions, are there, nevertheless, opportunities (for example, funding opportunities) that could be lost with inaccurate information? Or is the aim of collecting the information merely a general provision of useful material that needs to be broadly trustworthy, but not super-accurate?

Where knowledge technologies are taking data from a single source or type of source, then that source has to be trustworthy. In order to trust that source, the knowledge technology may need to gather some information to reduce uncertainty; this information, the meta-data of that source, should provide partial indications of the reliability of the source. The provenance of the source may be of a particular type (its address may be from the '.edu' range), or the source may make reference to other trusted sources. Of course, the meta-data and annotations themselves must be trustworthy, needing maintenance and curation as much as the top level information.

Branding of sites is important. For example, taking information about academic sites from a central government site, such as that of a research funding body, is better if that site has a good reputation for accurate collation of information. Such a reputation may well be encapsulated in a brand. Of course, symbolic shortcuts, such as brands, will be of much more relevance to the human intelligences guiding the machines than to the machines themselves. But the notion of creating an analogue of branding is intriguing. Correct identification of sites is important with any development of the brand model.

Where knowledge technologies are intended to facilitate knowledge sharing or discussion, there is an obvious problem of trust with respect to the person with whom one is sharing or discussing knowledge. If a novice persisted in firing off uninformed questions in a document discussion space, for example, much of the value of that space might be lost as a result of the necessity to reinvent the wheel for the purposes of the discussion, or the other interlocutors might lose patience with the whole process.

5.4.3 Trust in Process and Output

In terms of process and output, knowledge technologies must have reliable methods. Such methods as knowledge acquisition techniques, modelling languages and so on, must do what they advertise. But evaluation and testing of such methods is non-trivial (Shadbolt et al. 1999). For example, many knowledge technology methods are designed to work over the web scale. If the methods are not reliable, then the output of knowledge technologies will be correspondingly less trustworthy. For trust – which obviously depends on knowledge and publicity – such evaluations must be publicized and certified (or inspectable). For instance, a knowledge modelling method may need to provide links to academic papers describing the method and its results.

Similarly, where a knowledge technology manipulates knowledge (for example when it retrieves an answer from a repository, or when it repackages some knowledge for bespoke publication), then an important issue of trust is whether that manipulation preserves the important properties of the knowledge. So, for instance, if information is presented in personalized web pages, two different users must trust the knowledge technology to be presenting the same knowledge, even if in different forms (different languages, different levels of abstraction and so on). Good ontologies are important here; yet many ontologies may be generated automatically from combinations of smaller ones. There may be all sorts of problems with respect to issues like the integrity of referring expressions (Alani et al. 2002).

Explanation is very important. Knowledge technologies must be able to reduce the uncertainty of the users about their output. They must be open to interrogation, or provide explanation of their output, together with other useful meta-data such as margins of error. This entails the development of, for example, query languages to frame an appropriate interrogation.

One important aspect of trust in this context is privacy. Much privacy is preserved by the clear separation of sources of knowledge; placing two knowledge sources together can be invasive of someone's privacy by allowing a much greater range of inference about that person. For example, the inferences available about someone on the basis of their tax records combined with their bank account history massively outweigh those possible without cross-referring those two sources.

A related concern is that of the secondary use of data. One can hand over information for some purpose – to a funding body, to a law-enforcement organization – and then an important privacy question concerns what legitimately can be done with that data. The aim of many knowledge technologies, for example those that find and repackage information from the Web, is precisely to use data for secondary purposes.

There is an interesting distinction between the American and European models of privacy. The American approach is rights based and people are given rights to disclose or not to disclose information in various circumstances. Once information has been freely given away or published for some purpose by an individual, he or she has relatively few rights to prevent its secondary use. Europe has a data protection model where secondary use is regulated and restricted to so-called 'fair use' (that is, private data can only be used for the purpose for which the individual has given consent). Tailoring a knowledge technology to one or the other of these regulatory models may be non-trivial.

5.4.4 Agents

Much of the discussion on trust in the context of the Web, the semantic web and knowledge technologies is complicated by the fact that many agents – and indeed some principals – are artificial. When trust is taken functionally, as it almost always is in the literature, as a strategy for complexity reduction, then there may seem to be little difficulty in adapting what began as a human trait to the realm of the artificial. After all, the serious problem of bootstrapping – the key issue, for example, discussed in Hobbes's *Leviathan* – can be finessed much more easily with artificial agents than with recalcitrant humans.

However, though this is undoubtedly an advantage, humans are of course able to apply a great deal of flexibility to their trusting decisions and to balance their interests very finely (though equally their reasoning may be more bias-prone). In a network of heterogeneous agents, such as an online market might consist of, agents' decisions to trust other agents will depend on effective models of trust. Such models are a matter for experiment as to what best balances flexibility and an acceptable level of risk.

Furthermore, agent environments are inherently distributed and decentralized. Such potential security ideas as central databases listing security clearances are not going to be possible on large scales. Security must be achieved on the basis solely of an accurate evaluation of an agent's own credentials. And the dynamic nature of agent environments means that security policy will have to be dynamic too.

Artificial agents being dynamic and built for interaction, it may well be that virtual organizations are created and disbanded on the fly for particular tasks. Such organizations of agents may only be in existence for relatively short periods of time. Questions of trust will almost certainly arise about how such a mayfly organization can take responsibility for decisions or output, and how the user may place trust in it (see Section 5.5.4).

Humans will also have to learn to trust their artificial agents. Again, in many ways this issue is continuous with the issue of any principal trusting its agent. However, trusting an artificial agent involves being *au fait* with the properties of that agent and its suitability for the virtual environment or market in which it operates. For example, if the agent is a negotiating agent, the principal needs to know how advantageous the negotiation algorithm is and how suited it is to the market.

The extent of trust will of necessity vary, depending on the powers transferred from the principal to the agent. Variations on this theme include: What decision rights has the principal transferred to the agent? Can the agent gain access to the principal's resources? And, is the agent acting as principal to other agents?

5.5 TACTICS FOR TRUST

We move on now to a review of approaches to trust. First, in this section, we look at a number of basic approaches to the creation and sustenance of trust, what we have called tactics for trust. Then in Section 5.6, we look at how these tactics might be combined and deployed; in other words, we look at potential strategies for trust.

5.5.1 Transparency

The first tactic for trust that we consider is that of transparency. Here the tactic is for the agent to open up its activities to the scrutiny of the principal. If some black box processes are governed by the agent, then the agent can allow the principal access to the workings of the processes, opening up the black box.

The principal would not be assumed to be constantly observing these newly transparent processes. If the principal performed such rigorous oversight, then most if not all the gains of its trust strategy – complexity reduction, lowered transaction and information-processing costs – would be lost. The incentive for the agent to behave in a trustworthy way is that the principal could, at any time, check any of the newly transparent processes. Transparency is generally assumed to be a key strategy for trust.

There is some empirical evidence for this. For example, trust in automatic recommender systems can be increased by a conversational interface and the disclosure of the recommender's personalized user model (Corritore et al. 2003).

There are problems with the use of transparency to promote trust however. First, much depends on the complexity of the agent's services, and how likely the agent calculates it to be that the principal will discover any underhand practices. Second, and perhaps more importantly, is the effect that discovery of untrustworthy behaviour might have relative to the expectations of the principal. The problem here would be if the agent was using relatively unreliable sub-processes. For example, it might be employing heuristics or subcontracting work to a risky agent. This problem might also be compounded if the agent, in contact with subagents of its own, had access to the principal's resources.

It may be that the unreliability of these sub-processes would be unlikely, except in the extreme, to affect the successful outcome of the process as a whole. But if the expectations of the principal were unrealistically high, then it may withdraw trust from the agent. Transparency, in conditions of uncertainty, will always contain the risk of loss of trust as the flip side to its benefits.

5.5.2 Transfers of Ownership

A second tactic is to transfer ownership of certain processes to the principal.

The idea is that stakeholders take responsibility for processes or artefacts, rather than allowing experts or authority figures to adopt that responsibility themselves. An example would be where a community might take over ownership of knowledge-based resources, such as ontologies, from the knowledge engineers who might otherwise be able to impose those resources without significant input. The development of such resources might well be done properly, but the air of mystery might be off-putting for the stakeholders (Domingue et al. 2001).

The problem is that developing knowledge-based resources is a difficult and time-consuming job. The key is to create usable tools that allow resource development to take place in the absence, or relatively low profile, of a knowledge engineering expert. For example, Tennison's Adaptive Presentation Environment for Collaborative Knowledge Structuring (APECKS) tool allows collaborative asynchronous discussion and construction of ontologies (Tennison et al. 2002).

Another example is the use of open hypermedia to control associative linking from web pages, as, for example, in the Conceptual Open Hypermedia Services Environment (COHSE) (Carr et al. 2001). The use of embedded hyperlinks to simulate associative linking has always been a relatively odd strategy, as it is the author of the page that controls the associations. It is as if Proust's narrator had bitten into the Madeleine and found himself remembering, not his time at Combray with Aunt Leonie, but rather some episode from the baker's past (O'Hara 2004b). It has been argued that taking control of associative linking could increase trust, for example by allowing the principal access to alternative views not necessarily endorsed by the web page's author (Sunstein 2001; O'Hara 2002b).

A final example is to reduce the automation of processing, so that the principal does more of the processing itself. This involves a step back from the usual knowledge technology approach, which is to automate tedious though knowledge-based tasks. If we consider what this idea would involve we can imagine a search engine looking for web pages. At present, the engine would be expected to do some of the processing (as, for example, with Google's PageRank system, which orders the hits in a cogent way) and the principal does some more (as with Google, it is the user who looks through the hits and discards those that are of no use). The aim of knowledge technologies is to shift the balance towards automatic processing and away from the principal. If the balance goes too far the other way, towards processing by the principal, then the whole principle of knowledge technologies will be undermined, since all the knowledgeable processing will have been exported away from the technology. Indeed, this points to the downside to this tactic. If stakeholders take ownership of processes or resources, this means they take responsibility. This might transfer some risk to them, or it might commit them to providing resources of their own. In turn this may lead to a lack of enthusiasm, and it may be that fewer such resources are built successfully. As we have noted, the semantic web is at an early stage of development and this is one example where trust might profitably be sacrificed in the short term in order to secure the development of the semantic web into a medium with positive, visible and quantifiable benefits.

5.5.3 Exploiting Transitivity

Where trust already exists, a third tactic is to exploit transitivity of trust when it occurs; recall that trust is not genuinely transitive, though often takes on the properties of transitivity. That is, if A trusts B, and B vouches for C, this in itself provides a reason for A to trust C (not necessarily a decisive reason – hence, trust is not genuinely transitive). A related tactic, which we will not treat separately in this section (although much of the discussion implicitly applies), is to exploit the distributivity of trust. If A trusts a group X, then that may give it a reason to trust the X_is in X, though again this will be hedged around with many caveats. For example, what will A trust the X_is to do? The same thing in each case? Or particular subtasks of the global task? Distributivity is a more complex topic, and we focus here on transitivity.

There are advantages and disadvantages to this tactic. An advantage is that it does not rely on the creation of institutions. The Internet is remarkably institution-free, which is one reason why trust is so difficult to manage online (O'Hara 2004a). Despite the fact that the Internet is the global technology *par excellence*, trust online is actually very often local. Transitivity is rooted in direct personal acquaintance, and so a system that is based on transitivity can be grafted onto the local trust networks that one would expect to find online.

A related point is that there are remarkably few sanctions available to online institutions and so institutions are relatively unable to police their charges. An institutional approach will always be at something of a disadvantage online, although infrastructure changes may alter this (Lessig 1999). There is also some empirical evidence that institutional approaches, such as seals of approval or kitemarks, are not particularly exploited by users, at least in e-commerce contexts (Corritore et al. 2003). It may be intriguing to investigate the reasons for such a shying away from institutional approaches. One reason, in the context of European Union regulation, which was discovered from empirical analyses, is that mention of European Union regulation seems to produce a false sense of security (Spiekermann et al. 2001).

A disadvantage of exploiting transitivity is that it is inevitably limited.

Beyond more than a few links in the chain, the connection between principals, the Parsonian community of interests which those principals may feel that they have in common and which underpins their trust relations, will be very stretched indeed. In relatively small 'worlds', such as individual academic communities, this may not be too much of a problem. Certain prominent figures, either famous people or branded sites, might also ease the problem of the ebbing in transitive trust if they appear somewhere along a chain. If B (trusted by A) tells A that C (unknown to A) endorses X, then A may not be altogether inclined to trust X. But if B tells A that Tim Berners-Lee endorses X, the chain may not degrade quite as rapidly. Another disadvantage is that such transitive chains do depend on reasonably robust networks of trust being around in the first place; they do not address any bootstrapping problem.

A third disadvantage is that identity becomes essential as the chains of trust become very long; there must be some kind of certification procedure, otherwise the chains will degrade. This will require the inclusion of institutions and the consequent possibility of sanction, and so may only be possible in fairly specialized contexts. The Internet is generally opposed in ethos to too much of an institutionalized approach, and so systems of, for instance, digital signatures, though useful in many contexts, may meet resistance from many Net users (Lessig 1999). There is a definite and uncomfortable trade-off here; one of the charms of the Net is that on it 'no one knows you're a dog', but equally, it is useful sometimes to be able to prove you are not a dog.

Identity is also a problem in very short chains of trust, down to the limiting case of two actors, and ensuring identity is extremely important. The well-known issues of identity theft and dealing with multiple identities are as important with knowledge technologies and for the semantic web as with other areas of online interaction. The point we are making, however, is that as the chains get longer, it becomes increasingly difficult for a principal to manage its interactions (as it may then be going through a number of intermediaries, only one of which needs to be unreliable to scupper the entire interaction). In a world where chains of trust do get very long – and the semantic web is envisaged to be such a world – the institutional trade-off will appear to be more pressing.

James Hendler's 'web of trust' initiative (Golbeck et al. 2003) aims to exploit the transitivity of trust to create a social network that can extend beyond the immediate personal acquaintances of its members. They provide metrics for inferring trust at remote parts of the chain and use such algorithmic methods for generating meta-data for authentification. This approach has an interesting take on the bootstrapping problem, as it is intended to determine trust from annotations to documents that are not explicitly relevant to trust. However, a system of digital signatures is also required to authenticate entries. Various other network-based schemes are possible, for example as described by Richardson et al. (2003), or exploiting techniques for analysing networks determined by ontologies (Alani, Dasmahapatra et al. 2003).

The Friend-of-a-Friend (FOAF) system is an RDF schema that allows users to develop an interlinked set of statements about agents to build a web of acquaintances.[5] The identity problem is finessed by linking the descriptions with emails; again, a system of digital signatures is also required.

Yolanda Gil and colleagues (Gil and Ratnakar 2002) have suggested that an annotation system called TRELLIS[6] could be used to bolster trust. Documents and other information resources can be annotated by users, providing assessments about argumentative structures, the quality of the arguments within those resources and relations to other resources. Such assessments go towards the ability to suggest measures of credibility that are entered explicitly by individual users and then summarized (averaged) and presented to new users. This is another way of exploiting transitivity as the users will accept these credibility assessments if, and only if, they trust previous users. It is also a good example of the sort of exploitation that can be made of the semantic web.

Certification of identity is an important adjunct to the tactic of exploiting transitivity. We discuss this aspect more explicitly in the next section.

5.5.4 Provenance and Certification

Identity, provenance and certification together make up a big element of the likely direction of online trust management. The provenance of some information is the history of the item insofar as it can be traced, together with information about its originator (which will bring us to the problem of identity).

One example of the provenance problems that the semantic web will throw up can already be seen in the world of virtual organizations and also in grid applications. The semantic web is likely to see virtual organizations form dynamically, very possibly coming in and going out of existence in extremely short periods of time. The trust problem here is how a user can trust information released by such short-lived dynamic coalitions, given that data will be modified depending on what services the virtual organization performs. In other words, how can the user determine what process generated the resulting data when the virtual organization that produced the result may have ceased to exist?

Provenance may be seen as an annotation recording how some data were derived, showing how data were passed between services and altered as a result. The user may then be able to step through the process via the services. Some architecture must be in place to facilitate the recording of these decisions and actions, and this architecture should support reasoning or navigation through the workflow of a virtual organization, as well as storage of the annotations, that is, the provenance data. To achieve this some centralized architecture will be required to oversee authentification and non-repudiation (Szomszor and Moreau 2003).

Centralized architectures are also important for certification of identity. We have already seen, as for example with Hendler's 'web of trust', that certifying identity is crucial for the operation of many ideas. Note that with a certification approach, the certifier does not necessarily vouch for the agent's trustworthiness; the certifier merely certifies the agent's identity − from which the principal must deduce whether the agent should be allowed access to resources. Most certification approaches involve a two-step process: first the key is bound to the agent by the certifier; second the principal gives access rights to the agent, independently of the certifier.[7]

For example, in an open agent-based environment, as we have noted, agents must interact with agents whose identities they will need to verify, as they will not have come into contact with them before. Such agents, particularly when they control some of their principals' resources, and particularly in negotiating or commercial contexts, will have to decide whether to act on requests and how to assess assertions. This will require examination of other agents' credentials. Such credentials will include properties of the agent, such as membership of accredited organizations, age or host of the agent and recommendations from and delegations by other agents. In particular, delegations and recommendations (estimates of trust values) are passed about between agents in communities as ways of signalling their beliefs about the trustworthiness of third party agents.

All this must be able to be performed dynamically. Tim Finin and colleagues in Maryland (Kagal et al. 2002) have developed a dynamic framework, based in the semantic web language DAML+OIL (DARPA Agent Markup Language + Ontology Inference Layer) and a standard agent framework (such as developed by the Foundation for Intelligent Physical Agents; FIPA), which provides authorization and credibility assessments. The security framework is based very strongly on digital signatures, generated using public key infrastructure (PKI).

The advantage of this approach for an agent environment is that it is distributed. The agents can be held accountable for their actions because they have to sign all queries and requests with their personal key. This removes the need for a central database of security clearance which would not be appropriate in the decentralized agent world. Instead, an agent platform, associated with a security policy, is able to check an unknown agent's credentials whenever it tries to register.

So, simple verification of an agent's credentials works as follows. All the credentials that are relevant to the inquiry are presented at the time of request:

> In order to use its services, a requesting agent must send all required credentials along with the request for service. The service agent will check its knowledge base, and question other agents about their beliefs in order to verify the credentials. Suppose agent A has an alarm service which requires that requesters be AAAI members. The security policy of agent A also states that the agent XYZ should be trusted to verify AAAI certificates. An agent B sends A a request to use the service along with its certificate from the AAAI CA. This certificate states that the bearer of this certificate is a member of AAAI. Agent A asks agent XYZ to verify the certificate. If the certificate is valid then agent B is authorized to use the alarm service. If agent B did not send the required certificate or sent an invalid certificate, its request would be denied. (Kagal et al. 2002, p. 30)

An example of this is an agent-oriented PKI system described by Hu (2001). In this system, there are two types of certificate: identity certificates for humans and their agents; and authorization certificates, which represent authorizations by entities, including the public key for the granting entity, the public key of the entity that receives the authorization, the authorization itself and so on.

It should be noted that any trust policy that involves using certification systems or digital signatures, such as PKI, does not solve the trust problem, but it shifts it one step along. The user has to trust the certification system and the institutions that check the signatures; this localizes the trust issue and simplifies trust management – and is thereby extremely valuable in itself – but it does not remove the problem.

In this context, Marianne Winslett and colleagues' system, TrustBuilder, is an interesting approach. This exploits trust negotiation, where agents – strangers to each other – iteratively disclose credentials until sufficient trust has been built up to secure the transaction required. This has the happy effect of helping secure trust across domain boundaries so that agents subscribing to different trust systems can establish trust between themselves (Winslett et al. 2002; Grandison and Sloman 2000).

This is how such a negotiation might work:

> A service agent A only allows employees of XYZ Pvt. Ltd. to access its services, and accepts delegations from these employees. Agent B approaches agent A with a credential from AAAI. Agent A decides that the credential is not good enough and asks the agent B to prove that it is an employee of XYZ or if B has a delegation from an employee. Agent B possesses a delegation from Bob who is an employee of XYZ and sends this delegation to A. A verifies the delegation and the chain of

delegations and decides to authorize agent B's request. (Kagal et al. 2002, pp. 30-1)

Thought also needs to be given to how to manage certification obsolescence. It may be that certification systems used for trust management become obsolete or compromised, or are merely superseded by other systems. Or, in the case of networks of trusting agents, they may simply lose their critical mass and cease to be effective.

Principals who are exploiting certification systems need to have strategies for dealing with such obsolescence and managing the transition to new certification systems. This is particularly true when certified agents are of crucial importance in safety- or mission-critical applications, and where their *de facto* decertification might cause the whole application to crash. There is an intuitive distinction between certificate obsolescence and certificate revocation, but, equally, it may be hard for a principal to make that distinction.

5.5.5 Alternative Tactics of Restriction

So far we have been describing the tactics of restriction. The section on exploiting transitivity (5.5.3) explored the possibilities of restricting interactions with agents you 'don't know', while the section on provenance and certification (5.5.4) suggested restricting interactions with those who do not have the correct certification. There are other ways of restricting interaction with classes of agents that are possibly untrustworthy.

For example, the Advanced Knowledge Technologies project runs a semantic web application called CS AKTive Space (Shadbolt et al. 2004). This application takes information from a number of heterogeneous and distributed resources describing the state of the computer science discipline in the UK, continuously harvesting and screenscraping content, and maintaining a central store of information. The resulting snapshot of the discipline, mediated via an ontology, is then presented to users through various visualizations.

The reliability of this picture depends on the quality of the information gathered and the maintenance of the datastore. If information is gathered from an unreliable source, then the result would be untrustworthy information that might pollute the whole dataset. The solution pursued by AKT is to restrict attention to branded websites, that is, websites that are presumed explicitly to be trustworthy, such as the websites of relevant university departments (using the '.ac.uk' suffix as a brand), or the information gathered by research councils such as the Engineering and Physical Sciences Research Council (EPSRC). Using brands in this way, the domain of information can be usefully restricted. The development and monitoring of brands as vehicles of trust is extremely important (O'Hara 2004a).

Another example of a possible restriction would be to confine oneself to one's own research (or another) community. Communities of practice are seen as essential knowledge-managing entities (Wenger 1998). They are vital for training new practitioners and for maintaining corporate memories. As such, there has been a good deal of work on identifying communities – often reaching beyond one particular organization (Alani, Dasmahapatra et al. 2003; McDermott 1999). Communities identified by relatively mechanical methods – such as Ontocopi, which identifies communities based on analysis of domain ontologies (Alani, Dasmahapatra et al. 2003) – could be another basis for restriction of interaction, being more meaningful than anything exploiting transitivity and yet more open than a system based on brands.

5.5.6 Formality

A leading characteristic of the semantic web, and indeed the Web in general, is the scruffiness of the data and the heterogeneity of the users. Trust could be extremely problematic, simply on the grounds that anomalies may be extremely hard to spot. Policing the semantic web, therefore, may be difficult. Formal methods could be of some interest in the context of the semantic web. They are, without doubt, somewhat contrary to its spirit. Nevertheless, they might serve to restrict interactions to those that can be modelled and, therefore, are relatively predictable. They can be used to lead users away from the scruffier bits of the online world and towards more straightforward bits.

There has been a relatively small quantity of work in this field. However, the general approach has much in common with the subject of the next section, the development of 'calculi of trust'. Whereas the formal approaches we envisage are designed to model the domain, calculi of trust are designed to model the trusting behaviour itself.

5.5.7 Calculi of Trust

Calculi of trust are attempts to model trusting behaviour and, as such, have a particular relevance in the software agent world, where trusting behaviours have to be produced entirely artificially. However, it should be noted that primitive logical frameworks rarely have the expressive power to model the typically complex reasoning required to maintain trust relationships (Grandison and Sloman 2000).

Dimitrakos and Bicarregui (2001) for example, have set up the basic elements of a model in axiomatic form. They use multimodal and subjective logics to derive inferences. These axioms were drawn up in the particular context of e-services, with the hope that formal reasoning will facilitate formation of trust relationships and resolution of conflicts.

The model is interestingly complex and sensitive. The authors do not assume that trust or distrust are necessarily transitive. They have interesting methods for extending the discussion to consider the trusting of intermediaries; different relationships between the principal, the intermediary and the intermediary's agents (for example, does the principal even know of the existence of the intermediary's agents?) lead to very different trusting behaviour, and axiomatic analysis can expose interesting types of behaviour and isolate the possible types of intermediary.

For instance, Dimitrakos and Bicarregui suggest there are four types of intermediary. A transparent intermediary identifies the agents to the principal. A translucent intermediary identifies the existence of the agents to the principal, but not their identities (for example, telling the principal that its goods will be sent by courier without specifying which courier). An overcast intermediary hides the existence of the agents. A proxy intermediary actually acts as the agent itself, but does not reveal its own existence (that is, it acts in another's name without disabusing the principal of the assumption that the other is actually operating).

These categorizations then lead to various axioms (Dimitrakos and Bicarregui 2001). Examples include:

1. Trust (distrust) is not transferred along an overcast intermediary.
2. Trust is transitively transferred through transparent intermediaries.
3. Trust (distrust) in all subcontractors of a transparent intermediary is transferred to an inclination to trust (distrust) the intermediary.
4. Trust is transferred anonymously through translucent intermediaries.
5. Trust in an adviser is transferred to the recommended parties.
6. Distrust in recommended parties is transferred to an inclination to distrust the adviser.

Golbeck et al. (2003) use a method to compute trust. They create graphs of networks of trusting agents, developed using the FOAF schema (see Section 5.5.3). The method then computes measures of trust by looking at the strength of connections between the two relevant nodes (agents) on the graph. They are able to calculate a maximum and a minimum amount of trust between two agents; they also create a weighted average giving a recommendation for trusting. The algorithm for computing this searches the graph for paths between the two agents, taking the value of a direct edge connection as the trust value where such an edge exists and, where it does not, recursively determining a value of trust relationships between all the neighbours on a path. The algorithm ensures that no agent is trusted by a principal more than another agent closer to the principal on the graph.[8] The trick with any formal calculus of trust is to capture the richness of behaviour in the face of uncertainty.

5.5.8 Interrogation and Dialogue

Interrogation, conversation and dialogue have long been seen as keys to trust. Testimony on its own is rarely seen as a sufficient guide to controversial action; the author of the testimony must be cross-examined in order to establish his or her bona fides. The argument goes back to Plato, who gives Socrates the following passage in the *Phaedrus*:

> SOCRATES: You know, Phaedrus, writing shares a strange feature with painting. The offspring of painting stand there as if they are alive, but if anyone asks them anything, they remain most solemnly silent. The same is true of written words. You'd think they were speaking as if they had some understanding, but if you question anything that has been said because you want to learn more, it continues to signify just that very same thing forever. When it has once been written down, every discourse roams about everywhere, reaching indiscriminately those with understanding no less than those who have no business with it, and it doesn't know to whom it should speak and to whom it should not. And when it is faulted and attacked unfairly, it always needs its father's support; alone, it can neither defend itself nor come to its own support. (*Phaedrus*, 275de)

In other words, the written – because of the properties of written script – is not trustworthy. It cannot be restricted to those who should see it. It cannot be personalized to the reader. It cannot add anything, it cannot enlighten the reader any further. And it cannot argue, nor enter into a dialectic (O'Hara 2004a).

This sort of argument is still adhered to. In law courts, for example, a signed affidavit (that is, a written account of some event) is only permissible in a relatively small number of circumstances, such as when the content of the testimony is uncontroversial. Otherwise, witness testimony has to be given orally, and the witness must engage in a conversation with a properly accredited representative of the defendant. And so specialized has this conversational task become, that years of training are required, and those people (barristers) who possess the expertise can command huge salaries. Some even become media personalities – and all because there is a general presumption in society that Socrates' argument above is valid. Similarly, PhD candidates are examined orally, committee meetings depend on face-to-face discussion rather than on the submission of written argument that the chairperson can evaluate, and so on.

This is not to say that the written word is inherently untrustworthy; only that the spoken mode of communication includes many features that enhance trust. Interestingly, many of the developments of the semantic web allow precisely the sorts of dialogue and personalization of content that provide these features (O'Hara 2004b). In this sense, the semantic web actually blurs – as have earlier technologies – the boundaries between the spoken and the written. Dynamic content retrieval and publication reproduce the instantaneity of the spoken, and the responsiveness to an interlocutor. And as such, they allow certain types of interrogation that may well extend the boundaries of what we trust. Such interrogation allows interlocutors to rate the value of information the other provides, which is an important determinant of trust (Corritore et al. 2003).

For instance, D3E (Buckingham Shum and Sumner 2001) is a document discussion environment that allows structured discussion of a web page or document. This is a discussion that even the author can take part in. Artequakt provides personalized content for readers, synthesized dynamically from web documents – in its case, biographies of artists (Alani, Kim et al. 2003).

Another interesting example of blurring the spoken–written distinction can be found with the open hypermedia system – Conceptual Open Hypermedia Services Environment (COHSE) (Carr et al. 2001). COHSE allows the reader, rather than the author, to generate associations. Transferring control of associative linking from the author to the reader is a prime example of a technology of the written allowing the incorporation of some characteristic properties of the spoken (O'Hara 2004b).

5.5.9 Redundancy

Replicating processes and introducing redundancy is a further way to help promote trust. If some process is deemed risky, having several different agents run the process and then having a relatively transparent process of arbitration between them, is advantageous. Replication tactics work particularly well in a distributed or grid environment where different nodes of the grid will have different computational capabilities, nodes will not always be available and network connectivity may be relatively unreliable. In such a case, replicating computation on multiple nodes can improve performance and increase trust by ensuring that no one (possibly flaky) node will bear the full weight of responsibility for some piece of processing (Li and Mascagni 2003).

The severity of the downsides to a redundancy tactic will depend on the type of inference being replicated. First, there are obviously the excess costs introduced by replication, since the same processing has to be done more than once. However, if the processing is relatively straightforward and costs are low, then the tactic may be useful. On the model of a computational grid, for example, the paradigm is for powerful low-cost computation to come on stream as a result of the grid arrangement, in which case the costs of redundancy may well be outweighed by the benefits.

Second, there are areas where some intelligence or creativity might be exploited in reasoning. In this event, replicating processing might pull the net result to the centre, ruling out riskier, but possibly more creative solutions. On the other hand, if the processes are relatively straightforward, or if the creation of trust is more important than extracting value out of processes, then again the replication tactic might prove to be valuable.

5.5.10 Other Forms of Knowledge Management and Presentation

Finally, we must not forget other, perhaps more mundane, ways that knowledge technologies can increase trust and trustworthiness. Recall the knowledge life cycle (Section 5.4). The final knowledge challenge in that cycle is that of maintaining knowledge bases. Knowledge maintenance, which is greatly aided by knowledge technologies, will aid the process of keeping knowledge bases up to date and correct, and will therefore improve performance of that knowledge base.

For example, methods to model knowledge in order to anticipate what knowledge needs to be junked would be useful. Methods for determining inconsistencies are also of value. In short, merely ensuring that knowledge bases are kept trim will increase trust not only in them, but also in those knowledge technologies that use such knowledge bases as input.

Another knowledge challenge is that of publishing. Clever methods of presenting personalized knowledge to a user in a way that allows its significance to be gauged should also increase that user's trust in the knowledge. For instance, Gil and Ratnakar's (2002) TRELLIS system presents arguments about a document's veracity in a structured way. Buckingham Shum's D3E (Buckingham Shum and Sumner 2001) also allows a structured argument to develop about a text, which allows the reader to follow whether the document stands up to scrutiny. Indeed, in general, information content provides useful cues for users to assess trust, and provision of content that is appropriate and useful for the audience is very important for establishing trust (Shelat and Egger 2002; Corritore et al. 2003). Semantic web technologies to personalize content will clearly be of great importance here.

5.5.11 Summary

We summarize a number of tactics for establishing and/or extending trust in

Table 5.1. In the next section, we turn to the strategies for trust.

Table 5.1 Tactics for creating or sustaining trust

Tactic	Description	Costs
Transparency	Allow principal access to hitherto closed processes, black boxes	Potentially open to creating mistrust, if expectations are too high
Transfers of ownership	Allow stakeholders decision rights and responsibilities	Stakeholders may be more reluctant to put in effort than an agent
Exploiting transitivity of trust	Where a trust network already exists, extend it via transitive (or, on occasion, distributive) extensions	Neither transitivity nor distributivity are perfect models of trust. Plus this strategy cannot address any bootstrapping problem
Certification	Create some institutional support for digital signatures, thereby securing provenance	Institutional structures are contrary to the anarchistic value ethos of the Net, and thereby might work to reduce trust (cf Durkheim). Doesn't address bootstrapping, as the principal still has to trust the certification system and authorities
Restriction	Increase trust by policies designed to avoid interaction with the non-trustworthy	May be arbitrary. May be over-limiting. Hard to evaluate the efficacy of the tactic
Formal methods	Use formal methods to avoid dealing with the scruffier parts of the Web	High modelling overhead. Plus the whole development of the Web, with its heterogeneous users, has encouraged scruffiness. Many of the richer parts of the Web are scruffy
Calculi of trust	Use formal characterizations of trust relationships to govern when an agent should trust	Trust, being a second-order phenomenon, is hard to model successfully. Such a system is likely to lack the flexibility inherent in trust
Interrogation	Submit documents, web pages, etc, to interrogation and scrutiny	Technology in the early stages
Redundancy	Run processes several times in parallel	Extra computing costs. For certain types of process may be opportunity costs, producing 'safe' average results rather than risky, creative ones
Knowledge management	Use tools for knowledge management to maintain knowledge bases and keep them accurate, up to date and trustworthy	High maintenance overheads

5.6 STRATEGIES FOR TRUST

Trust management will continue to be very important on the World Wide Web. Developing strategies for trust, which might involve deploying some of the tactics mentioned in Section 5.5 in intelligent ways, and dynamically configuring various tactics depending on the context of the transaction, will be essential if trust is to be maintained as the Internet user community increases.

5.6.1 Trust Management

Policies governing trust and trust management are essential. In particular, security requires a wide understanding of the domain in question, together with specifications of how actions ramify (Schneier 2003), and should be high level, abstract and integrable with heterogeneous applications and platforms (Grandison and Sloman 2000). Indeed, attention needs to be paid not only to the relationships between the principal and the remote systems with which it communicates, but also to other components in the system such as the interactions over underlying systems, for example communications services (Grandison and Sloman 2000; Schneier 2003).

Such management models must be alert to the difference between a system designed to block some accidental incident and a system designed to block malicious action. The former should, if well designed, completely eradicate the type of accident it is meant to counter, although it could well have unintended consequences further along the line. The latter, however, is of necessity at risk from further malicious attempts to get around it.

We should also note the importance of human versus machine security. It is arguable that in many cases the unit of the trust relationship is neither the human user nor the artificial agent, but, in fact, the whole integrated system, human plus machine. According to the testimony of hacker Kevin Mitnick, it is the human element in a security system that is actually easiest to get round. Computer hackers who enjoy the challenge of getting round a technical fix are obviously a problem, but not necessarily the major security issue (Mitnick 2000).

Complexity of domains is obviously a serious difficulty. In general, any movement towards establishing or spreading trust on the Web or semantic web will necessitate a shift from transactions involving centralized information systems to distributed domains and organizations. The picture will be further complicated because all these different information sources will be trusted to varying degrees (Grandison and Sloman 2000). For instance, there are a number of perfectly sensible methods using system-based controls to verify the identity of an agent or a process. If such an agent or process wishes to get access to some resource, then a central database or repository storing access control information can be consulted. However, it is unlikely that such schemes, efficient though they are, will scale up to web dimension applications. For example, authorization cannot in such circumstances be divided up into authentication and access control. Therefore, a trust management system cannot rely on centralization and instead must be distributed like the system itself. Credentials provided by agents within the system, such as recommendations and delegations, become essential for making judgements about whether to trust (Kagal et al. 2002).

This is an example of a trust management issue. The question, in such a distributed system, is how to show that an agent is entitled to access a resource, given the necessary restriction of the information available to the system for verification of the certification (or whatever) that the agent carries with it. Credentials might include agent's properties, for instance membership of organizations, and delegations from other agents (see Section 5.5.4).

How might a delegation-based system work? An agent would have the ability to make a delegation of any rights that it possesses to use resources. It also could have the right to delegate delegated to it by another agent. In this case, assuming that the original delegation is legal, the agent could make any delegation that falls within the constraints of the rights it had been granted. A valid delegation will change the access rights of the agents in the system.

Problems might occur in such chains, for example when agents are created dynamically. An agent may be delegated a right by another agent, which then goes down. When the first agent asks to use the resource and presents its certification, there may be problems if the rights to delegate of the now non-existent delegating agent cannot be checked. Thus, there may be some requirement for a register of delegation certificates that will either have to be centralized or, alternatively, will need to be stored in some distributed fashion that still allows the owners of resources to get at the certificates easily (and still allows security of the certification process) (Kagal et al. 2002).

Given such a palette of information, trust management issues will include how to create security policies, what credentials to associate with what properties, and how to reason about credentials and properties to produce a set of decision and access rights. Because such reasoning is a basis for trust management, there will be requirements for such expressive formalisms as trust and security ontologies (Kagal et al. 2002).

Another important trust management issue is that of determining the nature of trust dynamically over time. Current solutions tend not to handle changes in trust, but typically one would expect one's attributions of trust to be altered as knowledge of the world changes, as new actions (which may or may not demonstrate the trustworthiness of agents) occur and as certification and other systems are perceived in different ways. Trust systems need to respond to environmental changes and to learn from agents' behaviour to change trust attributions where this is appropriate. Most current trust applications tend not to incorporate the experience of agents into decision making (Grandison and Sloman 2000). The value of particular trust policies also needs to be regularly assessed.

5.6.2 Meta-data for Trust

These trust management issues seem to suggest that there is an opportunity for toolkits and languages to aid the expression of and inferences about trust relationships, allowing such relationships to be established, analysed, evaluated, monitored and reasoned over (Grandison and Sloman 2000). This leads on to a further requisite for trust management, the languages and understanding required to create trustworthiness meta-data.

Much of the functionality of the semantic web is premised on the creation of rich sets of meta-data about objects – knowledge objects in particular, which will allow machines to reason about their content as much as their external characteristics. Meta-data about documents or agents will, by hypothesis, be around in large quantity if the semantic web takes off. In that case, it would be reasonable to expect much of that meta-data to be concerned with the trustworthiness of those objects, to allow reasoning about whether a source should be trusted, to what extent, with which resources, for which task.

Such meta-data, for example, are likely to be stored in any system recording provenance (see Szomszor and Moreau 2003). The annotations to data that enable the provenance of those data to be inferred are one example of meta-data that may be extremely important to collect and curate.

It is arguable that relatively little is known about why certain agents should be trusted, how to recognize trustworthiness and what information is factored in. Much of it will no doubt be similar to the information we have considered in this chapter, such as certification of identity or provenance. But equally, there may be other relatively complex factors that principals use in their trust management, and these should be representable via meta-data mark-ups. Ontologies of relevant concepts may be available to aid the expression of such meta-data and such ontologies are beginning to be seen (for example Kagal et al. 2002).

We have not considered risk in detail in this chapter. The relation between risk and trust, despite a superficial inverse pattern, is not trivial to describe. It seems clear that when calculating which agents or knowledge to trust, and how to mark up a source, risk factors will loom large. These factors include the value of the knowledge under examination, or the value of the services provided by an agent. Value will determine the extent to which trust will be extended; a principal might be more prepared to go out on a limb if the knowledge it was hoping to acquire were more valuable. In particular, value would be closely related to opportunity costs – in other words, what would the principal lose by eschewing the knowledge or services, and how cheap would the knowledge or services be when acquired from another (more trustworthy) source? Is the knowledge or service being obtained by exchange? If so, what is being exchanged and (if it is an excludable good) can the principal afford to lose it? And will the agent acquire access to any other resources of the principal?

Other factors influencing risk will include more obvious information such as: Who developed the knowledge or provides the service? Who certifies the knowledge? Does the knowledge or service have a wide user base? Is the principal acquainted with anyone in this user base?

It is important that principals should have (1) sufficiently expressive formalisms to enable them to specify precisely what their assessments of their sources are, and (2) sufficient understanding of their own trust requirements to enable them to make accurate assessments and to interpret meta-data provided by other principals (which will probably have different trust requirements). Both of these prerequisites imply at the least the development of useful and used ontologies for expressing trust and for expressing the characteristics of sources which go into a calculation of trust.

5.6.3 Trust and Trustworthiness

In considering strategies for trust an important problem concerns the creation of a formula for a type of behaviour or for a type of credentials management, in that if it becomes too formulaic there is a danger that it will be too imitable. The issue is the important distinction between trust and trustworthiness (O'Hara 2004a). As Corritore et al. (2003) argue, trust is an act by a principal; trustworthiness is a property of an agent. The agent is in control of its trustworthiness, but is not in control of whether it is trusted; that decision is out of its hands. This gap is essential to the system's working at all. However, if the agent comes to recognize how to influence the decisions of principals to trust it, then it may become able to close, or partially close, that gap.

Put another way, if an agent knows how to signal its trustworthiness, this then takes away all its incentives to be trustworthy. If the meta-data assigned to objects, for example, become too fixed or predictable, then the agent may be able to mimic these meta-data, to produce them via spurious routes.

Trust management needs to be active and dynamic. It needs managers to be constantly vigilant with respect to potential ways around strategies. Certification authorities and procedures need to be continually updated. Identities need to be monitored. Typical profiles of trustworthy agents or entities need to be treated with care. Equally, if particular strategies for trust management become entrenched (for example, certification of provenance), then such strategies will become overheads on knowledge technologies and web services. They will impose a cost and, in the event that they cease to ensure trustworthiness, that cost will be wasted.

For example, if a certification authority is acting as the means to ensure the provenance of information being used as input by a knowledge technology, then it is important to realize that this imposes three overheads on that knowledge technology. First, the knowledge technology must go through a process of verifying the certificate accompanying the information. Second, there will inevitably be trustworthy yet uncertified information (or maybe information certified, but not by a currently recognized authority), which the knowledge technology is unable to use. It is worth remembering in this context that in the fourth quarter of 2002, American online retailers lost an estimated US$160m through fraud. But they lost an estimated US$315m through rejecting legitimate sales that failed to satisfy rigorous security procedures (Gaudin 2002).

The third overhead is the constant effort that the managers of the knowledge technology must invest to ensure to their own satisfaction that the certification authority was efficient and accurate. As Schneier (2003) argues, overheads such as these must be balanced against a realistic assessment of the costs of failures of trust. There is a danger that trust and security systems become 'motherhood and apple pie' issues while merely imposing needless costs on a system.

5.6.4 Other Properties of Knowledge Technologies

Similarly, trust has to be balanced against other system properties. The semantic web is at a very early stage of development and the creation of usable techniques for the efficient production of interesting information may be of greater importance than the development of trust mechanisms. At a later stage, when more users need to be brought in to secure large-scale growth for the semantic web, such imperatives may be reversed. Corritore et al. (2003) also argue, as we have noted, that such usability itself contributes to trust. On the other hand, Fogg and Tseng (1999) argue that trustworthiness is a key component of credibility, but it is harder to see how this causative directionality can be sustained. In addition, the production of useful data abstracted or inferred from large-scale repositories of scruffy data may be inherently hard to achieve in reliable, trustworthy ways.

The development of trustworthy methods of mining data from large repositories is important, but the problem with scaling these methods up to the web scale may not be one of expanding the techniques to deal with more data. The problem may be retaining trustworthiness as the scale begins to outgrow the largest well-managed repositories. Beyond a certain level, data mining and other knowledge extraction techniques might have to work on scruffy and unmaintained datasets, in which case trust may be unable to depend on certificates or evaluations of formal models of reasoning. It may be that trust comes along with usable results, extracted from a wider range of individually less trustworthy datasets.

Using knowledge management techniques and knowledge technologies however, is a clear way forward to retaining trust while dealing with ever-scruffier datasets.

5.6.5 Privacy: The Power of Knowledge

Privacy is extremely important for trust. Data will not be released to technologies if those technologies cannot ensure fair use. Here, distinct legal discourses make a difference. A European use-based discourse is relatively restrictive, whereas a rights-based discourse may be more liberal. In the former, the individual can give information away for use for some particular purpose and then the recipient of the information will only be allowed to use it for that purpose. On a rights-based model, owners sign away their rights to control data about them, thereby opening up the possibility of future commoditization of those rights.

The major lines of privacy invasion in the US are based on four specific torts (Camp 2000): (1) intrusion upon seclusion; (2) appropriation of name and likeness; (3) false light, which is the publication of misleading information. The information may be true, yet is edited or presented placing the individual in a false light. A link to a commercial website, written as 'link to a fraudulent site' would, assuming the site to be above board, be an example of this; and (4) public disclosure of private facts.

One serious challenge for privacy advocates raised by the semantic web and knowledge technologies is the effect of aggregating knowledge. In practical terms, until recently invasions of privacy were monopolized by government and the media, because collection and publication of information were tough barriers to entry. New technologies have changed this radically. Surveillance is cheap and publication is trivial.

Data compilation is much more powerful than merely extracting information from individual datasets. Information about people's incomes may be harmless; information about people's tax records may be harmless. But put the two together and much criminal activity might be exposed.

The US has developed a Code of Fair Information Practice (Camp 2000), which sets out what is reasonable for the management of compilations and data collections. Examples of its recommendations are:

- Data compilations should not be secret.
- Individuals should have access to data collected about them.
- Individuals should be able to audit and correct data.
- Individuals should be able to prevent disclosure. Prevention of disclosure should be the responsibility of the organization with possession of the data.

Strangely, this code does not as yet apply to medical data. In the face of increasing pressure for data collection and the greater possibilities of data gathering and storage (New Scientist 2003) as studied, for example, in the Memories For Life Grand Challenge submission,[9] policies and technologies for ensuring privacy are becoming essential, and will be a key research area in the next few years.

5.7 OPPORTUNITIES FOR INTERDISCIPLINARITY

Trust is first and foremost a social phenomenon, and sociological studies are essential, first to map the properties and functions of trust (Misztal 1996), and second to detail the relationships between people and technology. It should be noted, however, that sociological monographs often have more or less overt political agendas behind them. Many discussions of trust extol the virtues of democracy, consultation, ownership and transparency, all of which are important, but all of which equally are ideologically enshrined in anti-authoritarian and anti-elitist thought, which is aimed explicitly at 'empowerment of the individual' and discounts the possibility that such empowerment might actually be detrimental to some individuals on some occasions (O'Hara 2004a). On the other hand, those discussions of trust that focus on social capital (Fukuyama 1995; Putnam 2000) are often driven by a neo-conservative agenda that is intended to minimize the participation of government in social life, arguing that formal governmental direction of informal social relations will of necessity undermine those very relations (O'Hara 2004a).

Another discipline that focuses on the relationship between people and technology is management science, including organizational science, behavioural science and other flavours. Ethnography also is important for mapping behavioural traits and is being used increasingly in a number of knowledge technology and semantic web-relevant projects (Cheverst et al.

2001). Psychology also joins the group of related disciplines that mine this seam. Semantic web technologies, such as ontologies and tools, need to be integrated into working practices in order to be taken up (Buckingham Shum 2004; Ellman 2004). Much trust will come 'for free' along with successful integration.

Philosophical analysis is interesting, particularly in the development of ideal theories of trust, which may feed into the calculi of trust that we have discussed. Furthermore, as trust is increasingly seen as an epistemological problem and/or strategy (Luhmann 1979), branches of philosophy such as epistemology, or scientific methodology, will make important contributions – though epistemology will need to be de-psychologized and made relevant to organizational contexts and artificial agents (O'Hara 2002a).

Linguistics has already proved extremely important in the development of new semantic web tools. Being able to extract usable information (knowledge) from the large legacy of plain texts that are available on the Web is already proving to be of crucial importance in enhancing the value of that knowledge. Interpretation of such texts is often contested and, therefore, constitutes a dangerous moment for trust; such natural language technologies may improve matters. We have also argued that interrogation and dialogue, using technology to give the written medium of the Web some of the properties of the spoken, will aid the development of trust. Linguistics has provided many interesting analyses of the effects of technology on language modes, and these are of major importance to this topic (Ong 1982).

Trust is based to a large extent on incentives, and economics provides perhaps the most intensive study of incentives. Economics, and related fields such as rational choice theory and game theory, should be able to provide theories of how to signal to individuals that trust is in their interests and how to devise systems in which trust is in the interests of the actors (see Chapter 12 in this volume).

Also, needless to say, computer science, cryptography and mathematics have a large part to play by providing the infrastructure for secure systems. Though, as we have argued, technological approaches finesse the problem of trust without necessarily solving it; users must still trust the technological fixes and the motives of those who pay for and police the new systems. In the terminology of O'Hara (2004a), global trust requires underlying local trust.

The reader will no doubt have spotted a number of areas where other disciplines have a role to play. In the following, we highlight areas where such opportunities lie. It should be noted that the scope of many of these extends beyond the area of knowledge technologies.

The following sets out some of the important general opportunities for interdisciplinarity.

5.7.1 Online and Offline Trust

We have made the assumption, common to many (Corritore et al. 2003), that online trust is broadly analogous to offline trust. This is an inviting idea, and there is no doubt that many of the properties of the two are the same. However, even ignoring the obvious point that offline trust is a highly heterogeneous social phenomenon (O'Hara 2004a), there are reasons for subjecting the assumption to a deeper examination. This is a project that would require at the least a deep conversation with those whose work it is to study offline trust, for instance anthropologists, sociologists, economists and philosophers.

In the first place, the Internet as a space has a number of properties broadly analogous to those of the 'real' world, but it also has properties that are not matched by the real world, such as a dramatic fluidity of identity of its denizens. To an extent, the nature of a space will determine the interactions that go on within it and, therefore, the differences between the Internet and other spaces may affect the trust relations that take place within it, making them importantly disanalogous to those of offline trust. An interesting line of research would be to map out the analogies and disanalogies of online and offline trust, and then to determine the significance of the disanalogies.

Secondly, in offline trust the agents involved are of course human. Online trust may involve: two human agents; a human and an artificial agent; two artificial agents; or one or more artificial proxies for human agents.

Clearly, the artificial element will have an effect on how analogous online and offline trust are. But the interesting options opened by the externalization of psychological faculties should not be discounted – the Internet appears to be having a similar effect to that of the spread of literacy and, because artificial agents become involved, that does not necessarily mean that 'trust' is an inappropriate concept here.

In short, the use of the term 'trust' for these online relations is obviously metaphorical. Overextending a metaphor can be disastrous if we take it too seriously. But equally, metaphors do suggest interesting correspondences that often can be detected in the metaphorical situation. The use of the term 'trust' in an online context has been fruitful so far and we should beware of being too cautious. This is a clear case of where interaction with sociology and related disciplines could prove to be very interesting.

Thirdly, as well as comparing and contrasting online and offline trust, we should also realize that the combination of online and offline trust into a single integrated technological system is also worthy of study. Sociologists of technology are interested in these issues. Important issues include the interface between the online and the offline aspects of the total system, how the online trust serves the purposes of the offline actors, how the assumptions made offline affect the online interactions, and how either the online or the offline trust mechanisms could override one another in any integrated application.

5.7.2 Trust as Utilitarian versus Trust as a Mark of a Moral Community

In the sociology literature, two related but different concepts of trust seem to be in operation. The first is a utilitarian concept, associated particularly with Niklas Luhmann (1979). This type of trust is an acceptance of collaborators' bona fides. Thus, the principal makes tangible gains from trusting. It cuts transaction costs, as it no longer has to investigate the agent or perform the subtask itself. It is therefore rational for the principal to trust. The direction of causality is from the agent to the principal; the agent's good behaviour leads the principal to trust it. The good behaviour is the cause of the trust; the trust is the effect of the good behaviour. This form of trust is most commonly associated with economic domains, such as e-commerce, and has been explicitly associated with online trust (Grabner-Kräuter and Kaluscha 2003).

The second is a more value-based trust concept, which comes about through a consensus of values. This is a more traditional notion of trust going back to Durkheim (1893) and Parsons (1949), although empirical analyses of survey data have been argued to support the assumption that this notion of trust is still prevalent in society (Uslaner 2002). Here, to trust someone is to accept them into one's moral community, where there may be fewer rational justifications for this to happen – indeed to do so may entail quite some risk for the principal. The direction of causality is precisely reversed – the principal's trust leads an agent to good behaviour. The trust is the cause of the good behaviour, the good behaviour the effect of the trust.

In the context of the Internet, this second notion of trust is interesting because – almost uniquely among technologies – the Internet is very value-laden. Hackers have a set of values that lead them to attempt to disrupt normal operations; they do not do it for gain in most cases (O'Hara 2004a). Scientists and academics have a knowledge-sharing, public-spirited set of values that have fostered, for example, the e-prints movement (Harnad 2003). On the other hand, Microsoft pioneered the idea of selling software by restricting access to source code, protecting and therefore creating the option of exploiting their intellectual property. The open source movement claims to produce better software, while exposing source code to view.

All these decisions are based on a set of values, and it is not hard to characterize Internet politics as a series of clashes of these value sets (see Lessig 1999). It would be interesting, therefore, to investigate, together with sociologists and other social scientists, which – in this context – would be the best notion of trust to deal with. In addition, there are several opportunities for interdisciplinary research that are specific to the knowledge technologies field.

5.7.3 The Nature of Knowledge Acquisition

The clear connection for knowledge technologies is with the field of epistemology. There are three major types of interaction that would be useful as a focus for research.

First, trustworthy knowledge technologies require trustworthy processes for producing knowledge from the input information. Therefore, the field of analytic epistemology should provide a useful set of guidelines for when knowledge acquisition processes are trustworthy – and collaboration could be envisaged with philosophers of science and theorists of probability.

Second, knowledge is also very powerful; possession of it (particularly monopolistic possession), or the perception of possession, can lead to the owner having a great deal of power. A Continental tradition of epistemology, based, for example, on the writings of such as Habermas ([1968] 1987) and Foucault and Lyotard (Lyotard [1979] 1984), while often anti-technology, provides important commentaries on the way knowledge is used to get things done and the legitimacy of the power thus created. These issues are very relevant to trust.

Third, applied epistemology, or the use of technology to create knowledge in a systematic way, has been a feature of the software industry for some time. For example, the field of knowledge acquisition was associated with the creation of knowledge bases for expert systems and the like from the late 1980s onwards. Knowledge acquisition, data mining and machine learning can shine very interesting light on the possibilities for knowledge technologies. At a higher level of abstraction, the areas of cognitive psychology that crucially informed these technologies are also of interest.

5.7.4 The Nature of Personalized Interactions

Interrogation and dialogue are important for establishing trust. We did not speculate in Section 5.5.8 on why this might be – is it the responsiveness of speech to interaction, or is it the greater bandwidth of communication that presence allows? However, if it would be possible, via collaboration with linguists or anthropologists, to establish the key trust-creating or trust-enhancing properties of oral communication over literate communication, then this would be of great help in designing semantic web tools and knowledge technologies that exploit those key properties.

5.7.5 Brands, Reputations and other Filtered Narratives

Selection of interlocutors is important, and if knowledge technologies can take input only from trustworthy sources, then we will be a long way towards ensuring the production of trusted knowledge from scruffy web scale sources. The main way to do this is to create a reputation, that is, a filtered narrative taken from past events involving the source, that signals trustworthiness (or untrustworthiness). Reputations can be fair or unfair, but they are important in reducing transaction costs (O'Hara 2004a).

Particular symbols of reputation that are very important repositories of trust are brands (O'Hara 2004a), and restricting knowledge acquisition to branded websites is obviously an important move, although it may be too restrictive in some circumstances, where the relative quantity of branded websites is low. Nevertheless, an interesting research collaboration would be with those disciplines studying branding as a phenomenon and as a mechanism for spreading trust, for example economics and business studies.

5.7.6 Effective Maintenance of Knowledge Bases

Finally, effective maintenance of knowledge bases and information sources helps of course to retain their trustworthiness. Knowledge maintenance is notoriously difficult because it involves a substantial overhead. Yet if maintenance became more of an accepted practice, a cost that information providers were more generally prepared to take on, then in general the amount of trustworthy knowledge available on the Internet would increase, and large-scale knowledge harvesting efforts would be that much more reliable.

An obvious set of collaborations, therefore, would be with the management science and knowledge management communities to try to establish sensible methodologies for knowledge maintenance that could be integrated with standard work practices without imposing too much of an overhead.

5.8 CONCLUSION

We have discussed a number of issues and open questions with respect to trust, its creation, propagation and conservation on the Internet and the World Wide Web, particularly bearing in mind likely technological developments to extend the Web. We have set out our understanding of trust and the likely technological developments of the semantic web and knowledge technologies.

Trust can be viewed at a micro or macro level. At the micro level, a series of tactics can, in various circumstances, help create or preserve trust. At the macro level, such tactics need to be combined into trust strategies. Various tactics were set out, some of which are variants on others. For example, there are many variations on the tactic of restricting those sources of knowledge that a knowledge technology uses, including relying on branded websites, and demanding verifiable certification of provenance. Managing trust is a key managerial requirement for the semantic web, and an interesting demand that has come to light is for informative meta-data about knowledge sources that can be used for assessing trustworthiness.

We have also discussed the contribution that can be made by various disciplines to the issues raised in this chapter. We highlighted a number of interesting potential research directions and ways of developing, monitoring and maintaining trust online. Several research strands look particularly promising.

Meta-data and provenance. The creation and curation of the meta-data that signal trustworthiness and provide evidence of a piece of information's provenance are very important. Issues to be addressed include the identification (possibly dynamically) of the meta-data most relevant to trust issues in a particular context, and methods of storing these meta-data in such a way as to maximize both security and ease of access for queries.

Trust management. Here the issues include how to provide a system that can deal with the trust issues as the agent communities scale up. Is it possible, for example, to keep track of a series of agents' delegation rights without a centralized authority, which, however, is likely to be overwhelmed by requests in an environment of the scale of the Web?

Transitivity. As we noted, trust is not strictly transitive. However, networks of actors making recommendations can be a very powerful method of spreading trust. Key issues include how to understand this process; trust in recommendations will naturally decay as the chains of recommendations shrink, but the rate of decay may well change from application to application.

Interrogation. Trust is enhanced when an agent can be interrogated, through dialogue, as opposed to merely presenting certificates that provide a fixed set of credentials. For knowledge technologies on the semantic web, such tactics are particularly plausible.

Knowledge management. Finally, given that we are focusing on knowledge technologies, managing knowledge effectively and presenting it in a timely way will have a strong effect on trust, even if that effect is only indirect. Various data management housekeeping issues will enhance both trust (because a principal can see that knowledge is being curated accurately and processed efficiently) and trustworthiness (because the technology's information processing should be more reliable).

APPENDIX 5.1 THE SEMANTIC WEB[10]

The World Wide Web is based on HTML (Hypertext Markup Language). Web pages are created by commands in HTML. Because HTML is the common web language, web pages are always more or less alike, and can all be seen by the main browsers. HTML tells the computer how to arrange all the information in a web page on a screen, where the text should go, how it should be formatted, where the pictures fit, how the different panels of text should fit together, and so on; it controls the look of the page.

Navigation through the Web is controlled by hyperlinks and search engines; however, this system is reaching the limits of its capacity, given that there are more than half a trillion web documents. The more information that appears on the web, the less useful a simple key word system, as used by search engines, is; it will give you too many irrelevant hits. The trouble with key words is that they are uninterpreted; if your key word is, say, Bush, a key word system is unable to tell the difference between George Bush, Kate Bush, the African bush or the metal lining of an axle-hole (known as a bush, believe it or not). Therefore, the semantic web is being developed.

Playing the HTML role in the semantic web is a language called XML, the eXtensible Markup Language. XML differs from HTML in that it allows users to define little sub-languages for describing objects. Whereas HTML tells the computer how to arrange the content on the page, XML allows you to tell the computer what the things named by the content are.

However, this is not enough. The computer can do very little more with that information than it could do before. Therefore the semantic web needs the Resource Description Framework (RDF). RDF is a framework that brings together three things: two objects, and a relation between them. So for example, the two objects might be 'University of Southampton', and a picture of the university buildings (which will be a file, perhaps called something like 'soton.jpg'). RDF enables you to tell the computer that there is a relationship between the two: the relation might be called 'picture-of', and so RDF lets us assert that 'soton.jpg picture-of "University of Southampton"' – that is, that the picture is of the University of Southampton.

XML lets you tell your computer what things are, and RDF lets you tell it how these things are related. A third element is still needed, because the computer still does not know (in a metaphorical sense of 'know') what these terms mean. This is achieved with the use of ontologies.

An ontology is a specification of the language and concepts of a restricted domain of discourse, and gives as it were the conceptual background to the words and phrases used in XML and RDF. These words and phrases are therefore defined in terms of each other, which specifies a little web of interrelated concepts. The technology is too weak to say that the computer understands anything (in other than metaphorical senses), but an ontology will provide the beginning of an interrelated web of terms in the sense of Quine and Ullian (1970). The computer could be told, for instance, that a university is a type of educational establishment, that it has students and lecturers, an address, a website, a telephone number, that the lecturers will include professors, senior lecturers and readers, that the students will include undergraduates and postgraduates, that the postgraduates will have degrees, that these degrees will be in subjects, and will have been awarded by educational establishments, and so on. The ontology links together all the concepts and terms that will help the computer to make holistic sense of the terms like 'university' that were being used in the XML specification of the web page.

In short, whereas in the World Wide Web, HTML told the computer how to arrange the content on the screen, in the semantic web, XML + RDF + ontologies tell it not only how to arrange the content, but also what it is all about. The effect is suddenly to provide the computer with a richer characterization of the domain. Figure A5.1-1 shows how the new expressivity can allow the computer to see much more.

Figure A5.1-1 From the World Wide Web to the semantic web

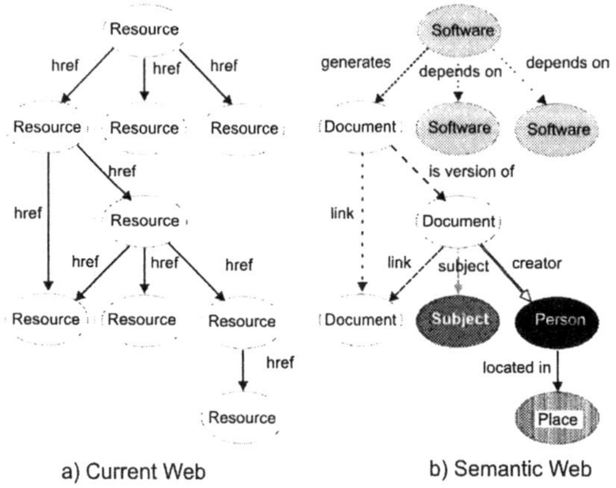

a) Current Web   b) Semantic Web

Source: Adapted from Koivunen and Miller (2002, p. 30).

On the left, we see the basic web view of the computing world; the resources are whatever is held at web addresses, and they are connected by hypertext links written in HTML. But on the right, the same domain is seen in much more detail. With an XML characterization of the domain, the computer can see that some of the resources are pieces of software, others are documents, others are persons and so on. The links are made more meaningful too by RDF. For instance, we can see that one document is a version of another, that the creator of one of the documents is a particular person, and so on. The formalisms of the semantic web allow you to tell the computer so much more about the domains you are describing.

If we now look at what is becoming the increasingly well-known layered model of the semantic web (Figure 5.3), how in the light of this discussion do we interpret these layers? At the bottom are Unicode (a standardized system for encoding data) and URIs (uniform resource identifiers – addresses of resources). These are the nuts and bolts of the semantic web. But there is no point having these unless you have XML to tell you what they refer to. And there is no point having XML unless you have RDF to tell you how those things relate to each other. Similarly, there is no point having XML and RDF unless you have ontologies to explain the significance of the XML classes and RDF relations. There is no point in having ontologies without a logic to provide methods of inferring one thing from another. There is no point inferring things without a theory of proof to tell you that the inferences are sound.

And finally there is no point in having a system of proof unless those who will use it (in the case of the semantic web, this means the 654 million Internet users) have confidence in it. Without the trust of the users in the system, the semantic web will never get off the ground.

NOTES

1   Thanks are due to anonymous referees for several improvements to this chapter.
2   See Misztal (1996) for a review of some of the best-known approaches.
3   See also the large empirical literature that they cite.
4   See www.aktors.org, accessed 17 April 2004.
5   See http://rdfweb.org/foaf/, accessed 17 April 2004.
6   See http://www.isi.edu/ikcap/trellis/, accessed 17 April 2004.
7   There are some exceptions to this, such as PolicyMaker, which binds access rights to the public key; see Blaze et al. (1996).
8   A similarly-inspired algorithm is exploited by Richardson et al. (2003).
9   See http://www.csd.abdn.ac.uk/~ereiter/memories.html accessed, 17 April 2004.
10 Adapted from O'Hara (2004b).

REFERENCES

Alani, H., Dasmahapatra, S., Gibbins, N., Glaser, H., Harris, S., Kalfoglou, Y., O'Hara, K. and Shadbolt, N. (2002), 'Managing Reference: Ensuring Referential Integrity of Ontologies for the Semantic Web', in A. Gómez-Pérez and V.R. Benjamins (eds), *Knowledge Engineering and Knowledge Management: Ontologies and the Semantic Web*, Berlin: Springer-Verlag, pp. 317-34.

Alani, H., Dasmahapatra, S., O'Hara, K. and Shadbolt, N. (2003), 'Identifying Communities of Practice through Ontology Network Analysis', *IEEE Intelligent Systems* Mar/Apr: 18-25.

Alani, H., Kim, S., Millard, D., Weal, M., Hall, W., Lewis, P. and Shadbolt, N. (2003), 'Automatic Ontology-based Knowledge Extraction from Web Documents', *IEEE Intelligent Systems* 18(1): 14-21.

Berners-Lee, T., Hendler, J. and Lassila, O. (2001), 'The Semantic Web' *Scientific American* May: 34-43.

Blaze, M., Feigenbaum, J. and Lacy, J. (1996), 'Decentralized Trust Management', in *Proceedings of the 1996 IEEE Symposium on Security and Privacy*, Washington DC: IEEE Computer Society, pp. 164-73.

Buckingham Shum, S. (2004), 'Contentious, Dynamic, Information-sparse Domains and Ontologies?', *IEEE Intelligent Systems* Jan/Feb: 80-81.

Buckingham Shum, S. and Sumner, T. (2001), 'JIME: An Interactive Journal for Interactive Media', *Learned Publishing* 14(4): 273-85.

Camp, L.J. (2000), *Trust and Risk in Internet Commerce*, Cambridge MA: MIT Press.

Carr, L., Bechhofer, S., Goble, C. and Hall, W. (2001), 'Conceptual Linking: Ontology-based Open Hypermedia', in *Proceedings of the 10th World Wide Web Conference*, New York: ACM Press, pp. 334-42.

Cheverst, K., Clarke, K., Cobb, S., Hemmings, T., Kember, S., Mitchell, K., Phillips, P., Proctor, R., Rodden, T. and Rouncefield, M. (2001), 'Design with Care', *New Technology in Human Services* 14(1/2): 39-47.

Corritore, C.L., Kracher, B. and Wiedenbeck, S. (2003), 'On-line Trust: Concepts, Evolving Themes, A Model', *International Journal of Human-Computer Studies* 58(6): 737-58.

Dimitrakos, T. and Bicarregui, J. (2001), 'Towards Modelling e-Trust', presented at the 3rd Panhellenic Logic Symposium, Anogia, Greece, http://www2.nr.no/coras/workshop_at_RAL/Dimitrakos_Modelling Trust/sld022.htm accessed 17 Apr. 2004.

Domingue, J., Motta, E., Buckingham Shum, S., Vargas-Vera, M. and Kalfoglou, Y. (2001), 'Supporting Ontology-driven Document Enrichment within Communities of Practice', in *Proceedings of the International Conference on Knowledge Capture*, New York: ACM Press, pp. 30-37.

Durkheim, E. (1893/1984), *The Division of Labour in Society*, London: Palgrave Macmillan.

Ellman, J. (2004), 'Corporate Ontologies as Information Interfaces', *IEEE Intelligent Systems* Jan/Feb: 79-80.

Fogg, B.J. and Tseng, H. (1999), 'The Elements of Computer Credibility', *Proceedings of CHI 99*, http://www-pcd.stanford.edu/captology/Key_Concepts/Papers/Credibility25.PDF accessed 17 Apr. 04.

Fukuyama, F. (1995), *Trust: The Social Virtues and the Creation of Prosperity*, New York: Free Press.

Gaudin, S. (2002), 'Online Fraud Growing in Scale, Sophistication', *Datamation*, 5 Dec, http://itmanagement.earthweb.com/ecom/article.php/1552921 accessed 17 Apr. 04.

Gil, Y. and Ratnakar V. (2002), 'Trusting Information Sources One Citizen at a Time', in I. Horrocks and J.A. Hendler (eds), *Proceedings of the First International Semantic Web Conference*, Berlin: Springer, pp. 162-76.

Golbeck, J., Hendler, J. and Parsia, B, (2003), 'Trust Networks on the Semantic Web', in M. Klusch, S. Ossowski, A. Omicini and H. Laamanen (eds) *Proceedings of Cooperative Information Agents VII (CIA 2003)*, Berlin: Springer, pp. 238-49.

Grabner-Kräuter, S. and Kaluscha, E. (2003), 'Empirical Research in On-line Trust: A Review and Critical Assessment', *International Journal of Human-Computer Studies* 58(6): 783-812.

Grandison, T. and Sloman, M. (2000), 'A Survey of Trust in Internet Applications' *IEEE Communications Surveys* 4th Quarter, www.comsoc.org/livepubs/surveys/public/2000/dec/grandison.html accessed 17 Apr. 04.

Habermas, J. ([1968] 1987), *Knowledge and Human Interests*, (translated by Jeremy J. Shapiro), Cambridge: Polity Press.

Hardin, R. (1999), 'Do We Want Trust in Government?', in M.E. Warren (ed.), *Democracy and Trust*, Cambridge: Cambridge University Press, pp. 22-41.

Harnad, S. (2003), 'Eprints: Electronic Preprints and Postprints', in M. Dekker (ed.), *Encyclopedia of Library and Information Science*, http://eprints.ecs.soton.ac.uk/archive/00007721/01/eprints.htm accessed 17 Apr. 04.

Hu, Y.-J. (2001), 'Some Thoughts on Agent Trust and Delegation', in *Proceedings of Autonomous Agents 2001*, New York: ACM Press, pp. 489-96.

Kagal, L., Finin, T. and Joshi, A. (2002), 'Developing Secure Agent Systems using Delegation Based Trust Management', in K. Fischer and D. Hutter (eds), *Proceedings of 2nd International Workshop on Security in Mobile Multiagent Systems (SEMAS 02), held with Autonomous Agent and Multiagent Systems (AAMAS-2002)*, Research Report RR-02-03, Kaiserslautern: Deutsches Forschungszentrum für Künstliche Intelligenz GmbH, pp. 27-34.

Koivunen, M.-R. and Miller, E. (2002), 'W3C Semantic Web Activity', in E. Hyvonen (ed.), *Semantic Web Kick-Off in Finland – Vision, Technologies, Research and Applications*, Helsinki: Helsinki Institute for Information Technology, pp. 27-44.

Lessig, L. (1999), *Code and Other Laws of Cyberspace*, New York: Basic Books.

Li, Y. and Mascagni, M. (2003), 'Improving Performance via Computational Replication on a Large-scale Computational Grid', in *Proceedings of the 3rd IEEE International Symposium on Cluster Computing and the Grid (CCGRID2003)*, New York: IEEE Computer Society, pp. 442-9.

Luhmann, N. (1979), *Trust and Power*, Chichester: John Wiley & Sons.

Lyotard, J.-F. ([1979] 1984), *The Postmodern Condition: A Report on Knowledge*, (translated by G. Bennington and B. Massumi), Manchester: Manchester University Press.

Malhotra, D. and Murnighan, J.K. (2002), 'The Effects of Contracts on Interpersonal Trust', *Administrative Science Quarterly* Sept.: 534-59.

McDermott, R. (1999), 'Why Information Technology Inspired but Cannot Deliver Knowledge Management', *California Management Review* 41: 103-17.

Misztal, B.A. (1996), *Trust in Modern Societies*, Cambridge: Polity Press.

Mitnick, K. (2000), 'Testimony to US Senate Committee on Governmental Affairs', March, http://www.senate.gov/~gov_affairs/030200_mitnick.htm accessed 17 Apr. 04.

New Scientist (2003), 'The Story of your Life … On a Laptop', 4 Oct., p. 28.

O'Hara, K. (2002a), *Plato and the Internet*, Cambridge: Icon Books.

O'Hara, K. (2002b), 'The Internet: A Tool for Democratic Pluralism?', *Science as Culture* 11(2): 287-98.

O'Hara, K. (2004a), *Trust: From Socrates to Spin*, Cambridge: Icon Books.

O'Hara, K. (2004b), 'Trust, Socrates and the Internet', in M. Toyota and J. Noguchi (eds), *Speech, Writing and Context: Interdisciplinary Perspectives*, Osaka: Intercultural Research Institute of Kansai Gaidai University (in press).

Ong, W.J. (1982), *Orality and Literacy: The Technologizing of the Word*, London: Methuen Co.

Parsons, T. (1949), *Structure of Social Action*, Glencoe IL: Free Press.

Povey, D. (1999), *Trust Management*, http://security.dstc.edu.au/presentations/trust/, accessed 17 Apr. 04.

Putnam, R. (2000), *Bowling Alone: The Collapse and Revival of American Community*, New York: Simon and Schuster.

Quine, W.V. and Ullian, J.S. (1970), *The Web of Belief*, New York: Random House.

Richardson, M. Agrawal, R. and Domingos, P. (2003), 'Trust Management for the Semantic Web', in D. Fensel, K.P. Sycara and J. Mylopoulos (eds), *The Semantic Web – ISWC 2003, Second International Semantic Web Conference*, Berlin: Springer, pp. 351-68.

Schneier, B. (2003), *Beyond Fear: Thinking Sensibly About Security in an Uncertain World*, New York: Copernicus.

Shadbolt, N., O'Hara, K. and Crow, L. (1999), 'The Experimental Evaluation of Knowledge Acquisition Techniques and Methods: History, Problems and New Directions', *International Journal for Human-Computer Studies* 51(4): 729-55.

Shadbolt, N.R., Gibbins, N., Glaser, H., Harris, S. and schraefel, m.m.c. (2004), 'CS AKTive Space, Or How We Learned to Stop Worrying and Love the Semantic Web', *IEEE Intelligent Systems* 19(3): 41-7.

Shelat, B. and Egger, F.N. (2002), 'What Makes People Trust Online Gambling Sites?', *CHI 2002 Abstracts*, http://www.ecommuse.com/research/publications/chi2002.pdf accessed 17 Apr. 04.

Spiekermann, S., Grossklags, J. and Berendt, B. (2001), 'E-privacy in 2nd Generation e-Commerce: Privacy Preferences versus Actual Behavior', *Proceedings of the 3rd ACM Conference on Electronic Commerce, Tampa*, New York: ACM Press, pp. 38-47.

Stanford, J., Tauber, E.R., Fogg, B.J. and Marable, L. (2002), 'Experts vs Online Consumers: A Comparative Credibility Study of Health and Finance Web Sites', *Consumer WebWatch*, 29 Oct., http://www.consumerwebwatch.org/news/report3_credibilityresearch/slic edbread_abstract.htm, accessed 17 Apr. 04.

Sunstein, C. (2001), *Republic.com*, Princeton: Princeton University Press.

Szomszor, M. and Moreau, L. (2003), 'Recording and Reasoning over Data Provenance in Web and Grid Services', in R. Meersman, Z. Tari and D.C. Schmidt (eds), *On the Move to Meaningful Internet Systems 2003: CoopIS, DOA and ODBASE – OTM Confederated Conferences*, Berlin: Springer, pp. 603-20.

Tennison, J., O'Hara, K. and Shadbolt, N. (2002), 'APECKS: Using and Evaluating a Tool for Ontology Construction with Internal and External KA Support', *International Journal for Human-Computer Studies* 56(4): 375-422.

The Economist (2003), 'The New Geography of the IT Industry', 19 July.

Uslaner, E.M. (2002), *The Moral Foundations of Trust*, Cambridge: Cambridge University Press.

Wenger, E. (1998), *Communities of Practice: Learning, Meaning and Identity*, Cambridge: Cambridge University Press.

Winslett, M., Yu, T., Seamons, K.E., Hess, A., Jacobson, J., Jarvis, R.,

Smith, B. and Yu, L. (2002), 'Negotiating Trust on the Web', *IEEE Internet Computing* Nov./Dec.: 30-37.

6 Trust in agent-based software

Sarvapali D. Ramchurn and Nicholas R. Jennings

6.1 INTRODUCTION

Many modern computer applications are open distributed systems in which the (very many) constituent components are spread throughout a network, in a decentralized control regime, and which are subject to constant change throughout the system's lifetime. Examples include the grid (Foster and Kesselman 1998), peer-to-peer computing (Gong 2002), the semantic web (Berners-Lee et al. 2001), web services (Cerami 2002), e-business (Deitel et al. 2001), m-commerce (Sadeh 2002; Vulkan 1999), autonomic computing (Kephart and Chess 2003) and pervasive computing environments (Schmeck et al. 2002). In all of these cases, however, there is a need to have autonomous components that act and interact in flexible ways in order to achieve their design objectives in uncertain and dynamic environments (Simon 1996). Given this, agent-based computing has been advocated as the natural computation model for such systems (Jennings 2001).

More specifically, open distributed systems can be modelled as open multi-agent systems that are composed of autonomous agents that interact with one another using particular mechanisms and protocols. In this respect, interactions form the core of multi-agent systems. Thus, perhaps not unsurprisingly, the agent research community has developed rich models of interactions including coordination (Jennings 1993; Durfee 1999), collaboration (Pynadath and Tambe 2002; Cohen and Levesque 1990) and negotiation (Rosenschein and Zlotkin 1994; Kraus 2001; Jennings et al. 2001). However, their application in large-scale open distributed systems presents a number of new challenges. First, the agents are likely to represent different stakeholders that all have their own aims and objectives. This means the most plausible design strategy for an agent is to maximize its individual utility (von Neuman and Morgenstern 1944).

Second, given that the system is open, agents can join and leave at any given time. This means that an agent could change its identity on re-entering and avoid punishment for any past wrong-doing. For example an agent could sell low-quality products, leave the system as soon as it gets paid (so avoiding retribution from buyers or authorities operating in the system) and then subsequently rejoin the system unscathed. Third, an open distributed system allows agents with different characteristics (for example policies, abilities, roles) to enter the system and interact with each other. Given this, agents are likely to be faced with a number of possible interaction partners with varying properties. For example, several agents might offer the same type of web service, but with different efficiencies (for example speed of execution) or degrees of effectiveness (for example providing richer forms of output).

Fourth, an open distributed system allows agents to trade products or services (for example through various forms of auctions or market mechanisms) and collaborate (for example by forming coalitions or virtual organizations) in very many ways. Therefore, agent designers are faced with a choice of a number of potential interaction protocols that could help them achieve their design objectives. Moreover, the choice about which interaction protocol (or mechanism) to adopt is important since each protocol may enforce a different set of rules of encounter and each protocol may result in a different outcome for the agents involved (for example auctions maximize the utility of only two agents, the auctioneer and the buyer, while voting maximizes the social welfare).

Specifically, we can characterize the key interaction problems in such contexts through the following questions:

- How do agent-based system designers decide how to engineer protocols (or mechanisms) for multi-agent encounters?
- How do agents decide who to interact with?
- How do agents decide when to interact with each other?

In formulating a protocol, it is intended that the sequence of moves of the agents, and the allocation of resources brought about by applying the protocol, are made in such a way that they prevent agents from manipulating each other (for example through lies or collusion) so as to satisfy their selfish interests. Therefore, having such protocols in place provides guarantees that should facilitate the choice of interaction partners at any given time. However, protocols may at times be subject to trade-offs among the rules they enforce in trying to achieve their objectives (Sandholm 1999) (for example in voting, while some constraints force truth-telling, they may lead to intractability). In such cases it is left to the agents to decide how, when and with whom to interact without any guarantees that the interaction will actually achieve the desired benefits. To make such decisions would require agents to be fully informed about their opponents, the environment and the issues at stake. Such information should enable agents to devise probabilities for particular events happening and allow them to act in a way that maximizes their expected utility (Savage 1954). Moreover, given such information, agents should be able to act strategically by calculating their best response given their opponents' possible moves during the course of the interaction (Binmore 1992).

However, both the system (enforcing the protocol) and the agents may have limited computational and storage capabilities that constrain their control over interactions. Moreover, the limited bandwidth and speed of communication channels limits the agents' sensing capabilities in real world applications. Thus, in practical contexts it is impossible to reach a state of perfect information about the environment and the interaction partners' properties, possible strategies and interests (Binmore 1992; Russell and Norvig 1995; Axelrod 1984). Agents are therefore necessarily faced with significant degrees of uncertainty in making decisions (that is, it can be difficult or impossible to devise probabilities for events happening). In such circumstances, agents have to trust each other in order to minimize the uncertainty associated with interactions in open distributed systems.[1]

In more detail, trust has been defined in a number of ways in different domains (see Falcone et al. 2001 for a general description). However, we find the following definition most useful for our purposes:

> Trust is a belief an agent has that the other party will do what it says it will (being honest and reliable) or reciprocate (being reciprocative for the common good of both), given an opportunity to defect to get higher payoffs. (Adapted from Dasgupta 1998)

Broadly speaking, there are two main approaches to trust in multi-agent systems.[2] Firstly, to allow agents to trust each other, there is a need to endow them with the ability to reason about the reciprocative nature, reliability or honesty of their counterparts. This ability is captured through trust models. The latter aim to enable agents to calculate the amount of trust they can place in their interaction partners. A high degree of trust in an agent would mean it is likely to be chosen as an interaction partner and (possibly) a reciprocative strategy would be used towards it over multiple interactions. Conversely, a low degree of trust would result in it not being selected (if other, more trusted, interaction partners are available) or a non-reciprocative strategy being adopted against it over multiple interactions (if there is no better alternative). In this way, trust models aim to guide an agent's decision making in deciding on how, when and with whom to interact. However, in order to do this, trust models initially require agents to gather some knowledge about their counterparts' characteristics, which can be done in many different ways (for example through inferences drawn from the outcomes of multiple direct interactions with these partners or through indirect information provided by others). The direct interaction case leads us to consider methods by which agents can learn or evolve better strategies to deal with honest and dishonest agents such that pay-offs are maximized in the long run. The indirect interaction case requires agents to be able to develop methods to reliably acquire and reason about the information gathered from other agents.

While trust models pertain to the reasoning and information gathering ability of agents, the second main approach to trust concerns the design of protocols and mechanisms of interactions (that is, the rules of encounter). These interaction mechanisms need to be formulated to ensure that those involved can be sure they will gain some utility if they rightly deserve it (that is, a malicious agent cannot tamper with the correct pay-off allocation of the mechanism). Thus, we expect agents to interact using a particular mechanism only if it can be trusted. For example, an English auction can be trusted (by the bidders) to some extent since it ensures that the auctioneer cannot tamper with the bids because these are publicly voiced. However, the same auction cannot be trusted (by the auctioneer) to elicit the bidders' true valuation of the auctioned goods (because the dominant strategy of this mechanism is to bid lower than one's true valuation of the goods and a little higher than the current asking price). This highlights the need for protocols that ensure that the participants will find no better option than telling the truth and will interact honestly with each other.

As can be seen, trust pervades multi-agent interactions at all levels. With respect to designing agents and open multi-agent systems we therefore conceptualize trust in the following ways:

- individual-level trust, whereby an agent believes its interaction partners are honest or reciprocative;
- system-level trust, whereby the actors in the system are forced to be trustworthy by the rules of encounter (that is, protocols and mechanisms) that regulate the system.

The above approaches can be seen as being complementary. Thus, while protocols aim to ensure the trustworthiness of agents at the system level, they cannot always achieve this objective without some loss in efficiency and, in such cases, trust models at the individual level are important in guiding an agent's decision making. Similarly, where trust models at the individual level cannot cope with the overwhelming uncertainty in the environment, system-level trust models, through certain mechanisms, aim to constrain the interaction and reduce this uncertainty.

Generally speaking, the various issues concerning trust at these two levels have been dealt with separately in the literature, each forming a different piece of the puzzle, without any consideration for how they all fit together. To rectify this position, this chapter presents a critique of the work that has been carried out on trust in multi-agent systems. More specifically, we evaluate the most prominent trust models that have been presented and show how they all fit together at the individual and at the system level. From this we develop a general classification of approaches to trust in multi-agent systems and outline the open challenges that need to be addressed in order to provide a comprehensive view of trust in computational systems.

The chapter is organized as follows. Section 6.2 deals with models that fit into the individual aspect of trust. We describe and evaluate the trust models that have been devised using learning and evolutionary techniques, reputation and socio-cognitive concepts. Section 6.3 deals with system-level trust where we illustrate different mechanisms that enforce certain properties of the interaction and hence the trustworthiness of agents involved. Section 6.4 concludes and outlines the key future lines of research.

6.2 INDIVIDUAL-LEVEL TRUST

Here we take the viewpoint of an agent situated in an open environment trying to choose the most reliable interaction partner from a pool of potential agents and deciding on the strategy to adopt with it (that is, the who, when and how of interactions mentioned in Section 6.1). As we have already indicated, there are a number of ways the agent can go about doing this. Firstly, it could interact with each of them and learn their behaviour over a number of encounters. Eventually it should be able to select the most reliable or honest agents from the pool or devise an appropriate strategy to deal with the less (or more) reliable ones. In this case, the agent reasons about the outcome of these direct interactions with others. Secondly, the agent could ask other agents about their perceptions of the potential partners. If sufficient information is obtained and if this information can be trusted, the agent can reliably choose its interaction partners. In this case, the agent reasons about interactions that others have had with its potential partners (indirect interactions). Thirdly, the agent could characterize the known motivations of the other agents. This involves forming coherent beliefs about different characteristics of these agents and reasoning about these beliefs in order to decide how much trust should be put in them.

Given the above, we can classify trust models at the individual level as either learning (and evolution) based, reputation based or socio-cognitive based. While the learning and evolutionary models aim to endow agents with strategies that can cope with lying and non-reciprocative agents, reputation models enable agents to gather information in richer forms from their environment and make rational inferences from the information obtained about their counterparts. Socio-cognitive models adopt a rather higher level view of trust that takes the knowledge of motivations of other agents for granted and proposes ways to reason about these motivations. The remainder of this section follows this classification and outlines the main models in each of the various categories.

6.2.1 Learning and Evolving Trust

In this section we consider trust as an emergent property of direct interactions between self-interested agents. Here we assume that the agents will interact many times rather than through one-shot interactions. This tallies with the concept of trust as a social phenomenon that is inherently based on multiple interactions between two parties (Molm et al. 2000; Carley 1991; Prietula 2000; Yamagishi et al. 1998; Dasgupta 1998). It is further assumed that agents have an incentive to defect (Dasgupta 1998). For example defecting in an interaction could mean that the agent does not satisfy the terms of a contract, sells poor-quality goods, delivers late or does not pay the requested amount of money to a seller. In these examples, defection could get higher pay-offs for the agent defecting (for example, the seller gets paid more than the actual value of the goods sold) and cause some utility loss to the other party (for example the buyer loses utility in buying a low-quality product at a high price). However, defection reduces the possibility of future interactions since the losing agent would typically attempt to avoid risking future utility losses. In contrast, if both interaction participants cooperate, we assume that they get an overall higher pay-off in the long run (Axelrod 1984). For example, a seller delivering goods on time or selling goods of an initially agreed quality may result in future purchases from the buyer. In all these cases, we are generally assuming that the agents already know the pay-offs associated with each of their actions.

If the pay-offs of each encounter are known, the agents can reason strategically by assessing the best possible move of their opponent and hence plan their own best response. This analysis falls within the realm of game theory (von Neuman and Morgenstern 1944), which regards all interactions as games with different pay-offs (for example winning or losing the game) for the individual players (that is, the interaction partners). Most games assume that the move of an opponent is not known in advance. In such one-shot games, the safest (that is, minimizing possible loss) and not necessarily the most profitable move will be chosen unless there can be some way to ascertain that the other party can be trusted.[3] Thus, if an agent believes its counterpart is reciprocative then the former will never defect, otherwise it will, and both could end up with lower pay-offs than if they trusted each other or learned to trust each other. This belief may only be acquired if the game is repeated a number of times such that there is an opportunity for the agents to learn their opponent's strategy or adapt to each other's strategy.

To this end we will first consider models that show how trust, through reciprocation (of positive deeds), can be learned or evolved over multiple direct interactions (Section 6.2.1.1). These interaction models, however, greatly simplify the interactions to extreme notions of cooperation and defection. In reality we believe these two extremes can rather be considered the two ends of an axis measuring the success of the outcome of the interaction. In this context, cooperation could mean, for example, that a seller actually delivers some of the goods (rather than not delivering all), but some slight delay in the delivery might still be considered poor cooperation (rather than complete defection). Hence, the perception of an agent of another party's trustworthiness is relative to the level of satisfaction of the outcome. We therefore consider, in Section 6.2.1.2, how the pay-offs in the individual interactions can actually be modelled in realistic applications.

6.2.1.1 Evolving and learning strategies

The most common example used to illustrate the evolution of trust or cooperation over multiple interactions is Axelrod's tournaments revolving around the prisoner's dilemma (Axelrod 1984).[4] Within very controlled settings, Axelrod's tournaments have shown that the tit-for-tat strategy was the most successful (reaping higher average points over all the encounters) relative to other selfish or nicer (that is, mostly cooperative) strategies. Tit-for-tat strategy cooperates on the first move and imitates the opponent's move in the remaining interactions. By adopting this strategy, agents are, in fact, trusting each other, but would punish untrustworthy behaviour should it ever happen (and also forgive if trustworthy behaviour were shown again). If two agents adopt tit-for-tat (or permanently cooperative strategies) it is shown that they end up with the highest pay-offs compared to all other strategies. However, when faced with other selfish strategies, tit-for-tat does not get the maximum pay-off, though it actually gets a higher pay-off than most other strategies. This is because tit-for-tat loses on the first encounter and actually never beats an opponent.

It is therefore required that an agent adapts its strategy according to the type of environment (agents therein) it encounters in order to minimize losses and foster cooperation. By allowing agents to adapt, Wu and Sun have shown that trust can actually emerge between them (Wu and Sun 2001). This means that the agents evolve a trusting relationship (that is, a cooperative strategy) by evaluating the benefit of each possible strategy over multiple interactions. A multi-agent bidding context, in which a number of seller agents bid for contracts in an electronic marketplace, is chosen to exemplify the concept. It is first shown that when agents are all nice (always cooperating) to each other, sellers tend to learn to exploit them. To counter this, the nice agents learn to use tit-for-tat to minimize their losses. As a result, the nasty sellers (exploitative agents) then learn to be reciprocative since cooperating would bring them more benefit than defecting in the long run. Thus, trust emerges as a result of the evolution of strategies over multiple interactions. This example also shows that the evolution of strategies allows nice agents to beat nasty ones in the long run. However, while strictly applying to the bidding context, Wu and Sun's model does not take into account the fact that there might be some utility loss (in the short run) in cooperating with the other party (for example giving away some resources).

In this respect, while acknowledging a cost to cooperation, Sen[5] demonstrates how reciprocity can emerge when the agents learn to predict that they will receive future benefits if they cooperate (Sen 1996). In a more recent set of experiments, Sen and Dutta (2002) give clear guidelines about evolutionary stable strategies (not necessarily tit-for-tat) in different types of environments (with different sorts of strategies). They show that collaborative liars (collaborating defectors) perform well whenever the number of interactions is small and the number of philanthropic agents (always cooperating) is large. However, reciprocative strategies performed better in all other scenarios they tested. Besides proving that reciprocation pays, these results show that the length and number of interactions matter when it comes to evaluating another agent's trustworthiness. If the number of interactions is too low, then trust cannot be built. This is corroborated by Mui et al. (2002) in their probabilistic trust model which identifies a threshold for the number of encounters needed to achieve a reliable measure of an opponent's trustworthiness based on performance appraisal.

In the case that this threshold cannot be reached, other techniques must be used to elicit trustworthiness. In this respect, Mukherjee et al. (2001) have shown how trust can be acquired if agents know their opponent's chosen move in advance. They show that, in the case where agents do not reveal or only partially reveal (only the first mover does) their actions before their opponent acts, no amount of trust is built since it is optimal for the opponent to always choose to defect. However, in the bilateral information revealing scenario (both agents reveal their actions), both agents trust each other through mutually learning to choose an action that results in higher outcomes than predicted for the non-learning situation. It is to be noted that their model (as well as Sen's), besides assuming a static environment, uses an arbitrarily defined function to calculate the cost of interacting and returns from future actions (the basis of which might need more investigation, but has proven to be quite successful in applications simulated). Also, the experiments carried out have shown conclusive results only with a particular pay-off matrix. Hence, more experiments would be needed to show the applicability of the results to the more general class of interactions with different pay-off matrices.

Up to this point, all the models deal strictly with the problem of cooperation between self-interested parties. However, not all multi-agent interactions are strictly competitive. For example, agents may be self-interested, but still may need to achieve a maximum pay-off as a group or society since the latter determines their individual pay-offs (for example individuals contributing an unspecified amount of money to build a road in their community – the total amount collected decides whether the road will be built, giving utility to the individuals, otherwise the money is used for a secondary purpose). This is the problem tackled by Birk (2000, 2001). It is thus shown that trust may not only emerge from the evolution of strategies (Birk 2000), but can also arise strictly out of learning (Birk 2001). The learning method Birk espouses uses a continuous case N-prisoner's dilemma as basis for simulation. This involves agents contributing to a common fund required for the society to achieve its goals, but each agent is tempted to contribute less than the equal split of the total investment required, in the hope that others will contribute more. In this context, a cooperative strategy (that is, contributing more than the equal split) gradually predominates in an environment where bad agents (that is, contributing less) are in the majority. This is because the low investment obtained by the society impacts negatively on the utility of each individual member as well, forcing these latter to learn to cooperate to get higher pay-offs. However, as the number of cooperative agents increases, the agents learn to defect again to get better pay-offs (this is similar to what Wu and Sun's model predicts). Birk's results additionally show that the society reaches an equilibrium with a high level of trust (or cooperation) among its members.

The above learning and evolutionary models of multi-agent strategic interactions assume complete information (for example, strategies, pay-off matrix) for the multi-agent learning algorithms to work. These results have typically been obtained through simulations using very strict assumptions and settings rather than real-life scenarios where the main assumption of complete information about pay-offs simply does not hold. Also, most of the learning models conceive the outcome of interactions as being bi-stable, that is, either a defection or cooperation. To be more realistic, we believe agents need to infer, from the information gathered through their direct interactions, how their opponents are performing and how their performance is affecting their goals. This leads on to devising realistic trust metrics.

6.2.1.2 Trust metrics

For an agent to computationally model its trust in its opponent, it is first required that the former can ascribe a rating to the level of performance of its opponent. The latter's performance over multiple interactions can then be assessed to check how good and consistent it is at doing what it says it will. Therefore, in addition to a performance rating, an agent also needs a means of keeping track of the performance of an agent (in its direct interactions with it). To this end, Witkowski et al.'s (2001) model proposes a trust model whereby the trust in an agent is calculated based on its performance in past interactions (the context is a trading scenario for an intelligent telecommunications network where bandwidth is traded, the quality and quantity of which is varied depending on the trust suppliers and buyers have in each other). The update to the trust value is different for the different types of agents defined in the system. Specifically, consumers update their trust value according to the difference between their bids and the received goods (bandwidth in this case). The better the quality (size) of the goods the higher the increase in trust, and conversely for low-quality goods. A higher trust in a seller would then result in it being chosen for future purchases (conversely for low trust). In contrast, the supplier agents update their trust in the consumers according to the extent to which the quality (size) of the goods (bandwidth) supplied has been exploited. If the quality offered was not fully used, then the trust goes down since it implies that the consumer has dishonestly asked for more than is actually needed. If the quality is fully exploited, the trust goes up. Results of the experiments show how trust (of consumers in suppliers) is effectively strongly dependent on the ability of suppliers to cope with the demand.

The model used by Witkowski et al. simplifies the calculation of trust through equations that deal with measurable quantities of bandwidth allocation and bandwidth use. Other models (such as Mui et al. 2002; Sen and Sajja 2002; Schillo et al. 2000) consider the performance of an agent to be simply a bi-stable value (good or bad). While these models achieve the objectives of the agents for the specific simulation settings studied, they cannot generally be used more widely because realistic interactions in an open distributed system involve richer outcomes (for example quality of goods traded, efficiency of task handling, duration of task). To overcome this, we need more generic means of assessing performance over time. To this end, Sabater and Sierra (2002) do not just limit the overall performance to a bi-stable value or to an efficiency measure (as per Witkowski et al. 2001), and rather attribute some fuzziness to the notion of performance. Thus, depending on the context, the performance of an agent can be subjectively judged on a given scale where -1 represents very poor performance, 0 represents neutral, and +1 represents being very good. The

REGRET system actually gives richer semantics to ratings (or impressions) by defining their particular characteristics. For example, an agent can express a satisfaction -0.5 for the delivery date of some goods and +1 for the price of the same goods. These impressions are then analysed and aggregated using fuzzy reasoning techniques to elicit a representative value for the overall impression (or trust) of one agent on another.

In contrast to Witkowski et al.'s model, REGRET's evaluation of trust is not only based on an agent's direct perception of its opponent's reliability, but it also evaluates its behaviour with other agents in the system. This is carried out because only perceiving direct interactions can pose a number of problems. For example, in an open system it would be very difficult for an autonomous agent to select an interaction partner if the agent itself had never interacted with another party (that is, it has no history to analyse). Moreover, the method opens itself to attack by strategic liars, who, knowing how they are rated by the other side, can adapt their behaviour (for example clients overloading their channels) to make the other party believe they are trustworthy (that is, fully using their bandwidth). In such cases an agent could be better off evaluating other environmental parameters (such as asking other agents about their impressions of each other) in an attempt to get a more reliable rating of its opponents. However, a number of problems arise in doing this. For example, information gathered from other agents could be wrong or incomplete. Such problems are exemplified and studied in Section 6.2.2.

6.2.2 Reputation Models

Reputation can be defined as the opinion or view of someone about something (Sabater and Sierra 2002). Here we consider that this view can be mainly derived from an aggregation of opinions of members of the community about one of them.[6] In multi-agent systems, reputation can be useful when there are a large number of agents interacting (for example online auctions, stock-trading). Reputation should, for example, enable buyers to choose the best sellers in the system. Moreover, reputation can induce sellers to behave well if they know they are going to be avoided by future buyers as a result of their reputation going down due to bad behaviour. These different aspects of reputation divide the field into the following lines of research:

- devising methods to gather ratings that define the trustworthiness of an agent, using relationships existing between members of the community;

- devising reliable reasoning methods to gather as much information from the aggregation of ratings retrieved from the community;
- devising mechanisms to promote ratings that truly describe the trustworthiness of an agent.

The last of the above items is dealt with in Section 6.3.2 (since it falls within the realm of system-level trust). For now we will be concerned with the first two items because these are at the level of individual agents.

In order to organize the retrieval and aggregation of ratings from other agents most reputation models borrow from sociology the concept of a social network (Burt 1982; Buskens 1998). Similar to human societies, this assumes that agents are related to each other whenever they have roles that interconnect them or whenever they have communication links (for example by observation, direct communication or as information sources) established between one another. Through this network of social relationships, it is assumed that agents, acting as witnesses to interactions, can transmit information about each other (Panzarasa et al. 2001). Information takes the form of a performance rating (for example, good or bad, seller delivers late, buyer never paid) as explained in Section 6.2.1.2. Such a rating could then be shared by the different nodes of the social network, thus giving rise to the concept of reputation.

6.2.2.1 Retrieving ratings from the social network
Yu and Singh (2002a) tackle the problem of retrieving ratings from a social network through the use of referrals. In this context, referrals are pointers to other sources of information similar to links that a search engine would plough through to obtain a web page or uniform resource locator (URL). Through referrals, an agent can provide another agent with alternative sources of information about a potential interaction partner (particularly if the former cannot handle the latter's request itself). Yu and Singh propose a method of representing a social network (based on a referral network; Singh et al. 2001) and then provide techniques to gather information through the network (Yu and Singh 2003). Specifically, they show how agents can explore a network by contacting their neighbours and can use referrals gathered from the latter to gradually build up a model of the social network. Furthermore, Schillo et al. (2000) enrich the representation of an existing social network by annotating nodes of the network to represent their particular characteristics. Thus, each node of the network holds two values: (1) the trust value, which describes the degree of honesty of the agent represented by the node; and (2) the degree of altruism (that is, being good to others even at the expense of one's own utility). Both of these values are used to deduce the trustworthiness of witnesses queried at the time of

calculating the reputation of potential interaction partners (see Section 6.2.2.2). From an established social network it is then possible to derive higher level concepts. For example, Sabater and Sierra (2002) and Yu and Singh (2002a) derive the concept of a group of neighbours from the social network by identifying those nodes (agents) that are close together (linked together). Thus, having a social network represented allows an agent to select and contact those agents it needs in order to get a proper measure of the reputation of another agent. For example, Yu and Singh's model takes into account ratings from those agents that are close (by virtue of the number of links separating them from a potential interaction partner) to choose witnesses for a particular agent. Underlying this is the assumption that closer witnesses will return more reliable ratings.

It is further assumed in all of the above models that witnesses share ratings freely (that is, without any profit). This is a relatively strong assumption, which can be removed if proper mechanisms are implemented (as will be seen in Section 6.3.2). Therefore, given that agents have represented their social network and properly extracted the ratings of their counterparts from the network, they then need to aggregate these ratings so as to form a coherent impression of their potential interaction partners.

6.2.2.2 Aggregating ratings

Several means of aggregating ratings in online communities already exist. For example, in eBay (2003), ratings are +1 or -1 values (in addition to textual information) that are summed up to give an overall rating. Such simplistic aggregation of ratings can be unreliable, particularly when some buyers do not return ratings (see Kollock 1999 and Resnick and Zeckhauser 2002 for a complete account of online reputation systems). For example, a sum of ratings is biased positively when there are fewer people not reporting bad ratings, even though these people have had bad experiences. Having no rating is considered neither as a bad rating nor as a good rating, and is simply discarded from the aggregation. Moreover, ratings are open to manipulation by sellers trying to build their reputation. While the latter problem can be dealt with by designing sophisticated reputation mechanisms (see Section 6.3.2), the former problem can be solved at the level of the agent's reasoning mechanism.

To this end, Yu and Singh (2002b) deal with absence of information in their reputation model. The main contribution of their work is in aggregating information obtained from referrals while coping with the lack of information. More specifically, they use the Dempster Shafter theory of evidence to model information retrieved (Yager et al. 1994). The context is the following: an agent may receive good or bad ratings (+1 or -1) about another agent. When an agent receives no rating (good or bad), how should it classify this case of no information? In Yu and Singh's model, a lack of belief (or disbelief) can only be considered as a state of uncertainty (where all beliefs have an equal probability of being true). Dempster's rule allows the combination of beliefs obtained from various sources (saying an agent is trustworthy, untrustworthy, or unknown to be trustworthy or not) to be combined so as to support the evidence that a particular agent is trustworthy or not. Moreover, together with a belief derived from ratings obtained, an agent may hold a belief locally about the trustworthiness of another due to its direct interaction with it. However, in such cases, the ratings obtained from witnesses are neglected. Nevertheless, their measure of reputation does not discredit nor does it give credit unnecessarily to agents (as eBay does) in the absence of information.

As can be seen, Yu and Singh do not deal with the possibility that an agent may lie about its rating of another agent. They assume all witnesses are totally trustworthy. However, an agent could find some benefit in lying about its rating of an opponent if it is able to discredit others such that it appears to be more reliable than them. In this respect, Schillo et al. (2000) deal with the problem of lying witnesses. They first decompose the rating into social metrics of trust and altruism (as discussed above – see Section 6.2.2.1). The latter metrics are used in a recursive aggregation over the network, taking into consideration the probability that the witnesses queried may lie to (or betray) the querying agent. In this way, the value obtained for the trust in an agent is more reliable than fully trusting witnesses as in the case of Yu and Singh's model (which assumes cooperative settings). The probability of a witness lying to the querying agent is actually learnt over multiple interactions in Schillo et al.'s model.

Similarly, Sen et al. (2000) extend this work and demonstrate how agents can cope with lying witnesses in their environment through learning rather than attributing subjective probabilities to the event of a witness lying (Sen and Sajja 2002). Specifically, they develop a reputation model which makes the same simplifying assumptions as those illustrated in Section 6.2.1. Their approach shows how the sharing of trust values (or reputation) can benefit reciprocative agents in the long run. In the short run though, selfish and lying agents still benefit from totally reciprocative agents. Furthermore, it is shown that over time, colluding agents cannot exploit reciprocative agents if these learn the behaviour of the former and share their experience with others of a similar type. The reciprocative agents then become selfish towards these lying and completely selfish agents so as to minimize utility loss in interacting with them. Their model, however, fails when the number of witnesses in the environment falls below a given threshold. This is because a sufficiently high number of witnesses is needed to report ratings about most lying agents in a population. If this is not the case, there is a higher probability of a reciprocative agent interacting with a lying one that has not been encountered by the witnesses previously.

While Yu and Singh's model demonstrates the power of referrals and the effectiveness of Dempster Shafter's theory of evidence in modelling reputation, Schillo et al.'s, and Sen et al.'s models show how witness information can be reliably used to reason effectively against lying agents. These models, however, greatly simplify direct interactions and fail to frame such interactions within the social setting (that is, relative to the type of relationships that exist between the witnesses and the potential interaction partners). To overcome this limitation, Sabater and Sierra (2002) adopt a (sociological) approach closer to real-life settings. Thus, the reputation value, which is representative of the trust to be placed in the opponent, is a weighted sum of subjective impressions derived from direct interactions (the individual dimension of reputation), the group impression of the opponent, the group impression of the opponent's group and the agent's impression of the opponent's group (together, all of these compose the social dimension of reputation). Now the weights on each term allow the agent to variably adjust the importance given to ratings obtained in these diverse ways. Moreover, older ratings, devised as shown in Section 6.2.2.1, are given less importance relative to new ones.

The strong realism of REGRET also lies in its definition of an ontological dimension that agents can share to understand each other's ratings (for example a travel agent being good might imply low price for one agent, but for another might imply good-quality seats reserved). However, REGRET does not handle the problem of lying (strategically) among agents. Ratings are obtained in a cooperative manner (from an altruistic group) rather than in a competitive setting (where witnesses are selfish). Moreover, the aggregation method REGRET uses can be sensitive to noise since ratings are simply summed up. In contrast, Mui et al.'s (2002) model calculates the probability of an agent being trustworthy on the next interaction by considering the frequency of (positive and negative) direct impressions conditional upon the impressions gathered from the social network. This approach, we believe, is less sensitive to noisy ratings from the network.

6.2.3 Socio-cognitive Models of Trust

The approaches to modelling trust at the individual level that we have considered in the previous sections are all based on an assessment of the outcomes of interactions. For example, learning models consider the pay-offs of each individual strategy, while reputation models assess outcomes of both direct and indirect interactions (that is, third-party assessments). However, in assessing the trustworthiness of an opponent, it may also be important to consider the subjective perception of the latter since it enables a more comprehensive analysis of the characteristics of the opponent (Dasgupta 1998; Gambetta 1998). For example, the tools and abilities available to the other party could be assessed to check whether or not the agent can indeed use these to carry out an agreed task. Such beliefs or notions are normally stored in an agent's mental state and are essential in assessing an agent's reliability for doing what it says it will (that is, being capable), or its willingness to do what it says it will (that is, being honest).

In this respect, we report the line of work initiated by Castelfranchi and Falcone (1998, 2000, 2001). In particular, they highlight the importance of a cognitive view of trust (particularly for Belief–Desire–Intention agents; Wooldridge 2002) in contrast to a mere quantitative view of trust (Sections 6.2.1 and 6.2.2). The context they choose is that of task delegation where agent x wishes to delegate a task to agent y. In so doing agent x needs to evaluate the trust it can place in y by considering the different beliefs it has about the motivations of agent y. They claim the following beliefs are essential (in x's mental state) to determine the amount of trust to be put in agent y by agent x (these have been adapted and summarized):

- Competence belief: a positive evaluation of y by x saying that y is capable of carrying out the delegated task as expected. If agent y is not capable there is no point in trusting it to accomplish the task fully.
- Willingness[7] belief: x believes that y has decided and intends to do what it has proposed to do. If agent y is not believed to be willing to do the task, it might be lying if it says it wants to do so. This would then decrease x's trust in y.
- Persistence[8] belief: x believes that y is stable enough about its intention to do what it has proposed to do. If y is known to be unstable, then there is added risk in interacting with y, hence a low trust would be put in y even though it might be willing to do the task at the point the task is delegated.
- Motivation belief: x believes that y has some motives to help x, and that these motives will probably prevail over other motives negative to x in case of conflict. This highlights the possibility for y to defect as argued in Section 6.2.1. The motives mentioned here are the same as the long-term gains obtainable in helping x achieve its goals. If y is believed to be motivated (to be helpful or positively reciprocative as in Section 6.2.1), then x will tend to trust it.

To devise the level of trust agent x can place in agent y, agent x would need to consider each of the above beliefs (and possibly others). These beliefs actually impact on trust, each in a different way, which needs to be taken into account in a comprehensive evaluation of all beliefs concerned. For example, the competence belief is a prerequisite for trusting another agent, while the motivation belief would vary according to the calculation of the future pay-offs to the agents over multiple interactions. This kind of strategic consideration becomes even more important when such beliefs are known to all actors (that is, the preferences of agents are public). For example, what could happen if agent y knows that x trusts it, or relies on it? The authors claim that this may increase the trustworthiness of x in y's mind, the self-confidence of y, or its willingness to serve x, which in turn change the trustworthiness of y. Agent x can then take into account the possible effects of its trust in y (even before performing the delegation) to support its decision of delegating. However, Castelfranchi and Falcone's approach is strongly based on humans who are not always rational beings (as opposed to what we expect agents to be).

In contrast to the cognitive approach of Castelfranchi and Falcone, Brainov and Sandholm (1999) support the need to model an opponent's trust (as described above) with a rational approach (they specifically target the context of non-enforceable contracts). They do so by showing that if an agent has a precise estimation of its opponent's trust (in the former), this leads to maximum pay-offs and trade between the two agents. However, if trust is not properly estimated, it leads to an inefficient allocation of resources between the agents involved (hence a loss in utility) since both underestimate or overestimate their offers on exchanged contracts. It is also shown that it is in the best interests of the agents, given some reasonable assumptions, to actually reveal their trustworthiness in their interaction partner (to efficiently allocate resources).

Although still in its infancy, the socio-cognitive approach to modelling trust takes a high-level view of the subject. However, it lacks the logical grounding (as shown by Brainov and Sandholm) in rational mechanisms which learning and reputation models (and mechanisms) provide. In effect, the socio-cognitive approach could exploit the assessment performed by these models to form the core beliefs illustrated above. Thus, speaking generally, all the individual models of trust could contribute to a comprehensive evaluation of trust at the individual level. This would take into account strategies learned over multiple interactions, the reputation of potential interaction partners, and finally the latter's believed motivations and abilities regarding the interaction. However, it can be computationally expensive for an agent to reason about all the different factors affecting its trust in its opponents. Moreover, as highlighted earlier, agents are limited in their capacity to gather information from the various sources that populate their environment. Given these constraints, instead of imposing the need to devise trust at the individual level, it can be more appropriate to shift the focus to the rules of encounter so that these ensure that interaction partners are forced to be trustworthy. In this way, these rules of encounter can, at times, compensate for limited applicability of individual-level trust models (conversely, whenever the rules of encounter cannot guarantee interacting agents will be trustworthy, we might need to resort to individual-level trust models to do this).

6.3 SYSTEM-LEVEL TRUST

In the context of open multi-agent systems, we conceive of agents interacting via a number of mechanisms or protocols that dictate the rules of encounter. Examples of such mechanisms include auctions, voting, contract-nets, market mechanisms and bargaining, to name but a few. These mechanisms take agents to be completely self-interested and, therefore, need to make sure that the rules of encounter prevent lying and collusion between participants. Generally speaking, such requirements impose some rigidity on the system (for example an English auction forces bidders to reveal their bids). However, these rules enable an agent to trust other agents by virtue of the different constraints imposed by the system. These constraints can be applied in a number of ways. Firstly, it is possible to engineer the protocol of interaction such that the participating agents find no gain in utility from lying or colluding. Secondly, an agent's reputation as being a liar (or truthful) can be spread by the system. Thus, knowing that their future interactions will be compromised if they are reputed to be liars, agents can be forced to act well, up to the point they leave a system. Thirdly, agents can be screened upon entering the system by requiring proof of their reliability through the references of a trusted third party.

Against this background, we subdivide system-level trust in terms of (1) devising truth-eliciting interaction protocols; (2) developing reputation mechanisms that foster trustworthy behaviour; and finally (3) developing security mechanisms that ensure new entrants can be trusted. This is the structure that we adopt in the following subsections.

6.3.1 Truth-eliciting Interaction Protocols

In order to ensure truth-telling on the part of agents involved in an interaction, a number of protocols and mechanisms have been devised in recent years (see Sandholm 1999 for an overview). These protocols aim to prevent agents from lying or speculating while interacting (for example lying about the quality of goods sold or proposing a higher price than one's true valuation for goods to be bought). They do so by imposing rules dictating the individual steps in the interaction and the information revealed by the agents during the interaction. Thus, by adhering to such protocols it is expected that agents should find no better option than telling the truth. Given the aim of this chapter, we do not wish to launch into a detailed explanation of all available protocols that have such properties and enforce them to a certain degree (see Sandholm 1999 for such an analysis). Rather we will focus on one such protocol (namely auctions, since these are the most widely used mechanism in multi-agent system applications).

As opposed to other mechanisms, such as voting which focuses on the social welfare, auctions focus on the benefit of only two agents – the auctioneer and the bidder. There are four main types of single-sided auctions, namely the English, Dutch, first-price-sealed-bid and Vickrey. In the English auction, each bidder is free to raise his bid until no bidder is willing to raise any further, thus ending the auction. The Dutch auction instead starts with a very high asking price and reduces it in steps until one of the bidders bids for the item and wins the auction. The first-price-sealed-bid involves agents submitting their bids without knowing others' bids. The highest bidder wins the auction. In the Vickrey auction, the bids are sealed but the winner pays the price of the second-highest bid.

In this context, the Dutch and English auctions enforce truth-telling on the part of the auctioneer (for example the winner and the winning price cannot be faked) since bids are made publicly, as opposed to Vickrey and first-price-sealed-bid auctions where the bids are hidden. However, the Dutch, English and first-price-sealed-bid auctions do not ensure that the bidders reveal their true valuation of the goods at stake. This is because the dominant strategy in these auctions is to reveal either a lower valuation (in the case of Dutch and first-price-sealed-bid) or to bid only a smaller amount more than the asking price up to one's true valuation (in the case of the English auction). In contrast, the Vickrey auction does enforce truth-telling by bidders. A bidder's dominant strategy is to bid its true valuation, since doing otherwise, given uncertainty about other bids and the final price to be paid, would result in some loss in utility. Bidding higher than its true valuation could end up with the agent paying more than its valuation, and bidding lower than its true valuation could make it lose the auction altogether.

As pointed out above, the main weakness of the Vickrey mechanism is that it does not ensure truth-telling on the part of the auctioneer. The latter could still lie about the winning bid since bids are private and known only to the auctioneer (and obviously to each of the bidders in private, unless there is some amount of collusion). The auctioneer could thus ask for a higher price than the second-highest bid (just below the highest bid) to the highest bidder. In so doing, the auctioneer reaps a higher benefit than it should, without the bidders knowing. In this respect, Hsu and Soo (2002) have implemented a secure (that is, ensuring the privacy of bids and the allocation of the goods to the true winner) multi-agent Vickrey auction scheme. The scheme differs from the original Vickrey auction in that it involves an additional step of choosing the auctioneer from among the bidders (advertised on a blackboard). The bidders submit their encrypted bids to a blackboard. The auctioneer is selected at random from the bidders and given a key to access all sealed bids and, using this key, it can only compare the bids' values. Thus, the auctioneer can only determine the order of bids and allocate the second-highest bid to the winner. This scheme also allows the auctioneer (also a bidder), the winner, and the second-highest bidder to verify the result by using their key to check the bids shown on the blackboard.

However, the Vickrey auction and the other main ones stated above are not collusion proof. This means that agents can collaborate to cheat the mechanism by sharing information about their bids. Collusion would first necessitate that the agents know each other before they place their bids and therefore arrange to place bids that do not reveal their true preferences (for example agents withholding their bids in a Dutch auction until the asking price has gone very low, or some bidders colluding with the auctioneer to artificially raise the asking price in an English auction to force others to pay a very high price, or bidders colluding to beat competitors in a Vickrey auction). To prevent this collusion from happening, Brandt (2001, 2002) extends the work of Hsu and Soo by devising a collusion-proof auction mechanism that ensures the privacy and correctness of any (M+1)st-price auction – that is, an auction where the highest M bidders win and pay a uniform price determined by the (M+1)st price. In this type of auction, bids are sealed and the highest bid wins the auction, but pays a price determined by the auctioneer (for example in the Vickrey auction the second-highest price is paid).

Only the auctioneer and the bidder know the highest bid. To allow bidders to verify whether the winning bid is actually the highest (hence checking the trustworthiness of the winner and auctioneer) the protocol devised by Brandt distributes the calculation of the selling price between the individual buyers using some cryptographic techniques. However, the only other agent, apart from the seller, able to calculate the exact value of the selling price is the winner of the auction. The protocol also ensures that bids are binding. These conditions, combined with the fact that the protocol can be publicly verified, allow the identification of malicious bidders that would have tampered with the bids, and prevent collusion from affecting a single bidder.

While being very powerful, the protocol is computationally expensive when a large number of agents is involved, but works well for small numbers.

As can be seen, most auctions are not robust to lying and collusion unless some security mechanism is plugged into them (that is, using cryptographic techniques). The protocols mentioned above, besides constraining interactions, neglect the fact that the agents in an open distributed system might want to interact more than one time. As was shown in Section 6.2.1, reciprocative or trustworthy behaviour can be elicited if agents can be punished in future interactions or strictly prevented from engaging in future interactions if they do not interact honestly. For example, if a winning bidder in an auction has been found to have lied about its preferences, it could be prevented from accessing future runs of the auction (Brandt 2002). If an agent knows it will lose utility in the future due to bad behaviour in the present, it will find no better option but to act in a trustworthy way. In this respect, earlier in the chapter (see Section 6.2.1) we showed how agents could learn to actually adapt their strategy (reciprocative or not) in order to maximize their long-term pay-offs against different strategies over multiple runs of an auction.

However, as pointed out in Section 6.1, open multi-agent systems allow agents to interact with any other agent in the environment. This could permit malicious agents to move from group to group whenever they are detected by a given group of agents and therefore exploit trustworthy agents as they move around. In order to prevent this from happening, agents can be made to share their ratings of their opponent with other agents in the environment once they have interacted with them. Techniques to allow agents to gather ratings and aggregate those in a sensible way were presented in Section 6.2.2. However, it was shown that these techniques do not consider the fact that we expect agents to share (true) ratings only if it brings them some utility. In open multi-agent systems, this can be achieved through reputation mechanisms which we discuss in the next section.

6.3.2 Reputation Mechanisms

As was seen in Section 6.2.2, the reputation models described do not take into account the fact that the agents are selfish and, therefore, will not share information unless some benefit can be derived from doing so. Furthermore, these reputation models (for example REGRET or Yu and Singh's model) do not motivate the use of reputation by some agents to elicit good behaviour from other agents. These models aim to endow agents with a better perception of their opponent and do not consider the effect of doing so on an opponent when the latter is aware of it. Given these shortcomings of reputation models, reputation mechanisms consider the problem of inducing trustworthy behaviour and modelling the reputation of agents at the system level. Reputation mechanisms can operate through centralized or distributed entities that store ratings provided by agents about their interaction partners and then publicize these ratings, such that all agents in the environment have access to them. In this case it is the system that manages the aggregation and retrieval of ratings, as opposed to reputation models, which leave the task to the agents themselves. In so doing, reputation mechanisms can be used to deter lying and bad behaviour on the part of the agents. Moreover, reputation mechanisms aim to induce truthful ratings from witnesses and actually make it rational for agents to give ratings about each other to the system. Such a mechanism, that makes it rational for participants to use it, is said to be incentive compatible (Resnick and Zeckhauser 2002).

More specifically, Zacharia and Maes (2000) have outlined the *desiderata* for reputation mechanisms, particularly with regard to how ratings are aggregated and how these impact on the behaviour of the actors in the system. They do not propose such requirements for agent-based reputation systems per se, but as we move into agent-mediated electronic commerce (He et al. 2003), it is obvious that such mechanisms will guide agent-based reputation systems. These *desiderata* are listed below:

1. It should be costly to change identities in the community. This should prevent agents from entering the system, behaving badly, and coming out of the system without any loss of utility or future punishment bearing upon them.
2. New entrants should not be penalized by initially having low reputation values attributed to them. If new entrants have low reputation they are less favoured, though they might be totally trustworthy. This actually makes the system less appealing to agents (with bad reputation) intending to (re)enter the system.
3. Agents with low ratings should be allowed to build up reputation similar to a new entrant. This allows an agent to correct its behaviour if it has been shown to be badly behaved in the past.
4. The overhead of performing fake transactions should be high. This prevents agents from building their own reputation.
5. Agents having a high reputation should have a higher bearing than others on the reputation values they attribute to an agent. This presupposes that agents with high reputation will give truthful ratings to others. However, this can be contentious if reputation determines the level of profit the agent acquires, since it could lead to the creation of monopolies or cartels in the market.
6. Agents should be able to provide personalized evaluations. This involves giving more than just a simple rating of +1 to -1 to allow a better evaluation of the reputation of another agent. For example, the REGRET system actually implements richer ratings that can be shared using the ontological dimension.

7. Agents should keep a memory of reputation values and give more importance to the latest ones obtained. This is needed to keep the reputation measure as up to date as possible and helps prevent an agent from building up positive reputation by interacting well and then starting defecting (the last defection having a greater effect than its past good behaviour).

With respect to the above requirements, Zacharia and Maes present two reputation systems (for example for chat-rooms, auctions and newsletters): SPORAS and HISTOS. While these are not strictly multi-agent systems, they present techniques to aggregate ratings intelligently and reflect the real performance of users in an online community. In both cases, the aggregation method allows newer ratings to count more than older ones. SPORAS, however, gives new entrants low initial reputation values and, therefore, reduces their chance of being selected as possible interaction partners. This is a trade-off afforded to prevent identity switching, because an agent having low reputation would not be any better off by re-entering the system with a new identity. HISTOS is an enhancement to SPORAS, which takes into account the group dynamics as in REGRET. In particular, HISTOS looks at the links between users to deduce personalized reputation values (that is, taking into account the social network). This enables an agent to assemble ratings from those it trusts already rather than those it does not know. Moreover, both HISTOS and SPORAS have been shown to be robust to collusion. This is because those agents that are badly rated themselves have a diminished effect on the reputation of others and those they might want to protect. However, as the authors themselves point out, the major drawback is that users are reluctant to give bad ratings to their trading partners. This is because there is no incentive to give ratings in the first place (that is, it is not incentive compatible).

In an attempt to make reputation mechanisms incentive compatible, Jurca and Faltings (2003) introduce side payments to make it rational for agents to share reputation information. Thus, agents can buy and sell reports to and from special information agents supplied by the system. Reports are values between 0 and 1, where 0 represents completely bad behaviour and 1 represents absolutely trustworthy behaviour. Agents are only allowed to sell a report for an agent when they have previously bought reputation information for that agent. This ensures that agents cannot sell reputation information they make up by themselves. They additionally propose two conditions to make a reputation mechanism robust to lying witnesses:

- agents that behave as good citizens (report truthfully) should not lose any utility;

- agents that give false reports should gradually lose utility.

In their model, they aim to fulfil the above conditions by implementing information agents which pay only for reports (to one agent) if they match the next report given by another agent (having interacted with the same agent as the previous one). In this way, the authors claim that agents revealing truthfully get paid and those that do not will lose money in buying reports and not getting paid on selling them. However, this method does not work if most agents lie about the reports or if they collude over giving false reports. Moreover, they assume that information agents already store some reputation information after bootstrapping the system. This overly simplifies the process of reputation management and, additionally, does not take into account the case of new entrants into the system. More work is therefore needed to make this model applicable to open multi-agent systems.

Jurca and Faltings's reputation mechanism actually aims to be generic, and as a result suffers the above shortcomings. It might be preferable instead to design reputation mechanisms that are tailored to individual protocols of interaction. In this respect, Dellarocas (2002) introduced 'Goodwill Hunting' (GWH) as a more realistic feedback mechanism for a trading environment. This system claims to:

- induce sellers of variable quality goods to truthfully reveal the quality of their goods;
- provide incentives to buyers to truthfully reveal their feedback.

The GWH algorithm uses the threat of biased future reporting of quality (of goods to be sold) in order to induce sellers to truthfully declare the individual qualities of their items. Specifically, the mechanism keeps track of the seller's 'goodwill'. This value represents the seller's trustworthiness. It is adjusted by the quality reported by buyers. Good reports bias goodwill positively and bad reports bias it negatively. To induce sellers to reveal the true quality of their goods, the goodwill factor is used to adjust the quality they wish to broadcast for the goods they wish to sell. Thus, if the seller has low goodwill, the quality of the goods it tries to publicize will be actually shown to have a lower quality by the system.

To induce buyers to report their ratings of sellers, they are given rebates on future transactions in the system. It is then shown that if buyers report untruthfully, they can drive out sellers of good-quality goods and, therefore, lose the opportunity of buying high-quality goods. However, the mechanism makes several somewhat unrealistic assumptions about real-life online markets. For example, it assumes that sellers are monopolists; that is, they are the only ones to sell a particular product (of varying quality). Also it assumes that buyers will interact with sellers only once. These assumptions are needed to simplify the analysis of the model. As Dellarocas points out, among other enhancements, it is still to be shown how the mechanism fares against strategic reporting from buyers whereby they force a seller to reduce the price of its goods by giving it bad ratings, hence damaging its reputation.

The reputation mechanisms detailed above and interaction mechanisms discussed in Section 6.3.1 actually try to enforce trustworthy behaviour by minimizing the opportunity for agents to defect to gain higher pay-offs (see our definition of trust in Section 6.1). As has been shown, more of these mechanisms still need to be developed. In the case where interaction protocols and reputation mechanisms cannot guarantee trustworthy behaviour, there still exists a need to give agents in an open system the possibility of proving their trustworthiness, and to enable other agents to recognize them as reliable interaction partners. One way this could proceed is by providing references from well-recognized sources. This is similar to the case of a job seeker providing credentials to a potential new employer. Note that this process is not the same as reputation building and acquisition, which pertains to the recognition of an entire community. Rather, credential assessment falls within the realm of network security, which we discuss next.

6.3.3 Security Mechanisms

In the domain of network security,[9] trust is used to describe the fact that a user can prove it is who it says it is (Mass and Shehory 2001). This normally entails that it can be authenticated by trusted third parties (that is, those that can be relied upon to be trustworthy and as such are authorities in the system; Grandison and Sloman 2000). At a first glance, this does not completely fit with our initial definition of trust, but it is certainly a basic requirement for the trust models and mechanisms described earlier to work (see Sections 6.2.1, 6.2.2, 6.2.3, 6.3.1, 6.3.2). This is because these models are based on the fact that agents can be recognized by their identity and would, therefore, require authentication protocols to be implemented.

To this end, Poslad et al. (2002) have recently proposed a number of security requirements that they claim are essential for agents to trust each other and each other's messages transmitted across the network linking them (that is, to ensure messages are not tampered with by malicious agents):

- Identity: the ability to determine the identity of an entity. This may include the ability to determine the identity of the owner of an agent.
- Access permissions: the ability to determine what access rights must be given to an agent in the system, based on the identity of the agent.
- Content integrity: the ability to determine whether a piece of software,

a message, or other information has been modified since it was dispatched by its originating source.

- Content privacy: the ability to ensure that only the designated identities can examine a message or other data. To the others, the information is obscured.

The authors specify these requirements for the FIPA (Foundation for Intelligent Physical Agents) (2001) abstract architecture. These basic requirements can be implemented by a public key encryption and certificate infrastructure (Grandison and Sloman 2000). A digital certificate is issued by a certification authority, or CA, and verifies that a public key is owned by a particular entity. The public key in a certificate is also used to encrypt and sign a message in a way that only its owner can examine the content and be assured about its integrity. The two most popular public key models are PGP (pretty good privacy) and the X.509 trust model (Adams and Farrel 1999). PGP supports a web of trust in that there is no centralized or hierarchical relationship between CAs, while the X.509 is a strictly hierarchical trust model for authentication (Grandison and Sloman 2000). However, these authenticating measures do not suffice for open multi-agent systems to ensure that agents act and interact honestly and reliably towards each other. They only represent a barrier against agents that are not allowed in the system or only permit their identification in the system. In order to enforce good behaviour in the system, it is instead possible that certificates are issued to agents if these agents meet specific standards that make them trustworthy.

In order to achieve this, trusted third parties are needed to issue certificates to agents that satisfy the standards of trustworthiness (that is, being reciprocative, reliable and honest). For example, agents would need to satisfy certain quality standards (for instance products stamped with the Kitemark or the 'CE' marking are assured to conform to the British standards and the European Community standards respectively) and terms and conditions for the products they sell (for instance sellers have to abide by a 14-day full refund return policy in the UK for any goods they sell). It is only upon compliance with these quality standards that the agent would be able to sell its products. To this end, Herzberg et al. (2000) present a policy-based and certificate-based mechanism that can assign roles to new entrants. A certificate in this work is signed by some issuer and contains some claims about a subject. There is no restriction on what the claims can be. For example, they may be claims about organization memberships (company employee and so on), the capabilities of the subject, or even the trustworthiness (or reliability) of the subject in the view of the issuer.

The mechanism in Herzberg et al. also enables a party to define policies for mapping new entrants to predefined business roles. Thus, an agent can ensure that a new entrant will act according to the settings defined by its role or access rights. The role assigned to an agent carries with it a number of duties and policies it needs to abide by. If the agent undertakes the role, it is forced to abide by the given rules of good behaviour. The process of role assignment and access provision is performed in a fully distributed manner, where any party or agent may be a certificate issuer. Moreover, it is not required that certificate issuers be known in advance. Instead, it is enough that, when requested, an agent that issues certificates provides sufficient certificates from other issuers to be considered a trusted authority according to the policy of the requesting party. This allows distributed trust build-up among parties in an open environment (Mass and Shehory 2001).

Mass and Shehory (2001) extend the work in Herzberg et al. (2000) to open multi-agent systems. Specifically, they take into account the fact that agents with reasoning or planning components can adapt their strategies rather than sticking to one strategy while maintaining their role (as discussed in Section 6.2.1). This means that an agent's role does not fully constrain its actions so as to prevent it from reasoning strategically about its interactions with other agents. An agent could thus learn how to adapt its strategy according to the role it has. For example, an agent bearing the role of accountant in a system could report fictitious profits, thus benefiting its company's share price, while still satisfying its role. To prevent such strategic defection or wrongdoing, the agent assigning the role to the new entrant is allowed to adjust its priorities or policy based on results from interactions with others dynamically. This presents a more realistic view of using trust (both at the individual and the system level) to decide how to constrain the actions (or strategies) of an interaction partner.

6.4 CONCLUSION AND FUTURE DIRECTIONS

This chapter has systematically analysed the issue of trust in open multi-agent systems. We have deliberately taken a broad-based approach in order to produce a comprehensive view of this multifaceted topic. In particular, we have related the different means of devising trust, firstly at the individual level and then at the system level. These two approaches lay the burden of computation on the agent and the system, respectively. In effect, they complement each other by minimizing risks in different circumstances differently and aim to solve the same problem of deciding the 'who, when and how' of interactions.

At the individual level, we have described learning and evolutionary models that show how agents could evolve or learn more reciprocative strategies in order to get higher pay-offs in the long run. Various means of characterizing the experience from individual interactions were presented and these were shown to lead to a measure of trust that enables an agent to choose future interaction partners and shape these interactions based on its personal experience with them. In contrast, reputation models have been shown to be efficient at gathering the experiences of others in various ways and using these to deduce the level of trustworthiness of another party. Various ways of gathering ratings from other parties using a social network were discussed. In so doing, we illustrated how the problem of lying witnesses can be dealt with using learning and probabilistic techniques and how agents can deal with the lack of ratings from the network. Having described the various ways of gathering information about direct and indirect experiences, it was then shown how an agent could use this information to form various beliefs about its counterparts. The socio-cognitive approach to trust also takes into account the fact that other beliefs about an agent's capabilities and motivations are essential in judging its trustworthiness.

Trust being enforced by the system was first discussed at the level of the interaction protocols and mechanisms themselves. We showed how the system can be devised so as to force the agents to be trustworthy. We particularly illustrated how auctions could be made secure and foster truth revelation on the part of bidders. We then showed how the threat of future punishment – through avoidance of or constraining interaction(s) – could be used by reputation mechanisms to prevent agents from lying about their preferences or force them to behave well in an open environment. Various methods of aggregating ratings and incentivizing agents to return ratings were discussed. The use of reputation through certificates was also shown to be an important solution in security mechanisms. The latter also ensure that agents are properly authenticated and therefore present a first line of defence against malicious agents in open multi-agent systems.

As can be seen from Figure 6.1, while the individual-level trust models enable an agent to reason about its level of trust in its opponents, the system-level mechanisms aim to ensure that these opponents' actions can actually be trusted. In more detail, using their trust models, agents can:

- reason about strategies to be used towards trustworthy and untrustworthy interaction partners (for example being reciprocative or selfish towards them) given a calculation of pay-offs over future interactions;
- reason about the information gathered through various means (for example either directly or through reputation models) about potential interaction partners;
- reason about the motivations and capabilities of these interaction partners to decide whether to believe in their trustworthiness.

Figure 6.1 A classification of approaches to trust in multi-agent systems

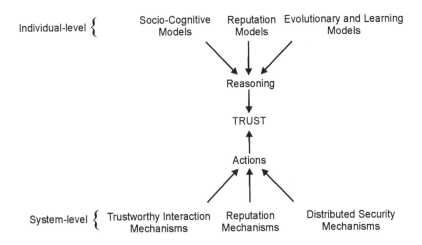

In contrast, the mechanisms and protocols described (that is, enforcing system-level trust) aim to force agents to act and interact truthfully by:

- imposing conditions that would cause them to lose utility if they did not abide by them;
- using their reputation to promote their future interactions with other agents in the community or demote future interactions whenever they do not behave well;
- imposing specified standards of good conduct that they need to satisfy and maintain in order to be allowed in the system.

Based on our survey of the state of the art, pertaining to both individual- and system-level trust in multi-agent systems, the key findings in this chapter are as follows:

- Various trust models have been developed based on sociology, machine learning techniques and game theory. These have been shown to be useful in helping agents interact better. However, these models each look at a different facet of the trust problem without relating to each other (a lacuna which we fill in this chapter).
- A very small number of interaction protocols have been shown to be trustworthy. The reason is that the computational complexity of interaction protocols can be a barrier to designing trustworthy interaction mechanisms.

- Security mechanisms provide a number of techniques to make interactions secure. However, they do not control the semantics of interactions beyond the line of defence provided by security policies and encryption techniques.
- Most trust models and interaction protocols do not cope effectively in the face of strategic lying. This means that agents can lie about their properties or the information they supply in order to exploit loopholes in the interaction protocol or in the decision making of their counterparts so as to gain more utility.
- Most trust models and interaction protocols are not collusion-proof. Agents can collude in order to exploit other agents or the system itself. Unless more attention is given to its detection and prevention, collusion could substantially alter the outcomes of interaction mechanisms and therefore damage open markets.
- While using game theory as a means of studying interactions, protocol designers and trust models make many unrealistic assumptions about the context comprising the environment and the social network. A more precise modelling of the context of interactions is needed. Trust models and interaction protocols should then be adapted to whichever (dynamic) context they are used in.
- With the advent of open distributed systems, agents representing different countries, institutions or societies will be interacting. This could give rise to a clash of norms and cultures (for example, laws, societal norms) which, in turn, will result in agents making the wrong assumptions about their counterparts, leading to distrust. Trust models should therefore conceptualize the difference in expectations arising from a difference in norms and cultures.

In the next subsection we outline future work that would be needed to completely define comprehensive trust models and mechanisms. Moreover, Appendix 6.1 provides a motivating scenario that shows how these abstract trust concepts can be grounded in a particular application context.

6.4.1 Research Challenges

We end our analysis of the state of the art in trust in multi-agent systems by outlining the key issues that need to be solved in order to have a comprehensive trust model for open multi-agent systems.

Computational complexity. Very few interaction protocols have been shown to elicit trustworthy behaviour from the interacting agents (for example, English auction, Vickrey auction). This is mostly because richer forms of interactions (for example combinatorial auctions) can become intractable or computationally expensive. In order to deal with this problem, better protocols, with minimum computational complexity, need to be devised to regiment the interactions of agents in open societies.

Security mechanisms. Security mechanisms provide a first line of defence against malicious attacks from outsiders. However, encryption and authentication tools do not control the semantics of direct interactions between agents in the system. To do so, security mechanisms would need to detect any unaccounted-for behaviour in the system and, combined with trust models, direct agents to the most appropriate remedies.

Strategic lying. While some reputation mechanisms and models try to deal with this problem (for example Schillo et al. 2000; Sen and Sajja 2002; Zacharia and Maes 2000), most models do not give a deep treatment of strategic lying. Strategic lies aim to trick agents into believing the liars are trustworthy while allowing the liars to exploit these unaware agents. A more thorough treatment is needed to address this shortcoming both at the individual level and at the system level of trust.

Collusion detection. Very few existing reputation or interaction mechanisms can prevent or deal with collusion (Sen and Sajja 2002; Brandt 2002). Moreover, while it has been shown how agents can learn to reciprocate good actions over time, it has not been shown how they could learn to collude, which is equivalent to reciprocating to only some agents and sharing false information about these accomplices to exploit others. We could expect agents to collude in an open environment and, if the system is to be robust and incentive compatible, collusion should be prevented. Otherwise, agents could end up trusting others that are exploiting them.

Context. Most trust models do not take into account the fact that interactions take place within a particular organizational and environmental context (with the exception of the socio-cognitive approach to some extent). If an agent has performed poorly due to changes in its environment, it should not be taken to be dishonest or a liar. Rather, there should be the possibility to take into account the environmental variables in deciding to trust another agent. This necessitates a better evaluation of risks present in the environment (Molm et al. 2000; Yamagishi et al. 1998). If risks are high due to the lack of stringent rules of encounter (for example preventing lying), an agent interacting honestly would then be considered to be more trustworthy than if the protocol of interaction dictated truth-telling for example. Thus, if rules prevent lying, there is no need to increase trust in interaction partners if they interact well, since there is no guarantee they would still do so if the rules were not present (Molm et al. 2000).

Expectations. None of the models surveyed showed how agents could convey their expectations (about the outcome of interactions) to each other (for example about the quality of goods exchanged or time of delivery). This we believe is important because, in an open environment, agents can have different concepts or ontologies that describe the expectations from an interaction. For example, 'high-quality service' could mean 'timely delivery of goods' for one agent while the other party implied 'good price' in the former's ontology. REGRET presents such an ontological dimension of trust ratings that are shared, but does not show how this dimension could be shared between interaction partners to better understand each other's expectations about the outcomes of the interaction. Understanding these expectations would enable an agent to satisfy them in the way that they are understood to be from the other side. Otherwise an agent could be deemed untrustworthy because of its ignorance of the real expectations of another party.

Social networks. While in most reputation models or security mechanisms (to some extent) it is assumed that there exists a social network, the connections between the nodes in the network are rarely, if at all, given a meaning (that is, the semantics of connections are not detailed). Connections have mostly been used to represent past interactions among the agents in the community (that is, a connection means that an interaction has occurred between the two nodes at its ends) or are simply given to the agents (Sabater and Sierra 2002; Yu and Singh 2002b; Schillo et al. 2000). A clearer definition of relationships (for example as collaborators, partnerships in coalitions, or members of the same organizations) defining the connections within the network would be needed. This, we foresee, should enable a better aggregation and evaluation of ratings, and hence trust.

APPENDIX 6.1

We choose the semantic web to illustrate the practical applications of trust for open multi-agent systems. This is because, while potential applications of agent-based systems such as ubiquitous computing and pervasive computing applications are still in their infancy, the semantic web is building upon the considerable success of the World Wide Web and technologies associated with it. Moreover, the semantic web is inherently strongly motivated by concepts in multi-agent systems (for example reasoning under uncertainty, ontologies, communication languages). It can therefore be considered that the semantic web will provide the test-bed for the first large-scale application of agent-based systems in everyday life. For these reasons, we provide the following vision of the semantic web (adapted from Berners-Lee et al. 2001) and detail the roles of trust models and interaction mechanisms within it.

Lucy and Pete have to organize a series of appointments to take their mother to the doctor for a course of physical therapy sessions. (We identify the need for trust at each step of the scenario in italics.)

At the doctor's office, Lucy instructed her semantic web agent through her handheld web browser. The agent promptly retrieved information about Mom's prescribed treatment from the doctor's agent, looked up several lists of providers, and checked for the ones in-plan for Mom's insurance within a 20 mile radius of her home and with a rating of excellent or very good on trusted rating services.

The first interaction between Lucy's agent and the doctor's agent should involve a secure authentication protocol (see Section 6.3.3) that would ensure that Lucy's agent is allowed to handle her Mom's data. This protocol would first verify the true identity of Lucy's agent and assign to it the proper rights to handle the data. Also, the trusted rating services could be based on reputation mechanisms (see Section 6.3.2). These reputation mechanisms could publish the ratings of health care providers and reward agents which return ratings with discounts on treatment costs to be paid to the advertised providers. This would make the mechanism incentive-compatible. Also, different providers could bid, via a trusted mechanism such as a secure Vickrey auction, to provide the requested service to Lucy's agent (see Section 6.3.1). Provider agents would need to bid their true valuation of the treatment plan requested to win the bid whereas Lucy's agent would act as the auctioneer in this case.

Lucy's agent then began trying to find a match between available appointment times (supplied by the agents of individual providers through their websites) and Pete's and Lucy's busy schedules. In a few minutes the agent presented them with a plan. Pete didn't like it: University Hospital was all the way across town from Mom's place, and he would be driving back in the middle of the rush hour. He set his own agent to redo the search with stricter preferences about location and time. Lucy's agent, having complete trust in Pete's agent in the context of the present task, automatically assisted by supplying access certificates and shortcuts to the data it had already sorted through.

The interaction between individual providers and the user agents (Lucy's and Pete's) needs a secure mechanism that ensures messages transmitted between all parties are not manipulated. Pete's agent could enhance the search for trustworthy potential providers by looking at its past interaction history with them (see Section 6.2.1) rather than looking at only the reputed ones (see Sections 6.2.2 and 6.3.2). It could also use referrals of other agents in the network to get in touch with a trustworthy agent it does not directly know.

Almost instantly the new plan was presented: a much closer clinic and earlier times, but there were two warning notes. First, Pete would have to reschedule a couple of his less-important appointments. He checked that they were not a problem. The other was something about the insurance company's list failing to include this provider under physical therapists: 'Service type and insurance plan status securely verified by other means' the agent reassured him. 'Details?'

> *Here the issue of reputation and distributed security is again raised (Sections 6.2.2 and 6.3.3). The 'other means' that helped to check the validity of the insurance company may pertain to an analysis of the certificates it provided that linked it to trusted sources. These certificates could provide evidence of the provider's compliance with laws and regulations of the country or certain quality standards that are equivalent to those needed by the insurance company.*

Lucy registered her assent at about the same moment Pete was muttering, 'Spare me the details', and it was all set. (Of course, Pete couldn't resist the details and later that night had his agent explain how it had found that provider even though it was not on the proper list.)

> *Here, the need for an agent to demonstrate how it could flexibly deal with different beliefs it acquired in the environment about potential interaction partners is highlighted (see Section 6.2.3). This implies a higher-level reasoning ability than just an evaluation reputation of providers for example. The agent should also be able to reason about the selected provider's location and treatment facilities to decide on whether to trust that provider in being able to supply the required services.*

NOTES

1   In agent-based systems, the network security issues associated with distributed systems (such as delegation, authorization) are not specifically dealt with. Some attempts are described briefly in Section 6.3.3 and we point to other relevant literature in the network security paradigm.

2   We here omit a third approach which is that taken in the mobile agent community. This focuses on identification issues (similar to network security approaches) and host–client interaction at the code-execution level rather than at the semantics of interactions, which we are more concerned with in most agent-based systems.

3   The moves chosen will also be dependent on the risk attitude (risk seeking, risk neutral or risk averse) of the agent. In this respect, we conceive of trust as a means to minimize the risk perceived by the agent (Yamagishi et al. 1998; Molm et al. 2000; Dasgupta 1998).

4   The prisoner's dilemma is a game involving two prisoners that have to decide whether to cooperate by not revealing their accomplice's deeds, or to defect by revealing this information. The dilemma arises as a result of each having to separately (in different rooms) decide to cooperate or not, resulting in some years of imprisonment (five for one cooperating and one defecting, three for both if they both defect and one for both if they both cooperate). In the face of such uncertainty the dominant strategy proves to be defection even though this does not lead to best outcomes (hence the dilemma).

5   For a wider reading on the problem of learning cooperative strategies in competitive settings, see Mukherjee et al. (2001), Biswas et al. (2000) and Sen (1996).

6   We here distinguish between trust and reputation in the sense that the former is derived from direct interactions while reputation is mainly acquired (by an agent about another) from the environment or other agents and ultimately leads to trust. This distinction is only made to facilitate the study of the different models presented rather than to prescribe such an approach to trust and reputation.

7   In order to have this belief, agent x needs to model the mental attitudes of agent y.
8   See note 7.
9   We do not wish to give a complete account of network security mechanisms since this is
     beyond the scope of this chapter. Rather, we will focus on the main concepts and models
     that strictly pertain to multi-agent systems. For a wider reading on network security for
     open distributed systems, see Grandison and Sloman (2000).

REFERENCES

Adams, C. and Farrel, S. (1999), 'RFC2510 Internet x.509 Public Key
    Infrastructure Certificate Management Protocols. Technical Report', *The
    Internet Society*,
    http://www.cis.ohio-state.edu/htbin/rfc/rfc2510.html accessed 12 Apr. 04.
Axelrod, R. (1984), *The Evolution of Cooperation*, New York: Basic Books.
Berners-Lee, T., Hendler, J. and Lassila, O. (2001), 'The Semantic Web',
    Scientific American 284(5): 34-43.
Binmore, K. (1992), *Fun and Games: A Text on Game Theory*, Boston MA:
    D.C. Heath Company.
Birk, A. (2000), 'Boosting Cooperation by Evolving Trust', *Applied
    Artificial Intelligence* 14(8): 769-84.
Birk, A. (2001), 'Learning to Trust', in R. Falcone, M.P. Singh and Y. Tan
    (eds), *Trust in Cyber-societies, Integrating the Human and Artificial
    Perspectives, Lecture Notes in Computer Science, Vol. 2246,* Berlin:
    Springer, pp. 133-44.
Biswas, A., Sen, S. and Debnath, S. (2000), 'Limiting Deception in Groups
    of Social Agents', *Applied Artificial Intelligence Journal* (Special issue
    on Deception, Fraud and Trust in Agent Societies) 14(8): 785-97.
Brainov, S. and Sandholm, T. (1999), 'Contracting with Uncertain Level of
    Trust', in *Proceedings of the 1st ACM Conference on Electronic
    Commerce*, New York: ACM Press, pp. 15-21.
Brandt, F. (2001), 'Cryptographic Protocols for Secure Second-price
    Auctions', in M. Klush and F. Zambonelli (eds), *Lecture Notes in
    Artificial Intelligence, Vol. 2812,* Berlin: Springer, pp. 154-65.
Brandt, F. (2002), 'A Verifiable Bidder-resolved Auction Protocol', in
    *Proceedings of the Workshop on Deception, Fraud and Trust in Agent
    Societies, The International Conference on Autonomous Agents and
    Multiagents (AAMAS)*, Bologna: AAMAS, pp. 18-25.
Burt, R.S. (1982), *Toward a Structural Theory of Action. Network Models of
    Social Structure, Perception, and Action*, New York: Academic Press.
Buskens, V. (1998), 'The Social Structure of Trust', *Social Networks* 20(3):
    265-98.
Carley, K. (1991), 'A Theory of Group Stability', *American Sociological
    Review* 56(3): 331-54.

Castelfranchi, C. and Falcone, R. (1998), 'Principles of Trust for MAS: Cognitive Anatomy, Social Importance, and Quantification', in *Proceedings of the 3rd International Conference of Multi-Agent Systems (ICMAS'98)*, 3-7 July, Paris: ICMAS, pp. 72-9.

Castelfranchi, C. and Falcone, R. (2000), 'Trust Is Much More Than Subjective Probability: Mental Components and Sources of Trust, in *Proceedings of the 33rd Hawaii International Conference on System Sciences* Vol. 6, Maui, 4-7 January, IEEE Computer Society, http://www.computer.org/proceedings/hicss/0493/04936/04936008abs.pd f accessed 17 Apr. 04.

Castelfranchi, C. and Falcone, R. (2001), 'Social Trust: A Cognitive Approach', in C. Castelfranchi and Y.-H. Tan (eds), *Trust and Deception in Virtual Societies*, Dordrecht: Kluwer Academic Publishers, pp. 55-90.

Cerami, E. (2002) *Web Services Essentials,* Sebastopol CA: O'Reilly & Associates.

Cohen, P.R. and Levesque, H.J. (1990), 'Intention is Choice with Commitment', *Artificial Intelligence* 42(2-3): 213-61.

Dasgupta, P. (1988), 'Trust as a Commodity', in D. Gambetta (ed.), *Trust: Making and Breaking Cooperative Relations*, Oxford: Blackwell, pp. 49-72.

Deitel, M.H., Deitel, P.H. and Nieto, T.R. (2001), *E-business and E-commerce: How to Program*, Princeton NJ: Prentice Hall.

Dellarocas, C. (2002), 'Towards Incentive-compatible Reputation Management', in *Proceedings of the Workshop on Deception, Fraud and Trust in Agent Societies, The International Conference on Autonomous Agents and Multiagents (AAMAS)*, Bologna: AAMAS, pp. 26-40.

Durfee, E.H. (1999), 'Practically Coordinating', *AI Magazine* 20(1): 99-116.

eBay (2003), http://www.ebay.com, accessed 17 Apr. 04.

Falcone, R., Singh, M.P. and Tan, Y. (eds) (2001), *Trust in Cyber-societies, Integrating the Human and Artificial Perspectives*, Lecture Notes in Computer Science, Vol. 2246, Berlin: Springer-Verlag.

Foster, I. and Kesselman, C. (eds) (1998), *The Grid, Blueprint for a New Computing Infrastructure*, San Mateo CA: Morgan Kaufmann Inc.

Foundation for Intelligent Physical Agents (FIPA) (2001), 'Abstract Architecture Specification, Version j', http://www.fipa.org/specs/fipa00001/ accessed 17 Apr. 04.

Gambetta, D. (1998), 'Can We Trust Trust?', in D. Gambetta (ed.), *Trust: Making and Breaking Cooperative Relations*, Oxford: Blackwell, pp. 213-37.

Gong, L. (2002), 'Tutorial: Peer to Peer Networks in Action', *IEEE Distributed Systems Online* 3(1), http://dsonline.computer.org/0201/ic/w1o2gei.htm accessed 17 Apr. 04.

Grandison, T. and Sloman, M. (2000), 'A Survey of Trust in Internet Applications', *IEEE Communications Surveys and Tutorials* 4(4): 2-16.

He, M., Jennings, N.R. and Leung, H. (2003), 'On Agent-mediated Electronic Commerce', *IEEE Transactions on Knowledge and Data Engineering* 15(4): 985-1003.

Herzberg, A., Mass, Y., Michaeli, J., Naor, D. and Ravid, Y. (2000), 'Access Control Meets Public Key Infrastructure, or: Assigning Roles to Strangers', in *Proceedings of the IEEE Symposium on Security and Privacy*, New York: IEEE Computer Society, pp. 2-4.

Hsu, M. and Soo, V. (2002), 'A Secure Multi-agent Vickrey Auction Scheme', in *Proceedings of the Workshop on Deception, Fraud and Trust in Agent Societies, The International Conference on Autonomous Agents and Multiagents (AAMAS)*, Bologna: AAMAS, pp. 86-91.

Jennings, N.R. (1993), 'Commitments and Conventions: The Foundation of Coordination in Multi-agent Systems, *The Knowledge Engineering Review* 8(3): 223-50.

Jennings, N.R. (2001), 'An Agent-based Approach for Building Complex Software Systems', *Communications of the ACM* 44(4): 35-41.

Jennings, N.R., Faratin, P., Lomuscio, A.R., Parsons, S., Sierra, C. and Wooldridge, M. (2001), 'Automated Negotiation: Prospects, Methods and Challenges', *International Journal of Group Decision and Negotiation* 10(2): 199-215.

Jurca, R. and Faltings, B. (2003), 'An Incentive Compatible Reputation Mechanism', in *Proceedings of the IEEE Conference on E-Commerce CEC03*, Newport Beach CA, 24-27 June, New York: IEEE Computer Society, pp. 285-92.

Kephart, J.O. and Chess, D.M. (2003), 'The Vision of Autonomic Computing', *IEEE Computer* 36(1): 41-50.

Kollock, P. (1999), 'The Production of Trust in Online Markets', in E.J. Lawler, M. Macy, S.T. Thyne, and H.A. Walker (eds), *Advances in Group Processes Vol. 16*, Greenwich CT: JAI Press, pp. 99-124.

Kraus, S. (2001), *Strategic Negotiation in Multi-Agent Environments*, Cambridge MA: MIT Press.

Mass, Y. and Shehory, O. (2001), 'Distributed Trust in Open Multi-agent Systems' in R. Falcone, M. Singh and Y.-H. Tan (eds), *Trust in Cybersocieties*, Berlin/Heidelberg: Springer-Verlag, pp. 159-73.

Molm, L.D., Takahashi, N. and Peterson, G. (2000), 'Risk and Trust in Social Exchange: An Experimental Test of a Classical Proposition', *American Journal of Sociology* 105(5): 1396-1427.

Mui, L., Mohtashemi, M. and Halberstadt, A. (2002), 'A Computational Model of Trust and Reputation for e-Business', in *35th Hawaii International Conference on System Science (HICSS 35 CDROM)*, IEEE

Computer society (online publication),
http://csdl.computer.org/comp/proceedings/hicss/2002/1435/07/14350188
.pdf

Mukherjee, R., Banerjee, B., and Sen, S. (2001), 'Learning Mutual Trust', in R. Falcone, M.P. Singh and Y. Tan (eds), *Trust in Cyber-societies, Integrating the Human and Artificial Perspectives, Lecture Notes in Computer Science, Vol. 2246*, Berlin: Springer, pp. 145-58.

Panzarasa, P., Jennings, N.R. and Norman, T. (2001), 'Social Mental Shaping: Modelling the Impact of Sociality on the Mental States of Autonomous Agents', *Computational Intelligence* 4(17): 738-82.

Poslad, S., Calisti, M. and Charlton, P. (2002), 'Specifying Standard Security Mechanisms in Multi-agent Systems', in *Proceedings of the Workshop on Deception, Fraud and Trust in Agent Societies, The International Conference on Autonomous Agents and Multiagents (AAMAS)*, Bologna: AAMAS, pp. 122-7.

Prietula, M. (2000), 'Advice, Trust, and Gossip among Artificial Agents', in A. Lomi and E. Larsen (eds), *Simulating Organizational Societies: Theories, Models and Ideas*, Cambridge MA: MIT Press, pp. 141-80.

Pynadath, D. and Tambe, M. (2002), 'Multi-agent Teamwork: Analyzing Key Teamwork Theories and Models', in C. Castelfranchi and L. Johnson (eds), *Proceedings of the First International Joint Conference on Autonomous Agents and Multi-Agent Systems, Vol. 2*, New York: ACM Press, pp. 873-80.

Resnick, P. and Zeckhauser, R. (2002), 'Trust among Strangers in Internet Transactions: Empirical Analysis of e-Bay's Reputation System', in M.R. Baye (ed.), *The Economics of the Internet and E-commerce, Advances in Applied Microeconomics, Vol. 11*, Amsterdam: Elsevier Science, pp. 127-57.

Rosenschein, J. and Zlotkin, G. (1994), *Rules of Encounter: Designing Conventions for Automated Negotiation among Computers*, Cambridge MA: MIT Press.

Russell, S. and Norvig, P. (1995), *Artificial Intelligence: A Modern Approach*, New York: Prentice Hall.

Sabater, J. and Sierra, C. (2002), 'Regret: A Reputation Model for Gregarious Societies', in C. Castelfranchi and L. Johnson (eds), *Proceedings of the 1st International Joint Conference on Autonomous Agents and Multi-Agent Systems*, New York: ACM Press, pp. 475-82.

Sadeh, N. (2002), *M-Commerce: Technologies, Services, and Business Models*, Chichester: Wiley Computer Publishing.

Sandholm, T. (1999), 'Distributed Rational Decision Making', in G. Weiss (ed.), *Multi-Agent Systems: A Modern Approach To Distributed Artificial Intelligence*, Cambridge MA: MIT Press, pp. 201-58.

Savage, L. (1954), *The Foundations of Statistics*, Hoboken NJ: John Wiley and Sons.

Schillo, M., Funk, P. and Rovatsos, M. (2000), 'Using Trust for Detecting Deceptive Agents in Artificial Societies', *Applied Artificial Intelligence, Special Issue on Trust, Deception, and Fraud in Agent Societies* 14(8): 825-48.

Schmeck, H., Ungerer, T. and Wolf, L.C. (eds) (2002), *Trends in Network and Pervasive Computing ARCS 2002, International Conference on Architecture of Computing Systems, Karlsruhe, Germany, April 8-12, Proceedings* (Lecture Notes in Computer Science, Vol. 2299), Berlin: Springer-Verlag.

Sen, S. (1996), 'Reciprocity: A Foundational Principle for Promoting Cooperative Behavior among Self-interested Agents', in *Proceedings of the Second International Conference on Multi-agent Systems*, Menlo Park CA: AAAI Press, pp. 322-9.

Sen, S., Biswas, A. and Debnath, S. (2000), 'Believing Others: Pros and Cons', in *Proceedings of the Fourth International Conference on Multi-Agent Systems*, Boston, 10-12 July, pp. 279-86.

Sen, S. and Dutta, P.S. (2002), 'The Evolution and Stability of Cooperative Traits', in C. Castelfranchi and L. Johnson (eds), *Proceedings of the First International Joint Conference on Autonomous Agents and Multi-Agent Systems, Vol. 3*, New York: ACM Press, pp. 1114-20.

Sen, S. and Sajja, N. (2002), 'Robustness of Reputation-based Trust: Boolean Case', in C. Castelfranchi and L. Johnson (eds), *Proceedings of the 1st International Joint Conference on Autonomous Agents and Multi-Agent Systems, Vol. 1*, New York: ACM Press, pp. 288-93.

Simon, H.A. (1996), *The Sciences of the Artificial*, Cambridge MA: MIT Press, (3rd edn).

Singh, M.P., Yu, B. and Venkatraman, M. (2001), 'Community-based Service Location', *Communications of the ACM* 44(4): 49-54.

von Neuman, J. and Morgenstern, O. (1944), *The Theory of Games and Economic Behaviour*, Princeton NJ: Princeton University Press.

Vulkan, N. (1999), 'Economic Implications of Agent Technology and e-Commerce', *The Economic Journal* 109(453): 67-90.

Witkowski, M., Artikis, A. and Pitt, J. (2001), 'Experiments in Building Experiential Trust in a Society of Objective-trust Based Agents', in R. Falcone, M.P. Singh and Y. Tan (eds), *Trust in Cyber-societies, Integrating the Human and Artificial Perspectives, Lecture Notes in Computer Science, Vol. 2246*, Berlin: Springer, pp. 111-32.

Wooldridge, M. (2002), *An Introduction to Multi-Agent Systems*, Chichester: John Wiley & Sons.

Wu, D.J. and Sun, Y. (2001), 'The Emergence of Trust in Multi-agent

Bidding: A Computational Approach', in *Proceedings of the 34th Hawaii International Conference on System Sciences (HICSS-34, CD ROM),* Vol. 1, IEEE Computer Society Press.

Yager, R.R., Kacprzyk, J. and Fedrizzi, M. (1994), *Advances in the Dempster-Shafer Theory of Evidence,* Chichester: John Wiley.

Yamagishi, T., Cook, K. and Watabe, M. (1998), 'Uncertainty, Trust, and Commitment Formation in the United States and Japan', *American Journal of Sociology* 104(1): 165-94.

Yu, B. and Singh, M.P. (2002a), 'Distributed Reputation Management for Electronic Commerce', *Computational Intelligence* 18(4): 535-49.

Yu, B. and Singh, M.P. (2002b), 'An Evidential Model of Reputation Management', in C. Castelfranchi and L. Johnson (eds), *Proceedings of the 1st International Joint Conference on Autonomous Agents and Multi-Agent Systems, Vol. 1,* New York: ACM Press, pp. 294-301.

Yu, B. and Singh, M.P. (2003), 'Social Networks and Trust: Searching Social Networks', in *Proceedings of the 2nd International Joint Conference on Autonomous and Multi-Agent Systems,* New York: ACM Press, pp. 65-72.

Zacharia, G. and Maes, P. (2000), 'Trust through Reputation Mechanisms', *Applied Artificial Intelligence* 14(9): 881-908.

Part 3   Experiencing cyberspace

William Dutton and Adrian Shepherd call the Internet an 'experience technology'. In Chapter 7 they set out results from the first 2003 Oxford Internet Survey that bear on questions of trust in the Internet. In Chapter 8 Jonathan Jackson, Nick Allum and George Gaskell review research on public perceptions of risk and suggest a framework for further analysis in the context of cyberspace. Charles Raab (Chapter 9) takes up issues of privacy protection, arguing for a shift away from the conventional privacy paradigm towards a consideration of equity in privacy protection. Cyberspace end-user considerations are the focus of Angela Sasse's contribution (Chapter 10), which draws on the literature on the computer usability field, while James Backhouse and his colleagues in Chapter 11 focus on organizational change management and behavioural approaches to security and information assurance. Part 3 is completed with Jonathan Cave's analysis of the way structure, conduct and performance theory shed light on the evolution of cyberspace markets and of the application of economic game-theoretic approaches to trusting behaviour in cyberspace.

7 Confidence and risk on the Internet

William H. Dutton and Adrian Shepherd[1]

7.1 INTRODUCTION

Trust in the Internet and related information and communication technologies (ICTs) – cyber trust – could be critical to the successful development of e-services ranging from electronic public service delivery to e-commerce. This chapter is anchored in a study conducted in the summer of 2003 that explored trust in cyberspace. This Oxford Internet Survey (OxIS) was conducted by the Oxford Internet Institute (OII) based on a multi-stage random sample of the population of Great Britain aged 14 and upward. The sample was designed so that the results of the survey could be projected to the country as a whole. It provides important new evidence that helps to illuminate the concept of trust and the determinants of its relationship to the Internet.

The chapter begins with an overview of these concepts. After describing the methodology and findings of the OxIS survey, analyses of the survey are drawn on to explore and refine key cyber trust issues. The potential for its findings to assist in shaping future directions for research and cross-disciplinary collaboration is discussed in the concluding section.

It is argued that cyber trust should be seen as referring to the everyday view of trust in general, as a confident expectation. In the case of cyber trust, this relates to expectations about the reliability and value of the Internet and related ICTs, such as the equipment, people and techniques essential to the use of online services.

The OxIS survey reveals wide variations in cyber trust between individuals in Britain. Few exhibit a blind faith in the Internet and all that it offers, but most people are reasonably confident, if guarded, in the information and people they are able to access over the Internet. Well over half (59 per cent) of the respondents to the OxIS use the Internet, suggesting that there is sufficient trust to support the continued diffusion of this technology, despite a general awareness of the potential risks entailed in exposure to unwanted mail, viruses and other specific risks. Variation across individuals in their levels of cyber trust supports the view that the Internet is an 'experience' technology. Generally, experience on the Internet tends to engender a higher level of cyber trust.

There are two general categories of cyber trust, which we have labelled 'Net-confidence' and 'Net-risk', that can assist in analyses of cyber trust. Specifically, they have helped this analysis of survey data to show that: (1) users of the Internet have more certainty and more confidence in the information and people they can access through the technology than do non-users, with many non-users having no opinion about its trustworthiness; and (2) greater proximity to the Internet tends to instil more trust, to some extent (where 'proximity' is indicated by the use of the Internet over more years, in more ways and with greater expertise). Trust appears to shape use of the Internet. Specifically, the presence of cyber trust is positively associated with the use of the World Wide Web for e-commerce. However, those who use the Internet more, for example for online shopping, are somewhat more likely to expose themselves to spam email and other bad experiences, which tend to undermine trust in the Internet and raise concerns over the risks.

Individuals with more formal education tend to be somewhat more sceptical of the information and people accessible on the Internet, but also somewhat less concerned about the risks entailed in Internet use. Therefore, education and exposure to the Internet might offer a general strategy for coping with the risks and threats to the trustworthiness of the technology. However, since education and exposure to the Internet and ICTs are skewed towards higher socio-economic groups, these strategies could reinforce the 'digital divide' in access to the Internet over time. This threat is somewhat diminished by the fact that the Internet is becoming so widely accessible in Britain, but advances such as broadband Internet will continue to raise issues of the digital divide in access and trust. The manner in which bad experiences on the Internet can undermine cyber trust suggests that initiatives to enhance the trustworthiness of the Internet are warranted. However, these efforts will create a tension, competing against other values such as privacy or access, which could be threatened by some trust-enhancing services.

7.2 THE SOCIAL DYNAMICS OF CYBER TRUST

The Internet, World Wide Web and related ICTs 'reconfigure access' to information, people, services and technologies (Dutton 1999; Dutton et al. 2003).[2] The use of the Internet, for example, not only enables people to get information, communicate with others, obtain services and use technologies in new ways, but it also reconfigures what users know, who they know and stay in touch with, what know-how they need, what they consume – and when and where they acquire and consume it.

This chapter is based on the Oxford Internet Institute's OxIS national survey of Great Britain, which focused on the use and non-use of the Internet. Conducted in May and June 2003, it found that nearly 60 per cent of a probability sample of individuals (14 years or older) said they used the Internet.[3] This represents a substantial increase over previous estimates of Internet access in Britain, suggesting that trust in the Internet remains high enough to continue supporting its diffusion. Trust in this new online cyberspace might well shape a person's decision to go online. It is also likely to shape what is done online, such as whether a person shops and banks electronically or cyberchats with others (Urban and Sultan 2000). In turn, users' experiences on the Internet might then raise or lower their level of cyber trust. However, there are many unanswered questions related to cyber trust:

- How much (dis)trust does the public place in cyberspace – the Internet's world of information, people, services and technologies?
- How does cyber trust shape use of the Internet?
- Does use of the Internet enhance or undermine that trust over time and with what effect on subsequent patterns of (non-)use?
- How do different social contexts (for example generational, educational and geographic) affect issues of trust and the design and use of trust-enhancing products, services and frameworks?
- How do skills in accessing, managing and interpreting information on the Web, and engaging in social interactions through the Internet, affect trust outcomes in relation to e-commerce?

7.2.1 Cyber Trust and its Determinants

Trust is a broad concept with application across many disciplines and subject areas, but with no commonly agreed definition. A review of the economic literature on trust found that the existence of uncertainty was one factor present in most definitions of trust (Guerra et al. 2003).

For example, a strict definition by some economists reads: 'a person trusts someone to do X if she acts on the expectation that he will do X when both know that two conditions obtain: if he fails to do X she would have done better to act otherwise, and her acting in the way she does gives him a selfish reason not to do X' (Bacharach and Gambetta 2001, p. 150). Within this definition, the people displaying or acting in trust – the trustors – must put themselves in a position where they would be worse off should their trust be violated. Furthermore, the people they trust – the trustees – should have some temptation to violate that trust. This creates uncertainty about the behaviour of both parties, providing economists with an interesting case of decision making under uncertainty.

However, conventional definitions of trust do not entail all of these conditions of uncertainty, exposure and temptation. The most conventional usage defines trust as 'a firm belief in the reliability or truth or strength etc. of a person or thing. ... a confident expectation. ... reliance on the truth of a statement etc. without examination' (*Oxford English Dictionary*). For example, when someone says they do not trust a story in the newspaper, they might mean that they are uncertain about its truthfulness, or they might be certain that it is biased or otherwise misleading. People define trust to suit their own perceptions and needs, not as economists, sociologists, political scientists or other social scientists might wish to define it. For this reason, survey research on trust needs to adopt the broad, conventional conceptual definition of a 'confident expectation' and specify it operationally by responses to particular survey questions. This definition has, therefore, been adopted for the study reported here.

On the assumption that ICTs might undermine the trust of their users, and prevent people from obtaining services over the Internet, many current and potential technology producers, providers and publishers are putting effort into technical, legal and social approaches to enhancing trust in online products and services, such as in devising e-commerce 'trustmarks' (Guerra et al. 2003). It is therefore important to understand the factors that shape trust in cyberspace in order to assess the merit of these initiatives and determine whether they are aimed at the right problems.

7.2.1.1 Trust deficits
A key assumption is that computer-mediated communication, such as over the Internet, will undermine trust because it eliminates face-to-face interaction. However, empirical evidence relating to the impact of ICTs on trust is still sparse and contradictory. For instance, some researchers (for example Wallace 2001) argue that trust might be undermined in electronic interactions and transactions because the reduced communication channel makes it harder to observe vital non-verbal physical cues, such as facial expressions and body language, which have traditionally been viewed as the prime means used by people to detect deceit. On the other hand, despite decades of research, there is no definitive research on the impact of different media – audio-only, video, computer-mediated communication and a mix of media – on one's trust in another person involved in interpersonal communication.[4] Moreover, there are strong arguments that trust can be enhanced by making effective use of the vast amount of information and new forms of online social networks available through Internet-based interactions (for example Ben-Ner and Putterman 2002).

7.2.1.2 Factors shaping trust in the Internet: the certainty trough

As features of online communication could erode or enhance trust, it would be valuable to understand what factors, if any, can ensure that users place the appropriate level of trust in this technology. Trust as conventionally defined is closely connected with a greater level of certainty or confidence in the reliability and security of the Internet, so it is likely that trust will be enhanced as a person learns more about the technology. However, information can create, rather than reduce, uncertainty. Donald MacKenzie's (1999, pp. 43-6) research posited a curvilinear relationship between information and certainty, which he called a certainty trough (Figure 7.1).

Figure 7.1 The certainty trough

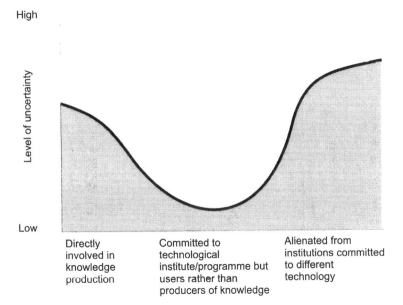

High

Low

Level of uncertainty

| Directly involved in knowledge production | Committed to technological institute/programme but users rather than producers of knowledge | Alienated from institutions committed to different technology |

Source: Adapted from MacKenzie (1999, p. 43).

At one extreme in Figure 7.1, those most socially distant from the Internet, with no knowledge of the technology or its use, are likely to be alienated from the technology and least certain about its role (MacKenzie 1999). Those people who learn more about the Internet, for instance by becoming a user, might obtain a higher level of certainty and trust in the technology. At the opposite extreme, those who are socially closest to the Internet – for example, web developers and content producers, and other ICT professionals – are likely to gain knowledge from which they have learned to have a higher level of uncertainty, as they understand the complex issues surrounding online reliability, security and privacy.[5]

The concept of a certainty trough not only challenges linear notions of the relationship between proximity and trust, but also raises questions about the appropriate level of trust. The most informed users and the producers might be less, rather than more, trusting. Scepticism or uncertainty can be positive. Of course, total trust or blind faith in technology could be risky.

However, proximity is one of many social and institutional factors that could play an important role in determining perceptions of trust.[6] So it is essential to understand how perceptions of trust might be modified or explained by different social backgrounds and contexts, whether generational, educational or geographic, which might yield patterned responses to the same technology, or technological risks in general.

It is critical that government, industry, business and other organized groups respond to concerns over trust with an understanding anchored in empirical research. Debate over cyber trust is long on speculation and competing conventional wisdom, but short on real data on the public's actual perception of the Internet and trust in cyberspace. For example, one Luxembourg Minister argued: 'consumers are still reluctant to purchase on the net and want these virtual transactions to have the same level of guarantee as those carried out in traditional commerce'.[7] He goes on to posit that: 'trustmarks, certificates, labels, on-line disputes resolution ... will re-establish consumer confidence'.

Much additional evidence and analysis is needed to gain more reliable insights into how Internet users and non-users differ in their levels of cyber trust, and how that shapes their involvement in e-commerce and other online activities. These and related issues are developed in this analysis within the broader context of research and understanding of the personal, social, institutional and economic changes tied to the growing use of the Internet and related ICTs.

7.3 TRUST IN CYBERSPACE: LEARNING LESSONS FROM EXPERIENCE ONLINE

7.3.1 Research on Trust in the Internet

Although the Internet emerged in the 1970s as the Advanced Research Projects Agency Network (ARPANET), its widespread use and the growing interest in e-commerce and cyber trust are much more recent phenomena. Few robust, in-depth and long-term studies of trust in the Internet are therefore available. However, some recent studies – mainly based on the US case – are developing an empirical base for grounding speculation about the use and implications of the technology (Lohse et al. 2000; Lunn and Suman 2002). We are not aware of systematic survey research on cyber trust among the general public in the UK, other than the OxIS study reported here.

7.3.2 The Oxford Internet Survey

In this chapter we address the cyber trust questions raised above through an analysis of the OxIS study: a current and comprehensive investigation of public attitudes in Britain toward the Internet. This examined levels of trust in various aspects of the Internet, including the reliability of information on the Web and opinions about people's perceived exposure to risks when online, such as a loss of personal privacy. Key questions included: Does experience generate more or less trust in the people and information accessed online? To what degree do people 'trust' online contexts more, or less, than other environments? How can ICTs be deployed to enhance rather than diminish trust? And, how does trust shape the use of the Internet?

The study entailed face-to-face interviews with its nationally representative random sample.[8] Personal interviews were conducted through household visits, based on a multi-stage sampling technique designed to provide a sample that could yield estimates for the population as a whole. A probability sample of households was drawn up as the basis for visits. Field staff then randomly sampled individuals within households to determine whom to interview. The aim was to obtain 2,000 completed interviews. An excellent response rate of 66 per cent of those contacted yielded 2,030 respondents from England, Wales and Scotland (Northern Ireland was not included in the population sampled). Appendix 7.1 provides a detailed explanation of the sample design.

The interviews lasted 30 to 35 minutes on average, covering a wide range of topics related to the Internet and the Web, as well as the background of the respondent. Non-users as well as Internet users were interviewed. Interviews began with general questions, such as attitudes towards the Internet and technology in general, before proceeding to detailed questions about patterns of (non-)use. The full interview questionnaire is available online.[9]

The key concepts developed in this analysis, such as proximity to the Internet, were all defined operationally by how respondents answered one or more specific questions in the survey. These operational definitions are explained here and when describing the results. A variety of multivariate statistical techniques was used to determine how individual questions should be grouped and whether differences reported are meaningful and statistically significant. Details are discussed in Appendix 7.2 with respect to measurement, and Appendix 7.3 concerning issues of statistical significance.

7.4 DIMENSIONS OF CYBER TRUST

The study identified, and described in some detail, wide variations in public perceptions in Great Britain of the trustworthiness of the Internet. This helped to show how levels of trust are related to an individual's patterns of (non-)use of the Internet over time. Several social background characteristics of users were related to their trust in the Internet, such as age. However, most predispositions to trust or distrust the Internet associated with these characteristics tend to be mitigated over time, and can be accounted for by the lessons learned from experience online.

Patterns of responses to the OxIS survey formed the basis for our definition of two general categories related to broad conceptions of trust, which we labelled 'Net-confidence' and 'Net-risk'.[10] These two types of trust are distinct. For example, a person can have very little confidence in the value of information on the Internet, but see few risks entailed in its use, or vice versa.[11]

7.4.1 Net-Confidence

Users of the Internet have more confidence in the technology and in the people they can communicate with on the Internet, than do non-users. They were also significantly more likely to think that information on the Internet is reliable.

This can be seen primarily through answers to three specific questions that operationally define Net-confidence (also see Appendix 7.2). One asked respondents to rate the quality of information on the Internet on a scale of 1 to 10, where 10 is 'totally reliable' and 1 is 'totally unreliable'. (As discussed below, respondents were also asked to rate the information found in newspapers and on television on the same scale.) Responses varied across the full range of the scale, but those who do not use the Internet were much more likely to say they did not know whether the information on the Internet was reliable or not (Figure 7.2).

About one-third (32 per cent) of non-users said they 'don't know' how reliable information is online. Former users express more certainty, but are significantly less certain than are current narrowband or broadband Internet users (Figure 7.2). The validity of attributing a higher level of uncertainty to those answering 'don't know' is reinforced by the patterns of responses from those who expressed an opinion.

Among those respondents who had an opinion, non-users were more likely to rate information on the Internet as less reliable than current users. Past users fall in between these two ratings (Figure 7.3).

Figure 7.2 Uncertainty over the reliability of information on the Internet (N = 2,029)

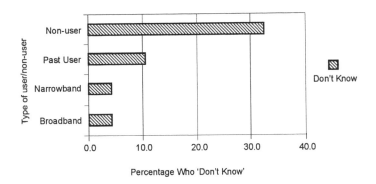

Percentage Who 'Don't Know'

Figure 7.3 Reliability of information on the Net (N = 2,029)

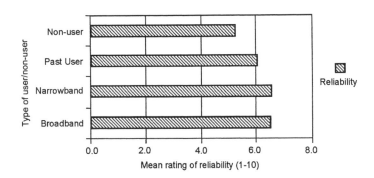

Mean rating of reliability (1-10)

There is no difference between narrow and broadband Internet users in the reliability they attribute to information on the Internet. Those who use the Net are, therefore, more confident about the reliability of online information. At the same time, Internet users are not blindly trusting of information on the Net. Their ratings average just over 6 on a 10-point scale, suggesting that they tend to be mindful of the potential for biased information, misinformation or weak sources.

A second indicator of Net-confidence is institutionally anchored. On this basis, users tend to be more institutionally trusting of the 'people' associated with the Internet. Respondents were told: 'Now I'd like to ask you about some institutions. Please tell me how much confidence you have in the people running each. Use a 5-point scale where 1 means you have no confidence at all and 5 means you have total confidence.' The list of institutions (major companies, the government, television news, newspapers and the Internet) was then read out. The order was rotated across interviews.

On this question, as in the case of confidence in information, non-users displayed far more uncertainty about the Internet, with just over one-third (35 per cent) saying they 'don't know' if they have confidence or not (Table 7.1). Those non-users who had an opinion were also more likely to have no confidence in 'the people running' the Internet (Table 7.1)[12]. Internet users were more confident, with broadband users being the most confident.

Table 7.1 Confidence in the people running the Internet by type (N = 2,030)

Level of confidence	Broadband %	Narrowband %	Past user %	Non-user %	Total %
Don't know	3	8	15	35	17
1. No conf.	4	5	8	23	11
2	16	14	15	15	15
3	33	36	34	20	30
4	35	30	20	6	22
5. Total conf.	9	7	8	1	5
Total %	100	100	100	100	100
No of resp.	232	978	117	703	2030

A third indicator concerns the people to whom users can gain access over the Internet, and vice versa. In parallel with the patterns above, users have more confidence than non-users in the people they can communicate with on the Internet. Respondents were given a card and told: 'Now I'd like to ask you about different groups of people. Please tell me how much confidence you have in the following groups of people. Use a 5-point scale where 1 means you have no confidence at all and 5 means you have total confidence'. The list of groups (scientists, doctors, most people I know, most people in this country, most people you can communicate with on the Internet) was read out, with the order rotated across interviews.

Once again, uncertainty is greatest among non-users, with about one-third (35 per cent) saying they 'don't know' what level of confidence they have in people online (Table 7.2). Non-users who express an opinion are less confident than are users 'in people you can communicate with' online, with current users being more confident.

That said, most users are not naive. No category of user was likely to say they had total confidence in people they could communicate with online. Only 3 per cent of all respondents expressed total confidence, suggesting that concerns in the press over meeting 'strangers' and 'bad people' online have created a healthy scepticism among nearly all users.

*Table 7.2 Confidence in most people you can communicate with on the
Internet, by type of (non-)use (N = 2,030)*

Level of confidence	Broadband %	Narrowband %	Past user %	Non-user %	Total %
Don't know	3	8	11	35	17
1. No conf.	14	13	22	26	18
2	27	26	31	16	23
3	35	33	29	19	28
4	18	17	4	2	11
5. Total conf.	3	3	3	1	3
Total %	100	100	100	100	100
No of resp.	232	978	117	703	2,030

7.4.2 Net-risks: A Second Dimension of Cyber Trust

A separate dimension or category of trust-related issues concerns risks to which Internet users might be exposed, such as losing their privacy, buying the wrong products or not being able to secure personal information (Appendix 7.2).

Generally, Internet users had more confident expectations – that is, they were less concerned about risks. They were less likely to think that people who went online put their privacy at risk and were less likely to think it was difficult to assess product quality online. They were also less likely to think that the Internet allows people to get personal information about them. As in the case of Net-confidence, Internet users were significantly more trusting – less concerned over Net-risks – than were non-users. Past users were generally positioned between current and non-users in terms of their concern over risks on the Internet.

Respondents were read a number of comments 'that people make about buying products or services through the Internet'. They were shown a card which had on it a set of response categories, so that they could indicate how much they agreed or disagreed with each of the statements. The statements included threats to their personal privacy as well as risks involved in shopping online, such as being deceived about the quality of a product. Respondents tended to agree: (1) that people who go online put their privacy at risk; (2) that being online could enable others to get personal information about them; and (3) that it is difficult to judge the quality of a product online (Table 7.3).

Table 7.3 Agreement to statements about risks on the Internet (N = 2,030)

Question	Strongly disagree %	Disagree %	Neither %	Agree %	Strongly agree %	Don't know %
'Going online puts privacy at risk'	2	13	15	44	10	16
'Permits people to get information about you'	3	13	19	34	7	24
'It's difficult to assess product quality'	2	11	16	38	10	23

However, individuals vary in their perceptions of risks, depending on their experience with the Internet (Figure 7.4).

Figure 7.4 Net-risks (N = 2,029)

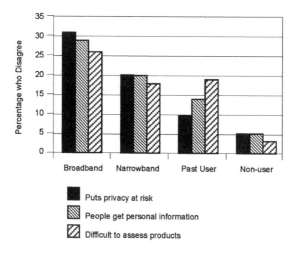

When read: 'People who go online put their privacy at risk', one-third (33 per cent) of users said they did not know, but non-users were also significantly less likely to disagree with this statement (Figure 7.4). Almost half of non-users (46 per cent) did not know if 'the Internet permits people to get personal information about you', but those non-users with an opinion were less likely to disagree with this statement. Likewise, nearly half (48 per cent) of non-users did not know if 'it's difficult to assess product quality online', while nearly half of those with an opinion said they agreed with this statement. Broadband users were most likely to disagree (Figure 7.4).

7.4.3 Diffuse Trust and Trust in the Internet

Some have argued that people who are more trusting in general, are more trusting about the Internet (Katz and Rice 2002). For example, in an essay on perceptions of risks from technical and environmental threats, Douglas and Wildavsky (1982) argue that there are individuals with general responses to risks, such as fatalism, that are shaped by the social and cultural setting in which they are located. A study drawing on US survey data found that individuals who are less trusting of people in general are more likely to perceive the Internet as threatening (Uslaner 2000).[13]

The OxIS research, however, indicates that Internet users in Britain are not more trusting in the Internet simply because they are more trusting of all institutions. First, Internet users are not significantly more confident in other media than are either non-users or past users. Confidence in the people running newspapers and television is the same for non-users and current Internet users (see Appendix 7.3). This reinforces the view that Internet users are not just more trusting in institutions generally, although broadband users were found by OxIS to be somewhat more trusting than non-users. For example, broadband users are slightly more confident in the reliability of information published in newspapers than are non-users and slightly more confident in the reliability of information broadcast on television as well (Figure 7.5), but these differences are quite minor and not statistically significant (Appendix 7.3).

Figure 7.5 Reliability of information (N = 2,029)

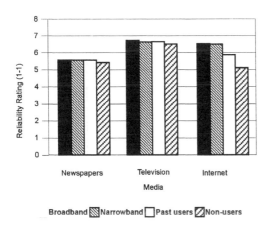

Broadband ▨ Narrowband □ Past users ▨ Non-users

Broadband and narrowband Internet users, however, are distinctive primarily in the reliability they assign to information on the Internet, which they rate almost as highly as they rate information on television, and more highly than they rate newspapers (Figure 7.5).

This potential of general attitudes shaping trust in the Internet was pursued in a variety of other analyses. Scales were created of trust in institutions, trust in the media, trust in other people and concerns over privacy. In each case, respondents who were more confident in institutions, the media and other people, and less concerned about privacy violations, tended to be more trustful of the Internet. However, these relationships did not account for the associations between use of the Internet and cyber trust.

7.5 FACTORS SHAPING CYBER TRUST

These patterns of relationships support the broad generalization that use of the Internet tends to engender cyber trust as they are associated with higher levels of Net-confidence and reduce the sense of Net-risk. It might be that use diminishes social distance and creates a higher level of certainty and confidence in the value of the Internet.

However, many factors are related to use of the Internet. For example, if better-educated individuals are more likely to use the Internet, and are more trusting, it could be that relationships between use and trust are spurious – explained by education. It is, therefore, important to control statistically for a range of variables that might explain levels of trust.

Table 7.4 provides the results of a regression analysis of factors related to Net-confidence. A large proportion of the variance in Net-confidence is not explained by any combination of these variables. However, the analysis suggests that gender, socio-economic status (SES)[14] and age are unrelated to Net-confidence, once use of the Internet is controlled. The most interesting background variable of relevance is education.[15] There is a statistically significant negative association between education and Net-confidence. That is, controlling for use of the Internet, better-educated people tend to be more sceptical of the information online, the people online and the institution of the Internet than are individuals with less schooling.

However, the stronger association is between use of broadband or narrowband Internet services and Net-confidence. Put simply, those exposed to the Internet gain more trust in the technology. Even past users – so-called Internet dropouts – have more confidence in the Internet than do non-users, who have no experience with the technology.

A similar pattern emerges with respect to perceived Net-risk, a scale combining perceptions that the Internet poses risks to privacy, the securing of personal information and to judging the quality of products online (Table 7.5). As in the case of Net-confidence, gender, socio-economic status and age variables are not significantly related to perceived risks, once other factors are controlled statistically.

Table 7.4 Regression coefficients on Net-confidence scale (N = 2,026)

Variable	B*	Std error*	Beta**	t	Sig.
Constant	-0.34	0.12		-2.78	0.01
Gender (F)	0.01	0.06	0.00	0.11	0.91
SES	-0.02	0.02	-0.03	1.20	0.23
Age	0.00	0.00	0.02	0.62	0.54
Education	-0.04	0.02	-0.05	-2.20	0.03
Broadband	0.71	0.08	0.23	8.87	0.00
Narrowband	0.71	0.06	0.36	12.78	0.00
Past user	0.39	0.10	0.09	4.02	0.00

*Unstandardized coefficients; **Standardized coefficients.*

Table 7.5 Multivariate regression coefficients on Net-risks scale (N = 2,026)

Variable	B*	Std. error*	Beta**	t	Sig.
Constant	0.24	0.13		1.90	0.06
Gender (F)	0.11	0.06	0.04	1.76	0.08
SES	-0.03	0.02	-0.04	-1.50	0.14
Age	0.00	0.00	0.01	0.44	0.66
Education	-0.04	0.02	-0.05	-1.91	0.06
Broadband	-0.53	0.08	-0.17	-6.35	0.00
Narrowband	-0.16	0.06	-0.08	-2.83	0.00
Past user	0.15	0.10	0.04	1.50	0.13

*Unstandardized coefficients; **Standardized coefficients*

Education has a non-significant association with trust, in the case of Net-risks, with better-educated individuals being somewhat less concerned about these risks. Proximity to the Internet – measured by the use of narrow or broadband Internet services – is inversely associated with perceived risks.

That is, those using the Internet tend to be less worried about the risks conventionally associated with Internet use. However, in this case, past users are more concerned about the risks than non-users. This relationship is not statistically significant, but it suggests that trust might be one factor that could explain why some users become Internet dropouts (Table 7.5).

7.5.1 Shaping Trust Among Users: Bad Experiences Online

There remains a great deal of unexplained variation in trust among those who use the Internet. Will bad experiences when using the Internet diminish trust, as suggested by the fact that dropouts tend to perceive greater risks?

Unwanted commercial email or spam is one of the most frequently cited problems tied to the use of email, and about half (47 per cent) of the email users in Britain say they receive 'too many' spam messages.[16] The longer a person uses the Internet, the more likely they are to have experienced one or more problems, such as with spam, a computer virus or fraudulent solicitations.

We asked users of the Internet to indicate whether they had problems with some of the negative Internet experiences that are frequently mentioned by others (Figure 7.6). Twenty-three per cent of British email users said they have received obscene or abusive email. Receiving a computer virus was cited by 18 per cent of users, and being contacted by someone from a foreign country suggesting an arrangement to make money, such as the infamous 'Nigerian fraud', was cited by 17 per cent of users (Figure 7.6). Another problem rated as highly, but still only mentioned by 16 per cent of users, was receiving mail 'not intended for you' (Figure 7.6). A worrisome, but relatively small, percentage of users indicated problems with excessive online bills, online purchases that were misrepresented, emails opened by someone else, or the theft of credit card details over the Internet. Less than 1 per cent of email users said that their credit card details were stolen by someone over the Internet. Just over half (54 per cent) of users did not experience any one of the problems listed in Figure 7.6.

Given news coverage about spam, obscene mail and viruses, for example, it is surprising that so many users do not have bad experiences with these. It is critical to remember that many use the Internet in a far more limited way than the heaviest users, such as those in academia and the computer industry. Survey research can correct some impressions driven by Internet commentators, who are among the heavy users. That said, those who use the Internet more might be a bell-wether for or early indicator of the problems likely to beset other users in due course. Therefore, these limited experiences with problems are not necessarily a reason for complacency. Furthermore, if experience with the Internet engenders trust, might it also be that bad experiences over time tend to erode that trust, creating a countervailing trust dynamic? Again, it is useful to look at the independent role of multiple factors that might explain differential levels of trust.

Figure 7.6 Bad experiences on the Net (N = 1,045)

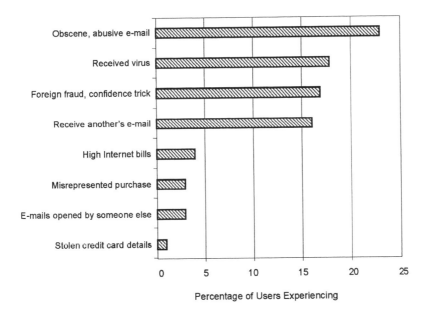

Percentage of Users Experiencing

7.5.2 Trust Among Users of the Internet

Does more experience with the Internet, for instance measured by years of experience and the range of uses, both of which relate to social proximity, help explain levels of trust? Is trust undermined by bad experiences online? Or is cyber trust anchored in more fundamental social determinants? For example, education and other social factors might lead to higher or lower levels of trust. In an attempt to sort out the independent role of a number of plausible factors, we conducted a multivariate statistical analysis.

For this analysis, broadband use was used as a dichotomous (yes or no) variable, capturing whether the respondent is currently using broadband Internet technology. The study included basic demographic variables, such as gender, age, socio-economic status and education. We also constructed a measure of involvement with, or proximity to, the Internet, which combines years of experience, a self-rating of expertise and the number of online activities, such as email, that a user engaged in for one hour or more per week. These three indicators were highly associated (see Appendix 7.2), supporting their use in a single scale. In addition, we created an index of 'bad Internet experiences', which is based on a simple count of the number of bad experiences, incorporating all of the items in Figure 7.6.

Table 7.6 shows the results of a multivariate regression analysis of Net-confidence on these variables for email users only. Just two variables have a statistically significant independent association with Net-confidence: education and bad experiences. Users with higher levels of education or schooling are likely to have somewhat less confidence in the Internet: they are more sceptical (Table 7.6), which is consistent with the findings across the entire sample (see Table 7.4). And those users who have had more bad experiences on the Internet are likely to be somewhat less confident (Table 7.6).

Proximity is not strongly associated with Net-confidence in a simple way (Table 7.6). There is a statistically significant negative association that suggests proximity tends to lower levels of Net-confidence, which makes those users more involved in the Internet more sceptical about it. This is in line with the concept of a certainty trough.

Table 7.6 Regression coefficients on Net-confidence for users (N = 1,045)

Variable	B*	Std error*	Beta**	t	Sig.
Constant	0.28	0.15		1.88	0.06
Gender (F)	-0.06	0.08	-0.02	-0.78	0.43
SES	0.01	0.03	0.01	0.28	0.78
Age	0.00	0.00	0.04	1.40	0.16
Education	-0.06	0.02	-0.09	-2.58	0.01
Broadband	0.03	0.07	0.01	0.39	0.69
Proximity	-0.20	0.10	-0.21	-2.11	0.04
SES* proximity	0.07	0.03	0.27	2.72	0.01
Bad Net experiences	-0.07	0.03	-0.08	-2.55	0.01

However, there is also a significant interaction between proximity to the Internet (more years of experience, a greater range of uses and more expertise) and socio-economic status (Table 7.6). For those in higher socio-economic groups, proximity to the Internet tends to diminish Net-confidence disproportionately. For those in lower socio-economic groups, proximity tends to increase confidence. Overall, it appears that proximity tends to undermine predispositions, whether positive or negative, and move all users closer to a learned level of confidence.

A different combination of factors is associated with Net-risk (Table 7.7). Those with a higher level of schooling are likely to be less concerned over Net-risk than those who use broadband Internet and have more proximity to the Internet.[17] This suggests that experience engenders trust. But there is a countervailing influence of bad experiences with the Internet, which tends to increase concern – Net-risk – as one would expect from other findings (Table 7.7).

Table 7.7 Regression coefficients on Net-risks scale for users (N = 1,045)

Variable	B*	Std error*	Beta**	t	Sig.
Constant	-0.09	0.17		-0.53	0.59
Gender (F)	0.07	0.09	0.02	0.84	0.40
SES	-0.02	0.03	-0.02	-0.50	0.61
Age	0.00	0.00	0.02	0.57	0.57
Education	-0.045	0.02	-0.07	-2.16	0.03
Broadband	-0.34	0.08	-0.13	-4.20	0.00
Proximity	-0.15	0.04	-0.13	-3.89	0.00
Bad experiences	0.16	0.03	0.18	5.57	0.00

*Unstandardized coefficients; **Standardized coefficients

7.5.3 Experience Technology or Certainty Trough

The concept of a certainty trough led to an exploration of proximity to the Internet as a factor shaping cyber trust. However, the findings are not entirely consistent with an explanation based on MacKenzie's notion of the certainty trough. First, those alienated from the technology, the Internet dropouts who have rejected the Internet, are more certain and more trusting than those with no experience with the Internet. This suggests that social proximity – experience – might be a more straightforward explanation of low certainty than alienation or a rejection of the technology. Secondly, we found no clear rise of uncertainty among the most experienced users, except as it might be connected with bad experiences online. This may be because we did not move to a high level of use, and look at actual producers – those closest to the technology.

Therefore, we developed a combined indicator of Internet non-users, consumers and producers to better represent MacKenzie's categories of those alienated (non-users and dropouts), users, and those directly involved, defined as those who have produced a web page (Figure 7.7).

It is useful to compare levels of confidence and risk across these categories of proximity. We compared the mean scores for 'Internet confidence' and 'Internet risk' across categories of non-users, users who have never produced their own website, and users who have created their own website. Figure 7.7 shows that website producers have slightly more confidence than Internet users, not less, which is a minor exception to the pattern expected by a certainty trough, but consistent with an experience technology. There is absolutely no evidence of a trough when it comes to concern about Internet risks. Instead, there is a monotonic decline in concern the more proximate the person is to the Internet, with the mean for producers significantly less concerned. Website producers are less concerned than Internet users, who are less concerned than non-users.

Figure 7.7 Trust by Internet non-users, consumers and producers (N = 2,029)

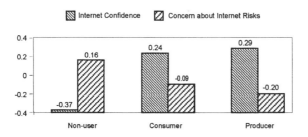

Thus, within the range of respondents surveyed, there is more evidence for the Internet as an experience technology – with proximity promoting more cyber trust – than as a curvilinear certainty trough. It might be that at the highest end of expert producers, such as in the case of computer scientists, there might be a diminishing level of trust or greater uncertainty. However, this is not the case in this more representative cross-sectional sample of Britain.

7.5.4 The Impact of Trust on Internet Use

Does trust matter in the subsequent use of the Internet? The analyses reported above found that Internet dropouts perceived somewhat greater risks in the use of the Internet, so distrust might help explain why some people stop using the Internet. The relationships found between use of the Internet generally, and levels of Net-confidence and Net-risk, are also likely to be in part two-directional. That is, use could engender trust, but trust could reinforce decisions to get online.

Therefore, there is some evidence to support the commonsense view that trust is an important factor in the future of the Internet. To explore this, Table 7.8 shows the degree to which trust is related to the use of the Internet for online shopping, one use of the Internet that has been associated with experience and trust (Lunn and Suman 2002). Respondents who use email were asked to indicate the approximate number of online purchases they made per month. Using this indicator as a dependent variable, Table 7.8 shows the results of a multivariate regression analysis, which sorts out the independent role of Net-confidence and Net trust in whether a person shops online.

Most variance in Table 7.8 is unexplained. However, in line with findings in the US, the strongest relationship is with proximity to the Internet (Lunn and Suman 2002). Those who have used the Internet for more years, who use it for more types of activities and have a higher level of expertise, are more likely to shop online. Those with more confidence in the reliability of information and people online (Net-confidence) are somewhat more likely to shop online, but this relationship is not statistically significant. However, perceived Net-risks are significantly and negatively associated with online shopping (Table 7.8). In short, it appears, as many suspect, that distrust of the Internet undermines e-commerce. Specifically, those who perceive greater risks on the Internet are less likely to shop online. In turn, perceptions of risks are associated with bad experiences online.

Table 7.8 Regression for online shopping among users (N = 1,045)[a]

Variable	B*	Std error*	Beta**	t	Sig.
Constant	-0.14	0.39		-0.37	0.71
Gender (F)	0.25	0.21	0.04	1.17	0.24
SES	0.13	0.08	0.06	1.75	0.08
Age	0.01	0.00	0.04	1.32	0.19
Education	0.10	0.06	0.06	1.76	0.08
Broadband	0.30	0.20	0.05	1.47	0.14
Proximity	0.42	0.08	0.16	4.87	0.00
Net-confidence	0.09	0.08	0.03	1.07	0.29
Net-risks	-0.25	0.07	-0.10	-3.38	0.00

[a] *Online shopping measured by number of purchases per month.*
* *Unstandardized coefficients; ** Standardized coefficients.*

Thus, two countervailing trends are shaping the future of e-commerce and, quite likely, other online services. As people get closer (more proximate) to the Internet – using it over more time, in more ways, and gaining expertise – they tend to gain, or learn, an educated level of cyber trust. However, with experience can come bad experiences – for example viruses, spam, obscene mail – which tend to increase one's sense of the risks entailed in the use of the Internet, and which undermine trust and confidence in use of the technology.

7.6 DISCUSSION AND FUTURE DIRECTIONS

A developing literature on trust and risk associated with ICTs is most often anchored in case studies and ethnographic approaches, which highlight the subtle, but no less real complexities of expert and public perceptions. Survey research can complement these studies in a variety of ways. First, surveys enable us to identify explanations that could evade case research, such as experience, which emerges from comparisons across many users at different stages of involvement. A number of more conventional explanations of public perceptions of risk, such as those tied to particular social groups, are not well supported by this study. Likewise, the certainty trough did not provide a valid interpretation of our findings, although it led us toward an alternative explanation, more consistent with our results. Secondly, survey data permit generalization to a wider population of the public. Nevertheless, there are limitations to surveys, particularly cross-sectional survey research, that arc important to recall.

7.6.1 Limitations of a Cross-Sectional Analysis

The OxIS study highlights issues concerning cyber trust for which more evidence and analysis is needed to gain a better understanding of the underlying social dynamics. Survey research is one of the few ways available to provide an indication of patterns and trends across a large population, like that of Great Britain. Also, by enabling multivariate statistical controls, survey data permit the exploration of underlying patterns that is impossible with small samples and qualitative observations. However, while they offer analytical advantages and provide a means to project to a larger population, surveys are weak in providing detailed contextual knowledge and in unravelling the full complexity of individual beliefs, motivations and actions. Therefore, these analyses could be complemented by more qualitative research.

The OxIS survey is also a snapshot at one point in time. Longitudinal surveys would enable stronger conclusions to be drawn about any causal relationships suggested by the associations identified in this chapter. For example, it is clearly important to follow changes in cyber trust over time, particularly given the degree to which trust appears to be anchored in experiences online. Will more users have more frequent negative experiences online, or will contemporary problems, such as with spam, diminish as they are taken more seriously and anticipated?

These limitations are mitigated to some degree by a degree of replication across surveys, some of which have relied on longitudinal data. For example, the findings from this survey analysis generally reinforce the findings of the major longitudinal study in the US (see Lunn and Shuman 2002). Other studies within the World Internet Project[18] hold out the potential for further replication across nations and over time.

7.6.2 General Patterns and Themes

7.6.2.1 Experience technology and the certainty trough
Most generally, experience with the Internet over time tends to shape trust, as indicated by perceptions of Net-risk and Net-confidence outlined earlier. As people use the Internet, they gain experience and skills and are more socially proximate – less distanced from – the technology. This tends to undermine distrust. However, those who are engaged in Internet use over more time and in more ways are likely to become more aware of the risks and more likely to be exposed to negative experiences, such as unwanted email, which can undermine trust.

This illuminates the view that the Internet can be called an 'experience' technology, as it is difficult for people to understand how the Internet and Web work until they use them. Non-users are among the more distrustful of the Internet. They have less confidence in information and people online, and in the institution of the Internet. They are also more concerned about the potential risks. Distant from the technology, they are most uncertain of its value.

Experience – use of the Internet – tends to shore up one's trust, boosting confidence in the Internet and undermining concerns over risks to privacy and security. In fact, the risks experienced in using the Internet are most often less than the risks imagined by non-users. As people use the Internet and gain expertise and capabilities and greater access to Internet resources, such as with the use of broadband, they are also likely to be less concerned over the risks of Internet use. That is not to say that they become naive or exhibit blind faith. Most people perceive risks attached to Internet use. However, people anticipate greater risks than they appear to encounter once they gain experience. Similarly, non-users often underestimate the benefits of the Internet, leading users to have more confidence than non-users. A number of patterns discovered in this analysis support this general theme.

However, it may also be difficult to appreciate the risks of Internet use until one suffers the effects of them. With use will come bad experiences online that undermine confidence in the technology and increase users' uncertainty over whether they can avoid the risks entailed.

In 2003, a significant, but surprisingly small, percentage of users had bad experiences on the Internet. This may account for the rather guarded but trusting attitude of most users. It might also suggest that it is timely, before problems with Internet use, such as with spam, become more widespread, to undertake initiatives to reduce the likelihood of more users experiencing greater difficulties.

A closely related pattern is the degree to which there is lower trust in the technology among categories of users, such as the less affluent, who have less access to the Internet. It is within these groups that real experience in using the Internet has a particularly disproportionate positive impact, increasing their trust in the Internet and lessening their preconceived concerns over risks.

These general findings fit key aspects of the certainty trough. Trust in the Internet shows some evidence of a curvilinear pattern, although our survey instruments lack the precision to trace that precisely. Non-users, distant from the technology, are the most distrustful. When people first become users, they gain trust and become more convinced of the Internet's value. Time and experience can temper this trust as they experience problems and become more sceptical. Over time, it may be that most users gain a more realistic view of the Internet, question the sources and credibility of information and are watchful in a bid to avoid the pitfalls of the Net.

Experience also provides a better interpretation than explanations anchored in categories of users, such as suggested by literature on risk cultures (Douglas and Wildavsky 1982). Proximity variables and levels of use, such as indicated by broadband use, were consistently significant in all the analyses while demographic variables – which might relate to cultural settings – were not. While social network and cultural settings might help account for differences in attitudes among non-users, such as across age groups, this does not help interpret findings across categories of users. The main influence on perceptions of trust in the Internet is experience with the technology.

7.6.2.2. Social issues of a 'trust tension'

The OxIS findings about the ways in which social distance and know-how relates to social inequities, suggest that cyber trust might reinforce the digital divide in the use of ICTs. People with the appropriate skills and resources to get online and to collate and interpret online information could enhance their ability to authenticate the value of products, services and information, thereby protecting themselves against cyber fraud and crime. However, others with less expertise remain offline, fail to experience the Internet and are more likely to distrust the technology.

The value to e-business and e-government of finding effective means of establishing identity and trustworthiness to overcome these fears has stimulated the development and application of many privacy-enhancing tools and services (Guerra et al. 2003), as well as interest in privacy regulations (for example OECD 2002) and cyber crime legislation. To the degree that these initiatives are effective in diminishing bad experiences online, they might help shore up levels of cyber trust.

However, these methods confront a tension between privacy concerns and the need to gather data to help confirm e-identities (Guerra et al. 2003). Finding an appropriate framework to address this 'trust tension', by balancing consumer protection with the free flow of traffic on e-networks, involves many interrelated uncertainties: economic, psychological, institutional, technical and legal. Unravelling and gaining a better understanding of these requires social and economic research with a broad perception of the co-evolutionary nature of human, organizational and technological systems.

7.6.3 Future Directions for Cross-Disciplinary Collaboration and Research

Many other significant social issues require investigation and clarification in developing effective policies towards cyber trust and crime prevention:

- *Learning global lessons from local contexts.* While acknowledging the importance of examining key influences on local contexts, policy makers also need advice on how to apply what works in one context or country to other situations. Such insights of global relevance often emerge by joining together and comparing analytically sophisticated and richly descriptive studies of local processes, which are then analysed using theoretically powerful concepts and frameworks that integrate the discussion of issues and policy. For instance, OxIS is associated with research underway in other nations involved in the World Internet Project. It will be important to explore the robustness of the findings reported here in other national settings.
- *Assessing the effectiveness of trust-enhancing products, services and regulations.* Survey research is unlikely to shed light on the impact of particular interventions, such as new, trust-enhancing products and services, unless it is targeted at the most sophisticated and experienced users. However, qualitative and experimental research could address the role of these new technologies.

In each of the above areas, assessments need to be made both of the relevance to e-networks of past research, and of the effectiveness of actual policies and techniques that have been applied in search of appropriate solutions to important social and economic challenges.

All technologies are inherently social, in that they are designed, produced, used and governed by people (for example Dutton 1999). This is particularly significant for complex technologies such as the Internet, the Web and the other ICTs that pervade most aspects of modern society. Understanding relevant social and institutional dimensions is therefore a key priority in addressing the way these technologies affect trust, crime and related issues.

APPENDIX 7.1 OxIS METHODOLOGY

The Two-Stage Sampling Design

The 2003 OxIS survey was based on a two-stage sampling design. In the first phase, a random sample of 175 paired enumeration districts (EDs), stratified by region, were selected. Within each selected ED, a random sample of ten addresses was selected from the Postal Address File. The selection of ED sample points was based on the following process:

1. Sampling points were allocated to each of the ten government regions in proportion to the population in each region. These regions (with proportion of sample achieved) were: North East (4 per cent), North West (11 per cent), Yorkshire and Humberside (10 per cent), East Midlands (5 per cent), West Midlands (8 per cent), Eastern (8 per cent), London (15 per cent), South East (12 per cent), South West (8 per cent), Wales (6 per cent) and Scotland (13 per cent).
2. In each government region all EDs were paired with an adjacent ED most similar in terms of its ACORN type.[19]
3. Within step 2 above, all paired EDs with a combined population of 60 or more people were listed in descending order of ACORN type, with the most affluent pair at the top of the list and the poorest pair at the bottom.
4. The populations of each set of paired EDs were accumulated down this list. Using a random start and fixed sampling interval the required number of paired EDs was selected. This gave each ED a probability of selection proportionate to its size.

In the second stage, interviewers within each selected ED were issued with ten randomly selected addresses from which they were expected to achieve a 60 per cent response rate. A further three addresses were issued to be used only if six interviews could not be achieved with the original ten addresses.

Out of a total of 3,500 addresses issued, 74 were in areas that interviewers felt unable to work in, such as very deprived inner-city areas with significant drugs problems. In all, 3,426 addresses were visited by ICM Research staff. The outcome of these visits is shown in Table A7.1-1.

Table A7.1-1 Outcomes of tracking addresses

Address occupied	90%	3,077
Property vacant/no longer a dwelling/new building not occupied	2%	80
Commercial property	1%	51
Interviewer unable to locate address	6%	200
Not stated	1%	18
Total	100%	3,426

In cases where the selected addresses proved to be vacant, demolished, or were commercial properties, interviewers were allowed to go to the closest inhabited dwelling. In all, out of 3,426 addresses visited by interviewers for the purpose of this research, 276 were substitute addresses used because the original address fell into one of these categories.

Selection of Respondent at Household Address

At each address, respondents for interview were selected by asking the person who answered the door if it would be possible to interview the person normally resident at that household (aged 14 or over) whose birthday was next in the household. A 'person normally resident' was defined as someone living in the household who was related to the person answering the door or living with someone in the household as a partner. In cases where the person answering the door did not know which household member had the next birthday, a respondent was selected according to the alphabetic position of the first letter of their first name. On the initial occasion this was encountered by the interviewer, the person with a starting letter nearest the beginning of the alphabet was selected; next time, a person with a first name starting with a letter nearest the end of the alphabet; and so on. In all, only 244 respondents were selected by the alphabet rule, rather than by birthday.

Outcomes of Interviews

The results of the contacts made at each address are shown in Table A7.1-2. The high response rate achieved in this survey was helped by respondents knowing that the research was being conducted for Oxford University and by the promise that the Red Cross would receive £1 for every successful interview. Reasons for the 674 refusals included: lack of interest or no wish to participate (63 per cent), too busy (22 per cent), ill or not feeling well (4 per cent), inadequate English (4 per cent) and absent or away for duration of fieldwork (1 per cent). 'Other reasons' accounted for 4 per cent. No clear reason was given for only 2 per cent.

Table A7.1-2. Interview outcomes at selected addresses

Addresses visited	100%	3,077
Productive interview obtained	66%	2,030
Refusal by person answering the door	18%	547
Refusal by selected respondent (incl. 4 interviews begun but terminated)	4%	126
Unable to contact after repeated visits to address during fieldwork period	11%	348
Not stated	1%	22

APPENDIX 7.2 INDICATORS AND INDEXES OF KEY CONCEPTS

Dimensions of Internet Trust

In order to move beyond a bivariate analysis to a more multivariate one, we attempted to reduce the number of indicators by collapsing items into more meaningful clusters of highly correlated indicators. Any single item or question includes considerable noise, such as errors due to respondents misunderstanding the question in idiosyncratic ways. By using several highly related items to form a scale or index, it is possible to reduce the level of noise in the underlying variable, as systematic covariance is identified in creating dimensions, and random noise is reduced.

Factor analysis, using varimax rotation, was used to identify these underlying factors. For this analysis, 'don't knows' and missing cases were given the median value on the scale. The analysis produced two clear dimensions with an eigenvalue of greater than one (Table A7.2-1).

Table A7.2-1 Dimensions of trust: factor analysis of component items

	Dimension	
Questionnaire Item:	Net-confidence	Net-risk
Reliability of information on the Internet	**0.76**	-0.08
Confidence in Internet	**0.84**	-0.04
Confidence in people you can communicate with on the Internet	**0.73**	-0.10
Puts privacy at risk	-0.06	**0.81**
Internet permits people to get personal information about me	-0.08	**0.77**
Difficult to assess product quality	-0.07	**0.67**

The factor analysis produces scores that locate each respondent on each of the dimensions. A high figure on dimensions 1 and 2 means that the respondent has high levels of trust. A high figure for dimensions 4 and 6 means that the respondent has high levels of concern about privacy.

Net-confidence

The first dimension loads heavily on confidence in the Internet, confidence in people you can communicate with on the Internet, and confidence in the reliability of information provided on the Internet. This defines the items we have called Net-confidence.

Net-risk

The second dimension is Net-risk as it loads heavily on whether the Internet endangers privacy, allows personal information to be obtained by someone else and causes concern that the respondent cannot ascertain product quality online.

Other Dimensions of Trust and Privacy Concerns

A number of other closely related indicators of trust emerged from the survey. They are defined by the factor analysis in Table A7.2-2 and include the following.

Institutional trust

The first dimension, called institutional trust, loads heavily on questions regarding confidence in companies, government, television news, scientists and doctors, and somewhat less on newspapers.

Media trust

The second dimension, called media trust, loads heavily on the reliability of information on television and in newspapers. It also loads on confidence in people running television and newspapers.

Social trust

Social trust, a third dimension, loads heavily on variables capturing 'confidence in people I know' and 'confidence in most people in this country'. It also loads somewhat on confidence in scientists, doctors and other people you can communicate with on the Internet.

Table A7.2-2 Factor analysis of general trust items: four dimensions

Item	1	2	3	4
Confidence in major companies	**0.64**			
Confidence in government	**0.61**			
Confidence in TV news	**0.58**	0.46		
Confidence in newspapers	0.44	**0.58**		
Confidence in scientists	**0.53**	0.40		
Confidence in doctors	**0.55**	0.47		
Reliability of information in newspapers		**0.84**		
Reliability of information on television		**0.77**		
Confidence in most people I know			0.75	
Confidence in most people in this country			0.70	
Concerned about threats to personal privacy				0.83
Information about me is being kept in a file				0.82
You should only trust what you verify yourself	0.40	-0.27	-0.26	
Eigenvalues	2.10	2.03	1.55	1.48

Privacy concerns

The fourth dimension loads heavily on concerns about privacy in Britain, and about whether information about the respondent is kept in a file somewhere. This 'privacy concern' dimension does not relate to the Internet specifically.

Social proximity: experience, time and expertise

Three variables were found to be highly correlated and, therefore, were used to create an indicator of social involvement with the Internet (Table A7.2-3). One is a measure of expertise, based on a self-rating of ability, which ranged from a low score of 5 for 'very bad' to a high score of 1 for 'excellent'. Another is a measure of the respondent's diversity of use, based on the number of activities on which they spend at least an hour a week, such as email. The third is an indicator of experience, based on the number of years that a person says they have used the Internet.

Table A7.2-3 Factor analysis of items composing social proximity scale

Item	Loading on factor
Self-rated ability	-0.78
No. of activities online	0.72
Experience	0.68

APPENDIX 7.3 NOTES ON STATISTICAL SIGNIFICANCE

Strategy for Initial Analyses and Tests

The initial analysis employs a bivariate approach to determine whether use of the Internet is associated with different attitudes towards the technology. We tested whether Internet users are more likely to have an opinion (versus responding 'don't know' to a question) on Internet-specific items. This test is carried out using a Pearson Chi-Squared test of significance, which determines whether the mean response (where the data are binary in nature) differs significantly across groups. We also tested whether, for those who gave a substantive response to the question, Internet users, on average, had a more or less trusting response than non-users. This test is carried out using an Independent Samples T-Test, which is used to ascertain whether the mean response (where the data are continuous in nature) to a question differs significantly across different groups. These analyses show that Internet users are more likely to give a substantive response indicating greater trust in the Internet than non-users.

For questions that are on similar topics, such as the reliability of information, but which do not pertain to the Internet, users' responses were very similar to non-users'. This shows that differences in levels of Internet trust between users and non-users are not part of a broader pattern of differences regarding trust, but are Internet-specific.

Detailed Findings

Confidence in the reliability of information on the Internet
Average evaluation of Internet information reliability on a scale of 1-10, where 10 indicates total confidence:

Broadband users	= 6.5
Narrowband users	= 6.5
Past users	= 5.9
Non-users	= 5.1

The differences were all significant at the .05 level between: broadband and past users, broadband and non-users, narrowband and past users, narrowband and non-users, and past users and non-users.

Percentage responding 'don't know'

Broadband users	= 4.3
Narrowband users	= 3.1

Past users   = 15.8
Non-users   = 36.3

The differences were significant at the .05 level for the likelihood of saying 'don't know' between broadband and past users, broadband and non-users, narrowband and past users, narrowband and non-users, and past and non-users.

Confidence in the Internet
Average confidence in the Internet on a scale of 1-5, where 5 indicates total confidence:
Broadband users   = 3.3
Narrowband users   = 3.2
Past users   = 3.1
Non-users   = 2.2

The differences in evaluation were significant at the .05 level between: broadband and narrowband users, broadband and past users, broadband and non-users, narrowband and non-users, and past and non-users.

Percentage Responding 'don't know'
Broadband users   = 2.6
Narrowband user   = 8.8
Past users   = 15.8
Non-users   = 36.0

The differences in likelihood of a 'don't know' response between all groups were significant at the 0.05 level.

Confidence in the people you can communicate with on the Internet
Average confidence in people you can communicate with on the Internet on a scale of 1-5, where 5 indicates total confidence:
Broadband users   = 2.7
Narrowband users   = 2.7
Past users   = 2.3
Non-users   = 2.0

The differences in evaluation were significant at the 0.05 level between: broadband and past users, broadband and non-users, narrowband and past users, and narrowband and non-users, and past and non-users.

Percentage responding 'don't know'
Broadband users   = 3.4
Narrowband users = 9.6
Past users   = 10.7
Non-users   = 37.8

The differences were significant at the 0.05 level for the likelihood of saying 'don't know' between: broadband and narrowband users, broadband and past users, broadband and non-users, narrowband and non-users, and past and non-users.

Putting privacy at risk on the Internet
Average agreement that going on the Internet puts privacy at risk on a scale of 1-5, where 5 indicates strong agreement:
Broadband users   = 3.1
Narrowband users = 3.4
Past users   = 3.7
Non-users   = 3.9

The differences in evaluation between all groups were significant at the 0.05 level.

Percentage responding 'don't know'
Broadband users   = 5.2
Narrowband users = 5.7
Past users   = 9.9
Non-users   = 34.2

The differences were significant at the 0.05 level for the likelihood of replying 'don't know' between: broadband and non-users, narrowband and non-users, and past and non-users.

Accessing personal information on the Internet with the individual's permission
Average agreement that going on the Internet permits people on a scale of 1-5, where 5 indicates strong agreement:
Broadband users   = 3.0
Narrowband users = 3.3
Past users   = 3.7
Non-users   = 3.8

The differences in evaluation were significant at the 0.05 level between:

broadband and narrowband users, broadband and past users, broadband and non-users, narrowband and past users, and narrowband and non-users.

Percentage responding 'don't know'
Broadband users   =   4.7
Narrowband users   = 10.6
Past users   = 22.5
Non-users   = 48.1

The differences in likelihood of replying 'don't know' between all groups were significant at the 0.05 level.

Difficulties in assessing product quality and descriptions when shopping online
Average agreement that it is difficult to assess product quality when shopping online on a scale of 1-5, where 5 indicates strong agreement:
Broadband users   = 3.2
Narrowband users   = 3.4
Past users   = 3.7
Non-users   = 4.0

The differences in evaluation between all groups were significant at the 0.05 level.

Percentage responding 'don't know'
Broadband users   =   6.0
Narrowband users   = 10.9
Past users   = 13.3
Non-users   = 48.1

The differences were significant at the 0.05 level for the likelihood of replying 'don't know' between: broadband and narrowband users, broadband and past users; broadband and non-users, narrowband and non-users, and past and non-users.

In the above items, which relate specifically to the Internet, there was a consistent pattern of broadband users being more confident in the Internet than narrowband users, who, in turn, were more confident than past users, who were more confident than non-users. There was also a consistent pattern in the way broadband users were more likely than narrowband users to give a substantive answer to the question (as opposed to 'don't know'). In turn, narrowband users were more likely to give a substantive response than past users, who were more likely to do so than non-users.

By contrast, on questions that do not relate to the Internet, Internet users and non-users show similar levels of trust, as Table 7.5 showed.

Confidence in the reliability of information in the newspapers
Average evaluation of newspaper information reliability on a scale of 1-10, where 10 indicates total confidence.

Broadband users   = 5.6
Narrowband users   = 5.6
Past users   = 5.7
Non-users   = 5.4

The differences in evaluation between all groups were not significant at the 0.05 level.

Percentage responding 'don't know'
Broadband users   = 2.2
Narrowband users   = 1.3
Past users   = 3.3
Non-users   = 2.1

The differences in likelihood of a 'don't know' response between all groups were not significant at the 0.05 level.

Confidence in the reliability of information on the television
Average evaluation of television information reliability on a scale of 1-10, where 10 indicates total confidence:

Broadband users   = 6.7
Narrowband users   = 6.6
Past users   = 6.6
Non-users   = 6.5

The differences in evaluation between all groups were not significant at the 0.05 level.

Percentage Responding 'Don't Know'
Broadband users   = 5.6
Narrowband users   = 2.3
Past users   = 5.8
Non-users   = 2.8

Broadband users were significantly more likely to reply 'don't know' to the above question than were narrowband users or non-users, and past users were significantly more likely to reply 'don't know' than were narrowband users. Although there are significant differences between the groups, they show a very different pattern of significance than the equivalent Internet-specific question, where non-users were most likely to reply 'don't know', past users the next likely, and so on.

NOTES

1   Earlier versions were presented at the Information, Communication, Society Symposium at the Oxford Internet Institute, Oxford, 17-20 September 2003, and the Society for Social Studies of Science (4S) Conference, Atlanta, Georgia, 15 October 2003. The authors thank Miles Yarrington, Robin Mansell, Richard Rose, Malcolm Peltu and several anonymous reviewers for their comments.
2   The concept of 'reconfiguring access' or 'shaping access' is developed in a synthesis of research on ICTs in Dutton (1999). A recent application of this concept to the context of broadband Internet is discussed in Dutton et al. (2003).
3   OxIS asked individuals: 'Do you yourself use the Internet at home, work, school, college or elsewhere or have you used the Internet anywhere in the past?' In response, 59 per cent said they currently use the Internet, 6 per cent said they had used it in the past, and 35 per cent said they have never used the Internet. A discussion of Internet adoption is provided by Rose (2003).
4   A growing literature is devoted to comparing the impact of alternative media on interpersonal communications. Early experiments comparing face-to-face with mediated communication failed to substantiate many conventional expectations about the superiority of face-to-face interpersonal communication (Short et al. 1976). The debate has continued since (see for example Rice 1984; Johansen 1988; Ben-Ner and Putterman 2002; Riegelsberger et al. 2003). Work is often focused on the social implications of computer-mediated communication (CMC), generating a huge body of research as well as journals dedicated to the topic, such as the *Journal of Computer Mediated Communication*. This literature conveys the contingency of any impacts, and counters overly simplistic views that Internet or other CMC is trusted less than face-to-face communication.
5   For example, early survey research on privacy attitudes tended to find that managers and professionals who simply use ICTs were less concerned about threats to privacy than those most informed about ICTs, such as computer experts, or those least well informed, such as the poor (Dutton and Meadow 1987).
6   A comprehensive overview of research on the factors related to the perception of risk generally is provided by Jackson et al., Chapter 8 in this volume. Also see Douglas and Wildavsky (1982).
7   Henri Grethen, Minister of the Economy of the Grand Duchy of Luxembourg, quoted in the preface to a 17-19 September 2003 Luxemburg conference on 'e-commerce trustmarks', see: www.e-trustmarks.lu (requires password).
8   Dutton is a co-principal investigator of the Oxford Internet Survey with Professor Richard Rose, director of OxIS at the Oxford Internet Institute. The sample design and field research were subcontracted to the London-based ICM Research (www.icmresearch.co.uk, accessed 17 April 2004), which provided valued input on question wording and survey design. The OII's work on it was supported by public and private sources, including sponsorship by the Broadcast Standards Commission and Freeserve.com. Sponsors of the Oxford Internet Surveys are provided a copy of the database at an early date. The OII retains full control over the design of the survey, sample, and the wording of all questions.
9   The OxIS questionnaire and additional information about the survey are available at http://www.oii.ox.ac.uk/research/?rq=oxis accessed 18 April 2004.
10 These two dimensions of trust were defined through a factor analysis of items judged most closely related to the study's broad conceptual definition of cyber trust (see Appendix 7.2).
11 These two dimensions of trust were defined through a factor analysis of items judged most

closely related to the broad conceptual definition (see Appendix 7.2).

12 This question is designed to conform to a traditional set of questions concerning trust in institutions. It is arguable, however, that there are no people who 'run' the Internet in the same way people run newspapers or the media. However, in pre-tests conducted prior to the study and in the survey interviews, this question did not surface confusion, and seemed to fit within the general scheme of institutional trust.

13 Respondents tended to agree that 'you can't be too careful in dealing with people'.

14 Socio-economic status was captured by the standard British social profile, which was coded 1-6, where 1 was assigned for the high socio-economic status, and 6 to those who rely on state income for support. Income was not used in the analysis as we had too many missing cases for this item. However, for those who answered the income question, we found a high correlation with our SES scale.

15 Education was coded 0 if the respondent had no qualification; 1 if they had a GCSE; 2 a vocational qualification; 3 an A-level; 4 a Bachelor's degree or equivalent; and 5 if they had higher than a Bachelor's degree.

16 Respondents who use email were asked: 'Which of the following most closely describes your attitude to receiving unsolicited email from people trying to sell you something, sometimes called spam?'

17 Given press attention to inappropriate content for children and to paedophiles attempting to meet children online, one might expect people living in households with children to be more concerned about risks or less confident in the Internet. We asked if there is anyone under 18 living in the person's household, and found this variable to be unrelated statistically within any of our models. Experience diminishes such concerns.

18 Recent World Internet Project reports include one by UCLA's Center for Communication Policy (CCP 2003). For information about WIP centres and reports, see http://www.worldinternetproject.net/published.html accessed 17 April 2004.

19 For a description of ACORN and other classifications of socio-economic status, see http://www.businessballs.com/demographicsclassifications.htm accessed 17 April 2004.

REFERENCES

Bacharach, M.O.L. and Gambetta, D. (2001), 'Trust in Signs', in K. Cook (ed.), *Trust in Society*, New York: Russell Sage Foundation, pp. 148-84.

Ben-Ner, A. and Putterman, L. (2002), 'Trust in the New Economy', *HRRI Working Paper 11-02*, Minneapolis/St. Paul MI: University of Minnesota, Industrial Relations Center.

CCP (2003), Center for Communication Policy, 'The UCLA Internet Report: Surveying the Digital Future: Year Three', Los Angeles, CA: UCLA Center for Communication Policy, http://ccp.ucla.edu/pdf/UCLA-Internet-Report-Year-Three.pdf accessed 17 Apr. 04.

Douglas, M. and Wildavsky, A. (1982), *Risk and Culture: An Essay on the Selection of Technical and Environmental Dangers*, Berkeley CA: University of California Press.

Dutton, W.H. (1999), *Society on the Line: Information Politics in the Digital Age*, Oxford and New York: Oxford University Press.

Dutton, W.H., Gillett, S.E., McKnight, L.W. and Peltu, M. (2003), 'Broadband Internet: The Power to Reconfigure Access', *OII Forum Discussion Paper No. 1*, Oxford: Oxford Internet Institute, University of

Oxford.

Dutton, W.H. and Meadow, R.G. (1987), 'A Tolerance for Surveillance: American Public Opinion Concerning Privacy and Civil Liberties', in K.B. Levitan (ed.), *Government Infostructures*, Westport CT: Greenwood Press, pp. 147-70.

Guerra, G.A., Zizzo, D.J., Dutton, W.H. and Peltu, M. (2003), 'Economics of Trust: Trust and the Information Economy', DSTI/ICCP/IE/REG(2002)2, OECD, Paris and OII Research Report No. 1, www.oii.ox.ac.uk accessed 17 Apr. 04.

Johansen, R. (1988), *Groupware*, New York: Free Press.

Katz, J., and Rice, R.E. (2002), *Social Consequences of Internet Use: Access, Involvement, and Interaction*, Cambridge MA: MIT Press.

Lohse, G.L., Bellman, S. and Johnston, E.J. (2000), 'Consumer Buying Behavior on the Internet: Findings from Panel Data', *Journal of Interactive Marketing* 14(1): 15-29.

Lunn, R.J. and Suman, M.W. (2002), 'Experience and Trust in Online Shopping', in B. Wellman and C. Haythornthwaite (eds), *The Internet in Everyday Life*, Oxford: Blackwell, pp. 549-77.

MacKenzie, D. (1999), 'The Certainty Trough', in W.H. Dutton (ed.), *Society on the Line*, Oxford and New York: Oxford University Press, pp. 43-6.

OECD (2002), *Guidelines on the Protection of Privacy and Transborder Flows of Personal Data*, Paris: OECD.

Rice, R. (1984), 'Mediated Group Communication' in R. Rice &Associates (eds), *The New Media: Communication, Research, and Technology*, Beverly Hills CA: Sage, pp. 129-54.

Riegelsberger, J., Sasse, M.A. and McCarthy, J.D. (2003), 'The Researcher's Dilemma: Evaluating Trust in Computer-Mediated Communication', *International Journal of Human–Computer Studies* 58(6): 759-81.

Rose, R. (2003), 'The Dynamics of Digital Choice', paper delivered at the Information, Communication, Society Symposium, Oxford Internet Institute, University of Oxford, 19 September.

Short, J., Williams, E. and Christie, B. (1976), *The Social Psychology of Telecommunications*, Chichester: John Wiley & Sons.

Urban, G.L. and Sultan, F. (2000), 'Placing Trust at the Center of your Internet Strategy', *Sloan Management Review* 42(1): 39-48.

Uslaner, E. (2000), 'Trust, Civic Engagement and the Internet', paper presented at the Joint Sessions of the European Consortium for Political Research, University of Grenoble, Switzerland, April.

Wallace, P. (2001), *The Psychology of the Internet*, Cambridge: Cambridge University Press.

8   Perceptions of risk in cyberspace

Jonathan Jackson, Nick Allum and George Gaskell

8.1 INTRODUCTION

This chapter reviews the social scientific literature on public perception of risk. We begin with a discussion of the concept of risk and its place in the social sciences. Then we outline psychological research on cognition and emotion and how laypersons appraise uncertainty. This highlights the different ways in which experts and the public often approach risk. After this discussion we turn to the issue of trust and risk perception – a concept particularly apposite for the consideration of cyber crime.

An important issue is the role of the social meaning of a given hazard, and how citizens approach, make sense of and respond to it. Group and cultural identities shape how individuals define risks – we review the pioneering cultural theory work of Mary Douglas and Aaron Wildavsky. But, more than this, people receive information about risks primarily from the mass media. Representations, imagery and symbols circulate in society, transmitted and transformed by multiple actors with a wide array of effects. We discuss the rich set of concepts contained in the Social Amplification of Risk Framework (SARF), along with the notion of stigma and how the media frame and anchor issues and events.

Overall, the literature suggests that the social meaning of a risk determines its salience – whether an individual focuses on one rather than another, and why – and how uncertainty is judged, interacting with cognitive and affective processes at an individual level. Concerns about risks also express underlying values and attitudes regarding blame, morality and the value placed on the outcome of an event.

We finish with some thoughts on cyber trust and crime prevention and, particularly, the applicability of key concepts to public confidence and perceptions of risk regarding information and communication technologies (ICTs) and cyber crime.

8.2 RISK: AN ISSUE FOR SOCIAL SCIENCE

Risk has become something of a buzzword for the social sciences in recent times. Ulrich Beck's (1992) *Risk Society* has received much attention, and this places notions of man-made risk in the foreground in an understanding of what Anthony Giddens (1991) referred to as 'high modernity'. In this view:

> To live in the universe of high modernity is to live in an environment of chance and risk, the inevitable concomitants of a system geared to the domination of nature and the reflexive making of history. Fate and destiny have no formal part to play in such a system ... (Beck 1992)

High modernity is characterized by the production and distribution of risks from an increasingly complex techno-scientific system. It is one where every citizen is exposed, to some degree, to technological dangers such as radioactivity, airborne and waterborne pollution, and hazards from mass transportation such as airline, automobile or train crashes. The nature of modern societies is such that risks multiply with the increasing 'complexification' of societal systems of production, consumption, governance and technological control.

Implicit also is the notion that more knowledge leads to more risk. Now, how can this be? As Douglas and Wildavsky (1982, p. 3) note: 'The advance of science increases human understanding of the natural world. By opening up new realms of knowledge, however, science simultaneously can increase the gap between what is known and what it is desirable to know'.

This hints at what underlies nearly all the social scientific interest in risk as a concept: whatever else risk may refer to outside technical definitions it is to some degree a social and psychological construct. A risk must be identified and appraised. Without human attention it is not a risk in the modern sense of the word. Risk is a measurement, an estimation of exposure, likelihood and extent of loss (Garland 2003). Attention and judgement create a risk in this sense; modern systems of risk assessment, that classify, select and respond, bring attention to bear on a danger and give the newly formed risk meaning and technical precision.

Just as science and technology open up new worlds of possibility, so science and technology reveal new risks. Many risks in late modern society conform to what Beck considers to be an ideal type (Beck 1992). Firstly, they are invisible and the consequences are likely to be irreversible. Secondly, risks are based on 'causal interpretations' meaning that, initially at least, they depend upon scientific knowledge claims that are, in principle, open and contested. They are thus particularly prone to construction and redefinition by the most important social actor groups – the mass media, the scientific and legal professions, and regulatory authorities – as well as by individuals. This phenomenon is amply visible in new media tags such as 'blame culture', used to describe the political wrangling and media interest that inevitably follow in the wake of what might formerly have been considered unavoidable accidents. *Daily Telegraph* columnist W.F. Deedes (2001), commenting on a recent spate of train crashes in Britain characterized this view succinctly enough:

> The blame culture has grown stronger since [the 1950s]. There is no such thing as an accident or mishap these days. Someone must have blundered, and so heads must roll ... . Our own inner philosophy has undergone a change. We find it harder to take in our stride the blows that life suddenly delivers. Science replacing religion has something to do with it. In our homes, in the air, on road and rail, we expect modern devices to afford us protection against life's hazards.

A risk by definition has consequences for humans and what humans value. As Douglas (1990, p. 10) says: 'risk is not only the probability of an event but also the probable magnitude of its outcome, and everything depends on the value that is set on the outcome. The evaluation is a political, aesthetic and moral matter'. Different individuals and different communities might judge a risk more or less seriously because they value the consequences differently – they value differentially what is being harmed and who is doing the harm. In this way, the identification of a threat or danger, and the appraisal of its possible consequences, is inherently moral. And this has wider consequences. The production of such knowledge creates a capacity to act according to principles, responsibility and accountabilities; more and more, risk carries connotations of accountability and blame (Douglas 1990, 1992).

Risk research within the social sciences, then, is 'alive and kicking'. Later we will discuss competing definitions and conceptions of risk. First, though, it will be useful to briefly outline the history of the usage of the word, its denotations and connotations up to the present.

8.3 ORIGINS OF 'RISK'

The word 'risk' derives from the early Italian word *risicare*, which means 'to dare'. It speaks to the idea of choices, decisions that may carry downsides, but are made in order to reap a possible gain. Bernstein (1996, p. 2) regards the connection between 'daring' behaviour and rational analysis as a central feature of modernity:

> The ability to define what may happen in the future and to choose among alternatives lies at the heart of contemporary societies ... the capacity to manage

risk, and with it the appetite to take risk and make forward-looking choices, are key elements of the energy that drives the economic system forward.

In his account of the origin of modern understandings of risk, Bernstein focuses on the development of probability theory. This he sees as the means by which social and individual decision-making has become more rational. He does not equate this with the idea that we as people are becoming more rational – rather, that 'our understanding of risk enables us to make decisions in a rational mode' (Bernstein 1996, p. 4).

By the middle of the eighteenth century, with probability theory developing, a flourishing insurance market had sprung up in London. In order to make money from insuring a vessel and its cargo, insurance underwriters needed a workable estimate of the probability that it would reach its destination intact. The realization that 'fate' and 'chance' were not entirely capricious was not lost on Leibniz, who wrote to Bernoulli that 'Nature has established patterns originating in the return of events, but only for the most part' (Bernstein 1996, p. 4). During the past 200 years, from Bernoulli's Law of Large Numbers to Bayes's theorem, Galton's regression to the mean and Markowitz's portfolio theory, this account of risk is synonymous with the development of techniques for rational decision making in the face of uncertain futures. As such, it is an account of the harnessing of 'upside' risk for economic and social gain.

A complementary story is told by Judith Green (1995). She traces 'the accident' as it has been constructed through history. Green defines accidents as misfortunes that satisfy two criteria. Firstly, the event must have been unmotivated (or at least seen as such). In other words, no person or agency willed the event to take place. Secondly, it must be unpredictable. If it were predictable and were also not intended, the accident would most likely have been prevented or the conditions for its existence would not come about.

So, while Bernstein characterizes risk chiefly as opportunity, Green looks at risk from the perspective of accidental losses. She traces a parallel story of risk that centres on historical discourses of accidents. The accident is not only a pivotal category of misfortune in contemporary times; it is also a blank slate on which various cultural concerns about uncertainty, responsibility and culpability are inscribed (Green 1995, p. 196).

Green follows Hacking's (1987) interpretation of the development of probability or 'chance'. Prior to 1650 in the West the accident, as we might understand the term today, simply did not exist. There was no room for chance in a universe governed by an omnipotent God. Indeed, its absence in the cosmologies of 'primitives' like those studied by Levy-Bruhl (Levy-Bruhl and Clare 1923) or Evans-Pritchard (1937) was seen as one of the defining points of difference between the 'primitive' and the 'modern' mind. For the primitive mind, every 'accidental' event is invested with ulterior meaning. Causes of misfortune are ascribed to angry gods, witchcraft or some such. Mere coincidence is not an admissible category.

After this time, Enlightenment thinking and its discourse of science transformed the notion of the accident. New ways of explaining the world, through deduction, evidence and, increasingly, statistical reasoning, meant that accidents came to mark the boundary of rational explanation. They represented, in some sense, a residual category of event, or, as Green (1995, p. 197) puts it, 'Rationality ... produced a space for accidental events at the margin of its explanatory reach'. By the end of the nineteenth century, the idea that some events like train crashes or being struck down by illness were inexplicable or, at least, random and unpredictably distributed, was a marker of modernity.

During the middle of the twentieth century, again there is a shift. Green suggests, again following Hacking (1987), that there was a probabilistic revolution in science and in the philosophy of science that filtered into other forms of discourse – business, government, legal. In this view, deterministic laws and ways of understanding the world are replaced by 'autonomous laws of chance' (Green 1995, p. 198). In this climate, discourses of risk management and containment flourish. Accidents become reconfigured as the outcome of complex sets of risk factors. The regulation of mass transport, energy and public health, for example, can all now be technically oriented around (among other things) the prevention of accidents. This is the point at which the accounts of Bernstein and Green converge. For Bernstein, profits and economic growth can be maximized through the use of quantitative models and probabilistic models. The same logic underpins the present state of risk management, where the 'accident' is coming to be seen as a failure of systems or individuals to take the necessary steps to prevent misfortune.

8.4 EMPIRICAL RESEARCH ON PUBLIC PERCEPTION OF RISK

Risk has thus become a fundamental aspect of modern life in the West. And, interestingly, if the analyses of Green and Bernstein hold, the present situation has almost led us back to Levy-Bruhl's primitive cosmology, superimposed on contemporary Western societies. In harnessing the power of probabilistic ways of viewing the world, we return to a state where all misfortunes have 'causes' where some person or agency is culpable. Add the factor of extensive media coverage of accidents, health scares, crime and the like, and one can clearly see why risk *qua* problem is a prominent political issue. This is reason enough for it also to be an issue for social scientists.

Having considered the concept of risk, we now begin the review of empirical and theoretical work on the public perception of risk. But before we do this, it is worth saying a few words about terms and definitions.

Research on risk is seen in economics, in political science, in psychology and in anthropology, among other social sciences. Many different definitions (implicit and explicit) have informed this work and Thompson and Dean (1996), to whom we will return, offer a useful framework in this regard. On the one hand, we have a probabilistic conception that broadly maps onto the scientific or quantitative approach. Risk comprises quantitative assessments of likelihood and consequence. Often research looks at how public perceptions differ from more technical estimates, which raises the unhelpful and evaluative notion of 'misperception'. On the other hand, there is a contextualist formulation of risk. This opens the door to a wide range of other questions that colour public understanding and response, including control, the cultural resonance of a risk and its consequences and aspects of trust and blame. All these may contribute to the definition and salience of a particular hazard.

Much of the work on risk refers to the 'perception of risk' by the public and by experts. The analogy of perception of an object (in this case an 'objective risk') is not always appropriate. However, in much of the literature, and especially in the early years, this phrase is used. For now, we note its inappropriateness, but for simplicity's sake risk perception will be used in the widest possible sense, to cover all possible connotations of 'risk'.

Let us turn to the literature review. The first port of call is psychological study into cognitive processes in judgements under uncertainty. As such, we begin with a narrower definition of risk as probability and consequence.

8.4.1 The Contribution of Cognitive Psychology

The following literature engages with uncertainty; it deals with how individuals approach probabilities of possible outcomes. Risk perception, thus conceived, is a matter of perception or judgement concerning an uncertain event – its likelihood and its consequences.

8.4.1.1 Heuristics and biases
The most complete summary of the approach of two influential psychologists, Tversky and Kahneman, is contained in the collection of articles reprinted in book form in 1982 (Kahneman et al. 1982). The main contention is that people do not follow the principles of probability theory when judging the likelihood of uncertain events. They rather employ heuristics or rules of thumb. Often these heuristics lead to fairly good estimates of the probability of an event. Often, though, they do not.

The procedure followed by Tversky and Kahneman is to use very simple examples where the statistical properties of the distribution are well known – for example tosses of a coin, the distribution of people's heights within the population – and compare subjects' estimations with those made according to the principles of probability theory. The heuristics and biases observed under these conditions are also thought to apply to the way people estimate the probability of events that cannot be statistically estimated. The most significant of these empirically observed heuristics and biases are now summarized.

8.4.1.2 Representativeness

People tend to evaluate the chance of X as originating from Y to the extent that X resembles Y. This tendency appears to act as a means by which probabilities are evaluated to the extent that other relevant information is overlooked. In one study (Kahneman et al. 1982) subjects were asked which of two sequences of births of girls and boys in a family is more likely – BBBGGG or GBBGBG. Subjects viewed the former as significantly less likely than the latter. The suggestion is that the latter sequence appears to be more representative of randomness, and this is why people judge it as the more likely sequence even though both are, in fact, equally likely. People have also been shown to ignore so-called 'base-rate information'. In one experiment subjects were asked to judge the likelihood that several individuals were lawyers or engineers, given a brief description of their personality. One group was told that the individuals whom they were asked to assess had been sampled from a pool of 70 lawyers and 30 engineers; for the other group the proportions were reversed. This information had little or no effect on the way subjects made judgements. The only substantial criterion employed appeared to be the extent to which the descriptions of the individuals resembled the stereotypes associated with lawyers and engineers. Even when given a neutral description that bore no relation to characteristics that might distinguish the two professions, people in both experiment groups judged it equally likely that the individual was an engineer or lawyer, ignoring the prior probabilities of 0.7 and 0.3 arising from the stated distributions of the sample population.

8.4.1.3 Availability

The size of a class tends to be judged by the ease with which instances of it can be retrieved from memory. This means that those events that are easily retrieved, that are vivid instances, are judged more numerous or more likely than those that are more difficult to retrieve. For example, an experiment was carried out in which lists of well-known personalities were read out. In some lists the male personalities were relatively more famous than the women; in others, the women were more famous. There were equal numbers of men and women in all lists. Subjects asked to judge whether there were more men or women in each list incorrectly judged that there were a greater number of the sex that included the more famous personalities (Kahneman et al. 1982). A similar phenomenon is observed when people try to imagine hypothetical risks. Where a particular danger is easy to imagine, perhaps because it has been discussed in the press in great detail, its probability of occurrence tends to be judged as higher than one that cannot be conceptualized so easily.

8.4.1.4 Prospect Theory

Kahneman and Tversky's (1979) 'Prospect Theory' elaborated a general framework for understanding why people's actual behaviour, in relation to risky decision making, departs from the predictions of rational choice theory. Prospect Theory includes both a probability weighting function and a weighting function for utilities. The probability function captures the findings on systematic biases of estimates of fatalities. We tend to over-estimate (weight) low-probability events and under estimate those with a high probability, essentially a regression to the mean effect. Although the availability or vividness bias is one possible explanation, in Prospect Theory it is proposed that over-weighting of low-probability events occurs regardless. That something is conceivable appears to be sufficient to give it a reality beyond its objective probability. The value function is defined in terms of gains and losses from a reference point or adaptation level. For gains, the function is concave and, while the same holds for losses, in this context the slope of the curve is much steeper. In other words, the utility weighting leads to an asymmetry between 'objectively' equivalent gains and losses. The pain from a small loss from one's current position will far outweigh the pleasure from an equivalent small gain.

8.4.2 The Psychometric Paradigm

During the period when Kahneman and Tversky's research programme was developing, Chauncey Starr (1969) published what became a seminal paper in the history of risk research, setting the terms of reference for what became known as the psychometric approach to the study of risk perception (Slovic et al. 1979). Early work by the Decision Research Group at the University of Oregon in 1978 showed that people's ideas of what is meant by risk and, consequently, what could be described as 'acceptable risk', were complex and multifaceted. The simple expedient of measuring risk magnitudes in terms of the number of fatalities per year was shown to be inadequate (Royal Society for the Prevention of Accidents 1992; Slovic 1987) as it failed to capture the way people – both experts and the lay public – actually understood the term. It was, during the late 1970s (and still is), possible to argue, as Kahneman and Tversky had originally done, that lay perceptions of risk are subject to biases akin to making systematic errors in estimating knowable probability distributions. However, the most important result of the psychometric programme of risk perception research has been 'to demonstrate that the public's viewpoint must be considered not as error but as an essential datum' (Royal Society for the Prevention of Accidents 1992, p. 91). There now follows a review of the important findings of this research, its methods and its scope.

The psychometric approach to risk perception research is an individual-based approach. It is a research paradigm that aims to elicit judgements about risks from individuals who are confronted by risk stimuli. In fact it is more appropriate to refer to these stimuli as hazard stimuli because one of the main objectives of risk perception research using this approach is to measure not only the quantitative judgements of persons about risks – for example how likely is the risk to lead to an undesirable outcome – but also the qualitative dimensions of what is subjectively understood by the term 'risk' in relation to one or more hazards.

In an empirical review, Rohrmann (1999) sees the psychometric approach as having four principal intentions:

- to establish 'risk' as a subjective concept, not an objective entity;
- to include technical and physical, and social and psychological aspects in risk criteria;
- to accept opinions of 'the public' (that is, laypeople, not experts) as the matter of interest; and,
- to analyse the cognitive structure of risk judgements, usually employing multivariate statistical procedures such as factor analysis, multidimensional scaling or multiple regression.

Hazards that have been rated vary according to the focus of the study. As already mentioned, the classic, and rather general, investigation of Slovic et al. (1980) presented respondents with 90 hazards. As can be seen from Figure 8.1, hazards included large-scale technologies whose risks might be perceived at the societal, environmental and personal level, such as nuclear power (this was a very 'hot topic' at the time when psychometric risk research was becoming established), fossil-fuelled electric power and space exploration. Transport hazards included motor vehicles, railways, jumbo jets and recreational boating.

As well as technological hazards, risks associated with personal behaviours were included, for example downhill skiing, smoking and sunbathing. Antisocial activities such as crime and terrorism were rated, as were various drugs and foodstuffs. Many of these hazards or risk sources have been used in later studies (for example Bastide et al. 1989; Brun 1992; Sjoberg 1996).

Figure 8.1 Qualitative dimensions of risk perception

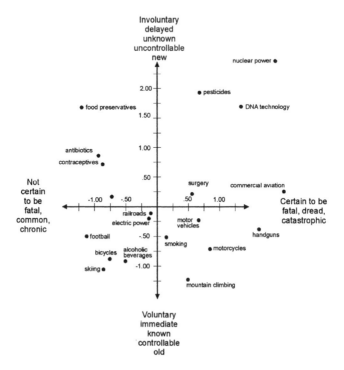

Source: Adapted from Slovic et al. (1980).

The figure depicts the range of hazards rated across different risk characteristics, shown at the base. Each hazard is mapped onto the space demarcated by the two factors that are derived from the collection of risk characteristics that were rated using factor analysis (a statistical technique that identifies underlying dimensions of data). What this diagrammatic representation clearly shows is that different types of risks are judged according to quite a complex set of qualitative dimensions. Clearly, the concept of risk means more to people than an estimate of its probability of occurrence. Starr (1969) had already noted that whether exposure to a risk is voluntary or involuntary is related to its acceptability. Here it can be seen that a much wider range of risk qualities is significant. The two factors shown have been labelled as 'dread' risk and 'unknown' risk by Slovic et al.

A third, 'exposure to risk', is not shown.

'Dread' risk is characterized by the perception of uncontrollability and the idea that the danger might be of a global catastrophic nature, fatal, a high risk to future generations, an involuntary risk and one that is perceived as affecting the perceiver. Also significant for this factor is whether or not the risk is seen as increasing, not easily reduced and inequitable. Hazards that score highly on this factor are, among others, nerve gas, nuclear weapons and terrorism; those at the other end of the scale include home appliances, sunbathing and cosmetics. The second factor, 'unknown' risk, is composed of qualities such as observability, whether a risk is known to those exposed to it or to science and whether the effect of a hazard is delayed or immediate. DNA research and space exploration are high on this factor, while handguns and fire fighting are low. The characteristics used to rate risks here have subsequently been widely used in psychometric risk studies. A number of these risk characteristics relate to whether the threat is to the individual or to many people simultaneously. This distinction is explicitly utilized in some studies where hazards are rated according to the risks they pose for the respondent personally, for people in general and for society as a whole.

From the large number of empirical studies carried out using this paradigmatic approach, some relatively common results emerge. The factor structure shown in Figure 8.1 shows two dimensions – 'dread' and 'unknown' risk. This correlational structure is found in many studies, although there are exceptions (Brun 1992; Johnson and Tversky 1984). Ratings about the magnitude of risks are systematically related to this structure. Higher ratings of risk magnitudes are associated with the top right quadrant of Figure 8.1.

It is possible to see that one or both of two superordinate classes of hazards are involved in most psychometric studies. One is the class of hazards involving personal or societal exposure to dangers to health and well-being, and to financial and physical assets. The other concerns environmental dangers that do not necessarily physically threaten people directly but threaten the state of the environment, possibly with consequences for future generations (Rohrmann 1999). In general, what constitutes an acceptable level of risk is higher for natural than for technologically induced risks. Personal, private risk-taking activities, such as driving or smoking, which are undertaken voluntarily and are more familiar, are still seen as less risky and more acceptable. Risks that are seen to have catastrophic potential, that are thought to impact unfairly on certain people and are unfamiliar to the public and scientists, all tend to be rated as 'riskier', more probable and more serious than others. People typically overestimate the dangerousness of air or rail travel and underestimate the dangerousness of cigarette smoking relative to the actual fatalities reported year on year.

8.4.3 Emotion and Risk Perception

The psychometric paradigm raises the issue of 'dread' – an affective appraisal of a risk. But these accounts lack theoretical underpinning. Analysis of the role of emotion in risk perception, which has received a good deal of attention recently, should therefore be welcomed.

The starting point of this work is the distinction between two modes of information processing. On the one hand is a formal, logical and numerical style of reasoning; on the other, a type of thinking that Epstein (1994, p. 710) calls 'intuitive, automatic, natural, non-verbal, narrative, and experiential'. For Slovic et al. (2004), this second system, which they term 'experiential', is affect-laden rather than formally logical like the 'analytic system'. It involves more rapid processing and the encoding of reality in images and metaphors rather than abstract symbols and numbers. And as Sloman (1996) suggests in an influential article, such associative processing probably operates by using more rapid pathways based on context and similarity rather than the conscious use of logic and evidence.

It is also important to note that psychological research has shown there to be much interplay between emotion and cognition. As Damasio (1994) demonstrates, good decision making often requires affect to direct reason and to provide basic motivation; a loss of emotional capability in patients who have suffered brain damage can reduce judgemental efficiency and accuracy. Affective reactions help us navigate a complex world, pointing out things we should quickly focus on in order to speed up action (Zajonc 1980; Bargh 1984). Emotions can also create and shape beliefs, amplifying or altering them and making them resistant to change (Frijda et al. 2000). They may provide information and guide attention, just as beliefs backed up by emotion direct attention towards belief-relevant information (Clore and Gasper 2000).

Paul Slovic has termed the role of emotion in risk perception the 'affect heuristic' (for example Slovic et al. 2002). A stimulus can evoke images that have affective and cognitive dimensions. When a representation becomes tagged with affect, giving it a good or bad quality, the overall affective impression can be more influential than more cognitive assessments. Furthermore, the affect heuristic, or short cut, may shape numeric assessments of risk and benefit. Readily available images of genetically modified (GM) food that are tagged with 'badness' for example, are more likely to increase judgements of riskiness and decrease the perceived level of benefit (Finucane et al. 2000). Similarly, a more immediate sense of danger shapes attention and increases likely threat assessment (Armony et al. 1997).

Strong emotions may have a greater impact. Borkovec (1994, p. 29) argues that long-term worrying can inhibit emotional processing and maintain 'anxious meanings', or negative thoughts and images. Worriers can be preoccupied with negative information and future unpleasant outcomes, be hyper-vigilant in scanning for salient material relating to threat (Mathews 1990), see ambiguous events as threatening (Butler and Mathews 1983, 1987; Russell and Davey 1993) and overestimate risk (Butler and Mathews 1983, 1987; MacLeod et al. 1991; Vasey and Borkovec 1993).

So, feelings about a risk object seem to infuse more formal and numeric appraisals. But the two systems can also diverge. Affective reactions may also be shaped by different things and may arise without cognitive mediation (Loewenstein et al. 2001) (see Figure 8.2). According to this model, cognitive evaluations tend to be composed of assessments of likelihood and cost, but emotional reactions also constitute factors such as the vividness with which consequences can be imagined, mood and prior experience with the event. Emotions can then directly influence judgement or behaviour. Furthermore, when cognition and affect diverge there is a tendency for feelings to hold sway; our evolutionary make-up strongly influences fear responses and threat appraisal.

Figure 8.2 Risk as feeling model

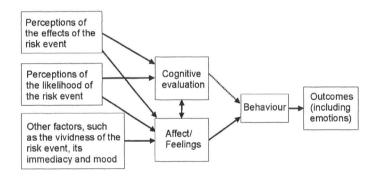

Source: Adapted from Loewenstein et al. (2001).

8.4.4 Competing Conceptions of Risk: Contrasting Expert and Lay Representations

In the following we consider the competing conceptions of risk that are found in the literature.

8.4.4.1 Debates about 'objective' and 'subjective' risk

So far we have considered research on risk as appraisal of an object or a potential event. Including subjective likelihood estimates, and consequences, familiarity and control, these appraisals have affective and cognitive components that can interact and diverge. Research has thus shown the complex and multifaceted ways the public gauge a risk event. As Slovic (1987) argues, risk means different things to lay people than it does to scientists: familiarity attenuates perceived risk; dread amplifies it.

Public opinion has often been contrasted with expert assessments of risk, with rather unproductive outcomes in many cases. In the area of crime, for example, survey data since the 1980s show that significant proportions of the UK population feel unsafe walking alone in their area after dark – more than have actually experienced crime (or a proportion higher than the average number of people who do fall victim in a given year). Indeed, women and the elderly feel least safe, on average. Yet at the same time, young males are most at risk of personal crime. During the 1980s these findings gave rise to what became known as the 'risk–fear paradox'.

This precipitated a response from the government of the day (for more details, see Jackson 2004). The early 1980s saw the Home Office deprecate the public concerns to which these survey findings attested, reflecting the orthodoxy that public fears were misplaced and exaggerated. It was: 'a serious problem which needs to be tackled separately from the incidence of crime itself' (Hough and Mayhew 1983, p. 26). The authors continued that 'excessive anxiety about crime not only impoverishes people's lives, but also makes it difficult to secure rational discussion of criminal policy' (pp. 33-4). If fear of crime exceeded reality then re-education and public involvement in community safety would become a serious and important objective. To downplay public concern could also be to downplay embarrassing levels of concern by a government proud of its 'Law and Order' image; it may be politically expedient to partly displace the problem of crime onto the fear of crime. But the deprecation was also partly a function of frustration that uninformed public opinion might deleteriously affect more reasoned Home Office policy, coupled with a sense that crime was not as serious a problem as public opinion might have it.

This dynamic has been evident in many high-profile debates. The philosopher Paul Thompson addresses the mismatch of perceptions between public and experts. He claims that at the root of this is serious dispute and confusion over 'competing conceptions of risk' (Thompson and Dean 1996, p. 1). The precondition for this type of dispute is, paradoxically, that when experts analyse risk, they appeal to what they assume are differences in interpretation that:

take the form of principled and reasoned disputes as opposed to simple misunderstandings. The claim that there are competing conceptions of risk implies that the concept of risk is like contested concepts such as 'causality', 'reality', 'justice' and 'truth', in that competing interpretations reflect philosophical differences that are long-standing and systematically linked. Such differences will not be settled merely by stipulating definitions for the disputed terms.

These differences, moreover, are highly relevant for understanding political disputes about risk in the public sphere. They are also significant for understanding how the communication of risk information can either clarify or confuse matters. The way risk is defined in the public sphere and within scholarship constitutes two related problems and, in response to this state of affairs, Thompson offers a framework for clarifying the risk concept.

8.4.4.2 The probabilist–contextualist dimension
At one end of this dimension, Thompson and Dean (1996) write, is the probabilist view of risk. From this standpoint, risk is purely a matter of the probability of an event or its consequences. The hazard that gives rise to the possibility of this event is real, independent of our perception of it. Any particular risk will be laden with other characteristics; for example GM food may engender fears about infection and illness, nuclear power risks may invite horror of environmental catastrophe. However, just as the colour of an eye plays no part in deciding whether something is or is not an eye, these 'accidental' attributes of a risk do not provide criteria in themselves for deciding whether something is, or is not, a risk.

From a purely contextualist perspective, at the opposite extreme of the dimension, risk has no single determining criterion. A risk will always be associated with a number of characteristics such as whether it is voluntarily undertaken, whether it is familiar or unfamiliar or whether it involves societal or personal danger. Probability, in this view, is simply one among other risk attributes, none of which is singularly a necessary condition for something to be classified as a risk. According to Thompson and Dean (1996, p. 1), the distinction between these poles is most apparent in informal discussion. When a probabilist talks of the 'risk of an earthquake' occurring, he or she really speaks of the probability of the event occurring. By contrast, a contextualist would speak of the risk of an earthquake according to the particular danger relevant from a given perspective. For example, the risk would be different for someone who had no choice but to live in the hazardous area compared to the risk as seen by a geologist who chose to move to the area in order to study it. The implication of the strong contextualist position is that probability estimation may be irrelevant to determining the existence of a risk, much less for understanding it or communicating related information to others.

The practical result of these competing conceptions of risk is that misunderstandings and disputes occur that are difficult to resolve. Within a more contextualist understanding of risk, it is apparent that people who raise questions about particular risks, for instance of violent crime or antisocial behaviours, may be using risk language to articulate all kinds of legitimate claims dependent on the context in which these claims are made (Thompson and Dean 1996). For the probabilist, such claims will likely as not make little sense because probability is the single essential component of any discussion about risk: that is, how probable is it that one will become a victim of such crime? Furthermore, it is generally experts that incline towards the probabilist pole. The communication of quantified probability estimates as input to public deliberations on such risks may sometimes, as a result, be simply irrelevant.

Thompson (1999) suggests that the language of risk has been adopted by scientists doing risk assessment and is, in general, functionally equivalent to the language of probability. The practical use for such language is in the field of decision making. Risk analysis utilizes mathematical and scientific techniques to arrive at the best estimate of the likely costs and benefits of any course of action. This process is highly deliberative, in the sense that people are engaged explicitly in evaluating and weighing the options.

But much human behaviour and cognition is not deliberative. It is habitual, even unconscious, that any particular course of action is being adopted. Risk in lay or everyday usage, Thompson argues, 'functions as a cognitive gatekeeper between the deliberative and the non-deliberative dimensions of practice ... in this respect, the concept of risk functions as a category for organizing or prioritizing the expenditure of deliberative resources' (Thompson 1999, p. 499). In this account, in the practice of risk assessment, once something is categorized as being a risk the deliberative process of determining probabilities and weighing costs and benefits begins. Where risk or risk language enters lay discourse, it can be dysfunctional in the sense that once something is categorized as risky, the layperson no longer acts as if there is zero or negligible risk, but often has neither the resources nor the information to arrive at a more 'rational' judgement.

8.4.5 Trust and Risk Perception

So far we have reviewed studies into cognitive and affective appraisals of uncertainty. The mismatch between public and expert perceptions has been discussed. We go on to explore how public perceptions often encompass wider social attitudes and values. But first we argue that how the public see experts and regulators might also be relevant to how risks are variously interpreted.

Work on risk perception has focused increasingly on the role of trust. In part this is due to the relative failure of risk communication strategies in relation to technological risks, most notably civil nuclear power, based on 20 years of research in the field (Cvetkovich and Lofstedt 1999). It is also a consequence of the gradual widening over time of the scope of explanations of perceptions of risk in the literature. Alongside the rather specialized academic field of risk perception research, the concept of trust has found its way into political and academic agendas in some more general contexts. For instance, Putnam's (2000) work on declining trust and social capital in the US and in Italy has been influential inside and outside academic circles. Putnam's thesis mainly concerns declining interpersonal trust, while trust in institutions is the prime focus of research on trust and technological risk. Public anxieties in the UK about GM food, bovine spongiform encephalopathy (BSE), rail safety, mobile phone transmitter masts and a host of other risks could be explained not so much by the particular characteristics of the hazards themselves, but by a lack of trust or confidence in those responsible (Poortinga and Pidgeon 2003). In some cases, it appears the relevant authorities have lost their very legitimacy in addition to being simply distrusted.

Empirical research on the role of trust in risk perception has been on the increase since the early 1990s. An early article by William Freudenburg (1993) looked at the effect of trust on the concerns of local citizens about the proposed siting of a nuclear waste facility in Nevada. Freudenburg additionally coined the term 'recreancy' as a specific form of mistrust relevant in cases of potential risk within complex technological systems. The concept of recreancy is intended to capture the idea that people in positions of responsibility with respect to potentially hazardous situations can sometimes fail to 'carry out their responsibilities with the degree of vigour necessary to merit the societal trust they enjoy' (Freudenberg 1993, p. 909). The idea is not necessarily that individual actors are incompetent, self-interested or villainous, but that the complex division of labour that characterizes modern systems of technological control makes disastrous outcomes possible even where no individual can be held fully culpable.

Slovic (1993) investigated the asymmetrical effects of trust-building and trust-destroying information. He notes that although the risks associated with medicines and X-rays are real, people tend typically not to have concerns about them because doctors and the medical professions are generally trusted. In the case of government and industry officials managing such industrial technologies as pesticides and nuclear power, there is little trust. Risks are concomitantly a greater source of concern (Slovic 1993, p. 676). Using questionnaire experiments, Slovic shows that the effect of negative information on 'trust destruction' is much greater than positive information on 'trust building'. The conclusion is that trust is difficult to earn, but easy to lose.

The empirical research points to trust as an important variable in relation to risk perception. Trust relates to beliefs and expectations that some possibly remote institution or actor will act in a particular way in a particular context. Luhmann has suggested that, from a functionalist perspective, social trust enables societies to tolerate increasing uncertainty due to progressive technological 'complexification'. Thus he states that trust 'reduces social complexity by going beyond available information and generalizing expectations of behaviour in that it replaces information with an internally guaranteed security' (Luhmann 1979, p. 93). Although Luhmann is writing about social systems, the idea that trust reduces the need for information can be just as relevant at a social psychological level too. By trusting someone else to make decisions on the basis of relevant information in situations of potential risk, one reduces one's own cognitive load.

Bernard Barber shares Luhmann's perspective on trust concerning its function – the reduction of complexity – but distinguishes between three types of expectation that comprise social trust. In his framework, trust as a general concept has more than one dimension. The first is value compatibility. The second is the expectation that actors or institutions will perform their role in a technically competent manner. The third is that actors or institutions will demonstrate 'fiduciary responsibility' (Barber 1983, p. 14). That is to say they are expected to act with special concern for others' interests above their own. In relation to risk perception, a lack of trust that leads people to see risks as greater could be based on expectations about risk managers' competencies or their fiduciary responsibility. It remains an empirical matter as to the relationship between these three attributes, both as public perceptions and in reality.

Another conception of trust has been proposed and tested empirically in a number of studies. Earle and Cvetkovitch (1995) share the general assumption of Luhmann and Barber that the function of trust is to reduce complexity. However, they point out that in Barber's conception of trust, people actually require rather a lot of information about actors and institutions in order to decide whether or not to grant trust. So, while the function of such trust may be a reduction of cognitive complexity, the basis on which it would be granted would itself require considerable cognitive effort. Earle and Cvetkovitch claim that social trust is based on what they call salient value similarity (SVS). This is a groundless trust, needing no justification. Rather than deducing trustworthiness from direct evidence, people infer it from value-bearing narratives. These could be information shortcuts, available images, schema and the like. Essentially, people trust institutions that tell stories expressing salient values that are similar to their own. Salient values consist of 'the individual's sense of what are the important goals (ends) and/or processes (means) that should be followed in a particular situation' (Siegrist et al. 2000, p. 355). This yields a general basis for trust only to the extent that situations are perceived as being similar. Hence, one might think that equal sharing is a salient value in relationships with family members, but that competitiveness is important in business situations. Similarity of values between trustor and trustee is inferred from the trustee's words, actions and perceived cultural and social group membership.

The key point is that trust is conferred not on the basis of a detailed appraisal of the likely competence and fiduciary responsibility of the actor, but on the perception of shared salient values. Interestingly, the SVS theory of trust is consistent with affective understandings of risk, as discussed earlier in this chapter. The perception of shared values and affective, emotionally tagged representations and associations both rely more for their transmission on cues and shortcuts than on in-depth cognitive processing.

8.4.6 Cultural Theory

Recall Thompson and Dean's (1996) assertion that the public use risk to articulate a range of connecting attitudes and values. Conceivably, risk might also express a lack of confidence and trust in the organizations supposedly regulating a risk, protecting certain groups from harm. This general idea was pioneered by the anthropologist Mary Douglas, and colleagues.

Mary Douglas offers an explanation for why different social groups have different attitudes towards technological and natural dangers. In earlier work, Douglas claims that the content of beliefs about purity, danger and taboo in any given culture are essentially arbitrary. Within a particular culture these arbitrary beliefs become fixed and henceforth serve to organize and reinforce social relations according to hierarchies of power. In her book *Purity and Danger* (Douglas 1966), she advances the idea that different cultures denote certain activities as taboo not because of objective harm that may arise from carrying out these activities, but as a way of maintaining and reinforcing the moral, political, religious or social order that binds members of that culture. She cites the example of the ancient Israelites who, on the command of Leviticus, prohibited the consumption of pork. Pork was not, in fact, dangerous to eat, but its prohibition served as means of reinforcing and maintaining a monotheistic society against the polytheistic nomadic culture that surrounded it (Douglas 1966; Rayner 1992). Douglas and Wildavsky (1982) cite the example of the Hima of Africa who think that it is risky for women to come into contact with cattle. This belief functions to maintain a set of hierarchical relations in that culture regarding the role of women, rather than reflecting any objective risks. In Western societies the picture is necessarily more complex but, according to Douglas and Wildavsky, the same principles apply. An individual's beliefs about what constitutes an important risk are, in part, indicative of their place in society.

Others, such as Rayner (1992), have argued that this phenomenon is true not only at the societal level, but can also be observed within smaller organizations such as firms, political parties and non-governmental organizations. The implication of this for the social study of risk is rather important because it shifts the emphasis away from individual differences or biases in perception of objective risks towards more fundamental types of inter-group cleavages. In the cultural theory view, people's conception of what constitutes danger or a risk varies according to the way their social relations are organized. People select risks as being important or trivial because in so doing they reinforce the established social relations within the culture in which they are located. Douglas and Wildavsky proposed four prototypical cultural types within modern industrialized societies. These are located along two dimensions that describe, firstly, the degree of social incorporation constituted within the culture and, secondly, the nature of these social interactions. This analytic framework is known as grid/group, where grid is defined as a measure of the constraining classifications that bear upon members of any social grouping, and group as the degree of social interaction and the extent to which people rely on social networks (Rayner 1992). The four cultural biases or stereotypes are summarized in Figure 8.3.

Figure 8.3 Cultural theory's four stereotypes

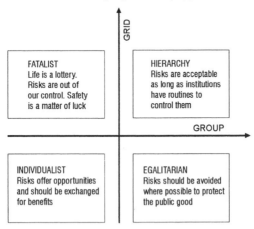

Source: Adapted from Douglas and Wildavsky (1982).

At high grid and high group, the modal form of organization is hierarchical, where all individuals are strongly reliant on others, but where movement between levels of authority is strongly constrained. In terms of risk perception, the key concern is for control and management. Rules and procedures are favoured responses to risk. For the egalitarian, there is an emphasis on strong cooperative relations and equality. The response to risk is highly precautionary, concerned to minimize possible harms by avoidance of risky activities rather than control and management

At low grid and group, the individualist sees risks as opportunities for gain. Market mechanisms are favoured, rather than bureaucratic regulation. Potential losses can be mitigated by insurance. Finally, the fatalist perspective is that of the atomized individual. Risks are seen as inevitable and whether or not one can avoid harm is simply a matter of luck.

Most of the empirical work that has been carried out using cultural theory has followed the example of Karl Dake who developed a set of questionnaire items designed to tap the four cultural biases (Brenot et al. 1998; Dake 1991, 1992; Langford et al. 2000; Marris et al. 1998; Sjoberg 1996). These have been used in many studies as independent variables, or as a way of classifying people into one of cultural theory's stereotypes. In most of these studies, people's scores on the scales designed to measure the four cultural biases tend to correlate weakly with perception of risks of various hazards. In general, environmental hazards are seen by egalitarians as more serious and more likely to cause damage.

Crime-related risks are seen as greater by hierarchists. Unfortunately, individualists and hierarchists are often empirically barely distinguishable, which calls into question the classificatory value of the theory. In fact, classification is never really achieved in these investigations, as most people exhibit some degree of concordance with all the beliefs expressed in the four scales.

So while it is clear that the values expressed in the cultural theory-inspired scales do tap into attitudes or values related to perception of technological and other risks, it is not clear what are the advantages or, indeed, the veracity of the four-way classificatory system proposed. There is a certain circularity of argument. For instance, egalitarians might perceive GM crops as more risky than individualists because they see nature as fragile (Adams 1995). But if one's worldview is that nature is fragile, it is almost tautologous to say that cultural theory predicts that such people will perceive more risk in tampering with nature. The prediction is at least partially entailed by the premise. In quantitative operationalizations it is difficult to avoid some semantic overlap between concepts. For an excellent review of these conceptual and methodological difficulties, see Boholm (1996).

8.4.7 Constructing and Communicating Risk: Social Amplification, Stigma and the Mass Media

It seems trivial to say that people get their information about risk and risk events from somewhere – most likely from the mass media, interpersonal interaction and through personal experience.

However, it is important to take account of the transmission mechanisms through which representations, beliefs and attitudes about societal risks are propagated in different social and cultural contexts. Social meaning infuses appraisals of a perceived threat or an uncertain event, and places risk objects within a cultural context. And as Douglas reminds us, group and cultural identities shape what people value and so permeate what they see as threatening.

8.4.7.1 The social amplification of risk framework
The collection of (loosely related) concepts best placed to encompass such cultural significance, and how information and images circulate through society, can be found in the SARF. This was proposed in the late 1980s (Kasperson et al. 1988) partly to integrate aspects of the psychometric and cultural theory paradigms, and work is continuing. For Pidgeon et al. (2003, p. 2):

> [it] aims to examine broadly, and in social and historical context, how risk and risk events interact with psychology, social, institutional, and cultural processes in ways that amplify and attenuate risk perceptions and concerns, and thereby shape risk behavior, influence institutional processes, and affect risk consequences.

In the most recent formulations (Kasperson et al. 2003; Rosa 2003), the starting point is this. Risks have ontological status; they are events that occur that have consequences for humans and for what humans value. But they are uncertain – they must be appraised. It is our attention and scrutiny that bring them into focus, with attempts to identify and measure risks being necessarily imperfect, even with the most precise analytical tools at hand. They thus have, in Rosa's words, 'epistemological lability' (Rosa 2003, p. 50). Moreover, what the public and experts decide to concern themselves with is shaped by social and political factors. And, of course, in the public sphere, risks would be irrelevant unless they were communicated.

Heated debates between experts and laypersons are inevitable perhaps, given the uncertainty surrounding a risk, and varying judgements about what is at stake, with outcomes that are themselves uncertain. Debates between paradigms in the risk field are essentially debates about knowledge claims. But rather than propounding a relativistic stance, the assumption is what Rosa (2003, p. 62) calls a 'hierarchical epistemology', where some claims to knowledge are valued more highly than others, but none offers direct access to reality.

Kasperson et al. (2003, p. 15) describe SARF thus, and it is difficult to improve on their summary:

> as a key part of [the] communication process, risk, risk events, and the characteristics of both become portrayed through various risk signals (images, signs, and symbols), which in turn interact with a wide range of psychological, social, institutional, or cultural processes in ways that intensify or attenuate perceptions of risk and its manageability ... . The experience of risk therefore is not only an experience of physical harm but the result of processes by which groups and individuals learn to acquire or create interpretations of risk. These interpretations provide rules of how to select, order, and explain signals emanating from the physical world (Renn, Burns, Kasperson et al. 1993, p. 140). With this framework, risk experience can be properly assessed only through the interaction among the physical harms attached to a risk event and the social and cultural processes that shape interpretations of that event, secondary and tertiary consequences that emerge, and the actions taken by managers and publics.

Figure 8.4 replicates the SARF from Kasperson et al. (2003, p. 14). The goal then is to understand why some hazards and events come to be of social and political relevance, even while experts judge them to be relatively unimportant (risk amplification). Conversely, why do other events (to experts, more serious) induce comparatively low levels of concern and activity (risk attenuation)?

But this should make one pause. For what indeed is being amplified or attenuated? Rayner (1988) argues that the framework implies there is a baseline of objective risk portrayed by experts, which then gets distorted in the public sphere. And Petts et al. (2001, p. 2) argue that:

> in policy circles, social amplification is often alluded to in traditional technocentric language – i.e. it is seen as giving credence to the perceived irrationality of lay public responses to risk issues, providing a means of explaining behaviour and identifying what communication is required, as opposed to a means of understanding the reasons for responses and perceptions.

But Kasperson et al. (2003, p. 37) reply that there is no such intention. Rather, they emphasize that all perspectives on risk entail some degree of judgement and approximation:

> the observation that experts and public sometimes disagree about risks is compatible with the claim that different groups may filter and attach salience to different aspects of a risk or a risk event. Amplification and attenuation, then, refer to the processes of signal interpretation, transformation, intensification, and dampening as the dynamics of risk consideration proceed iteratively in society.

Figure 8.4 The social amplification of risk framework

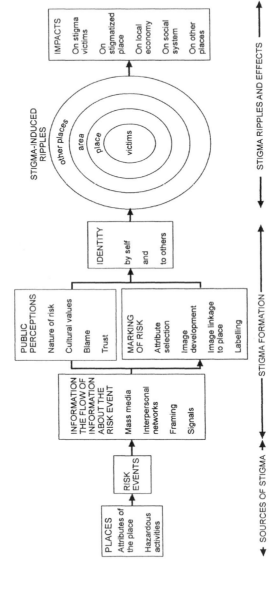

Source: *Adapted from Kasperson et al. (2003).*

Perhaps the greatest strength of the SARF is its attention to processes of communication, and we will return to this issue. The framework states that risk signals are received, interpreted and passed on at a series of 'amplifier' stations and diffused through different channels. While the media are primary amplifiers, stations can also include individuals, groups and organizations, such as activist groups of government agencies, driven by their interests and functions. The results are signals that are increased or decreased in intensity and transformed in their cultural content.

The framework distinguishes between social and individual stations. The first consists of opinion leaders, cultural and social groups, government agencies, voluntary organizations and news media. While these groups consist of individuals, the institutional structure and function will direct how risks are dealt with. At the second class of individual and station, the social processing of risk will be more affected by risk heuristics, qualitative aspects of risk documented by the psychometric paradigm, and attitudes, values and beliefs specific to cultural affiliations that are non-organizational. Here the set of behaviours that responds to perceived risk might include a whole host of secondary and tertiary ripple effects, including public outrage, demands for regulatory action, stigmatization and economic consequences.

8.4.7.2 Technological stigma

In the preface to their edited volume, Flynn et al. (2001, p. xi) state that: 'technological stigmatization is a powerful component of public opposition to many technologies, products, and facilities and an increasingly significant factor in the acceptance of scientific and technological innovations'. For these scholars then, stigma is about public concerns about human health and ecological risk that have been amplified by the mass media. In this way, laypersons come to have knowledge about a risk. But they also come to see certain places, products and technologies as hazardous or unduly dangerous. Stigma is something:

> that is to be shunned or avoided not just because it is dangerous but because it overturns or destroys a positive condition; what was or should be something good is now marked as blemished or tainted ... . A critical aspect of stigma is that a standard of what is right and natural has been violated or overturned because of the abnormal nature of the precipitating event (crude oil on pristine beaches and the destruction of valued wildlife) or the discrediting nature of the consequences (innocent people are injured or killed). As a result, management of the hazard is brought into question with concerns about competence, conflicts of interest or a failure to apply proper values and precautions. (Gregory et al. 1995, p. 220; reprinted in Gregory et al. 2001, pp. 3-4)

The impetus for stigmatization is often some signal event, where 'negative imagery and negative emotional reactions become closely linked with the mere thought of the product, place, or technology, motivating avoidance behavior' (Gregory et al. 2001, p. 3). Stigmatized things tend to share features. They have 'dreaded' consequences and involuntary exposure (which, in general, tend to contribute to high perceptions of risk). They have impacts that are inequitably distributed across groups or geographical areas. And they have impacts that are unbounded (magnitude or persistence over time is not known).

The process of marking refers to how the label of 'deviant' on a person, place or technology can have devastating effects. This mark need not be physical, of course – symbolically designating devalued status can arouse strong feelings in observers and interpreters and also become linked to attribution and responsibility. The imagery and label can become embedded and intrinsic to that person, place or technology – and, indeed, autonomous from the event that generated it. As such, it helps form a narrative, condensing and typifying the story around the event.

8.4.7.3 Representations of risk and the mass media: framing and anchoring

Murdock et al. (2003), but see also Petts et al. (2001), develop the account of the mass media's role in risk communication. To mix metaphors slightly, they remind us that the media are not a single black box and that messages are not magic bullets. Rather, a plural set of media can amplify or attenuate risks if they resonate with public feelings and mood – if the symbols and representations deployed capture existing public concerns and frames of reference. Furthermore, many consumers are sophisticated readers of multiple media messages. They understand hype and drama. Laypersons try to make sense of things by 'integrating the media's diverse and divergent arguments and anchors with their own interpretive grids underpinned by direct and local knowledge, experience and formal education' (Petts et al. 2001, p. 94).

The mass media are important agenda setters and providers of information though, especially when the public has little direct experience of an issue. A key concept here is framing. Issues are more likely to receive media attention if they can be easily integrated into a narrative that motivates interlinked processes: (1) connecting; (2) contextualizing; and (3) anchoring. In the first, links are made between new events and already familiar instances and narratives, providing a readily available frame within which to understand novel phenomena. In the second, links are made to more abstract, but still resonant, contemporary issues; in the third, the imagery and connotations of an event are placed within popular anxieties and fears.

In this type of account, symbols are important in shaping and reproducing the social meanings attached to risks. One interpretive account of lay perceptions can be found in Horlick-Jones et al. (2003). They are interested in the thick descriptions (Geertz 1973) that communicate, for them, so much of the meaning and interpretation present in how people make sense of risk. Qualitative methodologies elicit stories involving symbols and images, which are situated accounts of the risk. For example, a risk issue might stimulate a set of concerns and debates quite apart from a narrowly conceived idea of the risk object itself. This is because the issue might involve a set of 'symbolic tangles' (Horlick-Jones et al. 2003, p. 284).

Wiedemann et al. (2003) adopt a similar approach, but this time stressing the narrative structure. They argue that experts see risks as chains of cause and effect and are interested in the nature of the hazard, the dose needed to induce harm, the exposure to that dosage and the extent of the potential damage caused. By contrast, laypersons see risks 'primarily in a social and relationship-oriented context ... based on common patterns for interpreting events, which are heavily influenced by the media, such as scandal stories, investigative exposés, tragedies, and disaster reports' (Wiedemann et al. 2003, p. 289). At the heart of such narratives is a range of regularities, they argue. These include: the designation of heroes and villains to actors; the assignation of intentions and motives; dramatizing the conflict by filling out a logic to its build-up; drawing out a moral of the study, particularly around the consequences; and bringing in other instances that strengthen and clarify the 'moral of the story'.

Using the notion of risk signatures, Petts et al. (2001) show how patterns of talk and structures of accounts are at the heart of lay interpretations of a risk. These draw upon both the interpretive work of individuals and the information and imagery received from the mass media and direct experience. Risk signatures can be more or less grounded in everyday experience, and the more they are grounded, the more they are seen as a personal and credible threat. But they also see trust to be a key underpinning of a particular risk signature. Not only does a lack of trust raise issues of vested interests – for example that companies or industries are only chasing things that profit them and their interests; a lack of trust also creates discord between the values and interpretive practices of the public (what a risk means and symbolizes for them) and the information they receive from the mass media, government and industry.

8.5 RISK, CYBER TRUST AND CRIME PREVENTION RESEARCH

In this final section, we suggest some implications of the risk perception literature for crime and, particularly, for the less researched area of public perception of cyber crime.

8.5.1 Risk and the Individual

8.5.1.1 Judgemental biases: crime and risk perception
Available research on judgemental biases and risk perception suggests several fruitful possibilities for future research into cyber crime.
Judgements based on availability. A well-publicized, dramatic instance of crime or cyber crime may engender vivid images that are easy to retrieve in the public mind. This would then elevate estimates of the probability of that event occurring. Mass media reporting of just one particularly dramatic and resonant episode might have extensive consequences for public assessments of threat. For example, a case involving paedophilia and chat rooms might instil the sense that such incidents are widespread. Policy makers must be sensitive to such possibilities, understanding why the effects can be so wide-ranging, and stress the unusual nature of episodes if this be the case.
Judgements based on representativeness. Because of the importance of individual events, people are less persuaded by expert assessments of probability or likelihood. The individual experience of various forms of cyber crime, as well as stereotyping of perpetrators, contexts and places, will have a greater impact on people's perception of cyber crime than any expert reassurance that, on average, people are very safe. And it may be noted that it is thus very difficult to change public perceptions.
Judgements of gains and losses. Prospect Theory shows that losses and gains are asymmetric. The pain from a loss is far more than the satisfaction from an equivalent amount of gain. The imagined instance of falling victim, of losing property or experiencing psychological or physical pain, is weighted as extremely serious. For cyber crime, there are benefits to using information and communication technologies (ICTs). However, perceived losses will affect the overall evaluation more keenly than perceived benefits. This may influence the extent of people's trust in cyberspace supported by a wide variety of digital technologies and applications.

8.5.1.2 The 'qualities' of the risk of crime
There seem to be individual differences regarding feelings of control over the risk of criminal victimization. Some people may be more familiar with particular environments, feel more able to avoid dangerous situations and be more physically suited to conflict. They may feel that the risks are voluntary, in the sense that they can avoid certain areas and situations. Others may have a more emotional sense of risk, having felt anxious or worried in the past. These differences may impact on where certain crimes appear on the factor space of the psychometric paradigm and, thus, shape how individuals define particular risks. The notion of outrage has been barely explored, yet seems a promising line of enquiry. Crime is most often a deliberate act to deprive

someone of something – individuals are thus directly to blame and the act is intentional. This raises issues of blame – the 'how dare they' factor – and responsibility, which may raise the salience of a particular risk.

In the case of ICT and cyber crime, many intensive users of ICTs might have a sense of familiarity, of control and clear benefits. Such competence might act as a hurdle, inoculating against a sense of risk. For these people, ICT is a familiar technology: it has been absorbed into everyday life. But there may also be a sense of complacency that criminals may take advantage of. Other ICT users might be less familiar, less confident and have lower trust in the system. They may be more open to a set of negative connotations, images and representations of the technology.

Cyberspace is disembodied – a space in which we come to 'know' unknown people and make judgements about their motives and intentions. Once one opens up the sense of risk, there are many uncertainties and limitless aspects and these need to become the subject of research which, in turn, would inform strategies of crime prevention.

8.5.1.3 Emotion and risk perception
A number of studies have examined emotion and risk perception in the context of the fear of crime, using some of same ideas contained within the psychometric paradigm. While these studies have not considered cyber crime, the results are likely to be transferable. It is worth summarizing the key points in order to highlight which ideas might transfer.

Worry about crime is shaped by the perceived likelihood of victimization, the perceived consequences of victimization and feelings of control over its possibility (Jackson 2003). Perceived control shapes subjective probabilities of crime. Someone who feels in control worries less because they perceive the chances of victimization to be lower. Moreover, being familiar with one's environment – feeling able to spot potential signs of trouble, in essence being able to 'read the environment' – shapes perceived self-efficacy.

Similarly, judging the consequences to be serious also increases the perceived likelihood of the event, because such a judgement is likely to include emotional, vivid and easily accessible representations of the event and its aftermath. Indeed, encounters with disorderly aspects of the social and physical environment also seem to increase the vividness of the image of oneself becoming a victim of personal crime, which then raises the perceived probability of victimization (Jackson in press).

High levels of anxiety can lead individuals to attend to threat-related stimuli in the environment, increase the tendency to regard ambiguous stimuli as threatening and retrieve threat-related information from memory more readily. The implication is that an anxious person walking through a particular area after dark is more likely to scan for certain threat-related information based on cues defined by an existing set of cognitive representations. They are also more likely to interpret such symbols as indicating a threat of victimization. Thus, emotional and cognitive appraisals might themselves be critical to the upkeep of a sense of threat that directs attention and interpretation of relevant stimuli.

These observations may apply in the case of cyberspace and suggest the need for research on people's attentiveness to threat-related stimuli in these environments. Firstly, worry and anxiety are shaped by issues of control, consequences and perceived likelihood. Among other things, this raises the issue of how feelings of control arise. Experience and the ease of system use are likely to be at the heart of this with regard to ICTs. Secondly, once an individual is worried or anxious, the emotion colours their perceptions and interpretations. Not only do they see things as more threatening, but emotion can also amplify estimates of likelihood and the severity of perceived consequences, as well as attenuating a sense of self-efficacy.

8.5.2 Risk and Society

8.5.2.1 The expressive function of risk
Research into public perceptions of crime has begun to explore how fear and anxiety express a range of social, moral and political attitudes related to the issue of crime and articulate underlying values regarding society and law and order (Girling et al. 2000; Jackson in press; Farrall et al. in press). What has been called expressive fear serves to articulate more generalized, broader attitudes and values. Crime acts as a lightning rod, a metaphor for social changes and problems that are specific both to the local community and to wider society.

Attitudes toward crime thus constitute and express a range of complex and subtle lay understandings of the social world. These include broader social values and attitudes about the nature and make-up of society and community, the value placed on crime in its symbol of deterioration, and all the implications that flow from both its prevalence and its impact, including social cohesion and stability, a predatory, uncaring and fractured society.

These issues need investigation in the context of concerns about cyber crime. For example, the perceptions of the risk of the Internet with regard to sexual offences may serve to express a range of underpinning values and attitudes about the vulnerability of children, the lack of protection and what these dangers say about the society – the 'symbolic tangles' of Horlick-Jones et al. (2003, p. 284). The cultural resonance or significance of a particular risk raises its salience – the expression of concern about that risk then articulates values that underpin interpretations of cultural significance. Relevant research might use qualitative methodologies in order to produce stories that are situated accounts of the risk, a set of concerns and debates quite apart from a narrowly conceived idea of the risk object itself.

8.5.2.2 Trust and crime

Trust is a means for alleviating risks. But on what bases are we prepared to trust others? There are many cues and preconditions that indicate that we can trust the other. For example familiarity, the person having the appropriate credentials, competence, dress and manner of speaking and the existence of sanctions for misdemeanours. Theorists of trust, such as Barber or Earle and Cvetkovitch, capture the basic expectations that underlie trust – value similarity or compatibility, competence, and public or fiduciary responsibility. In other words, does an organization or system accord with our values? Are those running it competent to enact their roles in the system, and in their actions are they motivated to take the public interest into account?

In terms of trust, the cyber user confronts a system independent of the provider of a particular service. Hence, trust is predicated on the establishment of preconditions regarding the technology and the other – the service provider. System trust is a prerequisite, for without this even the most trustworthy service provider cannot offer basic protection. Many contingencies of the system may act to obstruct trust building – hearing about hackers, experience of viruses and worms and so on. And even if the system is believed to be watertight, what assumptions are made about the service provider?

Since low trust implies high risk perception, the key to reducing risk perception may not be risk communication strategies, but rather trust building. And trust is not built by strategic communication directed toward the other, or the demanding of trust. On the contrary, trust is built in the other by working on oneself, as an individual or organization. Individuals and organizations have to demonstrate by their actions that they merit the other's trust. These observations raise issues of reciprocity in cyberspace, identity and certification procedures and the way they may or may not facilitate trust in the other.

8.5.2.3. Social amplification of risk and crime

The SARF is a very inclusive set of rather loosely related concepts. In many ways it brings together all the other work within risk perception. But this ambition is tempered somewhat by the lack of specificity in content and process. In particular, it is unclear whether the SARF can be used as a successful tool of prediction; perhaps it is too fuzzy a framework for this, its value being more as a way of explaining something after it has occurred.

Yet despite these problems, a SARF approach to crime and cyber crime would seem to offer much. At the least it would provide an overarching framework within which to position particular studies on risk perception. But, more ambitiously, the use of cyber crime as a case study of the SARF might have clear value for public policy making. Research could elucidate an account of the communication of the risk of cyber crime, attending to how symbols and imagery shape public perception and how various institutions handle and disseminate risk information. In particular, research might lead to the identification of signal events; for example an instance of cyber crime comes into the public domain, is transformed as it is communicated through mass media channels and shapes public perception of risk.

REFERENCES

Adams, J. (1995), *Risk*, London: University College London Press.

Armony, J.L., Servan-Schreiber, D., Cohen, J.D. and LeDoux, J.E. (1997), 'Computational Modeling of Emotion: Explorations through the Anatomy and Physiology of Fear Conditioning', *Trends in Cognitive Sciences* 1(1): 28-34.

Barber, B. (1983), *The Logic and Limits of Trust*, New Brunswick NJ: Rutgers University Press.

Bargh, J.A. (1984), 'Automatic and Conscious Processing of Social Information', in R.S. Wyer Jr and T.K. Srull (eds), *Handbook of Social Cognition* (Vol. 3), Hillsdale, NJ: Lawrence Erlbaum, pp. 1-43.

Bastide, S., Moatti, J.-P., Pages, J.-P. and Fagnani, F. (1989), 'Risk Perception and Social Acceptability: The French Case', *Risk Analysis* 9(2): 215-25.

Beck, U. (1992), *Risk Society: Towards a New Modernity*, London: Sage.

Bernstein, P.L. (1996), *Against the Gods: The Remarkable Story of Risk*, New York: John Wiley & Sons.

Boholm, A. (1996), 'Risk Perception and Social Anthropology: Critique of Cultural Theory', *Ethnos* 61(1-2): 64-84.

Borkovec, T.D. (1994), 'The Nature, Functions, and Origins of Worry', in G.L. Davey and F. Tallis (eds), *Worrying: Perspectives on Theory, Assessment, and Treatment*, Chichester: John Wiley & Sons, pp. 5-34.

Brenot, J., Bonnefous, S. and Marris, C. (1998), 'Testing the Cultural Theory of Risk in France', *Risk Analysis* 18(6): 729-39.

Brun, W. (1992), 'Cognitive Components in Risk Perception: Natural versus Man Made Risks', *Journal of Behavioural Decision Making* 5: 117-32.

Butler, G. and Mathews, A. (1983), 'Cognitive Processes in Anxiety', *Advances in Behaviour Research and Therapy* 5(1): 51-62.

Butler, G. and Mathews, A. (1987). Anticipatory Anxiety and Risk

Perception. *Cognitive Therapy and Research* 11(5): 551-65.

Clore, G.L. and Gasper, K. (2000), 'Feeling is Believing: Some Affective Influences on Belief', in N.H. Frijda, A.S.R. Manstead and S. Bem (eds), *Emotions and Beliefs: How Feelings Influence Thoughts*, Cambridge: Cambridge University Press, pp. 10-44.

Cvetkovich, G., and Lofstedt, R. (1999), *Social Trust and the Management of Risk*, London: Earthscan.

Dake, K. (1991), 'Orienting Dispositions in the Perception of Risk - An Analysis of Contemporary Worldviews and Cultural Biases', *Journal of Cross-Cultural Psychology* 22(1): 61-82.

Dake, K. (1992), 'Myths of Nature - Culture and the Social Construction of Risk', *Journal of Social Issues* 48(4): 21-37.

Damasio A.R. (1994), *Descartes' Error: Emotion, Reason and the Human Brain*, New York: Grosset/Putnam.

Deedes, W.F. (2001), 'In the Blame Culture There is No Such Thing as an Accident', *Daily Telegraph,* 21 June.

Douglas, M. (1966), *Purity and Danger: Concepts of Pollution and Taboo*, London: Routledge and Kegan Paul.

Douglas, M. (1990), 'Risk as a Forensic Resource', *Daedalus* 119(4): 1-16.

Douglas, M. (1992), *Risk and Blame: Essays in Cultural Theory*, London: Routledge.

Douglas, M., and Wildavsky, A. (1982), *Risk and Culture: An Essay on the Selection of Technical and Environmental Dangers*, Berkeley CA: University of California Press.

Earle, T. and Cvetkovich, G. (1995), *Social Trust: Toward a Cosmopolitan Society*, Westport CT: Praeger.

Epstein, S. (1994), 'Integration of the Cognitive and Psychodynamic Unconscious', *American Psychologist* 49(8): 709-24.

Evans-Pritchard, E. (1937), *Witchcraft, Oracles and Magic Among the Azande*, Oxford: Oxford University Press.

Farrall, S., Jackson, J. and Gadd, D. (in press), 'Filtering Fear: On the Use of Filter and Frequency Questions in Crime Surveys', *Journal of Quantitative Criminology*.

Finucane, M.L., Alhakami, A.S., Slovic, P. and Johnson, S.M. (2000), 'The Affect Heuristic in Judgments of Risk and Benefits', *Journal of Behavioral Decision Making* 13: 1-17.

Flynn, J., Slovic, P. and Kunreuther, H. (2001), *Risk, Media and Stigma: Understanding Public Challenges to Modern Science and Technology*, London: Earthscan.

Freudenberg, W.R. (1993), 'Risk and Recreancy: Weber, the Division of Labor, and the Rationality of Risk Perceptions', *Social Forces* 71(4): 909-32.

Frijda, N.H., Manstead, A.S.R. and Bem, S. (2000), 'The Influence of Emotions on Beliefs', in N.H. Frijda, A.S.R. Manstead and S. Bem (eds), *Emotions and Beliefs: How Feelings Influence Thoughts*, Cambridge: Cambridge University Press, pp. 144-70.

Garland, D. (2003), 'The Rise of Risk', in R.V. Ericson and A. Doyle (eds), *Risk and Morality*, Toronto: University of Toronto Press, pp. 48-86.

Geertz, C. (1973), *The Interpretation of Cultures*, New York: Basic Books.

Giddens, A. (1991), *Modernity and Self-Identity: Self and Society in the Late Modern Age*, Stanford CA: Stanford University Press.

Girling, E., Loader, I. and Sparks, R. (2000), *Crime and Social Control in Middle England: Questions of Order in an English Town*, London: Routledge.

Green, J.M. (1995), *Risk, Rationality and Misfortune: Towards a Sociology of Accidents*, London: University College London Press.

Gregory, R., Flynn, J. and Slovic, P. (1995), 'Technological Stigma', *American Scientist* 83: 220-3.

Gregory, R., Flynn, J. and Slovic, P. (2001), 'Technological Stigma', in J. Flynn, P. Slovic and H. Kunreuther (eds), *Risk, Media and Stigma: Understanding Public Challenges to Modern Science and Technology*, London: Earthscan, pp. 3-21.

Hacking, I. (1987), 'Was there a Probabilistic Revolution 1800-1930?', in L. Kruger, J. Daston Lorraine and M. Heidelberger (eds), *The Probabilistic Revolution*, Cambridge MA: MIT Press, pp. 45-55.

Horlick-Jones, T., Sime, J. and Pidgeon, N. (2003), 'The Social Dynamics of Environmental Risk Perception: Implications for Risk Communication Research and Practice', in N. Pidgeon, R.E. Kasperson and P. Slovic (eds), *The Social Amplification of Risk*, Cambridge: Cambridge University Press, pp. 262-58.

Hough, M. and Mayhew, P. (1983), 'The British Crime Survey: First Report', *Home Office Research Study no. 76*, London: HMSO.

Jackson, J. (2003), 'Developing a Social Psychological Perspective on the Fear of Crime', manuscript submitted for publication, London School of Economics and Political Science.

Jackson, J. (2004), 'An Analysis of a Construct and Debate: The Fear of Crime', in H. Albrecht, T. Serassis, and H. Kania (eds), *Images of Crime Volume II*, Freiburg: Edition Iuscrim (Max Planck Institute).

Jackson, J. (in press), 'Experience and Expression: Social and Cultural Significance in the Fear of Crime', *British Journal of Criminology*.

Johnson, E., and Tversky, A. (1984), 'Representations of Perceptions of Risks', *Journal of Experimental Psychology* 113(1): 55-70.

Kahneman, D., Slovic, P., and Tversky, A. (eds) (1982), *Judgment Under Uncertainty: Heuristics and Biases*, Cambridge: Cambridge University

Press.

Kahneman, D. and Tversky, A. (1979), 'Prospect Theory: Analysis of Decision under Risk', *Econometrica* 47(2): 263-91.

Kasperson, J.X., Kasperson, R.E., Pidgeon, N. and Slovic, P. (2003), 'The Social Amplification of Risk: Assessing Fifteen Years of Research and Theory', in N. Pidgeon, R.E. Kasperson and P. Slovic (eds), *The Social Amplification of Risk*, Cambridge: Cambridge University Press, pp. 13-46.

Kasperson, R.E., Jhaveri, N. and Kasperson, J.X. (2001), 'Stigma, Places, and the Social Amplification of Risk: Toward a Framework of Analysis', in J. Flynn, P. Slovic, and H. Kunreuther (eds), *Risk, Media and Stigma: Understanding Public Challenges to Modern Science and Technology*, London: Earthscan, pp. 9-27.

Kasperson, R.E., Renn, O. and Slovic P. (1988), 'Social Amplification of Risk: A Conceptual Framework, *Risk Analysis* 8(2): 177-87.

Langford, I., Georgiou, S., Bateman, I., Day, R. and Turner, R.K. (2000), 'Public Perceptions of Health Risks from Polluted Coastal Bathing Waters: A Mixed Methodological Analysis using Cultural Theory', *Risk Analysis* 20(5): 691-704.

Levy-Bruhl, L. and Clare, L.A. (1923), *Primitive Mentality*, London/New York: George Allen and Unwin Ltd/The Macmillan Company.

Loewenstein, G.F., Weber, E.U., Hsee, C.K. and Welch, E.S. (2001), 'Risk as Feelings', *Psychological Bulletin* 127: 267-86.

Luhmann, N. (1979), *Trust and Power*, Chichester: John Wiley & Sons.

MacLeod, A.K., Williams, M.G. and Bekerian, D.A. (1991), 'Worry is Reasonable: The Role of Explanations in Pessimism about Future Personal Events', *Journal of Abnormal Psychology* 100(4): 478-86.

Marris, C., Langford, I.H. and O'Riordan, T. (1998), 'A Quantitative Test of the Cultural Theory of Risk Perceptions: Comparison with the Psychometric Paradigm', *Risk Analysis* 18(5): 635-47.

Mathews, A. (1990), 'Why Worry? The Cognitive Function of Anxiety', *Behaviour Research and Therapy* 28(6): 455-68.

Murdock, G., Petts, J. and Horlick-Jones, T. (2003), 'After Amplification: Rethinking the Role of the Media in Risk Communication', in N. Pidgeon, R.E. Kasperson and P. Slovic (eds), *The Social Amplification of Risk*, Cambridge: Cambridge University Press, pp. 159-74.

Petts, J. Horlick-Jones, T. and Murdock, G. (2001), 'Social Amplification of Risk: The Media and the Public', *Health and Safety Executive Contract Research Report 329/200*, Sudbury: HSE Books.

Pidgeon, N., Kasperson, R.E. and Slovic, P. (eds) (2003), *The Social Amplification of Risk*, Cambridge: Cambridge University Press.

Poortinga, W. and Pidgeon, N. (2003), *Public Perceptions of Risk, Science*

and Governance: Main Findings of a British Survey of Five Risk Cases, Norwich: Centre for Environmental Risk, University of East Anglia, January,
http://www.uea.ac.uk/env/pur/Final%20Report%20Risk%20Survey%202
002.pdf accessed 17 Apr.04.

Putnam, R.D. (2000), *Bowling Alone: The Collapse and Revival of American Community*, New York: Simon & Schuster.

Rayner, S. (1988), 'Muddling through Metaphors to Maturity: A Commentary on Kasperson et al. "The Social Amplification of Risk"', *Risk Analysis* 8(2): 201-4.

Rayner, S. (1992), 'Cultural Theory and Risk Analysis', in S. Krimsky and D. Golding (eds), *Social Theories of Risk*, Westport CT: Praeger, pp. 83-116.

Renn, O., Burns, W.J., Kasperson, J.X., Kasperson, R.E. and Slovic, P. (1993), 'The Social Amplification of Risk: Theoretical Foundations and Empirical Applications', *Journal of Social Issues* 48(4): 137-60.

Rohrmann, B. (1999), 'Risk Perception Research: Review and Documentation', RC Studies No. 48, Julich Research Centre, Julich, Germany.

Rosa, E. (2003), 'The Logical Structure of the Social Amplification of Risk Framework (SARF): Metatheoretical Foundations and Policy Implications', in N. Pidgeon, R.E. Kasperson and P. Slovic (eds), *The Social Amplification of Risk*, Cambridge: Cambridge University Press, pp. 47-79.

Royal Society for the Prevention of Accidents (1992), *Risk: Analysis, Perception and Management*, London: ROSPA.

Russell, M. and Davey, G.C.L. (1993), 'The Relationship Between Life Event Measures and Anxiety and its Cognitive Correlates', *Personality and Individual Differences* 14(2): 317-22.

Siegrist, M., Cvetkovich, G. and Roth, C. (2000), 'Salient Value Similarity, Social Trust, and Risk/Benefit Perception', *Risk Analysis* 20(3): 353-62.

Sjoberg, L. (1996), 'A Discussion of the Limitations of the Psychometric and Cultural Theory Approaches to Risk Perception', *Radiation Protection Dosimetry* 68(3-4): 219-25.

Sloman, S.A. (1996), 'The Empirical Case for Two Systems of Reasoning', *Psychological Bulletin* 119(1): 3-22.

Slovic, P. (1987), 'Perception of Risk', *Science* 236: 280-85.

Slovic, P. (1993), 'Perceived Risk, Trust, and Democracy', *Risk Analysis* 13(6): 675-82.

Slovic, P., Finucane, M.L., Peters, E. and MacGregor, D.G. (2004), 'Risk as Analysis and Risk as Feelings: Some Thoughts about Affect, Reason, Risk, and Rationality', *Risk Analysis* 24(2): 311-22.

Slovic, P., Finucane, M., Peters, E. and MacGregor, D.G. (2002), 'The Affect Heuristic', in T. Gilovich, D. Griffin and D. Kahneman (eds), *Heuristics and Biases: The Psychology of Intuitive Judgment*, New York: Cambridge University Press, pp. 397-420.

Slovic, P., Lichtenstein, S. and Fischoff, B. (1979), 'Which Risks are Acceptable?', *Environment* 21(4): 17-20.

Slovic, P., Lichtenstein, S. and Fischoff, B. (1980), 'Facts and Fears: Understanding Perceived Risk', in R.C. Schwing and W.A. Albers (eds), *Societal Risk Assessment: How Safe is Safe Enough?,* New York: Plenum, pp. 67-93.

Starr, C. (1969), 'Social Benefit versus Technological Risk', *Science* 165: 1232-38.

Thompson, P. (1999), 'The Ethics of Truth-telling and the Problem of Risk', *Science and Engineering Ethics* 5(4): 489-510.

Thompson, P. and Dean, W. (1996). 'Competing Conceptions of Risk', http://www.piercelaw.edu/risk/vol7/fall/thompson.htm accessed 17 Apr. 04.

Vasey, M.W. and Borkovec, T.D. (1993), 'A Catastrophising Assessment of Worrisome Thoughts', *Cognitive Therapy and Research* 16(5): 505-20.

Wiedemann, P.M., Clauberg, M. and Schutz, H. (2003), 'Understanding Amplification of Complex Risk Issues: The Risk Story Model Applied to the EMF Case', in N. Pidgeon, R.E. Kasperson and P. Slovic (eds), *The Social Amplification of Risk*, Cambridge: Cambridge University Press, pp. 288-301.

Zajonc, R.B. (1980), 'Feeling and Thinking: Preferences Need no Inference', *American Psychologist* 35(2): 151-75.

9 The future of privacy protection

Charles D. Raab[1]

9.1 INTRODUCTION

Protection against the privacy-invasive processing of personal information, as well as protection with regard to spatial and other forms of intrusion, has gained in prominence as a social and political issue in recent years, posing challenges for policy makers and inviting a variety of analyses of problems and their possible solutions. Whilst it is tempting to attribute the increased salience of privacy issues and anxieties to the advent of 'technology', this would be to fix on a single opaque cause without much theoretical or empirical persuasiveness. It is possibly because we do not understand technology very well that it is so often demonized. Equally – and equally misleadingly – one might point to 'e-commerce', 'e-government', 'law enforcement' and a host of other applications of whatever is meant by 'technology'. But, for that matter, how well do we understand these? For the general public as well as large swathes of the policy classes, these governmental and commercial processes are as mystifying as 'technology'. What baffles us often frightens us. What frightens us often stimulates, as well as feeds on, lack of trust in whatever it is that causes us to worry about our privacy. Alongside other objects of distrust, it is said that a lack of trust in the way our personal data are handled threatens to impede the full realization of goals that are predicated on the successful exploitation of new, technologically assisted ways of transacting business, delivering public services and maintaining public order.

In the face of these circumstances, states, firms, technologists and civil society groups have sought remedies in a host of solutions to the problem of privacy invasion, particularly concerning information or data privacy. This chapter aims to provide an overview of a number of central issues involved in this constellation of perceived problems and their solutions. It also aims to offer some new ideas to the policy debate about privacy in the 'information age', with a view to the future. It cannot hope to be a comprehensive or nuanced treatment of this subject, but it will canvass and comment upon conceptual understandings that have shaped privacy as a public and political issue that has arisen concerning processes that use information and communication technologies (ICTs) to negotiate cyberspace. It will reflect upon the inadequacy of this conventional wisdom for the development of a fuller range of policy objectives related to a different valuation of privacy. It will then review and question the robustness of the variety of protective instruments that have been developed over the period since the 1970s within the terms of the accepted paradigm. These instruments face new tests that stem in large part from the globalization of the information processes that constitute the perceived 'problem'.

This chapter will also consider new approaches and developments that offer to meet the challenge at the transnational level and in regard to protective strategies that emphasize precaution as much as, or instead of, remedy. It will underscore the importance of better knowledge and understanding of privacy and the threats to its realization as a human value, as well as the importance of creating new avenues for the exercise of power and influence at several levels of the regime for protecting privacy. The aim of this chapter is to inform readers about these problems, issues and solutions, and to stimulate further debate about them.

9.2 THE PRIVACY PARADIGM

A good place to start this excursion is by considering the conceptual underpinning of the conventional approach to the diagnosis of privacy threats and to the actions that might cope with them. This approach rests on assumptions derived from liberal political philosophy and epistemology, and entails a number of policy implications. Some of these assumptions require reformulation as a result of changes in the nature and scope of the privacy issue under conditions of globalization, involving recent technological developments and trends in the use of personal data in the economy and the state.

Stated crudely, the conventional privacy paradigm – a set of assumptions about a phenomenon or area of study, which are generally unquestioned – rests on the conception of a civil society comprised of relatively autonomous individuals who need privacy in order to be able to fulfil the various roles of the citizen or consumer in a capitalist, liberal-democratic state. Further, it rests on the notion that individuals are the best judge of their own privacy interests or claims, and that these may differ from person to person. Individuals should be allowed a private sphere untouched by others; there is a boundary between the individual and other individuals, and between the individual and the state. Warren and Brandeis (1890, pp. 219-20) comment in their seminal article on the right to privacy (defined famously as 'the right to be let alone'), 'the protection of society must come mainly through a recognition of the rights of the individual. Each man is responsible for his own acts and omissions only'.

More recently, Westin (1967, pp. 31-2) identifies four 'states' of privacy – solitude, anonymity, intimacy and reserve – and eloquently states the importance of privacy for democratic societies. In contrast to totalitarian regimes:

> [A] balance that ensures strong citadels of individual and group privacy and limits both disclosure and surveillance is a prerequisite for liberal democratic societies. The democratic society relies on publicity as a control over government, and on privacy as a shield for group and individual life. (Westin 1967, p. 24)

The way the balance between privacy and community obligations and duties is struck within different societies is likely to vary according to different cultural traditions, but surveys on privacy in many countries suggest that populations generally have high and increasing levels of concern about privacy. These seem mainly to be driven by fears about new ICTs and by people's distrust of public and private institutions to use these with sufficient respect for individual liberty (Bennett and Raab 2003; Bennett 1992).

Privacy protection, therefore, is typically justified in individualistic terms in academic writing and in the popular mind. We each have a right or claim to be able to control information that relates to us. Privacy has an affinity with individual autonomy and dignity. It is politically justified as promoting the institutions of liberal democracy, and it has a number of utilitarian values in terms of the responsible use of personal data (Sieghart 1976). Privacy is taken to be something that 'we' once had, but that is now being denied us by public and private organizations employing the latest ICTs.

Popular culture and the mass media amplify these themes, forming part of the social context for e-commerce and e-government. Horror stories about the intrusive nature of modern technology, about the abuse and misuse of personal data and about the size and interconnectedness of contemporary information systems have affected public and political consciousness (Smith 1993). Dystopian 'Big Brother' imagery, as well as reportage of how the powerless are denied rights and services through the wrongful collection, use and disclosure of personal data, make good copy; they also make good films. The message is that privacy (as typically defined) is something of the past: to paraphrase the chairman of Sun Microsystems, 'privacy is doomed ... get used to it' (*The Economist* 1999, p. 16). Whilst the popularity of voyeuristic, 'reality' television programmes like Big Brother has cast some doubt on the public's embrace of privacy as a cultural value, the erosion of information privacy through the formation and manipulation of databases by government or business, or on the Internet, is still seen as regrettable by large proportions of survey respondents.

9.3 THE PRIVACY PARADIGM'S IMPLICATIONS FOR POLICY

This paradigm has had a number of political and policy implications since the 1970s. The overall policy goal has been to give individuals greater control of the information about them that is collected, stored, processed and disseminated by public and, in some cases, private organizations. Policy development has come to rest on a set of assumptions, among which four can be highlighted.

The first is that privacy is a highly subjective and variable value. Policy is therefore based on procedural rather than substantive tenets. It can implant the mechanisms, such as the availability of legal remedies and channels for complaint, by which individuals can assert their own privacy interests and claims, and it can impose obligations on those that use personal data. Yet laws have also defined a few categories of inherently 'sensitive' data worthy of greater protection, and have also created regulatory roles and structures to enforce the law and to promote privacy as a value.

A second assumption stems from the observation that personal information cannot easily be regarded as the individual's property. It was once considered that the power of the state to gather and process personal information posed the most significant challenge to privacy. Consequently, information privacy was generally defined more as a problem to be solved by public policy than as an issue for market choice. It is only more recently that private sector, commercial practices have arisen as an equally pressing concern, giving rise to a number of market-based solutions (Laudon 1996; Rule and Hunter 1999; Lessig 1999).

A third assumption concerns the relationship between information privacy and information security: it is that the quality of data is crucial to privacy protection. Security is necessary, but far from sufficient, to ensure privacy. Computer scientists and others often take 'privacy' to mean (only) 'data security' against risks of unauthorized access, physical damage to databases or transmissions, and the like. However, it is no comfort to a privacy-aware individual to be told that inaccurate, outdated, excessive and irrelevant data about her are encrypted and stored behind hacker-proof firewalls until put to use by (say) a credit-granting organization in making decisions about her.

A fourth assumption is predicated upon a distinction in role between the data controller (or user) and the data subject, in which both are conceived in terms only of bundles of rights and obligations that should be addressed by legal prescriptions and proscriptions. The consensus is that the focus of data protection laws and other instruments should be the individual, or the 'natural person' rather than some other entity, such as groups and organizations, and that the individual has only a legal personality abstracted from any social, cultural or other factors that might seek to influence the canons of protection policy and its armoury of instruments.

These assumptions set privacy protection policy on a particular course towards regulatory responses, in which the doctrine of 'fair information principles' (FIPs) is inscribed, establishing consensual norms for the responsible processing (that is, collection, retention, use, disclosure and destruction) of personal information. The principles are codified within all national data protection or information privacy laws, including the UK's Data Protection Act (DPA) 1998, and appear in voluntary codes and standards (for example, CSA 1996) as well as in international agreements. These include the 1981 Guidelines of the Organisation for Economic Co-operation and Development (OECD 1981), the 1981 Convention of the Council of Europe (CoE) (1981), and the European Union's Data Protection Directive 95/46/EC (EU 1995). Paraphrasing the FIPs, an organization:

- must be accountable for all the personal information in its possession;
- should identify the purposes for which the information is processed at or before the time of collection;
- should only collect personal information with the knowledge and consent of the individual (except under specified circumstances);
- should limit the collection of personal information to that which is necessary for pursuing the identified purposes;
- should not use or disclose personal information for purposes other than those identified, except with the consent of the individual (the finality principle);
- should retain information only as long as necessary;
- should ensure that personal information is kept accurate, complete and up to date;
- should protect personal information with appropriate security safeguards;
- should be open about its policies and practices and maintain no secret information system;
- should allow data subjects access to their personal information, with an ability to amend it if it is inaccurate, incomplete or obsolete.

Of course, privacy is not an absolute right; it must be balanced against other rights and obligations. A second prominent feature of the regulatory response, therefore, is the paradigm of practice that has entrenched an assumption of balance in the rhetoric and work of privacy and data protection regulators. However, for several reasons, this concept is problematic (Raab 1999). Although the concept is related to the terminology of judicial decision, the achievement of a balance may ultimately be a matter of political negotiation, perhaps arriving at a consensus or, alternatively, of authoritative assertion.

9.4 CRITIQUES OF THE PRIVACY PARADIGM

The paradigm has served privacy well for a long period of time, generating much valuable policy and practice. How well it may continue to do so, however, is a pressing question. A lively, but often sidelined, critique of liberal political theory as a basis for privacy comes from at least four overlapping positions. A first one rejects the perhaps selfish, possessive-individualist, antisocial implications of a privacy that allows people to conceal information and to mislead others (Arndt 1949; Posner 1978). A second argument points to the problematic distinction between public and private, which are complex concepts that operate on different dimensions. Feminists, for example, have rejected the reified distinction between a private, domestic (female) world and a (male) public sphere (Pateman 1983; Allen 1985; Boling 1996). A third school sees liberal democracy as only one kind of democracy; it holds that the test of a democracy is not the protection of individual rights, but rather the degree of participation, cooperation, community consciousness and so on – values that are not necessarily promoted by asserting the 'right to be let alone'.

A final critique arises from postmodernist scepticism about the premise of the central autonomy of the subject. As Lyon (1994) puts it, the more profound question for the post-modern era is nothing less than 'where the human self is located if fragments of personal data constantly circulate within computer systems, beyond any agent's personal control' (Lyon 1994, p. 18). The 'decentring' of the individual and of her privacy is part of the essence of this critique of the importance of selfhood and of the very definition of the self (Giddens 1991).

The liberal political theory that underpins FIPs and promotes balance banks heavily on procedural and individual remedies to excessive privacy intrusions. But some would contend that they serve to legitimize new personal information systems and thus extend social control in surveillance societies (Flaherty 1989, p. 384). Running alongside the literature on privacy is a large literature on surveillance, which is seen as a contemporary condition within advanced industrial societies and which is sometimes conceptualized rather differently from, and more subtly than, the usual, mass media conception of surveillance as a 'snooping' process involving what 'they' do to 'us' based on high-tech information-gathering tools. The latter include the interception of communications, video monitoring, the tracking of movement and the analysis of data trails left in the course of daily life. Perhaps Foucault's (1979) point, reflected in Lyon (2001), about the ubiquitous and everyday nature of power relations in which individuals unwittingly subscribe to their own surveillance within the panopticon, provides the key insight, albeit perhaps too sweeping as an explanation.

The essential problem is the inherent tendency of bureaucratic organizations to want to amass more, and increasingly more detailed, personal information (Rule et al. 1980). Other writers analyse surveillance in other domains: for example undercover policing (Marx 1988, 1999) and profiling or social sorting (Gandy 1993; Bowker and Star 1999). These domains continually seek to identify, classify and evaluate individuals according to ever more refined and discriminating forms of personal data. Sorting is a highly potent set of socio-technical practices with political and social-control implications.

For all their differences, the privacy and surveillance literatures can often be seen as two sides of the same coin. Most of the literature shares the following four assumptions:

- that privacy is an individual right;
- that privacy is something that we once had and is now being eroded;
- that the source of the privacy problem is structural, lying in impersonal and remote forces that contribute to the declining ability of individuals to control the processing of information that relates to them; and
- that privacy-invasive organizations can be observed, resisted and regulated because they are subject to obligations that stem from principles embodied in the laws of discrete, bounded, liberal-democratic states.

Questions can be posed about each of these assumptions; brevity and relevance militate against a discussion of more than the first and fourth (for the rest, see Bennett and Raab 2003), from which may emerge new perspectives on the concept of privacy and on the practice of privacy protection.

The privacy paradigm encourages the view that individual privacy and social values such as sociability, internal security, social welfare or government efficiency are necessarily antithetical. The problem with this is not only the deeply contested and ambiguous quality of these concepts, but also that the promotion of privacy can itself be socially important. It can be argued that, for instance, excessively intrusive CCTV surveillance, involving mistaken identification with adverse consequences, is bad not only for individuals, but also for society. We might properly question the quality of a society in which cameras record our every movement, enabling the compilation of comprehensive records of what we do, with whom, when and where. Moreover, such surveillance may have a 'chilling' effect on associational activity and political participation. Two of Westin's (1967) four states of privacy – intimacy and anonymity – imply the ability of the individual to engage with others, rather than withdrawing from social contact. This relationship between privacy and political or social participation opens an avenue, even within the conventional paradigm, for considering privacy as a value for democratic society beyond the single individual or aggregate (Raab 1997a). Moreover, excessive surveillance can lead to the erosion of trust and to social inequities, which, however, can be addressed when privacy protection is viewed as social policy (Bennett and Raab 2003), as will be argued later.

In response to the fourth assumption, personal information knows neither organizational nor national attachments. Yet the privacy paradigm tends to be state-centric, whilst ICTs, and systems and practices involving personal data, have changed dramatically over the years. Personal data routinely flow around the world. The problem, therefore, must be redefined, and frameworks for protection, including new policy instruments and combinations of old ones, must be found to cope with these globalized conditions (Bennett and Raab 2003). This, too, will be discussed later.

9.5 PRIVACY PROTECTION AS SOCIAL POLICY

The paradigmatic emphasis on procedural due process and on an individualist construct of the value of privacy militates against raising distributional issues of privacy protection. The conception of privacy as a right rather than as a preference does provide a better basis on which to strengthen privacy's claim to be taken seriously in the 'balance'. But to the extent that little is understood about the distribution of privacy, it is all the more difficult for equity to enter into consideration as a policy value. Comprehending privacy in terms of equity strengthens the need to argue the grounds on which an unequal distribution can be justified.

Even to the extent that privacy is a value for individuals to enjoy, it would still be relevant to ascertain who enjoys what privacy, and why, and who does not. However, the knowledge basis for informing privacy policy is underdeveloped, although unequal distributions, if they exist, can be construed as worrisome. By failing to consider the social distribution of privacy, the conceptual apparatus and the paradigm it sustains are deficient. Is an uneven distribution of data protection justifiable on social and political grounds? Is everyone's privacy of equal worth to protect, or should some receive greater protection than others, and how? There are few arenas in which such queries can be addressed.

We can comprehend the effects on privacy that innovations will have: for instance mobile telephony, data matching, genetic screening, video surveillance or identity cards. But the conventional paradigm makes it all but impossible to ask what categories of persons risk what privacy invasion and receive what privacy protection. That is because the paradigm conceives of persons as undifferentiated 'data subjects' or 'citizens', making it more difficult to tailor privacy protection to the needs of different population segments. The abstract data subject needs to be made more three-dimensional. Persons and categories differ in terms of the extent and frequency of their exposure to information processing systems. Therefore, it is reasonable to suppose variation and inequality in the quality of their privacy. Whether such inequality is so serious or so structural, amounting to 'privacy classes', as to warrant remedy beyond individual redress is a political question.

The entrenched conceptual framework is not illogical given its underpinning assumptions, but it fails to address wider issues of the distribution of privacy protection in terms of gender, ethnicity, social class, age, income or other typical socio-economic and demographic categories. Knowledge about data subjects' privacy circumstances could inform ways of levelling the playing field between data controllers and data subjects. Privacy regulators are better organized and have better 'detectors' (Hood 1983) to comprehend the activities of the former in the great variety of 'sectors' in which they operate, than they are to understand the circumstances of the persons whose data are processed. When regulators do distinguish among data subjects, it is mainly to see them in terms of data controllers' sectoral categories, as credit-seekers, depositors, welfare recipients, online consumers, students, suspects and the like. Outlooks, interests and socio-demographic characteristics are often left on one side. Ironically, many data controllers themselves construct finely differentiated categories of members of the public in order to 'know' their customers and to target these market segments rather than to protect their privacy (Gandy 1993). Classification schemes are potent (Bowker and Star 1999): they lay down the tramlines for the way organizations understand things, and for the way in which people understand themselves and their relations with institutions. They also affect the whole gamut of human values.

Regulatory agencies have little incentive and few resources to gain more systematic knowledge about the privacy dimensions of the social, economic and other behaviour of those whose privacy they protect. It is therefore difficult for regulators to target their assistance. Regulatory practices instead focus upon broad, often low-level, objectives. This is not to be disparaged, but a better understanding of these distributions could sustain discussion about their causes, about whether inequalities can be justified and about the capacity of public policy and its implementation to alter them. Privacy protection would thus become more clearly part of social policy, debated – as in the case of welfare, education or health – in terms of alternatives such as public or private provision, costs and benefits, responsibilities and entitlements and the best way to 'deliver' privacy. Seen in this way, this conception of privacy would instigate a rethinking of the role of the regulatory agency in championing privacy protection, and of the responsibilities of government agencies in at least mitigating the adverse effects on privacy that their policies and practices might induce.

Distributional questions may be less easy to avoid if it can be argued that privacy has a social value in addition to its value to the individual (Regan 1995). Regan (1995, 2002) has gone the furthest to develop the theory of privacy as a value for entities beyond the person (see also Schoeman 1992). She maintains:

> that privacy serves not just individual interests but also common, public, and collective purposes. If privacy became less important to one individual in one particular context, or even to several individuals in several contexts, it would still be important as a value because it serves other crucial functions beyond those that it performs for a particular individual. Even if the individual interests in privacy became less compelling, social interests in privacy might remain. (Regan 1995, p. 221)

As a collective value, privacy cannot easily be provided to one person without its being enjoyed by others. Rather like street lighting, to provide for one is to provide for all. Regan (1995, p. 230) also observes that 'some minimum level of privacy may be indivisible' because of the way information and communication systems are designed. Beyond this, individual privacy may only be truly achievable in a society in which privacy is considered socially valuable and which reflects that esteem in its collective decision making. The question is how societal arrangements can promote privacy in this sense. Morally, this might mean that any citizen should so recognize the importance of privacy to other citizens, and to society as a whole, that she would support the protection of their privacy even if she does not value it for herself and – more controversially – even if particular instances of its enjoyment by others interfered with the full satisfaction of her own interests.

Although many ICT systems exacerbate social differences, Regan (1995, p. 237) shows how the creation of 'privacy haves' and 'privacy have-nots' can be inhibited. This social division is likely to happen unless privacy's collective value is explicitly recognized in organizational practice and built into the construction of technical systems. However, this value could be subverted if the main way in which privacy could be protected were the acquisition of protective ICTs for personal use, in keeping with the individualist paradigm. Despite the inherently collective-value nature of some information systems, the opportunities for social division, if not exclusion, could win out in the era of e-commerce and of ideologies and technologies of tailor-made privacy preferences. These offer individuals the real possibility of uncoupling 'their' privacy from that of everyone else. Yet there are strong constraints on realizing this in practice. Moreover, it may be chimerical if the neglect of privacy as a social value were to negate individual privacy as well, for the two are related. Market solutions, which involve choice of privacy 'levels', assume a well-informed consumerate, but it is likely that such knowledge and awareness would be unevenly distributed unless supported by effective and deliberately egalitarian policies of consumer or citizen education.

It is taking a further step to consider privacy not only as a collective or social value, but also as an egalitarian one. In this idiom, unequal distribution is seen as a societal problem, to be handled by a range of remedial or preventive policy options and by considering where responsibility should lie for effecting them. To date, none of these departures has been undertaken within the communities involved in the policy process, for privacy-as-social-policy has not yet seriously entered the conceptual and practical thinking of the privacy policy community of policy makers, regulators, privacy advocates or academia. Therefore, we are nowhere near what may be called the 'social democracy of privacy protection'. But, stemming from an analysis of surveillance rather than privacy as such, Lyon (2001) highlights the way in which social sorting creates or reinforces situations of inclusion and exclusion, advantages and deprivations, and discrimination. 'Surveillance', he writes (Lyon 2001, p. 151), 'has become an indirect but potent means of affecting life chances and social destinies ... it can display unjust and antisocial features even when privacy policies are in place'.

This is not to foreclose a debate over conceptions of 'equality of opportunity' and 'equality of result'. It may only be possible to entertain the former conception, especially if the latter cannot be so easily measured. But equality of opportunity is more likely to be approached where under-empowered individuals are not left entirely to their own devices to protect their information, for some are better able to look after themselves, to know and exercise their rights, than are others. In the UK and in many other countries where data protection regimes exist, individuals do – in principle and to some extent in practice – receive protection through the actions of others that have the effect of improving privacy protection. This is why protection, and indeed the question of equal protection, through 'devices' or privacy instruments beyond those wielded by individuals for themselves are important in the light of equity considerations. It leads to a consideration of the instruments that are available within the data protection regimes that have developed over many years.

9.6 PRIVACY INSTRUMENTS

Predicated largely upon the liberal democratic model and its assumptions about individual rights, four broad classes of information privacy instruments have emerged and are described below (see Bennett and Raab 2003). These instruments have influenced, and are comprehended within, the system of information privacy protection in the UK as well as in all other national jurisdictions that have reasonably fully developed protective regimes. Beyond these instruments, a relatively new one, privacy impact assessment (PIA), is an analytical technique that is attracting interest in many policy quarters; it will be discussed later. In addition, there are other strategies as well as players in the regulatory field. They include pressure group activity by privacy advocates and civil society groups, and the media, which are not discussed here. Citizen and consumer education, which has featured in the practice of a number of regulatory and other bodies and market-based 'property' practices, are also not covered here. Contracts as a safeguard for flows of personal data have played an important part, but space does not permit their consideration in this chapter.

9.6.1 International Instruments

Reference was made earlier to the 1981 OECD Guidelines, the 1981 Convention of the Council of Europe and the European Union's Data Protection Directive 95/46/EC, and the principles laid down in these influential documents were listed. As of May 2004, 37 of the Council's 45 members had signed the Convention, and 31 had ratified it, signifying that they have incorporated its principles into national law, allowing citizens of one country to seek redress in another. The Convention sought to establish an equivalent level of protection among contracting parties, assuring the free movement of personal data among them. It was the prospect of being shut out of these transborder flows of data – so essential to economic prosperity – which prompted the passage of the first UK Data Protection Act in 1984. But data transfers to non-ratifying states are left up to national law, and the Council of Europe has no supranational legal structure to ensure the enforcement of the principles. Yet the Convention serves as a beacon for newly democratizing states and it supports the protection of personal data within European inter-state arrangements such as Europol. The Council has also adopted many influential privacy-related recommendations with respect to a range of practices and technologies, and has developed a Model Contract for international data flows.

The OECD, too, has played a major early role in the development of data protection. In the late 1970s, issues of global market dominance and trade protection pervaded the negotiation of the Guidelines (Bennett 1992). The OECD's basic principles resemble those of the Council of Europe's Convention. The OECD went further in 1985, when its countries adopted a Declaration on Transborder Data Flows (OECD 1985) as a harmonized way of tackling the policy issues arising out of trading activities, intra-corporate flows, computerized information services and scientific and technological exchanges amongst diverse participants. The OECD has also promulgated guidelines for the security of information systems (OECD 1992) and for cryptography policy (OECD 1997), the latter after years of intense controversy over the export of cryptographic products.

By the late 1980s, it became obvious that the Convention was not serving to harmonize European data protection law, and that the Guidelines seemed to be more a way of justifying self-regulatory approaches than a route to the promotion of good data protection practices. The EU saw an urgent need to harmonize data protection law for the creation of the Internal Market, envisaged for 1992. Five years of difficult negotiation, in which the UK government as well as British business interests were among the keenest opponents of a strong Directive, resulted in the most influential international policy instrument to date: the Directive on the Protection of Personal Data with Regard to the Processing of Personal Data and on the Free Movement of such Data (EU 1995). Member states have some latitude in the details of their implementing legislation. The Directive is a complicated legal instrument, but it is innovative, abandoning some outdated concepts such as the distinction between public and private sector data processing and covering both automated and manual data processing. Like the Convention, the Directive makes specific provisions for 'sensitive' forms of data. It eschews distinctions between information collection, use and disclosure by defining 'processing' as embracing all these phases and more. The EU Directive set up Brussels-based machinery: an advisory Working Party (Article 29) and a body simply called 'The Committee' (Article 31), giving the Commission an instrument for adopting further decisions and regulations. The post of EU Data Protection Supervisor was established and its first incumbent was installed, charged with the responsibility for ensuring the compliance of European Union institutions with data protection law. A complementary telecommunications privacy directive was adopted in 1997 (EU 1998) based on the general Directive; this was repealed and replaced by an electronic communications Directive in 2002 (EU 2002).

9.6.2 Privacy Protection Through Legislation

A state's enactment of data protection laws is not the only legal route to regulating privacy. Constitutional provisions (for example the Fourth Amendment in the US), privacy torts, contract law remedies and privacy-protective restrictions in other laws (for example for the control of wire-tapping) have been important. Nevertheless, comprehensive national data protection laws have been regarded as essential, starting with Sweden in 1973 (Bennett and Raab 2003, Table 5.1).

In recent years, EU member states, including the UK with its Data Protection Act 1998, have rewritten their national laws to conform to the more stringent requirements of the Directive, and Greece and Italy have passed laws for the first time. In EU candidate countries, new legislation has been passed with an eye on the Directive. The elevation of data protection more prominently on political and legislative agendas also occurred in the 1990s in the Asia-Pacific region and in North and South America. Canada and Australia have had long experience of public sector laws overseen by independent Privacy Commissioners, but they have now extended data protection rules to the private sector. Generally, the perceived weaknesses of existing kinds of self-regulation, pressures to harmonize public and private sector standards, and concerns about the extra-territorial effect of the EU Directive – especially the Article 25 requirement that non-EU 'third' countries provide 'adequate' data protection for EU citizens' data when sent to those countries – have produced legislative action.

In the US, the adoption of general legislation for the private sector is strongly resisted. The US Privacy Act of 1974 (Public Law 93-579) applies only to the federal government, and not the private sector, and its implementation has been limited in the absence of a 'dedicated' authority to oversee and enforce compliance. Although there are many sectoral privacy laws, large areas of data processing go unregulated, resulting in a confusing pattern in which data protection has become 'fragmented, incomplete, and discontinuous' (Gellman 1993, p. 238); individuals' rights, therefore, are difficult and costly to pursue. Influential interests often argue that privacy can be better protected at the sectoral level or through self-regulation. Sectoral laws can coexist with comprehensive legislation, as they do in many European countries. In a sectoral approach, policy and legislation tend to be reactive, and enforcement machinery is often not available. But a sectoral approach may also mean that privacy regulations are inserted into other laws or policies in which personal data processing is part of the state activity that is being empowered: the *vires* may constrain what public organizations can do with personal data. Sectoral laws may clarify rights and responsibilities, but they may also limit the application of privacy principles in order to advance preferred policies such as combating welfare fraud or terrorism. Data protection laws rarely interfere very much with policing and state security, and laws in those sectors may weaken privacy protection.

In future, countries with comprehensive laws may well find that more specific laws covering sectors or particular information practices, such as data matching and data sharing, offer a more flexible and focused approach. But, as with comprehensive statutes, their oversight and implementation remain the key to their effectiveness, and in these tasks the role of public agencies is central. The most important are supervisory bodies; in the UK, this is the Office of the Information Commissioner, which was created by the Data Protection Act 1998 in succession to the Data Protection Registrar created by the Data Protection Act 1984. These bodies each perform a range of functions that appear in various mixes, and with different emphases, in different regimes. They thus have roles as ombudsmen, auditors, consultants, educators, negotiators, policy advisers and enforcers (Bennett and Raab 2003; Raab 1996, 1993). The existence of active supervisory authorities has been regarded as essential to good privacy protection, as laws are not self-executing and the maintenance of a privacy culture needs an authoritative champion (Flaherty 1989). The EU Directive enjoined these bodies to cooperate with one another. Indicative of their existing and perhaps future importance in global regulatory regimes, agencies have developed relationships and activities at the international level and in smaller regional groupings, where they discuss and concert their approaches to issues such as the regulation of the Internet, cyber crime and the availability of cryptography.

There is an intricate and growing global network of privacy commissioners that has met annually for the past 25 years, as well as more frequently in smaller regional, functionally specific, or less formal contexts. These include, for instance, the commissioners of the EU meeting in the Directive's Article 29 Working Party mentioned above. There is also, in Europe, Europol's Joint Supervisory Body, which supervises the work of the European Police Office; the Data Protection Common Control Authority, established to oversee arrangements for the sharing of police data under the Schengen Convention; and a Customs Information System, which began operations on 24 March 2003. A telecommunications privacy grouping has also been active, and fruitful collaboration has occurred between the commissioners' offices in the Canadian province of Ontario and the Netherlands over the development of research and appraisal of technologies for protecting privacy (Ontario 1995, 1999); Ontario and Australia have also jointly analysed online web seal programmes (Ontario 2000). Asia-Pacific countries take part in a Forum on Privacy and Data Protection, and are active in devising region-wide approaches. Whether a global regulatory regime will emerge from such developments cannot be foretold. The question of whether the world's, or even Europe's, commissioners can and should take a collective stand on public issues has itself been contentious, including the question of the future of privacy protection following 11 September 2001 and the expectation of intensified counter-terrorism surveillance and the interception of communications.

9.6.3 Privacy Protection Through Self-Regulation

'Self-regulation' is an omnibus term for a variety of tools that include privacy commitments, codes of practice, adherence to standards, and online tokens or 'seals'. Regarded as 'voluntary' instruments, self-regulation does not necessarily release organizations or industries from the requirement to comply with laws. Self-regulation normally pertains to the private sector, although codes, commitments and the like appear in the public sector to cover practices such as video surveillance, online delivery of public services and others. The Trust Charter or Guarantee proposed by the Government (PIU 2002; DCA 2003) to reassure the public about government data sharing is a UK example of the latter. Self-regulation can play an important role alongside statutory measures, helping to implement or supplement legislation. However, in other contexts they have been promoted in order to avoid or to anticipate legislation.

In the absence of general legislation, the Safe Harbor agreement between the US and the EU, concluded in 2000 after an arduous and conflict-ridden transatlantic process of negotiation, is intended to fill the gap for the private sector (Charlesworth 2000). American companies that gain entry to the Safe Harbor are thereby deemed to provide adequate protection for the personal data of EU citizens that are transferred to the US, for they agree to be bound by a set of privacy principles that are overseen and enforced by the Federal Trade Commission (FTC). But, in the first place, their subscription to the Safe Harbor is voluntary; moreover, the number of subscribers has not been impressive and the FTC's enforcement activity has been small.

Beyond mere commitments to protect customers' or citizens' personal information – which are often perfunctory public relations exercises although arguably a necessary first or supplementary step – privacy codes of practice are the most complex and varied of the range of self-regulatory instruments. Codes enjoin employees, members or member organizations to adhere to a set of rules, and provide important guidance about correct procedure based on a version of FIPs.

Five kinds of privacy code can be distinguished (Bennett and Raab 2003; Bennett 1995). The organizational code applies to one firm or agency – typically, a large and prominent one (for example American Express) – that is bounded by a clear organizational structure. Perhaps a more important category is that of the sectoral code developed by an industry (for example banking) for adoption by their member organizations. A sectoral code therefore tailors general rules to an industry's circumstances. Internationally, sectoral codes have begun to be developed within industries that operate on a global scale (for example airline transport). However, trade associations do not always fully represent the whole sector, and may be dominated by one or two large players. Some associations apply serious sanctions to non-compliant members, whilst others do not. The nature of relationships between industry and government may be important. For example, in Japan close ties between industry associations and the Ministry of International Trade and Industry (MITI) enabled MITI to promulgate privacy guidelines in 1997 on the content and procedures of industry codes of practice (MITI 1997).

Functional codes are defined less by economic sector and more by the practice in which the organization is engaged. The direct marketing associations in the UK and in many other countries have responded to long-standing concerns about direct marketing by developing privacy codes of practice, which have now moved to the international level. Telephone, mail and email preference services run by these associations allow consumers to remove their names from the members' marketing lists; in the UK, the Direct Marketing Association has been active in this. As new, potentially intrusive technologies have emerged, so a fourth type, technological codes, has developed. They typically apply to the governance of new applications, such as electronic funds transfers and the issuance of debit cards and personal identification numbers. Smart card technology in use across sectors and functions also lends itself to specific codes. Finally, professional codes have been developed for information-processing professionals, for survey researchers, for market researchers, for librarians and for a range of health- and welfare-related professionals. They are created by professional associations and can be reinforced by some significant disciplinary measures entailing a loss of professional reputation. They may also be incorporated into larger sets of ethical guidelines and codes of conduct. The National Health Service provides an important UK example of these developments (Department of Health 2003).

Privacy codes have been formulated with varying amounts of care and analysis and have no consistent format. Procedures for implementation, complaints resolution and communication differ. Privacy codes operate within a complicated set of incentives that vary between, and even within, sectors, professions and the like. Without an external regulatory framework to impose sanctions for non-compliance, they generally suffer from the reasonable public perception that those that have the most to gain from the processing of personal data arbitrate the individual's privacy rights. The role of codes in fostering and maintaining public trust is germane; the UK's proposed Trust Guarantee, mentioned earlier, is an attempt to grapple with this issue.

The adoption of specific privacy standards has been seen by many as a major way forward for privacy protection. Proponents argue that an international privacy standard would carry greater weight in both Europe and the US, giving business outside Europe a good way of demonstrating their conformity to international data protection standards, and providing a better mechanism for the implementation of Article 25 of the EU Directive concerning third-country 'adequacy'. Required registration to a standard, and obliging independent and regular auditing, would provide greater certainty that 'adequate' data protection is being practised by the data-receiving organization.

Information security standards have played a role in privacy protection for some years, with the adoption in December 2000 of the International Organization for Standardization (ISO) ISO 17799; it was preceded by the British Standard BS 7799. In the 1990s, however, the idea of a more general management standard for the complete set of privacy principles emerged onto the international agenda, stemming largely from the negotiation in Canada of the 'Model Code for the Protection of Personal Information' under the auspices of the Canadian Standards Association (CSA 1996; Bennett and Raab 2003). The development process first involved the International Organization for Standardization, and then more specifically the European Comité Européen de Normalisation (CEN) began to study the feasibility of an international privacy standard, supported by the EU Directive's Article 29 Working Party. Three paths were identified: a general data protection standard which would set out practical operational steps to be taken by an organization in order to comply with relevant data protection legislation, principally the EU Directive; a series of sector-specific initiatives in key areas such as health information and human resources management; and task-specific initiatives mainly related to the online environment (Dumortier and Goemans 2000). But powerful multinational firms, which regard these paths as imposing a regulatory burden with important implications for international trade, have resisted standards; their future is therefore insecure.

Turning more specifically to the online environment, the recent development of privacy seals as an instrument of self-regulation reflects the Internet's inherently global nature, and the growing prominence of online commercial transactions. Some of the most notable schemes have been developed by the TRUSTe organization, by the Better Business Bureau (BBB) and by WebTrust.[2] Websites can display a symbol indicating that they have been certified or registered as adhering to certain privacy protection practices and policies. Online customers can then exercise choices on an informed basis. The schemes, however, differ in terms of their stringency, the nature of any audits of practice, the dispute-resolution procedures they provide for consumers and their helpfulness for consumer choice. No scheme has yet achieved general recognition and credibility, and the proliferation of schemes may leave consumers confused. It is difficult for any system to gain a pre-eminent reputation.

9.6.4 Privacy Protection through Privacy-enhancing Technologies

If some part of the 'privacy problem' is caused by properties inherent in the design of information technologies, then it appears that the same technologies can be effectively configured to protect privacy, rather than to invade it; for instance if the default is the collection of no personal information (Chaum 1992). Public-key or asymmetric cryptography builds anonymity into information systems without reducing the ability of organizations to verify identity (Diffie and Landau 1998). Thus, technologies themselves are becoming a potent policy instrument that is considered by many to be particularly well suited to the global environment of information processes.

Privacy-enhancing technologies (PETs) come in a variety of overlapping forms. Systemic instruments arise from the decisions of the engineers that design networks, machinery or computer code, and from the technical standards and protocols that are devised to enhance network efficiency. These instruments correlate with Reidenberg's (1998) conception of Lex Informatica and Lessig's thesis about the regulatory effects of computer code (Lessig 1999). Collective instruments are created as a result of government policy, and are authoritative policy applications where government or business makes explicit decisions to build privacy protection into the technical systems for the provision of services and goods. Prominent examples are the attempts to develop public key infrastructures for government service delivery, and certain configurations of smart cards. The Dutch 'Privacy Incorporated Software Agent' (PISA), converting identities into pseudo-identities, is another example (Borking and Raab 2001).

Instruments of individual empowerment require explicit choices by individuals who activate the PET by choosing a measure of privacy enhancement in their online transactions. Proprietary encryption instruments, devices for anonymity and pseudonymity, filtering instruments and privacy management protocols are members of this family. The most prominent initiative is the Platform for Privacy Preferences (P3P), constructed by the World Wide Web Consortium (W3C). Persons can use their browsers (enabled with P3P readers) or other software tools to read the site's privacy policy, and receive automatic notification about whether the policy matches their privacy preferences, so that they can decide whether to engage in online transactions. P3P has been incorporated into Microsoft's recent Internet browsers enabling users to set their browser to one of five degrees of privacy. In terms of the earlier discussion of the social distribution of privacy, those who have the financial and other means to take advantage of PETs may be better able to protect their privacy, and to levels of their own choosing. There is room for debate here, not only on technical grounds, but in terms of public policy and the nature of privacy as a value (Charlesworth 2003; Catlett 2000).

PETs may complement existing regulatory and self-regulatory approaches; they may act as a condition or standard for service delivery; or they may be an alternative to legislation or other forms of regulation. The wide variety of available applications and their variable quality will continue to militate against neat generalizations concerning PETs' effectiveness. The tendency to see PETs as a magic bullet solving the privacy problem is regrettable. They may be necessary for certain types and media of transaction, but insufficient; legal, organizational and cultural conditions cannot be left out of account in designing a PET approach to privacy protection (Borking and Raab 2001).

9.7 PUTTING THE INSTRUMENTS TOGETHER

A consensus has emerged which holds that data protection requires something more than a monotechnic, one-size-fits-all solution, and that laws are insufficient. The complexity, dynamics and diversity (Kooiman 2003; Raab 1993) of data processing suggest the desirability of forging new relationships between state regulation and societal forms of privacy protection. Good privacy protection has been said to involve several instruments comprising a privacy toolkit, a mosaic of solutions, or a regulatory mix (for example Industry Canada 1994 and Cavoukian and Tapscott 1996).

'Toolkit', 'mix' and 'mosaic' are suggestive metaphors for combined approaches to data protection. Each has a somewhat different implication, but they are misleading because they cannot adequately describe the actual or preferred relationship among the instruments in practice. Each policy instrument tends to be thought of as a supplement, complement or substitute for others, without seriously investigating clashes and compatibilities. Yet each country's system of data protection relies on a more integrated, but often not rationalized, combination of different instruments. In Australia, practical discourse has centred on a co-regulatory approach. This involves a legislative context for flexible industry codes of practice, developed in conjunction with the Privacy Commissioner. In the EU, one effect of the Directive has been to establish common criteria for the powers of a supervisory authority to enhance the blending of instruments in each country. The evolution of regulatory practice has also pointed in the direction of complex relationships within privacy protection regimes. In the UK for example, the Information Commissioner has powers regarding the promotion and promulgation of codes of practice, but also contributes to policy and statute formation within government where the protection of personal data is at stake. The Information Commissioner's roles, enumerated earlier, bring that office into important relationships with the media, pressure groups, technology designers and others whose activities, in various ways, affect privacy outcomes.

Reidenberg (1997) describes comprehensive privacy regimes by identifying specific interactions among state, business, technical and citizen mechanisms. Writing of 'co-production', Raab (1997b) observes that the combination of privacy protection instruments is more than incidental to their effectiveness. To varying degrees, these instruments are interdependent, and their users often know and emphasize this. Privacy commissioners, for example, acknowledge the importance to their own work of a public that is educated about data protection. Privacy advocates want laws that bring sanctions to bear on those that breach self-regulatory codes. Resisting laws, self-regulating organizations may think that the market and customer-controlled PETs will work effectively alongside codes or commitments to help give people the privacy they want. These observations suggest that attempts to analyse and to design a regime should be alert to synergy in involving broader and multiple relations within and across jurisdictions, organizations and instruments.

The perception of interdependence among actors and instruments opens up possibilities for devising comprehensive policy approaches that transcend both action at single jurisdictional levels – potentially to reach a global dimension – and actions undertaken by only one type of actor or stakeholder. This points towards a holistic conception of regulatory policy and practice. That approach (see Bennett and Raab 2003) makes it feasible to interpret the governance of data protection in terms of complex regimes, and helps us to understand the intricate processes through which privacy protection is provided. This is not a matter of orchestration from a central point, nor indeed of automatic harmony, for there are many conflicts among these actors and interests. Nonetheless, considering them more explicitly as interactive agents opens up a richer conceptualization of privacy protection as something more than, and perhaps other than, the mechanical application of a toolkit.

The nature of contemporary and future information flows means that it is by now well understood that privacy cannot be adequately protected at the level of the single national jurisdiction. We have already seen the range of international instruments that have guided information privacy from the outset, and the EU Directive has exerted a powerful influence on the shaping of national laws and other arrangements, such as the Safe Harbor, towards greater similarity, at least on many essential elements. The Directive (Article 27) also encourages the development of transnational codes of practice. Many firms and some industries operating at the global level have indeed produced codes that span more than one country. The standardization movement faces strong obstacles, but is still under way. PETs are capable of operating on a global level, as do online commitments and seals. Transnational groupings have emerged in regions, of which the EU – now expanded – and Asia-Pacific have been the most evident. Official regulators combine, learn from each other, compare experiences, fulfil obligations for mutual assistance and participate together in some supervisory activities. However, the quality and effects of these interactions, including conflicts, have not yet been systematically studied or evaluated.

An historical pulsation of periods of convergence and divergence in data protection (Bennett 1992) may be entering new phases beyond the reconvergence that the EU Directive aimed to achieve. Whilst it would be delusionary to be sanguine about the prospects for the transnational and perhaps global reach of privacy protection in a joined-up fashion, there are, nevertheless, a number of pointers in that direction. These include a transnational policy community, a discourse, common principles and similar instruments inscribed into law and practice. To be sure, none of these 'straws in the wind' suggests anything like uniformity or a high degree of articulation, but they are not negligible as foundations for further development, partly through political will and deliberate policy design.

9.8 PRIVACY IMPACT ASSESSMENT AND THE QUESTION OF RISK

Recently, a further 'tool' has emerged – privacy impact assessment (PIA). This has elicited considerable interest in many countries, leading towards a possible consensus on how it should be implemented. It also holds the potential for divergence once again as different examples proliferate, but proliferation is arguably beneficial if it means the tailoring of PIAs to different sectors and contexts; no one would seriously argue for the rigid, mechanical application of an inappropriate template. The New Zealand Privacy Commissioner's Office, through its Assistant Commissioner, (Stewart 1996) has had a seminal influence on shaping this analytical approach, and there have been other powerful New Zealand contributions to the PIA movement (for example Longworth 1996). It has been developed, and probably practised most frequently, in Canada (White 2001; Ontario 2001; Stewart 2003) and was mandated for new federal programmes in Canada and by the US E-Government Act of 2002 (OMB 2003).

Many examples of PIAs, and much promotional and practical literature (for example Hong Kong 2001; Flaherty 2003) as well as many templates and tools for conducting them, have been put forth by privacy commissioners and other government agencies (for example Alberta OIPC 2001; British Columbia Ministry of Management Services 2003; Ontario 2001; New Zealand 2002; Treasury Board of Canada Secretariat 2002). In the UK, they have attracted the attention of the Performance and Innovation Unit (PIU; now the Prime Minister's Strategy Unit) in their report on privacy and data-sharing (PIU 2002), and this approach remains on the agenda for further policy development on that topic (DCA 2003) although statutory enactment is unlikely. We are likely to see PIAs proliferate as privacy consultants as well as other governmental and non-governmental organizations position themselves to offer proprietary PIA services.

It is too soon to say whether this will simply create a bewildering welter of incommensurable tools, or contribute a valuable new instrument to the privacy protection armoury. Yet perhaps one value of PIAs is their adaptability to the variety of projects and initiatives in many parts of the private and pubic sectors, online and offline, thus contributing to raising the level of awareness, and of informed debate, of privacy issues amongst technologists, systems managers, policy makers and data controllers generally. The corpus of PIA literature is emphatic that the routines of applying a PIA force the promoters of initiatives to understand, in detail, the flows of data in and around their systems and to address a range of issues beyond mere legal compliance, although a typical PIA routine uses FIPs as the basis for deriving more detailed questioning. PIA can thus play an important part in raising awareness of the effects of existing and new developments on privacy and in developing practical solutions. For this reason, PIA advocates argue that the assessment should ideally be carried out by an in-house team rather than be performed by outside consultants.

PIAs come in a variety of forms, but a basic definition of a PIA is that it is 'an assessment of any actual or potential effects that an activity or proposal may have on individual privacy and the ways in which any adverse effects may be mitigated' (Stewart 1996, p. 61). PIAs are project based (PRIVA-C™ 2003), and most PIAs have been performed in the public sector, especially in health information systems. They have been carried out in regard to new and revamped information systems, database linkages allowing remote access, establishing identification practices and the central accumulation of data (Stewart 2003). PIA should be distinguished from a privacy or a compliance audit, which usually considers existing information systems and is mainly concerned with whether or not they comply with legal requirements. In contrast, PIAs, which have an affinity with environmental impact assessments, assess the likely privacy impact of technology applications or new information systems in the future and take more than the law into consideration. In subscribing to the view that it is better to build privacy in than to bolt it on, they share a common outlook with PETs.

A further definition of PIA illustrates an important dimension:

> [PIA] is an analysis of how information is handled: (i) to ensure handling conforms to applicable legal, regulatory, and policy requirements regarding privacy; (ii) to determine the risks and effects of collecting, maintaining and disseminating information in identifiable form in an electronic information system, and (iii) to examine and evaluate protections and alternative processes for handling information to mitigate potential privacy risks. (OMB 2003, Sec. II.A.6)

This definition explicitly makes the linkage between PIA and risk assessment, placing the concept of risk at the centre of the process (Raab 2003). This is a brave step, given that this concept is itself the subject of widespread debate concerning its objective or subjective dimensions, and concerning the way in which risks can be measured in the case of privacy, in which the questions of conceptualization and measurement are very difficult.

Implicitly or explicitly, a good deal of privacy and data protection discourse is taken up with the concept of risk. The idea of 'sensitive data' implies that individuals would suffer greater damage through misuse of such data than they would through misuse of their name, address or other less 'sensitive' information. But some have argued that sensitivity depends more upon the contexts in which pieces of personal information are processed or communicated.

To some extent, we may infer the risks to privacy that come from security breaches or breakdowns of information equipment (Neumann 1995), but beyond that the issue is clouded.

For a more precise analysis of risk, the paradigmatic concept of the abstract 'data subject' is of little help. This legal term needs to be understood from a social scientific perspective in terms of the different characteristics of individuals, or of categories of individuals, who experience different kinds and degrees of privacy breaches and who enjoy different levels and forms of privacy protection (Raab 1995). This links to the earlier discussion of the distribution of privacy. We are as yet unable to say who gets what protection against what privacy risks, or which data of person A are more at risk of breaches of privacy than which data of persons B, C, D ... X. The uniform, legal construction of the 'data subject' is not fleshed out by understandings of the various kinds of data subjects, by explanations of what differentiates them – for instance their involvement with different intensities in different commercial or government sectors in which their data are used – and by a recognition of the different consequences they experience through involvement in the variety of information processes that put them at risk or that protect them.

A further important issue is whether we are talking about objective or subjective dimensions of the concept of risk; or rather, the relationship between the two. Debates about risk analysis in a wide range of fields – for example nuclear hazards, traffic accidents, environmental pollution and many others – have tried to understand the probabilities of the occurrence of events, the magnitudes of their consequences and the effects of human activity and responses to the risks involved in these phenomena (for example Adams 1995; Beck 1992; Royal Society 1992). But it is difficult to distinguish between 'real risks' and 'mistaken perceptions', in which science can supposedly determine the former and discount the fallacies of the latter. This may be particularly so in fields such as information processing in which human perception and 'agency' shape the situations in which personal data are collected or transmitted, and in which regulation must be geared to people's perceptions and fears as much as – or more than – any 'objective' calculation of risk, even if the latter were to be conceptually and empirically possible. On the other hand, even if we are unable to estimate different degrees and kinds of privacy risk, to say simply that 'cookies pose a threat to privacy', or that 'people's privacy is at risk if databases are inaccurate' – however true – does not get us closer to a more nuanced understanding of what is more serious and what is less serious, or what is perceived to be the case and why, on which to base regulatory policy.

PIA methodology prompts an important question, one which is not often asked in this field, although it is ubiquitous with regard to, for example, genetically modified foods, environmental pollution and nuclear energy: should we see ICTs and practices as safe until proven dangerous, or dangerous until proven safe? PIA may require a reasonable demonstration of the latter; laws and litigation for violations of privacy may be based on the former. These are alternative, not necessarily competing, strategies, but there has been little explicit exploration of their relationship, which would bring to the surface many implicit and perhaps erroneous assumptions about the nature of risk and about the way in which individuals act to avoid or accept it in particular types of information transactions. PIAs may help, therefore, to concentrate minds upon the question of the privacy risks people face from new technological innovations or applications. If such questioning can take the practice and theory of privacy protection beyond the stage of the merely casual use of the term 'risk', it could perform an overdue service.

Looked at in the light of the above question, data protection laws that require, for example, an element of 'prior checking' by regulators before a data controller's practice is deemed to be compliant implicitly involve some test of risk. How this is to be achieved is not always clear, but it points in the direction of a proactive, rather than a reactive, regulatory system (Tait and Levidow 1992), one in which the role of the 'precautionary principle' in privacy protection is made more explicit. Indeed, it already exists in the FIPs, in laws, in codes of practice and in PETs. Remedies, to be sure, are available for breaches of privacy regulations, and complaints about violations of privacy rules are at the heart of existing regulatory systems. Privacy protection in the US private sector is especially reliant on these provisions more than on the premise of enforcement by regulatory bodies, but even in the US we find the application of FIPs as a preventative means of making information systems privacy-friendly and less 'dangerous'. A more explicit acknowledgement of the precautionary approach, how and when to apply it (and how and when to eschew it) would be a constructive spin-off from PIAs.

Whatever the ambiguity of applying risk analysis to the privacy implications of technological design and application, risk assessment may thus help data controllers, regulators, PIA practitioners and the public to a better understanding and to a more fully informed debate about privacy. It is perhaps not so much the bottom line of a risk analysis or a PIA – the verdict on the particular technology or information practice under investigation – that is important, but the process of examining the issues, debating the criteria and forming judgements. In the final analysis, however, it may be a question of how risk assessment can be brought into the processes of policy making and governmental decision making more effectively: the timing, the institutional machinery and so on.

9.9 THE QUESTION OF TRUST

The foregoing are matters that the PIA technique itself cannot determine; they depend on political will. They may also depend upon how seriously governments take the question of public trust and confidence in ICTs and their application in e-commerce and e-government. Strong signals have been given in many advanced industrialized countries and in international organizations that trust is a crucial factor in arbitrating the future of electronic transactions (Raab 1998; PIU 2002). However, the examination of trust as a concept and as an interactive social process, and its application to the question of privacy, is not well developed; it could be better informed by a growing body of recent literature (for example O'Neill 2002; Misztal 1996; Fukuyama 1995; Giddens 1991; Gambetta 1988; Barber 1983; Luhmann 1979).

The concept of trust is at the centre of recent research (6 1998) which argues that more needs to be known about the public's worries about how their personal information is used and protected. There has been much survey research, albeit of very variable quality, into attitudes towards privacy and the processing of personal data (Bennett and Raab 2003). A UK example is a MORI (2003) survey, which revealed considerable public ignorance about what happens to personal data as used by public agencies. Better, more comparable and systematic evidence is needed about why people trust organizations, what specifically they trust organizations to do or not to do, how attitudes relate to risk perception and how people evaluate the trustworthiness of various public and private organizations. Improved knowledge of how privacy invasions, risk and fears are distributed across a population is important not only for a clearer understanding of the role of ICTs in society, but for more effective regulation. Such knowledge could help privacy regulatory bodies to rationalize the application of their limited resources in implementing the law. It could also help them to monitor the effectiveness of their efforts in order to retarget their efforts. Commercial and other organizations that control and process personal data might gain a clearer indication of how far they are gaining the trust and confidence of customers or clients and on what factors their reputation for trustworthiness as data-controlling organizations rests. More might be learned about how damaged reputations can be regained.

These matters are important, because the trustworthiness of many institutions is perceived to be low just when it needs to be high in order to provide a reputational platform for new applications of information systems that employ personal data. Laws, technologies and institutional infrastructures for conducting 'safe' electronic transactions explicitly aim at creating a trusted environment in which privacy concerns play an important part. Innovations such as TRUSTe and other seals, and the inclusion of privacy statements on websites, point to the importance of trust as a factor, or perhaps as an emblem, although little is known about their likely credibility and effectiveness. Sociological and psychological research could play an important part here.

Relevant questions abound: on what grounds do people trust organizations which say they are trustworthy, especially if there is evidence (or folklore and rumours) that could undermine such claims? Should one trust the ICTs used by governments whose reassurances about other technologies have been shown to be misleading? Would companies as well as proprietary seal or trustmark providers benefit by having to adhere to an established standard, accredited by a reputable standards organization, to back up the programme and provide a high level of trust? Or does a company's adherence to its industry's code of practice actually enhance people's trust that they are dealing with a reliable merchant? To what extent does such enhancement depend on whether the code is actually complied with in practice by firms in the industry, and on the industry's mechanisms of enforcement and sanctions for breach of the code? Does the combination or collaboration of several instruments of privacy protection, as outlined earlier, serve to increase the likelihood of public trust in the use of ICTs that depend on personal data? Why should one trust organizations that say they provide good privacy protection through self-regulatory mechanisms? But equally, why should one trust in the protection that laws are supposed to provide it and in the workings of the regulatory authorities that enforce it?

9.10 CONCLUSION

These questions are perhaps a good way to end this commentary on concepts, practices and instruments of privacy protection in the 'information age'. This chapter has highlighted a number of issues involved in the discussions of the recent past and present. To recapitulate, and to go beyond what has been said: among the most important issues that might bear upon current and future policy development in the UK, the first is a reconsideration of the individualist assumptions upon which privacy protection law and practice has been based. To be sure, law and practice has not capitulated to a purely market-based paradigm, for there are many processes that are predicated on the assumption that privacy protection is a matter of public policy, which includes principles and rules to be followed by those who control data. Law itself betokens the public policy nature of the privacy issue. Moreover, this assumption has generated at least one prominent institution (the Information Commissioner's Office) that plays a variety of roles of importance in terms of society, the culture of privacy and of governance in general beyond whatever importance it may have for assisting individuals to assert their claims and rights. Codes of practice also implicitly acknowledge institutional responsibilities towards citizens or customers beyond the simple responsiveness to individual complaints. However, if the conventional paradigm were to be altered in the direction of recognizing the social importance of privacy more explicitly, it would create a more secure space for policy making – informed by research – aimed at addressing the distributional question, 'who gets privacy?' in much the same way as social policy addresses questions of deprivation and inequality. This shift in focus might bring into the privacy debate a wider array of interests and voices and would establish a new set of criteria against which the performance of privacy protectors – in business, in government and in regulatory bodies – could be judged. It would also bring to the fore new thinking about responsibilities and accountability.

A second and related issue is the relationship between privacy and its protection and the broader treatment of surveillance in modern society. According to some, privacy is not the main concern, but surveillance, and the effects it has – both positive and negative – on human values, relationships and daily practice, should command more attention as a way of assessing the implications of processes and technologies outwith the question of how they affect individual privacy.

Third, the outline of policy instruments has served to show that the governance of privacy is not best conceived of as the application of one 'tool' or another, each doing a specific job (as tools do), or as interchangeable multi-purpose devices (as tools generally are not), but as an integrated combination of instruments as well as roles. The problem here is that the manner of their combination – or, in the case of roles, the interaction of the persons or institutions involved – has not been fully worked out in practice and may only partly be capable of design rather than evolution within and across jurisdictions. Yet some of the interdependence of this governance can already be appreciated: for example privacy regulators cannot work effectively without a certain level of public awareness and complaints, without a certain level of compliance and self-regulation amongst data controllers, and without a mass media capable of communicating messages and information about privacy protection. Nor can members of the public have their privacy protected without laws that enjoin data controllers to perform in certain ways and without regulators or civil society groups to champion their interests.

Technology developers, for their part, need greater understanding of the privacy (or surveillance) implications of what they design, and need it early enough to allow the incorporation of protections in their products and services; the repository of such understanding lies largely outwith the technology community, in the regulatory, advocacy and academic worlds. On the transnational level, privacy protection in one country is no longer a feasible strategy in the age of globalized information flows, for regulators need each other and are enjoined, in some legislation, to help each other, and they need transnational self-regulatory associations as well. These are only sketchy indications of how a realization of the way in which instruments relate to one another could assist towards a clearer view of the aims, objectives and means of providing privacy protection.

A fourth set of issues that require clearer conceptualization and practical thinking concerns the nature of risk and trust, and the relationship between them. Everyone says that trust is crucial for e-commerce and e-government, and something is known, through surveys and focus group research, about who trusts which organizations to do what, and why, yet exploration of how trust works as a process is not far advanced. Moreover, how much trust is enough to sustain transactions in cyberspace? How can the requisite level be achieved and who should be responsible for helping to achieve it, given the broad value of these transactions for economies and governments and not merely for the suppliers of goods and services? How can trust be regained once it has been lost by (say) governments and online merchants? As for risk, it seems important to get beyond simple divisions of situations into those that are risky and those that are not, or even a conventional high/medium/low assessment. It is rarely clear how such determinations are arrived at; nor is it clear who should be responsible for making them. Moreover, in the terms of privacy protection as social policy, we are hampered in our ability to understand the social distribution of these privacy risks and, therefore, to argue for a more equitable redistribution. Certainly, the question of risk is extraordinarily difficult to apply in many fields, not least in that of privacy protection; yet in the absence of an attempt to do so more coherently, privacy-invasive practices whose proponents can point to the benefits to be gained, and who can put monetary or political value on these benefits, are far more likely to be persuasive in thus trumping privacy. To the extent that this remains so, it constitutes a policy problem in a liberal-democratic society which, like others, subscribes to internationally recognized principles of human rights.

In this connection, PIA could play an important role in addressing issues of risk inherent in information systems and practices and, by extension, in having an effect on the confidence or trust in which the managers of those systems and practices are held by members of the public whose data they process. Depending on its rigour – and in the current state of its development as a technique, there is no universal standard – PIA could prove to be too inconvenient and contestable to constitute an acceptable and valuable addition to a privacy regime. On the other hand, the value of PIA may lie in the questions it requires proposers of new ICT and systems applications to answer in some detail, and to take action upon if the answer so indicates; questions which would arguably not be posed in the absence of a requirement – whether mandated or by self-regulatory policy – to do so. In particular, the embedding of PIA in the precautionary principle is likely to prove controversial; but this principle is already inherent in many aspects of privacy protection law and practice.

This chapter has thus tried to suggest some new ways of looking at the subject and to explore the practical potential of new ways of constructing regulatory regimes for privacy protection. As mentioned earlier, regulatory problems and issues increasingly fall to the development of transnational institutions and processes, although those of particular jurisdictions, including the UK, are not obsolete. This is in part because they may be indispensable platforms for transnational action and in part because information privacy problems of domestic provenance will remain matters of concern for populations, perhaps especially in the realm of e-government and the public sector. It may be insufficient to train our analytical lenses on the national level, or to concentrate on the improvement of regulatory practice within the borders of the UK alone, but it is far from irrelevant. Either way, national policy making and adjudication are likely to play a major part in the protection of privacy in cyberspace.

NOTES

1   This chapter draws upon Bennett and Raab (2003), which should be consulted for a more detailed discussion of issues and developments.
2   See www.truste.org; www.bbbonline.org; and www.webtrust.org, all accessed 17 April 2004.

REFERENCES

Adams, J. (1995), *Risk*, London: UCL Press.

Alberta OIPC (2001), 'Privacy Impact Assessment: Full Questionnaire', Office of the Information and Privacy Commissioner of Alberta, www.oipc.ab.ca/pia/ accessed 17 Apr. 04.

Allen, A. (1985), *Uneasy Access: Privacy for Women in a Free Society*, Totowa NJ: Rowman & Littlefield.

Arndt, H. (1949), 'The Cult of Privacy', *Australia Quarterly* 21: 69-71.

Barber, B. (1983), *The Logic and Limits of Trust*, New Brunswick NJ: Rutgers University Press.

Beck, U. (1992), *Risk Society: Towards a New Modernity*, London: Sage.

Bennett, C. (1992), *Regulating Privacy: Data Protection and Public Policy in Europe and the United States*, Ithaca NY: Cornell University Press.

Bennett, C. (1995), *Implementing Privacy Codes of Practice: A Report to the Canadian Standards Association*, Canadian Standards Association, PLUS 8830, Rexdale.

Bennett, C. and Raab, C. (2003), *The Governance of Privacy: Policy Instruments in Global Perspective*, Aldershot: Ashgate.

Boling, P. (1996), *Privacy and the Politics of Intimate Life*, Ithaca NY: Cornell University Press.

Borking, J. and Raab, C. (2001), 'Laws, PETs and Other Technologies for Privacy Protection', *The Journal of Information Law and Technology* 1, elj.warwick.ac.uk/jilt/01-1/borking.html accessed 17 Apr. 04.

Bowker, G. and Star, S. (1999), *Sorting Things Out: Classification and its Consequences*, Cambridge MA: MIT Press.

British Columbia Ministry of Management Services (2003), *Privacy Impact Assessment (PIA) Process*,
www.mser.gov.bc.ca/foi_pop/PIA/piaPrint.asp accessed 17 Apr. 04.

Canadian Standards Association (CSA) (1996), *Model Code for the Protection of Personal Information*, CAN/CSA-Q830-96, Rexdale: CSA.

Catlett, J. (2000), 'Open Letter to P3P Developers and Replies', in *CFP2000: Challenging the Assumptions, Proceedings of the Tenth Conference on Computers, Freedom and Privacy*, New York: Association for Computing Machinery, pp. 155-64,
www.junkbusters.com/ht/en/standards.html, accessed 17 Apr. 04.

Cavoukian, A. and Tapscott, D. (1996), *Who Knows? Safeguarding Your Privacy in a Networked World*, New York: McGraw-Hill.

Charlesworth, A. (2000), 'Clash of the Data Titans: US and EU Data Privacy Regulation' *European Public Law* 6(2): 253-74.

Charlesworth, A. (2003), 'Information Privacy Law in the European Union: E Pluribus Unum or Ex Uno Plures?', *Hastings Law Journal* 54: 931-69.

Chaum, D. (1992), 'Achieving Electronic Privacy', *Scientific American* 267(Aug.): 96-101.

Council of Europe (CoE) (1981), *Convention for the Protection of Individuals with regard to Automatic Processing of Personal Data (Convention 108)*, Strasbourg: Council of Europe.

Department for Constitutional Affairs (DCA) (2003), 'Response to the Consultation Paper, For Your Information: How Can the Public Sector Provide People with Information on, and Build Confidence in, the Way it Handles their Personal Details?', London: Department for Constitutional Affairs,
www.dca.gov.uk/consult/datasharing/datasharcrcsp.htm accessed 17 Apr. 04.

Department of Health (2003), *Confidentiality: NHS Code of Practice*, London: Department of Health.

Diffie, W. and Landau, S. (1998), *Privacy on the Line: The Politics of Wiretapping and Encryption*, Cambridge MA: MIT Press.

Dumortier, J. and Goemans, C. (2000), 'Data Privacy and Standardization', discussion paper prepared for the CEN/ISSS Open Seminar on Data Protection, Brussels 23-24 March, www.law.kuleuven.ac.be/icri/publications/90CEN-Paper.pdf accessed 17 Apr. 04.

European Union (EU) (1995), *Directive 95/46/EC of the European Parliament and of the Council on the Protection of Individuals with regard to the Processing of Personal Data and on the Free Movement of Such Data*, OJ L281, 23 November, Brussels: EC.

European Union (EU) (1998), *Directive 97/66/EC of the European Parliament and of the Council Concerning the Processing of Personal Data and the Protection of Privacy in the Telecommunications Sector,* OJ L24, 30 January, Brussels: EC.

European Union (EU) (2002), *Directive 2002/58/EC of the European Parliament and of the Council Concerning the Processing of Personal Data and the Protection of Privacy in the Electronic Communication Sector,* OJ L201, 31 July, Brussels: EC.

Flaherty, D. (1989), *Protecting Privacy in Surveillance Societies: The Federal Republic of Germany, Sweden, France, Canada, and the United States*, Chapel Hill NC: University of North Carolina Press.

Flaherty, D. (2003), 'Privacy Impact Assessments (PIAs): An Essential Tool for Data Protection', (revised version of paper first published in S. Perrin, H. Black, D. Flaherty and T. Rankin (eds), *The Personal Information Protection and Electronic Documents Act: An Annotated Guide*, Toronto: Irwin Law, 2001.

Foucault, M. (1979), *Discipline and Punish: The Birth of the Prison*, New York: Vintage Books.

Fukuyama, F. (1995), *Trust: Social Virtues and the Creation of Prosperity*, New York: Free Press.

Gambetta, D. (ed.) (1988), *Trust: Making and Breaking Cooperative Relations*, New York, NY: Blackwell.

Gandy, O. (1993), *The Panoptic Sort: A Political Economy of Personal Information*, Boulder CO: Westview Press.

Gellman, R. (1993), 'Fragmented, Incomplete and Discontinuous: The Failure of Federal Privacy Regulatory Proposals and Institutions', *Software Law Journal* 6(2): 199-231.

Giddens, A. (1991), *Modernity and Self-Identity*, Stanford CA: Stanford University Press.

Hong Kong (2001), *E-Privacy: A Policy Approach to Building Trust and Confidence in E-Business*, Hong Kong: Office of the Privacy Commissioner for Personal Data, www.pco.org.hk/textonly/english/publications/eprivacy_1.html accessed 17 Apr. 04.

Hood, C. (1983), *The Tools of Government*, London and Basingstoke: Macmillan.

Industry Canada (1994), 'Privacy and the Canadian Information Highway: Building Canada's Information and Communications Infrastructure', Information Highway Advisory Council, Industry Canada, Ottawa.

Kooiman, J. (2003), *Governing as Governance*, London: Sage.

Laudon, K. (1996), 'Markets and Privacy', *Communications of the Association for Computing Machinery* 39(10): 92-104.

Lessig, L. (1999), *Code and Other Laws of Cyberspace*, New York: Basic Books.

Longworth, E. (1996), *Notes on Privacy Impact Assessments*, Christchurch, NZ: Longworth Associates.

Luhmann, N. (1979), *Trust and Power*, Chichester: John Wiley & Sons.

Lyon, D. (1994), *The Electronic Eye: The Rise of Surveillance Society*, Minneapolis MN: University of Minnesota Press.

Lyon, D. (2001), *Surveillance Society: Monitoring Everyday Life*, Buckingham: Open University Press.

Marx, G. (1988), *Undercover: Police Surveillance in America*, Berkeley CA: University of California Press.

Marx, G. (1999), 'Ethics for the New Surveillance', in C. Bennett and R. Grant (eds), *Visions of Privacy: Policy Choices for the Digital Age*, Toronto: University of Toronto Press, pp. 38-67.

Ministry of International Trade and Industry (MITI) Japan (1997), *Guidelines Concerning the Protection of Computer Processed Personal Data in the Private Sector*, Tokyo: MITI.

Misztal, B. (1996), *Trust in Modern Societies: The Search for the Basis of Social Order*, Cambridge: Polity Press.

MORI (2003), *Privacy and Data-Sharing: Survey of Public Awareness and Perceptions*, Research Study Conducted for Department for Constitutional Affairs, London: Market and Opinion Research International.

Neumann, P. (1995), *Computer-Related Risks*, New York: ACM Press/Addison-Wesley.

New Zealand (2002), *Privacy Impact Assessment Handbook*, Office of the Privacy Commissioner, Auckland, www.privacy.org.nz/comply/pia.html accessed 17 Apr. 04.

Office of Management and Budget (OMB) (2003), *OMB Guidance for Implementing the Privacy Provisions of the E-Government Act of 2002*, M-03-22, Memorandum for Heads of Executive Departments and Agencies, Office of Management and Budget, Executive Office of the President, Washington, DC.

O'Neill, O. (2002), *Autonomy and Trust in Bioethics*, Cambridge: Cambridge University Press.

Ontario (2001), *Privacy Impact Assessment: A User's Guide*, Information and Privacy Office, and IT Strategy, Policy, Planning and Management Branch, Office of the Corporate Chief Strategist, Management Board Secretariat, Toronto.

Ontario (1995), Office of the Information and Privacy Commissioner and Netherlands Registratiekamer, *Privacy-Enhancing Technologies: The Path to Anonymity*, Toronto: Information and Privacy Commissioner and Registratiekamer.

Ontario (1999), Office of the Information and Privacy Commissioner and Netherlands Registratiekamer, *Intelligent Software Agents: Turning a Privacy Threat into a Privacy Protector*, Toronto: Information and Privacy Commissioner and Registratiekamer.

Ontario (2000), Office of the Information and Privacy Commissioner and Australia, Office of the Federal Privacy Commissioner, 'Web Seals: A Review of Online Privacy Programs', a Joint Paper by Ontario's Information and Privacy Commissioner and the Federal Privacy Commissioner of Australia, for Presentation to the 22nd International Conference on Privacy and Personal Data Protection, Venice.

Organisation for Economic Cooperation and Development (OECD) (1981), *Guidelines on the Protection of Privacy and Transborder Flows of Personal Data*, Paris: OECD.

Organisation for Economic Cooperation and Development (OECD) (1985), *Declaration on Transborder Data Flows*, Paris: OECD.

Organisation for Economic Cooperation and Development (OECD) (1992), *Guidelines for the Security of Information Systems*, Paris: OECD.

Organisation for Economic Cooperation and Development (OECD) (1997), *Cryptography Policy: The Guidelines and the Issues*, Paris: OECD.

Pateman, C. (1983), 'Feminist Critiques of the Public/Private Dichotomy', in S. Benn and G. Gaus (eds), *Public and Private in Social Life*, New York: St. Martin's Press, pp. 281-303.

Performance and Innovation Unit (PIU) (2002), *Privacy and Data-Sharing*, London: PIU, Cabinet Office.

Posner, R. (1978), 'An Economic Theory of Privacy', *Regulation* May/June: 19-26.

PRIVA-C[TM] (2003), *Privacy Impact Assessments: A Guide to the Best Approach for Your Organization*, Fredericton, New Brunswick: PRIVA-C[TM], www.priva-c.com, accessed 17 Apr. 04.

Raab, C. (1993), 'Data Protection in Britain: Governance and Learning', *Governance*, 6: 43-66.

Raab, C. (1995), 'Connecting Orwell to Athens? Information Superhighways and the Privacy Debate', in W. van de Donk, I. Snellen and P. Tops (eds), *Orwell in Athens: A Perspective on Informatization and Democracy*, Amsterdam: IOS Press, pp. 195-211.

Raab, C. (1996), 'Implementing Data Protection in Britain', *International Review of Administrative Sciences* 62(4): 493-511.

Raab, C. (1997a), 'Privacy, Democracy, Information', in B. Loader (ed.), *The Governance of Cyberspace*, London: Routledge, pp. 155-74.

Raab, C. (1997b), 'Co-Producing Data Protection', *International Review of Law, Computers and Technology* 11(1): 11-42.

Raab, C. (1998), 'Electronic Confidence: Trust, Information and Public Administration', in I. Snellen and W. van de Donk (eds), *Public Administration in an Information Age: A Handbook*, Amsterdam: IOS Press, pp. 113-33.

Raab, C. (1999), 'From Balancing to Steering: New Directions for Data Protection', in C. Bennett and R. Grant (eds), *Visions of Privacy: Policy Choices for the Digital Age*, Toronto: University of Toronto Press, pp. 68-93.

Raab, C. (2003), 'Privacy Impact Assessment: The Question of Risk', paper presented to the International Workshop on Privacy Impact Assessment, Office of the Privacy Commissioner, Auckland, NZ, 16 Sept.

Regan, P. (2002), 'Privacy as a Common Good in the Digital World', *Information, Communication and Society* 5(3): 382-405.

Regan, P. (1995), *Legislating Privacy: Technology, Social Values and Public Policy*, Chapel Hill NC: University of North Carolina Press.

Reidenberg, J. (1997), 'Governing Networks and Rule-Making in Cyberspace', in B. Kahin and C. Nesson (eds), *Borders in Cyberspace*, Cambridge MA: MIT Press, pp. 84-105.

Reidenberg, J. (1998), 'Lex Informatica: The Formulation of Information Policy Rules Through Technology', *Texas Law Review* 76(3): 553-85.

Royal Society (1992), *Risk: Analysis, Perception and Management*, London: The Royal Society.

Rule, J. and Hunter, L. (1999), 'Towards Property Rights in Personal Data', in C. Bennett and R. Grant (eds), *Visions of Privacy: Policy Choices for the Digital Age*, Toronto: University of Toronto Press, pp. 168-81.

Rule, J., McAdam, D., Stearns, L. and Uglow, D. (1980), *The Politics of Privacy: Planning for Personal Data Systems as Powerful Technologies*, New York: Elsevier Science.

Schoeman, F. (1992), *Privacy and Social Freedom*, Cambridge: Cambridge University Press.

Sieghart, P. (1976), *Privacy and Computers*, London: Latimer.

Smith, R. (1993), *War Stories: Accounts of Persons Victimized by Invasions of Privacy*, Providence RI: Privacy Journal.

Stewart, B. (2003), 'Classification of Known Privacy Impact Assessments', document prepared for the International Workshop on Privacy Impact Assessment, Auckland, NZ, 16 September.

Stewart, B. (1996), 'Privacy Impact Assessments', *Privacy Law and Policy Reporter* 3-4(July): 61-4,
www.austlii.edu.au/journals/PLPR/1996/39.html accessed 17 Apr. 04.

Tait, J. and Levidow, L. (1992), 'Proactive and Reactive Approaches to Regulation: The Case of "Biotechnology"', *Futures* 24(3): 219-31.

The Economist (1999), 'End of Privacy', 351(8117): 16, 105-7.

Treasury Board of Canada Secretariat (2002), *Privacy Impact Assessment Policy*,
www.tbs-sct.gc.ca/pubs_pol/ciopubs/pia-pefr/paip-pefr-
PR_e.asp?printable=True accessed 17 Apr. 04.

Warren, S. and Brandeis, L. (1890), 'The Right to Privacy', *Harvard Law Review* 4(5): 193-220.

Westin, A. (1967), *Privacy and Freedom*, New York: Atheneum.

White, F. (2001), 'The Use of Privacy Impact Assessments in Canada', *Privacy Files* 4(7): 1-11.

6, P. (1998), *The Future of Privacy, Volume 1: Private Life and Public Policy*, London: Demos.

10 Usability and trust in information systems

M. Angela Sasse

10.1 INTRODUCTION

The need for people to protect themselves and their assets is as old as humankind. People's physical safety and their possessions have always been at risk from deliberate attack or accidental damage. The advance of information and communication technology (ICT) means that many individuals, as well as corporations, have additional ranges of physical (equipment) and electronic (data) assets that are at risk. Furthermore, the increased number and types of interactions in cyberspace have enabled new forms of attack on people and their possessions. Consider grooming of minors in chat-rooms, or Nigerian email cons: minors were targeted by paedophiles before the creation of chat-rooms, and Nigerian criminals sent the same letters by physical mail or fax before there was email. But the technology has decreased the cost of many types of attacks, or the degree of risk for the attackers.

At the same time, cyberspace is still new to many people, which means they do not understand these risks or recognize the signs of an attack as readily as they might in the physical world. The ICT industry has developed a plethora of security mechanisms, which could be used to mitigate risks or make attacks significantly more difficult. Currently, many people are either not aware of these mechanisms, or are unable or unwilling to use them. Security experts have taken to portraying people as 'the weakest link' in their efforts to deploy effective security (for example Schneier 2000). However, recent research has revealed that at least part of the problem may be that security mechanisms are hard to use or are ineffective. This chapter summarizes current research on the usability of security mechanisms and discusses options for increasing this usability and the effectiveness of these mechanisms.

Most security mechanisms are based on access control and checking of credentials, and often users are told 'not to trust anyone in cyberspace'. Most people would agree that minors in chat-rooms should not unquestioningly trust that their conversation partners are who they say they are, and that recipients of con emails should not believe the stories put forward as lures. But the solution to the threats from cyberspace cannot simply be 'don't trust anyone'. Trust is an integral part of our social and business interactions: trust that is warranted will, over time, lead to an increase in social capital and a decrease in the cost of economic systems. The review in this chapter points out the underlying dilemma between the need for trust in human interactions and the dangers of misplacing trust in the electronic domain. Finally, this chapter identifies some usability issues connected to privacy, which is closely linked to security and trust.

10.2 USABILITY

Usability of security mechanisms was, until recently, an under-researched area. Zurko and Simon (1996) were the first to point out that current security mechanisms make unreasonable demands on many stakeholders. Users, system administrators and system developers struggle with the workload created by many current security mechanisms, and are overwhelmed by the increasing complexity involved in securing systems at all possible levels (hardware, operating system, network, applications). The problems of system administrators and developers will be briefly considered in the conclusions to this section. The main part of the chapter, however, focuses on usability of security mechanisms for users.

The definition of a usable system (based on Shackel 1975) requires that:

- the intended users can meet a desired level of performance operating it (task performance);
- the amount of learning and practice required to reach that desired level of performance is appropriate (learnability);
- the system does not place any undue physical or mental strain on the user (user cost); and
- users are satisfied with the experience of interacting with the system.

These considerations have traditionally been applied to an individual user interacting with the technology. However, most interactions between users and security mechanisms take place in the context of a socio-technical system (for example, a corporate environment) with different stakeholders (Checkland 1999). These stakeholders have different goals and views, which sometimes conflict – for example the organization may put the task performance of the organization as a whole before satisfaction of the individual user. While outside the corporate context, users may have some degree of choice about security mechanisms and whether they employ them, organizations set security policies, which not only govern the selection of security mechanisms, but also specify the behaviour that users are expected to exhibit. Another issue is that key usability principles (for example providing feedback or forgiveness) are currently not applied to design of security mechanisms, because help offered to the user could also be exploited by a potential attacker. Usability and security are often seen as competing design goals and it is thus not surprising that the results of the few empirical studies that have looked at usability of security mechanisms have been rather damning. Security mechanisms that have been studied include authentication mechanisms, email encryption and web security; the remainder of this section summarizes the findings and discusses how usability of these specific mechanisms could be improved.

10.2.1 Authentication Mechanisms

Authentication is a cornerstone of most security systems today, and most users interact with these mechanisms on a daily basis. The login is usually a two-step procedure:

- identification (entering the user_id or account), followed by
- verification (matching the password stored for that account to what the user enters).

Some mechanisms can operate as a one-step procedure of identification or verification only.

There are three types of authentication mechanisms:

- knowledge-based authentication (passwords and passphrases, PINs, graphical passwords);
- token-based authentication (physical tokens such as smart cards or badges); and
- biometric-based authentication (using users' physical characteristics such as fingerprint, hand geometry, iris pattern or face).

Some security mechanisms may combine two of these mechanisms as part of the two-step procedure (for example bank card and PIN).

The vast majority of empirical studies on usability and security have looked at authentication mechanisms. This review uses those findings to ground a detailed discussion of the causes of usability problems with security mechanisms and what options are available for improving that situation.

10.2.1.1 Knowledge-based authentication

Knowledge-based authentication is by far the most common security mechanism used in ICT today. The cardinal rule of knowledge-based authentication is that the verification item (password or PIN) should exist in two places only: in the system (in encrypted form) and in the user's mind, and should not be externalized (written down) or disclosed to anyone else.

Passwords and passphrases. Passwords consist of strings of alphanumeric characters. To prevent cracking attacks,[1] security experts advise that users must have strong passwords (a non-meaningful string of characters drawn from a large character set, mixing letters, numbers and symbols, and upper and lower case) and many company security policies (see also section on user interfaces) mandate the use of strong passwords. Unfortunately, the functioning of human memory makes strong passwords more difficult to recall. In the study by Adams and Sasse (1999), users reported that they had an increasing number of passwords to remember and regularly encountered problems, particularly for infrequently used passwords.

Sasse et al. (2001) confirmed this with a set of objective data on password performance and concluded that the way in which passwords are currently implemented (non-meaningful items, changed regularly, with many similar competing items) conflicts with the characteristics of human memory (items decay over time unless recalled frequently; cannot forget on demand; similar items compete), especially for infrequently used passwords.

Brostoff and Sasse (2000) provide some insight into failed logins based on empirical data:

- 52 per cent of failed logins are due to users entering the wrong password (37 per cent entered their old password for the same system, instead of their current one, 15 per cent entered their password for another system).
- In 12 per cent of failed logins users seemed to have recalled the correct password, but mistyped it on entry.
- 20 per cent of failed logins were due to the users entering the wrong user_id (account name), rather than the wrong password.

Users' inability to cope with the current number and form of passwords is further confirmed by the quality of passwords users chose. In a survey of 1,200 users of bank access control systems (Petrie 2002):

- 90 per cent of respondents reported having passwords that were dictionary words or names; with
- 47 per cent of the sample using a name (their own name or names of their partners, children or pets); and
- only 9 per cent of respondents reported using cryptographically strong passwords, as recommended by security policies.

Yan (2001) points out that weak passwords, as used by 90 per cent of respondents in this study, hugely reduce the time and computing power required to crack passwords.

Even in organizations that explicitly instruct users on how to select strong passwords, many do not comply: Yan et al. (2000) report that 32 per cent of students at Cambridge University had passwords that could be cracked with a quick dictionary attack. Dhamija and Perrig (2000) report that despite instruction and admitting to 'knowing better', participants in their study at the University of California at Berkeley picked weak passwords.[2] Similar results have been reported by studies run in corporate environments, for example Sasse et al. (2001). Other pertinent findings on password quality from this study are that:

- most users try to increase the memorability of passwords by using one password for several systems;
- more than half of passwords consist of a word with a number at the end;
- users only change passwords when forced to; and
- most 'change' the password by increasing the number by one.

Personal identification numbers (PINs). PINs are used to secure access to applications, either in combination with a token for two-step identification (for example for cash dispensers), or as a one-step authentication (for example mobile phones, home burglar alarms). Given their wide usage, the lack of available (published) empirical evidence is disconcerting; many financial institutions conduct internal research, but the findings are never published for fear of damaging customer confidence or reputation. There are informally reported data, for instance, that one-third of users use their birth date as their PIN (Anderson 2001). There are anecdotal reports that users write the PIN on the card itself, or other materials carried in the same wallet; some banks have also discovered PINs scratched into cash dispensers or materials surrounding them.

This indicates that PINs are even harder to remember than the standard computer password, which also tallies with results from general research on human memory (Schacter 2002). Sasse et al. (2001), comparing problems reported with passwords and PINs in the same corporate environment, conclude that:

- infrequently used PINs are extremely vulnerable to being forgotten;
- even frequently (daily) used PINs are forgotten by the majority of users after very short periods (one week) of non-use; and
- managing multiple PINs, and/or PINs that are frequently changed, creates even more usability problems than managing multiple passwords.

Graphical passwords. Increasing problems with passwords and PINs have led to a spurt in the efforts to provide more usable knowledge-based authentication mechanisms. Psychological research on human memory (Schacter 2002) has established that:

- human performance at recognition is far superior to unaided recall;
- images are processed and stored differently from words, and are easier to recall.

This knowledge has been applied to the design of graphical user interfaces (GUI) since the 1980s, and more recently has been applied to developing graphical passwords, which authenticate users through recognition of images, or features of images. The two leading examples of such systems are *Déjà Vu* (Dhamija and Perrig 2000) and Passfaces™ (Passfaces 2003). With *Déjà Vu,* users select their clues from a set of random art (randomly generated computer art), and on login select their images from a set of distractor images. Passfaces™ is based on a large image base of human faces.[3] Users select one face from each of four panels of nine faces and recognize these images from eight distractor faces on login.

Initial evaluation of these systems indicated huge advantages in memory performance compared to standard passwords. Dhamija and Perrig (2000) report that an initial evaluation of *Déjà Vu* demonstrated much better performance than for passwords. A laboratory-based study of Passfaces™ (Valentine 1999a, b) found extremely good recall rates (over 95 per cent successful logins within three attempts), even after a three-month period of non-use.

These results indicate that graphical password systems have a significant performance advantage for infrequently used authentication. Informal reports from commercial trials, however, indicate that this performance advantage disappears rapidly when users have multiple logins using the same type of image or when the images or faces are changed.

Graphical passwords are not suitable for frequently used authentication because they tend to be slow – graphics slow down the login procedure – and to decrease the chances of an attacker guessing the right cue, users have to go through a minimum of three or four rounds of selection. Brostoff and Sasse (2000) report that logins by students to a coursework server dropped by 70 per cent compared to the standard password login, because the graphical login took 30 to 90 seconds to complete, as opposed to five seconds for the password login. Also, frequent use of graphical passwords in public or semi-public environments (such as public libraries or Internet cafes) increases the chances of shoulder-surfing attackers.

Empirical evidence on knowledge-based authentication. Knowledge-based authentication in the form of passwords and PINs is by far the most widely used security mechanism today. From a technical point of view, password systems are cheap to set up. However, empirical research has shown that the cost of operating this mechanism is unacceptable for individual users and organizations alike:

1. The user cost associated with current password systems is unacceptable for most individual users. There is a high mental workload associated with memorizing and recalling multiple passwords, and cost associated with failed logins. Additional user cost arises because many users worry about not being able to recall passwords, which leads to stress, and this, in turn, often creates negative perceptions of, and attitudes to, security mechanisms and organizational security in general (Adams and Sasse 1999).
2. When legitimate users fail to authenticate, they are unable to carry out the work activity or gain access to resources or services. Thus, low task-performance on the login task impacts on performance of the production task. This means individual users are prevented from reaching their goals, which is irritating at best, and very distressing if the goal is important and/or users are under time pressures. In corporate environments, failure to complete production tasks has a negative impact on the productivity of the overall organization.
3. There are further costs to the individual user and the organization when passwords have to be reset following a failed login. The user has to construct, memorize and recall a new password. The organization incurs further costs because the resetting of passwords has to be done by system administrators or via specialist helpdesks; some organizations now expend significant resources on resetting passwords (Sasse et al. 2001). Many organizations use automated password reminder systems, which minimize the costs for both the individual user and the organizations, but reissuing rather than resetting passwords contravenes standard security

guidelines (FIPS 1985). Automated credential recovery systems (CRS) can be used to reset passwords without a human operator (Just 2003), but the cost of setting up a secure CRS, and registering credentials, is high for both organization and user.[4]

The attitude of many security experts is that good security does not come cheap. The results from empirical research on knowledge-based authentication show, however, that the strategies that users employ to cope with the 'inhuman' workload that knowledge-based authentication creates makes these systems largely ineffective. The vast majority of users do write some or all of their passwords down – and some security departments even encourage their users to do so in a secure manner.[5]

Another, less often discussed, threat arises from users' attempts to increase memorability by using the same password across several systems. Whilst the increase in risk from doing this may be low in many corporate contexts (where reuse of passwords may be allowed for low-risk systems), Anderson (2001, p. 39) points out that many users do not consider the consequences in every circumstance: 'the password you use to authenticate [yourself as] the customer of the electronic banking system ... is quite possibly known to a Mafia-operated porn site as well'.

Similarly, users may see little wrong with disclosing the PIN used on a shared office or mobile phone. But if this is the same PIN as used with their bank card, this practice greatly facilitates theft by colleagues or family members. Given that individuals who are victims of bank fraud are very likely to have been defrauded by somebody known to them, the need for individuals to protect themselves on shared devices, such as home PCs and mobile phones, is overriding.[6]

Any knowledge-based authentication mechanism will create a certain amount of mental workload for individual users, but the workload is manageable if the number of items is kept low, or if items are frequently used (in which case recall becomes automatic). The problems observed arise from the fact that each user interacts with many systems and devices that have to be protected, and their numbers are likely to increase significantly over the next ten years.

Research on memory (see Schacter 2002 for a summary) suggests that recalling more than two or three strong passwords is beyond the ability of human memory, and even those would be difficult to recall if used infrequently. Possible interventions include:

1. *Reducing the number of passwords.* In corporate environments, a deliberate strategy to reduce the numbers of passwords and PINs is employed. Some companies are deploying single sign-on, for an

example, see V-Go (2003). Even simple measures such as standardizing individual users' user_id across different systems can help to reduce users' mental workload and numbers of failed logins.

2. *Provide training and support.* If security needs are such that users have to manage a number of strong passwords, specialist instruction and training on how to construct and memorize passwords, for example on how to construct passwords or passphrases with a high degree of personal entropy (Ellison et al. 2000), can improve their performance. Passphrase (longer, and hence harder to crack) passwords allow users to use meaningful content (Schneier 2000). This increases memorability, but also the chance of mistyping; given an appropriate number of attempts (see below), passphrases would seem particularly suitable for infrequently used authentication. Other types of support could be allowing users to store hints with a high degree of personal entropy (including images and sounds) in a CRS or personal password manager on a device users carry with them (for example, a personal digital assistant (PDA) or mobile phone).

3. *Recognition rather than recall.* The characteristics of human memory mean it is far easier to recognize an item (aided recall) or action than to recall it (unaided recall). This design principle is pervasive in the design of current-generation GUIs (where users recognize the correct command from a limited set of menu items or icons), and there have been attempts to apply this principle to authentication mechanisms using graphical passwords. Such mechanisms are likely to work particularly well for infrequently used systems, provided the number of clues used is low, or multiple cues are very distinct. The principle can also be applied to text-based knowledge-based systems: for example, through associative passwords (see Zviran and Haga 1993) or challenge-response authentication.

4. *Move away from 'all-or-nothing' authentication.* Current password logins fail unless the password is entered 100 per cent correctly; they are not forgiving to user error. Rather than drawing a complete blank, most logins fail because users mistype passwords, or enter an old password, or the password for a different system. A key usability principle is to provide feedback to users when their actions are unsuccessful. Current password systems do not provide any feedback about why the login failed and possible actions the user could take to recover, because this could help the attacker. Nevertheless, authentication mechanisms can be made more forgiving. Text-based challenge-response systems, for instance, can be set to pass the user on three correct answers, or four correct and one incorrect and so on. Multilevel authentication (Zviran and Haga 1990) can make systems more forgiving by providing back-up

when access by password and/or PIN (see below) fails; typically, the user will be taken through an automated or human-interaction credential recovery process. This method is widely used in telephone banking, for instance, but many of these systems are vulnerable because they use publicly available knowledge (for example mother's maiden name) as credentials, as opposed to 'secrets' (Schneier 2000).[7] Even the usability of standard password authentication can be improved by relaxing some policies. Brostoff and Sasse (2003) conducted a three-month trial in which users were free to have as many login attempts as they wanted and could at any stage ask for a password reminder. They found that when the initial login attempt failed, only 53 per cent of users managed to recover within three attempts, but almost all users (93 per cent) would persist and manage to login in ten attempts or less. Increasing the number of login attempts increases the threat of password guessing by a fellow insider (who may also employ shoulder-surfing), but makes no difference to the threat of password cracking by an outside attacker (which is what most firms worry about).

In the light of usability problems with PINs, it is worrying that manufacturers of smartcards and other forms of token-based authentication systems seem to favour using tokens in combination with a PIN, and that PINs have been proposed as a back-up for biometric authentification.

10.2.1.2 Token-based authentication
Whilst knowledge-based authentication is currently the predominant mechanism, token-based authentication has been widely used in the physical domain. Tokens can be used as a one-step process, for example swipe cards for door access, but this is a fairly weak mechanism since a token may be stolen or found by a potential attacker, who can use it until the loss or theft is discovered and the token is revoked. Therefore, tokens are more often combined with another method in a two-step process, the combination of bank cards and PINs for cash dispensers being the most widely used example. Tokens are becoming increasingly popular, with the token used for authentication, and the knowledge-based item (PIN) for verification, thus reducing the memory load compared to a two-step knowledge-based procedure. There is no published research on usability issues with tokens or smart cards. Tokens such as the SecurID have been used, with apparent success, for remote access by financial institutions. On the other hand, the high cost of replacing lost tokens and/or lost working time has led companies in other sectors to abandon it.

The city of Turin is currently undertaking the first large-scale attempt to issue smart cards to citizens for access to services and payment of local taxes

(Torinofacile 2003). Based on 2,655 smart cards issued, the number of tokens that were lost in the post or stolen in the first six months was low (16). The majority of citizens who registered for the card were male, well educated and aged between 19 and 45; the number of cards issued to males was three times higher than for female citizens. Since most home and small business PCs are currently not fitted with smart card readers, the trial issued digital certificates for users who needed them. The initial phase has seen a high number of calls to the helpdesk, the majority of which (83) were due to problems with using these digital certificates. The second most frequent problem was that personal details registered about the owners of the cards were incorrect.[8] These insights offer some pointers as to logistical aspects and the costs that are likely to be associated with issuing such tokens to a large number of citizens. At the same time, small businesses, single traders and professionals report significant time savings and benefits from online access and payments compared to paper-based systems and access restricted to office hours.

Smart cards can offer additional usability benefits: once the login procedure is completed, the token can be used to carry sessions from one machine to another, thus removing the need to log out or lock the screen when leaving the machine unattended for brief periods. They can also offer additional security features for applications such as credit cards.

One usability concern arising from the increasing popularity of tokens is that users may end up being 'weighed down' by a collection of tokens that they find hard to manage. There are two possible ways in which this might be prevented:

1. Single tokens carrying multiple credentials. A single token, such as a smart card, could be used to store users' credentials for multiple systems. The single token could either store data for multiple identification and verification mechanisms operated by different organizations (providing the user with a personal 'credential/password manager'), or have a single strong verification (providing the user with a 'magic key'). Both approaches would require an open standard for credentials, and the second would also require agreement on a single form of authentication and a high degree of trust between participating organizations. The 'magic key' model would create least work for the user, but also create a single point of attack.

2. Miniaturization of tokens. Organizations continue to issue their own tokens and decide their own access control mechanisms, but the tokens are so small (for example radio frequency identification (RFID) chips) that users can keep all of their tokens on them at all times, for example in a smart card-type device to which individual chips can be added.

10.2.1.3 Biometric authentication

Biometric authentication uses a physical characteristic (the most commonly used ones being a fingerprint, iris recognition, hand geometry and face recognition) to identify or verify individuals. Since biometrics use physical characteristics, they are generally perceived to provide a strong form of identification or authentication. However, many usability experts (for example Schneier 2000) dismiss biometrics as an ineffective security mechanism because, unlike knowledge-based items, biometrics are not secret: systems can be attacked by harvesting characteristics from legitimate users (for example 'lifting' a fingerprint from a surface or taking a picture of the eye). As a heuristic, the better that systems protect against such attacks, the more expensive they are.

Most biometric solutions are designed to operate in the traditional two-step mode: the user identifies herself using a token or user_id, and then presents her biometric characteristic, which is compared to a previously stored template: access to cash dispensers for instance, could be secured with a card and fingerprint. Templates are reduced versions of the biometric characteristic, mapping a certain number of key data points. As a rule of thumb, the more data points a template has, the more accurate the recognition, and the more expensive the application is to procure and run. Accuracy of identification has implications for both usability and security: lack of accuracy leads to false rejection (keeping legitimate users out, which reduces usability) or false acceptance (letting in an unauthorized user, or mistaking one user for another), which reduces security. For any particular application with given levels of accuracy, the operators have to make a trade-off: minimizing the number of false acceptances made by the application will lead to a higher number of false rejections. Effectively, operators have to make a trade-off between usability and security. Schneier (2003) cites a study that estimates that even a false rejection rate of 1 per cent could increase the average throughput time for each passenger through airport security by 45 minutes.

An assumed usability advantage of biometrics is that, since individuals always carry their characteristics with them, there is no token that users can forget, lose or have stolen and this therefore minimizes the memory load on the user and supports the usability principle of universal access[9] (Fairhurst et al. 2002)[9]. The reality is that biometric security solutions raise a raft of usability issues, for individuals and organizations alike. A significant number of users are temporarily or permanently unable to register a particular biometric. For instance, 5 per cent of people are estimated not to have readable fingerprints,[10] and blind users cannot register iris images. Temporary inability to register or use a biometric can result from cuts or burns on fingers for fingerprints, or pregnancy or certain types of medication for iris recognition. While temporary inability to use a biometric application might lead to mere delays (decrease in task performance) or annoyance (decrease in user satisfaction), permanent inability to use the system would violate the principle of universal access. Since exclusion of certain user groups is not feasible or acceptable for a wide range of applications, operators have to provide a contingency authentication system (for example a PIN, though this is likely to cause problems, or staff checking written credentials). The cost of operating a contingency authentication system can increase the cost of the biometric application significantly.

More than any other security mechanism, biometric authentication raises the question of acceptability. For certain reasons, some user groups are not comfortable with the use of biometrics, or with the use of biometric authentication in general, for example:

1. Religious reasons. Some religions prevent their members from having their face or eyes photographed, others prohibit touching of artifacts that have been touched by a member of the opposite gender.
2. Safety concerns. Some people fear they might be maimed or killed by criminals trying to obtain their biometric. This seems to be particularly prevalent in individuals who have had no personal experience with biometrics (BIOVISION 2003), since for these individuals, the perception of biometrics is fed by depictions in films (for example of removing eyeballs or hands to overcome biometric access control systems in *Minority Report* or *Die Another Day*).
3. Privacy concerns. Some biometrics, such as face recognition, can also be used in a one-step identification process. An issue here is that they can be used covertly (without the individual being aware that she is being identified), for example in combination with security cameras, to detect known shoplifters, football hooligans and so on. A key concern for many users is whether their biometric data are 'safe'. This concern can be decomposed into two questions:
   (i) How safe are my biometric data? The concern is whether data can be copied or changed.
   (ii) How are my biometric data used? The concern is whether the operator, or anyone else, can use the data for purposes other than those advertised, for example for tracking users' movements.
   Users weigh these concerns against benefits to themselves and others.
4. Labour relations. In corporate environments, biometric authentication is often used as a means of exerting control over employee behaviour – for example biometrics on a time and attendance monitoring system prevent 'buddy-punching'. Employees have fewer issues with the system provided it works well enough, and they trust the operator of the system

(usually their employer) (BIOVISION 2003). However, most people dislike the idea of being constantly monitored and tightly controlled, which is a particular concern with fine-grained monitoring of behavioural biometrics (for example monitoring keystrokes on a keyboard) (Henderson et al. 1998). Constant worry about not performing, or how behaviour is being interpreted by the 'watchers', can be a significant source of stress.

These concerns will need to be balanced by significant real and perceived benefits to make the technology useful and acceptable. Data from surveys and interviews with individuals and organizations reviewed in the EU Roadmap Project on Biometrics (BIOVISION 2003), indicate that this balance will be hard to achieve for large-scale public security deployments of biometrics. The performance that can be achieved with current systems is not sufficient, the cost of deployment and operation is high and most users currently have no security needs that are addressed by these systems. The perceived benefits are seen as being for 'government', with the 'citizen user' shouldering the cost in terms of use and increased cost of identification documents.

In marked contrast, acceptability of biometric solutions was high for applications in areas with a perceived security need (such as access control for neonatal wards in hospitals) or if users experienced a reduction in physical or mental workload (such as fingerprint logins replacing multiple passwords and PINs). In general, acceptability of biometric solutions is higher amongst those with first-hand experience of biometric applications or those that have a relative or friend who has such experience.

BIOVISION (2003) identified many commercial applications of biometrics that are likely to succeed. Some of these applications will be in areas with high security needs, where performance with a limited number of registered users can be achieved at acceptable cost. Most manufacturers focus on the financial sector and fraud reduction as the most likely application areas (Coventry et al. 2003). The Director of the US National Biometric Test Center, James Wayman, suggested as early as 1998 that 'The technology now exists to replace pass codes [PINs] with biometric measures without a substantive decrease in security protection' (Wayman 1998).

However, many banks have ruled out use of biometrics on cash dispensers in the foreseeable future, partly because of concerns about how customers will respond to false rejection,[11] and partly because the cost of the technology is too high. In the UK, the Nationwide Building Society has investigated the potential costs and benefits of biometric applications over a number of years. Trials with fingerprints and iris recognition showed good usability[12] and user acceptance, but the increased cost of cash dispensers (25 per cent) does not make the widespread introduction of such systems viable (McClue 2003). A German study also raised the additional cost of the secure registration process (which has to be performed by trained and trustworthy staff), and the technical and organizational measures required to safeguard customers' biometric templates as key reasons against use of biometric authentication. The same study also concluded that reliability of biometrics was such that customers would have to be issued with a PIN as a back-up (Thiel 2001), which is likely to lead to significant usability problems. The entertainment industry employs biometrics for convenient verification (as opposed to strong identification): Disney registers hand geometry with season tickets to stop travel agents misusing season tickets for tour groups, and lap dancing clubs register fingerprints with credit cards on entry and request that customers confirm each order (which will appear on their bill) with a fingerprint.

These developments indicate that even though biometrics is generally perceived as a security technology, it may be more likely to succeed in areas where it enables business process improvement, leading to improved productivity of services or cost reduction. An example is the use of dynamic signature recognition (DSR), which authenticates users based on the shape of their signature and characteristics of their signing pattern. In contrast to most other biometrics, providing a dynamic signature is also a declaration of will in the legal sense (BIOVISON 2003). DSR means contracts can be kept in electronic form, thus allowing companies to finally enter the long-promised age of the paperless office. The Nationwide Building Society, for instance, is deploying DSR in its branches and aims to store all mortgage agreements in electronic form only, and forecasts significant cost savings (BBC 2002).

10.2.2 Summary: Authentication Mechanisms

Passwords and PINs were first introduced when computers were expensive and scarce, and anyone attempting unauthorized access had to have physical access to a machine. With the exception of a few professionals, such as systems administrators, each user only had a few items to recall. The arrival of networking technology has increased the number of attacks and attackers that each system faces, and the proliferation of devices that have to be protected means that each user has to manage a multitude of knowledge-based items. In this context, knowledge-based authentication in the form of passwords and PINs as the general authentication mechanism has become unusable, both from an individual user's and an organization's point of view.

At the same time, as this chapter points out, there are a number of usability issues with other authentication mechanisms, and – given that most of these are relatively new and largely untried – further issues are bound to emerge with more extensive use. To anticipate usability issues, we have to consider not only the immediate task of using the security mechanism, but also the question of universal access. Knowledge-based authentication inconveniences many users, but presents an insurmountable access hurdle for only a relatively small number of elderly users and some users with learning difficulties. These user groups would have even bigger problems with token-based authentication, which requires them to look after the token, plus usually to have more technical skills. Biometric identification has potentially the lowest mental workload, but any specific biometric technique bars some users because they cannot register the biometrics – in the case of fingerprinting, favoured by many politicians because of its success in the context of law enforcement, the number is around 5 per cent. Authentication of multiple characteristics would solve this problem, but is currently prohibitively expensive; the development of smart cameras, which can capture and process a range of biometric characteristics, would make it feasible.

To conclude that because fingerprint matching works in a law enforcement context it will also work for biometric authentication, is misguided: the techniques employed and context of operation are very different.[13] The general public is as unaware of these subtle differences as are many politicians – many find fingerprinting unacceptable precisely because 'it is something you do to criminals'. More than any other mechanism, biometrics face acceptability issues, not only because of such misconceptions and Hollywood depictions, but also because individuals have to place a great deal of trust in the operator of the technology to safeguard their biometric templates and their privacy. If biometric templates are compromised, the consequences for individuals can be severe, particularly if one characteristic is used in a variety of applications. Biometric authentication can afford invasions of privacy if technology is set up to collect data beyond the immediate purpose of authentication – for example to determine who goes where, when, and in the company of whom. BIOVISION (2003) reports that (particularly young and technically knowledgeable) users oppose the use of biometric characteristics on id_cards and passports because they perceive governments would most likely succumb to the temptation of 'function creep'.

Any of the alternative mechanisms will increase the cost of authentication, in some cases substantially, and the question is who will bear the cost. Individual customers are usually not inclined to pay more for better security. In corporate environments, the cost will be weighed against the losses (in tangible financial terms, and/or intangibles such as reputation). This section has pointed out that application of biometrics, for instance, can be used for business process improvements that reduce cost. For a pure security application, a good cost–benefit ratio will be much harder to achieve.

The answer to the question of which is the most usable authentication mechanism is that 'it depends' – on the characteristics of the user group, and the task, and the physical and social context in which users and the security mechanism interact.

10.2.3 Security and Tasks

The notion of task is key to considerations of usability in general, and performance in particular. Human behaviour is largely goal-driven, so the effective and efficient execution of tasks that help us attain goals is important. The discussion so far has shown that usability of knowledge-based authentication differs for frequently and infrequently performed tasks. In addition to minimizing the physical and mental workload for users, a well-designed mechanism needs to maximize effectiveness and efficiency of task execution. A mechanism must support the desired outcome, and it must be configured for efficient task execution. An example would be providing a hands-free access control mechanism on a door when there is a need to carry things, or the use of speaker recognition as a means of authentication in a system accessed by telephone.

A further notion of key importance is the distinction between production tasks and supporting tasks. Security – like safety – is a supporting task; for instance it is not on the critical path to attaining the goal. This means that performance in terms of efficiency is even more critical than for the production task, on which users are focused. If a supporting task conflicts with a production task, users will attempt to work around it or cut it out altogether. If a supporting task requires significant extra effort, and/or interferes with the production tasks (and this is often the case with security and safety measures), users need to understand the reason for this, and be motivated to comply. Failure to provide users with the necessary understanding, training and motivation will result in human error (Reason 1990). The current reality is that security is badly integrated with production tasks, and individual users are often left to make a choice between complying with security regulations or getting their job done – with predictable results. The conclusion is that the selection of a security mechanism and how it is configured cannot be left to security experts; rather, such decisions need to be made in the context of business processes and workflow (Brostoff and Sasse 2001).

10.2.3.1 User motivation
Many users are not motivated to comply with security regulations. Beyond the conflicts with production tasks, Weirich and Sasse (2001) identified the

following key factors in a survey on user motivation and security:

1. Users do not believe they are personally at risk.
2. Users do not believe they will be held accountable for not following security regulations.
3. The behaviour required by security mechanisms conflicts with social norms.[14]
4. The behaviour required by security mechanisms conflicts with users' self-image. The perception is that only 'nerds' and 'paranoid' people follow security regulations.

There can be no doubt that security in general, and ICT security in particular, currently suffer from an image problem. Education campaigns (similar to those employed in health education) can be effective, provided they make users believe that they are at risk,[15] but good security behaviour also needs to be re-enforced on a regular basis. The recent notion of persuasive design of technologies (Fogg 2003) offers techniques for designing systems that intrigue, persuade and reward users for good security behaviour.

10.2.3.2 Security policies and security culture

At an organizational level, a key change that companies need to undertake is to integrate security into their business processes. This means that the habit of copying 'standard' security policies and mandating 'maximum strength' security irrespective of security needs, should be replaced by risk and threat analysis appropriate to the business. Many companies already do this, but as Schneier (2003) points out, the interests and needs of all stakeholders are rarely considered, and the economics of security are generally not well understood.

Once security aims appropriate to the organization have been established, role models are essential to change behaviour and rebuild the security culture. This will require buy-in from the top (senior management often exhibit the worst security behaviour because they believe they are too important to bother with 'petty' security regulations), and making secure behaviour a desirable trait, for example by making it part of professional and ethical norms (Sasse et al. 2001).

Brostoff and Sasse (2001) point out that in many Western countries, health and safety regulations have led to significant changes in organizational culture with respect to employee safety, and that Reason's (1990) approach for designing safety as a socio-technical system offers a blueprint for a similar approach in the security domain.

10.2.3.3 User interfaces to security tools and user-centred design

Many security researchers and practitioners see usability of security as a user interface problem. The most widely known and cited paper on usability and security – 'Why Johnny Can't Encrypt' (Whitten and Tygar 1999) – reports that a sample of users with a good level of technical knowledge failed to encrypt and decrypt their mail using PGP 5.0, even after receiving instruction and after practice. Whitten and Tygar attribute the problems they observed to a mismatch between users' perception of the task of encrypting email, and the way that the pretty good privacy (PGP) interface presents those tasks to users. There can be no doubt that the security community has not paid much attention to usability until recently and, consequently, few tools have interfaces that fulfil usability criteria. Well-designed user interfaces can reduce users' workload significantly: the AT&T Privacy Bird,[16] for example, alerts users when a site does not match their specified P3P (platform for privacy preferences), which relieves users from inspecting the privacy policy of each site they interact with.

User-centred design of security mechanisms, however, is more than user interface design. The case of PGP (Zimmermann 1995) presents a good example. The problem lies less with the interface to PGP than with the underlying concept of encryption (which pre-dates PGP), and how it functions. The concept of encryption is complex, and the terminology employed is fundamentally at odds with the everyday meaning of the terms: a cryptographic key does not function like a key in the physical world, and people's understanding of 'public' and 'private' is different from how these terms are applied to public and private keys. While some security experts advocate educating all users on how encryption works so they can use it properly, this author argues that security systems should be designed to make it easy for users to do the right thing, with a minimum amount of effort and knowledge.

There are examples showing that this is possible: statistics suggest that only 10 per cent of installed burglar alarms are armed when they should be, because they are too difficult to use. In the Channel 4 TV series, *Better by Design*, designers Richard Seymour and Dick Powell addressed the problem by applying the successful and well-understood car central locking mechanism to the house burglar alarm. The resulting alarm is extremely easy to operate (the system is armed and de-armed with a single key-press), and the device is light and visually appealing, so users can carry it on a keyring (Seymour Powell 2000). Another example of a step in the right direction is Friedman and Felten's (2002) application of the user-centred approach for their Cookie-Watcher, which was designed to match users' actual needs and values for privacy (as opposed to security experts' prescriptions of how users should manage cookies). While users of the AT&T Privacy Bird still have to understand P3P in all its complexity to use it effectively, the Cookie-Watcher only presents users with the information they want, when they want it, and allows them to make decisions about whether to accept cookies. Given that most users' perception of threats and risks is not accurate, user needs and preferences will need to be complemented by, and reconciled with, output from an expert risk analysis.

10.2.4 Trust

In the past, interactions between strangers who never met face to face used to be rare events. Today, new technologies support an ever-increasing number of interactions between strangers: people who have never met 'in real life' buy and sell goods from each other on eBay, spend hours playing against each other on Xbox-live and date via instant messaging. These interactions involve different types and levels of risk, and they are only possible if actors have trust in each other and in the systems they use to meet, communicate and transact. Yet, in many recent applications, this essential ingredient has proved difficult to attain: lack of trust in e-commerce applications for instance, causes many people to stay away from these systems (Consumer WebWatch 2002).

Since trust is a critical factor for user acceptance of cyber-systems and their long-term success, it has prompted a spate of research on human–3computer interaction (HCI) and computer-meditated communication (CMC). Most of this research aims to help those designing or deploying such systems: the focus is on increasing users' trust perceptions, rather than allowing users to make correct trust decisions. The recent surge of empirical studies on trust has also produced a large number of definitions and operationalizations of trust. Given that trust is an everyday term that applies in many different situations, this is not surprising. Several researchers have recognized the need for a trust framework and presented candidates. However, these models address only one type of trust-requiring online interaction (for example e-commerce Corritore et al. 2003; Egger 2001; Riegelsberger and Sasse 2001) or focus on trust as a psychological construct (McKnight and Chervany 2001-2). There is a need to unify these different perspectives on trust and – more importantly – to link them to structural dimensions that differentiate situations that require trust. The following provides a summary overview and discussion of the factors that have been identified.

Trust is only required in situations characterized by risk and uncertainty. Only if something is at stake, and only if the outcome is uncertain, do we need to trust to engage in the situation. The simplest possible trust exchange involves only two actors – the trustor (the trusting actor) and the trustee (the trusted actor). Normally, both have something to gain by conducting the exchange – this might involve money, but also information, time or other goods that have value to the actors. Prior to the exchange, trustor and trustee have information about each other before they engage in the exchange. In interactions in cyberspace, many of these interactions are disembedded (Giddens 1990), since the actors are not in the same physical or time context. In e-commerce, for instance, the trustor may have to wait for days or weeks to take possession of the goods and check that they are to her satisfaction. Because of disembedding, interactions in cyberspace are riskier and require more trust than similar interactions in a physical context. In addition to having to trust the trustee, users have also to be prepared to trust the technology that mediates interaction (for example the Internet), and their own ability to use both the underlying technology and the specific application (for example the e-commerce website) correctly. For the last two factors, usability is a key prerequisite.

Whether users are prepared to trust and engage in an exchange, additionally depends on a number of other factors that characterize the interaction. Factors that have been identified include:[17]

1. the number of actors involved in the exchange (ranging from dyads to potentially millions in public good dilemmas);
2. the actor type (individuals, organizations, technology such as an e-commerce website);
3. whether there is synchronous or asynchronous trust exchange (asynchronous exchanges create higher strategic insecurity);
4. whether the user can identify trust-warranting properties;
5. the type of signals employed to communicate trustworthiness (symbols and symptoms of trustworthiness, identity and property signals);
6. the trustor's propensity to trust;
7. the trustor's knowledge of the situation;
8. the trustor's prior experience;
9. the potential benefits expected by the trustor; and
10. the risk to the trustor's risks (enacted as 'trusting action').

This summary illustrates how pervasive the need is for trust in technology-mediated interactions. Since the technology that mediates interactions in cyberspace is novel and complex for most users, their willingness to trust will be mostly influenced by previous experience with a particular trustee and situation (factors 2, 7 and 8) and assessment of the trust-warranting properties (factors 4 and 5). For interactions with low numbers of actors (for example e-commerce transactions), it will, therefore, be important that users can reliably (1) identify the actors, for example, that it is easy to determine whether an email purporting to be from my bank is really from my bank; and (2) identify and interpret the trust-warranting properties in an interaction: for example, are the hundreds of positive votes or reviews I see honest reviews from real customers. Currently, the technology makes it easy to fake identities and trust-warranting properties in cyberspace; consequently, the trust basis for interactions in cyberspace is rather fragile.

10.2.5 Privacy

Safeguarding privacy is a key concern for many users in cyberspace. On the one hand, security mechanisms can be an essential tool for protecting privacy, for example because they prevent unauthorized access to data. On the other hand, a security technology can enable invasions of privacy, for example because it becomes possible to monitor an individual's behaviour closely, or track her movements.

Much of the published literature on privacy concentrates on protecting certain types of data without establishing what people regard as private information (Davies 1997). Expert opinion on what is invasive is a necessary, but not sufficient basis for designing technology that is acceptable in use. Adams and Sasse (2001) found that users' perceptions and values differ from the legal perspective in that:

1. People do not classify data as 'private' or 'not private' – rather, they rate the sensitivity of their information on a continuum.
2. The sensitivity of a particular data item will vary over time and in response to events.
3. The sensitivity of a particular data item will vary depending on who is using the information that can be derived from the data, and for what purpose.
4. Users are less concerned about securing access to data, and more concerned about protecting themselves from the adverse effects that may result from having the information that can be derived from the data used against them.[18]
5. Data do not have to identify an individual to be perceived as private: individuals regard some usage of information about a family unit, a geographic area, or demographic, racial, social or interest group as an invasion of privacy.

Essentially, most peoples' attitude to privacy is pragmatic rather than dogmatic. Rather than treating privacy as an absolute value to be protected, people weigh the risks to their privacy (see point 4 above) against potential benefits that might be derived by providing the data. For instance, in the presence of a perceived safety need (for themselves or significant others), privacy usually becomes a secondary concern. People's decisions to disclose information are mediated by the degree of trust they have in the receiver of the data.

However, this 'pragmatic' attitude should not be confused with privacy not being important. Firstly, the ability to disclose information selectively, depending on perceived risks and benefits and the degree of trust in the receiver, is key to users 'feeling in control' in cyberspace. Secondly, there are many legitimate and beneficial interactions (such as self-help groups, role-playing and games), where anonymity or the ability to adopt multiple personae is seen as essential or important.

10.3 CONCLUSION

This chapter has revealed the range of usability issues that current security mechanisms raise. It has also shown that usable security is not simply an issue of 'fixing' user interfaces to current mechanisms; rather, a change in how individuals, organizations and governments think about security is required. Usable security means appropriate security, and effective security is an integral part of the socio-technical system it is supposed to protect. Effective security has to take into account the needs of all stakeholders, acknowledge that their needs sometimes conflict, and find a solution that is acceptable for all stakeholders in ongoing use.

The review has highlighted issues affecting individual users and organizations. There are other stakeholders in the design and operation of security whose needs have not been explicitly discussed. System developers and system administrators are critical of effective security, but currently often make mistakes because of the number and complexity of security issues they have to consider (Zurko and Simon 1996; Flechais et al. 2003). The needs of administrators could be addressed by reducing the amount and complexity of data they have to contend with. Machine learning and agent technologies could be used to summarize and filter information, and data visualization can be employed to help them interpret data and identify critical events.

To address the problems of developers, security needs to be integrated into current development approaches (for example it should be part of the software engineering documentation developers work with, rather than in a separate document). Design decisions must consider the mental and physical workload mechanisms impose on system administrators as well as end-users, and provide them with tools that support their decision making. The safety community has devised methods for developing systems that do exactly that, and security developers could harness and adapt their approaches.

While the review emphasizes the urgent need to put users' needs and values at the centre of security design, one caveat must be added: most users are not knowledgeable about security, nor do they want to be. Motivational approaches can be employed to change underlying perceptions about security and a limited set of key behaviours, but they will not motivate the majority of users to become security experts. Most users' perceptions of security threats and risks to their assets are highly inaccurate, and input from security experts is required to make sure they protect their assets effectively. Security experts, in turn, need to be prepared to design security that is appropriate for, and can work in, a particular social and organizational context, and incorporate basic ergonomic and economic principles in their considerations.

Only systems that support the exchange of reliable trust cues – and thus allow for correct trust attribution – will be viable in the long run. If users find that they cannot rely on their trust perceptions when ordering goods or taking advice via video conferencing, trust in the technologies and application domains may be lost, or result in a system burdened with costly regulation and control structures. What is sometimes described as a 'lack of trust' in e-commerce or free-riding in peer-to-peer systems is not an unavoidable consequence of technology-mediated exchanges; rather, it is a symptom of difficulties in adapting traditional ways of trustworthiness signalling and trust formation to new structural conditions. This should, however, not be interpreted as 'in time, the trust problem will disappear because people will learn' – negative trust experiences can cause long-term damage to the technologies and/or application domains involved. The damage will not only be to commercial companies – technology providers and organizations offering innovative services – but may also deprive individuals and society of the benefits the technology or service could offer. Such developments would disenfranchise those who can least afford to take financial risk, and/or lack in-depth knowledge and the technical savvy to distinguish trustworthy actors from untrustworthy ones.

Safeguarding privacy is a key concern for many users in cyberspace. On the one hand, security mechanisms can be essential tools for protecting privacy, for example, because they prevent unauthorized access to data. On the other hand, a security technology can enable invasions of privacy, for example because it becomes possible to monitor an individual's behaviour closely, or track her movements. Biometric technologies, seen by many governments and some security experts as the solution to providing 'strong' authentication, raise particular concerns in this respect. To make biometric applications acceptable, these applications will need to address a perceived security need, or offer other tangible benefits to users.

NOTES

1 In a cracking attack, the attacker downloads the encrypted password file and tries all possible 'key combinations' to reveal the password. Such 'brute force' attacks take a lot of computing power, or a very long time. Attackers can improve their chances by trying more 'likely' combinations (such as common words) first. Many users do not understand how cracking works, and assume passwords are 'cracked' by an individual trying to 'guess' their password (Adams and Sasse 1999).

2 The reasons for lack of compliance are discussed later.

3 Human memory performance for human faces is even better than for other images.

4 An additional issue is that since credential recovery occurs infrequently, the clues used would have to be extremely memorable and, at the same time, what Zviran and Haga (1990) call spouse-proof, that is not guessable by someone who knows the user well.

5 Even though writing down passwords is forbidden in most security policies, the security research community is divided on this issue. Schneier (2000) endorses 'secure writing down' (in his case, in a file protected with a long passphrase) as the only way of managing a plethora of passwords, and makes fun of the 'kneejerk' reaction that traditional security has against it. However, writing the password down violates the cardinal assumption of knowledge-based authentication (that the password should never be externalized in plain text). There are plenty of anecdotal reports and observations that users do externalize passwords and PINs for their own benefit in a way that significantly assists attackers (see section on PINs). Also, since writing down is a form of disclosure, permitting some form of disclosure whilst punishing others makes it harder for users to distinguish between bad and good security behaviour.

6 This issues also reiterates the need for spouse-proof authentication, see note 4.

7 The use of credentials which are not secrets is becoming increasingly untenable in cyber-society. Users with some technical savvy recognize that such credentials could be used for identity theft, and use fake answers in an attempt to protect themselves. Unless this is done with careful planning (and possibly writing the credentials down), however, fake credentials are extremely vulnerable to being forgotten.

8 Based on statistics compiled by researchers at the University of Bologna accompanying the trial.

9 A key usability principle championed, amongst others, by the EU's IST programme.

10 Because some people do not have hands, or because their fingerprints are genetically indistinct or have been worn down by manual labour or exposure to chemicals (*The Economist* 2003).

11 Most users are more likely to blame themselves for failure to memorize a PIN, whereas failure to authenticate on a biometric system is perceived as a failing of the technology.

12 A caveat that has to be added here is that the users were Nationwide employees, and the machines were situated indoors.

13 Fingerprinting usually matches 'found' fingerprints against scanned full images of rolled fingerprints (usually taken of all ten fingers, with expert handlers checking the prints on registration, and no time limits during registration or retrieval), as opposed to matching a template of a partial fingerprint against a registered template. A key usability issue is that the user has to present the part of the registered finger that matches the stored template and that many authentication systems have to work very fast to be effective.

14 Trust is a particularly interesting and relevant example of such a social norm. A user may not want to upset a colleague by locking their screen when they leave the office, because this may be interpreted as a lack of trust. Mitnick (2002) points out that social engineering attacks often exploit the users' reluctance to declare or signal that they do not trust the attacker.

15 In a context of high security awareness and shared security goals (for example during the Second World War), campaigns with simple reminders of how an individual's behaviour puts them and others at risk may suffice. If people do not believe they are at risk, campaigns need to make the risks and consequences tangible – see, for instance, the current anti-smoking advertisements using real people, dying as a result of smoking, and

other graphic imagery illustrating the consequences. Social marketing can have some effect, but changes in behaviour come about mostly when undesirable behaviour is confronted directly by other people.

16 http://www.privacybird.com/ accessed 17 April 2004.
17 These factors interact with each other, for example a user's previous experience can raise or lower her general propensity to trust.
18 An example would be that an organization obtains data about a person from several sources by legal means, and then uses the information that can be derived from the data to classify the person without their knowledge.

REFERENCES

Adams, A. and Sasse, M.A. (1999), 'Users Are Not The Enemy', *Communications of the ACM* 42(12): 49-64.

Adams, A. and Sasse M.A. (2001), 'Privacy in Multimedia Communications: Protecting Users, Not Just Data', in A. Blandford, J. Vanderdonkt and P. Gray (eds), *People and Computers XV - Interaction without frontiers. Joint Proceedings of HCI2001 and ICM2001*, Lille, Sept., Berlin: Springer, pp. 49-64.

Anderson, R. (2001), *Security Engineering*, Hoboken NJ: John Wiley & Sons.

Axelrod, R. (1980), 'More Effective Choice in the Prisoner's Dilemma', *Journal of Conflict Resolution* 24(3): 379-403.

BBC (2002) http://news.bbc.co.uk/1/hi/technology/2420143.stm accessed 17 Apr. 04.

BIOVISION (2003) – *Final Report*, http://www.eubiometricforum.com/biovision/index.htm accessed 17 Apr. 04.

Brostoff, S. and Sasse, M.A. (2000), 'Are Passfaces More Usable than Passwords? A Field Trial Investigation', in S. McDonald, Y. Waern and G. Cockton (eds), *People and Computers XIV - Usability or Else! Proceedings of HCI 2000*, Berlin: Springer, pp. 405-24.

Brostoff, S. and Sasse, M.A. (2001), 'Safe and Sound: A Safety-critical Design Approach to Security', in *Proceedings of the New Security Paradigms Workshop 2001I*, 10-13 September, Cloudcroft NM, New York: ACM Press, pp. 41-50.

Brostoff S. and Sasse M.A. (2003), '"Ten Strikes and You're Out": Increasing the Number of Login Attempts can Improve Password Usability', paper presented at the CHI Workshop on Human-Computer Interaction and security systems, Ft Lauderdale, April 1-6, http://www.andrewpatrick.ca/CHI2003/HCISEC-papers.html accessed 17 Apr. 04.

Checkland, P. (1999), *Soft Systems Methodology: A 30-year Retrospective*,

Chichester: John Wiley.

Consumer WebWatch (2002), 'A Matter of Trust: What Users Want From Web Sites', Consumer WebWatch, Yonkers, NY, http://www.consumerwebwatch.org/news/report1.pdf accessed 17 Apr. 04.

Corritore, C.L., Kracher, B. and Wiedenbeck, S. (2003), 'On-line Trust: Concepts, Evolving Themes, A Model', *International Journal of Human Computer Studies* 58(6): 737-58.

Coventry, L., De Angeli, A. and Johnson, G. (2003), 'Honest it's Me – Self-Service Verification', paper presented at the CHI Workshop on Human-Computer Interaction and security systems, Ft Lauderdale, 1-6 April, http://www.andrewpatrick.ca/CHI2003/HCISEC-papers.html accessed 17 Apr. 04.

Davies, S. (1997), 'Re-engineering the Right to Privacy, in P.E. Agre and M. Rotenberg (eds), *Technology and Privacy: The New Landscape*, Cambridge MA: MIT Press, pp.143-66.

Dhamija, R. and Perrig, A. (2000), '*Deja Vu*: A User Study. Using Images for Authentication', in *Proceedings of the 9th USENIX Security Symposium*, Aug. 2000, Denver, Colorado, pp. 45-48, http:/www.usenix.org/events/sec2000/dhamija.html accessed 17 Apr. 04.

Egger, F.N. (2001), 'Affective Design of E-Commerce User Interfaces: How to Maximise Perceived Trustworthiness', in M. Helander, H.M. Khalid and Tham (eds), *Proceedings of CAHD 2001: Conference on Affective Human Factors Design*, Singapore, 27-29 June, London: ASEAN Press, pp. 317-24.

Ellison, C., Hall, C., Milbert, R. and Schneier, B. (2000), 'Protecting Secret Keys with Personal Entropy', *Future Generation Computer Systems* 16: 311-18.

Fairhurst, M.C., Guest, R.M., Deravi, F. and George, J. (2002), 'Using Biometrics as an Enabling Technology in Balancing Universality and Selectivity for Management of Information Access', in N. Carbonelle and C. Stephanidis (eds), *Universal Access: Lecture Notes in Computer Science 2615*, Berlin: Springer, pp. 249-59.

Flechais, I. Sasse, M.A. and Hailes, S.M.V.H. (2003), 'Bringing Security Home: A Process for Developing Secure and Usable Systems', paper presented at the ACM/ACSAC New Security Paradigms Workshop, Switzerland, August, http://www.cs.ucl.ac.uk/staff/I.Flechais/downloads/nspw2003.pdf accessed 17 Apr. 04.

FIPS (1985), 'Announcing the Standard for PASSWORD USAGE', Federal Information Processing Standards Publication, 112, US Department of Commerce, National Bureau of Standards, http://csrc.nist.gov/publications/fips/fips112/fip112-1.pdf accessed 17 Apr. 04.

Fogg, B.J. (2003), *Persuasive Technology. Using Computers to Change What We Think and Do?* San Francisco CA: Morgan Kaufmann.

Friedman, B. and Felten, E. (2002). 'Informed Consent in the Mozilla Browser: Implementing Value-Sensitive Design', *Proceedings of the Thirty-Fifth Annual Hawaii International Conference on System Sciences*, Abstract, p. 247,
http://www.ischool.washington.edu/networksecurity/outcomes.html accessed 17 Apr. 04.

Giddens, A. (1990), *The Consequences of Modernity*, Stanford CA: Stanford University Press.

Henderson, R., Mahar, D., Saliba, A., Deane, F. and Napier, R. (1998), 'Electronic Monitoring Systems: An Examination of Physiological Activity and Task Performance within a Simulated Keystroke Security and Electronic Performance Monitoring System', *International Journal of Human–Computer Studies* 48(2): 143-57.

Just, M. (2003), 'Designing Secure Yet Usable Credential Recovery Systems with Challenge Questions', paper presented at the CHI Workshop on Human–Computer Interaction and security systems, Ft Lauderdale, 1-6 April, http://www.andrewpatrick.ca/CHI2003/HCISEC-papers.html

McClue, A. (2003), 'Nationwide Ditches Iris and Fingerprint Biometrics', 23 September,
http://www.silicon.com/software/security/0,39024655,10006129,00.htm accessed 17 Apr. 04.

McKnight, D.H. and Chervany, N.L. (2001-2002), 'What Trust Means in E-Commerce Customer Relationships: An Interdisciplinary Conceptual Typology', *International Journal of Electronic Commerce* 6(2): 35-59.

Mitnick, K. (2002), *The Art of Deception*, Hoboken NJ: John Wiley & Sons.

Passfaces™ for Windows (2003), http://www.realuser.com/cgi-bin/ru.exe/_/homepages/index.htm accessed 17 Apr. 04.

Petrie, H. (2002), 'Password Clues, CentralNic',
http://www.centralnic.com/page.php?cid=77 accessed 17 Apr. 04.

Reason, J. (1990) *Human Error*, Cambridge: Cambridge University Press.

Riegelsberger, J. and Sasse, M.A. (2001), 'Trustbuilders and Trustbusters: The Role of Trust Cues in Interfaces to e-Commerce Applications', in B. Schmid, K. Stanoevska-Slabeva, and V. Tschammer (eds), *Towards the E-Society. Proceedings of I3E 2001*, Zurich, 3-5 October, Norwell MA: Kluwer, pp. 17-30.

Sasse, M.A., Brostoff, S. and Weirich, D. (2001), 'Transforming the "Weakest link": A Human–Computer Interaction Approach to Usable and Effective Security', *BT Technology Journal* 19(3): 122-31.

Schacter, D.L. (2002), *The Seven Sins of Memory: How the Mind Forgets and Remembers*, Boston MA: Mariner Books.

Schelling, T.C. (1960), *The Strategy of Conflict*, Oxford: Oxford University Press.

Schneier, B. (2000), *Secrets and Lies: Digital Security in a Networked World*, Hoboken NJ: John Wiley & Sons.

Schneier, B. (2003), *Beyond Fear: Thinking Sensibly about Security in an Uncertain World*, New York: Copernicus Books.

Seymour, R. and Powell, D. (2000), 'Better by Design – The Burglar Alarm', http://www.designcouncil.org.uk/betterbydesign/security/challenge.html accessed 17 Apr. 04.

Shackel, B. (1975), *Applied Ergonomics Handbook*, Guildford: IPC Science and Technology Press.

The Economist (2003), 'Prepare to be Scanned – Will Biometric Passports Improve Security?', *The Economist Technology Quarterly* 6 Dec.: 20-22.

Thiel, C. (2001), 'Voraussetzungen für den Ersatz der PIN bei Geldausgabeautomaten: bankfachliche Anforderungen', paper presented at BIOTRUST Workshop June 5, University of Giessen-Friedberg.

Torinofacile (2003), available at: http://www.torinofacile.it/ accessed 17 Apr. 04.

Tucker, A. (1995), *A Two-person Dilemma*, Stanford CA: Stanford University Press.

V-GO SINGLE SIGN-On (2003), at http://www.passlogix.com/ accessed 17 Apr. 04.

Valentine, T. (1999a), 'An Evaluation of the Passfaces Personal Authentication System', Technical Report, Department of Psychology Goldsmiths College, University of London.

Valentine, T. (1999b), 'Memory for Passfaces after a Long Delay', Technical Report, Department of Psychology Goldsmiths College, University of London.

Wayman, J. (1998), 'Biometric Identification and the Financial Services Industry', http://financialservices.house.gov/banking/52098jlw.htm accessed 17 Apr. 04.

Weirich, D. and Sasse, M.A. (2001), 'Pretty Good Persuasion: A First Step Towards Effective Password Security for the Real World', in *Proceedings of the New Security Paradigms Workshop 2000*, Cloudcroft NM, 10-13 September, New York: ACM Press, pp. 137-43.

Whitten, A. and Tygar, D. (1999), 'Why Johnny Can't Encrypt: A Usability Evaluation of PGP 5.0' in *Proceedings of the 8th USENIX Security Symposium*, Washington DC, 23-26 August, http://www.usenix.org/publications/library/proceedings/sec99/whitten.html accessed 17 Apr. 04.

Yan, J.J. (2001), 'A Note on Proactive Password Checking', in *Proceedings of the New Security Paradigms Workshop, 2001*, Cloudcroft NM, 10-13 September, New York: ACM Press, pp. 127-36.

Yan, J., Clackwell, A., Anderson, R. and Grant, A. (2000), 'The Memorability and Security of Passwords - Some Empirical Results', Technical Report No. 500, Computer Laboratory, University of Cambridge, http://www.ftp.cl.cam.ac.uk/ftp/users/rja14/tr500.pdf accessed 17 Apr. 04.

Zimmermann P.R. (1995), *The Official PGP User's Guide*, Cambridge MA: MIT Press..

Zurko, M.E. and Simon, D. (1996), 'User-Centered Security' in *Proceedings of the 1996 Workshop on New Security Paradigms Workshop*, Lake Arrowhead CA, New York: ACM Press, pp. 27-33.

Zviran, M. and Haga, W.J. (1990), 'Cognitive Passwords: The Key to Easy Access Control', *Computer and Security* 9(8): 723-36.

Zviran, M. and Haga, W.J. (1993), 'A Comparison of Password Techniques for Multilevel Authentication Mechanisms', *Computer Journal* 36(3): 227-37.

11 Risk management in cyberspace

James Backhouse,
with Ayse Bener, Narisa Chauvidul-Aw,
Frederick Wamala and Robert Willison

11.1 INTRODUCTION

This chapter addresses the social aspects of the information systems security and risk agenda. It counterposes the prevailing focus on technical issues by reviewing research undertaken using a social science perspective. Underpinning this account is a belief that information systems are essentially social systems that rely on an important technical component, and that security is likewise dependent on social behaviour. End-users who are appropriately trained and predisposed towards securing information offer a direct solution to a great many security problems; on the other hand, systems that fail to take account of end-users and their behaviour inevitably contribute to the creation of more vulnerabilities.

It might be natural to assume that a focus on social risks associated with electronic delivery of products and services is an established reality. On the contrary, the prevailing concern is over technical, not social, risks. This chapter seeks to draw attention to the behavioural issues that surround the deployment of information and communication technology (ICT) in organizations and an assessment of the present risks and the viability of countermeasures, if they are appropriately managed. The notion of cyberspace does not now smack of its former connotations associated with hacking or with terrorism. Today it refers to interconnected networks or the space within which electronic communications take place and it has become interchangeable and merged with the Internet and World Wide Web (Skibell 2002). This merged notion is adopted for the purposes of this chapter.

Security managers address information systems issues from three aspects: technical, formal and informal. The formal element contains the rules and policy that govern the functioning of the information system (IS) and the informal element connotes actual practice and behaviour. Simply focusing on technical problems and solutions can miss the point about how end-users actually form part of the system and how their contributions can spell success or failure – for instance security can be threatened if users share passwords or choose easily guessed examples. The fruits of risk management activities are embodied in the formalities of a security policy, essentially a set of rules; while the informal system needs to be addressed by means of awareness campaigns and education of users about the importance of security. A culture of security means that end-users, and maybe customers, take on the responsibility themselves for monitoring risk and taking appropriate action. We need to understand more about the interplay of technology, security and risk in the context of cyber operations.

Information security professionals use risk analysis to justify the cost of designing and implementing security on the information system (IS). Courtney (1977) and Fitzgerald (1978) were among the first to develop risk analysis methods and by the 1980s, the US government had adopted risk analysis as a standard for security mechanism design. Courtney (1977) defined risk as the 'product of probability of an exposure occurring a given number of times per year (P) and the cost (or loss) (C) attributed to such exposure'. Therefore, risk (R) is $R = P \times C$. In this insurance-based approach there is an assumption that appropriate statistics are available to perform the calculation. In a social science approach where cultural perceptions are critical, it may be that before counting individual examples there is a great deal of work to be done to agree on the nature of the exposure and what constitutes a risk event in the first place. As the information society cuts through time and space to gather ever more actors in its embrace, the question of the social and cultural basis of information and risk urgently needs addressing. An analysis of the dialectic of theory and practice in information security can be helpful in avoiding the one-sidedness of basing policy on abstract theories about risks in cyberspace and the rejection of the lessons from theory by practitioners.

This chapter draws on organizational studies performed between 1998 and 2004 into the behavioural and organizational aspects of risk and security in the context of global companies whose use of web-based technology is critical to both their front and back offices. Each study focuses on different aspects of security and risk in information systems and adopts a different perspective for the purpose. The first study, undertaken in a global bank, demonstrates how, despite a collective aim to deliver a new Internet banking product, different perceptions of risk and security flourished within the same project team. Insights emerge into how the various actors construct the trustworthiness that lends credibility to communications and the role of the medium chosen. A second study explores the role of criminal opportunity as a concept for analysing IS security situations, taking the perpetrator's context as a rogue insider as the analytical focus. A third study focuses on internal control issues in the context of a geographically dispersed corporation and shows how cultural issues can drastically affect the expectations–reality equation of control exercised from a distant Western headquarters. As back-office financial sector work is shifted towards developing countries, the risk and security implications are highlighted. The fourth study compares how public key infrastructure (PKI) was introduced in an oil company and a global bank and recounts the critical role of institutional factors in determining the success of the deployment. There are important implications for all enterprises seeking to create secure interoperability internally or externally. A discussion follows in Section 11.6 on the lessons to be drawn from the review of the cases.

Using a social science approach to security permits the adoption of a range of perspectives, rooted in different theories and frameworks and in their respective disciplines. For understanding and managing the technical aspects of information security, an engineering and computer science background remains essential, but for dealing with the pragmatic and semantic aspects of information security, other forms of preparation are required which can offer legal, political, sociological and economic insights.

Our general aim is to demonstrate that IS security and risk research must go beyond the usual prescriptive and technical advice where IS security is seen as a purely technical concern (Wood 1995; Parker 1997; Osborne 1998; von Solms 2001). Since information systems are viewed here as more than merely technical systems, this body of research is able to address that part of the security risk agenda that might formerly have been dismissed as a troublesome 'people problem' and hence not of prime concern.

11.2 RISK PERCEPTION AND COMMUNICATION

At the core of risk management in any social or organizational context lies the issue of how social actors discern risks and enter into communication about them and how they may be addressed. In this first case study Bener (2000) researched risk in a project that aimed to launch an Internet banking product in a top-tier global bank (NIMETBANK in her study) and provided interesting findings directly relevant to risk perception, risk communication and trust and credibility. A field study and a supporting customer survey confirmed that individuals and institutions processed messages they received and developed their perceptions of these messages according to their previous experiences, the social and economic climate, their cultural backgrounds and the trust they placed in the messages and their sources.

The stakeholders in the project management team included representatives from three broad categories in relation to the Internet banking product within the global bank – the UK Business and the Bank Information Security Office (users), the US-based Advanced Technologies Group (ATG) (supplier), and the information technology infrastructure, operations risk, corporate audit, project risk review, teams and so on (support).

11.2.1 Stakeholders Defined and Perceived Risk Events Differently

The priorities of the stakeholder groups reflected their cultural backgrounds as described by Douglas (1985). They were largely influenced by the organizational structure, and the findings confirmed that institutional structure is the ultimate shaper of risk perception. Each unit in the project at NIMETBANK brought its own view of risk and organizational imperatives clearly shaped by their attitudes and beliefs. Risks were overlooked if they conflicted with the goals of the stakeholders. Since stakeholders had different priorities, they also attenuated or intensified certain aspects of risks according to their own priorities.

For example, the goal of the UK business unit was to have more functionality in their product in order to be ahead of their competitors, and they saw no security risk in delivering on the Internet. By contrast, the bank information security officer thought, unsurprisingly, that security on the Internet was the biggest problem. He doubted that the risk could be covered even by security measures, but that if a customer lost money because of a security breach, the terms and conditions should protect the bank against claims by the customers: 'Hackers are always ahead of the others and therefore it is difficult to protect the bank from them. Therefore, my main objective is to draft the terms and conditions properly and tight enough to protect the bank from suing customers' (Bener 2000, p. 151).

In all, six major risk events were discussed among members of the project team, and they crystallize the divisions and differences among the units on the perception of risks.

Personal identification number (PIN). In view of the security concern perceived by an audit team member: 'Security is the single most important thing to look for in the Internet banking project. Customers will be able to transfer money all over the place and if they can access their bank account from their homes, anyone else can' (Bener 2000, p. 149).

The audit team suggested a six-digit rather than four-digit PIN, a proposal eventually overruled on the grounds of lack of conformity with competitors' banking products.

Private dial-up network. The ATG suggested that if the security of the Internet was an issue a private dial-up network could be established for the customers of NIMETBANK. The idea was supported by the technology infrastructure group and others. However, after lengthy arguments between the business units and the information security office, the UK marketing director explained:

> when we had to make a decision to go on the Internet we consulted ATG. They gave us pros and cons of both options honestly. In regards to the Internet they did ring the alarm bells, therefore we decided against the dial-up since its cost did not justify its benefits. (Bener 2000, p. 167)

Delivery time. UK business saw time to market as critical for them: 'The only risk in this project I could imagine is the time for delivery. Getting it up and running and the web site. Just the risk of the schedule' (Bener 2000, p. 154).

Operational risk. UK operations had to incorporate some of the new features of the product into their host system. They also had to prepare for the expected increase in customer volume and, hence, an increase in transaction volumes. For them, 'the riskiest factor has always been, besides time and quality, that not everyone does things in the same way in the technology department' (Bener 2000, p. 156).

Additional product feature. The current Internet banking product did not allow for a prospective customer to open an account with the bank in an online manner. UK business thought that online account opening was a critical competitive advantage as well as a significant cost saving for the operations. However, ATG declined to modify the existing product on the grounds that it did not have a secure solution to implement this change in the given time frame.

Co-brand agreement. UK business aimed at acquiring new customers with the Internet banking product, and entered into an agreement with a local internet service provider (ISP) to offer free Internet access to its customers. However, the technology infrastructure team raised a concern on the grounds that this was a major breach of security as far as the information security policies of the bank were concerned. The European audit manager explained: 'we also sent a memo that the business units could not enter into marketing arrangements with local ISPs in their respective countries since the ISPs could tap into the bank's backbone and this would be a major security breach' (Bener 2000, p. 152).

11.2.2 Importance of the Social Climate for Risk Perception

The prevailing social climate (of the late 1990s) had a positive impact on the stakeholders of the project team and the customers of the NIMETBANK towards Internet usage. Stakeholders based their decisions on consideration of the social issues beyond those internal to the bank. Key issues here were the stiff competition from other well-known UK banks who were bringing

Internet banking to millions of customers and the growth in popularity of the Internet for financial and commercial transactions. A third issue was the increasing publicity being given by the media to incidents concerning Internet and information systems security, raising the stakes for Internet ventures of this kind. All three issues played a part in shaping perceptions of risk.

11.2.3 Trust Established through Competence

Openness and objectivity in the risk communication on its own was not enough to establish trust between the parties. Trust was only established through the competence of the source or transmitter in the message process. Several findings confirmed that as long as the transmitter was competent, the receivers paid less attention to the source of the message, and vice versa. Another conclusion was that the personality of the communicator, with attributes of ability and integrity, was also important in establishing trust. Trust was seen to be placed in those who had delivered in the past. Those units associated with the delivery of technology were well regarded and trusted. A UK business manager explained her trust in the ATG:

> I trust ATG very much. They were very successful lately in the implementation of the PC banking product. Not only that, ATG has been successful all around the World. They manufactured and installed all of the more than 3,000 NIMETBANK automated teller machines in many countries, including the UK. My experience has always been very good when working with them. I am sure they will be successful in implementing the Internet banking product here. (Bener 2000, p. 165)

By contrast, where there were doubts, they were driven by organizational rivalries, for example the UK marketing director recounted that:

> we just ignored what they [technology infrastructure] said since they could not explain why we were at risk, and then, we started thinking that the reason they were pushing so hard was to get us on the global ISP contract they signed last year so that they could take the whole credit. (Bener 2000, p. 167)

11.2.4 Risk Communication

The matter of how to communicate risk issues has been a vital concern for business and government alike, whether it relates to cyber risks or more traditional risks:

> Risk Communication is an interactive process of exchange of information and opinion among individuals, groups and institutions. It involves multiple messages about the nature of risk and other messages, not strictly about risk, that express

concerns, opinions and reactions to risk messages or to legal and institutional arrangements for risk management. (National Research Council 1989, p. 21)

Researchers such as Fesseden-Raden et al. (1987) and Krimsky and Plough (1988) have taken this definition further, so that risk communication consists not only in the exchange of information among the parties involved, but also in the wider institutional and cultural contexts within which risk messages are articulated, transmuted and embedded. Risk communication represents a 'tangled web' of messages, signs and symbols. Besides the intended risk message, other unintended messages may be transmitted through signs and symbols and, hence, result in outcomes that are unpredictable. Moreover, because most hazards have a history, this too influences the receivers' interpretations of the messages.

The basic communication model describes three roles in the process: sources of a message, transmitters of a message and receivers of a message. Interactions about risk issues may serve to amplify or attenuate communication signals. Social amplification of risk suggests that during the communication among stakeholders, whichever role they may take, source or transmitter, the communication process either intensifies or attenuates certain aspects of risk because of cultural factors.

Generally, because of distance, communication between members of the teams took place through email or telephone. However, inter-team communication was usually face to face at scheduled or informal meetings. The interviews for this study revealed that email was a very dominant communication medium for NIMETBANK employees. It was observed that, even among the members of a team who were located in the same building, email was used very frequently with reasons cited such as:

information can be disseminated to many receivers in a more efficient way ...

communication gets recorded and senders and receivers do not forget what was said ...

it's easier to remember what you've said; what you've asked [others] to do, what they've promised or undertaken to do for you and what they've done ... (Bener 2000 p. 151)

There were conflicting messages received from the employees interviewed about the effectiveness of methods of communication within NIMETBANK. Most employees said that face-to-face communication was best, but because of time constraints, email, telephone and teleconferencing were used the most. Almost all the employees affirmed that sometimes more emails than necessary were generated. One employee from ATG said, 'It's got to be a mix between email, telephone, teleconferencing and face-to-face communication; coming up with the right mix is very difficult. If you have the wrong mix, you can waste a lot of time, not get the job done. I don't know what the right mix is' (Bener 2000, p. 158).

The credibility of communicators is critically dependent upon the trust placed in them. In other words, in order for us to trust the message, we need first to trust the communicator of that message. Credibility of information sources is a key factor in risk communication such that credible sources are those that shape risk and security policies within the organization.

In summary, the findings of the study are as follows:

* Risk perception: different stakeholders hold different perceptions about what risks exist and this has implications for risk management.
* Trust and credibility: trust is given to those who have 'delivered' in the past.
* Risk communication: trusted sources are critical in risk communication, amplification and attenuation are endemic, and email is the dominant medium.

While none is surprising, the importance for risk management is not to overlook them. Risk perception, communication and trust all nestle in the bosom of socially constructed information systems that must be constantly reinterpreted if security is to be achieved.

11.3 OPPORTUNITY: PERCEIVING CYBER CRIME AND SECURITY

This section focuses on the concept of criminal opportunity and information security based on a case study by Willison and Backhouse (2003). More precisely, it questions the nature of this phenomenon with regard to the organizational context and the considerable threat posed by dishonest staff. One alternative approach to help mitigate the risks associated with rogue employees is to reduce their opportunities for computer abuse. To this end, a model to help understand the relationship between such staff, their environment and opportunity is advanced. In the literature that directly addresses the issue of opportunity, the focus divides into two distinct areas: opportunity both as a motivator of criminals and as an outcome of deficient security.

A few writers have discussed opportunity in terms of the motivational impact it may have on individuals (BloomBecker 1984; Forester and Morrison 1994; Hitchings 1995). In an early paper on the issue for example, BloomBecker cites eight types of motivational factors. One of these is 'the land of opportunity', where rogue employees exploit security loopholes spotted during the course of their daily work activities. However, other writers who discuss the relationship between opportunity and motivation merely mention this phenomenon in passing: 'Experts on computer fraud attest to the fact that opportunity more than anything else seems to generate this kind of behaviour' (Forester and Morrison 1994, p. 41).

With the aim of raising practitioners' awareness, the UK Audit Commission has been eager to spread the message regarding the relationship between poor security and opportunity. Its report, *Opportunity Makes a Thief* (Audit Commission 1994), indicates that one of the primary reasons for 'computer abuse' is a disregard for basic controls. More precisely, this disregard manifests itself in a failure to implement and maintain such controls. These findings are mirrored in the Commission's next report *Ghost in the Machine* (Audit Commission 1997), which finds 'little improvement' with regard to the provision of internal controls. Furthermore, this intransigence is reflected in the 2001 report which states: 'Auditors and security specialists continue to stress the need for proper control and security measures. Nevertheless, the majority of breaches of IT security are still caused by a lack of the basic fundamental controls and safeguards' (Audit Commission 2001, p. 17).

This view is supported by other writers in the field who have additionally and explicitly pointed to how poorly implemented and enforced controls might engender opportunities (Bologna 1993; Comer 1998; Stevenson 2000). Indeed, both Comer and Bologna stress how opportunities form one of the two key elements – the other being motivational factors – that must be addressed when combating computer fraud in organizations. But what exactly are the factors that lead to the absence and poor maintenance of safeguards?

11.3.1 Complacency

Complacency about IS security is a primary reason for the absence of the appropriate safeguards (Audit Commission 1997; Hinde 2001). As noted, this manifests itself in the failure of some organizations to implement even the most basic controls, leaving their systems vulnerable and possibly forming the conditions that create opportunities. The three UK Audit Commission reports cited above clearly demonstrate this. A key control, for example, is a security policy (Dorey 1994; Backhouse 1997; Osborne 1998; Nosworthy 2000). In 1994 and 1998 the Commission reports indicated that of the 1,073 and 900 organizations surveyed, one-third failed to implement this safeguard. While this position had improved by 2001, one-quarter of the 688 organizations still had failed to pay heed to the alarm bells.

11.3.2 Failure of Focus

While companies may fail to appreciate the value of information security, they may also fail to recognize potential threats (Parker 1997; Hinde 2001; Riem 2001; Wright 2001; Yapp 2001). A 2002 global security report reveals in a survey of 459 organizations:

> Yet again we see greater concern about vulnerability to external attack (57%), than internal (41%), and yet leading research groups continue to confirm that more than three quarters of attacks originate from within organisations ... an alarming amount of evidence remains that organisations are lacking fundamental management information about security breaches. (Ernst & Young 2002, pp. 8-9)

This is confirmed by Parker (1997) who argues that the 'distorted image' of security held by top-level business people is often 'informed' by trade publications such as the *Wall Street Journal* and *Forbes*, whose focus is more on the newsworthy than on the mundane. Additionally, the distorted image of security held by managers is often related to a myopic understanding of the problem area and how it should be addressed. Several writers have confirmed that in many organizations IS security is often perceived as a purely technical concern (Wood 1995; Parker 1997; Osborne 1998; von Solms 2001). The downside of this perspective is that it fails to encompass the whole of the problem domain and, hence, fails fully to appreciate all the components that constitute an information system with its technical, formal and informal elements.

11.3.3 Interrelated Controls

One problem often overlooked when safeguards are introduced is their interrelated nature. Security is very much like a house of cards: inadequate consideration for one area will impact on another, possibly creating conditions that help form an opportunity. One safeguard, for example, is an information security policy. The 2001 Audit Commission report revealed that 25 per cent of the 688 surveyed organizations still had no security policy. Through the creation and maintenance of a security policy, management can provide support and direction for information security in an organization. There is no denying the importance of a security policy as a cornerstone in the development of an organization's control environment (Dorey 1994; Backhouse 1997; Osborne 1998; Nosworthy 2000). However, unless the policy is brought to life through education and awareness programmes, then all the work undertaken to create a policy will ultimately have been a waste of time (Spurling 1995; Thomson and von Solms 1998; Nosworthy 2000).

11.3.4 Implementation of Inappropriate Controls

Even prudent companies that wish to establish effective security across the board may unwittingly create the conditions that help to form opportunities through the implementation of inappropriate controls (Warman 1993; Olnes 1994; Luzwick 2001). If the introduced safeguards provide a sub-standard level of security then the IS will be left vulnerable. However, the same is also true if the safeguards are perceived by staff as unworkable in the organizational context. One of the perennial problems for IS security is its uneasy relationship with business objectives. Although there is an obvious need to reduce the risks to an IS, the respective countermeasures are often seen by users as a constraint, given the range of tasks required to fulfil the objectives. If the safeguards are perceived to be too heavy-handed or impractical (or both), staff may circumvent the controls just to make their lives easier, or they may even rebel against such controls as in the recent case at British Airways, where security tokens were introduced to monitor staff without adequate canvassing of staff opinion.[1] Again, non-compliant behaviour leaves systems vulnerable, possibly providing opportunities for rogue employees. In this sense, although safeguards are obviously introduced to reduce risks, with a heavy-handed approach they may in reality create them.

11.3.5 Implementing Safeguards

Aside from the inappropriate nature of safeguards, a related issue concerns the implementation of controls. Poor implementation can negate improvements in security for which a safeguard was designed. Schneier (1998) discusses cryptographic systems as a case in point. He notes several problems pertaining to the poor implementation of this safeguard. With some systems, the plain text which the user wishes to encrypt is not destroyed after the process takes place. Other systems use temporary files on a computer in case of a system crash. While this is prudent, if these systems are wrongly implemented, the plain text is left on the hard drive. Schneier further notes how some poorly implemented systems can even leave the cryptographic keys on the hard drive.

11.3.6 Compliance Review

A key prerequisite of IS security is the need to confirm on a routine basis that the existing controls are working effectively. One of the messages repeated in several UK Audit Commission (1994, 1997, 2001) reports is that many organizations are failing to check whether their controls are operating as intended. As a consequence those safeguards that are failing to perform are leaving IS vulnerable. Furthermore, these vulnerabilities may persist for considerable periods of time, given the failure of some companies to monitor their controls.

11.3.7 Opportunity Structure: A Model for Security?

The Crime Specific Opportunity Structure (Clarke 1995), recognizing the threat from dishonest insiders, focuses on the opportunities afforded the potential perpetrator with regard to the organizational context.

Figure 11.1 Crime specific opportunity structure

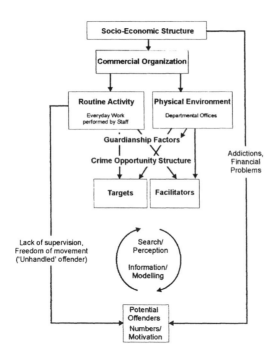

The model set out in Figure 11.1. draws on a number of criminological theories such as Situational Crime Prevention (Clarke 1997), the Rational Choice Perspective (Clarke and Cornish 1985, 2000), Environmental Criminology (Brantingham and Brantingham 1991), Routine Activity Theory (Hirschi 1969; Felson 1992), and Lifestyle Theory (Hindelang et al. 1978). It attempts to provide a new perspective and fresh insights into this opportunity risk.

This model can support information security work by exploring the constituent elements that together may afford an opportunity to the criminal and permits an examination of how safeguards interact to form a coherent control environment. Within the 'Opportunity Structure for Crime', the physical environment affords both targets and facilitators, for example, easily-guessed passwords or PCs left unattended that facilitate access to valuable transaction data that can be modified to the advantage of the rogue insider. Furthermore, lifestyle and routine activities also influence the number of targets. The behaviours inscribed in lifestyle and routine activities, that is, work, leisure, residence and shopping, can either enhance or hinder guardianship and can supply victims.

At a macro level within the structure, the socio-economic structure influences the lifestyle and routine activities and the physical environment. The former includes demography, geography, industrialization, urbanization, welfare and health, education and legal institutions. The socio-economic structure also partly determines the number of potential offenders through sub-cultural influences, such as neglect and lack of love, alienation and so on (identified by traditional criminology), and partly through lifestyle and routine activities. Classic fraud profiles point to a different set of socio-economic factors that may motivate an offender. These include addictions in their various guises, marital breakdown, financial problems and the like (Bologna 1993).

Routine activities and lifestyle can influence the degree of social control afforded by intimate handlers, leading to a possible lack of supervision and freedom of movement. The number of potential offenders is also partly determined by routine activities in terms of the degree of supervision afforded by managers or security-minded peers, leading to either handled or unhandled staff and, hence, to potential offenders. In the normal context there usually will be a capable guardian, possibly a supervisor or a fellow employee, whose presence dampens the ardour of perpetrators to commit their crimes. An interesting issue arises with teleworking where the guardian functions are embraced by an increasingly invasive technical infrastructure.

The opportunity structure addresses the interactions between potential offenders, facilitators, targets and victims. These interactions suggest the nature and scale of the opportunities for crime. Furthermore, the interplay between these entities largely takes place in the 'action' and subsequently 'awareness' spaces of offenders as indicated by the search/perception – information modelling sections of Figure 11.1 and as highlighted by Environmental Criminology. The offender's perceptions – highlighted by the Rational Choice Perspective and also by Environmental Criminology – of the risks, efforts and rewards associated with such spaces play a crucial role in defining the opportunity structure.

The Crime Specific Opportunity Structure model has been applied to analyse the Barings Bank disaster using the reports supplied by the Bank of England and SIMEX, the Singapore Exchange (Willison 2002). The issues raised by the model of lack of supervision and freedom of movement were reflected accurately in the Leeson affair. From the start of Leeson's career at Barings Futures Singapore there was confusion about who actually managed him: 'some members of management believed that responsibility for certain activities rested with other managers, who deny they had such responsibility' (Board of Banking Supervision 1995, para 2.28).

The absence of an 'intimate handler' meant that Leeson was able to undertake the fatal unauthorized trading. Furthermore, the little supervision actually exercised came from managers in Barings who did not understand the trading of futures and options, for example James Bax and Ron Baker. Of course where there is an inability to understand the work being supervised, there remains only trust as a support, in the Leeson case, decidedly misplaced – for it is 'extremely difficult to impose control systems that are so draconian that people who have the responsibility to act in a trustworthy fashion should nonetheless have people looking over their shoulders on a minute by minute basis, to make sure they don't conceal the evidence of their transactions'.[2]

11.4 INTERPRETING CONTROL RULES

Another perspective on social risks in a world where ICT is gradually defeating the imperative of distance has been developed by Chauvidul (2003). Using a semiotics framework, in this, the third of the case studies presented here, she examined the relationship between formal systems and informal norms in internal control systems in a global bank. She argued that the global policies and standardized manuals and procedures of multinational firms cannot be internalized and interpreted in the same way in every branch, as anticipated by the management. The risk under scrutiny is the breakdown of control systems in contexts where ICT has enabled a globalized and distributed organization. The main objective was to analyse in depth the interaction between formal and informal systems. The focus of the study was on the people who played a significant role in the control systems. In pursuing this aim, an interpretive case study of a global bank was conducted in two branches, London and Bangkok. Four themes are of particular interest with regard to risk management in such organizations.

11.4.1 Organizational Structure

Transnational companies, especially in the finance sector, have increasingly adopted the matrix system of management, eschewing the traditional multi-level hierarchical approach. With pervasive ICT to support decision making and given the benefits of a 'flatter' control pyramid and devolution of power away from the centre, such a development is not surprising. However, interviews in Thailand revealed discomfiture with the new structure. One implication was that the attitude towards written guidelines was 'don't bother to check it'. Local guidelines were not being updated and were being ignored. As one Western staff member working in Thailand put it: 'I think the guidelines are useful as a reference source, but at the end of the day, someone who knows their job won't really need the guidelines. They can think creatively, conceptually and rationally' (Chauvidul 2003, p. 121).

11.4.2 Control Structure

The loss of the powerful figure of the bank manager and the replacement by a matrix reporting system cut against the grain of the prevailing Thai culture, whereas the organizational impact of the new system in London was minimal. Many Thai staff felt that they no longer had support and back-up from management in their branch. The result was reduced motivation and general low morale. This confirms the findings of researchers who examine transnational companies who argue that managers in such companies should be responsive to individual companies and different cultural contexts (Wasilewski 2002; Bartlett and Goshal 1989). Local factors should be explored when implementing policies and procedures and internal control systems. Many of the 25 interviewees agreed that under the matrix system, there are more problems of communication and coordination:

> There is no one at a high level in the branch who has the final say whether one thing should be done or not because now they rely on communication – who has the best ability to make a better presentation. This is because those who have the final say are not in the Bangkok branch and so they would not know the local environment. (Chauvidul 2003, p. 134)

11.4.3 Globalization and Cultural Context

The 'one size fits all' approach was also demonstrated to be inappropriate in the case of the ABC Bank. One of the biggest challenges for multinationals using ICTs is how to manage global policies with appropriate consideration for the norms of specific cultural contexts (Bartlett and Goshal 1989;

McDonald 2000; Thorne and Saunders 2002). The global policies of multinationals usually reflect embedded Western values and culture and may not easily be institutionalized in other contexts where personnel have their own deeply held beliefs. Failure to acknowledge the existence and diversity of different cultures can disrupt control systems and, hence, give rise to new 'social' risks. For example, an analysis using a framework from Hofstede (1991) revealed nine separate dimensions of this kind of 'social risk', three of the most interesting in the context of this chapter are as follows:

Face saving. Where some staff members feel embarrassed about asking a question or imposing themselves on someone else. The risk here is that employees will not share their new ideas with their boss or colleagues. When they do not understand certain rules, they may make wrong judgements.

Criticism avoidance. Thai employees like to avoid criticism and confrontation. They do not want to change the way they do things because they do not like to hear negative comments. The risk is that when the bank tries to change or introduce different ways of doing things, this can sometimes lead to low motivation levels and general unhappiness on the part of Thai staff.

Kreng-Jai. Thai employees do not like to say 'I cannot do it'. Honest opinions or straight answers are hard to elicit from Thai staff. Auditors receive an inaccurate picture of the state of play (Chauvidul 2003, pp. 40, 184).

11.4.4 The Relationship between Formal and Informal Systems

ABC London is a rule-based branch with a culture common to the head office. Here the normal situation is for staff to follow rules and update their guidelines. When ambiguities arise, staff use personal judgement to make the best decision. In some areas there may only be norms rather than rules, and the guidelines or formal systems will be appropriately updated. In the Thai branch the status of the formal rules had been undermined by the organizational changes. Many of the key operating procedures just did not seem to apply in a developing country and, with demotivation winning the day, the formal system became discredited. Staff would resort to personal judgements in the absence of appropriate rules and, in this context, such practices presented increased risk for the bank.

One staff member of the Thai back office declared that when she needed to ask about the interpretation of particular rules, because of the matrix system she had to consult someone from head office in Singapore. However, staff in Singapore complained that she asked too many questions: 'they asked me why I did not use my common sense. Actually I wanted my work to follow the global standard, that's why I asked them. I do not want to use my own interpretation' (Chauvidul 2003, p. 196).

In a broad sense internal control can be considered as a part of IS security, which involves minimizing risk arising from inconsistent and incoherent behaviour of actors with respect to compliance with internal control systems. As ICT facilitates ever larger global networks of organizations, the danger is to assume that the individuals who interact with the technical system all hold the same values and interpret control information in the same manner. Cultural differences will impact increasingly on organizational security as ICT becomes more pervasive. The key insights from this case study are that:

- interpretation of formal rules is mediated into behaviour through local cultures;
- local cultures may clash with head office values and intentions, creating insecurity; and
- the 'view from the bridge' may just be a mirage.

11.5 INTEROPERABILITY IN TWO GLOBAL ORGANIZATIONS

Interoperability is one of the biggest problems facing public and private entities that use the Internet for commerce, business or government – how to assess 'stranger' identities in an 'open' environment where the burning questions are which online identities can be trusted, and how much. Deploying digital certificates and PKI is one way in which identity management has been tackled across the globe. The X.509 standard has been widely promoted as the *de facto* model for underpinning PKI because of its potential for eradicating interoperability problems between 'stranger' infrastructures (Chokhani and Ford 1998). The standard is an offshoot of the grand attempt in the 1980s to create a global directory of named persons and entities under the ITU-X.500 project (Ellison 1997). Nevertheless, the idea of a linked global directory failed because organizations refused to publish the names of their employees in this repository, thus dealing a blow to PKI interoperability. As a result, the search to link up multiple stranger PKIs has been a major preoccupation of the security community for many years. This section presents the fourth case study, which underlines the organizational issues that prevent interoperability as compared to the considerable emphasis that is given to technical standards and protocols.

11.5.1 PKI to Secure Online Working

Using a power analytical framework drawn from political science (Clegg 1989), research was undertaken in two global companies in the oil and finance sectors (Wamala 2002), Oilcom and Bankrecht, respectively. Oilcom is a large and diverse energy firm and is among the world's biggest oil companies. Oilcom operates in over 135 countries. Bankrecht is one of the world's largest and most influential financial institutions with assets worth over £428 billion and a workforce of over 70,000 working in 1,500 offices:

> Once upon a time Oilcom in common with other big companies had a closed network, which was opened selectively under very strict controls. What we now have is an open internal network, which we selectively close … . One method of selectively closing this network is providing strong authentication, identification, non-repudiation and all these good things which you get from PKI – if you do it properly. (Wamala 2002, p. 5)

In the recently merged Bankrecht the reason for the adoption of PKI was very straightforward:

> With the PKI our goal was that all communication should be encrypted so that even the so-called administrators cannot see any of the data …. The law here is that you must be physically in the country to access the data. PKI gives us a way of ensuring that the information is not revealed easily. (Wamala 2002, p. 10)

Both these assertions are sound, yet a detailed social and organizational study revealed the underlying risk of failure in the valiant search for security and interoperability.

11.5.2 Critical Role of Institutional Arrangements

The critical observation that arises from these two cases is that the relative success of Oilcom's PKI as compared to the problems experienced at Bankrecht was due neither to the technical efficacy of the product nor to its cost. The success of PKI in Oilcom appeared to be due to its supporters' engagement in a shrewdly orchestrated campaign to knit it with the existing institutional order. Because of this alignment, PKI has become an accepted part of organizational life at Oilcom without much ceremony. Why was this possible?

Centralizing tendency. Oilcom introduced PKI at a time when there was a drive to achieve more consistency in its global operations. The firm not only drafted policies to support this goal, but also put in place global ICT systems including a global desktop (GD) that supported this principle. Among other objectives, the GD was aimed at increasing the number of PCs under the control of the central information technology (IT) division from 69 per cent to 100 per cent. Furthermore, when Oilcom moved to its new Active Directory (AD), it simply replaced another enterprise-wide X.500 directory.

Security token use was established practice. Moreover, badges and smart cards had already been institutionalized in the organizational life at Oilcom over the years and building designs assumed their use.

Shrewd systems design. The factor that ultimately clinched the institutionalization of PKI at Oilcom was the smart card design, which combined physical access, network log on, lunch pass and document-signing capacities. Employees used the card to accomplish many of their everyday organizational tasks.

By contrast, at Bankrecht none of these conditions was in place.

Recent merger not fully digested. Because the company was still in the aftermath of a merger it did not have a widely accepted institutional order. The firm was in the throes of an open culture clash between the two groups of employees.

Weakened IT division. One of the biggest losers in the merged entity was the IT division because it ceded the command of financial resources to the business divisions. The business divisions effectively took over the governance of IT. They chose which projects to pay for and often excluded large infrastructure projects that they suspected would threaten their autonomy. The situation is summarized by a PKI engineer as follows:

> I am not aware of any common IT services. ... we don't have an IT team within Bankrecht that tries to enforce common practices within the divisions. ... At the moment, it is the business divisions that have the money to pay for IT projects so centralizing the service will involve moving the money away from them. (Wamala 2002, p. 14)

The *common directory problem.* The tussle over resources between the business divisions and Bankrecht head office negatively affected the take-up of PKI. This is clear in the stalemate over a common directory. One of the reasons for the relative success of PKI at Oilcom was the deployment of a common active directory (AD). Bankrecht has been unable to implement a common AD because this was at odds with the autonomous operations of its business divisions. The absence of a common directory was not the only factor impeding efforts by Bankrecht to create a single domain. It also accentuated the proliferation of PKI islands, as one PKI engineer lamented:

> One of the key things that I think is gonna affect the ability of Bankrecht to function as a group is the failure to deploy group-wide Active Directory. Over the future that will be significant. That failure was basically due to some technical issues within the product, and political issues. (Wamala 2002, p. 14)

There are problems in using a centralized directory running an AD solution. The biggest problem is that it assumes a unified, all-powerful and well-financed IT division. However, in many large global organizations, the IT division lacks such power because of the absence of a common account to pay for infrastructure projects. Many organizations such as Bankrecht simply do not have such a division. Perhaps even more critical is the assumption implicit in AD that organizations have distinct groups of employees that do not overlap. As observed by a PKI engineer, in practice, Bankrecht, in common with other global organizations, has many overlaps between geographical and functional roles:

> Bankrecht has six, seven, eight, nine subdivisions? I do not know how many! You see where my problem begins? There are official and non-official subdivisions. How do you classify those? Because what a PKI can allow you to do is by creating groups, you can make people have access only to certain data. If you say everyone is a Bankrecht employee then you do not have that finer granularity that the application offers to have more inbuilt security. (Wamala 2002, p.15)

Because the group was still integrating newly acquired businesses in the US and in its home base country, it would take some time for clearly defined groups to emerge. Bankrecht was not ready for interdomain interoperability since it had failed to consolidate its own internal PKI initiatives. The absence of a central IT function in a large organization generally means that problems arise with interoperation because different business divisions are likely to implement different technologies. Even in cases where the same technology has been implemented group-wide, such as at Oilcom, there often are significant modifications to the infrastructure in different parts of the world to appease dissenters in far-flung divisions and to cut out the more centralizing features of an AD that demands a robust telecommunication infrastructure. These compromises complicate PKI deployment and increase future interoperation costs.

11.5.3 PKI Islands put Interoperability at Risk

Potentially a more critical risk to Oilcom's future interoperability is the emergence of PKI islands within the outside-facing trust services. Individual business units have continued to spend on external PKI services with serious consequences, as observed by a security consultant:

> We lack coordination around the external uses of Trust Services. ... That is the worry because we will get to a situation where we will need to be looking into Microsoft, Entrust, Baltimore, Entegrity, RSA technologies and certificate provisions from a whole variety of different providers and we will have to somehow integrate all those into our technical infrastructure. .... We must understand policy and procedural implications as well because we have to tie our internal processes to these external requirements. Maybe islands of PKI is all we can achieve with external PKI. (Wamala 2002, p.17)

The accumulated effect of the absence of a consistent approach is the creation of islands that have to be expensively harmonized in the future. Consequently, Oilcom and Bankrecht were inadvertently moving from interoperable domains to islands representing a combination of sub-domains. These global, heterogeneous and distributed organizations are not using the PKIX[3] model with its assumption of a central or root certification authority. Instead, they are depending more on the 'circles of trust' approach by participating in closed trade bodies such as Trade-Ranger and Identrus. These bodies are informal in their origins, but are semi-formalized through the use of contractual agreements. The downside of the use of contracts is that organizations become involved in multilateral agreements that grow exponentially because each time a new member is added they have to sign individual agreements with all other existing members. Contracts demand constant changes in processes and policies to accommodate different relationships and, moreover, they tend to nullify the biggest advantage of e-commerce, that is, the conduct of transactions in real time.

In summary, it is clear that:

- PKI technology needs centralized directories and hence power to be successful;
- in the absence of a powerful IT department, PKI projects may be led by the businesses;
- interoperability is jeopardized by piecemeal approaches necessitated by power conflicts; and
- institutionalization is eased by linking identity tokens with realization of routine behaviours.

11.6 SOCIAL RISK MANAGEMENT REVIEW

As the information society unfolds, more social risks are destined to make themselves felt. Prudent governance of a society predicated on cyber operations will demand that these risks be acknowledged and that at least some of them be attended to.

The following section recapitulates the issues examined in the four case studies and sets out some of the questions that emerged.

Perception and communication. Drawing upon cultural and communication theory, the first study in Section 11.2 opened up the dimension of risk perception and communication. In the context of the risk society, it is increasingly urgent that more research be undertaken into the criticality of risk perception for both business and social affairs. How are cyber risks conceptualized at both organizational and societal levels? Who are the sources and transmitters of cyber risk communications? How does the choice of medium influence the perception of cyber risk? For the cyber organization, how can the various stakeholder views be appropriately reconciled and fed into security policies and procedures addressing those risks? Different perceptions can be a source of strength in the analysis phase, but not once policy has been decided. What emerges from the first study is a basis for rejecting the idea of objective risk and for developing a concept of many subjective understandings of risk. The issue for the organization is how to reconcile the different perceptions into an input into a single policy vehicle to deal with contingency and security. A further issue lies in deciding the most effective means of communication of risk, balancing, for example, effective but costly face-to-face models with efficient but impersonal emails. To what extent does the medium impact on the risk message positively or, indeed, negatively? These matters should figure large in the calculations of a government faced with managing the perception and communication of risk on a society-wide scale.

Opportunity and security. New technology is often associated with new risks and opportunities. Understanding what the new opportunities might be for the rogue insider or for the criminal outsider with access to IS makes the work of confounding their efforts much easier. The opportunity model discussed in Section 11.3, the second study, could be used in staff education and awareness programmes by emphasizing their role in supporting guardianship. One of the problems faced by organizations is gaining employee cooperation in maintaining effective security. Lack of cooperation is often the result of staff failing to appreciate the vital role they play, especially when they perceive security as solely the task of those people directly responsible for security (Wood 1995). However, one of the facets of the opportunity model is its ability to emphasize the centrality of staff behaviour in providing effective guardianship over an IS. This suggests that education programmes could, for example, be used to highlight the need for compliance with local security policies. Such a relationship could be described in terms of simple offender, target and guardianship relationships. Examples could be imported from criminology (for example guardianship over property and personal belongings) to help highlight the 'informal' role people can play in crime prevention programmes.

The Crime Specific Opportunity Structure model is a conceptual tool that can enable organizations to identify elements that may afford a collective control environment and to highlight the relationships between the components of the collective. This perspective provides a potential alternative to technocratic approaches to IS security. Further research is required to assess the feasibility of this model, but introducing a criminological perspective opens the way for transfusions into security thinking from insights from social science research. The opportunity structure model permits a systematic and coherent framework to be introduced, linking all those organizational functions whose work is central or tangential to security: risk, IS security, audit, compliance, human relations and so on, fostering an integrative or joined-up approach to the management of risks. Working in isolated 'silos' has been a problem for modern corporate functional divisions of labour, when information flows 'up' functions, rather than 'across' them, thereby hindering coordinated attacks on the problems.

Internal control systems. In the context of large-scale relocation of company operations to developing countries such as India and Thailand, the issues of internal control and security are key ones. In Section 11.4, the third study, within an audit approach to internal control a semiotic framework was applied to reveal important issues about control in decentralized organizations relying on a pervasive technical infrastructure. As the tentacles of cyber organization reach ever further into the recesses of the global environment, the issue of control looms ever larger. Empirical research is needed on the trade-off between the facility with which the technical side of cyber systems can be developed, and the more difficult establishment of operational norms among different participant cultures and sub-cultures. Formal rules developed in the corporate headquarters may not be implemented or inscribed into the informal systems of the operations in other countries in the manner expected. A focus on developing management tools and techniques drawing insight from a variety of theoretical frameworks must be a priority if control systems are to be strengthened in the future.

Interoperability. As the growth of networks supports greater interaction among businesses and government bodies, the question looms as to the security of the systems and procedures of potential collaborators. This is explored in Section 11.5, case study four. Not only must there be the technical capacity to interoperate, there needs to be interoperation at the level of the institution, its policies and practices. Collaboration usually requires giving access to users whose identities have been authenticated elsewhere and whose access rights must be reconciled with those of the 'home' organization. The technical problems have not been simple to resolve, but the institutional trust issues are proving even more intractable. The study of the take-up of PKI reveals the labyrinth of issues that arise within the confines of two global corporations. Both these organizations participate in many initiatives aiming to develop industry interoperability, yet both have had considerable problems in achieving that goal internally. The obstacles were never simply technical, but always involved the cultural and political dimensions of the organizational information systems. There has been an evolution in security issues from concern about technical devices, such as cryptography and firewalls, to management issues. This evolution is evidenced in the success of the code of information security management BS7799, and ISO17799, the international standard that it spawned. The next phase of security approaches is likely to focus on the interoperation of management policy. This will require new theoretical frameworks that can address the issues.

11.7 CONCLUSION: SOCIAL SCIENCE CONTRIBUTIONS

The failure of the *c:cure* accreditation scheme (Backhouse et al. 2003) and, arguably, the muted success of *tScheme*,[4] the UK's supervisory scheme for trusted third parties, underline the problems of approaching policy issues in security from technical and regulatory angles without considering sufficiently the social and political agendas. Although there was strong support for the use of PKI and digital certification to underpin identity management in the West (NIST 2000), nothing like the progress expected has been achieved. The social sciences have a contribution to make in framing the problem and offering solutions. Security issues are never simply technical questions that can be underpinned by law and regulation. In the area of web services and identity and authentication, a range of (technical) protocols is being established that are predicated on an entity accepting the trusted credentials from another.[5] What is missing are the business and trust protocols to provide the institutional level of mutual confidence. In the near future, it is likely that ratings service providers, such as Standard & Poor's and Moody's, will offer credit rating-style operational risk ratings to short-cut the process of deciding at what level to trust certain counter-parties. This may be followed by cyber risk ratings for insurance purposes along the lines of the operational risk ratings that are emerging with respect to Basel II Capital Accord.[6] Making a market in security risk might prove to be the quickest route to enabling interoperability of electronic identities. Longer-term security planning is likely to require that a variety of insights from the social science disciplines is brought to bear on the problems raised by identity and authentication issues.

11.7.1 Cross-disciplinary Focus

Opportunities need to be created for cross-disciplinary collaboration on the topic of security and risk. Traditional IS security research groups work will need to work with entities such as the Jill Dando Institute and University College London, with their focus on crime reduction. The Institute focuses on the application of criminology to reduce crime and includes eminent scholars such as Ron Clarke, who has been a pioneer in the development of the 'criminal opportunity' approach discussed in Section 11.3. A current proposal is to develop the criminal opportunity model for application to information systems security risks, building from the work of Willison (2002), in an effort to design crime out of systems and procedures. A suitably tested and researched model might be the basis for a risk management framework that could be taught to managers as 'best practice' in the area. As e-government and e-business take off, there will be greater opportunities for criminals to insinuate themselves into the crevices of such systems. They will seek to exploit design loopholes and to profit from tactics such as identity theft, the supply of false credentials and the like. If systems and procedures are conceived *ab initio* as 'low criminal opportunity zones', then significant reductions could be achieved in cyber crime. Many electronic systems are now being devised to take advantage of cyber working so there will be scope to deploy collaborations of this kind.

11.7.2 Qualitative Research in Security

Qualitative research of the kind reviewed here has an important role to play in information security. Yet the preconception that real security is about technology continues to linger. The realization that secure systems rely as much on social as technical factors is only slowly being established in the research and practitioner community. Qualitative, interpretive research can be rigorous and it addresses the recognition, meaning and interpretative aspects of risk. These are the baseline competences for contingency planning, security awareness and prompt preventive action. In a complex social system, a technically conceived security system will never replace the richness of a human and informal system, augmented by a formal control framework and supported by pervasive ICT. As the concern of business, government and the practitioner community focuses on the development of an appropriate culture of security, social science research will need to be undertaken to provide practical frameworks based on the results of theoretical and empirical work.

11.7.3 Future Research Topics

A number of possibly fruitful research topics emerge from this review and with consistent methodologies would yield useful results for those concerned about cyber risks and cyber security.

The semantics of security. To aid the sharing of data on security and the interoperability of policy, some fundamental concepts of the subject need to be properly mapped out and a logic of security behaviour determined. Currently terms such as 'risk', 'attack', 'event', 'threat' and 'vulnerability' mean different things to different entities. An interpretive or hermeneutic study aimed at analysing the meaning of these terms and the development of an ontology of the discourses employed in security debates would facilitate communication and policy development.

Signalling security and trustworthiness. A detailed analysis of how security and trustworthiness is signalled successfully in an open global environment still remains to be undertaken. Application of semiotics and signalling theory from economics would be a most valuable support to research in this area.

The well-chosen epigram - 'Security ... depends on balancing cost and risk through the appropriate use of technology and policy',[7] which captures the essence of the pragmatic approach subscribed to in this chapter, suggests two further areas for research.

One focuses on the notion of balancing cost and risk and, increasingly, reward – where, for example, a successful Basel II rating frees up risk capital for use in the business. Here, we could imagine a methodology for investigating the effects of different (portfolio) management strategies applied in the search to avoid underprotecting assets or overspending on countermeasures.

The other research area centres on the interplay between technology, policy and, arguably, informal culture and tries to develop, with an interpretivist study, greater understanding of the term 'appropriate' and so inform management who must decide about such trade-offs.

11.7.4 Emphasizing the Social Context of Security

Rejecting the view that security problems in cyberspace are caused by fallible humans and resolved by infallible technology, the aim in this chapter has been to draw attention to the social context in which security risks arise and may be resolved. While new technology always alters the social context in which it is introduced and triggers new risks, the accumulated evidence of qualitative research suggests that gradually efforts are made to accommodate the benefits and mitigate the disadvantages of the technology by altering behaviour appropriately. Security managers must grapple with the best combinations of technology, policy and behaviour. Good progress has been made on the first two – the greatest need now is to turn attention to the last member of this trinity.

NOTES

1 See Morgan (2003).
2 Baring (1995).

3 The PKIX Working Group was established in the Autumn of 1995 with the intention of developing Internet standards needed to support an X.509-based PKI, http://www.ietf.org/html.charters/pkix-charter.html accessed 17 April 2004.
4 At the present time only five Approved Services have been accredited, the first one dating from 11 February 2002, http://www.tscheme.org/directory/index.html, accessed 17 April 2004.
5 For example www.projectliberty.org or www.pingid.com both accessed 17 April 2004.
6 See http://www.aba.com/Industry+Issues/RiskBasedCapital2.htm accessed 17 April 2004.
7 See *The Economist* (2002).

REFERENCES

Audit Commission (1994), *Opportunity Makes a Thief: An Analysis of Computer Abuse*, London: Audit Commission Publications.

Audit Commission (1997), *Ghost in the Machine: An Analysis of IT Fraud and Abuse*, London: Audit Commission Publications.

Audit Commission (2001), *Your Business@Risk: An Update on IT Abuse 2001*, London: Audit Commission Publications.

Backhouse, J. (1997), 'Information@Risk', *Information Strategy Online* 4(Jan.): 33-35.

Backhouse, J., Hsu, W.Y. and McDonnell, A. (2003), 'Toward Public Key Infrastructure Interoperability' *Communications of the ACM* 46(6): 98-100.

Baring, P. (1995), *Financial Times*, 28 February.

Bartlett, C. and Goshal, S. (1989), *Managing Across Borders: The Transnational Solution*, Boston MA: Harvard Business School Press.

Bener, A. (2000), 'Risk Perception, Trust and Credibility: A Case in Internet Banking', Department of Information Systems, London School of Economics and Political Science.

BloomBecker, B. (1984), 'Introduction to Computer Crime', in J. Finch and E. Dougall (eds), *Computer Security: A Global Challenge*, Amsterdam: North-Holland/Elsevier.

Board of Banking Supervision (1995), 'Report of the Board for Banking Supervision Inquiry into the Circumstances of the Collapse of Barings', London: HMSO.

Bologna, J. (1993), *Handbook on Corporate Fraud*, Boston MA: Butterworth-Heinemann.

Brantingham, P.J. and Brantingham, P.L. (1991), *Environmental Criminology*, Prospect Heights IL: Waveland Press.

Chauvidul, N. (2003), 'Formality and Informality in Internal Control Systems: A Comparative Study of Control in Different Social and Cultural Environments in a Global Bank', Department of Information Systems, London School of Economics and Political Science.

Chokhani, S. and Ford, W. (1998), 'Internet X.509 Public Key Infrastructure Certificate Policy and Certification Practices Framework', RFC 2527, http://www.faqs.org/rfcs/rfc2527.html

Clarke, R. (1995), 'Situational Crime Prevention' in M. Tonry and D. Farrington (eds), *Building a Safer Society. Strategic Approaches to Crime Prevention. Crime and Justice: A Review of Research*, Chicago IL: University of Chicago Press, pp. 91-150.

Clarke, R. (1997), *Situational Crime Prevention: Successful Case Studies*, Albany NY: Harrow and Heston.

Clarke, R. and Cornish, D. (1985), 'Modelling Offender's Decisions: A Framework for Policy and Research', in M. Tonry and N. Morris (eds), *Crime and Justice: An Annual Review of Research*, Chicago IL: University of Chicago Press, pp. 147-85.

Clarke, R. and Cornish, D. (2000), 'Rational Choice', in R. Paternoster and R. Bachman (eds), *Explaining Crime and Criminals: Essays in Contemporary Criminological Theory*, Los Angeles CA: Roxbury Publishing Company, pp. 23-42.

Clegg, S.R. (1989), *Frameworks of Power*, London and Newbury Park CA: Sage.

Comer, M. (1998), *Corporate Fraud*, Vermont VA: Gower.

Cornish, D. and Clarke, R. (1986), 'Situational Prevention, Displacement of Crime and Rational Choice Theory', in K. Heal and G. Laycock (eds), *Situational Crime Prevention: From Theory into Practice*, London: HMSO, pp. 1-16.

Courtney, R. (1977), 'Security Risk Assessment in Electronic Data Processing', *AFIPS Conference Proceedings of the National Computer Conference*, Arlington VA: AFIPS Press, pp. 97-104.

Dorey, P. (1994), 'Security Management and Policy', in W. Caelli, D. Longley and M. Shain (eds), *Information Security Handbook*, London: Macmillan, pp. 27-41.

Douglas, M. (1985), *Risk Acceptability According to the Social Sciences*, New York: Russell Sage Foundation.

Ellison C. (1997), 'What Do You Need to Know About the Person With Whom You Are Doing Business?' Written testimony of Carl M. Ellison to the US House of Representatives Science and Technology Subcommittee, Hearing of 28 October 1997: Signatures in a Digital Age, http://world.std.com/~cme/html/congress1.html accessed 13 Nov. 2003.

Ernst & Young (2002), 'Global Information Security Survey Presentation Services', Ernst & Young, London.

Felson, M. (1992), 'Routine Activities and Crime Prevention: Armchair Concepts and Practical Action', *Studies on Crime and Crime Prevention* 1(1): 31-4.

Fesseden-Raden, J., Fitchen, J. and Heath, J.S. (1987), 'Providing Risk Information in Communities: Factors Influencing What is Heard and Accepted', *Science, Technology and Human Values* 12(3/4): 94-101.

Fitzgerald, J. (1978), 'EDP Risk Analysis for Contingency Planning', *EDP Audit Control and Security Newsletter* 6(Aug.): 1-8.

Forester, T. and Morrison, P. (1994), *Computer Ethics: Cautionary Tales and Ethical Dilemmas in Computing*, Cambridge MA: MIT Press.

Hinde, S. (2001), 'The Weakest Link', *Computers & Security* 20(4): 295-301.

Hindelang, M., Gottfredson, M. and Garafalo, J. (1978), *Victims of Personal Crime: An Empirical Foundation for a Theory of Personal Victimisation*, Cambridge MA: Ballinger.

Hirschi, T. (1969), *Causes of Delinquency*, Berkeley and Los Angeles CA: University of California Press.

Hitchings, J. (1995), 'Deficiencies of the Traditional Approach to Information Security and the Requirements for a New Methodology,' *Computers and Security* 14(5): 377-83.

Hofstede, G. (1991), *Cultures and Organisation – Software of the Mind. Intercultural Cooperation and its Importance for Survival*, Columbus OH: McGraw-Hill.

Krimsky, S. and Plough, O. (1988), *Environmental Hazards: Communicating Risks as a Social Process*, Dover MA: Auburn House.

Luzwick, P. (2001), 'Security? Who's Got Time For Security? I'm Trying to Get my Job Done', *Computer Fraud and Security* 1: 16-17.

McDonald, G. (2000), 'Cross-Cultural Methodological Issues in Ethical Research', *Journal of Business Ethics* 27(1/2): 89-104.

Morgan, O. (2003), 'Swipe Strike Cost BA £50M', *Observer/Guardian*, http://observer.guardian.co.uk/business/story/0,6903,1006430,00.html accessed 17 Apr. 04.

National Institute for Science and Technology (NIST) (2000), 'Federal Agency Use of Public Key Technology for Digital Signatures and Authentication', National Institute of Standards, NIST Special Publication 800-25, October, http://csrc.nist.gov/publications/nistpubs/800-25/sp800-25.pdf accessed 17 Apr. 04.

National Research Council (1989), *Improving Risk Communication, US Committee on Risk Perception and Communication*, Washington DC: National Academies Press.

Nosworthy, J. (2000), 'Implementing Information Security in the 21st Century – Do You Have the Balancing Factors?', *Computers and Security* 19(4): 337-47.

Olnes, J. (1994), 'Development of Security Policies', *Computers and*

Security 14(8): 628-36.

Osborne, K. (1998), 'Auditing the IT Security Function', *Computers and Security* 17(1): 34-41.

Parker, D. (1997), 'The Strategic Values of Information Security in Business', *Computers and Security* 16(7): 572-82.

Riem, A. (2001), 'Cybercrimes of the 21st Century', *Computer Fraud and Security* 4: 12-15.

Schneier, B. (1998), 'Security Pitfalls in Cryptographic Design', *Information Management and Computer Security* 6(3): 133-7.

Skibell, R. (2002), 'The Myth of the Computer Hacker', *Information, Communication and Society* 5(3): 336-56.

Spurling, P. (1995), 'Promoting Security Awareness and Commitment', *Information Management & Computer Security* 3(2): 20-26.

Stevenson, G. (2000), 'Computer Fraud: Detection and Prevention', *Computer Fraud and Security* 11: 13-15.

The Economist (2002), A Survey of Digital Security, *The Economist*, 26 Oct.

Thomson, M. and von Solms, R. (1998), 'Information Security Awareness: Educating Your Users Effectively', *Information Management and Computer Security* 6(4): 167-73.

Thorne, L. and Saunders, S.B. (2002), 'The Socio-Cultural Embeddedness of Individuals' Ethical Reasoning in Organisations', *Journal of Business Ethics* 35(1): 1-14.

von Solms, B. (2001), 'Corporate Governance and Information Security', *Computers and Security* 20(3): 215-18.

Wamala, F. (2002), 'Comparing Public Key Infrastructure Institutionalisation in Two Global Organisations', The Fiducia Project, Department of Information Systems, London School of Economics and Political Science.

Warman, A. (1993), *Computer Security Within Organisations*, London: Macmillan.

Wasilewski, N. (2002), 'An Empirical Study of the Desirability and Challenges of Implementing Transnational Marketing Strategies', *Advances in Competitive Research* 10(1): 123-49.

Willison, R. (2002), 'Opportunities for Computer Abuse: Assessing a Crime Specific Approach in the Case of Barings Bank', Department of Information Systems, London School of Economics and Political Science.

Willison, R. and Backhouse, J. (2003), 'Understanding Criminal Opportunity in the IS Context', paper presented at the Information Systems Research Seminar in Scandinavia IRIS 26 Conference, 9-12 August, Haikko, Finland.

Wood, C. (1995), 'Writing InfoSec Policies', *Computers and Security* 14(8): 667-74.

Wright, M.A. (2001), 'Keeping Top Management Focussed', *Computer*

Fraud and Security 5: 12-14.

Yapp, P. (2001), 'Passwords: Use and Abuse', *Computer Fraud and Security* 9: 14-16.

12 The economics of cyber trust between cyber partners

Jonathan Cave[1]

12.1 INTRODUCTION

This chapter considers some aspects of the intersection of trust and economics through the application of economic tools to the analysis of trust and the delineation of trust issues in the analysis of economics. As far as possible, the development of the argument will be related to trust in electronic contexts, though the former deals with more abstract issues that are necessarily less directly influenced by the specific features of electronic interactions than the latter.

This chapter is divided into two parts. The first part (Sections 12.2 and 12.3) applies game-theoretic tools to specific aspects of trust, while Section 12.4 presents a brief survey of trust in industrial organization economics (because this is the most appropriate context for cyber trust, and highlights trust considerations relating to, for example, e-commerce) with just enough model development to indicate a 'road map' for further development.

Section 12.2 develops some simple, essentially static game theoretic models of specific aspects of trust to analyse their equilibrium and efficiency outcomes. Section 12.3 examines the evolution of trust as a 'convention'. The game-theoretic analysis points up certain abstract implications that transcend the directly economic setting, but are less precise and less faithful to institutional detail. The supporting models shed light on the potential tension between efficiency and equilibrium, in terms of both the prevalence of trust behaviour and the network of relationships to which the need to trust others gives rise.

The models also identify conditions under which different levels of trust may 'prevail' (be widespread) and conditions under which a diversity of behaviour is likely. One consequence is the existence of 'catastrophes' – discontinuous jumps in the level of trust in response to small changes in underlying conditions. This can give rise to cyclic behaviour. Another use of the models is identifying low-cost ways for policy to exploit the evolutionary nature of trust in order to promote efficiency.

The purpose of the summary of more conventional economic analysis in Section 12.4 is twofold: to develop implications of existing economic models for trust and, conversely, to show how trust considerations have modified analysis of industrial structure, conduct and performance. In addition, this summary identifies places where game-theoretic analysis can usefully contribute to more practical policy problems. Section 12.5 concludes, developing policy implications and suggestions for further work.

12.1.1 Methodology

Several methodological points should be made at the outset. The game-theoretic models in Sections 12.2 and 12.3 seem more abstract than the economic models in Section 12.4 – but both approaches are theoretical and, in all cases, alternative models and conclusions are possible. None of the results should be taken as assertions about the way the world is or should be. Rather, the analysis starts from plausible representations of aspects of trust and derives conclusions using standard tools – the conclusions are only as empirically valid as the model's assumptions.[2]

The language of theory is necessarily condensed and may strike many readers as opaque, so details[3] of the models, derivations and computations have for the most part been placed in an appendix. The utility ultimately lies in a positive contribution: if we conceptualize trust in a given way, certain implications follow. The material in the Appendix is intended to indicate how the argumentation runs, so that its strengths and weaknesses and potential for development in more specific situations can be assessed.

The game-theoretic approach starts from specific stylized aspects of trust:

- one's own level of trust should match one's environment;
- opportunistic or criminal behaviour and carelessness or suspicion have different impacts on trust;
- trust creates linkage and link formation requires trust;
- the value of a trusted relationship may be affected by the partner's other trusted relationships;
- costly trust-enhancing activities may offer external benefits;
- individuals may be able to do similar things in high- and low-trust environments;
- there are unobserved individual differences in the subjective importance of trust;
- 'network externalities' (remote effects of trust linkages) can affect the dynamics of trusting behaviour; and
- trust can be viewed as a societal convention or norm.

Such models can illuminate such abstract features as:

- multiple stable outcomes;
- the dynamic evolution of trust (resilience, jumps, cycles and so on);
- connections between trust behaviour and the social fabric;
- the tension between stability and efficiency; and
- the scope for policy to exploit evolution and encourage efficient trust.

The economic analysis of industrial organization addresses the relations among economic actors and the degree to which competition and its efficiency consequences are affected by institutional, technological and informational factors. This offers ample scope for 'trust metaphors'. In contrast to abstract game-theoretic treatments of trust these tend to focus on concrete economic interactions, for example some form of contract and/or market. The economic analysis sheds light on how trust affects the operation of these institutions and on how economic considerations in turn affect the level of trust. Specifically, industrial economics considers:

- Reputations among economic agents that are linked:
  - horizontally – as competitors in markets;
  - vertically – as buyers and sellers of goods and services;
  - in networks – as producers and users of complementary goods and services.
- Standards relating to trust.
- The economics of security and security-enhancing technologies.
- Assurance and market mechanisms for signalling and providing it.
- Liability and its effect on the efficiency and equity of precaution and risk-bearing.

The analysis is tied to specific market features and thus provides more concrete ways to take account of trust in economic policy and of economic factors (especially profit) in policy relating to trust.

The mapping between issues and models is not one-to-one: many aspects of cyber trust are not addressed by the models and many phenomena with which the models are concerned (particularly in Section 12.3.4) have only an indirect connection to trust, or the specific implications of the Internet. However, some connections are stronger than may at first appear, and we attempt to draw out the interpretation of models in terms that relate to trust. This indirect approach reflects the inherent complexity of trust and attempts to balance tractability with conceptual relevance.

12.1.2 Trust and Trusting

Trust is a matter of expectation – extrapolations to other times and contingencies. A trusting individual has some view of what might happen, how likely the various possibilities are and the impact of current choices. These assessments may not follow expected utility theory: likelihoods may be more subjective than objective, outcome and likelihood may not be separable and the contingent future may be described in deliberately 'fuzzy' language. Within the expected utility framework, individuals may ignore the variance of outcomes. Finally, trust may involve different degrees of consequentialism – expectations may be bound up with process as well as outcomes. For example, an online customer may trust a transaction without distinguishing reliability of merchants, payment and/or delivery services and legal mechanisms that provide compensation in the event of loss. Others may evaluate a purchase quite differently, being reluctant to disclose payment details to some agents (but not all) even while maintaining the same beliefs about the likelihood of different outcomes.

Trust has proven a difficult concept for economics to clarify (see Hollis 1998), but its influence is widely acknowledged. Much analysis in the economic literature follows one or more dichotomies.[4] Several considerations follow from these distinctions.

The participation decision (if alternatives are available) is essentially to trust that the game is as described, that the other players will behave as expected and so on. This trust is essentially an expectation – an assessment of what will happen in the future and in different contingencies. To the extent that individuals regard the rest of the world as unmotivated or unresponsive to their own choices, the economics of incomplete information are appropriate. To the extent that the results of individual conscious choices are seen as interdependent, the appropriate approach is game-theoretic.

As a first consideration, it is fruitful to distinguish trusting – whether to trust another entity (person, group, institution and so on) – from trustworthiness (whether another entity should trust me). This distinction points the way for motivated and rational individuals to modify or facilitate the evolution of the rules of the game. In particular, choices of whom to interact (play) with and whose expectations to fulfil, disappoint or ignore determine the 'network structure' of the game.[5]

A second consideration is how the design of the game itself embodies trust. An important strand of the literature places trust in a contractarian setting. Bowles and Gintis (2000) relate trust to contractual incompleteness, which allows parties to economize on the information required to completely specify all contingencies and the obligations attached to them. As Bacharach et al. (2001) point out, this applies to default contracts – thus, trust is essential to the functioning of norms that allow markets to operate.[6] Fukuyama (1995), Puttnam (2000) and Politt (2001) extend this, placing trust at the heart of social capital. This view is not uncontested.[7] Some see an inherent conflict between contract (formal specification of transactional rights and obligations) and trust (informal or tacit surrender of powers or actions supported by expectations). Others make the pragmatic point that trust in incomplete contracts involves acting on incomplete information; some 'trust-enhancing' measures add information and thus weaken trust. Finally, the specific legal context of contracts provides for monitoring, verification and enforcement in the event of breach; this argues for looking at, for example, hierarchies of trust.[8] These discussions go beyond the simple trust models considered here.

Trust is reflected in all the underlying data of the game: the set of 'players'; their strategies or powers of action; their information; their motivations or pay-offs; and the solution concept used to summarize the information in the game.

Social games identify specific people 'trusted' to make decisions (play the game) and the decisions they are 'trusted' to make – drinking, driving, voting, making contracts and so on. This applies to acting on one's own behalf, working with others, participation in collective activity and even (especially in the contract case) whether one is allowed to trust others or occupy a position of trust. Second, most decisions are made under uncertainty. In distinguishing objective from strategic uncertainty, and uncertainty from risk, we trust that objective uncertainty is not rationally motivated and can be taken as exogenous, that other players are rationally motivated and can be understood by considering their preferences and beliefs, and that important elements of these uncertainties can be reduced to risk[9] and adequately described by equations and formal models.

Much recent work (including the present chapter) represents trust as a strategic choice.[10] An alternative aspect of trust is credibility: trusting information received and being believed by others (for example threats and promises). Another strand of work (Bacharach and Gambetta 2001) attributes trust to motivational factors outside the rational behaviour framework. The foregoing considerations are summarized in Table 12.1.

Trust (trustworthiness and trusting behaviour) is valuable in complex interactive systems, but not necessarily good in aggregate. Rather, the distribution of trust can ensure sound expectations and an appropriate alignment of information, motivation and power to act. For this reason, a simplistic objective of maximizing trust can be myopic or even counterproductive. To clarify this observation, it is useful to distinguish relations of trust between people, systems and organizations as shown in Table 12.2.

Table 12.1 Modelling aspects of trust

Aspect	Formal representation	Meaning
A decision to interact	Network structure	Choosing with whom to transact, trade or play.
Simplified societal mechanisms	Incomplete contracts, norms, conventions	Save 'costs' of covering all contingencies, potential 'partners'.
A collective good	Rules of the game, social capital, mechanism design.	The environment within which we negotiate and act
Being trusted	Players	Who gets to decide
Delegation	Strategies	What they can choose
Expected results of actions	Nash equilibrium	Trust in self-confirming beliefs or norms, even when held by others
Intention vs accident	Uncertainty, rationality	Trust in models
A conscious decision	Trust as a specific strategy, precaution	Choosing to delegate, keep promises
Credibility	Revision of beliefs, incomplete contracts	Willingness to rely on information received
A private good	Reputation	Connection between what I say I will do and what I am expected to do, inference drawn from my actions

Table 12.2 Trust and trusting

		Trusted party		
		People	Systems	Organizations
Trusting party	People	Societal trust (Fukuyama)	Agency, privacy, accuracy	Reputation, assurance
	Systems	Fault-tolerance	Complex system reliability	N/A
	Organizations	Agency	Reliance	Firm networking

Table 12.3 shows some advantages of coordinated trusting behaviour.

Table 12.3 Advantages of matching trust behaviour

	Trustworthy	Untrustworthy
Trusting	Appropriate delegation, specialization	Enforcement costs, costs of adverse incidents
Untrusting	Excess contracting, monitoring costs; race-to-the-bottom.	Lost gains from trade, inappropriate risk allocation

While it is advantageous, for example, for customers to trust e-commerce systems, it does not follow that more trust is better, or that it falls to firms or governments to build this trust, since due vigilance by customers is both empowering and efficient. On the other hand, many customers are unaware of the need for vigilance, or view the costs (including effort and knowledge acquisition) as too high. The analysis below recognizes that efficient vigilance may involve only a proportion of the population taking precautions and, hence, that the efficiency of the equilibrium outcome may be merely fortuitous – due to the natural tendency of individuals to avoid burdensome precautions and the (real or perceived) possibility of 'free-riding' on the diligence of others – in short, trust may be an undersupplied public good. Efficiency of risk allocation also underpins policy favouring market competition over price regulation and negotiated reallocation of liability in tort systems.

On the narrow issue of trust between individuals and information and communication technology (ICT) systems, we may distinguish:

- Whether people trust ICT systems:
  - to act for them (agency);
  - with information about themselves (confidentiality, privacy);
  - to provide information that they can safely act on (accuracy, currency, authentication, identity, integrity, etc.).
- Whether trust among people or civil/private sector entities:
  - is helped or hindered by new systems;
  - improves or weakens approaches to crime (for example Neighbourhood Watch).
- Whether trust between people and government reduces and improves the incidence of the impacts of crime and the burden of crime reduction.

This chapter does not consider crime directly.[11] From the contractarian perspective, crime is breach of an (incomplete) social contract. The critical issue, addressed to some extent in the models in Section 12.2, is how individuals distinguish mistakes from crimes and whether they accurately attribute unanticipated and adverse events to specific actors and adjust levels of trust accordingly.

12.2 TRUST GAMES

12.2.1 Specific Game Theoretic Models

In this section, trust is analysed through some specific game theoretic models. Table 12.4 summarizes these and the aspects of trust they are intended to illuminate.

Table 12.4 Trust games

Aspect of trust	Game(s)
Trust as a collective norm	Coordination[a]
Fear of crime as distinct from lack of trust	Coordination and crime[b]
Joining a network as a form of trust	Direct network games[c]
Indirect vulnerability (the trusting nature of those we trust)	Indirect reliance
Need for vigilance	Interdependence
Social value of free-riding on costly vigilance	Vaccination
Optional availability of trusted channels or 'safe environments' and network externalities	Hybrid game
Trust is learnt from one's own experience and incomplete information about others	Sampling

a – See Kandori et al. (1993); b – See Young (1998); c – See Jackson (2003).

Before proceeding, it is necessary to acknowledge specific features of some models: limited (usually pairwise) interaction; symmetry in pay-offs and strategies; 'coordination' structure (players prefer to adopt the same behaviour *ceteris paribus*); the possibility of trust as equilibrium behaviour; 'rational actors' (self-regarding preference); and perfect information. At first sight, these seem highly restrictive, and the theorist's preference for the simplest possible model might seem inadequate. However, in addition to simplifying the exposition, these assumptions are not as strict as may at first appear; below, we discuss these assumptions and acknowledge alternative approaches. The Appendix briefly indicates the implications of the analysis for alternative formulations.

Trust in two-person settings differs in important respects from trust in multi-person settings. Trusted interactions expose players to indirect interactions with others and players engage in multiple pairwise interactions with a range of more-or-less identifiable partners – this is partially addressed in some of the models used in this chapter (the indirect reliance, interdependence, vaccination and hybrid games). The third is beyond the scope of this chapter – trust relations between groups and individuals or among groups may differ in kind from those among individuals – for example because group membership involves trust.[12]

Symmetry might seem to present a more serious limitation. In commercial transactions the roles of buyer and seller are not directly interchangeable (though typically conflated in general equilibrium models).[13] While buyers certainly have to consider whether to trust sellers, sellers may have far less need to trust buyers. This applies more to retail transactions and irrevocable sales of goods and services than to business-to-business (B2B) transactions and exchange of information in general communication networks. As 'final-sale' retail transactions increasingly give way to 'lease' arrangements (Rifkin 2000) liability does not pass irrevocably from seller to buyer. The continuing quality of the match between buyer's need and seller's offer, resulting two-sided moral hazard and adverse selection problems and transactions and opportunity costs of dissolving relationships, encourage the parties to consider trustworthiness before making a deal. This can already be seen in changing retail contracts; as public policy pushes back the boundaries of *caveat emptor*, limitations and protections built into commercial contracts (for example software licences) increase despite empirical evidence that they are not very important to consumer choice. Section 12.3.4 applies the same methods to non-symmetric settings.

The coordination framework models situations where the parties must consider each other's actions in choosing their own and where there are multiple equilibria. Anecdotally, it can be suggested that both high-trust and low-trust outcomes can be stable. This class of games includes those where equilibria can be Pareto-ranked[14] and those where players prefer different equilibria.[15] This chapter primarily considers the Pareto-ranked setting and adopts the convention that the parties prefer the high-trust to the low-trust equilibrium. The analysis in Section 12.3.4 considers issues of horizontal trust in a collusive setting; this can give rise to coordination-game pay-offs by including legal or reputation costs or retaliatory commitments. Specifically, a model of 'price-matching' oligopolists would have both a 'competitive' low-price equilibrium and a 'tacitly collusive' high-price equilibrium preferred by all parties.

The key qualitative features of the coordination game (multiple, Pareto-ranked equilibria) apply even to the one-sided retail setting. There are always alternatives to e-commerce transactions, and often varying degrees of 'depth', which can make things two-sided. For instance, if an online buyer chooses to provide lots of information, the seller could realize further gains from trade via personalized transactions that benefit both of them. The seller does not 'trust' the buyer, but trusts the information provided enough to expend resources in devising and making targeted offers in the hope of future trades.

Of course the stakes are not the same on both sides. Even when buyers and sellers reallocate risk and return through negotiation and market pressure, liability should depend on (asymmetric) ability to reduce and/or bear risk. But such pay-off differences typically make only a quantitative, not a qualitative change to Nash equilibrium.

The games considered here model trust as a strict Nash equilibrium. An extensive literature[16] on trust is built around an asymmetric game between a trustor and a trustee, which does not have a trust equilibrium. In its starkest form, the trustor makes an unsecured transfer to the trustee – this amount is magnified (either in the transfer or by the trustee's action) and a portion returned to the trustee. In the one-shot version of this game, played by purely self-interested rational actors, it is weakly dominant for the trustee to return nothing, so the equilibrium transfer is nothing as well. The inefficiency of this equilibrium can be remedied in various ways, for example repetition, reputation, precommitment, third-party intermediation, auditing and other- or process-orientated preferences.[17] Most lead to equilibrium trust but retain the original, low-trust equilibrium. Because the former Pareto-ranked equilibria dominate the latter, they give rise to (possibly asymmetric) coordination-game 'reduced forms'.[18]

The games also assume perfect information: the critical uncertainties concern the opponent's action. This does not cover the trust issue as laid out in Section 12.1.2. Consider an ongoing interaction among players with different information. If player A does not do what player B expects, B's trust in the expected action was misplaced – B may respond by concluding that:

- A made a mistake (and B may form a belief about whether this will happen again).
- A was trying to send a message:
  - A may be sending a costly signal of willingness to switch to a better equilibrium;
  - A may be signalling private information ignored by the current equilibrium.
- B may have wholly misunderstood the game, or made some fundamental mistake in the chain of inference that led the current belief.[19]

- A may be trying to convince B that B has misunderstood the game.

This raises intricate epistemological issues beyond our current scope, but a simple example is briefly discussed in the Appendix. The basic contributions of game theory in this area are suitable 'reduced forms' for incomplete information games and more discriminating solution concepts that take account of knowledge, belief and inference.[20]

The models developed here do not distinguish large and small players: all players are in the same situation as regards any other player to which a link is formed. This asymmetry is not addressed by rescaling, particularly not where link formation is concerned. However, the concept of trust as a convention (see Section 12.3) mitigates this in the asymmetric retail context, if the costs of contract negotiation favour use of standard-form contracts. Because such standard forms are incomplete on both sides and uncontracted contingencies are pay-off relevant for both parties, trust is again two-sided; because they are standardized, there is at least a bit more symmetry across players and (for each player) across their partners.

The games considered here do not attempt formally to distinguish trusting from trustworthiness (Büschken 2000; Ben-Ner and Putterman 2001). Moreover, while the models are used to examine both trust as a norm and the indirect provision or erosion of trust through network interactions, they do not deal with third-party certification used to reinforce trust (or provide it more efficiently), but rather use a simple social capital metaphor. Other chapters in this book consider social capital in more detail – for the present, it should merely be noted that it is particularly relevant in communication networks.

Finally, in recent years a richer theory of networked behaviour has begun to emerge which allows for greater asymmetry and richer structures of interaction (Page et al. 2002). This points the way to a direct theory of trust relations involving more than pairwise interaction, and is clearly a fruitful area for further research.

12.2.2 Trust Games

In this section we describe some simple games representing stylized views of trust and their associated equilibria. This style of analysis is suited to the static assessment of trust. We consider three classes of game: trust modelled directly as strategic behaviour; games that focus on network formation – and thus on linking as a form of institutionalized trust; and hybrid games combining elements of both approaches.

Direct coordination games. The simplest case is a 'coordination game' where players choose between high-trust and low-trust strategies. In addition to any interactions with 'trusted' systems and other parts of the environment where individual strategic considerations do not apply, they interact with their network neighbours. We assume that individuals choose a single strategy for all interactions; the more general case where strategy (trust) depends on reputation is considered below (and see Appendix 12.1 for mathematical details of models).

Strategies in this coordination game are complementary – player 1's adoption of high trust increases player 2's pay-off from adopting high trust, and conversely for low-trust. The pay-offs are thus assumed to be:

		Player 2	
		High trust	Low trust
Player 1	High trust	5, 5	A, B
	Low trust	B, A	3, 3

By complementarity A <3 and B <5 (there are positive network externalities; adoption of different trust levels is not profitable). Different interpretations of the strategies (and the parameters A and B) correspond to different notions of trust.

One formulation deals with accidents and uncertainty. In this view, the low-trust strategy involves costly precaution taken to stave off costly losses. Losses are also influenced by neighbours' precautions (positively or negatively). In a second contractarian view, high trust corresponds to a willingness to make (and entertain) many offers, to engage in incomplete contracts and to join contracts for complements. Offers from trustworthy people will be rewarding, relatively cheap to monitor and enforce, and mutually-reinforcing. The third interpretation focuses on trustworthiness: low trust corresponds to sharp practice.

The parameter A is the consequence of trusting a low-trust person – if this means that advantages of trust are not realized or that one is taken advantage of, then A should be low. On the other hand, if a low-trust person takes extensive precautions that also provide benefits to his partners, then A should be relatively high. The parameter B is the consequence of not trusting a high-trust person. If this means foregoing the advantages of a mutually trusting relationship, or if the trusting partner also trusts untrustworthy third parties and thus jeopardizes the partnership, B could be low. On the other hand, if the partner's trust leads to more efficient delegation of work or provides indirect connection to mutually trusting groups (whose interactions economize on monitoring and enforcement costs) then B could be relatively high. These interpretations are developed at greater length in Section 12.3.2 and especially Section 12.3.3, where different scenarios corresponding to these interpretations are considered.

All individuals prefer the high-trust equilibrium, but they can get 'locked in' to the low-trust outcome. If each player interacts with all others (fully connected network) the two possible (pure-strategy) equilibrium outcomes are homogeneous: all play H or all play L. If players are locked into the low-trust equilibrium, they can escape if a sufficient number jointly switch to the high-trust strategy – for instance if they are temporarily indemnified against losses, or if policy measures reduce the cost of signalling (for instance by raising A). In the formal equilibrium analysis, however, this requires a 'leap of faith' – even foresight will not necessarily induce signalling behaviour if the players take no account of the past. On the other hand, the less players discount the future, the more likely they are to try to escape the low-trust equilibrium by making unprofitable defections to the high-trust strategy. This is particularly likely:

- When one or more play as 'Stackelberg leaders' – assume other players will respond optimally to their choice of strategies.
- When the geometry of connection creates 'hubs' – players to whom most players are connected by direct linkages or players whose behaviour is held up as exemplary. Hub players in such 'star-shaped' societal networks can be sure that changes will lead a critical mass of other players to re-examine their expectations.

The above analysis can be extended without much additional difficulty to distinguish fear of crime from lack of trust by adding a 'criminal' strategy (C). Assume that in the long run 'crime does not pay' – that is, H and L remain symmetric equilibria – but also that unilateral honesty does not pay when crime is conventional (C is also a symmetric equilibrium). The pay-off matrix might look like:

	High Trust	Low Trust	Crime
High Trust	5, 5	A, B	-4, 3
Low Trust	B, A	3, 3	0, 0
Crime	3, -4	0, 0	1, 1

As before $5 > B$ and $3 > A$ and the same interpretations of A and B apply.

A game of indirect reliance
The consequences of trust include the indirect impact of links to third parties trusted by the partner (see Appendix 12.1, Section A12.1.4). To examine this, we 'step back' from the specifics of network behaviour and simply

assume that the ability to verify trustworthiness decreases as connections become less direct, since verification must rely increasingly on hearsay and reputation. In other words, the value of trust decreases with 'distance' (the number of intervening links). We further assume that direct links are costly to maintain.[21] It is natural to define a network as efficient if it maximizes total pay-off to the players and Pareto-efficient if any change makes at least one worse off. In this model, efficiency depends on the relation of link costs to value:

- if costs are high the only efficient network is the 'empty' one with no connections (or where no use is made of this form of interaction), corresponding to no trust;
- with intermediate costs star-shaped networks are efficient; and
- if costs are low the fully-connected network is efficient.

Players form trusted relationships where both players agree, and break them when at least one player wishes to do so. In the intermediate cost case, players only trust those that have trusted relationships with others, but no player wishes to trust more than two others in view of the costs. A network in which each player trusts exactly two others is a collection of separate rings. A ring cannot be part of equilibrium since each player could improve his pay-off by breaking one link. The only equilibrium network (the 'no-trust' one) is not even Pareto-optimal since a line offers both end and middle players strictly more.

A game of interdependence
A related game looks at the concentration of trust partners on each others' needs. For instance, the added risk or dilution due to 'outside entanglement' makes the value of trust between partners depend inversely on the number of trusted relations each party has and (because at least one should concentrate on protecting the relationship) inversely on the product of these numbers (see Appendix 12.1, Section A12.1.5). Again, equilibrium networks are typically inefficient. In simple cases, only the 'full-trust' network is efficient, but players could unilaterally improve by splitting into disjoint pairs.

A vaccination game
The previous games illustrate a basic 'paradox' of trust: each of us wishes to be trusted, but those who trust us might trust others whom we would not trust, or whose trustworthiness extends only to their direct partners (see Appendix 12.1, Section A12.1.6). This suggests that trust 'flows through' societal networks so there may be value in having some form of precaution to stop the spread of criminal or unreliable behaviour. This can be

represented in a simple vaccination game: each player can choose whether to take a costly precaution. If either party to a pairwise interaction has taken precautions, both are protected; otherwise, both suffer. In a fully connected network the equilibrium level of p is only efficient if the level of cost is 'just right'. Network formation is rather trivial: any incautious player wishes to link to any cautious player and does not mind linking to other incautious players. Any cautious player wishes to link to all other players, so the fully connected network is (at least weakly) an equilibrium. Clearly, this set-up should be extended to a more realistic specification.

The hybrid game
The 'value of trust' specifications (the indirect reliance and interdependence games above) can be interpreted as trust strategy games (the coordination games) by assuming that trust attitudes are prescribed or unobservable (and therefore equivalent to their expectations). All assume a single environment, where the pay-offs can be interpreted in terms of the differential advantage to using the high-trust strategy (see Appendix 12.1, Section A12.1.7). This section uses this approach to consider a 'trusted' environment available alongside the 'game' environment. Players have unobserved differences in the degree to which they are willing to rely on the trusted channel. We begin by analysing equilibrium behaviour in terms of underlying attributes of trust (risk and exposure). This strategic model is then compared with an incomplete information approach in which players learn by sampling the population; the two models can be distinguished empirically.

Description of the one-sided model. Consider a population of linked, but heterogeneous individuals, each of whom can choose between a high-trust and a low-trust strategy. Players evaluate the high-trust option according to 'net benefits' minus expected 'risk cost' (which includes any costs of switching to the high-trust strategy). The net benefits term is weighted by the player's relative preference or taste for the high-trust channel, which is not observed by others. It contains a fixed component (for example, reduced transaction costs associated with trusting certified public channels) and a term that varies with the number of other high-trust individuals with whom the player interacts and with the 'strength' of network externalities among players. The analysis assumes that idiosyncratic preferences are distributed according to a unimodal (single-peaked) distribution. This set-up can give rise to multiple equilibria and this possibility may be related to underlying parameters representing the strength of network effects and the level of risk.

Equilibrium behaviour. Nash equilibrium (best replies to rational expectations about the behaviour of others) implies that the high-trust will be all those whose relative taste for the high-trust strategy is 'sufficiently high' – the cut-off value is increasing in risk cost and falling in net benefit. When network effects are small there is a unique equilibrium prevalence of trust (*h*), which is decreasing in risk cost and increasing in network effects. When network effects are strong there are three solutions (as shown in Appendix 12.1, under Equilibrium Behaviour). The highest and lowest solutions are stable and decreasing in both risk cost and network effects; the middle, unstable solution is increasing in both parameters. The overall picture is shown in Figure 12.1, with 'trusting' (*h*) measured on the vertical axis.

This picture illustrates the central characteristic of the model: when network effects are weak, trusting behaviour decreases continuously as perceived risk rises. As network externalities become more important, multiple solutions appear and gradually diverge. A similar result can be obtained from a model in which the risk parameter measures the likelihood of an abuse of trust and the network parameter is replaced by a measure of exposure or the likely loss from an abuse of trust.[22]

Figure 12.1 Equilibrium trust as a function of risk and network externalities

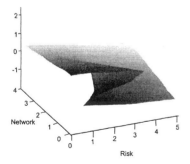

A two-sided version. The above shows the dependence of equilibrium trust on perceived risk. To close the loop, we fix the strength of network effects and assume risk responds instantaneously to the prevalence of trusting behaviour. One extreme assumption is opportunism: risk rises or falls according to whether *h* is above or below a critical value *h** at which expected returns to abuse of trust just balance expected costs (including punishment). If network effects are small enough for trust to respond continuously to risk, the model converges monotonically to *h** and the corresponding risk level. If network effects are 'too large' the system will cycle (clockwise) in a hysteresis loop.

The polar extreme is reassurance: risk falls or rises as *h* is above or below

h^*, and the system tends to a high-trust or low-trust corner solution. The same result is obtained in Section 12.3.2 for evolutionary dynamics in a fully connected network (except that only one – risk-dominant – corner is stable). This result also emerges from a Bayesian model with partial adjustment of subjective risk estimates.

An incomplete-information model. Qualitatively similar results (roughly S-shaped time-paths for creation and erosion of trust) can be obtained from a simple incomplete information model where individuals sample trust through a random 'word of mouth' process. The dynamics depend critically on the credibility of this information (whether reports of the general level of trustworthiness are themselves trusted) and bias in the reporting of relevant information (for example information selected by media or government to highlight negative or positive outcomes). In this model, high-trust individuals at any given time are a representative sample of the full population rather than an 'upper interval'.

Comparison. We can compare average trust per capita in the two models to track its response to a secular decrease in perceived risk brought about by, for example, government policy – which is equivalent to a fall in the critical taste parameter at which the individual is indifferent between high and low trust (see Table 12.5).

Table 12.5 Response of trust to fall in perceived risk

	Equilibrium	Incomplete information
No network externalities ($\nu = 0$)	Fall	Constant
Peer-to-peer ($\nu = 1$)	Rise, then fall	Rise

12.3 TRUST AS A CONVENTION

12.3.1 The Evolutionary Perspective

We now turn from the equilibrium to the evolutionary perspective. Evolution is the result of three coincident processes: variation, selection and heredity. As applied to conventions, variation results from natural mistakes: either conventional behaviour will be misinterpreted, or individuals will depart from convention. Selection is the result of mutual approval or rational recognition that the new behaviour may be better. Heredity is the result of societal learning and codification of behaviour into norms. To prevail, a pattern of behaviour should be self-reinforcing (or cohesive) and stable; variations should be small-scale, haphazard and not overly vulnerable to contagion.

Following the approach started by Kandori et al. (1993) and Young (1993, 1998), we consider a game played by a large, connected population, each of whom plays against all the others. For each potential convention (symmetric equilibrium), we use the size of spontaneous[23] deviations that could lead the players to wish to change their behaviour to assess its 'resistance' to contagion: the stable convention(s) are those against which other behaviours have the least resistance.

The following sections apply this to the direct coordination and criminal behaviour games described in Section 12.2.2 that are idealized representations of the 'coordination' aspect of trust. As argued above, the qualitative features of this representation are fairly general. The quantitative aspects (in particular the values of the parameters A and B) are not, so the following analysis considers how conventional behaviour varies with these parameters.

12.3.2 Stable Conventions in the Coordination Game

This section uses an evolutionary network approach to examine the emergence or disappearance of trust (see Appendix 12.1, Section A12.1.8). Each player plays against his or her 'neighbours' – the people to whom he or she is linked. Periodically, behaviour is reassessed and (subject to external shocks) revised. In consequence, actual behaviour depends on cohesion and contagion.

A fully-connected network

Here we use the direct coordination game from Section 12.2.2 – a player will want to switch to the high-trust strategy if a sufficient fraction $\left(\dfrac{3-A}{8-A-B} \right)$ of his or her neighbours do. A fully-linked group subject to random shocks will converge to high trust in the long run if this fraction is less than ½ – in other words if high trust is risk-dominant (better than low trust against a random opponent). The low-trust equilibrium can be stable even though it is not efficient. This simple model shows a 'cheap' way to escape low-trust equilibrium: in a non-evolutionary model, it would be necessary to indemnify victims of low trust by raising A to at least 3, whilst in the networked model it suffices to raise A to the lower level B-2. Figure 12.2 shows the stable conventions as a function of the parameters A and B.

Figure 12.2 Stable conventions in the coordination game

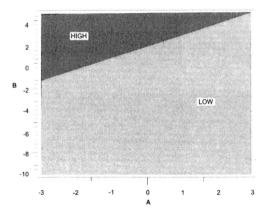

The influence of geometry

The analysis extends to clusters or 'small worlds' where a limited set of close neighbours interact (Watts 1999; Jackson and Watts 2002). Given appropriate structure, such clusters can support stable diversity – both high- and low-trust conventions can prevail locally, even though only the 'risk-dominant' one would survive in a fully connected world. The same result is reached if the players are arranged in a circle; because each cares only about the actions of two neighbours, a player playing the risk-dominant strategy would only switch if both neighbours switch to the other strategy, while one who joins his neighbours in playing the other strategy would switch if even one neighbour switches. The same is true in any regular network where all players have the same number of neighbours – a player is 'less likely' to switch away from the risk-dominant strategy because this requires simultaneous deviation by more of his neighbours than a change towards the risk-dominant strategy.

By contrast, asymmetric networks (such as star networks where all players share a common hub, as in the case of trusted services delivered from a central point) can support diverse outcomes. Consider three players linked to a common hub: each cares only about what the hub is doing, and the 'spokes' will copy any deviation of the hub. Any change by a spoke player in the direction of the risk-dominant strategy will lead to all players eventually following suit. Of course, there are 'more' paths leading towards the risk-dominant equilibrium, but where the risk-dominant equilibrium is inefficient, this can be offset by farsightedness (Page et al. 2002) on the part of the hub player – or some suitable liability arrangement.

One final note concerns the speed of adjustment: as Ellison (1993) shows, local interactions accelerate the diffusion of conventions through a social network – small groups are relatively easy to saturate. Thus, 'insularity' generally means more rapid convergence to the risk-dominant equilibrium, and therefore may be regarded as good or bad depending on whether risk dominance coincides with efficiency.

12.3.3 Stable Conventions in the Face of Criminal Behaviour

In this game, the behaviours that might prevail in the long run in a highly linked society are the symmetric outcomes (see Appendix 12.1, Section A12.1.9). The stochastically stable conventions, following Young (1993), for games with more than two strategies are those for which the 'resistance' of each convention to shocks that might 'tip' it towards another convention is greatest.

These shocks might be direct (for instance, if enough of one's neighbours switch from high to low trust, one will follow suit) or indirect (if an intermediate number of one's neighbours switches from crime to high-trust behaviour, one would wish to switch to low-trust behaviour, and the population as a whole might follow suit). To identify the stochastically stable convention, we sum the resistances associated with all transitions towards each convention; the stable convention has the lowest sum.

High trust is the unique stable convention if the pay-off to low trust in partnership with a high-trust player (B) is small, but low trust may be stable if both B and the payoff to a high-trust player facing a low-trust player (A) are large. Roughly, B can be large if the precautions accompanying the low-trust strategy are relatively costless for players transacting with high-cost players, or equivalently where most of the benefits of a high-trust relationship accrue if at least one of the parties is trusting or trustworthy. A is large if the costs of signalling willingness to trust are relatively low.

It is again cheaper to stabilize high trust than to force unique high-trust equilibrium. Network geometry matters – a densely connected network may require quite a few 'mutations' to flip behaviour, while a network of 'small world' neighbourhoods can 'escape' from the low-trust or criminal conventions relatively easily.

A parametric analysis of stability for different values of A and B is shown in Figure 12.3.

For the sake of comparison, the diagonal line shows the separation between low-trust and high-trust behaviour from the coordination game. We can make the following observations:

- In both games, low-trust behaviour is more likely as the consequences of trusting a low-trust person fall relative to the consequences of not trusting a high-trust person.

- Criminal behaviour can be stable under two circumstances: if the risks of being victimized by trusting a low-trust person are modest, but the loss involved in failing to trust a high-trust partner is substantial, or if there is no loss in trusting a low-trust person and a modest gain to a low-trust person when his or her partner switches from low to high trust.
- The introduction of criminal behaviour mostly works to destabilize high-trust conventions (except for the area above the diagonal line).
- Policies that try to stabilize high-trust behaviour by reducing *B* are less likely to work when there is a possibility of criminal behaviour – especially when *A* is low (that is, when there are substantial losses to trusting a low-trust partner).

Figure 12.3 Stable conventions in the crime game

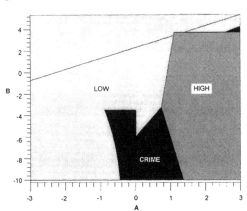

12.3.4 Stable Conventions in Other Games

As mentioned in Section 12.2.1, the model used here is highly specialized. Alternative formulations can be used to investigate the robustness of the analysis and represent different aspects of trust. In this section, three alternatives are briefly contrasted to the symmetric direct coordination game introduced in Section 12.2.2.

	HT	LT
HT	(5, 5)	(A, B)
LT	(B, A)	(3, 3)

Symmetric coordination [5 > B; 3 > A]

	HT	LT
HT	(5, 10)	(a, b)
LT	(c, d)	(10, 5)

Battle of the Sexes [5 > c, d; 10 > a, b]

	HT	LT
HT	(e, f)	(5, 3)
LT	(3, 5)	(g, h)

Costly Precaution [3 > e, f; 5 > h, g]

	HT	LT
HT	(e, f)	(3, 5)
LT	(5, 3)	(g, h)

Localized Precaution [5 > e, f; 3 > h, g]

The Battle of the Sexes may be interpreted in terms of complementary but costly precaution, differing levels of risk aversion or differing tastes for trust. Imbalanced levels of trust lead to, for example, litigation that is costly to both parties, but in the absence of litigation player 1 (2) prefers the high (low) trust outcome.

In the Costly and Localized Precaution games, exactly one player should take precautions; if both do the result is costly duplication; if neither does they suffer excessive damage. In Costly Precaution the careful player does worse (analogously to the vaccination game). In Localized Precaution vigilance is costless, but offers imperfect spillover protection to the other player (an extreme form of the indirect reliance game).

Exact numerical symmetry is irrelevant (for instance, the payoff to (HT, HT) in the coordination game could be changed from (5, 5) to (6, 8) without affecting the result). In each game pay-offs can be modified so that the equilibrium pay-off set is asymmetric.

Section 12.2.2 showed how players could get locked in to the inefficient low-trust equilibrium. In the Battle of the Sexes, pure-strategy equilibrium necessarily favours one or the other player, even if, for example, a = 9 = b, in which case (HT, LT) would be both equitable and Pareto-optimal – but not an equilibrium. The Precaution games have asymmetric pure strategy equilibria. The disequilibrium low-trust outcome may be Pareto-optimal in Costly Precaution and the disequilibrium high trust outcome may be Pareto-optimal in Localized Precaution.

The more interesting results concern the stable conventions. The following summarizes the conditions under which high trust is stable:

Game	High-trust player(s)			
	Both	*Player 1*	*Player 2*	*Neither*
Symmetric coordination	$2 > B\text{-}A$	NA	NA	$2 < B\text{-}A$
Battle of the Sexes	$a\text{-}c > 5 > b\text{-}d$	NA	NA	$b\text{-}d > 5 > a\text{-}c$
Costly Precaution	NA	$h\text{-}f > 2 > g\text{-}e$	$g\text{-}e > 2 > h\text{-}f$	NA
Localized precaution	NA	$h\text{-}f > \text{-}2 > g\text{-}e$	$g\text{-}e > \text{-}2 > h\text{-}f$	NA

12.4 CYBER TRUST AND CRIME PREVENTION, AND MARKET STRUCTURE

12.4.1 Structure, Conduct and Performance

Trust is essential to commercial transactions where costs of contractual completeness are high or legal frameworks for contract enforcement are unreliable. Trust among firms has traditionally been associated with collusion, but increasingly (in the so-called new economy) also with informal 'networking' arrangements that economize on transactions and communications costs and improve collective efficiency. Trust between consumers and firms also provides transaction cost savings and may provide incentives for competition and innovation leading to improved price and quality, but equally, trust constitutes a barrier to customer switching (to the extent that it is relation-specific) and thus weakens competition.

This section addresses two connections between industrial structure, conduct and performance and the constellation of issues around cyber trust and crime prevention: the impact of market failure on levels of trust and the reciprocal impact of trust on market structure and conduct.

12.4.2 Competing for Trust

Structure, conduct and performance (SCP) analysis can usefully be applied to these issues in several ways. The literature has extensively developed the theory of reputations in terms of both price and quality. A firm's market power may derive from its reputation; conversely, market power can allow the firm to signal its quality and build reputation more effectively. Because reputation and trust influence consumer decisions, they, in turn, alter incentives to use trust as a way of creating or consolidating market power.

Reputations

The most obvious representation of trust in the analysis of commercial transactions is the game-theoretic treatment of reputations. The starting point is the existence of relationships where the parties' interests may diverge, and where informational asymmetries and/or prohibitive costs of reliable contractual protection make it difficult to reap the benefits of interaction without informal trust-like mechanisms.

Horizontal trust

Such mechanisms are used among groups of horizontally related firms that trust each other to cope with an uncertain world or to counter specific challenges. The object of such trust may be market allocation, prices and quality of even the provision of information. Firms wishing to reach agreement on these strategies in pursuit of mutual interest face legal obstacles to formal contracting – hence the uses of the term 'trust' to refer to cartels at the turn of the nineteenth century. To overcome this inability to contract and the combination of temptation (profitable unilateral defection) and exposure (negative externalities), firms have developed a range of trust-enhancing strategies, including social contacts, interlocking directorates and most-favoured customer clauses. As a matter of definition, we should regard practices that facilitate collusion as 'trust based' to the extent that they are not directly enforceable, or sanction activities that cannot be directly verified. The cyber environment modifies the received thinking in a variety of ways. Most obviously, firms competing in electronic marketplaces have expanded opportunities for using anonymity to cloak departures from collusive agreements and, in some cases, a global platform for their activities. This could be seen as increasing the likelihood of defection – and thus for an increased need to rely on trust. The same factors also suggest an expanded scope for market-sharing agreements[24] as opposed to classical price fixing. A second cyber influence is the scope for rapid and effective response to defection and the relative ease with which extensive information could be provided – this may enhance the extent to which firms are able to trust each other. Finally, the emergence of new forms of market contact[25] that reduce search and transactions costs, which may simultaneously affect the potential impact of defections on other cartel members, influences the likelihood of effective detection and the power, speed and credibility of retaliation.

Vertical trust

Trust may also be critical in vertical relationships, such as input markets, providing access and retail or sales to consumers. Here, the impact of cyber technologies on trust and market power can be seen at various stages of the transaction: search, payment, fulfilment and follow-up.

At the search stage, new technologies can provide more information and 'broader' information (for example quality attributes or other non-price comparators). This, in turn, can sharpen consumer search – at least up to the point where effective comparison becomes impossible due to a glut of rapidly changing information. This could lower the cost of differentiating products from each other (rendering competition monopolistic and inefficient); alternatively, it could create a niche for information intermediaries (such as comparative search engines) that sharpen price competition – typically at a modest cost in deadweight loss. However, it is not obvious that the 'power' of search engines is entirely benign. While they do aggregate comparative information, they also order it, and there is no *a priori* reason to suppose that the ordering serves the interests of some (or even all) consumers, or provides open access to consumers by small-scale producers. In terms of trust, the question raised is the following: if consumers are inclined to trust large firms on the assumption that untrustworthy firms (or products) could not sustain prominence in the market, under what conditions should they trust the information intermediaries responsible for that prominence – since typically search engines assume no liability for the accuracy of the information provided to them or for the quality of goods purchased on the basis of this information (even in the case of electronic markets such as eBay) when intermediation extends beyond information to brokerage? The information itself may involve (or give the impression of involving) less commitment.[26] In particular, whether customers will trust comparative search engines to identify good buys[27] and whether the excess of information thus provided increases or reduces customers' feelings that they have selected a best buy[28] are matters that must be determined empirically and, as yet, the theory of vertical separation between sellers and information intermediaries is in its infancy (Bailey 1998; Bakos 1997). Certainly there is clear evidence that markets for information are even more prone to concentration than the up- and down-stream markets for 'real' goods and services (Brynjolfsson and Smith 2000). At this stage, it seems reasonable that the new technologies are more likely to enhance trust for standard commodities than for highly personalized or differentiated ones.

In cyber environments, payment typically involves one or more financial intermediaries. The most critical aspects of trust here are connected with the provision of (limited) access to financial assets and information; both parties need to be assured of each other's identities, to have confidence that payment and fulfilment will proceed in real time once the electronic transaction is completed, and that opportunities for repudiation are limited to those permitted in the contract. In addition, the paying party will need assurance that financial information will not be used to make further, unauthorized transactions. These issues have been discussed at length in the literature. We merely point out that, in contrast to product search – where multiplicity and competition are the most trusted sources of assurance – in the payment area there are advantages to prominence and a certain degree of concentration. However, with prominence may come increased risk – consumer concerns include dangers from mistakes, malfeasance by trusted parties or intermediaries, and insufficient precaution in guarding transaction details – and insufficient precaution, at least, may increase as a financial service provider's reputation and market share increase, if these signs of success make it a more attractive target.[29]

In the fulfilment phase, the impact of the new technologies is felt primarily through the globalization of commerce – the selling party may be located in another (even an unknown) jurisdiction, and pursuing consumer rights may be difficult or expensive. It may be that the prominence that comes with a dominant position can tie performance to reputation sufficiently to reinforce trust.

As regards follow-up, the analysis of reputations and quality emphasizes the importance of signalling. In particular, high quality can be signalled (and specific trust enhanced) by providing verified information (for example quality certification by independent third parties) or assurance. The efficacy of the former strategy may be limited by psychological factors – in particular, provision of information relating to risk may heighten risk awareness. This is particularly true where the effect of providing information is to shift either the effective or the perceived allocation of risk – typically, decisions and consent have more weight and attract more liability the greater is the information provided in advance.

In oligopolistically competitive environments, firms may attempt to signal their relative trustworthiness by talking up problems encountered by their competitors, but this may reduce trust in the market as a whole, particularly when the problems arise outside or among the firms. Certification is an attractive alternative, but depends again on the reliability of the certifying authority. Much of the recent literature on, for example, cyber-notaries or Internet governance is concerned with the relative merits of competitive and coordinated certification, and it is fair to say that at the moment the question remains unresolved.

One final comment concerns the evolving nature of goods and services delivered over the Internet. Increasingly, these have a heavy information content and run into the classic problem of asymmetric information – the buyer and seller cannot assess the suitability of the match between the supplier's offering and the customer's need without an exchange of information, following which the buyer (or indeed the seller, in the case of personally identifiable information) has an incentive to exploit the information without commensurate payment. To fit such transactions into the relatively anonymous framework of retail commerce, a fair amount of trust is required – perhaps on both sides. If the information is to be reused in some way, a further question arises regarding the allocation of any resulting loss (or gain). Put simply, it may be difficult to set appropriate limits on the provenance or use of information without introducing such heavy informational and contracting requirements that mutually beneficial transaction may not occur.

This is analogous to the agency situation pertaining between patient and health care provider – without an exchange of information (the patient describing symptoms and the provider describing treatments) effective treatment decisions cannot be made by either side. The traditional approach to preventing abuse in this situation of local monopoly[30] is to use a one-sided liability approach – trust is tied to certification of health care providers, backed up by the apparatus of tort law. However, these arrangements have not survived technological advances, including the availability of more effective treatments (which providers may not have incentives to provide) and increased consumer information (in no small part due to health-related information available on the Internet). The point of direct relevance is that the provision of information to the 'principal' (the patient) has undermined the former relationship of trust; patients no longer trust providers' expertise and providers no longer trust patients to follow advice or refrain from litigation.

Network externalities
The third type of relationship connects economic entities that produce complements rather than substitutes or inputs. The world defined by new technologies is increasingly a networked one. The simplest view of networks is of groups – trading partners, users of specific products, members of communities. Complementarity is perhaps the defining characteristic of such group-orientated economic relationships (Katz and Shapiro 1994). A more sophisticated view considers the geometry of networks, distinguishing indirect from direct connections (and thus potential from immediate interactions). In this approach, the very act of joining a network involves trust – the joining party must trust that indirect connections will not damage his interests, and incumbents must trust each other not to form damaging links. To make matters concrete and focus on market failure, let us consider the provision of software services, which may include some degree of security. For informational goods marginal costs of production are very low and the initial purchase or decision to adopt may involve a commitment to further purchases or adoption of software products – often from other producers. The net present value to the firm of its customer base equals the customers' aggregate switching cost (Anderson 2003). The impact of

competition is that incumbents try to maximize and potential entrants try to minimize switching costs. Both types of strategy impose costs on the market as a whole. Moreover, 'churn' can undermine trust in the stability of the market and reduce suppliers' incentives to invest in durability and continuity. As applied to complements, this further implies that incumbent firms have incentives to 'lock-in' suppliers of complementary products as a way of ultimately locking in consumers. In the specific context of security, this may mean lowering interoperability hurdles for 'compatible' products – effectively using the potential for attack at the interstices between software products as justification for extending the 'trusted zone' to enclose producers of complements.

Another implication of the network perspective is that these software products are used to mediate transactions and communication between other people, so the creation of proprietary standards builds a network externality among users of extended systems – the value to each person of using the system increases with the proportion of his or her contacts that use that system. Again, the strategy of a dominant incumbent is to attempt to maximize such network externalities. This in turn leads to U-shaped adoption curves, 'tipping equilibrium' (capture of the whole market by a single 'extended standard') and to abrupt jumps and local irreversibility leading either to cyclic variation or to dominance that endures radical changes in technology.

The implications for market structure are that the first-mover advantage and the need to capture suppliers of complements lead firms to reduce security barriers to developers, to share information with them and to shift the cost, complexity and liability burdens of security to customers. The implications for trust depend on the ability of customers to determine whether security provisions are effective (and appropriate). If customers cannot identify 'good' security, a form of Gresham's Law will operate, and inferior security precautions will drive out good ones. Continuing demand must then be sustained by exaggerating threats. Finally, it should be noted that even effective security precautions may merely displace risk.[31]

Consumer protection
Quality can also be signalled by assurance – usually taking the form of a warranty or compensation scheme tied to breakdowns of trust. In contractarian terms, this is analogous to penalties or liquidated damages.

At the most practical level, work on product safety and reliability has distinguished two strategies that can be used to signal quality and build trust – despite being opposites, both may coexist in equilibrium. A firm wishing to convince customers of the quality of its products can provide either extensive or minimal warranty protection. In the former case, the firm credibly signals product quality because the warranty would be too expensive to offer if quality were poor. In this case, the customer does not need to trust the firm,[32] but the firm may need to trust the customer not to make frivolous claims. A well-known firm can also credibly signal quality by providing unusually low levels of protection, since it is placing its reputation on the line by doing so.[33] In this context, we are essentially dealing with trust in the informational sense, since the consumer does not have much control over the extent of risk transfer, merely the choice of whether to buy (or lease) or not. Note also that the signalling value of trust-enhancing actions is relative to expectations – in other words, to the prevailing conventions regarding behaviour. This will be taken up next.

Liability

A final area where the industrial organization perspective is relevant is the economics of liability rules. Wherever trust and crime are important there are, by definition, externalities, which can be mitigated by precautions taken by the affected parties. The recommended collective response (in civil, criminal or contract law) is to allocate liability for consequences. If negotiation is costly, the allocation must balance welfare considerations of efficiency and equity (here, fairness). In some cases, the externality seems to be fairly one-sided (in other words, it is for me to trust you rather than for us to trust each other) as are the prevailing liability rules (*caveat emptor* or the complementary strict product liability). According to standard practice[34] for efficiency's sake (and 'natural justice') liability should fall on the least-cost avoider (sometimes least-cost insurer) of a particular harm. In cases where both parties make substantial contributions, or where avoidance costs are fairly symmetric, the same argument gives rise to the sort of 'relative negligence' rules used in transportation settings (for example automobile or marine liability). An extreme case is the 'eye-for-an-eye' rule in which all parties bear full liability: this ensures efficiency *ex ante* (people take efficient precautions), but is not efficient *ex post* (people collectively pay the damage several times over). This case corresponds to a situation of criminal law – the criminal is penalized for his actions, but the victim is not (or not fully) indemnified for her loss. If parties can bargain costlessly over liability, and if the total loss taking into account the liability system does not exceed the original harm, then efficiency can be achieved regardless of how liability is assigned – but in this case rules like the eye-for-an-eye rule lead to too much precaution.

These considerations seem particularly applicable to risks such as those associated with computer viruses, spam and harmful or illegal content, since a wide range of people can take precautions with varying degrees of efficiency. In addition, precautionary activities themselves have externalities:

some have the effect of protecting others (for example by shutting down the offending communication at the source), some do not affect risk to others (for example protecting one's own machine) and others may even transfer the risk or costs to others (for example refusing to communicate with those who appear to have sent offending messages, but whose identity has been stolen and then used to send such messages).

These considerations loop back into industrial organization because the 'ownership' of risks and precautionary activities – and thus the trust placed in the system by participants (whether end consumers or B2B partners) – are affected by the degree of monopolization, the prevalence, adequacy and ownership of standards, and the 'networking' among market participants. This is a two-way connection: industrial organization economics can be directly applied to the study of trust and crime – especially in commercial relationships – and considerations of cyber crime and trust can focus the development of industrial organization to deal with a range of 'new economy' issues. One specific area of application might be the economics of information assurance.

12.5 CONCLUSION

12.5.1 What Does Economic Theory Tell Us About Trust?

Economic analysis tends to endogenize trust – to treat it as an aspect of the functioning of economic systems whose roots are hard-headed calculations far from the intuitive notion of trusting behaviour. The individual's decision to trust or be trustworthy is analysed in terms of expected costs and benefits. Thus, person A will trust person B to capture gains from trade; B may have more relevant information, or greater powers of action, or the costs of fully negotiating and specifying the joint activity desired by A and B may be too great. A must assess both his exposure and B's temptation, and decide not to use all relevant information or to proceed in the absence of relevant information.[35] From this perspective, trust and identity services (as provided by, for example, cyber-notaries and trusted third parties) are valuable products of the economic system. Because such entities provide information goods the relevant economics is the analysis of incomplete information. These models show that institutions that permit credible or verifiable signals (assurance) and informal institutions (for example reputations) can improve efficiency; and that specific contractual forms can align incentives in cases of hidden information (adverse selection) and hidden action (moral hazard).

But trust is also a public good. Partially, this is because the acts of trusting, refusing to trust, fulfilling promises and breaking promises have both positive and negative externalities, from which it may not be possible to exclude others. In addition, it may not always be possible to distinguish individuals, or to fully anticipate the vulnerabilities to which a decision to trust exposes one – this is particularly true of the complex transactions of the cyber world. Thus, a person cannot fully 'own' trust or exact payment for it and it is possible to 'free-ride' on the trust or trustworthiness of others. To the extent that trust is costly, it will thus be underprovided.

12.5.2 Comments on the Analysis

The game theoretic analyses shed light on trust as a public good (especially the vaccination game). Efficient allocation depends on both the total and the incidence of costs and on the power to avert damage (or contribute to trust). Some of these can be measured, aggregated and traded, but others cannot. Other problematic possibilities suggested by the vaccination analogy include free-riding (the 'tragedy of the commons' if trust is congestible) and enclosure (the creation of trust 'clubs' from which others are excluded).

The analysis has also highlighted some common features that may be more broadly applicable. Chief among these is the S-shaped adoption curve, which also occurs in another guise in the discussion in Section 12.4.2 with respect to competing for trust. The curve reflected the impact of interoperability, and described the time-path of adoption of a trust-enhancing technology: initially, when adoption is low, the interoperability advantages are also low, and only early adopters use the new technology. As the number slowly grows, so do the advantages of joining, and the rate increases, until virtually the entire 'group' has joined.

This sort of behaviour results from two dynamic forces: the increasing strength of network externalities and the decreasing pool of 'outsiders' available to join. Superficially, the adoption of societal norms, the formation of expectations (for example of trustworthiness or reciprocity), the accumulation of market power and the accumulation of experience (and the related concentration of a market ruled by an 'experience curve'), would seem to follow a similar pattern. However, the S-shaped pattern runs deeper still – the time-path is based on the assumption of convergence to a prevailing norm. In the cyber trust world, this may apply more directly to the small-scale dynamics of the formation of specific groups and oscillation (as illustrated by the hybrid model) between high and low levels of trust. Throughout, the perspective has been on the evolution and dynamics of trust rather than on its static or equilibrium properties.

Another general conclusion is that there may well be a tension between stability (equilibrium) and efficiency. This may seem surprising from the standpoint of competitive economics, but is consistent with both the view of trust as a matter of externalities and with a series of results showing the generic inefficiency of (usually mixed-strategy) Nash equilibrium.[36]

From the SCP point of view, the need to rely on trust can reinforce the 'tipping' tendency towards market dominance and thus limit the effectiveness of competition. Similarly, competition to provide trust (or trust enhancement and assurance) can compensate for public good underprovision of precaution, the natural disinclination of many stakeholders to take appropriate precautions, and the consequent inefficient allocation of risk. In information markets, the struggle to lock in customers can affect quality, the extent of information assurance and information security – for example when bottleneck suppliers of ICT services or software reduce internal security barriers to 'capture' producers of complementary products and impose those costs instead on consumers.

Because trust is bound up with expectations, incompleteness of information, of markets and of contracts is critical. This suggests a role for policy that supports self-regulatory mechanisms (for example open standards, reputations) or provides for appropriate allocation or low-cost trading of liabilities. Other aspects of trust enhancement should be provided by public bodies or not-for-profit, open self-regulatory bodies. Because technology strongly affects trust, but is also liable to foreclosure through intellectual property rights systems, the terms of reference should probably favour institutional over technological specificity.

Ownership of technical standards, while both inevitable and appropriate, should carry a 'price' in terms of money, liability or responsibility – the role of government may simply be to oversee the markets on which this price is determined and paid and/or to certify that the price has been paid. Finally, the sustainability of trust relationships may depend on asymmetry among the participants – in such cases, 'improvements' that reduce this asymmetry (for example the provision of identical information to both sides) may actually undermine trust.

APPENDIX 12.1 MATHEMATICAL DETAILS OF MODELS

To simplify the exposition, mathematical details of some of the models are included in this Appendix.

A12.1.1 The Fundamental Trust Game and its Reduced Form

A 'fundamental' trust game used in experimental and theoretical analyses (see, for example, references in note 16) involves a trustor with wealth of, say £10, who allocates to a trustee $\sigma_1 \leq £10$. The money is doubled en route by the effort of the trustee, who can then decide to return $\sigma_2 \leq 2\sigma_1$ to the trustor. The pay-offs are $(U_1, U_2) = (10-\sigma_1+\sigma_2, 2\sigma_1-\sigma_2)$ – the only subgame perfect equilibrium is the inefficient no-trust outcome $(\sigma_1, \sigma_2) = (0,0)$. However, there are many ways out of this 'trap' – for instance, if player 2 (the trustee) can precommit to a strategy, efficient outcomes become far more likely – specifically, suppose $\sigma_2(\sigma_1) = 2\alpha\sigma_1$ if $\sigma_1 > s_1$ (and 0 otherwise). The trustor's best reply is shown in the following matrix.

	$\alpha < \frac{1}{2}$	$\alpha = \frac{1}{2}$	$\alpha > \frac{1}{2}$	$\alpha = 1$
$s_1 = 0$	No trust	No trust or any amount $\geq s_1$	Any amount $\geq s_1$	Any amount $\geq s_1$
$0 < s_1 < 10$	No trust	No trust or any amount $\geq s_1$	Maximum trust	Maximum trust
$s_1 = 10$	No trust or minimal trust	No trust or any amount $\geq s_1$	Maximum trust	Maximum trust

From this, it is clear that if the trustee precommits to a $= \frac{1}{2}$ the trustor is indifferent as to how much he commits, so the trustee should further stipulate $s_1 = 10$.

If we fix the player's strategies in advance (so that (σ_1, σ_2) are constants), and impose feasibility we obtain the following 2x2 game:

Trustor	Trustee	
	σ_2 (fulfil)	0 (violate)
σ_1 (trust)	$10-\sigma_1+\sigma_2, 2\sigma_1-\sigma_2$	$10-\sigma_1, 2\sigma_1$
0 (withhold)	10, 0	10, 0

If $\sigma_1 < \sigma_2$ we get the 'standard trust game' in which fulfilled trust is not an equilibrium (because the violate strategy is weakly dominant). If $\sigma_1 > \sigma_2$ we get a weak prisoner's dilemma. A staggered prisoner's dilemma can give rise to the standard trust game if appropriate tit-for-tat (TFT) strategies are used. Indeed, we can interpret trust as cooperation and apply Axelrod's (1984) experimental results.

For instance, if players remember only the other player's previous move, successive elimination of weakly dominated strategies eliminates all but two strategies for each player; tit-for-tat (trust/fulfil at the beginning, then trust/fulfil if the opponent played fulfil/trust last time) and the 'greed' (G) strategy (always withhold/violate). Using the long-term average pay-offs corresponding to full cooperation and equal division of gains ($\sigma_1 = 10$, $\sigma_2 =$

15) in the first matrix below, tit-for-tat weakly dominates greed. However, this rests on the assumption that players facing greed are indifferent between their strategies. An alternative would be to modify the pay-offs slightly to represent psychological attitudes.

The middle game below embodies a feeling of righteousness that comes from behaving in a reasonable way against an intransigent opponent. This is not a naive reliance on trust, since the tit-for-tat strategy does meet like with like. The first game represents an attitude of 'fool me once, shame on you; fool me twice, shame on me'.

	TFT	G
TFT	(15, 5)	(10, 0)
G	(10, 0)	(10, 0)

Weak dominance

	TFT	G
TFT	(15, 5)	$(10+\varepsilon, 0)$
G	$(10, \varepsilon)$	(10, 0)

Relative righteousness

	TFT	G
TFT	(15, 5)	(10, 0)
G	(10, 0)	$(10+\varepsilon, \varepsilon)$

'Fool me once'

Relative righteousness makes TFT dominant – at least in a world with only TFT and G. By contrast, the 'fool me once' game is a coordination game – and TFT-type trusting behaviour is risk-dominant (stable in a symmetric network) if $5 > \varepsilon$.

A12.2 A Simple Trust Dilemma in an Extensive Form Game

One simple illustration of the complexity of trust is the question of rational play in the centipede game:

- Player A is offered repeated (say 100) opportunities to end a game.
- If he ends the game at the first opportunity, players A and B each get £1 million.

- Each time A lets the game continue, this amount decreases by £10,000; thus on the 100th opportunity ending the game gives each player £10,000.
- If A allows the game to continue on the 100th round, the choice of whether to continue passes to player B. If she ends the game, each gets £200; if she allows the game to continue, player A receives a final choice: either each gets £500 or each gets £10.

The problem for player B is that, if she trusts in 1's rationality, she should allow the game to continue, thus getting the same £500 A will choose 'for himself'. On the other hand, the mere fact that she has to move is evidence that player A has deviated from rationality not once, but 100 times. Should she 'trust' the internal logic of backward induction or the external logic of the game? It could be, for instance, that A puts lexicographic priority on prolonging the game (which he enjoys) and only then wants to maximize pay-off – in which case she should allow the game to continue (while wishing, perhaps, that he was more mercenary). On the other hand, it could be that A does not care about money at all – or actively hates it, or wants to minimize B's pay-off, all of which should lead her not to 'trust' A with a further move.

A12.3 Costly Alternatives to Trust

One final example of trust in an imperfect information setting examines a situation in which the trustor does not necessarily know whether his trust has been betrayed – in this setting we can ask 'how far' the trust extends; in other words the form of the contract between trustor and trustee.[37] The example is a modification of the fundamental trust game of Section A12.1.1. The trustor can give a fixed amount to the trustee, which increases to a random amount $I(\omega)$, where the 'state' ω is observed by the trustee but not by the trustor. The trustor believes that the state ω is distributed according to a (common-knowledge) prior distribution $p(\omega)$.

To keep things simple, assume that the states are ordered in such a way that I is increasing in ω. The trustee 'should' return an amount $R(\omega)$ to the trustor. Even if $I(\omega)$ is always bigger than the original transfer ω, this game shows the basic trust problem: the trustee will always return the smallest possible amount – the amount corresponding to the worst outcome. But suppose that the trustor can 'audit' the state for a payment of $\alpha > 0$ and thus enforce the contract. To complete the model, let us assume that both parties are risk-neutral, and that the trustee cannot be forced to pay more than $I(\omega)$. The 'trust contract' specifies the set of states A in which the trustor calls in the auditors and the amount $R(\omega)$ that the trustee is supposed to return to the trustor. Finally, suppose the trustor can design an optimal contract – one that maximizes the trustor's pay-off subject to the participation of the trustee and the limitation that auditing is costly. Alternatively evolutionary pressures (competing trustees) may lead to an optimal contract.

Suppose the true state is ω; the trustee will only report a different state ω' if this does not lead to an audit (ω' is not in A) and if it does increase the trustee's pay-off ($R(\omega) > R(\omega')$). Therefore, any two states not in A must stipulate the same repayment. Denote this constant repayment as R^*. It is easy to show that in the optimal contract, A is precisely the set of states where the trustee cannot afford this repayment (that is, where $I(\omega) < R^*$), and moreover that when the auditors are called in, the trustee should be made to return the entire remaining amount ($R(\omega) = I(\omega)$ for ω in A). This means that the stipulated repayment, R^* completely determines the trust contract. A higher R^* leads to more frequent auditing; a lower R^* leads to a smaller return on trust. Ignoring the trustee's willingness to participate, there is thus an 'interior' level of R^*. If the trustee has a lucrative 'outside option' the actual level of R^* will be determined by the condition that accepting the trust compensates the trustee for foregoing the outside option.

This model can be expanded to take account of differences in the productivity of different trustees, the interaction among trustors (in other words, a given trustee's outside option for accepting one person's trust is, at least in part, determined by the reward for accepting another's), 'distance-related' costs (hence networking) and changes to the auditing cost (reflecting for instance different costs of monitoring and enforcement in an electronic world).

A12.4 Game of Indirect Reliance

Let N be the set of players, $N_i(\Gamma)$ those directly trusted by player i in network Γ and d(i,j) the minimum length of a path from i to j.[38] The benefit to i of connection to j is:

$$b_i^j = \begin{cases} \delta_{ij}^{\ d(i,j)-1} - c_{ij} & \text{if } j \text{ is connected to } i \\ 0 \text{ otherwise} \end{cases}$$

The basic value, δ, of trust combines both the value of the exchange and the assurance that the other party is trustworthy. We assume δ < 1, so the expected value of indirect trust falls with distance. The value to i of a network Γ is thus:

$$v_i(\Gamma) = \sum_{j \in N} \delta_{ij}^{\ d(i,j)-1} + \sum_{j \in N_i(\Gamma)} c_{ij}$$

A network is efficient if it maximizes the total pay-off of the players and Pareto-efficient if any change makes at least one player worse off. Efficiency depends on the relation of links' costs to value:

- If costs are high ($c > \delta + \delta^2/2$ in a setting with four individuals), the only efficient network is the no trust 'empty' network.
- With intermediate costs ($\delta < c < \delta + \delta^2/2$), star-shaped networks are efficient.
- If costs are low ($\delta > c$), the fully connected network is efficient.

Players form trusted relationships where both players agree, and break them where at least one player wishes to do so. In the intermediate cost case, players only trust players who have trusted relationships with others ($\delta < c$), but no player wishes to trust more than two others in view of the costs. A network in which each player trusts exactly two others is a collection of disjoint rings – but a ring cannot be an equilibrium since each player gets $2\delta + \delta^2 - 2c$, but could improve his payoff to $\delta + \delta^2 + \delta^3 - c$ by breaking one link. The only equilibrium network is the 'no-trust' one, but this is not Pareto optimal let alone optimal, since a line offers each end-player $\delta + \delta^2 + \delta^3 - c > 0$ and each middle player $2\delta + \delta^2 - 2c > 0$.

A12.5 A Game of Interdependence

The value of trust between i and j depends inversely on the number of trusted relations each player has (for instance, because 'outside entanglement' brings added risk), and (to reflect the need to have at least one party concentrating on protecting the relationship) inversely on the product of these numbers:

$$b_i^j = \frac{1}{\#N_i(\Gamma)} + \frac{1}{\#N_j(\Gamma)} + \frac{1}{\#N_i(\Gamma)\#N_j(\Gamma)},$$

so

$$V_i(\Gamma) = 1 + \sum_{j \in N_i(\Gamma)} \frac{1}{\#N_j(\Gamma)} + \frac{1}{\#N_i(\Gamma)\#N_j(\Gamma)}$$

Again, equilibrium networks are typically inefficient: the only efficient network in a four-person game is the 'full-trust' one (in which $\#N_i(\Gamma) = 3$ for all players), which pays each player $7/3$. If the players broke into disjoint pairs (so $\#N_i(\Gamma) = 1$ for all players) they would each get 3 – truly a case where 'two's company and three's a crowd'.

A12.6 A Vaccination Game

Each player chooses whether to take precautions that cost c.[39] If either or both parties to a pairwise interaction have taken precautions, both receive pay-offs of 1; otherwise, both get 0. Thus, in a fully connected network in which p of the n players have taken precautions, each cautious player gets $n-1-c$ and each incautious player gets p, for a total pay-off of $(2n-1-c)p - p^2$, so in an efficient network $p = \frac{1}{2}(2n-1-c)$. In such a network, the (pure-strategy) equilibrium level of p satisfies $p > n-1-c > p-1$; it is only efficient if $c = \frac{1}{2}$. Network formation is rather trivial: any incautious player wishes to link to any cautious player, and is indifferent as to whether he links to another incautious player. Any cautious player wishes to link to all other players, so the fully connected network is (at least weakly) an equilibrium configuration. Clearly, this set-up should be extended to a more realistic specification.

A12.7 The Hybrid Game

Description of the one-sided model
Consider a population of linked, but heterogeneous individuals, each of whom can choose between a high-trust and a low-trust strategy. Preferences are parametric – it should be clear how they can be derived from, for example, the coordination game (Section 12.2.2 in this chapter). Define:

Variable	Definition
Δ_I	The pay-off advantage to player i of using the high-trust strategy
ρ_I	Player i's perceived risk-cost from using the high-trust strategy
h_i	The proportion of i's neighbours using the high-trust strategy
θ_I	Player i's idiosyncratic taste parameter, independently and identically distributed according to density $f(\theta)$ and *cdf* $F(\theta)$
v	The strength of the 'network externality' among high-trust players

We assume players have the following evaluation of the high-trust option:

$$\Delta_i = \theta_i [1 - v + vh_i] - \rho_i$$

The 'taste' parameter θ_I measures the relative value of these benefits compared with the expected costs ρ_i, which include the cost of switching to the high-trust strategy.[40] θ is independently and identically distributed on a compact interval $[\theta^-, \theta^+]$.

The 'benefits' term includes both a fixed component (for example, the reduced transaction costs associated with trusting certified public channels) and a term that varies with the number of other high-trust individuals with whom player i interacts.

We assume a fully connected network involving a large population, so h_i = h, where h is the proportion of individuals employing the high-trust strategy. v measures the strength of the network interaction: if $v = 0$ there is no network externality, while $v = 1$ corresponds to the 'peer-to-peer' case where only network interactions matter. There is no asymmetry in risk cost assessments, so $\rho_i = \rho$ for all i.

Equilibrium behaviour
Nash equilibrium implies the set of high-trust players is $[\theta^*, \theta^+]$, where the cut-off value, θ^*, satisfies:

$$\text{Indifference: } \theta^* = \frac{\rho}{1 - v + vh},$$
$$\text{Consistency } \theta^* = F^{-1}(1 - h)$$

The graph below (Figure A12.1-1) plots these equations for $\rho = 1$, $v = 0.91$ and $\theta \sim N(0.87, 3.6)$.

Figure A12.1-1 Trust – indifference and consistency curves

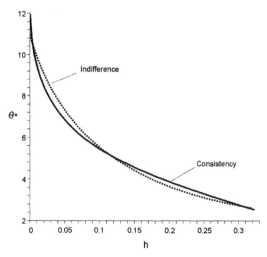

Figure 12.1 in the text plots the equilibrium values of h against ρ and v.

A two-sided version

Assuming fixed network effects, risk responds instantaneously to the prevalence of trusting behaviour: $d\rho/dt = \phi(h)$.

For predation or opportunism $d\rho/dt$ is positive or negative if h is larger or smaller than a critical value h^* where expected returns to abuse of trust just balance expected costs. If network effects are small enough for trusting to respond continuously to risk ($n < n^*$), the model converges monotonically to $v = v^*$ and $\rho = [1-v+vh^*]F^{1}(1-h^*)$. If network effects are 'too large' the system cycles (clockwise) in a hysteresis loop.

For reassurance $d\rho/dt$ is positive or negative if h is above or below h^*. In this case, the system tends to one of the two corner solutions: high-trust ($h = 1$ and $\rho = 0$) or low-trust ($h = 0$ and $\rho = 1$). This result can also obtained from a Bayesian model in which subjective risk estimates are adjusted according to a dynamic equation:

$$\rho_t = (1-\lambda)\rho_{t-1} + \lambda h, \text{ or } \dot\rho = \lambda(h-\rho)$$

An incomplete-information model

Qualitatively similar results (roughly S-shaped time-paths for creation and erosion of trust) can be obtained from a simple incomplete information model where individuals become aware of current differential pay-offs to trusting behaviour by sampling the population. Dynamics depend critically on credibility and any bias in this information. One interesting feature is that S-shaped adoption paths can result from a uniform distribution of prior beliefs.[41] Using the above notation, the population of high-trust individuals at any give time is a representative sample of the distribution of tastes θ rather than an 'upper interval' of the form $[\theta^*, \theta^+]$.

A more explicitly dynamic story would model strategy choice as a two-armed bandit problem, in which the value of information is traded off against current pay-off.

In the equilibrium model sketched above, average trust per capita is given by

$$\tau = \frac{\int_{\theta^*}^{\infty} [1 - v + v(1 - F(\theta^*))] \theta f(\theta)d\theta}{\int_{\theta^*}^{\infty} f(\theta)d\theta}$$

which for $\theta \sim N(\mu, \sigma^2)$ gives

$$\tau = [1 - v + v(1 - F(\theta^*))]\frac{\theta^* \sigma^2 f(\theta^*)}{1 - F(\theta^*)}$$

By contrast, in the epidemiological model with the same normal distribution, each type θ's propensity to use the high-trust strategy is:

$$\tau = \theta\left[1 - v - vh^*\right],$$

so per-capita average trust is:

$$\bar{\tau} = \mu\left[1 - v - vh^*\right].$$

We can compare these two expressions to track the response of trust to a secular decrease in perceived risk – equivalent to a fall in the critical taste parameter θ^* at which the individual is indifferent between high and low trust (cf Table 12.5).

Change in τ as θ^* falls	Equilibrium	Incomplete information
No network externalities ($v = 0$)	$\dfrac{\sigma^2 f(\theta^*)}{1 - F(\theta^*)}$	μ
Peer-to-peer ($v = 1$)	$\sigma^2 f(\theta^*)$	μh^*

A12.1.8 Network Dynamics in the Coordination Game

We use the game from Section 12.2.2 of this chapter – if a fraction γ_H of a player's neighbours uses the high-trust strategy, she or he will also play high trust if $\gamma_H > \dfrac{3 - A}{8 - A - B}$. A fully-linked group of $n+1$ players subject to random shocks will converge to high trust in the long run if $\dfrac{3 - A}{8 - A - B} < \dfrac{1}{2}$ – in other words if high trust is better than low trust against a random opponent $\left(\dfrac{5 + A}{2} > \dfrac{B + 3}{2}\right)$.

Note the low-trust equilibrium can be stable even though it is not efficient. Figure 12.2 in this chapter shows the stable conventions as a function of the parameters A and B.

A12.1.9 Network Dynamics with Criminal Behaviour

We use the game from Section 12.3.3 in this chapter – the stochastically stable conventions[42] for games with more than two strategies are those for which the 'resistance' of each convention to shocks that might 'tip' it towards another convention is greatest.

These shocks might be direct (copying one's neighbours) or indirect (responding to changes in partners' behaviour by adopting a third strategy).

The following matrix shows the resistance[43] associated with each transition.

Transition	Direct resistance	Indirect resistance	Minimum
H→L	$\max\left\{\dfrac{5-B}{8-A-B}, \dfrac{3-B}{6-B}\right\}$	$\dfrac{5-B}{9-B}$ if $B \le \dfrac{17}{5}$	See below
H→C	$\max\left\{\dfrac{2}{7}, \dfrac{B-3}{B-2}\right\}$	$\dfrac{2}{8-A}$ if $A < \dfrac{6(B-2)}{B-3}$	See below
L→H	$\dfrac{3-A}{8-A-B}$	N/A	$\dfrac{3-A}{8-A-B}$
L→C	$\dfrac{3}{4}$	$\dfrac{3}{6-B}$ if $A < \dfrac{24}{B-3}$	See below
C→H	$\max\left\{\dfrac{5}{7}, \dfrac{4}{9-B}\right\}$	N/A	$\max\left\{\dfrac{5}{7}, \dfrac{4}{9-B}\right\}$
C→L	$\dfrac{1}{4}$	N/A	$\dfrac{1}{4}$

The minimum resistance for the transition H→L is

$\dfrac{5-B}{8-A-B}$ if $\dfrac{6}{B-3} \le A \le -1$ or $B > 3.4$

$\dfrac{3-B}{6-B}$ if $A \le \dfrac{6}{B-3}$ and $B > -3$

$\dfrac{5-B}{9-B}$ if $B \le 3.4$ and either $B < -3$ or $A > -1$

The minimum resistance for the transition H→C is:

$$\frac{2}{7} \qquad \text{if } B \le 3.4 \text{ and } A > 1$$

$$\frac{B-3}{B-2} \qquad \text{if } A \ge 1 \text{ and } B \le \frac{20-3A}{6-A}$$

$$\frac{2}{8-A} \qquad \text{otherwise}$$

The minimum resistance for the transition L→C is:

$$\frac{3}{4} \qquad \text{if } B < 2 \text{ or } A > \frac{24}{B-3}$$

$$\frac{3}{6-B} \qquad \text{otherwise.}$$

To identify the stochastically stable convention, sum the resistances associated with all transitions towards each convention; the stable convention has the lowest sum:

Convention	Resistance	
	if $B < 3.4$	if $B \ge 3.4$
H (high-trust)	$\dfrac{32-13A-7B+AB}{(8-A-B)(9-B)}$	$\dfrac{61-12A-5B}{7(8-A-B)}$
L (low-trust)	$\dfrac{28-A-5B}{4(8-A-B)}$	$\dfrac{29-5B}{4(9-B)}$
C (crime)	$\dfrac{28}{29}$	$\dfrac{7B-18}{4(B-2)}$

Graph	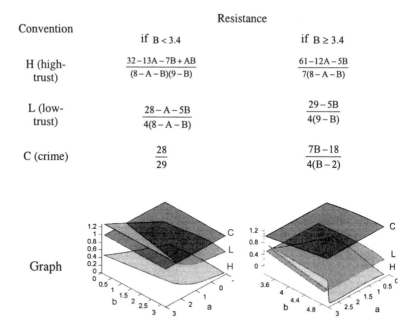

A complete parametric map of the stable conventions is shown in Figure 12.3 in this chapter.

NOTES

1   The author would like to acknowledge the support of the Department of Trade and Industry and stimulating conversations with members of the Foresight Cyber Trust and Crime Prevention project team (especially Miles Yarrington, Robin Mansell and Claire Craig), colleagues at RAND Europe (especially Maarten Botterman and Lorenzo Valeri) and the University of Warwick (especially Bhaskar Dutta and Myrna Wooders), seminar participants in Bled, Oxford, London and Warwick and the helpful comments of anonymous referees. Of course, they bear no responsibility for any errors or omissions.

2   Testing the model is at best a matter for econometrics, but in practice many of the phenomena here cannot be measured and/or depend on individual and collective perceptions that may be hard to measure separately from the behaviour that the models attempt to describe.

3   The analyses are condensed (especially in Section 12.2) for focus. More detailed treatment is available from the author on request.

4   For example trusting behaviour vs trustworthiness, trust as a public or a private good; a matter of credibility or of delegation.

5   In classical game theory, all 'players' interact with each other. More recently, these tools have been extended to take account of patterns of local interaction, see for example Morris (2000), Jackson and Watts (2002).

6   These norms include billing later for services, acceptance of fiat currency, self-reporting in transactions.

7   See for example David and Spence (2003).

8   The sociological literature has extensively developed such trust architectures, see for example Eisenstadt and Roniger (1984). The computing literature, has further elaborated these constructs to assist communication in insecure environments.

9   See Knight (1921).

10   For example Hardin (1991), Bowles and Gintis (2000) and Guerra and Zizzo (2002).

11   A partial exception is made in the 'crime game' examined in Sections 12.2.2 and 12.3.3.

12   Kasher and Rubinstein (1998) differentiate group identification based on individual affiliation, group inclusion and third-party labelling.

13   Asymmetry with regard to roles (for example buyer and seller) is perfectly compatible with symmetry across members of a society. If a strategy is described as a prescription for how a person should behave in a given situation and if any person might be in any position, symmetric equilibrium is much less restrictive (since the play between different roles can be asymmetric).

14   Including team working games like 'Stag Hunt'.

15   Like 'Battle of the Sexes'.

16   For example Bacharach. and Gambetta (2001), Bacharach et al. (2001), Bohnet et al. (2001), Bohnet and Zeckhauser (forthcoming 2004).

17   On this point, see esp. Bowles and Gintis (2000) and Ben-Ner and Putterman (2001).

18   These possibilities are sketched in the Appendix. In any case, the use of simplified representative or reduced form games has a long history: see for example Axelrod (1984), Morris (2000), Young (1993, 1998).

19   For instance, A might have different preferences than B believed (reputation – see Section 12.4.2.2), darker motives, a steeper discount factor and so on.

20   See for example Hintikka and Sandhu (1996) on the epistemic and semantic issues, and Harsanyi (1973), Cho and Kreps (1987) on game-theoretic approaches. These approaches are combined to provide a framework for trust issues in Bacharach and Gambettta (2001).

21   We could equivalently assume that direct trust exposes a party to risk from all those trusted by his partner(s), but this would complicate the exposition without compromising the basic tension between efficiency and equilibrium.

22   Bacharach and Gambettta (2001) identify these as salient characteristics, though the underlying game and analysis are different.

23   If the network is not fully connected, the possible trajectories may be more complex, since some players will face different circumstances.

24 See for example Belleflamme and Bloch (2001), which characterizes efficient and stable market sharing networks in which firms agree not to compete with their 'partners'. Efficient networks in symmetric industries involve all firms having the same number of agreements; in stable networks completely-connected 'clusters' of a minimum size form – these clusters are typically too small to maximize industry profit and larger than would be socially optimal. Stable networks in asymmetric industries may be incomplete and fail to provide socially optimal levels of connection.

25 For example electronic input markets such as Covisint or MyAirline.com and an ever-expanding range of other B2B e-commerce markets. Many such markets have been set up by either the buyer or the seller side; the remarks above are concerned with their impact on trust among players on one side of the market only.

26 There is some evidence that it is relatively easy to attract customers to websites, but much harder to retain them compared with offline channels.

27 By providing complete, accurate, reliable and durable information.

28 In other words, whether search results in greater satisfaction or a higher possibility of regret.

29 As demonstrated by recent 'phishing' attacks on online banking sites and transactions service providers such as Paypal, see http://news.independent.co.uk/digital/features/story.jsp?story=473895 accessed 17 April 2004.

30 Effective consumer search is inhibited by information asymmetry, and the provision of comparative information inhibits treatment of difficult or doubtful cases, leading to a classic 'lemons market'.

31 Anderson (2003) cites the case of mobile telephones, where anti-cloning precautions led to increases in theft of 'legitimate' phones – and thus to an increase in physical risk accompanying financial risk.

32 At least, providing the 'hassle costs' of obtaining warranty performance are not too high. This is certainly an issue in the cyber world, where much of the 'protection' takes the form of customer service or advice, which may take a long time to obtain and comes without further warranty for consequential damage.

33 Relevant articles include Shapiro (1982, 1983).

34 Calabresi (1970).

35 This is connected to the analysis of incomplete rationality and the insight that it can be Pareto-improving to commit to not using all relevant information, not auditing in every case where it is possible to do so and not retaining extensive records of past behaviour. See for example Jensen and Meckling (1976) or Murphy (1999) for examples from financial economics.

36 See for example Caillaud and Jehiel (1998), Fischer and Kakkar (2000), Geanakopolos et. al. (1990), Jehiel and Moldovanu (1996), Jehiel et al. (1996) and Kubler and Schmedders (2003).

37 This is a simplified example of an optimal incentive contract – see Laffont and Tirole (1993).

38 We also assume $d(i,i) = 0$ and that $d(i,j)$ is infinite if i and j are unconnected.

39 Again, players could incur cost for each pairwise trust relationship, but this adds little to the indirect reliance analysis.

40 An equivalent formulation would assume quadratic utilities; treat r_i as the (subjective) variance of returns, and q_i as an inverse measure of risk aversion.

41 Jensen (1982) obtains a similar result in a technology diffusion model.

42 Following Young (1993).

43 Formally, the resistance is the proportion of 'mistakes' by neighbours needed to induce a player to make the indicated transition. For instance, if the current convention is C, a player will switch to L if at least ¼ of the other players deviate to L (direct resistance) or if at least $1/(B-2)$ of the other players deviate to H (indirect resistance; in this case the proportion playing H must not be larger than $4/(9-B)$) – since $B < 5$, the 'threshold' associated with the indirect transition is higher than that associated with the direct transition.

REFERENCES

Anderson, R. (2003), 'Cryptography and Competition Policy: Issues with "Trusted Computing"', Cambridge University Working Paper, http://www.ftp.cl.cam.ac.uk/ftp/users/rja14/tcpa.pdf accessed 17 Apr. 04.

Axelrod, R. (1984), *The Evolution of Cooperation*, New York: Basic Books.

Bacharach, M. and D. Gambetta (2001), 'Trust in Signs' in K. Cook (ed.), *Trust in Society*, New York: Russell Sage Foundation, pp. 148-84.

Bacharach, M., Guerra, G. and Zizzo, D. (2001), 'Is Trust Self-fulfilling: An Experimental Study', Oxford University Department of Economics Working Paper 76.

Bailey, J. (1998), 'Intermediation and Electronic Markets: Aggregation and Pricing in Internet Commerce', unpublished PhD dissertation, Program in Technology, Management and Policy, Massachusetts Institute of Technology.

Bakos, J. (1997), 'Reducing Buyer Search Costs: Implications for Electronic Marketplaces', *Management Science* 43(12): 1676-92.

Belleflamme, P. and Bloch, F. (2001), 'Market Sharing Agreements and Collusive Networks', University of London Queen Mary College Working Paper 443, http://www.econ.qmul.ac.uk/papers/docs/wp443.pdf accessed 17 Apr. 04.

Ben-Ner, A. and Putterman, L. (2001), 'Trusting and Trustworthiness', *Boston University Law Review* 81(3): 523-51.

Bohnet, I., Frey, B. and Huck, S. (2001), 'More Order with Less Law: On Contract Enforcement, Trust and Crowding', *American Political Science Review* 95(1): 131-44.

Bohnet, I. and Zeckhauser, R. (2004 forthcoming), 'Trust, Risk and Betrayal', *Journal of Economic Behavior and Organization*.

Bowles, S. and Gintis, H. (2000), 'Optimal Parochialism: The Dynamics of Trust and Exclusion in Networks', Santa Fe Institute Working Paper.

Brynjolfsson, E. and Smith, M. (2000), 'Frictionless Commerce? A Comparison of Internet and Conventional Retailers', *Management Science* 46(4): 563-85.

Büschken, J. (2000), 'Reputation Networks and "Loose Linkages" Between Reputation and Quality', Katholischen Universität Eichstätt, Wirtschaftswissenschaftliche Fakultät Ingolstadt, Working Paper, http://www.ku-eichstaett.de/Fakultaeten/WWF/Lehrstuehle/MKT/ downloads accessed 17 Apr. 04.

Caillaud, B. and Jehiel, P. (1998), 'Collusion in Auctions with Externalities', *Rand Journal of Economics* 29(4): 680-702.

Calabresi, G. (1970), *The Costs of Accidents: A Legal and Economic Analysis*, New Haven CT: Yale University Press.

Cho, I. and Kreps, D. (1987), 'Signaling Games and Stable Equilibria', *Quarterly Journal of Economics* 102(2): 179-221.

David, P. and Spence, M. (2003), 'Towards Institutional Infrastructures for e-Science', Oxford Internet Institute Research Report No. 2, http://www.oii.ox.ac.uk/resources/publications/OIISP_BailliolOII.pdf accessed 17 Apr. 04.

Eisenstadt, S. and Roniger, L. (1984), *Patrons, Clients and Friends*, Cambridge: Cambridge University Press.

Ellison, G. (1993), 'Learning, Local Interaction and Coordination', *Econometrica* 61(5): 1047-71.

Fischer, E. and Kakkar, E (2000), 'On the Evolution of Comparative Advantage', http://econ.ohio-state.edu/efisher/evolution.pdf accessed 17 Apr. 04.

Fukuyama, F. (1995), *Trust, the Social Virtues and the Creation of Prosperity*, New York: Free Press.

Geanakopolos, J., Magill, M. Quinzii, M. and Dreze, J. (1990), 'Generic Inefficiency of Stock Market Equilibrium When Markets are Incomplete', *Journal of Mathematical Economics* 19: 113-51.

Guerra, G. and Zizzo, D. (2002), 'Trust Responsiveness and Beliefs', Oxford University, Department of Economics Working Paper No. 99.

Hardin, R. (1991), 'Trusting Persons, Trusting Institutions', in R. Zeckhauser (ed.), *Strategy and Choice*, Cambridge MA: MIT Press, pp. 185-209.

Harsanyi, J. (1973), 'Games With Randomly Disturbed Payoffs: A New Rationale for Mixed Strategy Equilibrium Points', *International Journal of Game Theory* 2: 1-23.

Hintikka, J. and Sandhu, G. (1996), 'Game-Theoretical Semantics', in J. van Benthem and A. ter Meulen (eds), *Handbook of Logic and Language*, Amsterdam: Elsevier, pp. 361-410.

Hollis, M. (1998), *Trust Within Reason*, New York: Cambridge University Press.

Jackson, M. (2003), 'The Stability and Efficiency of Economic and Social Networks', in S. Koray and M. Sertel (eds), *Advances in Economic Design*, Heidelberg: Springer-Verlag, pp. 319-62.

Jackson, M. and Watts, A. (2002), 'On the Formation of Interaction Networks in Social Coordination Games', *Games and Economic Behaviour* 41: 265-91.

Jehiel, P. and Moldovanu, B. (1996), 'Strategic Nonparticipation', *Rand Journal of Economics* 27(1): 84-98.

Jehiel, P. Moldovanu, B. and Stacchetti, E. (1996), 'How (Not) to Sell Nuclear Weapons', *American Economic Review* 86(478): 814-29.

Jensen, M. and Meckling, W. (1976), 'Theory of the Firm: Managerial Behavior, Agency Costs and Ownership Structure', *Journal of Financial*

Economics 3(3): 305-60.

Jensen, R. (1982), 'Adoption and Diffusion of an Innovation of Uncertain Profitability', *Journal of Economic Theory* 27(1): 182-93.

Kandori, M.G., Mailath, G. and Rob, R. (1993), 'Learning, Mutation, and Long Run Equilibria in Games', *Econometrica* 61: 29-56.

Kasher, A. and Rubinstein, A. (1998), 'On the Question "Who is a J?" A Social Approach', Tel Aviv Foerder Institute for Economic Research and Sackler Institute for Economic Research Working Paper: 20/98.

Katz, M. and Shapiro, C. (1994), 'Systems Competition and Networks Effects', *Journal of Economic Perspectives* 8: 93-115.

Knight, F.H. (1921), *Risk, Uncertainty and Profit*, Boston MA: Riverside Press.

Kubler, K. and Schmedders, K. (2003), 'Generic Inefficiency of Equilibria in the General Equilibrium Model with Incomplete Asset Markets and Infinite Time', *Economic Theory* 22(12): 1-15.

Laffont, J.-J. and J. Tirole (1993), *A Theory of Incentives in Procurement and Regulation*, Cambridge MA: MIT Press.

Morris, S. (2000), 'Contagion', *The Review of Economic Studies* 67(1): 57-78.

Murphy, K.J. (1999), 'Executive Compensation', in O. Ashenfelter and D. Card (eds), *Handbook of Labor Economics*, Volume 3B, New York and Oxford: Elsevier Science, pp. 2485-563.

Page, F., Wooders, M. and Kamat, S. (2002), 'Networks and Farsighted Stability', University of Warwick Economics Research Papers No. 621.

Pollitt, M. (2001), 'The Economics of Trust, Norms and Networks', Judge Institute of Management Working Paper, Cambridge University, http://www.econ.cam.ac.uk/electricity/people/pollitt/economicstrust.pdf accessed 17 Apr. 04.

Puttnam, R. (2000), *Bowling Alone – The Collapse and Revival of American Community*, New York: Simon & Schuster.

Rifkin, J. (2000), *The Age of Access*, New York: JP Tarcher/Putnam.

Shapiro C. (1982), 'Consumer Information, Product Quality, and Seller Reputation', *Bell Journal of Economics* 13(1): 20-35.

Shapiro C. (1983) 'Premiums for High Quality Products as Rents to Reputation', *Quarterly Journal of Economics* 98: 659-80.

Watts, D. (1999), *Small Worlds: The Dynamics of Networks between Order and Randomness*, Princeton NJ: Princeton University Press.

Young, P. (1993), 'The Evolution of Conventions', *Econometrica* 61(1): 57-84.

Young, P. (1998), *Individual Strategy and Social Structure*, Princeton NJ: Princeton University Press.

Part 4 Commentary on ethical, market, legal and regulatory issues

The three short chapters in Part 4 – two by academics and one by a lawyer – are discussion documents commissioned to address gaps that arose during the course of the Cyber Trust and Crime Prevention project in the coverage of issues.

Chapter 13 by Edward Steinmueller complements Jonathan Cave's paper (Chapter 12). Steinmueller provides a map and explanation of the range of approaches to the economic analysis of trust, including those offered by Cave. In Chapter 14, Kieron O'Hara sets out some of the principal ethical issues in the area of crime prevention including trust, security, rationality and value, and liberalism and liberty. Finally, this volume is completed with a paper by John Edwards, based on consultation with a group of lawyers that he convened. In Chapter 15 the main focus is on measures to combat opportunistic crime on the Internet.

13 Cyberspace markets, social capital and trust

W. Edward Steinmueller

13.1 INTRODUCTION

This short contribution outlines several economic approaches to the issue of trust in cyberspace interactions ranging from e-commerce to interpersonal communication. The purpose is to illustrate some practical contributions that specific areas of economic analysis can make to the analysis of behaviour and to the setting of policies and rules. The focus is on instrumental or 'purposive' transactions rather than 'expressive' or 'associational' interactions. Thus, the word 'trust' in this contribution is used in a narrow sense – for example this contribution is concerned with the question: is it appropriate for an individual to rely upon another individual or organization not to exploit potentials for opportunistic financial gain that would be of harm to the individual advancing 'trust'? By considering only opportunism related to financial gain at another's expense, many issues related to trust are excluded from the analysis. Such issues include interpersonal relationships – emotional attachment, affiliation or issues of identity that are part of our everyday understanding of trustworthiness. This limitation is the most straightforward way to link issues of trust to the logic of economics, which generally either explicitly excludes non-rational elements of human behaviour from analysis or attempts to make them conform to a rational calculus.

A second guiding principle for this short contribution is to identify issues of trust that include, but also extend beyond individual decision-making processes. Thus, while the contribution begins by considering decision making at the level of the individual in Section 13.2, it also recognizes that individuals operate within a social context with institutional features such as norms, standards and rules that provide a governing structure for individual decision-making. These institutional issues are considered in Section 13.3. This discussion skates to the edge of the 'thin ice' of economic analysis to the extent that it implies there might be 'something more' to transactions than simply the rules of the game – social reputation or responsibility are rarely used in the economics literature. The larger issues of social influences on behaviour include those identified in the emerging literature on social capital, see Section 13.4, in which not only reputation, but also other forms of ties (strong and weak) link the individual to a larger social context and constrain (or sometimes enhance) the individual pursuit of satisfaction.

For economists, the principal concerns with issues of cyberspace security are directly linked to economic 'transactions', the process of voluntary exchange underlying market economies. In short, economists are interested in how the processes of voluntary exchange may be reproduced, be adapted or may evolve in cyberspace. The analytical tools that economists employ to examine more traditional transactions are assumed to be relevant to cyberspace. This is because in economic analysis, the physical location and methods of communication between economic agents are generally thought to be irrelevant except inasmuch as they may affect the costs of a transaction. If methods employed in cyberspace alter the costs of transactions, economic analysis will be relevant. Costs here are understood to include not only direct costs, but also the indirect costs implied by timeliness and various understandings of quality.

In analysing transactions, the two key benchmark assumptions that economists employ are 'complete contracts' and 'perfect information'. Complete contracts exist when the terms of exchange are completely specified and all states of the world are included so that there are no uncertainties regarding the exchange. Perfect information is the benchmark assumption that economic agents engaged in a transaction have symmetrical knowledge of what is being exchanged (for example the qualities of a good or service) and that no other relevant economic agent has 'better' knowledge. Under the conditions of complete contracts and perfect information, the term 'trust', as it is employed by other disciplines, has no relevant meaning in economics and is therefore not employed in economic analysis (Blomqvist 1997). Transaction decisions are made solely in terms of what is on offer and the offer price.

The issue of 'trust' is relevant when alternatives to the benchmark assumptions of economic analysis are introduced. A principal motive for introducing alternative assumptions is that they may more realistically represent actual market and transaction conditions than the benchmark assumptions. Whether 'realism' per se is a desirable goal for economic studies is debatable. (The question of realism in economic theory is an ongoing controversy with the most influential contribution being Friedman 1953, which argued against the principle that one should adopt 'realistic' assumptions because of their realism, a principle that has become the generally followed practice of economists.) In some cases, however, such alternative assumptions may be essential for an accurate analysis. Thus, despite economists' wariness of considering 'states of mind' such as trust as determinants of behaviour, some ideas related to 'trust' have been introduced to economic analysis.

13.2 TRUST AND INDIVIDUAL DECISION MAKING

Two basic approaches have been employed in introducing 'trust'-related ideas in economics with a third bidding for attention in recent years. The first, which partially corresponds to the individual psychology of learning and decision making, takes trust to be part of the 'preference structure' of economic actors. The level of trust in the agent making an 'offering' is embedded as a characteristic of the good or service (commodity) on offer. In this framework, examined further in Section 13.2.1, trust is equivalent to other characteristics such as the perceived quality of the commodity in determining whether a transaction occurs (Daspupta 1998). The relevant economic theories for analysing this definition are non-cooperative game theory and information economics. The second approach to introducing trust into economic analysis, examined in Section 13.2.2, is to view interactions between economic agents as offering a choice between opportunistic and cooperative behaviour. In other words, allowing agents to recognize their interdependence and to modify their behaviour accordingly. This approach employs the economic theory of cooperative game theory. Third, and finally, ideas about the interdependence of the economic agents have produced a new set of ideas in which economic agents may seek to influence how they are perceived through signalling behaviour, a new branch of information economics, which is considered in Section 13.2.3.

13.2.1 Non-Cooperative Game Theory Approaches Related to Trust

Despite the potential relevance of beliefs about agents making offers, works in information economics rarely employ the term 'trust', as their primary aim is to understand the analytical consequences of replacing the benchmark perfect information assumption with assumptions about 'asymmetric information'. In this context, trust can be thought of as 'expectations' regarding the unknown reliability of the 'offering' party (with regard to either their trustworthiness or the veracity of their claims). Expectations are formed that determine the decision or outcome of the transaction. One means for forming expectations is past experience with the offering agent. While they use the term 'beliefs' rather than trust, Fudenberg and Levine (1993) model the formation of these expectations as a Bayesian learning process, which they demonstrate converges towards a Nash equilibrium (a fundamental result in non-cooperative game theory in which an agent's decisions are made under the assumption that other agents are also attempting to maximize the value of the outcomes of the process). This approach is critically assessed in Mailath (1998). A similar approach can be employed in designing economic experiments in which human subjects are given the opportunity to receive real monetary rewards for decisions and results from this approach are summarized in Camerer (2003). In the context of cyberspace transactions, the behaviour that is exhibited in real time auctions online bears great similarity to the predictions of economic theory and the results of economic experiments concerning non-cooperative behaviour.

Non-cooperative game theory is of considerable use for analysing behaviour that violates rules (laws), norms and standards such as cyberspace fraud. Rational actors are expected to assume the possibility of fraud (a form of opportunistic behaviour) in cyberspace transactions and to make their decisions based upon the possibility that fraud is possible. This is one reason that 'indemnification' from fraud is a central component underlying the use of credit cards for Internet transactions – without such indemnification it would have been necessary to develop alternative mechanisms for minimizing the losses from fraudulent transactions. The model of the human being that economics presents is strongly bounded by rationality assumptions – 'trust no one' is a starting and often an ending point in economic analysis; all ideas about trust are provisional and trust is only offered in the contemplation of the possibility of its being broken.

13.2.2 Cooperative Game Theory Approaches to Trust

Alternatively, and superficially more akin to sociological approaches, it may be assumed that the transaction has a cooperative element – there may be outcomes in which both agents can benefit from cooperation, but in which there is also the possibility of opportunistic behaviour. In this case the relevant approach is cooperative game theory which is often explored using experimental methods (for example Glaeser et al. 2000 and Anderhub et al. 2002). These methods have close connections to Axelrod (1984) who pioneered the study of the development of cooperation by considering extensions to the prisoner's dilemma.

The prisoner's dilemma is the classical framing problem for cooperative game theory in which two individuals accused of a crime are separately questioned. Each individual has a choice between maintaining innocence or admitting guilt. If only one admits guilt he or she goes free, while the other receives a long prison sentence. If both maintain their innocence, they will both receive a short prison sentence. If both admit guilt they will both receive a medium-length prison sentence. In the absence of knowledge about the other's choice, what decision should an individual make? If this type of game only occurs once, each prisoner has a strong incentive to admit guilt in the hope that the other prisoner will deny involvement and in the fear that they will confess. Police interrogation practice of implying to each prisoner that the other is cooperating is an attempt to heighten the incentives for both to confess. Similarly, the social norms among criminals never to cooperate are a simple statement of the optimal 'joint' solution to the game from the criminal viewpoint.

This basic framework may be extended to consider a multiple period game in which cooperation or defection is a choice in each period for each player. Defection is highly rewarded, but at a cost to the other player, while if both players cooperate a smaller mutual gain is possible. Axelrod and others have employed this framework, both theoretically and experimentally, to discover the existence of 'robust' strategies for 'cooperation' and found that (among others) a tit-for-tat strategy emerges in which defection in one period is punished by defection in the next period by the other player. Cooperation is re-established and maintained as a stable outcome after some further periods of playing the game. In the context of cyberspace transactions and indemnification, it is possible for a buyer to renege on payment for commodity purchases (such as online entertainment) where it is costly to 'prove' that the commodity has been received. Repeated fraudulent claims of 'non-receipt' are likely to invoke tit-for-tat behaviour such as investment of resources in proving the fraudulent nature of claims. In a similar fashion, filtering of unwanted content transmitted by others (such as spam) may rely upon individual or collective tit-for-tat behaviour in blocking such content or pursuing its originators.

13.2.3 Signalling and Filtering

A further extension of the theory of individualistic behaviour related to trust in information economics is the role of signalling and filtering. Signalling and filtering theories attempt to answer the question, 'Faced with uncertainty concerning the inherent characteristics of a commodity (conditions giving rise to distrust), how will markets operate?' Vickrey, Akerlof and Spence, three Nobel Prize-winning economists, in separate lines of investigation develop answers to these questions (Riley 2001). Spence's contribution, in particular, was to ask whether it might be possible to invest in some signal that would encourage the other party to respond more favourably – for example, investing in a 'secure' Internet connection may signal the desire to maintain confidentiality for the entry of personal details such as credit card information for electronic payments. Correspondingly, which signals might be selected as relevant suggests a theory of 'filtering'. Obviously, certain signals, such as the secure Internet example, may become overused and, hence, ineffectual over time (for example fraudulent sites may also signal secure connections to extract credit card information). Despite the importance of signals and filters in the development of cyberspace institutions, very little work has been done so far in this area.

13.3 NEW INSTITUTIONAL ECONOMICS AND TRUST

The second approach for introducing trust-related issues into economics is related to the institutional structures (rules, norms and standards) that are generally applicable and, hence, govern transactions (Williamson 1975). In this case, specific departures from the 'benchmark' standard of perfect knowledge and enforceability of the terms of exchange need to be specified. The relevant body of economics for analysing this definition is transaction cost economics or the new institutional economics (Williamson 2000). A basic result from this literature is that long-term contracts are often incomplete because the parties are mutually dependent on the maintenance of business ties – as with the repeated prisoner's dilemma situation, there is a strong incentive not to defect and behave opportunistically. Relying on this incentive amounts to what some would call trust.

Given the economist's aversion to using the word 'trust', however, the term 'incentive compatible' is employed to describe situations in which defection and opportunistic behaviour are likely to meet with unfavourable responses. In other words, economists would focus on the costs of breaching trust as the principal motive for maintaining it. Williamson (2000), for example, draws directly on the sociological contribution of Macaulay (1963), to conclude: 'Businessmen operating in competitive industries in a high trust culture who insist on contractual completeness and exacting execution will find that such transactional *attitudes* result in excessive costs and render their businesses nonviable' (emphasis added, p. 107). In other words, acting 'as if' one is trusting is best. Note that Williamson feels it necessary to add the phrase 'in a high trust culture' (ambiguous as to society or specific industry), thus reserving the question of whether trust is a prevailing characteristic or not in a particular context. He also demonstrates the economist's distaste for the analysis of internal states of mind by associating attitude with dysfunctional behaviour while it is clear, in the context that he is describing, that the formation of specific social norms and individual attitudes is equally relevant in supporting an environment of incomplete contracts and some permissiveness with regard to contract execution.

In the area of transaction cost economics and the new institutional economics, which Williamson and others have developed, trust serves as a lubricant in markets, reducing transaction costs and assuring something closer to perfect competition. Instead of focusing on trust as an attitude, however, transaction cost economics focuses on the structure of institutions (rules, norms and incentives) that align the behaviour of actors towards 'incentive compatibility', where it may be expected that economic agents will act according to expectation rather than opportunistically. This expectation approaches, but clearly is distinguished from, a sociological understanding of trust as an inherent characteristic of a relationship.

The establishment of an institutional framework for cyberspace transactions directly addresses transaction cost economics issues. This institutional framework involves technical methods for user authentication, time-stamping and electronic signatures, as well as accompanying norms or standards, such as indemnification from fraud, reducing the costs of transactions and, hence, making them more likely to occur.

13.4 TRUST AND SOCIAL CAPITAL

A third approach to introducing trust into economic analysis is currently being negotiated. This approach stems from the idea of 'social capital' developed by Bourdieu and Passeron (1977) as a means for modernizing Marxist concepts of 'class' as reflecting relational capital of elites. The social capital idea has received considerable attention due to the efforts of Putnam (1993) to explain economic performance distinctions between Northern Italy and the mezzogiorno and between different regions within the US (Putnam 2000), as being the result of differences in the nature and density of non-economic relational associations in society.

Economists have been sceptical of the 'social capital' idea, for example Sobel (2002), because of the causal ambiguity in the relation between non-economic social relations and economic performance – while Bourdieu and Putnam argue that the causation runs from social relations to economic performance, economists would begin with the premise that causation operates in the opposite direction, from performance to relationships. This has not prevented some economists from embracing the social capital idea as a reason to explore the more familiar agenda of 'trust' as a feature of preferences. For example, Glaeser et al. (2000) cite the findings of Knack and Keefer (1997) that the absence of government corruption has a positive influence on economic growth for analysing the behaviour of Harvard undergraduates in an experimental setting involving trust formation.

Assuming that Bourdieu and Putnam's ideas of causal direction are correct, a case can be made for linking trust with non-economic social relations, which would suggest, for example, that societies that engender and support a more complex and dense pattern of networked social relations may benefit from lower transaction costs and more robust assumptions concerning the unlikelihood of opportunistic behaviour. This approach bridges the contentious issue of how trust can be extended between parties that are ostensibly capable of opportunistic behaviour – creating a 'web' or 'network' of trust (Mansell et al. 2000). A further extension would be to suggest that explicit policies aimed at supporting the development of virtual communities in cyberspace (for example such as those advocated in Mansell and Steinmueller 2000 for somewhat different reasons) would have a positive pay-off in economic performance.

13.5 DISTINGUISHING BETWEEN PREFERENCE AND INSTITUTIONAL APPROACHES

Finally, it may be useful to distinguish economic concepts of 'trust' that are based upon incomplete information and incomplete contracts (including business relationships that involve repeated transactions) from economic concepts of trust that are based upon preferences. Figure 13.1 does this, noting the strong link between game-theoretic approaches, which may proceed from either premise while positioning the other approaches discussed above in relation to a series of questions about the context of the transaction.

The one issue that was not discussed above is the situation where trust is taken as an inherent feature of preferences, but in which neither prior experience nor signals and filters can be taken as relevant to making a decision. Under these conditions, the decision maker considering a transaction can only take account of general issues of risk in resolving whether to make the transaction or not. The analysis of risk, including the prevailing 'expected utility theory' in which choices are made based upon the statistically expected value of their outcomes, continues to be developed in economics in both theoretical and empirical contexts (see Starmer 2000). The issue of generalized risk can be thought of as a comparison between cyberspace and more traditional transaction methods and thus can be linked to findings from other disciplines regarding attitudes and preferences of individuals and organizations in terms of the 'safety', 'reliability' or 'value' of cyberspace transactions.

In summary, game-theoretic approaches are central to the economic analysis of individual decision making when issues of trust are involved. The cyberspace applications of these theories are direct applications of existing theories in which trust is either an inherent characteristic of an economic agent or where trust is the result of formation of expectations based upon interaction between agents. An area in which more research is needed is the use of signals and filters in a cyberspace context to attempt to influence expectations concerning trust.

Figure 13.1 Economic analysis related to trust

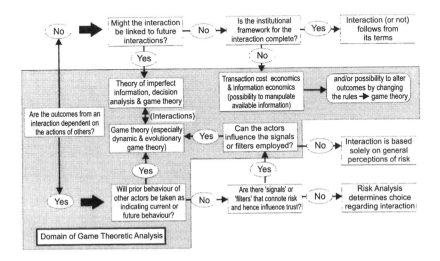

Economists are also willing to consider whether expectations concerning trustworthiness may exist within a specific social or business context, providing a context for interactions, and influencing transaction costs (and hence the willingness to make transactions). In the first instance this context may be set by institutional features of a particular market or group of economic actors – their standards, norms and rules may effectively govern the formation and maintenance of trust. Economists will, however, always be looking at the penalties for opportunistic behaviour and assuming that 'cheating' will occur when it brings economic gains. More generally, and still not well accepted within economics, the entire constellation of social ties that bind the individual to society or meaningful associations may also govern the formation and maintenance of trust. Whether the creation of a richer network of such ties is a cause or effect of the purposive exchange behaviour upon which economists focus remains in question, but provides a rich agenda for research and interpretation in the cyberspace context.

REFERENCES

Anderhub, V., Engelmann, D. and Güth, W. (2002), 'An Experimental Study of the Repeated Trust Game with Incomplete Information', *Journal of Economic Behavior and Organization* 48(2): 197-216.

Axelrod, R. (1984), *The Evolution of Cooperation*, New York: Basic Books.

Blomqvist, K. (1997), 'The Many Faces of Trust,' *Scandinavian Journal of Management* 13(3): 271-86.

Bourdieu, P. and Passeron, J.-C. (1977), *Reproduction in Education, Society and Culture*, translated from the French by Richard Nice, London: Sage.

Camerer, C.F. (2003), *Behavioural Game Theory*, Princeton NJ: Russell Sage Foundation and Princeton University Press.

Daspupta, P. (1998), 'Trust as a Commodity', in D. Gambetta (ed.), *Trust: Making and Breaking Co-operative Relationships*, Oxford: Blackwell, pp. 49-72.

Friedman, M. (1953), *Essays in Positive Economics*, Chicago IL: University of Chicago Press.

Fudenberg, D. and Levine, D. K. (1993), 'Steady State Learning and Nash Equilibrium,' *Econometrica* 61(3): 547-73.

Glaeser, E.L., Laibson, D.I., Scheinkman, J.A. and Soutter-Glaeser, C.L. (2000), 'Measuring Trust', *Quarterly Journal of Economics* 115(3): 811-46.

Knack, S. and Keefer, P. (1997), 'Does Social Capital have an Economic Payoff?', *Quarterly Journal of Economics* 112(4): 1251-88.

Macaulay, S. (1963), 'Non-Contractual Relations in Business', *American Sociological Review* 28(1): 55-70.

Mailath, G.J. (1998), 'Do People Play Nash Equilibrium? Lessons from Evolutionary Game Theory', *Journal of Economic Literature* 36(3): 1347-74.

Mansell, R., Schenk, I. and Steinmueller, W.E. (2000), 'Net Compatible: The Economic and Social Dynamics of E-commerce', *Communications and Strategies* 38(2): 241-76.

Mansell, R. and Steinmueller, W.E. (2000), *Mobilizing the Information Society: Strategies for Growth and Opportunity*, Oxford: Oxford University Press.

Putnam, R. (1993), *Making Democracy Work: Civic Traditions in Modern Italy*, Princeton NJ: Princeton University Press.

Putnam, R.D. (2000), *Bowling Alone: The Collapse and Revival of American Community*, New York: Simon and Schuster.

Riley, J.G. (2001), 'Silver Signals: Twenty-Five Years of Screening and Signaling', *Journal of Economic Literature* 39(2): 432-78.

Sobel, J. (2002), 'Can We Trust Social Capital?' *Journal of Economic Literature* 40(1): 139-54.

Starmer, C. (2000), 'Developments in Non-Expected Utility Theory: The Hunt for a Descriptive Theory of Choice Under Risk', *Journal of Economic Literature* 38(2): 332-82.

Williamson, O.E. (1975), *Markets and Hierarchies: Analysis and Antitrust Implications*, New York: Free Press.

Williamson, O.E. (2000), 'The New Institutional Economics: Taking Stock, Looking Ahead', *Journal of Economic Literature* 38(3): 595-613.

14 The ethics of cyber trust

Kieron O'Hara

14.1 INTRODUCTION

This chapter discusses ethical aspects of efforts to secure cyber trust. It is less than a decade since the Internet became a major medium for communication and a major space for political and commercial action, beyond the academic enclave. In so short a time, it is unsurprising that ethical considerations have yet to be well worked through, never mind to have yielded a consensus. Numerous open questions remain about the type of space the Internet provides, the type of medium it is and the nature of the harms that can be perpetrated on it.

Furthermore, answers to these questions depend on (at least) three sets of orthogonal issues. First, we must look to the field of ethics, where there is of course a body of work stretching back over two and a half millennia. The main issue here is the mapping between standard ethical concepts and the 'new world' of the Internet. Second, there are the technical structures, the architecture, of the Internet itself, which will enable or restrict what types of action are available. Third, there are the social aspects of actions, the sociological distinctions and ramifications that follow from whether an action is, say, commercial, or criminal or knowledge sharing.

These issues are complicated by feedback between them. Regulating architectures will impact on who uses the Internet and why. Trying to alter social usage (for example to try to breach the 'digital divide') will have effects on the harms that may be caused, and so on.

This brief comment will look to apply relatively well-known ethical positions to the new environment and try to suggest issues that will arise given potential policy decisions. The aim is not to provide solutions, which in any event can only arise after properly informed debate; rather the aim is to provide an indication of likely ethical minefields, the beginnings of a framework for understanding the ethical ramifications of attempts to secure cyber trust.

14.2 TRUST AND SECURITY

The first issue concerns the definition of trust itself and its relationship with the idea of security. One of the many uses of trust is as an epistemological tool; trust enables a principal to cut transaction costs by foregoing various levels of security. If an agent claims to be able to perform service X, then the principal will save resources if it takes the agent's word for it. If it does not, then it will need to investigate the agent's abilities, investigate the agent's incentives and also decide whether to share its own resources with the agent if necessary. The more trusting an agent is, the greater the savings in the costs of setting up the transaction.

Trust is required in situations of uncertainty. Hence reducing uncertainty reduces the requirements for trust. Removing uncertainty is of course easier said than done. An enticing alternative is to impose security systems, which does not remove the need to trust, but rather shifts its object to the systems. This will make a failure of trust more traumatic, but equally requires trusting many fewer agents.

Ethically, the issue here is the spread of such security infrastructure. What avenues will be cut off for those who do not wish to employ it? For example, most security systems require some kind of pinning down of identity; however, for many users, the charm of the Internet is precisely the ability to get away from, or play with, one's identity.

As liberal political philosopher Bruce Ackerman puts it, we must ask of every exercise of power: why? (Ackerman 1980). The analysis of power becomes a dialogue, with an extension of power always responded to with a requirement for justification. In the online world, it is the code of the Internet that controls the architecture and, therefore, what actions are permissible or not. Code writers become lawmakers; their decisions determine what is allowed. Hence the issue here revolves around the architectures that get put into place and their questioning (Lessig 1999).

If we are to be able to question the extension of security online, there needs to be some forum where the sceptical can table their requirement for justification. This leads to a requirement at the very least for an open and democratic debate. Most commentators, of course, would agree with this proposition and many initiatives are designed expressly for this purpose. However, given the multinational flavour of the Internet, and the fact that security issues cross jurisdictions, then getting a full cross-section of users – including those who currently are unable to use the Internet, but may be able to do so soon – will inevitably be very hard.

It may be that a sensible strategy is to place the burden of proof on those who wish specifically to alter the principles upon which the Internet was founded and which brought it about, namely liberty and openness. On the other hand, an argument might be taken from John Stuart Mill's (1869) work *On Liberty*, which holds that liberty and openness are the essentially important values after a certain level of cultural development has been achieved, and we have pulled ourselves away from barbarism. Taken from its nineteenth century context and applied to the Internet, the argument could suggest that first of all it is essential to provide an architecture in which particular privileged activities can flourish (for example science, e-commerce) and only then should liberty become an overriding value (the decision about exactly which activities are privileged is a political one and will depend on who has the legitimate power to enter the debate).

14.3 RATIONALITY AND VALUE

A second issue is the type of trust envisaged. Trust is an extremely multifarious phenomenon, and academic practice has often been to narrow the definition (O'Hara 2004, pp. 21-2). This facilitates study by scoping enquiry, but has a tendency to warp the phenomenon itself by focusing on one or two of its properties.

In particular, in the context of the Internet, there are two readings of trust that suggest themselves. The first is a utilitarian notion of trust developed by Niklas Luhmann (1979; O'Hara 2004, pp. 64-6), which sees trust as a way of reducing complexity by accepting the bona fides of agents rather than investigating them. The second is a moral notion of trust, that dates back to the nineteenth century pioneer of sociology Emile Durkheim (1893), which sees trust as an inclusion into a value-laden society; if I trust you, I accept you as one who shares my values (O'Hara 2004, pp. 52-5). Durkheim's view is optimistic and conservative; Luhmann's is rooted in self-interest. There is some evidence from value surveys that the Durkheimian view is more widely held in society as a whole (Uslaner 2002). Note, incidentally, that the Durkheim view is more amenable to culture-relative interpretation, whereas the Luhmann view has far more universalizing tendencies.

With regard to trust, these views have differing corollaries. The Luhmann view is that trust is the effect of good behaviour and, therefore, ensuring trust requires providing incentives for good behaviour. The Durkheim view is that trust is the cause of good behaviour, and that the best strategy to ensure that people behave well is to trust them and make it clear to them what behaviour is acceptable.

This argument is important in the context of the Internet in that it mirrors a major ethical debate about the purpose of the Internet and the limits of its regulation. On the one hand, there are people who consider that the Internet is just a new type of space that must develop its own limits and types of action (which will include, for example commercial actions and surveillance). On the other, there are those who note that the Internet is the creation of scientists and hackers and that this historical fact is essential in planning the regulation of the Net.

So when we consider the governing values of the Internet, liberty and openness, the former group think that they mark a stage through which the Internet had to move, but which may be transcended to allow other forms of online life to develop. The latter think that liberty and openness are essential and non-negotiable. The former are Luhmannian and want to ensure trust by altering architectures to make bad behaviour more difficult. The latter are Durkheimian and want as much as possible to be allowed in order to imbue the Internet with their libertarian values. This entails, for example, the downplaying of commercial applications, as these – with their discounting of trust and focus on security – create incentives for bad behaviour.

The two different notions of trust available help to explain why these two groups of people often talk past each other. The difference between them might be put like this. Both groups agree that it is in one's interests to trust if and only if society is well-behaved enough to ensure that in general most agents are well disposed and act in good faith. But because they disagree about what constitutes good behaviour and good faith, they then disagree about when it is in one's interests to trust.

14.4 TRUST AND RATIONALITY

If we take this thought a little further, we might note that there is a spread of views about trust and rationality. The reciprocity required by trust is part of the uncertainty that trust tries to dispel. Consequently, there is a long and interesting literature about when and whether it is rational to assume that reciprocity will be respected. In other words, whether you perceive it as rational to trust may depend on existing social structures. In the online world, of course, many of those 'social structures' will actually be aspects of the Internet architecture.

The more narrow the conception of when it is rational to trust, then the lower the level of trust in a society and also the lower the level of betrayal. Some indicative positions include the following. Table 14.1 suggests six possible positions, together with a major thinker who held (more or less) that position, and a brief sketch of the implications. As we go down the table, the positions become more forward-thinking and less egoistic. Note that the representative thinkers are all from the eighteenth century or earlier – very little new has since been added to this debate (Hollis 1998; O'Hara 2004, pp. 42-9).

Table 14.1 Alternative conceptions of when to trust

Position	Representative	Implications
Law of the jungle		In this position, trust depends entirely on the principal's assessment of the agent. As there is little or no comeback for the principal if the relationship goes wrong, then trust may be slow to develop. However, it does of course depend on the type of relationship. Relationships that thrive on openness and selflessness (such as friendship, e.g. in a chatroom or a MUD or MOO) will be well-placed here, whereas those in which the protagonists have more of a distance, such as commercial relationships, will not thrive.
Leviathan	Thomas Hobbes (1588-1679)	Hobbes suggested a strong state, which he called Leviathan, will provide an important resource for the bootstrapping of trust. A central authority with stern powers of sanction will tilt the balance of probabilities towards trustworthy behaviour, and away from betrayal. Although, here, people may still betray if they think they can get away with it.
Preference models	David Hume (1711-1776)	The idea here is that the important psychological vectors are preferences and calculation. We form preferences, and then we calculate how best to achieve them. One thing that may help trust, then, is if we can theorize about and calculate others' preferences. In such an event, then we can work out when particular solutions are to the advantage of all.
Out of equilibrium play	Adam Smith (1723-1790)	There are many difficulties in the above positions, and many (including Hume himself) are sceptical that they could sustain or nurture trust. What Smith in effect calls for is the game theoretic notion of 'out of equilibrium play', or making the strategic choice that is not the best answer to your opponent's move. In this case, the actors need to have alternative motives to simple desires or preferences; they also need to be motivated by views about outcomes that are best for others. They need to be impartial between themselves and others.
Fairness	Immanuel Kant (1724-1804)	Extending this Smithian argument, a Kantian idea would be to insist on fairness across agents. One should not treat another any differently from the way one would have oneself treated.
The General Will	Jean-Jacques Rousseau (1712-1778)	Rousseau argues that any kind of individual rationality cannot support trust. Instead, he argues that people generally will judge their interests in terms of the interests of their society (which may, for example, be an online community). In that case, free riding will be a relatively small problem, in that most people most of the time will allow the interests of the community to trump their own personal egotistic interests.

Source: Based on Hollis (1998).

When we survey these positions, what we see is that they are all defined in terms of how egotistical the actors are and, therefore, what counts as a motivation. In other words, it goes to the heart of what counts as an identity.

But then we can see that this issue – complicated enough in the real world – is doubly difficult online; firstly, because identity itself is highly fluid (O'Hara 2004, pp. 106-9) and secondly, because how identity is conceived goes a long way towards defining different attitudes towards the Internet and its governing values. Those who value retaining the liberty and openness of the system, for instance, already think that online identity should be as fluid and unfixed as possible; those who wish to move beyond the Internet's starting position will be much happier about introducing stringent architectures for identity tracing.

14.5 LIBERALISM AND LIBERTY

The final issue concerns the question of how much Western bias is detectable in the debates and policies. There is no doubt that the Internet as a whole has its roots in particular Westernized views of the world. For example, the idea of environments as being definable in terms of local features (all of which may be virtual) stems from the philosophy of Descartes. The idea of people as individuals – and therefore of identity as something that can be fluid and self-defined – is notably Western. Many have argued that such positions cannot ultimately be sustained without threat of severe social breakdown, and that the social context of an interaction must be taken account of (Gray 1995; Mahbubani 2002).

The positions outlined in Table 14.1 are all characteristically Western liberal positions, in that they either treat people as egotistical, and as supremely self-interested, or try to ensure people are treated as being of equal value, that everyone is the same. The arguments against Western liberal hegemony deny that either position is realistic and claim that society must be based on some intermediate position. They would point to the apparent unsatisfactoriness of each position in the table as evidence of the ultimate bankruptcy of the Western liberal view.

There are a number of responses that could be made, but three are highlighted here. One response is a principled one, which is of the school of a liberal like Ackerman (1980) or John Rawls (1972). This states that the essential aim of the authorities, the maximally liberal position, should be to allow any actor to pursue his or her own conception of the good (with the proviso that this does not interfere with others). In Internet terms, this would mean ensuring that architectures allow maximal freedom. This may include, in certain societies, the freedom to be illiberal. In Saudi Arabia, for example, there is an Internet censor, who uses Western technology to block offensive sites. But the censor does not have that much to do: private Saudi Internet users send the censor 500 suggestions per day of sites that should be closed down (Manasian 2003). Even so, the Internet has proved something of a boon to Saudi businesswomen, who can use the impersonality and the fluid identity of the Internet for communications that would be forbidden in face-to-face contact, for example women are not allowed to drive in Saudi Arabia (*The Economist* 1999).

This liberal position argues that liberalism is a universal ideology, because it alone can act as a fair referee between other ideologies. Liberalism ensures maximal freedom for alternate views to express themselves. This is a Western-centric idea, but, say the liberals, obviously the fairest.

The second response is to argue pragmatically and conservatively that liberal culture dominates the Internet, both in terms of its development history and of its current and likely future user base. In that case, departing from liberal Western principles would be a nod too far towards a multicultural agenda. Hence Western concerns, for example about organized crime or cyber terrorism, or even just the growth of e-commerce, should come first, even if other users are to be respected.

The third response is to make a compromise position. One problem with liberalism is that its conception of the good is rooted in rights. This is fine if the content of the rights is agreed with all parties, but with non-Western cultures they may not be. By retreating from the rights-based discourse favoured by philosophers such as Rawls, the issue of what privileges people should have becomes a political problem, and therefore ripe for compromise, rather than the legalistic, all-or-nothing position characteristic of rights.

Under such a compromise, it is essential to allow access for non-Western bodies to negotiations over how to promote cyber trust. Negotiations may then be messy and bad-tempered, but compromises may well be discovered. The obvious problem is that many alternative cultures find the trade-off between privacy and security much less difficult than do most Western liberals – they will be more likely to go for security. Any move away from the Western liberal model of interaction is likely to drag the Internet further away from the anarchistic ideals of its founding fathers.

REFERENCES

Ackerman, B. (1980), *Social Justice in the Liberal State*, New Haven: Yale University Press.

Durkheim, E. (1893/1984), *The Division of Labour in Society*, London: Palgrave Macmillan.

Gray, J. (1995), *Enlightenment's Wake: Politics and Culture at the Close of the Modern Age*, London: Routledge.

Hollis, M. (1998), *Trust Within Reason*, Cambridge: Cambridge University Press.

Lessig, L. (1999), *Code and Other Laws of Cyberspace*, New York: Basic Books.

Luhmann, N. (1979), *Trust and Power*, Chichester: John Wiley.

Mahbubani, K. (2002), *Can Asians Think? Understanding the Divide Between East and West*, South Royalton VT: Steerforth Press.

Manasian, D. (2003), 'Caught in the Net', *The Economist*, 23 Jan.

Mill, J.S. (1869), *On Liberty*, London: Longman, Roberts & Green (republished New York: Bartleby, Com 1999,
http://www.bartleby.com/130/ accessed 17 Apr. 04.

O'Hara, K. (2004), *Trust: From Socrates to Spin*, Cambridge: Icon Books.

Rawls, J. (1972), *A Theory of Justice*, Oxford: Oxford University Press.

The Economist (1999), 'How Women Beat the Rules', *The Economist*, 30 Sept.

Uslaner, E.M. (2002), *The Moral Foundations of Trust*, Cambridge: Cambridge University Press.

15 Cyber trust and crime prevention: towards generally accepted digital principles

John Edwards[1]

15.1 INTRODUCTION

During the course of the Foresight Cyber Trust and Crime Prevention project a group of lawyers was convened to discuss some of the legislative and regulatory issues that are likely to emerge as cyberspace continues to develop. We met several times and took soundings from others. A short report was prepared for wider consideration by those participating in the Foresight project and the observations it contained are summarized in this brief commentary.

We considered the legitimate concern that there might be an explosion of opportunistic crime following ubiquitous online activity. We did not consider aspects of, or methods for, combating organized crime, whether it be drug rings, money laundering, paedophile activity or whatever. Therefore, there was no consideration of steps that might be necessary to combat highly resourced offenders at a level where national security considerations might come into play.

We did consider the steps needed to establish a regime that would materially reduce, though perhaps not entirely eliminate, opportunistic or lower-level 'organized' crime, seeking to find a balance between ubiquitous, free-flowing online behaviour on the one hand, and heavy-handed, intrusive enforcement on the other.

We believe that the establishment of cyber trust, through the widespread (eventually near-universal) adoption of secure means for communications and transactions, coupled with rigorous authentication processes, could achieve both these objectives.

We did not focus on the role of online systems in crime prevention that allow improved policing. This commentary is confined to consideration of the prevention of crime occurring in the course of, or even being facilitated by, the use of online means.

15.2 TOWARDS 'APPROPRIATE' ONLINE ACTIVITY

In this context, we would see the primary driver towards online security as being the development of 'appropriate' online activity. We can perceive several distinct communities that would have an interest in such development or within which such development might take place. These include:

1. governments
2. banks
3. insurance companies
4. auditors
5. Internet service providers
6. manufacturers and suppliers of information hardware, software and systems.

All these groups would have an interest in ensuring that all online activity in which they engage would incorporate 'Generally Accepted Digital Principles'. These principles, which have yet to be devised, should establish standards for acceptable levels of security for online communications, transactions and authentication and should be suitable for application and adoption internationally.

A partial precedent is the OECD's (2002) 'Guidelines for the Security of Information Systems and Networks: Towards a Culture of Security'. This is an interesting and valuable document, but sets out the issues at a high level. The principles we are proposing would be more granular, at a level comparable to BS7799, the British Standards Institute's (1995) code of practice for information security management, and PD0008, the Institute's (1999) code of practice for the legal admissibility and evidential weight of information stored electronically, particularly the latter. They would be open principles, not linked to nor incorporating any proprietary features. The various communities might begin the task of developing the idea of these Generally Accepted Digital Principles in the ways described below.

1. The government's role could be that of example, facilitation and exhortation, all of which can be particularly efficacious. Government could, for example, ensure that its procurement programmes conducted electronically complied with these Principles and did not allow any contractor not adopting those Principles to win business. Inter-governmental bodies would act to diffuse and promote the Principles

internationally.

2. Banks would adopt all these Principles in their dealings with customers and in support of all other transactions.

3. Insurance companies would not only adopt such Principles themselves but also would ensure that insurance cover was closely linked to their adoption, with the penalty for non-adoption or loose adherence being demonstrated in significantly higher premiums.

4. Auditors would be given additional duties requiring them to report on information assurance as an aspect of corporate governance, which would involve compliance with Generally Accepted Digital Principles.

5. Internet service providers would provide services only after proof that they and their customers all complied with the required Principles.

6. Manufacturers and suppliers would incorporate the Principles in the products and services they supplied. Indeed, the Principles might even embrace generally accepted standards for software design and development. Whilst a false claim of compliance (or even failure to comply) would be a trading standards offence, the main driver for the spread of the Principles would need to be reputation and trading advantage, which cross boundaries more easily.

Once such standards of behaviour were established, attention would need to be paid to their maintenance. In our view, an individual licensing scheme analogous to the requirement for a driving licence, whereby a licence would be needed before any online activity could take place, would be too prescriptive, and involve a level of bureaucracy and expense that could not readily be supported. There would also be the danger that such a regime might largely fail, bringing the whole concept into disrepute. Nonetheless, there will have to be some acknowledgement of responsibility for 'online driving'. Perhaps common law would extend the civil law duty of care to online behaviour. It might be preferable, however, that rather than relying on judicial initiative and the occurrence of a precedent, this duty of care should be explicitly extended by legislation to online behaviour. However, civil liability and responsibility for online misbehaviour would need to be accompanied by action to maintain the trust in the online network.

We anticipate that autonomous software would be available, which under the supervision of a new agency would roam the network constantly, to monitor online conduct. The model for this autonomous agent should be the Automobile Association – AA Man, rather than Robocop. Upon detecting online performance failing to meet the required Generally Accepted Digital Principles, it would interact with the malfeasant and seek to suggest and encourage adoption of a remedy. Failure to improve would result in the autonomous agent placing a caution on the malfeasant's digital certificate.

This would be open to examination by anyone considering transaction with the malfeasant. Subsequent adoption of the remedy would allow the malfeasant to interact with the autonomous agent for removal of the caution from the digital certificate. Random checks by the autonomous software agent might also need support from the police in the physical world in order to validate the registration process in certain particulars.

A mechanism for a malfeasant to appeal against the lodgement of such a caution would need to be established. Legislation might be required to create the appeal function, which in the UK could be an extension of the duties of the Information Commissioner or otherwise would be entrusted to a new body.

Extending the driving analogy, the accumulation of a certain number of cautions upon the digital certificate would result in removal of digital privileges. This would result in the digital certificate being abolished and details of that abolition and the individual involved placed on public record accessible to all. Complete exclusion from online activity would not be feasible since a minimum level of online capability (digital 'bread and water') would be needed to support life. This community, spurning the advantages of compliant online behaviour (most meaningful events and transactions will be expected to have migrated to the use of the Generally Accepted Digital Principles) might continue in its digital backwater, as a matter of personal preference. Access to the autonomous agent would continue to be available, allowing adoption of the Principles at any time.

In an era of ubiquitous online activity, with continuous maintenance and monitoring behaviour, it would be important that the community at large had confidence in the checks being undertaken and were aware of their purposes. This might require the creation of a new body with powers of scrutiny and review, probably staffed from the judiciary, with manifest independence and considerable autonomous power. This must clearly be, and be seen to be, completely independent of the government of the day: existing institutions do not approach the required standard of independence, profile and transparency. Any new body would need considerable powers of investigation and the authority, upon discovering abuse of powers, not only to prosecute the malfeasant, but also to award compensation, limited to due damages, to those suffering from the abuse of power. Such a new body would itself of course also be subject to review by the courts.

15.3 CORE ISSUES FOR CONSIDERATION

In the course of formulating the above ideas, several core issues were identified and considered further.

Our first core issue was the idea of a system of centralized regulatory appraisal of online performance, perhaps accompanied by a facility for open recorded comment, similar to what can be seen on eBay. Further consideration of this issue however, clearly suggested that there may be no need for such a centralized system and the accompanying expense and bureaucratic burden. The proposed Generally Accepted Digital Principles would accomplish most of the objectives of such a system.

The second core issue was the idea of a licence to allow an individual to operate online, possibly carrying with it a duty of care in so doing. The desirability of avoiding unnecessary regulation if objectives can be met in other ways suggested that an individual licence is unnecessary and can be replaced by a duty of care for operating online, which might, in any event, be a natural extension of existing common law.

We considered the need for a base standard or criterion against which trustworthiness could be judged. Any rigid standard with perhaps a single electronic passport was in the end thought not to be practicable and the adoption of some Generally Accepted Digital Principles – not directly enforced by law – was thought to be preferable domestically and potentially internationally.

A third core issue that was examined was the notion of the multinational user group. Further reflection made it clear that the natural organic growth of online communities would be one way of exporting desirable standards insofar as appropriately secure behaviour was to be a feature of each of those communities. It also emphasized the limited utility of national court action.

The fourth core issue examined was legal liability for agents. Existing common law responsibility of a principal for its own agent seemed to answer this strict issue. However, there may be unresolved questions relating to identification of the principal of any agent.

15.4 CONCLUSION

All lawyers who considered these core issues were unanimous about the need for trusted government. However, the online communities are structured for the future, it clearly will be necessary for law enforcers to have extensive powers to monitor online activities. In the context of the need to guard against not only organized crime, but any explosion of opportunistic crime, the citizen is likely to accept that requirement.

Clearly, though, citizens must receive assurance that those powers will be both proportionate and properly used. To this end some obvious and external mechanisms will be needed to enable the population to feel comfortable with such powers, have confidence in them and not, as a result of alienation from them, to seek to undermine their operation. Hence, the suggestion to establish an entirely different kind of surveillance regulator, one with exceptional powers as described above and with a public face that would be widely known, easily accessible and, to the extent necessary, proactive in the prevention of abuse of investigative powers.

NOTE

1   This brief note is a product of consultations with a group of lawyers who were convened for the purpose. Thanks for their contributions go to Mark Turner of Herbert Smith, Tony Wales of AOL, Jeremy Barnett, Chair of Bar Council IT, Anthony Sylvester of Gilbert & Tobin, Peter Sommer of the London School of Economics and Jacqueline Reid of 11 South Square.

REFERENCES

British Standards Institute (1995), 'BS 7799 Code of Practice for Information Security Management', London.

British Standards Institute (1999), 'PD0008 A Code of Practice for Legal Admissibility and Evidential Weight of Information Stored Electronically, 2nd edn, London, April.

OECD (2002) *Guidelines for the Security of Information Systems and Networks: Towards a Culture of Security,* Paris: OECD.

Index

Adaptability 81
Advanced Knowledge Technologies
   project 137
Agents 128, 166, 193, 443
Ambient intelligence 13
AMSD 61, 65
ARPANET 212
Auctions 183
Audit Commission (UK) 357
Authentication 23, 92, 321
Autonomic computing 36, 67, 81

Barings Bank 362
Biometric authentication, 102, 330-
   33
Brands 155
British Standards Institute 451
Broadband 220, 223

CCTV 43
Certainty trough 211, 225-6, 229
Certification 134
   Authority 99, 190
Collusion 195
Combined data authentication 100
Computer games 31
Consumer protection 407-8
Contextualist theory 259
Contracts 121
Council of Europe 293, 294
Crime
   Crime   Specific   Opportunity
   Structure 360-62, 370
   prevention, 24
   risk of 272-5
Criminal
   behaviour 399-400, 421-2
   opportunity model 25
Cultural theory 263-5
Customs Information System 296

DARPA 67

Data Protection
   Data Protection Act (UK) 293,
   295
   Data Protection Common Control
   Authority 296
   Data Protection Directive (EU)
   293, 294, 303
Department of Trade and Industry
   (UK) 21, 61
Dependability 63
Dependable software 18, 77
Dialogue 140
Digital rights management 24, 109
DIRC (UK) 82, 85
Document authentication 100
Dutch auction 183
Dynamic data authentication 100

eBay 31, 177
e-Europe 60
E-Government Act 2002 (US) 304
Electronic   Communications
   Directive (EU) 295
Encryption 23
English auction 183
EPSRC (UK) 82, 85, 137
Equilibrium behaviour 394-5
Error 64
ESRC (UK) 85
Ethics 32, 442-8
Europol 296

Failure 64
Fair Information Principles 286
Fault 64
   Fault prevention 68
Federal Trade Commission (US) 297
Forensics 27
Formal methods 79
Foundation for Intelligent Physical
   Agents 190